GURU TO THE WORLD

GURU

TO THE

WORLD

THE LIFE AND LEGACY OF

VIVEKANANDA

Ruth Harris

The Belknap Press of Harvard University Press
Cambridge, Massachusetts
London, England
2022

First printing

Library of Congress Cataloging-in-Publication Data

Names: Harris, Ruth, author.
Title: Guru to the world : the life and legacy of Vivekananda / Ruth Harris.
Description: Cambridge, Massachusetts : The Belknap Press of Harvard
University Press, 2022. | Includes bibliographical references and index.
Identifiers: LCCN 2022006018 | ISBN 9780674247475 (cloth)
Subjects: LCSH: Vivekananda, Swami, 1863–1902. | Vivekananda, Swami,
1863–1902—Political and social views. | Gurus—India—History—19th century. |
Hindu philosophy. | Civilization, Western—Hindu influences. |
Hindu philosophers—History—19th century.
Classification: LCC BL1280.292.V58 H37 2022 | DDC 294.5/55092—
dc23/eng20220525
LC record available at https://lccn.loc.gov/2022006018

For Iain

Contents

Preface

Authors always like to construct retrospective accounts of why they chose their subjects and how they crafted their historical questions. Although such stories are generally too smooth to be truly believable, they reassure readers (and sometimes the author) that the book has direction and, hopefully, true purpose. In the past, I have felt that I had a clear and consistent understanding of my reasons for choosing a topic, and what themes and ideas I wanted to explore. But in the case of *Guru to the World,* I found that my relationship to both the work and its principal subjects shifted constantly and remained fluid till the end.

Perhaps I am simply more clear-eyed in accepting now that I have no straightforward tale to tell about the genesis of this book. This project surprised and dismayed both friends and colleagues who found it difficult to understand why I had chosen to leave behind three decades of work in French and European history to plunge into a study of Indian religion and the Atlantic world.

There are strands of continuity. I have always been fascinated by the fin de siècle and topics where science, religion, and healing mingle with politics and the lives of individuals. But I have never practiced meditation with any seriousness and have had no luck with yoga as a form of physical strengthening or spiritual advance. However, I did have very close American friends who had long abandoned conventional Jewish or Christian beliefs for yoga, mindfulness, and Hindu- and Buddhist-inspired ideas and practices, spiritual notions that were matched by a preoccupation with wellness and optimum health. I began to wonder how and why these women—nearly always women—came to such ideas and what they meant in their lives. Their interest was all the more surprising given that only a few had ever been to India. This realization led to the question of how and why Westerners, and particularly Americans, could become interested in Eastern spirituality without having any deep matching interest in the East itself.

The intellectual/professional inspirations were not only more specific but also more far-reaching. Years ago, I wrote about the miracles and apparitions at Lourdes and investigated the religious experience of Bernadette Soubirous, whose visions of the Virgin occurred in 1857. After this study, I examined the life and work of Nobel Prize–winning intellectual Romain Rolland. Few realize that he spent a decade writing about both Ramakrishna and Vivekananda before introducing Gandhi to the French-speaking world. In reading Rolland's study of Ramakrishna, I was struck by the parallels between the Indian mystic and Soubirous, the French saint. Not only was the moment of their first visions almost simultaneous; both Bernadette and Ramakrishna were illiterate, of poor background, and regarded as expressing some authentic, even primordial, truth about the divine beyond the grasp of the better educated. Moreover, their seemingly untainted religious experience inspired religious renewal in places where the local population felt downtrodden and immiserated. Both, too, were taken up by a cultivated audience.

Such links should not be overdrawn, but when I noticed the coincidences, they became crucial in prompting me to engage with global and transnational history, to look at parallel and virtually simultaneous happenings in new ways. My vantage point in Oxford—which has so many students from both India and America—was a wonderful meeting ground for these two global cultures. Of course, my association with the United States was simple because of my American origins, even though I left my country long ago; encountering the depth and range of Indian scholarship was far less familiar and exhilarating. The realization of the often hidden impact of India on the West was enticing precisely because Eastern spirituality, yoga, and meditation became part of global culture at the very moment when Christian missionizing and Western imperialism were at their height.

After I encountered Vivekananda, the secondary question emerged of how a man who is a household name for millions of Indians around the world could be virtually unknown in the West, despite his enormous impact. I became even more aware of this discrepancy when speaking with Indian colleagues and friends who knew immense amounts about Spinoza, Mill, and Darwin while their associates in the West knew little of Indians, except perhaps Gandhi and Nehru, but certainly not Vivekananda.

My concerns at the beginning of this project lay mostly in exploring the reception of Indian ideas among "alternative" Western spiritual seekers. I soon realized, however, that this approach would once again prioritize the Western arena. For me, nothing was more humbling than my novice attempts at understanding Indian metaphysical thinking and historiography. I can only say that my colleagues—historians of India in Europe and America and especially Indian colleagues—were astonishingly generous, tolerant, and helpful in steering me through the brambles and pitfalls while urging me onward.

Since then, I have begun to share my thoughts, and the process has been both warm and welcoming as well as bracing and questioning. Vivekananda has become highly controversial as a historical figure with a major contemporary political and religious presence in Indian politics. He remains an important figure in the inner lives of friends and colleagues who have both confirmed and challenged my conclusions when I have lectured or given papers. Responses from both sides have, I feel, strengthened my arguments, but I am aware that some readers will find my account too celebratory, and others will find it too critical.

Nonetheless, it has been a rare honor—and the most invigorating intellectual experience of my life—to have written a book that I hope will engage people's emotions, intellects, and political sensibilities. All I can say is that I have striven to bring some balance to our historical understanding of global Vedanta and the extraordinary people who engaged in a rare, difficult, and sometimes confusing attempt to build bridges across cultural divides.

Note on Transliteration

Indic languages include some letters with no equivalents in English. I have avoided the use of diacritics in this book because the general reader in India or anywhere else in the world is rarely helped by them and the scholarly expert will not require them. In addition, many place names and geographical landmarks, as well as orthographic conventions, have changed in the last few decades. Names of cities and towns, as anyone familiar with South Asia knows, continue to change. I have done my very best to standardize orthography and usage, and to make it as easy as possible for readers to locate the people and places in reference books and library catalogs.

GURU TO THE WORLD

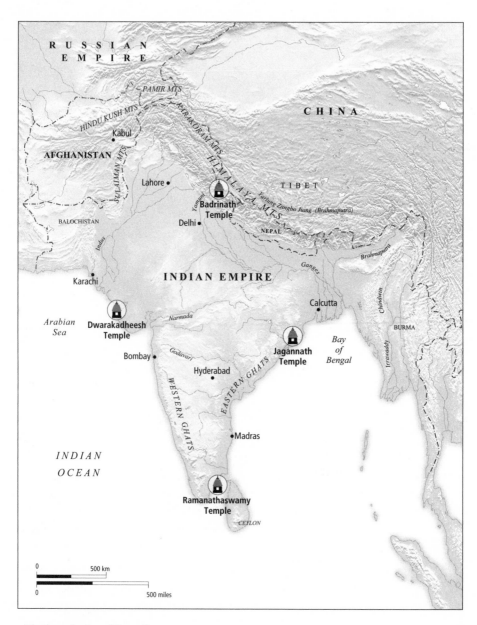

The four abodes of the gods

INTRODUCTION

Nothing is more difficult to disentangle than the history of a
definite religious idea.

—Margaret Noble, *The Complete Works of Sister Nivedita*, 1905

✦　✦　✦

IN JANUARY 1897, a young monk known as Vivekananda returned to India
after almost four years in the West. Greeted as a conquering hero, he first
stopped at Colombo, where "all classes . . . Hindus or Buddhists, forgot their
differences" and gathered to welcome him at the landing stage.[1] Before entering Jaffna, the crowds "met him ten miles from the town and escorted
him in twenty carriages."[2] For two miles, there was a grand procession, with
"[f]ifteen thousand persons [taking] part, all on foot except the Swami and
party."[3] As the returning hero made his way north to Madras (now Chennai),
crowds stood in ovation at the train halts and princes celebrated his home-
coming by feeding the poor.[4] Once in the city, the "horses were unyoked and
enthusiasts pulled the vehicle."[5] Children climbed to the treetops and families hailed him from their balconies as he made his way to the early Victorian Castle Kernan, where he was housed in princely fashion. When he arrived in Calcutta (now Kolkata), his hometown, "20,000 lined the route"
and the lecture halls overflowed with people.[6] Schoolboys were almost
trampled in the crush, and the Maharaja of Khetri "prostrate[d] himself before the Swami and offered flowers and other Pujah [offerings] articles on
his feet."[7]

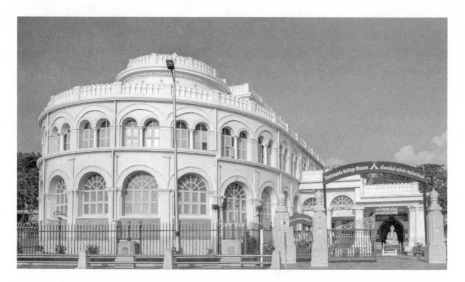

I.1. Castle Kernan, Madras, built 1842

⁕ ⁕ ⁕

Vivekananda received this welcome after crisscrossing the Western world to assert the value of Hinduism and Indian thought, winning admirers in the heartland of India's oppressors. An unknown from a poor and subjugated nation, he vaulted to fame in September 1893 at the World's Parliament of Religions in Chicago. This gathering was organized by progressive Protestants to coincide with the Columbian Exposition, an extravaganza of science, technology, and culture that a third of all Americans came to visit. Although claiming to promote a benevolent dialogue with "inferior" faiths, the Parliament—and the Exposition—aimed to signpost America's self-perception as *the* emerging world power.

Vivekananda rejected both the intent and the message. Instead of showing gratitude for being allowed to speak at all, he addressed his audience as "sisters and brothers" rather than as masters, and later criticized and even scolded them in his impeccable English. He wore a distinctive scarlet robe and orange turban, a costume of his own devising, and carried himself with a regal air. He condemned Western missionaries, and implied that Hinduism was superior to Christianity because, as he said, "We believe not only in universal toleration, but we accept all religions to be true."[8] Words, bearing, and character signaled a rejection of Western hegemony. More remarkable still was the way

I.2. Vivekananda at the World Parliament, Chicago, 1893

his ideas of religious universalism and anti-imperialism were met with wild applause by Westerners, who found themselves in (momentary) agreement.

From then on, his fame spread, to the point that he is today one of India's "fathers." In the Indian diaspora, he is eulogized as "One of the greatest Indians of the last millennium" and a "true rock star," the first to tell the "civilizational story of India" to an ignorant West, wrongly inclined in those times to view itself as the personification of modernity.[9]

He is often regarded as central to Hindu resurgence and has become linked to a populism that challenges the liberal global order.[10] India's current prime minister, Narendra Modi, regularly pays his respects to Vivekananda and does his utmost to mold his image to fit that of Vivekananda, while linking himself and Hindu nationalism to the swami.[11] He presents himself as a world teacher treading the same path as his revered predecessor, arguing not only for India's burgeoning power but also for almost supremacist civilizational values. Because Modi's party has sought to bind Hinduism so closely to its definition of Indian identity and destiny, aspects of Vivekananda's broad vision, especially in his own times, have been obscured. The rendition of selected passages, especially on self-reliance and India as the "Mother of Spirituality," can undoubtedly be made to serve a narrow vision of religious nationalism, and such associations in recent decades mean that many Indians and Western scholars of India may feel any revisionist interpretation of Vivekananda is wrongheaded, perhaps even irresponsible.

Despite these concerns, however, I aim to restore an understanding of Vivekananda's complexity by suggesting that making a direct link between the swami and the current politics of Hindu nationalism is both reductive and dangerously misleading.[12] His legacy was as various as his interventions in debates over spirituality, politics, nationhood, and experience. Certainly, Vivekananda has been claimed by Hindu right-wing extremists, but others just as readily cite him as a key influence in their turn to socialism and do so despite his unconventional but robust defense of caste.[13]

These different legacies suggest that history rarely contains lessons in inevitability; they also warn us against the dangers of reading back from current characterizations and the urgent need to return Vivekananda to his late-nineteenth-century context. This is no easy venture; it is difficult now to retrieve the many unfamiliar currents of fin de siècle "globalism," during which Boston ladies studied the *Sacred Books of the East* in their drawing rooms, English-educated Calcuttans perused Emerson's essay on the "Over-

I.3. Modi pays his respects to Vivekananda, 2017

soul," and distinguished scientists all over the world took spiritualism seriously. Science, religion, and the occult swirled in eddies that flowed into one another, all against the backdrop of the harsh imperial realities in which nascent anticolonial feeling surged.

Vivekananda's statements about Indian spiritual superiority must be seen as an attempt to instill pride and to provide solace in the face of the constant colonial humiliations. They also aimed to make Westerners aware of traditions that they normally received only through orientalist scholars, who rarely noticed the burgeoning transformations within contemporary Indian religion. Moreover, Vivekananda's nationalism was balanced by powerful universalist and idealist values, by a belief in a "Universal Self" that became important to his Western audience. As others have suggested, this vision of universality was inextricably tied to the project of national regeneration, to a vision of India that could embrace, comprehend, and even enhance other faiths with its special spiritual insights.[14] He was not, therefore, merely a shaper of a rein-vigorated Indian self-identity, nor even an influence on the Western intellectual and spiritual tradition. Rather, he helped create an important global amalgam that demands further investigation on its own terms.

Western ignorance of Vivekananda is perhaps as troubling as current Indian stereotypes of his life and thought. Why is Gandhi the only Indian who has widely penetrated Western consciousness, even though Vivekananda is now—for the reasons previously outlined—considered by many to be as important, if not more so, in today's India? For me this question is fundamental, for his impact on our thought and practice is profound and diffuse.[15] This obscurity is all the more perplexing given that up to 36 million Americans today claim to practice yoga regularly, and Vivekananda did more than anyone to introduce it, publishing the first manual in English on the subject in 1896.[16] Most are aware of yoga's Asian origins, but it has now been a part of our spiritual landscape for so long that the details of its arrival have been lost, while few realize how much Western journeys of "self-realization" owe to Vivekananda's efforts. Fewer still recognize that he fostered Eastern meditation as part of an explicit attempt to tame the spiritual, moral, and intellectual coercion that he associated with imperialism. Nor was his impact evanescent. Today, there are now 221 affiliated Vedanta Societies of the Ramakrishna Order and Mission around the world, which serve both Indians outside India as much as non-Indians of every nationality.

Do I, then, intend to write a long-overdue history of a "great man," seeking to group Vivekananda with the likes of Tolstoy, Marx, or Freud? Perhaps as a postcolonial project, such a work *might* be justifiable, but this is not my aim. Certainly, I want to reflect anew on Vivekananda, yet I do not wish to sponsor his election to a rebalanced pantheon or to compose a hagiography. Nor did Hindu Universalism in India belong to Vivekananda alone, and it could be expansive, ecumenical, and aggressive, depending on individuals, groups, and context.[17] In Vivekananda's hands, it was international and innovative, but also insistent and at times defensive. To understand it better, I will analyze a world convergence in spirituality, political activism, and intellectual endeavor by writing a new kind of transnational and global history where the key protagonists—other than the man himself—are often women, both Eastern and Western. I thus hope to reconceive the emergence of what is now often described as "Hindu Universalism," so that people of wildly dissimilar cultural and social backgrounds are recognized as central to its formulation. In this way, I intend to provide an integrated and interpretive history of Vivekananda's global project.

◆ ◆ ◆

Concentrating on the World Parliament—as most Western historians do—unduly emphasizes the Western arena and suggests that its Indian beginnings were merely a backstory to a more important Western intervention. However, Vivekananda's impact in Chicago resulted from years of apprenticeship in India under the guidance of his unconventional Bengali guru, Ramakrishna; extensive travel in South Asia; and engagement with its religious, ethnic, and linguistic diversity. He had met mystics, princes, intellectuals, the British, as well as the English-educated Hindu middle class, the cadre to which he belonged.[18] Moreover, he was already familiar with many Western ideas—Christianity, transcendentalism, homeopathy, spiritualism, evolution and more—from his youth in Calcutta, the cosmopolitan hub that was his birthplace. For this reason, the book begins in India and ends there, for his homeland generated the insights that he deployed to urge his Western audience to greater self-examination and recognition of non-Western forms of the universal.

If Western audiences need to know more about the Indian context, Indians, I hope, will learn more about the Anglo-American world. When Vivekananda first arrived, he met people very different from the supercilious and harsh masters of English schools and officialdom that he had known in British India. Instead, he encountered "alternative" Westerners, men and women interested in what was called New Thought. This movement ranged from theosophy and vegetarianism to mesmerism and homeopathy, as well as absorbing more orthodox scientific ideas from modern biology, physics, and psychology. Many of Vivekananda's concepts concerning selfhood, consciousness, reality, and truth, for example, seemed tailor-made to address the philosophical, spiritual, and personal concerns surrounding "subjectivity" that fascinated his Western turn-of-the-century audience. As idealists who had rejected both conventional Christianity and scientific positivism—but who were enthralled by the "sciences of mind" emerging in psychology and anthropology—they regarded his insights on perception, experience, and states of meditation as a spiritual and intellectual boon.[19]

Looking at Vivekananda's Hindu Universalism also provides a means to reconsider the "feminization of religion" in the nineteenth century, a term ordinarily applied to the armies of female activists and missionaries who worked at home and in the colonies to promote Christianity.[20] But his enterprise strikingly inverted the normal alliances, with Western women coming to *oppose* Christian missionaries, and Indian female figures becoming the new saints of his form of Hindu Universalism. By forming such strong connections with women both in India and in the West, Vivekananda brought their worlds together—indeed, the internationalization of his enterprise demanded that he do so and, of all his projects, few were so significant or potentially contradictory. Early on in India, he was reluctant to undertake new ventures without the support of Ramakrishna's widow, Sarada Devi, requiring her permission before leaving for America. Equally important was Margaret Noble, a Hinduized European who both embodied his synthesis and extended it. Of Scots-Irish descent and an educator and reformer in London's avant-garde, Noble followed Vivekananda to Calcutta. He christened her the "Dedicated One," or Sister Nivedita, and she set herself the task of articulating his world significance and embedding aspects of his theology into a nascent Indian nationalism.

Sarada Devi and Margaret Noble perfectly exemplify the transnational endeavors that linked philosophy, spirituality, politics, and healing that are the focus of this book.[21] Such collaborations were central to what historians have called the global idealist moment, a synthesis that had a profound (even transformative) impact on twentieth-century thought.[22] Vivekananda contributed to this moment by arguing that modern science reinforced the ancient wisdom of India concerned with processes of creation and destruction, and especially karma—the idea that our present thoughts and actions shape our character and future lives. He sought to spiritualize science and scientize religion. His Western hearers, in contrast, drew on their own religious ideas—which ranged from orthodox Protestantism to New Thought—to translate Indian notions into Western spiritual categories and practices.

Part of this global idealism was to promote a vision of universal "tolerance," which Vivekananda now claimed for Vedanta and insisted was inherent in Hinduism. In deliberate contrast to Christian missionaries, he sought no converts, distanced himself from formalized church building (while creating Vedanta Societies), and scorned the divisive "sect-making" of American Protestantism. He also accused Christians of creating an unworthy "shopkeeper religion" that bargained with God for favors, especially for redemption.[23] He stressed instead that his goal was only to make "the Methodist a better Methodist; the Presbyterian a better Presbyterian; the Unitarian a better Unitarian."[24] He was realistic in realizing that he could not compete with established Christian churches. His open-ended and open-minded strategy contributed to his appeal; and yet it might also help explain why he is so little known in the West: he sought influence, but not obvious power, preferring to exemplify the tolerance that, for him, was the essence of Hinduism.

Although he recoiled often from the word "tolerance," which suggested a condescension he deplored, he used it at times as a way of passing over the reality of Hindu sect-making and Indian traditions that, as much as their Western counterparts, implored the divine for favors. It obscured how he borrowed and enfolded other traditions within the Hindu arena. Moreover, his seemingly benign vision of Hinduism's expansiveness hid the sense of threat Vivekananda felt when Hindus converted to Islam.[25] Despite his openness to many creeds, he was still a Hindu monk, concerned with Hinduism's reinvigoration.

Although I will give space to Vivekananda's unvoiced assumptions, I am more interested in analyzing the tensions in his emotional world and the sometimes contradictory spiritual message that he constantly recalibrated for different individuals and publics.[26] His reliance on the orientalist cliché of "Eastern wisdom," which essentialized India as "good" and Western materialism as "bad," aimed to counter perceptions of Hinduism as heathenish, infantile, and even nihilistic, while promoting new syntheses grounded in Indian self-belief.[27] And yet, as will be seen, he was also an astute critique of such stereotypes, while reinforcing them in other ways. He was thus obliged to struggle mightily with questions of caste and widow remarriage that Westerners traduced without a thought, and often refocused debate by scolding them for the cruelties of their own civilization and for inflicting them on others.

◆ ◆ ◆

Guru to the World benefits from recent work in global history, which has been extraordinarily productive in shifting some aspects of a Eurocentric approach to history. By providing new perspectives on markets, migrations, commodities, cities, transport, politics, war, and culture (especially ideas), it has emphasized movement and connection.[28] Vivekananda, in traveling around the world—and visiting China, Japan, Egypt, and several countries in Europe—seems to exemplify this emerging "global" arena. And yet, even this seemingly obvious designation raises difficulties. Despite his exposure to many countries and cultures, he relied mostly on the communication and knowledge networks of the imperial/Anglophone world. When he spoke of the "East" he generally meant India; but as a native of Calcutta, he knew only too well that there was a lot more East to be had. So, while I have titled the book *Guru to the World,* the historical conjuncture this volume analyzes concentrates mostly on the British Empire, as much as on emerging America. The title remains, however, as the presence of Vedanta Societies in many other continents today suggest the truly international influence of his ideas and Indian spirituality more broadly. The global history of Vedanta—and its entanglement with the Indian diaspora—still awaits a serious historian. My aim is to examine the history of the often ambivalent personal, cultural, and political consequences of laying claim to becoming the world's spiritual teacher, both in Vivekananda's own time and shortly after his death.[29]

These caveats aside, my approach takes a different tack from most global history, which has tended to leave the subjective dimensions of individuals only half-explored, or otherwise semihidden, either because the conceptual focus is elsewhere or because of the type of evidence available.[30] A long line of men such as Vivekananda have been called "counterpreachers," a term that underscores their iconoclasm but leaves unanalyzed the emotional drives behind such advocacy.[31] Interpreted as "social mediators" or "cultural translators," labels that sometimes veil individuality, their relationships are explored as "encounters" that often underscore tropes of empire and race.[32] I also touch on these issues while remembering that ideas spread through the interactions of real people, with inner lives, fears, and desires; and I try to link their emotional worlds to broader intellectual trends.

The people Vivekananda encountered responded so strongly because his ideas helped shape their vision of human-supernatural connection. At heart, this book is about problems associated with attempts at union between the "soul" and the "Absolute." It is also, however, about attempts at human connection—the making of soul mates—love stories so intense that they pervade the intellectual, cultural, and political life discussed here. It is a project in the history of global thought underpinned by an analysis of relationships between people. In short, it is a history about the power—and inadequacies—of love.

The work is therefore book-ended by two tales of such connection—the first between Ramakrishna and Vivekananda, the second between Vivekananda and Margaret Noble. Ramakrishna enables us to situate Vivekananda in his homeland, to recover the many spiritual tendencies of the early and mid-decades of the nineteenth century, and to analyze his metamorphosis from a skeptical, British-educated Hindu reformer into a man keen to reinterpret traditions he had once disdained. If Vivekananda was Ramakrishna's favored "son," Margaret Noble was Vivekananda's Western "daughter," who helped extend his legacy for early Indian nationalism as well as reshaped Hindu Universalism for Western avant-garde intellectuals up to the First World War.

These three people provide the temporal, affective, and intellectual arc of the narrative. For this reason, I discuss Ramakrishna's teachings and example substantially before I begin to analyze Vivekananda's relationship to his guru. And Vivekananda's death is recounted in a chapter devoted to Nivedita, a strategy designed to underscore the continuation of the story, even after the demise of the "great man."

Ramakrishna, Vivekananda's guru, and inspiration, sets the stage for stories of fusion and absorption through his ecstatic mystical trials and fantasies. His devotion to the Hindu diety Kali often combined childish surrender with transgressive drives to explore the creative and destructive qualities of the cosmos. His relationship to Vivekananda was sometimes tumultuous, for Ramakrishna embraced a disciple who was so very different in temperament. Their connection developed in a world of male intimacy, where an apparently childlike and certainly unconventional guru held sway over a bevy of young disciples, and where the dialectic of the two personalities generated a remarkable creative tension.

I could not have written about Ramakrishna without the insights of Bengali and Indian historians, Indologists, anthropologists, and specialists in Indian religious thought whose pioneering scholarship over the last twenty-five years at least opened up their world to me.[33] Without their work, I might never have understood how the mystic's apparent rustic authenticity helped educated young men of Calcutta reconsider their relationship to the religious traditions they had spurned. This scholarship began my interest in how the connection between Ramakrishna and Vivekananda transformed the latter's theological preoccupations and self-vision.[34] I will add new elements to the well-studied discussion of service, activism, and what Vivekananda called "man-making," but will spend as much time analyzing how he retained Ramakrishna's childlike qualities of humor and what has been seen as spiritual "quietism"; constantly revisited notions of femininity and masculinity; and sought to balance head and heart in his new synthesis. Exploring these oppositions provides a way of understanding not only Vivekananda's intricate emotional life and experimental relationships everywhere, but also suggests why it is so difficult to develop an interpretation that encompasses his paradoxes and tensions.

Following the first part of the book that concentrates on Ramakrishna and Vivekananda, the last third examines the relationship between Vivekananda and Margaret Noble. This connection was necessarily different because it was between an Indian man and a Western woman. By remaining sexually closed, Vivekananda had freedom of a special kind—he accepted hospitality all over the world and enjoyed interactions with people in all walks of life. For such intimates as Nivedita, his outsize personality and behavior were both difficult and rewarding.[35] They were also utterly life-changing, as she abandoned her desire for the "ordinary" love between a man and woman to dedicate herself to spiritual and political ideals. Moreover, their relationship underscores how such Western acolytes as Noble transformed Vivekananda as a guru, while raising questions about what "discipleship" might mean beyond Hindu societies.

Necessarily, the connections were paradoxical, ambivalent, confused, and confusing, as the protagonists sought to break down the barriers between the personal and the universal. But the human love they experienced could only ever be a pale reflection of the spiritual ideal, revealing as it did the insecurities, misunderstandings, and relations of power that are inescapable in human affairs. Like all things of substance, the love had its shadows; understanding this darkness will be as important as uncovering its radiance.

The work is also about forms of relativism that come from different perspectives. Although my starting point is India, Vivekananda's response to America and Europe will, I hope, allow Western readers to see the world through his eyes as they read his sometimes acerbic, and often funny, observations. Nivedita's later response to India provides, in turn, a unique perspective on spirituality, culture, and identity. At first glance, her earnest character should have predisposed her to Western platitudes about Indian inferiority and reinforced in her a desire to "uplift the natives." But instead, she became a sophisticated anti-imperialist, her views informed by many up-to-date sociological, scientific, and economic trends; she was even eager to defend what was indefensible in the West and explain the past immolation of Hindu widows as a form of radical sacrifice. In doing so, she embraced ideas that sometimes shocked, and even appalled, her educated Calcutta associates. The comparison between them will lay out how, as outsiders, both she and Vivekananda developed original, if sometimes contradictory and troubling, understandings.

◆　◆　◆

Although these three people provide the book's shape and direction, there are many others, of both East and West, who appear—hence their inclusion in the Dramatis Personae at the end of this book so that Western readers may keep track of the unfamiliar Indians, and Indian readers of the many unknown Westerners. In traveling to Hollywood, San Francisco, Thousand Island, Green Acre, St. Louis, Calcutta, Delhi, and Belur, I have conversed with the Ramakrishna monks and nuns—both Indian and Western—as well as lay helpers, devotees, and archivists; and have used sacred texts, newspapers, biographies, speeches, memoirs, reminiscences, and especially letters.

The variety of documents has made me think anew about texts. Ramakrishna never wrote about himself. We have only secondhand retrospective accounts which, as others have explained, are not always easy to interpret.[36] I also consulted many spiritual biographies and pious works of the Ramakrishna Mission that many secular historians have eschewed. These studies are crammed with important detail and chronology, even if one disagrees with the encompassing spiritual message they seek to convey. Because they prize the emotional and human dimensions of this story, they offer details of spiritual trials, family antagonisms, and institutional conflict. Their approach is not necessarily detrimental to historical interpretation, but rather can provide a gateway into discussions of devotional practices, mysticism, and forms of sanctity essential for probing a religious culture.

Equally difficult but fascinating are the reminiscences of people who knew Vivekananda or were his disciples. Many have a triumphal quality, as they share their views on him from the perspective of his later renown. At one moment, they seem predictably adulatory, but in the next, startling in offering impressions outside of hagiographical conventions. They drop important hints about how Vivekananda adapted his ideas and practices—especially about spiritual direction—in different contexts.

My main source, however, remains letters and, although I acknowledge their capacity for self-invention, I see them above all as creations central to relationships-in-the-making. They often reveal aspects of personality that published works obscure: Vivekananda was both funnier and harsher in his letters than in his public pronouncements, whereas Nivedita's account in her correspondence—later idealized in *The Master as I Saw Him* (1910)—is sometimes so emotionally raw that it feels almost intrusive to read. They are highly fashioned but also provide details of daily existence and anxieties that illuminate the nitty-gritty of life away from home, information essential to a study of cross-cultural spirituality and politics. Many have been in print for years, but have been used mainly to fix chronology, illustrate character and ideas, but not as the conceptual basis of historical study. By using them as an interpretive tool, I hope to break down the dualism between thought and feeling that so complicates any enquiry that treats spirituality as a worthy subject of analysis.

As I will show, Vivekananda's Western interventions as well as his anti-imperialism in India derived from a theology that was shaped by personal experience, even though it also prioritized the most intellectually prestigious tradition within Indian religion, Advaita Vedanta. This monistic school built on Upanishadic teachings that emphasized the underlying unity of all being.[37] In the West, Vivekananda conveyed this cardinal precept through such terms as the "realization of the self" and "consciousness of God," which he regarded as two sides of the same coin. He thus championed forms of spirituality that sought to challenge the monotheistic, and in this case, Christian view of a God as distinct from humanity and his creation.

To make himself understood in different contexts, he deployed key bridging concepts, especially the notion of "experience," a word that contemporaries endlessly employed to denote a shift away from dry intellect and philological exegesis to forms of understanding that connected individuals to the divine. Experience was important not just to Vivekananda and Nivedita, but to visionaries and monks, authors and actors, politicians, and theologians as well as the ordinary men and women drawn to his teachings. Its centrality can be gauged by the way the illiterate Ramakrishna prioritized his mystical experiences over sacred texts; and how William James emphasized it in his groundbreaking *The Varieties of Religious Experience* (1902), a cardinal book in the study of comparative religion and psychology.

By emphasizing experience, all underscored subjective understanding and their inner worlds, the joys as much as the ordeals.

The paradox of "self" and "nonself" that Advaita Vedanta explored was translated through the "experience" that both Vivekananda and James constantly, and imprecisely, evoked. Advaita had a long and venerated metaphysical pedigree in India before Vivekananda reworked it by linking it to a form of detached worldly activism. James, among many other Western spiritual investigators, also began to emphasize a vision of selfhood that explored mystical experience.[38] In both the East and West, they posited the "subject" not as a free-willed agent (of a Cartesian cogito), but one that recognized that "experience" signified possibilities beyond the world of objects and rational deduction. This intuition may explain, moreover, why feminine experience was often central to apprehending what was deemed beyond the "masculinized" domain of reason—hence James's recourse to female mediums and Vivekananda's acknowledgment of women's spiritual power.

However, I will also use the notion of experience in a more quotidian manner. New forms of intercourse, communication, and travel changed "experience." For example, Vivekananda's evolving perception of India owed much to his youthful pilgrimages to the sacred sites of gods and goddesses, but those same journeys were changed when he went by rail. Trains and ocean liners brought the ideas that confounded North American women with ideas about God that diverged from their childhood Christianity and exposed them to the first reasoned cases against imperialism and their own civilization. Educated Indians who had forsworn Shakti worship (practices involving worship of the Mother goddess) as primitive in the face of British contempt, were now confronted by Margaret Noble, a European woman, who traveled to Calcutta and lectured on the majesty of the cults they were abandoning. Such examples show how East and West—in a way not dissimilar to the paradox of Advaita—could seem to cancel each other out into an apparent unity.

Vivekananda linked self and nonself to other kinds of inarticulate and embodied experience. Ramakrishna's body was often the wellspring of his profoundest discoveries, its sensations and malleability a source of both spiritual delight and mystical agony, his apparent loss of bodily boundaries deemed crucial to his union with the divine. Both public and private remarks about Vivekananda stressed his physical presence, beauty, and manner. He cultivated a masculinity that his Western audience perceived as "authentic," a surprising judgment given that he felt the need to appear publicly in turban and scarlet coat to project a novel image of a cerebral, but also unfamiliar, spiritual teacher. Vivekananda was chronically ill for much of his adult life, and so his body also intruded on his spiritual mission; to him and to those (female) acolytes who sought to ease his pain, debates over healing and spiritual therapies were not mere abstractions. His sicknesses—and theirs—involved them in exchanges of mutual solicitude. Moreover, his observation of bodily habits while abroad was vital to the way he introduced yoga to the West, a discipline designed to introduce suppleness to what he considered the dry and brittle bodies (and minds) of his Western acquaintances.

The paradox of self and nonself emerged in discussion of the guru-disciple relationship. Western devotees responded variously to his spiritual direction, but some felt uncomfortable with the need to surrender the ego and the separateness that they saw as integral to their individuality. But rather than desisting, Vivekananda was forthright in claiming a spiritual authority that inverted colonial hierarchies to guide and instruct them. These interactions concentrated on the opposition between surrender and mastery also reified the new possibilities in play for Indian activists in devising anticolonial politics.[39]

I also focus on science and religion, with Vivekananda's interventions suggesting how this debate was hardly limited to Europe and America but also involved important South Asian participants and audiences.[40] Psychology and anthropology emerged through forms of encounter in the nineteenth century, be they with psychoanalysts, physicians, and healers treating their generally female patients; ethnologists studying colonial "natives"; sociologists observing urban, working-class "savages" in European cities; and orientalists examining Eastern languages and texts.[41] Much of this work, however, has focused on making others, on processes of distancing and objectification key to understanding relations of power.[42]

In looking at Vivekananda's world, I highlight instead the evanescent sense of drawing closer that such exchanges could also produce, while also exploring the disappointments when hope evaporated. In doing so, I use psychology and anthropology, the very disciplines whose history I am simultaneously exploring. This observation is a disclaimer as much as a profession of faith, and an implicit assertion of the vital continuities between past and present. It is also a way of approaching intellectual history differently. Hence, it concentrates on the healing rapport in psychology; the relations between art history, national symbolism, and anthropology; the history of bioscience and physics in relation to human holism; and the importance of Indian thought to debates over science and religion in the fin de siècle. Not surprisingly, such topics mean that path breakers—William James, sociologist Patrick Geddes, physicist Jagadish Chandra Bose, Rabindranath Tagore, and art historian Okakura Kakuzo—appear in these pages, and the list of men reveals how extraordinary Margaret Noble was in becoming a key female figure in debates over science, spirituality, economics, aesthetics, and politics.

Both she and Vivekananda show how gender must loom large at each level of the analysis. European dominance was predicated on the supposed need for "masculine" tutelage of a "femininized" India, and so Vivekananda famously propagated a gospel of "man-making" as vital for Indian nationalism. Nivedita became a worshipper of Kali and linked the sacrificialism of this devotion to what she called "aggressive Hinduism." Forms of maternal spirituality are central to Hindu Universalism, which, in turn, is inexplicable except against the backdrop of the global feminization of religion.

But by far, the most important "experience" lay in the way imperialism, race prejudice, and gender hierarchies impinged on every aspect of life. Because Indian indentured labor was commonplace in many parts of the British Empire but not in America, the United States allowed Vivekananda to dissociate himself from this humiliated population.[43] Nevertheless, he could not check into hotels in the American South and needed his female devotees to protect him against assaults on the street. In Britain, he was at first entranced by the English appreciation of Indian culture, but later worried that, by cooking for friends in London, he might be seen as just another brown underling. If Nivedita saw Vivekananda as occasionally harsh, he, in contrast, was vigilant against attempts by his American "mothers" to patronize and direct him. Aggression and defensiveness on both sides could not be avoided; such "experience" was vital to people's outlooks and, especially in Nivedita's case, important to their later political hardening in India.

Finally, the title of this book is deliberately ambiguous. Of course, it refers to Vivekananda, though he never described himself in this way. He was hardly the first Indian teacher to travel west, but he was unusual in his impact and global reputation. It also suggests Nivedita's equally ambitious plan to "make men" and transform the world. Both were synthesizers, but she attempted to enlarge Vivekananda's vision for a new generation, an achievement obscured by the fact that she was both a woman and an outsider. She readily allowed Indians to take the lead, which they did with growing frequency, power, and radicalism. But Vivekananda suggested that India itself was the world's teacher, the "mother of spirituality," which had lessons not only for the materialistic West but for emerging Asian nations as well, especially Japan.

Becoming the world's guru thus entailed a political as well as spiritual message, one that promised much but was also perilous. For disciples who judge their teachers as being intent on maintaining submission rather than encouraging self-realization, the guru-disciple relationship may be devastating; while a vision of India itself as the "guru to the world" may at times contain a dangerous model for Indian politics, catering to views of intrinsic spiritual superiority. Above all, however, I hope that this book will help readers understand that India's turbulent transformation through imperialism also entailed the transformation of the western world, even if this impact was only partly realized and very poorly understood. Vivekananda's audacious journey west was a self-conscious attempt to change the direction of influence and re-creation; it should be reconsidered not as power politics alone, but as a personal exploration of the shifting boundaries between ascendency and subordination, fusion and fragmentation.

PART ONE

INDIA

1

EARLIEST DAYS

The surest way to corrupt a youth is to instruct him to hold
in higher esteem those who think alike than those who think
differently.

—Friedrich Nietzsche, *The Dawn of Day*, 1881

◆ ◆ ◆

SWAMI VIVEKANANDA, né Narendranath Datta, was born January 12,
1863, in Calcutta, but our grasp of his early life is hampered by the hagiographical quality of many biographies. He came from the Kayasthas of he-
reditary government officials, a so-called service caste formed around the
thirteenth century; these were largely destined to staff Muslim princely
courts, and valued above all for their language skills.[1] Vivekananda's
father, Vishwanath, an attorney in the Calcutta High Court, was fluent in
Persian and hence epitomized the talents of the Kayasthas' upper echelons,
who came to prominence under the Mughals for their facility with Persian,
the linguistic glue that bound together people as far away as Ethiopia, Af-
ghanistan, and Arabia. From humble village accountants to Mughal court
readers, the Kayasthas of the higher ranks were proud of the cultural refine-
ments that Persian literature, poetry, and court culture bestowed.[2]

Persian was no longer the lingua franca of India by the time of Vivekananda's birth, but Vishwanath also knew English and could quote the
Bible as readily as he could Persian poets—evidence, for the critical, of an
unwholesome lack of orthodoxy.[3] He was an educated, professional man

and a bon vivant known for his cooking and generosity, characteristics that his son inherited. Given his father, it is not surprising perhaps that Vivekananda also had a talent for cultural mediation. But for upper-caste orthodox Hindus, such gifts did not cancel out the son's origins. In the *Kathamrita,* which claims to recount Ramakrishna's conversations, an unnamed "fat brahmin" wondered how the mystic could waste his time on a Kayastha boy: "'Sir, he's only moderately educated. Why do you get so restless for him?'"[4] The remark ridicules the Brahmin for caring that Vivekananda was not high caste enough, but also suggests the enduring importance of such distinctions. Vivekananda's origins were often misunderstood; when he returned to India, he defended himself against detractors who portrayed him as low caste. "I read . . . that I am called a Shudra [lowcaste] and am challenged as to what right a Shudra has to become a Sannyasin. To which I reply: I trace my descent to . . . the purest of Kshatriyas [warrior caste]."[5] He thus rejected prejudice against Shudras but was determined not to be dismissed as one. In India, even today, he is occasionally described as an upper caste Kshatriya, more easily associated with his apparent "man-making" mission, and conquering persona. In America, moreover, he was often wrongly identified as a Brahmin because of his intellectual prowess, eloquence, and demeanor.

Despite professional success, Vishwanath was a subordinate in the extended household in which Vivekananda's uncle was the patriarch, while his wife, Bhunvaneshwari Devi, was of second rank in the extended family hierarchy.[6] She is eulogized as belonging to the "old tradition of Hindu womanhood," and Vivekananda is said to have remembered her piety, storytelling, and devotion to housewifely duty.[7] She was literate and intelligent, and also known for her regal bearing and beauty. She had three sons and four daughters, two of whom the family lost when still young, and some of whom will appear intermittently in this story. When she became pregnant for the sixth time, she was said to have "observed religious vows, fasted, and prayed, so that she might be blessed with a son" and asked a relative living in Varanasi to worship at the Atma Vireshwar temple to honor Shiva, the Hindu god of asceticism.[8] Today, Vivekananda's renovated ancestral home has a lingam, a symbol of divine generative power, which marks her devotion to Shiva: "one night she dreamt that this supreme Deity aroused himself from his meditation and agreed to be born as her son. When she awoke she was filled with joy."[9] On January 12, 1863, she gave birth in the open-roofed courtyard, in accordance with contemporary custom. The baby was named Narendranath (or retained the name Vireshwara, depending on the account).[10]

Whatever the factual basis of these divine harbingers, Vivekananda remained devoted to the omniscient yogi who endures austerities on Mount Kailash in Tibet; he reminisced about how as a child of only two, he would play at being a renouncer, "clothed in ashes and *Kaupina* [loincloth]" like the great god.[11] And he told his disciple Sister Nivedita (Margaret Noble) that, as a child, his family even believed that he had lived in Tibet with the great god, but was now banished from Shiva's presence for a time.[12] Shiva's power was invested as much in this god's uncultivated wildness, as in his capacity to slay demons.[13] Vivekananda's mother's invocation hinted therefore at both his future vocation as a renouncer, and his turbulent nature. All the tales stress how, as a child, he mixed gentleness with tempestuousness, and mention that his tantrums could leave broken furniture in their wake.[14] It is said that Bhunvaneshwari had to "put his head under the cold-water tap, repeating Shiva's name, which apparently always produced the desired effect."[15] Throughout his life, Vivekananda called on Shiva—as his mother had—both when meditating and when angry. His poem "Shiva in Ecstasy" suggests his identification with the god's destructive power:

> Shiva is dancing, lost in the ecstasy of Self, sounding his own
>   cheeks.
> His tabor is playing and the garland of skulls is swinging in
>   rhythm.
> The waters of the Ganga are roaring among his matted locks.
> The great trident is vomiting fire, and the moon on his forehead is
>   fiercely flaming.[16]

Americans later also witnessed this wildness when Vivekananda erupted in the summer of 1893 in Massachusetts. He had just described India's English rulers as vampires, who "suck[ed] the last drop of our blood for their own pleasures."[17] He then "cast his eyes up to the roof and repeated softly, 'Shiva! Shiva!' and the little company, shaken and disturbed by the current of powerful feelings and vindictive passion which seemed to be flowing like molten lava beneath the silent surface of this strange being, broke up, perturbed."[18]

Nor was Vivekananda above claiming Shiva's yogic powers, though he was skeptical of occult pretensions—both abroad and in India—and often distanced himself from such "degraded" beliefs.[19] When trying to fall asleep, the young Vivekananda "would see between his eyebrows a ball of light of changing colours, which would slowly expand and at last burst, bathing his whole body in a white radiance."[20] Sometimes, he claimed he had known places and people before being acquainted with them, and could describe the interior of a house before visiting it: "Later he concluded that before his birth he must have had previsions of the people, places, and events that he was to experience in his present incarnation; that was why, he thought, he could recognize them as soon as they presented themselves to him."[21]

Years later, he explained to Westerners how karma governed individuals; how thoughts, impressions, and actions in previous lives touched the future. He claimed, too, that as a more "knowing man," able to look beyond the illusion of quotidian reality, he could discern the effects of karma in his present existence.[22] He was thus unruffled by Western psychic and telepathic phenomena, but rather bemused by what he considered to be the spiritually infantile interpretations placed on them by his American hosts.

*   *   *

If such hagiographical accounts suggest a young person devoted to spiritual reflection, the reality was different: "From my boyhood I have been a dare-devil; otherwise could I have attempted to make a tour round the world, almost without a penny in my pocket?"[23] Vivekananda grew up in a boisterous extended household where there were children of many ages. Episodes that presage later qualities abound, with one biographer claiming he was a natural leader at school: when playing "'King of the Court,' he would assume the role of the monarch and assign to his friends the parts of the ministers, commander-in-chief, and other state officials."[24] Such works maintain that he loved the outdoors, founded a gymnasium, and "took lessons in fencing, wrestling, rowing and other manly sports."[25] He was naturally athletic, with considerable physical presence. Sports later became central to the creed of the "Gita" and the "biceps" that he would intermittently espouse and promote among young Indians in his last years.[26] But in the early 1890s, physical prowess and spiritual patriotism were not yet firmly linked; rather, it was clear only that the muscled and intermittently portly Vivekananda was different from the hollow-cheeked ascetic beloved of imperial ethnography.[27]

Accounts of his character were shaped to highlight a combination of courage, practicality, and solicitude. Another story tells how, in setting up a heavy trapeze in a gymnasium, he asked a passing British sailor to help him. The contraption collapsed and the sailor was knocked unconscious. While everyone else ran away, Vivekananda stayed to bind the wound and revive the man, and then spent a week nursing him back to health. He apparently saved his theosophist friend Miss Müller from a raging bull when his British companions fled.[28]

He was also deemed to have both practical and artistic talent, building an imitation gas works and a factory for aerating water, innovations that had recently arrived in Calcutta; such projects hinted at his later interest in applied science, engineering, and innovation. He founded an amateur theatrical company at home, although it is not known what plays he produced before his uncle apparently destroyed the stage.[29] Clearly, while in the West, he had an aptitude for performing in public and even appeared in costume, either in an orange turban and scarlet robe, or in a more sober, almost clerical, black coat. He became a proficient musician and poet—talents central to his bond with both Ramakrishna and his American devotees, who were surprised by his quickness: in the summer of 1899, while staying in Upstate New York, Vivekananda became skilled in drawing after a few lessons from the society painter Maud Stumm.[30]

He was also said to have a "brilliant and energetic mind."[31] Again, it is unclear precisely how true these later stories are, but "before he reached the age of five, he could recite all the aphorisms of Sanskrit grammar" and had memorized an "entire musical composition of the *Ramayana*" by the age of six.[32] Nor was he modest about his abilities. He is reported as saying, "Just two or three days before the entrance examination I found that I hardly knew anything of geometry. So I began to study the subject, keeping awake the whole night, and in twenty-four hours I mastered the four books of Geometry."[33] His memory was compared to that of a *shrutidhar*, someone able to remember everything after only one hearing, and was an aspect of the aura of almost supernatural ability that came to surround him.[34]

There were many tales of his prodigiousness. Even as a child, his meditation was said to have been undisturbed when a cobra showed its hood.[35] At fifteen, he experienced his first ecstasy when journeying to Raipur through a narrow pass in a cart; the beauty of the landscape stunned him into unconsciousness.[36] He also said to have become increasingly serious in his intellectual pursuits, reading not only sacred Hindu texts, but also Mill, Descartes, Hume, Bentham, Spinoza, Darwin, Comte, Spencer, Fichte, Hegel, Schopenhauer, and Hamilton.[37] These authors reveal a heady eclecticism but were later deployed to assert the lack of originality in Western thought. He wrote in 1894, for example, that "Hindus were Spinozists 2,000 years before the birth of Spinoza," insisting that the philosopher's critique of Cartesian mind-body dualism had been pioneered in India.[38] He often took the same line with evolutionary theory, and later when he became familiar with Hegel, Kant, and Schopenhauer. He also loved poetry and knew Milton by heart. Certainly, Vivekananda's intellectual range went far beyond anything that Ramakrishna, yet to be encountered, possessed.[39]

· · ·

Vivekananda grew up in Calcutta, an imperial city even older than many of the New England towns—also founded by settlers of the British Empire—that he later visited on the other side of the globe. Stretching along the east bank of the Hooghly River, Calcutta was created when the Nawab of Bengal granted the East India Company a trading license in 1690; it became an important trading post, with British military, commercial, and administrative activities focused on the massive Fort William. By 1800, the city blended old and new; its riverside villages continued under the patronage of local families, while the City of Palaces housed rich Indian zamindars (landowners) and merchants. Cosmopolitan from the outset, Calcutta became the capital of British India, with enclaves of Muslims, Armenians, Jews, Christian, Jains, Parsis, Marwaris, and Hindus.[40] By the time of Vivekananda's youth, its large thoroughfares were dominated by recently constructed neoclassical and neo-Gothic British edifices. For its Indian inhabitants, Calcutta had none of the venerable associations of Lucknow or Varanasi, though its elite intellectuals created a forceful cultural pedigree in the nineteenth century. Its famous novelists or memoirists did not, however, create a mystique of modernity, despite a cityscape increasingly crowded with mercantile and government offices.[41]

Still, the looming foreign presence meant that Vivekananda could learn a lot about Western ideas and British associational life without needing to travel; when he first visited New England, he would be surprised, even shocked, by its dour provincialism and narrowmindedness in comparison to his hometown.[42] When his father prodded him to join the Freemason Anchor and Hope Lodge near Park Street—the first to accept Indians—he encountered its peculiar blend of esotericism, fraternal association, theism, and philanthropy in an organization famed for its global networks.[43] We can only wonder whether his masonic network was important in helping him contact elite Indians (especially the princes), when traveling around India.

Calcutta also supplied cultural amusements, including museums, musical events, and theater. Moreover, he was *au fait* with the intellectuals, reformers, literati, and scientists who met in the literary circles and discussion groups dotted around the city and its environs. The list includes Calcutta "superstars," such as reformers Raja Ram Mohun Roy (1772–1833) and Keshub Chunder Sen (1838–1884); novelist and polemicist Bankim Chandra Chattopadhyay (1838–1894); polymath and Sanskritist Ishwar Chandra Vidyasagar (1820–1891); and the Tagores, who all impinge on Vivekananda's story. Vivekananda seems to belong naturally in this group, but he was also notable for breaking away from his Bengali homeland to create pan-Indian and international institutions.[44]

For decades, such luminaries have been associated with the "Bengali renaissance," which underpinned a critique of Indian "backwardness."[45] The term "renaissance" seeks to capture these Indians' striking achievements, but also disconcertingly prioritizes the aspects of their thinking that confirm a progressive (in other words, seemingly Western) vision of Indian culture. It has also distracted historians from the social and economic disarray increasingly afflicting the wider Indian population. Vivekananda was certainly a legatee of this "awakening," but he was also a casualty of growing immiseration. As will be seen, his early adulthood was altered forever by reverses of fortune that became much more common, even in this educated and privileged stratum.

Despite the cultural effervescence, Calcuttans did not see their own time as one of rebirth. In fact, the city was often traduced as degraded or "primitive," with Vivekananda's brother Mahendranath among the many who bewailed its drunkenness, deceit, and even spiritual savagery.[46] Rather than feeling pride in the fifteenth-century origins of the Kalighat Kali Temple, for example, "enlightened" Hindus tended to regard the animal sacrifices conducted there as proof of spiritual decline. Indeed, Kalighat was held to typify the "Kali-yuga," the current epoch of degenerate ideas and base instincts.[47]

The British agreed wholeheartedly, pointing to the worship of Kali—the goddess of death and destruction as well as time—as evidence of the worst evils of Hindu idolatry and heathenism.

❖ ❖ ❖

Vivekananda's parents wanted Vivekananda to have the most advanced education possible. They therefore enrolled him at the Metropolitan Institution in 1871, recently founded by Ishwar Chandra Vidyasagar as one of the first private and secular schools in India staffed by Indians. Vidyasagar has been called India's Erasmus, a title that tries to express to Westerners his broad learning and significance.[48] But despite these promising beginnings, Vivekananda's early education was disrupted. After a two-year hiatus that lasted until 1880 when he lived with his family in Raipur, he went for a short time to Presidency, the city's premier school, then moved a year later to the General Assembly Institution (now known as the Scottish Church College), the oldest liberal arts and sciences college in India.

This connection underscores the significance of Christianity in Vivekananda's development. Founded in 1830 by Alexander Duff, the first Church of Scotland missionary in India, the school offered English instruction, including lessons from the Bible.[49] Duff was a major figure in the endless debates concerning "native" education. Even though Western orientalists sang the praises of Indian poets and dramatists (particularly the classical poet Kalidasa, one of Vivekananda's favorites) the British proscribed such works as too "exotic," "romantic," and "erotic" for Indian youth.[50] In contrast to the secular curriculum prescribed in the government institutions, Duff's church school emphasized Christian scripture; there, both Duff and his successor, the Reverend William Hastie (Vivekananda's teacher), prioritized English romantic poetry; they believed such readings would enlarge the virtuous and sentimental imaginings of young Indians and ready them for an appreciation of the Bible.[51] In touching the heart and not the head, such verse was crucial. But along with these lessons, Vivekananda's move to the General Assembly Institution meant that he was also confronted by the full force of Calvinist ideas of sin, duty, and hellfire, an early training that may explain his later distaste for certain aspects of Protestant theology.

He was thus formed in institutions that underscored these young men's status, but that also asserted Christian and British culture over Indian traditions. Vivekananda became culturally ambidextrous, gaining a facility with the English language that would impress Westerners with his fluency, literary reference, and endless wordplay. His experience also turned him into an unwilling expert in comparative religion: when he went to the West, he knew the Gospels as well as did many a Christian. This knowledge certainly empowered him in debate and dazzled his audiences; and yet, we can only imagine how the mounting pressure of this internal dialogue may have contributed at moments to resentment. His grasp of English literature contributed to his aura of intellectual refinement among his Western acolytes, but also underscored the power of British cultural hegemony.

Of equal significance, however, was Brahmoism, a reform movement that shaped some of the greatest figures in the Bengali elite, and which had generated its own variation of "Hindu Universalism." By the time he met Ramakrishna in 1881, Vivekananda was the outspoken product of three generations of Brahmo ideas and spiritual questioning. However, its early founders had so stripped Brahmoism of much Hindu thought and practice that opponents did not regard it as Hinduism at all. Certainly, Brahmoism abandoned caste, but it also dispensed with the images and Puranic tales that were integral to popular worship, and therefore retained an intellectual and exclusive aura. Roy's vision of Hindu Universalism was one of "subtraction," a means of disposing of what was "false" and "superfluous"; hence his *Religious Universalism* (1829) drew mainly on Hindu examples.[52]

By becoming a Brahmo, Vivekananda rejected polytheism, image worship, divine incarnation, and the guru cults of contemporary Indian spirituality. Indeed, because of his apparent skepticism, he seemed destined to enter and then stay in its ranks. Brahmoism would not have precluded Vivekananda from becoming much like his father, a householder and maybe a legal advocate, but perhaps with greater intellectual and political drive. For our purposes, this movement's significance lies in the way Vivekananda came to Ramakrishna as a young man deeply marked by its teachings and outlook.

Like other Calcutta youths, he was indebted to the "father of modern India," Raja Ram Mohun Roy; Roy remained a hero for him, and when Vivekananda taught his American disciples in the summer of 1895, he lauded the "great Hindu reformer" for his "unselfish work," and devotion to India.[53]

The founder of the Brahma Sabha [Assembly of God], Roy had condemned both Hindu polytheism and Christian Trinitarianism in the early

1.1. Raja Ram Mohun Roy, 1833

part of the nineteenth century and argued for a "purification" of the subcontinent's traditions.[54] His great erudition (Roy knew Arabic, Persian, Sanskrit, Bengali, and English) enabled him to engage with Muslim monotheism, while also poking fun at the conceits of both Hinduism and Islam. He unusually joined critical theology to the managing of religious difference through ethical reasoning, and later learned Hebrew to combat Christian missionaries.[55] In his Bengali writings, he emphasized a single all-pervading Lord from the Upanishads, the ancient Sanskrit texts.[56] While this view of God also existed in the Tantras and the Puranas—the large body of Hindu myth and legend—Roy rejected these as corrupted accretions, and focused instead on the last and, in his view, highest stage of Vedic antiquity in a hoped-for return to origins. He also repudiated *avataras* (incarnations of a deity), integral to the stories of Hindu gods (and Ramakrishna's life); and condemned Bengali image worship, seeking to sweep away the devotions to Kali, Krishna, Rama, and Durga that animated the festivals and temples of the region.[57] Once again, however, such views did not entail abandoning spiritual devotion, but rather aimed to transform it.

Like many educated Indians, Roy welcomed the British, and hoped they would root out the abuses of Mughal rule.[58] His trajectory exemplified the wideranging interests of Bengali intellectuals, though many of his positions have been inappropriately confined within anachronistic and Eurocentric labels, such as "cosmopolitanism, Anglophilia . . . proto-nationalism; neo-Hinduism, ecumenicism, or proto-secularism," to name only a few.[59] Although Roy held many liberal views, he was hardly "liberal" in the modern sense, but rather styled himself as an *ancien régime* raja, with title, turban, and palatial lifestyle, complete with courtiers and disciples. He created an entourage of devoted and influential followers and drew as much, if not more, from Indian traditions as from European ones. All too often, however, his religious ideas have been reduced primarily to a reaction to Christianity's critique of Hinduism.

For Vivekananda, Roy was more than some Western-styled Enlightenment deist, but an Indian "father." He applauded Roy's understanding of Vedanta and of Islam, his cosmopolitanism, and refusal to be intimidated by Western learning, positions that Vivekananda sought to live up to.[60] He also agreed with aspects of Roy's anti-Brahminism, when he rejected the spiritual prerogatives that Hindu priests kept for themselves.[61] Like Roy, he urged everyone to seek "God knowledge," a spiritual ideal that Vivekananda would enlarge and universalize.[62] And Vivekananda paid homage to Roy's pioneering campaign against *sati*, whereby widows were burned on the funeral pyre of their husbands, a stand that brought Roy to international attention.[63]

Like many of Brahmo contemporaries, Vivekananda also wanted to remove "the incrustations of the ages," but what this undertaking entailed shifted constantly.[64] Certainly, Brahmoism created new kinds of family and personal tension. Parents felt betrayed when their sons left the orthodox fold, sometimes even to the point of disinheriting them.[65] Beloved childhood rituals, collective festivals, and household gods associated with family tradition were often cast aside. Even for many of those dedicated to reform, Roy's prescriptions proved too austere and distant and inevitably became tied up with a defense of Indian society and its beliefs. With time, Brahmos answered Christian critiques more forcefully and became less willing to accept missionary characterizations of Hindu culture.

Vivekananda knew Debendranath Tagore, the father of Nobel Prize-winning poet Rabindranath, and leader of the Brahmo Sabha.[66] Debendranath's importance and longevity—he died in 1905 at the age of eighty-seven—meant that Vivekananda even made a courtesy visit in 1898 to the Brahmo scion.[67] Debendranath shared Roy's dislike of "idolatry," but stressed facets of Hinduism that focused on an awed appreciation of God's creation and began a sustained study of the Upanishads.[68] He rejected the Advaitic monism that merged the atman (soul) and Brahman (absolute) and instead described a God who offered divine care to all his creation through "such firm laws that the world can never be destroyed by their change."[69] He inspired the young Vivekananda, who later described how he had "practised meditation with a few friends according to the instruction of Maharishi Devendranath."[70] In particular, Vivekananda responded to the way the maharishi had rearticulated the importance of spiritual wonder and scriptural antiquity, views that Vivekananda never abandoned.

Debendranath was also unafraid to reconsider Hindu social prescriptions and discuss their spiritual intent. For example, in his Brahmo-Dharma (1848), he attempted to codify a rejuvenated theology to combat the evangelism of such Christians as Alexander Duff by discussing topics that ranged from marriage and funeral rites to dietary restrictions and wifely conduct.[71] However, he and other Brahmos also engaged seriously with Western science, ideas that fed into their theology. Despite his veneration of the Upanishads, for example, Debendranath knew their contradictions and argued against any fundamentalist acceptance of sacred texts. Thus, while the pressure of Christian missions may well have prompted revisions, he clearly continued to work "within the Hindu fold."[72] Vivekananda adopted a similar stance when criticizing Biblical literalism, citing both science and historical philology against Christian "dogmatism" and "fanaticism."[73]

Debendranath's importance, moreover, was reinforced by the impact he had on a young disciple, Keshub Chunder Sen, another product of the elite Hindu College (known as Presidency after 1855), and the most prominent—and controversial—Brahmo during Vivekananda's coming of age. Sen had scandalized middle-class opinion when he refused to be initiated by his Brahmin father's guru and instead accompanied his "new father," Debendranath, on a prohibited sea voyage to Ceylon.[74] Sen's life became very public, his course—at least for a time—illustrious. He met Queen Victoria and breakfasted with William Gladstone on a journey to Britain in 1870, thus continuing the Brahmo tradition of traveling that had made Roy so well known.[75] Sen was, moreover, famous for his efforts to educate women and the poor, organize relief, and oppose child marriage; as a skilled orator, he spoke eloquently to both English and Indian audiences.[76]

While Roy wore his raja's turban, and Debendranath withdrew for a time to the Himalayas, Sen, according to his Brahmo biographer Protap Chunder Mozoomdar, was moralistic, and "his religion . . . [as] stern, stoical, and colourless [as] his morality."[77] For the first time, therefore, a Brahmo leader adopted a personal style that may have appeared more Protestant Christian than Hindu, at least for a while. Sen disconcertingly fell into prayer without warning and was deeply influenced by Christian ideas of sin—notions which may have contributed to the depression he suffered at the Hindu College. He turned later to Unitarianism, and particularly Theodore Parker, an American Unitarian and transcendentalist. Vivekananda's brother Bhupendranath wrote disapprovingly of the unaccustomed "puritanism" that Sen brought to Calcutta with a branch of the Band of Hope, an organization that opposed tobacco and alcohol, and which may even have attracted Vivekananda to some of its meetings.[78] Sen also daringly broke with Debendranath in 1865 over Christian practices (the maharishi deplored them, whereas Sen thought them necessary to enliven Indian spirituality) to create the Adi Brahmo Samaj. Nor was this the only innovation he favored, as he implored his new ministers, often Brahmins, to cast aside their sacred thread (the mark of their distinction) and encouraged intercaste marriages.[79]

However, after his journey to Britain, Sen began a spiritual and intellectual journey that seemed to go into reverse, a trajectory that, as a young Brahmo, Vivekananda was well placed to observe.[80] Sen fell increasingly "out of love" with Britain—no longer believing in liberalism's promise and having been appalled by the poverty he had seen there.[81] But the imprint of British culture could not be so easily effaced. When Sen founded the Bharat Ashram, a kind of communal boardinghouse, he imposed an English work ethic and domestic orderliness on the twenty-five families that shared his collective "spiritual trial."[82] At the same time, however, he promoted Hindu asceticism and posed for photographs on a tiger mat with the single-stringed *ektara*, an instrument that exemplified traditions of "primitive simplicity."[83] He also fostered Brahmo street processions, recasting Vaishnava traditions of collective hymn singing, often intense devotional displays that honored the Hindu deity Vishnu. After March 1875 and a visit from Ramakrishna, Sen increasingly referred to "madness," "primitive

1.2. Keshub Chundra Sen with his disciples and *ektara*

faith," and "inspiration" to explain his search, words that evoked Ramakrishna's now-famous spiritual trials. Indeed, through his publications, Sen was responsible for eulogizing Ramakrishna as a saint, publicity that drew such curiosity-seekers as Vivekananda to a new temple north of Calcutta in Dakshineswar.[84] As Sen's friendship with Ramakrishna developed, Sen wrote about the mystic in late 1881 and early 1882, explaining that the "venerable Paramahamsa of Dakshineswar is serving as a marvelous connecting link between the Hindus and the Brahmos. . . . What this spiritual fusion and living union may lead to in the end who can divine?"[85]

Despite the talk of union, Sen had once again split the Brahmo movement in 1878, which prompted Vivekananda to join the Sadharan Brahmo Samaj, a splinter group that resisted what was seen as Sen's one-man rule.[86] When Sen's devotees erupted in "tears, and sobs" and fell into "fits of unconsciousness" during mass meetings, the Brahmo leader was criticized for creating a personality cult that betrayed the sedate Brahmoism of previous leaders.[87] Rabindranath Tagore later argued that Sen never understood the sober piety of his father, Debendranath, that Sen had "appropriated the emotional ecstasy that characterized Shakta [worship of the goddess Shakti] and Vaishnava religious traditions."[88] If Debendranath found Sen's growing exaltation objectionable, his response to Ramakrishna's rustic exterior and uncouthness was equally skeptical.[89] In contrast, he approved of Vivekananda, who he thought had the eyes of a yogi—large, slightly bulging—and luminous.[90] This anecdote underscores the continuing tension over "correct" religious style and sensibility.

In the early years of his visits to Ramakrishna, Vivekananda continued to associate with Brahmo friends, an indication of how he tried for a time to straddle both outlooks and perhaps did not even feel at this juncture that they were irreconcilable. He later explained that, while agreeing "on points of social reform" with the men at the Sadharan Brahmo Samaj, he was nevertheless pulled to Ramakrishna by spiritual idealism.[91] Sen's path exemplified how tumultuous the Brahmo journey could be. In little more than two decades, he had experimented with aspects of Unitarianism, the Brahmo Samaj, Debendranath's spiritual tutelage, ashram living, novel devotions, Ramakrishna's mysticism, evangelism, and elements of religious universalism. If Sen thought, however, that his ecstatic displays and the singing of Vaishnava hymns would generate a mass movement, he was wrong. If anything, they isolated him still further; indeed, while Ramakrishna was praised for appearing "authentic," Sen was disparaged for shaving his head and dressing like a mendicant.[92]

Vivekananda always respected aspects of Sen's legacy. After all, like the older man, Vivekananda fought against what he saw as Hinduism's "inertia" and what Sen called the "reign of quietism," in which meditation triumphed over activism.[93] Vivekananda also engaged with science and Darwinism, even if neither accepted that science and religion could be teased apart.[94] He gladly adopted Sen's emphasis on traveling the world and learning about other cultures, which once again reflected Brahmo cosmopolitanism.

This telling of Vivekananda's development, however, suggests an underlying paradox. If Brahmoism was so important in shaping his outlook, then perhaps Ramakrishna's influence was not as great as Vivekananda claimed? Of course, there is no denying the fluidity in these milieus, especially after Sen's encounter with Ramakrishna. However, Sen's spiritual search highlighted the limitations of Brahmoism precisely *because* he could not do without Ramakrishna's experiential spirituality and devotional enthusiasm. Divested of tradition, and seen as lacking authenticity, Sen's growing authoritarianism tended to confine rather than liberate his disciples, his movement becoming little more than a sect with an ashram.

In 1881, Sen created yet another Brahmo offshoot, the New Dispensation (Naba Bidhan), a "church" devoted to religious universalism, with "missionaries" who preached under a banner bearing a crescent, a cross, and a trident—symbols testifying to the unifying truths in Islam, Christianity, and Shaivism [worship of Shiva].[95] In contrast to Ram Mohun Roy's process of taking away what was "false," Sen's vision added unfamiliar realms to Brahmoism.[96] Vivekananda rejected Sen's claims to originality in devising the "religious universalism" of the New Dispensation, remarking that the idea was "stolen" from Ramakrishna. As will be seen, Ramakrishna's view of what it meant was in fact rather different, but Vivekananda's objections suggest his growing disenchantment with a figure who had been important in his youth.[97]

* * *

As with other young men, Brahmoism was no longer enough when Vivekananda finally met Ramakrishna in late 1881. Like him, these men were professionals, mostly educated and usually high-caste or of merchant origin, but despite their status, their families struggled to maintain their economic and social positions. Connected through cultural interests, family ties, schools, and religion, they knew only too well that, despite their hard-won academic success, they were swimming against a powerful tide of British exclusion and imperial privilege.[98]

This is the backdrop to Vivekananda's first encounter with the mystic of Dakshineswar, all related in Swami Saradananda's *Sri Ramakrishna and His Divine Play,* written over twenty years after his death.[99] The account illustrates how entwined these societies were, with Sen, a Scottish missionary, a family member, and a notable householder all given credit for the introduction. One story holds that the Reverend William Hastie, Duff's successor at the General Assembly College, read Wordsworth's poem "The Excursion" with his Indian students, and explained the stanza concerning the poet's "trances" by referring to the ecstasies of a new saint not far away at the Dakshineswar Kali Temple.[100]

This version, which again underscores the importance to Hastie of the English romantics, suggests that he believed Ramakrishna to be an exalted example of contemporary yogic culture. Hastie, it seemed, attempted to "translate" between the two heritages by linking Ramakrishna to Shelley and Wordsworth, whose descriptions of the British landscape were said to recall aspects of rural Bengal.[101] Vivekananda's brother Bhupendranath seconds this story, and suggests that Hastie had probably learned of Ramakrishna through Sen.[102] But the story is odd—Wordsworth's poem does not deal with mysticism per se, but rather with the nature of the self, the passage of time, the relationship between memory and history, and the grief of loss.[103] It signaled more Wordsworth's abandonment of radical politics in favor of introspection, rather than his relations with the supernatural.[104] Moreover, Hastie aimed to convert the young Indians to Christianity with such poetry, not encourage them toward Indian mysticism; he thus seems a strange candidate to appreciate Ramakrishna, who was a Kali worshipper. Indeed, Hastie was famous for his attacks against "heathen idolatry," and in turn was roundly condemned in famous polemical letters by Bankim Chandra Chattopadhyay, the most illustrious Bengali novelist of the day.[105]

If Hastie did not cause them to go to Dakshineswar, then Sen may have done so. This story, as suggested, revealed Ramakrishna's capacity to win over a learned elite. In the third story, lay people also appear—this time Vivekananda's uncle, grieving over the loss of children, who asked Vivekananda to accompany him to Dakshineswar. In this version, Vivekananda did not go as he opposed Kali worship, a tale that suggests how the uncle sought Ramakrishna's spiritual comfort, whereas his nephew remained true to Brahmoist beliefs. Surendra Nath Mitra, a generous householder disciple of Ramakrishna, is often believed to be the obvious candidate responsible for the first encounter. He asked Vivekananda to sing devotional songs at a festivity at his home, which Ramakrishna visited in November 1881.[106] In this tale, music and devotion, rather than doctrine and ritual, connected master and disciple for the first time.

Whatever the circumstances of the meeting, Vivekananda's ultimate decision to visit Ramakrishna suggested the beginnings of a change of heart. Despite his solitary attempts to "see" God (in this period he had meditated and fasted), Vivekananda found himself in a spiritual cul-de-sac. He finally went to Dakshineswar with a friend in December 1881. Although excursions to Ramakrishna now had become almost fashionable, the spark between the two men, at least for Vivekananda, was wholly unexpected. His book-learning, "rationalism," and independent-mindedness proved no defense: he was quickly enchanted by the combination of love, spiritual power, and native intelligence that Ramakrishna demonstrated. The visionary seemed able to help Vivekananda find a way to the mystical immediacy that the young man craved more than anything else, and which he felt he could not find in Calcutta. Vivekananda did not lose his rationalism, but he was about to change direction radically.

2

RAMAKRISHNA

And I have felt
A presence that disturbs me with the joy
Of elevated thoughts; a sense sublime
Of something far more deeply interfused,
Whose dwelling is the light of setting suns,
And the round ocean and the living air,
And the blue sky, and in the mind of man:
A motion and a spirit, that impels
All thinking things, all objects of all thought,
And rolls through all things.

—William Wordsworth, "Tintern Abbey," 1798

◆ ◆ ◆

VIVEKANANDA'S APPRENTICESHIP to Ramakrishna was about recovery and discovery. He learned again about what he had lost through Brahmoism and discovered a new world of mysticism, discipleship, and sensibility from a rare and inventive guru of exceptional charisma. Every "superstition" that Brahmoism had condemned was thus reclaimed, reenchanted, and often reconceived. He confronted Kali worship—the bane of Calcutta's educated elite—the mysteries of tantra, Radha's passion, and the blissful unity of Advaita Vedanta. Rather than teaching the exclusivity of sect, Ramakrishna built on Vedanta by insisting that all spiritual paths led to God, even Islam and Christianity, linked to conquest though these were. He was a different kind of teacher, one who acted like a needy baby yet who also bravely explored primordial Hindu traditions in a way that sent him almost mad.

The story of their relationship reified every cliché about the attraction of opposites—the urban and rural worlds, learnedness and naïveté, abstraction and experientialism, rationality and mystical sensuality.[1] Only by delving into Ramakrishna may we learn what Vivekananda sought to learn and encompass, as well as his deeper, inarticulate longings that belied the contrasts to reveal unexpected spiritual affinities. Vivekananda's relationship to Ramakrishna was the younger man's *experiential* embrace of Advaita, of the unity of opposites that he thereafter sought to explain both at home and in the West.

◆ ◆ ◆

If Vivekananda's childhood was framed by wealth, education, and privilege (despite the British), Ramakrishna's background encompassed loss, illness, and lack of opportunity.[2] Swami Saradananda's *Sri Ramakrishna and His Divine Play* recounts Ramakrishna's early life and the story of rural eviction, penury, and injustice perpetrated against his Brahmin family. And yet, despite dire poverty, this high-caste family still seems to have had laborers to till their tiny plot.[3] Although hagiographical, Saradananda's account never hides Ramakrishna's fragile humanity and his extreme spiritual experimentation; in fact, the work deftly uses his singular vulnerability to deploy a dialectic of naturalistic psychology and miraculous happenings that underpin the claim that Ramakrishna was a man-god, an avatara.[4]

This notion of the avatara, which Brahmoism had also rejected, denotes "divine descent," and perpetuates the connection between the human and divine. For example, Vishnu, the Supreme Being in the Vaishnava tradition, has over twenty avatars in the Bhagavata Puranas, the Sanskrit text devoted to this divinity.[5] Saradananda used these traditions when he recorded portents of Ramakrishna's greatness: his mother, Chandramani, when praying to Shiva, saw a "divine light emanating from the image" of the great Hindu diety and realized she was to give birth to a "Great Soul."[6] His Brahmin father was a devotee of Raghubir, another incarnation of Lord Rama; and when he found a *shaligram,* a fossilized stone that was a reminder of Vishnu, he regarded it as a harbinger of a special child.[7] Ramakrishna's spiritual name was a combination of the two most important Vishnu avatars, Rama, the perfect man—respectful polite, humble—and the hero of the great epic, the Ramayana; and Krishna, the cowherd boy and charming truant who mesmerizes with his flute-playing in the forest of Vrindavan. No Indian would have missed these associations.

But Ramakrishna, who abhorred sects of any kind, was not to belong to any one tradition, an attitude that the *Divine Play* reinforces by highlighting his wide-ranging spiritual inheritance. His home village was at the crossroads of both the Shaivite and Vaishnava pilgrimage routes as well as local divinities, while his family's spiritual proclivities demonstrated an appreciation of different deities. His community was alive with the Puranic tales and Hindu epics, especially in village theater where the boundaries between collective devotion and entertainment were porous.[8]

He was the youngest in a large family, his father in his sixties; his mother, twenty years younger. From infancy, therefore, he was surrounded by adults, and his theology focused on inventiveness, whimsy, and play. Play objects—dolls, kittens, and kites—feature prominently in his talk, and often underlay his most effective aphorisms. Saradananda titled his work *Lilaprasanga* because *lila* encompasses spontaneity, drama, and even sport. It linked Ramakrishna's playfulness to a mysticism that emphasized the connections between the absolute and the world of maya, that illusory existence of everyday life. The word "lila" suggests that everything we believe to be reality is conjured into existence by God's "play," obscuring the true reality that lies beyond, while also underscoring a divine capriciousness that sports with hapless humanity.

Like Vivekananda later, accounts of his youth were searched for signs of prodigiousness—Ramakrishna was said to have had a remarkable memory (associated with gurus who developed mental concentration and yogic gifts), an engaging personality, and artistic talent.[9] Both loved to perform, though the older man was more obviously "artistic," sensual, and concrete in his spirituality.[10] In a manner similar to Vivekananda's initial ecstasy, Ramakrishna was said to have had his first encounter with divine bliss when, quite literally, he was struck unconscious by beauty.[11] This portrayal of this experience has been quoted and requoted around the world:: "I was following a narrow path between the rice fields . . . I saw a great black cloud spreading rapidly. . . . Suddenly at the edge of the cloud a flight of snow-white cranes passed over my head. The contrast was so beautiful that my spirit wandered away."[12]

Saradananda places another trance after the death of the young mystic's father in 1843 and describes it as a creative response to loss amidst the difficulties of supporting a fragile and bereaved mother. Ramakrishna had sought out monks and ascetics and even returned home one day "besmeared with ashes; another day . . . with a mark on his forehead . . . and a loincloth around him."[13] His mother had feared he would follow Shiva's example and leave her. Indeed, his first spiritual vision, according to Saradananda, occurred in 1845, during a festival of Shiva, when he assumed Shiva's guise during a play and "lost outer consciousness."[14] After this incident, he skipped school (he had been briefly educated at the landlord's house) and rejected worldly knowledge; and yet, he showed an uncanny ability to teach abstruse theology to villagers and offered solutions to their problems in simple and compelling language.[15] He became part of the women's world, reading and singing from the Puranas, the writings on Hindu mythology. They believed that baby Krishna lived within him, that his body and spirit held this divine child.

He also put on women's clothing and jewelry and became so like the "aunties" of his village that, when in full costume, onlookers took him for one of them. Nor was this display of femininity held against him. For Bengalis, Ramakrishna was like Radha the milkmaid, Krishna's consort in the forest of Vrindavan, a familiar, venerated Hindu goddess, and still a living presence in Vaishnava liturgy and practice.[16] Indeed, Vivekananda valued this inheritance when he spoke of Ramakrishna as the champion of women.[17]

Other aspects of his story, however, were more unusual and began after his elder brother Ramkumar summoned him to Calcutta. In his search to make a living—made more difficult by Ramakrishna's unwillingness to engage in worldly affairs—Ramkumar turned to Rani Rashmoni, a well-to-do widow. She was the first of many remarkable women in a story replete with such figures. Celebrated for caring nothing about glory—she had resisted authority by fighting against British officialdom to defend the river rights of poor fishermen—Rani Rashmoni's vision and ambition were nevertheless immense.[18] Despite her wealth and philanthropy, however, as a Shudra, a low-caste widow, she was deemed unworthy by Brahmin pandits (scholars) to make food offerings to Kali, her favorite goddess.[19] Ramkumar suggested that a solution could be found if she donated property to a Brahmin for a temple, a gift that would enable high-caste people to take food offerings without "demerit."[20] Prepared by Brahmin priests who cooked and blessed it, such "sacrifices" would feed the deity and then be eaten by worshippers.

When she agreed to these conditions, she displayed a savviness in working around the rigidities of caste privilege while ostensibly adhering to its restrictions. She bought a large piece of land on the Hooghly River at Dakshineswar, building a nine-spired temple in a large courtyard where pilgrims could congregate to catch a glimpse of the goddess.[21] The compound contains not only the Kali Temple but twelve Shiva temples, another to Radha-Krishna, as well as the traditional platform for bathing. When Rashmoni installed the black Kali image on the last day of May 1855, Ramkumar became her chief priest. From the beginning, therefore, Dakshineswar accepted strict adherence to Brahmanical authority, but also found a way to accommodate the spiritual desires of a rich Shudra widow. Ramakrishna thus entered a world that was not only about retrieving an array of religious legacies, but also became one of her dependents.

Ramakrishna initially perceived such patronage as an affront to his dignity and reminded his brother that their Brahmin father had never "officiated for lower castes."[22] Moreover, there were moments when he asserted his spiritual primacy even over Rashmoni: on one occasion, because her "mind was elsewhere," he unashamedly "slapped her twice."[23] Such behavior suggests that, as a Brahmin, he may have felt entitled to discipline, teach, and conduct spiritual experiments in ways unimaginable to others in lower castes. Vivekananda explained in 1896 to audiences in New York and England that, for Ramakrishna, becoming a temple priest meant making "merchandise of sacred things."[24] And yet, such stories also underscored the transformation that Ramakrishna was about to undergo: later lore recounts how he abandoned caste rules by going into the house of a temple sweeper and cleaning it with his hair.[25] No longer was he afraid to "defile" himself, but rather eager to use his body to purify the abode of an "untouchable," the derogatory term used in the nineteenth century to signify those outside of the caste system and called today Dalits.

Part of his duties was to dress Kali, developing an intimacy with the goddess by feeding and clothing her. At Dakshineswar she was splendid like a queen, garbed in a gorgeous Benarasi sari—though otherwise she is usually depicted as semi-naked—and decorated with jewels, bangles, armlets, and tinkling anklets.[26] Believed to erupt from the head of Durga, Kali fights demons and evil. She is Shakti, the power that emerges from the primeval world, responsible for time and hence for the cycle of destruction and creation. She even generates Brahma, Vishnu, and Shiva, the three great deities of the Hindu pantheon. She makes them pass a test to win her as their bride, appearing with a gaunt countenance and fangs. Only Shiva can abide her presence, and so becomes her consort. She cavorts happily in cremation grounds, gets drunk on her victims' blood, and dances like a madwoman.[27]

2.1. Dakshineswar Temple, Calcutta

And so, in many Bengali depictions, she appears with protruding tongue and wild hair, a garland of skulls around her neck and severed hands dangling from her belt.[28] Kali's preference for the polluted cremation grounds symbolizes her distance from ordinary society. But Ramakrishna's devotion combined a recognition of her power with a belief in her maternal solicitude and tenderness, especially in his own case.

2.2. Kali statue,
Dakshineswar
Temple

2.3. Kali and
Shiva, Bengali
illustration,
c. 1885–1890

Saradananda describes the death of Ramakrishna's brother in 1856 as a cruel emotional blow. Indeed, it seems that Ramkumar was not only like another father, but also the unconscious facilitator of his sibling's mysticism, having undertaken the unholy work of creating Dakshineswar with a Shudra widow and servicing, against family tradition, low-caste devotions. After his death, a devastated Ramakrishna is portrayed entering another mystical stage, leaving the temple to meditate naked under a tree in a patch of jungle known as the Panchavati, casting aside his sacred thread, the mark of Brahmin status, as a fetter and "vainglory."[29] The "madness" of spiritual ecstasy that ensued permitted a remarkable freedom, releasing Ramakrishna from social constraint, and permitting him to make barbed remarks about government officials and worthies of all kinds. He later remarked: "I would tell the truth to everybody. I did not care about one's position and was not afraid of men of power."[30]

It is claimed that he immersed himself in mystical creativity for twelve years, when he almost "drown[ed] in ecstasy," thrusting aside "hatred, shame, family status, good conduct, fear, fame, pride of caste and ego."[31] He not only meditated, but also cleaned latrines, ate the leftovers of beggars, and touched excrement with his tongue.[32] So degrading for Brahmins, these trials were designed to "eradicate conceit and ego from his mind" and show that all things were mere "manifestations . . . of the Divine Mother."[33]

Ramakrishna's passion exemplified bhakti (devotion to a deity) mixed with the taboo-breaking practices of tantra, to be discussed later in greater detail. The term is variously used to characterize "love," "homage," and "worship," and in this context, "bhakti" describes both the devotee's passionate reverence and God's attachment to humanity. Ramakrishna's pining to "see" the Mother was an attempt to "behold" the divine, a favor only rarely bestowed on a determined supplicant. Known as *darshan*, such visual contemplation was often deemed essential to spiritual connection and explains why Vivekananda asked Ramakrishna whether he had actually "seen" God.[34] Intent on darshan, Ramakrishna ate little and slept even less. He wept and his chest turned crimson, the blood under the skin pulsating in longing. When his pleas went unanswered, he tried to kill himself with a sword, but he believed Kali saved him when he experienced a sense of "oneness" that brought him to her:[35] "I saw shining waves, one after another, coming towards me to swallow me up. . . ."[36] He then saw the Mother in an ocean of light.

From then on, he experienced the statue as a "living presence," felt her breath when he put his finger under her nostrils and listened to her anklets jingling in the darkness.[37] He prostrated himself with offerings of food and flowers; climbed onto the altar to chuck her under the chin; and talked to her before putting her to bed. His odd behavior brought officials to the temple to stop the scandal, "but when confronted by the master's god-intoxicated form . . . they were stupefied with fright" and did nothing.[38]

Ramakrishna also enacted other incarnations of Vishnu, seeking visions of Rama or Ramachandra, the seventh avatar, who killed Ravana, the demon king of Lanka and the subject of the epic tale told in the Ramayana.[39] In this mystical mood (*bhava*), Saradananda claimed, Ramakrishna became Hanuman, a Hindu deity in the form of a monkey, who devotes his life to aiding Rama's exploits. He tied a loincloth around his waist to have a tail, and moved like a monkey, jumping and eating only fruits and roots. He even urinated from a banyan tree as only a cheeky monkey could.[40]

Such scenes suggest everything that Brahmoism foreswore with disgust. But while some disapproved, others thought his behavior recalled Chaitanya, the late fifteenth-century Bengali saint, another legatee of Vaishnava bhakti and famous for his chant "Hare Krishna" that would later become internationalized in another form of "Hindu Universalism."[41] Chaitanya is seen as the "father" of the many currents of ecstatic religiosity associated with what is called Gaudiya Vaishnavism or even Bengali Vaishnavism.[42] For his devotees, Chaitanya was a golden-hued reincarnation of Krishna, whom Ramakrishna adored especially for embracing everyone, even Dalits; the mystic kept the saint's picture in his room and made a pilgrimage to his birthplace, Nadiya, in 1870.[43] In 1884, he even visited Calcutta's Star Theatre to watch the performance of *Chaitanya Lila*. Ramakrishna was "as happy as a child," going in and out of ecstasy during the performance.[44] Chaitanya's legacy was vital in framing Ramakrishna's experience.[45]

The search for unity with the divine was so intense that sometimes Ramakrishna's bodily boundaries softened, as his pores oozed blood and his joints became so supple that he was purged of a "red-eyed man of black complexion."[46] What remained, Saradananda tells us, was only goodness. He submerged himself in water to stop the burning, while birds nested in his hair during periods of prolonged stillness. He would remember the agony of these searches and the persistence and courage they demanded: "An ordinary man could not have borne a quarter of that tremendous spiritual fervour . . . I could forget my indescribable pangs only by seeing the Mother. . . . Otherwise this body could not have survived. I had no sleep at all . . . My eyes lost the ability to blink. . . . then

2.4. Chaitanya Mahaprabhu: Statue in Mayapur Temple,
West Bengal

at rare intervals my attention would fall on the body . . . I was frightened by its
condition. . . . I would say: 'Let it be as You [Kali-Ma] wish. Let this body go to
pieces, but don't leave me. . . .'"[47]

Ramakrishna was in such a state in 1858 that he was taken to Kamarpukur, his home village in West Bengal, where his mother summoned a
doctor and then an exorcist to relieve him. His visions of Kali returned,
however, when he sought out the jackals in the cremation grounds. His dis-
traught family married him to a six-year-old girl, Sarada Mukhopadhyay,
in the hope that domesticity would ground him. Ramakrishna was twenty-
three at the time. This celibate union, as will be seen, was deemed exemplary
despite the age difference, and would become central to Vivekananda, his
message, and the Ramakrishnan Mission.[48]

Ramakrishna returned to Dakshineswar, which, like his boyhood village,
was awash with many different spiritual tides. Rashmoni's temple attracted
pilgrims of every sort, and Ramakrishna met there the mysterious Bhairavi
Brahmani around 1861, who would become his guru. She not only reassured
him that his visions and ecstasies were not madness, but also taught him

tantra. Adepts believed that these disciplines of transgressive nonconformity freed them from the obligation to observe ordinary morality, and he now turned to this wandering yogini for instruction.[49] In Sanskrit, *tantra* literally means the "warp of reality" and suggests how adepts "stretch" to the limit trials of self-perfection.[50] The "left-handed" path was no orgiastic free-for-all, but rather an arduous discipline, often filled with technical instruction, during which the practitioner took prescribed quantities of "transgressive substances," such as fish, meat, parched grain (a kind of hallucinogen), and alcohol.[51] Under her guidance, Ramakrishna was asked to worship a beautiful (undressed) girl, and then to sit on her lap.[52] In addition, he "heroic[ally]" witnessed the union of a man and a woman, but perceived only the "divine sport of Shiva and Shakti" before going into ecstasy.[53] Saradananda tells us that his purity was such that he only needed to imagine the "horror" of physical intercourse to gain the spiritual prize.[54] He also said his mantra in the temple's garden between the skulls of men and animals, a ceremony that embraced Tantric imaginings of Kali.[55] Vivekananda later largely publicly disowned Tantra (he recognized it was a path only for exceptional aspirants), and later denounced its teachings in India, but he always recognized Ramakrishna's ability to undertake these unusual trials, and commended his tenacity and fearlessness.[56] The trials of tantra seemed to have helped Ramakrishna understand how "the whole world is filled with God alone."[57]

Ramakrishna also linked emotional and transcendent states when he recast the epic storytelling of the Ramayana, and the Mahabharata enacted in the village plays of his youth, again within Vaishnava traditions. Love, these "moods" suggest, was hardly simple, its many manifestations showing how ordinary, even humble, human relations provided searching models for connection with the Divine.[58] He spent his days in altered states of consciousness, dramatizing different forms of reverence; he was thus a subject to a ruler; a servant devoted to a master; engaged in reciprocal love as a friend; lived the love of a parent to a child; and behaved as a maidservant.[59] He contended, for example, that those who cared for children were little more than attendants, as all children belonged to Krishna. Parenthood was an illusion (maya), a prod to detachment precisely because such love generated an overwhelming emotional "lock."

Famously, he also explored the orgiastic connection between Krishna and his consort Radha. The mythology explains that the married Radha begins an illicit love affair with the irresistible youth, experiencing both a life beyond so-

2.5. Ramakrishna

cial norms and the torture of Krishna's infidelity. Ramakrishna thus followed
in the footsteps of Chaitanya, who enacted the Radha state so common in Bengali Vaishnavism, in which the frenzy of ecstasy alternates with the torment of
intermittent parting.[60] Saradananda related that Ramakrishna donned a wig,
wore gold jewelry, and put on "a beautiful and expensive sari from Varanasi"
when this mood overtook him.[61] Even his body began to function as a woman's,
so that every month, drops of blood would ooze from the pores "for three days,
like a woman's monthly cycle." He wore a loincloth so that his clothes would
not be soiled.[62] Such experientialism was necessary to attain the selfless, divine
love of *prema,* deemed far greater than "sexual pleasure."[63] Ramakrishna described how Radha "smel[ed] the sweet fragrance of [Krishna's] body," how she
developed a sexual organ of "ecstatic love."[64] Ramakrishna—who claimed to

abjure sexual thoughts—nevertheless had to resort to the language of the body to approximate his spiritual vision.[65]

He spoke openly about the spiritual possibilities that crossing gender boundaries allowed: "You can change your nature by imitating something . . . if you cultivate a feminine nature, you gradually slay enemies like lust. Then you begin to act just like a woman."[66] Ramakrishna believed he had overcome that part of the "I," or ego, which designated the self as "masculine" or "feminine," his torso thereafter permanently retaining something of the womanliness of Krishna's beloved.

He especially valued the feminine and believed himself to have a feminine nature. The *Divine Play* records a moment when Girish Ghosh, a disciple and actor, asked whether he was a man or a woman. Ramakrishna replied, "I don't know." It was not surprising perhaps that the self-sacrificing goddess of the Ramayana, Sita rather than Rama, luminously appeared before him and merged into his body.[67] Saradananda wondered if perhaps he had "realized the sexless Atman," the soul who knows no difference between man and woman, or whether it was simply that he recognized that he contained both "male and female characteristics."[68]

Almost a quarter of a century ago, Jeffrey Kripal asked whether Ramakrishna's mysticism and spiritual creativity could be better comprehended if they were linked to homoeroticism and / or homosexual desire.[69] As has been seen, aspects of Hindu theology engaged with sexuality but these were unconcerned with "homosexuality."[70] Even if it was not Kripal's intent, for many readers and especially Indians, the interpretation was seen to resonate with the pathological taint of nineteenth-century European sexology; it also, perhaps, risked a certain retrospective "knowingness" about sexual orientation that the historical actors did not themselves perceive or acknowledge. In this regard, the question of Ramakrishna's possible homosexuality remains an empirical cul-de-sac.

In my view, studying Ramakrishna helps us grasp instead the spiritual possibilities of sexual ambiguity and gender fluidity, which the focus on Radha-Krishna in Indian religion has long venerated. Ramakrishna was remarkable precisely because he assumed aspects of maleness or femaleness as his mystical imagination demanded, a rejection of the oppositions that underlined his belief in a universal "self." He consciously refused to be confined or captured by either identity or any single spiritual tendency, as his engagement with Shaktism, Tantra, and Vaishnavism suggest. A careful reading of Vivekananda, moreover, shows that even he played with this "moveable feast," becoming a man or a woman in his imaginings and in his letters.[71]

* * *

Ramakrishna's striking enactment of Radha came at the moment that British missionaries denigrated Vaishnava piety as part of Hinduism's "degeneracy."[72] Vivekananda's distrust of such celebrations was shared by many prominent Bengali families—zamindars, princes of ancient lineages, and even the Tagores—who had once been proud Vaishnavas and had patronized the massive Durga pilgrimages in honor of the Divine Mother before turning to Brahmoism.[73] But their abandonment of this heritage had not eradicated the popular songs and dances to Radha-Krishna central to Bengali culture.[74] Ramakrishna, through his evocation of Chaitanya, both embodied this tradition and became a part of a larger process of recuperation for urban elites, an important reminder of "golden Bengal" and of a cultural heritage, both urban and rural, under attack.[75] This process was also integral to Gaudiya Vaishnaivsm's reformulation which, perhaps ironically, increasingly valued the Bhagavad Gita's august characterization of Krishna as rational counselor over the seductive whimsicality of the cowherd deity who frolics with Radha.[76]

In teaching that "all religions are only different paths," Ramakrishna compared his ideas to the tenderness of a mother who "prepares exactly what they like, exactly what agrees with their stomachs." And as was his wont, he described the individual dishes, that she makes: "Pulao [one-pot rice] with fish for one, fish with sour tamarind for another . . . and fried fish for still another."[77] In October 1884, he explained that women possessed an intuitive discernment that men did not have, and so he turned to them for spiritual inspiration: "Bhakti is a woman. So she has access to the inner apartments. Jnana [wisdom] can only go to the visitor's room. (Everybody laughs.)"[78] Ramakrishna's personification of bhakti as a woman was striking, as his disciples' merriment suggests. When Vivekananda went to the West, this feminized spirituality in Hinduism was crucial when appealing to women, despite his widespread reputation for "man-making."

* * *

These religious traditions were not the only things that Vivekananda recon-sidered at Ramakrishna's side. Although he meditated, like Debendranath before him, Ramakrishna was *the* master of meditative consciousness, where paths of concentration, insight, and the acceptance of random im-pressions all required different techniques.[79] He slipped easily into *samadhi* (trance) that took other adepts years to realize. Rather than characterizing his experience according to complicated scriptural genealogies or schools of meditative practice, however, he preferred to focus on divine incarnations, be they Kali, Shiva, Krishna, Radha, or Rama, to center his concentration. Nor is it clear whether he saw "form" as a necessary stage before under-taking a higher understanding of nonduality, or the link between atman (soul) and Brahman (the absolute). There is little evidence that Ramakrishna saw Advaita, the union of "self'" and "nonself," as necessarily more spiritu-ally advanced in the way that Vivekananda later would.

Nevertheless, Ramakrishna sought this last state with the same determi-nation that he had applied to all his searches, showing a rare ability to reach both the ecstatic heights of bhakti as much as the highest meditative tran-scendence. He called on the help of an itinerant guru, the monk Tota Puri, who bowed down to no image and believed that Kali was little more than maya. Tota Puri arrived in Dakshineswar at the end of 1864, stayed for eleven months, and initiated Ramakrishna into *sannyasa* (renouncer status) for the first time. Under Tota Puri's instruction, Ramakrishna is said to have tried to empty his mind, but the image of Kali Ma remained and, after three days of intense mental concentration, she stood before him still "radiant with Pure Consciousness," unwilling to budge.[80]

Ramakrishna's struggle supported the widely held view that Advaitic realization was by far the hardest discipline to achieve. Exasperated and defeated, he told Tota Puri he could go no further. In response, Tota Puri found a shard of broken glass and "stuck its needle-sharp point between [Ramakrishna's] eyebrows," telling the visionary to fix his mind on the wound. When Kali appeared, Ramakrishna "mentally cut" her image in two, and, at that moment, "all distinctions disappeared from [his] mind, and it swiftly soared beyond the realm of name and form."[81] The story may also have had symbolic associations, as Ramakrishna became like the sword-wielding Kali herself. He thus achieved a state of transcendence that had taken Tota Puri years to accomplish, attaining a sense of absolute unity.[82]

2.6. Tota Puri

Ramakrishna used a metaphor to describe this state of ego-less bliss. He spoke of a salt doll, a recurring image in Hindu and Buddhist fables, which entered the limitless waves not realizing that there was no difference between itself and the water around it: "Once a salt doll went to measure the depth of the sea. No sooner did it enter the water than it dissolved. Now who could tell how deep the sea was? The one who was to tell had itself dissolved."[83]

The salt doll, not human but with human arrogance, thinks that it can measure the ocean when it can do no more than become subsumed by its infinity. This parable and its oceanic associations would later become crucial to Western understandings of Hindu transcendence.

For three days and nights, Ramakrishna entered that ocean and dissolved, then returned to this state intermittently for months, finding that as atman and Brahman joined, he came to realize his past lives. Saradananda insists that as he reached this utterly desireless state, he also realized the need to protect his body enough to continue his exertions; otherwise, the spiritual trials might kill him.

He then began to focus on religions other than traditions within Hinduism.[84] These forays into lesser-known spiritual terrain suggest how, for Ramakrishna, the distinctions between Hindus, Muslims, and Christians often seemed little different to those separating Shaktas and Vashnaivas, for example.[85] He associated with Govinda Roy, a Hindu of the Kshatriya (warrior) caste who had converted to Islam. Govinda was attracted by Sufism, Islamic practices of mysticism and asceticism, and became "absorbed day and night in practising the devotional moods of the Dervishes, devotees of that Sect." There were constant interchanges between yogis and Sufis, and Govinda's "conversion" was one example. Ramakrishna asked Govinda to initiate him into the Islamic path of "divine play"; at the end of 1867, he began to practice Islamic prayers and concluded that "the infinitely sportive Divine Mother has shown Herself to many people through this *sadhana* [spiritual trial]." And so, he repeated the name of Allah, "dressed like the Muslims, and said their prayers several times a day." He even had a vision of a "radiant Being, who looked grave and had a long beard."[86]

Ramakrishna's command of Islamic spirituality was less profound than his knowledge of Hindu traditions—Saradananda noted, for example, that Govinda was not fully aware of "Islam's social rules and customs."[87] But Ramakrishna "entered into Islam" to experience its mystical possibilities with the same gusto as when undergoing tantric, Vaishnava, and Advaitic trials. Until a disciple asked him to stop, it was reported that he thought of eating beef, and during his "Islamic" period, he even stayed away from the courtyard of his beloved Kali temple.

Ramakrishna's mysticism also encompassed Christianity, and in 1874, he became intrigued by the painting of the Madonna and Child in the parlor of an acquaintance: "Rays of light emanated from the bodies of Mother Mary and the child Jesus, entering the Master's heart and revolutionizing his mental attitudes." When this occurred, his love for the Hindu gods dissipated, and he was left only with "his heart . . . filled with faith in and reverence for Jesus and his religion." He then saw Christian clergymen praying in front of Jesus in a church. For three days, he remained in this state, until a "beautiful but unfamiliar godman with a fair complexion came to him."[88] Ramakrishna heard a voice tell him: "'[t]his is Jesus Christ, the great yogi, the loving Son of God who is one with the Father, who shed his heart's blood and suffered torture for the salvation of humanity.' Then the godman Jesus embraced the Master and merged into him. In ecstasy, the Master lost external consciousness."[89]

Whereas in the Islamic example, Ramakrishna had Govinda to inspire if not guide him in orthodoxy, his experience with Christianity was spontaneous. But Saradananda's portrayal of the visions were almost caricatures—the bearded prophet and the fair-skinned savior—but they underscored, yet again, how easily Ramakrishna connected with the supernatural.

Ramakrishna "saw" Jesus near the end of his trials, and from 1875, the year he met Keshub Sen, he devoted himself to his disciples, to the Dakshineswar community, and the many visitors and curiosity seekers—both men and women—who came to see him. One of these would be a skeptical Vivekananda.

◆ ◇ ◆

Ramakrishna was a rare guru. He rejected the roles of distant and authoritative father or guru of patriarchal Hindu society; neither did he accede to "modern" notions of an intimate paternity that slowly permeated upper-caste sensibilities in late-nineteenth-century advice manuals.[90] He is said to have remarked: "I don't initiate with a mantra. When you initiate a person, you have to take on yourself the sins of the disciple."[91] He remained determinedly childlike, sometimes maternal: "There are three words that prick me—guru, doer and father."[92] Instead, he focused on playfulness, on an inventiveness that is conveyed in Mahendranath Gupta's five-volume "Gospel of Sri Ramakrishna" (*Kathamrita*), and which provides a counterpoint to Saradananda's more conventional hagiography.

Another Brahmo "convert" from Presidency, Gupta was from a Baidya family of doctors, a subcaste of immigrant origin which associated with Brahmins and shared many of their privileges.[93] Like many disciples, Gupta turned to Ramakrishna in a moment of family crisis, and it was apparently he who saved the young man from suicide: "Just as a weak child holds to his mother with all its strength, Mahendranath . . . thought of Thakur [the title of 'Lord' used for Vishnu] as his only refuge, the most desirable goal, and the one aim in life. He had become one with Thakur [The Lord]."[94]

They met in 1882 (around the same time as Vivekananda), when Gupta spent hours writing down the conversations after purifying rituals, meditation. and fasts in an effort to dispense with "his own individual and independent thinking."[95] How much was an accurate recording of Ramakrishna's words and how much were Gupta's own remains unclear, but the *Kathamrita* is the closest we have to a "stenographic" account of Ramakrishna's teaching.[96] The five volumes often refer to different events in the same time frame, providing a more disjointed record than Saradananda's carefully constructed and largely linear compendium. They are dialogical, but peculiarly so, with Ramakrishna's poetic "rusticity" counterbalanced by the formal Bengali of the educated middle classes, especially those forced into office work. As Sumit Sarkar suggests, they also contained a conversation within a conversation.[97] Gupta seemed to want to assure readers that Ramakrishna's metaphysics were comparable to Western philosophy.[98]

But despite this elaborate literary construction, the *Kathamrita* cannot and should not be reduced to a form of middle-class "appropriation." It conveys something of Ramakrishna's magnetism and differentiates the voices of the disciples, while providing a rich and shifting landscape of classes, castes, and psychological tendencies, including suicidal candidates (like Gupta himself), betrayed lovers, schoolboys, childless widows, the elderly, students, and small businessmen.[99] Although the divide between householders and would-be disciples remained, many of the former came from different ranks of society and stages in the life cycle. Indeed, their presence showed Ramakrishna's wide embrace. His example at Dakshineswar may well have been a proving ground for the relationship between the "self" and the "greater self" that Vivekananda seems to have applied later when thinking of India.[100]

Neither Saradananda's nor Gupta's account, however, can be credited with historical accuracy—they were both involved, perhaps, in different forms of legend-making, and yet they remain the closest sources of Ramakrishna's teachings while also serving as historical evidence. Gupta, much more than Saradananda, conveyed Ramakrishna's homespun artistry— offerings of "green coconut and sugar"; fables of dogs, bullocks, and elephants; tales of the Ganges ferrymen and fish.[101] When talking of the difficulties of attaining spiritual perfection in November 1883, for example, Ramakrishna hit on a metaphor of milk: "The mind is like milk. If you keep it in the water of the world, the milk will get mixed with water. You must transform the milk into curds in a lonely corner to take the butter from it. When, by practising spiritual disciplines in solitude, you've taken out the butter of spiritual knowledge and love for God from the milk of the mind, then that butter can easily be kept in the water of the world."[102]

Ramakrishna's "simplicity" often drew its force from unspoken associations with Vaishnavism. As a little boy, Krishna entered the houses of his village and stole butter, a lila for which he was known forever more as the "Makhan Chor" (butter thief). In this way, he became the "ruler of hearts," which he hoped would be as soft as butter.

Ramakrishna's teaching was therefore so powerful because it differed from that of the philosopher or pandit. He did not hide his lack of learning (though assertions of his illiteracy are perhaps exaggerated and his passionate if intermittent interest in religious doctrine evident). He even dismissed sacred texts at times: "the Vedas, the Puranas, the Tantras, and other scriptures may be said to have been defiled because they are recited by the tongues of men."[103] With such remarks, he also rejected the caste prerogatives of Brahmins in charge of these writings.

When speaking of "householders," he referred to the "four stages of life" (ashramas) central to Hindu society. In this idealized vision, the celibate student (the first stage) then undertook marriage, reared children, and supported a family (second stage). Only when the next generation was launched could s/he withdraw from the world into the so-called hermit (third) stage to undertake austerities and penance; at the end of life, s/he was permitted to embrace renunciation and search for God (the final stage). Hinduism thus recognized the right of householders to retire from worldly existence, but only *after* having shouldered their responsibilities.

Ramakrishna encouraged householders to enrich their spirituality without having to wait, but above all, urged celibacy so disciples would not be distracted by social demands. His ideal was radical experientialism: "But what Brahman is, nobody has yet been able to express in speech. . . . Only he knows who has experienced it."[104] He also scoffed at his followers' learning, afraid that it might lead to restlessness, if not godlessness. The *Kathamrita* is thus full of the tension between the learned and the naive, orality and print, which pervaded the psychic, intellectual, and social heart of this Bengali world.[105] Formal education was meant to bring social ascent along with responsibilities, but since the British took all the high-ranking posts, Ramakrishna's disciples realized they might never achieve their goals.

Indeed, many of Vivekananda's guru-brothers were harried into British offices and became the clerks Ramakrishna despised. He said, "A clerk is jailed. He is bound, chained," retaining the "clerk" mentality even when set free.[106] He was in general dismissive of work, for it mired the individual in contaminating "worldly activities."[107] For this reason, though he intermittently recognized his dependence on others, he was not overly concerned. When one devotee told him that the "Westerners urged [them] to work more and more," Ramakrishna replied that they should pray, "O Lord, lessen my work."[108]

This injunction against long office hours was more, however, than a protest against exploitation and the demands of punctuality, which Vivekananda also always regretted. Rather, such endless "slaving" took time away from the spiritual marking of the life cycle, worship ceremonies, purification rituals, and ancestor rites integral to Bengali upper-caste society.[109] Ramakrishna feared that the neglect of such duties would turn his disciples into the British, who he believed were heedless of the divine:[110] "These days one slaves for others [like the British masters]. It is said that if you slave like this for twelve years or so, . . . you imbibe the qualities of those for whom you have been slaving for so long."[111]

Moreover, he understood their continued social insecurity, a theme that shadows all five volumes of the *Kathamrita*. We sense Ramakrishna's anxiety when Vivekananda falls on hard times; he learns that Vivekananda's family is "very cross with him," his aunt angry that he has borrowed money to take a carriage.[112] And Ramakrishna asks a superintendent in the Comptroller General's Office to find Vivekananda a job (no doubt as a clerk).[113] This ironically suggests that Ramakrishna may well have been a patron who might command enough influence to find positions for impoverished disciples. Although he makes the proposal, Ramakrishna also shames Vivekananda: "I said to myself, 'His mind is now set on finding a job, so his singing is dull.'"[114] Although Ramakrishna worried about Vivekananda's future, he feared even more that the young man would become just another householder, whose spiritual yearnings would be extinguished by the "slavery" he warned against.

And all around were British temptations and taunts. When riding in Calcutta with Ramakrishna and some disciples, Gupta tells us that the "[c]arriage rolls along the beautiful main thoroughfare of the English neighbourhood. Lighted mansions adorning both sides of the road seem as if they are in repose in the mellow, serene rays of the full moon. Near the main gates are gaslights. In almost every home, English ladies are singing to the accompaniment of the harmonium or piano."[115] It is not clear whether the Indians consciously felt excluded from the domestic glow, or whether this luminous, luxurious, and, above all, leisurely tableau of British wealth and security merely reminded them of the foreign domination of the city.[116]

*   *   *

If Ramakrishna feared that his disciples would become clerks under the British, he equally dreaded their loss to women—in his view, the most potent lure away from spiritual liberation. He reminded his followers that even the most beautiful was nothing more than "bones, flesh, fat, urine and excreta."[117] He also warned disciples against wanting to enjoy bodies that "contained all kinds of impurities—worms, pus, phlegm."[118] Such remarks were a classic trope of monastic Hindu (and Buddhist) texts that for millennia had tried to kill the desire for the female body. But the slavery of modern clerkship and the demands of wives and children gave these warnings a novel edge: "Lust and greed bind a man. One loses one's freedom. When there is a woman, you need 'gold,' and for that, you have to be a slave to another person."[119] He was, moreover, almost as fearful of men's lust as he was of women's "enticement": all bodies were dangerous because of their desire for pleasure. And so, he "shiver[ed] . . . as if stung by a singi fish" (Indian catfish) when he touched a woman.[120] Precisely *because* he identified so strongly with women (he had experienced both Radha's torments and her passionate arousal), he also understood the intensity of their allure. He even described their appetizing qualities: "Look, just by talking of tamarind pickles, my mouth has begun to water! (*all laugh*). You all know what happens when they are within reach. For men, women are the pickled tamarind."[121]

This taste summed up women's exotic complexity, the chile's heat in the pickle adding yet another dimension to their warmth and passion. He grasped the deep drives that attracted his disciples to women and resisted adult sexuality of any kind. He was furious with Pratap Hazra, a difficult and often mischievous disciple, for suggesting that he worried too much about "Narendra and the other young men." If this was a suggestion of same-sex erotic connection, it made Ramakrishna bridle—"that rascal has defiled my mind!"[122] Ramakrishna thus may have admitted the possibility but dismissed it as untrue. He was no prude—but he remained undisturbed when a disciple burst out laughing when he described the "sexual organ of ecstatic love."[123] Often as naked as a baby, with his loincloth tossed aside, he could become annoyed when questions of sexuality were raised.

Ramakrishna's child-bride, Sarada Devi, may have posed special difficulties for him; her story, and Vivekananda's special regard for her, is crucial to understanding how he envisaged the "maternal" in his theology. Like Ramakrishna, Sarada Devi was born into a pious but poor Brahmin family and lived a life of "sorrow and hardship."[124] Although her relationship is known largely through secondhand accounts, her early years of marriage evidently left her deeply insecure. She had no choice over whom she married and expected none. The poverty of her parents meant that Ramakrishna's family—hardly wealthy themselves—paid the dowry, but his reputation as an addled temple priest meant he was no great catch either. She did not stay with him in Kamarpukur, but rather traveled back and forth between her home village and his. During the twenty-six years of marriage, they lived together for only ten of them.

Ramakrishna's intermittent carelessness toward her is striking. From the beginning, he rejected the idea of children, with one witness describing the scene when he explained that family was a painful worldly goal: "One day the Master pointed to. . . . Sarada and said: 'What good is there in giving birth like dogs and jackals to a whole brood of children? You raised your young brothers and sister tenderly; you witnessed how deeply your parents lamented. . . . Why should you bother with it? Without any such trouble, you look like a goddess now and you will always remain a goddess.'"[125]

When Ramakrishna suggested that Sarada was a goddess, he implied that he wanted her to remain an unmarked, untouched, spiritual vessel—worshipping virginal innocence, and little girls as goddesses, was an important feature of Bengali devotion.[126] He remained intransigent despite her distress, and she lived with her parents from 1867 to 1871, mocked in the village as an abandoned wife. When she heard of his apparent madness in 1872, she went to Dakshineswar for the first time, a journey fraught with the fear of rejection. Because Ramakrishna had taken monastic vows from Tota Puri in 1864, she worried that he might send her away and was forever grateful that he had instead welcomed her. Now eighteen and considered fully mature, she became his first disciple, learning to be meticulous in domestic matters. She continued to challenge him, however, asking how he viewed her—he responded that she was the "embodiment of the blissful Mother of the Universe."[127] Although they slept in the same room for nearly eight months—living, in his words, as "maid companions of the Divine

2.7. Sarada Devi

Mother"—their union remained unconsummated.[128] In wanting children, she showed that she was not averse to sexual intimacy, yet we will never know how she felt about his insistence on celibacy.

Ramakrishna spiritualized their union through ritual. On June 5, 1872, he orchestrated a ceremony to Kali in her third incarnation as Shodashi, the pure maiden.[129] During this worship, he intended to make Sarada his Shakti (divine feminine energy), to remain together always in consciousness. Like other practitioners of Shakta and Tantra, he believed she provided the means through which he could unite with Kali, this time in her virginal guise.[130] "First he painted my feet with *alta* [a red dye], put vermilion on my forehead, and clad me in a new cloth. He then fed me with sweets and a betel roll. I saw him doing all this, but . . . I was in an ecstatic state and completely oblivious to the world."[131] Ramakrishna thus "remade" Sarada. A later hagiographer wrote that "she had inherited the richest spiritual wealth without any. . . . endeavour on her part" and participated in a nonsexual union that represented marital consummation.[132]

At night, she was said to have watched his ecstasy, fearing his spiritual transports but always present when he returned to the material world. During this period, she once again asked, "If there is no child, how will the family continue?" The query hints at the continued "ordinariness" of her outlook, but he reassured her that she would "have so many sons and daughters that [she would] be exhausted looking after them."[133] Later, he remarked that "[t]he mother who is in the Kali temple is the same Mother who dwells within this (pointing to his own body), and the very same Mother dwells by my side (as the Holy Mother)."[134]

Her future lay in embracing what he saw as her divinity. It took time before her standing improved—she continued to live in a tiny room in the northern balconied building where musicians played for temple pilgrims in Dakshineswar, a room that was "barely fifty square feet, the ceiling nine feet high, and the door so low that Sarada Devi knocked her head against the doorpost many times."[135] Although helped by one or two of Ramakrishna's disciples, she was effectively cloistered in a tiny space:[136] "I would stand for hours behind a small hole in the screen of my porch and listen to his singing. I got rheumatism from standing for long hours."[137] She was saved from this claustrophobia in 1874 not by her husband, but by a wealthy disciple who built her a cottage.[138]

Her humility always remained, as did her seclusion, but after Ramakrishna's death, she lived very much as he had foreseen. He had said that different religions were like different dishes that a mother cooked to show special love for each child. Despite the tremendous labor, Sarada took on this role with creativity, and became known for loving all the disciples equally, even when they transgressed. She did indeed end up with many sons and daughters, to whom she responded with advice, guidance, and the example of her own life.[139] She became a goddess in her own right, revered as the Holy Mother and able to bestow sannyasa (renouncer status). Her tranquility and self-abasement gave her a degree of spiritual dominion which Vivekananda believed was essential to everything he did. He later promoted these qualities as integral to his vision of her divinity.

*   *   *

Despite Tota Puri's instruction on Advaita, Ramakrishna remained loyal to the goddess. For him, Kali remained the "Eternal consort of the Infinite" when "neither sun, nor moon, nor planets" existed. She was the Tantric goddess, Kali the Destroyer, who lives with the "spirits of destruction," and who delights in impurity and decay.[140] Since the eighteenth century, Kali had also become less forbidding and more like an "ordinary" mother, her fury tamed by putting her crying children to her breast.[141] In the worst of times—during "epidemics, famine, earthquakes, drought, and floods"—she was the Preserver, "taking the jumbled leavings after the holocaust and bringing back life:[142] "Housewives do have a pot like that. Inside, she keeps . . . small bundles of seeds of cucumber, pumpkin and gourd. . . . —using them when needed. The Divine Mother collects such seeds after the dissolution of existence. The primordial energy remains latent in the world after creation! She gives birth to the world, she stays within it."[143]

Childish surrender to this transcendent Mother was the bhakta's aim, like a kitten who "knows only how to cry out to its mother, 'Mew, mew.'" Rather than taking the initiative, it waits for the mother, knowing that "she comes when she hears its mewing."[144] Although he does not mention her, he may have been thinking of Shashthi Devi, the popular goddess of children, who, like Kali, also protects her "kittens."

Ramakrishna celebrated the kitten because it waited until "the mother will put it in her mouth and place it anywhere she likes."[145] The monkey, in contrast, was like a *jnani,* the spiritual aspirant who sought the divine through wisdom. People were often like monkeys—they chattered too much and were endlessly "busy." Because he had lived as Hanuman, Ramakrishna knew that monkeys were clever, even remarkable: "Hanuman," he explained, set "fire to the golden city of Lanka" and "people were amazed that a monkey could burn the whole city."[146] Vivekananda, of course, was a jnani, and Ramakrishna recognized the power of this path in certain individuals. But bhakti was the devotional model for the age, its possibilities open to all—rich and poor, women and men. Once again, Ramakrishna opted for a form of universalism.

But Kali-worship was not just about becoming like the mewling kitten, but being courageous enough to face horror and transgression without recoiling. Ramakrishna explained that he was willing to die to realize his mystical longings that the secrets of Kali-love bestowed.[147] With Vivekananda present, he described devouring the mother, of taking her into his "net." At the end of September 1884, Ramakrishna said, "I would open my mouth wide as if it would touch both heaven and the nether world. And I would utter, 'Ma,' [Mother] as though I were pulling the Mother inside just as the fishes are pulled along with the net."[148]

Rather than taking food from Kali Ma, she became his food, in the same way that his mouth encompassed "both heaven and the nether world."[149] These fantasies were hardly original, but rather came from Ramprasad's poetry, the eighteenth-century Shakta saint who Ramakrishna adored as much as Chaitanya. The folk song "Ebar Kali, Tomaey Khabo" ("Now Kali, I'll eat you") expressed this desire that no other goddess inspired. With Kali worship, Ramakrishna entered a mystical realm that permitted the goddess's ingestion and signified his own intrepidity, for he insisted he would not be "in trouble by . . . by eating Kali."[150] Nor was he afraid of defilement, terrible for a Brahmin: "I will snatch the string of skulls . . . and make a sour broth with it," a desire intensified when he sang, "This time either You will eat me, or I will devour You and thus the two will become one."[151]

These aggressive fancies were as childlike as Ramakrishna's equally strong desire to sit in Kali's lap, or to be nothing more than a mewling kitten; and were as much about trusting surrender as they were about unfettered empowerment. Here, the daring of Tantra was directly related to the aggressive imaginings of childhood, a mysticism which sought to encompass "self" and "other," "son" and "mother," but in a way pointedly different from the reverie surrounding the salt doll with its soft melting away into oceanic infinitude. Instead, Ramakrishna spoke of a giant maw that was able, in one voracious bite, to take in heaven, earth, and the underworld. His mysticism presented a compelling, even fierce, vision of unity. His special gift was to encompass such intense desires and drives—the nightmares of infancy, childhood, mythology, and cradle tales—and embed them solidly in a theology of love: "I was like one gone mad. Such madness results from deep longing."[152] Divine play often encompassed what was harrowing and edgy, hence the allusions to insanity and experiments that imperiled both body and mind. This, again, was "heroism," a form of fierce determination that Vivekananda may even have sought to retain, in a different way, when describing the passionate need to love and serve the poor.

For Ramakrishna, moreover, the universal meant unity as much as difference. The metaphor of the salt doll permitted a soft dissolution, while ingesting could sharpen difference. For example, Sarada Devi was venerated because she cooked different dishes for different disciples, so they might flourish—her activity a perfect metaphor for the different ways people worshipped (and "took in") God. Thus, Ramakrishna suggested that universalism did not just accommodate difference, but often was difference. When Vivekananda came to America, he used both ideas, but when he spoke of Hindu Universalism in public, he often highlighted the second in railing against Christian intolerance. When such notions were recast in "aggressive Hinduism," however, this story of encompassment stressed the different, often fiercer sense of unity over diversity. As will be seen, Ramakrishna's theology—and both his "quiescent" and "aggressive" childlike emphases— was deployed in different ways by those who came after him. Like Kali, his ideas could be put to both destructive and creative use.

* * *

By rejecting householder duties and embracing both Kali and celibacy, Ramakrishna pursued the theology of childhood. Perhaps no word appears as often in the *Divine Play* and in the *Kathamrita* as "child." He is once reported as saying: "When one has attained the highest spiritual knowledge, one's nature becomes that of a five-year-old child. Then one no longer distinguishes between a man and a woman."[153]

He admired especially the way a "child has no attachment. It makes a doll house and if anybody touches it, it begins to cry loudly. Later, it breaks the doll's house itself."[154] Rather than condemning such temper, Ramakrishna saw the jnani in such childish destruction, an assault on material objects and the false conviction that valued them.[155] He regards the smashed doll's house as the spiritual lesson of a childish sage and sought no theory of infantile aggression and/or sexuality that so changed Western perceptions of childhood during the "psychoanalytic revolution."

And so, Ramakrishna acted like a child, hiding his sweets from his disciples, going into samadhi, begging peevishly for a meal, and fretfully demanding tending when he hurt his hand. Like him, children were passionate in their play, but innocent because they understood neither the etiquette nor desires of the adult world: "A person who has seen God develops the temperament of a child ... He seems to make no distinction between purity and impurity."[156] Children were thus uniquely beyond good and evil: "This 'I' is not to be counted as ego. Like sugar candy which, though sweet, is not like other sweets. While other sweets bring indigestion, sugar candy brings relief."[157]

He asserted that to be like an ego-less child was to enter a playful divine state. Studies of children aim to uncover the "authentic self" in which play reveals what is "real" in contrast to the "false self" that adapts to adult demands.[158] For both the religious mystic and the child psychoanalyst, playfulness was more "real" than the "real" life of adult responsibility.[159] There was a difference, however, between an adult professing to be a child, and the world of childlike play. Ramakrishna may have been childlike, but he strove after complex understandings and expressed them in imaginative, lyrical language, seeking a sense of childlike abandonment but, above all, absorption through stringent adult discipline: he exemplified a mystical arduousness and adventurousness very different from the crushing monotony the British demanded in their offices.[160] To accomplish his aims, moreover, he felt he must deny the needs of others by shirking familial duties, as when he resisted Sarada's entreaties to have a child, consigning such desires to the realm of maya. He acknowledged, though, that his spiritual trials had demanded a tremendous sacrifice, which took a heavy toll on his health.

To put forward such a case, however, suggests an equally unprovable interpretation—that Ramakrishna's rejection of adult sexuality "sublimated" erotic drives. In construing his quest in this way, we may risk misunderstanding the nature of mystical desire and the lessons that inspired Vivekananda. Ramakrishna summoned imaginative powers that destabilized gender and drew on feelings that remain difficult to explain. Indeed, his experience may involve a conception of self-understanding that constitutes an important counterexample to psychoanalytic universalism. This remark is offered as nothing more than a suggestion for further reflection; neither is it a call for a religious explanation. Whatever the answer, spiritual childishness was his aim, and he rejected every attempt to make him into an "omniscient father," rejecting the role of "guru" as much as husband.

Although he was every bit a guru despite his protests, he wanted to be one that emanated innocence, and so he celebrated "silliness" and nakedness.[161] His acts were shocking or awe-inspiring depending on point of view, but he certainly provided a vivid and spiritualized expression of babyhood. He forced his audience to see how infants had a unique call on the love of the older generation, and especially on their mothers, who wiped them clean without rebuke. It was precisely this form of unconditional, reflexive love that he hoped to inspire in others and to which Vivekananda, despite his many doubts, ultimately turned.

3

RAMAKRISHNA AND

VIVEKANANDA

S[wami]. How I used to hate Kali and all Her ways. *That* was my 6 years' fight, because I would not accept Kali.

N[ivedita]. But now you have accepted her specially, have you not, Swami?

S. I *had* to—Ramakrishna Paramahamsa dedicated me to her. And you know I believe that She guides me in every little thing I do—and just does what She likes with me.

Yet I fought so long.—I loved the man you see, and that held me. I thought him the purest man I had ever seen, and I knew that he loved me as my own father and mother had not power to do.

N. But when *you* doubted so long—with all your chances—what wonder if Brahmos still doubt? . . .

S. His greatness had not dawned on me then. That was afterwards, when I had given in. At that time I thought Him simply a brain-sick baby, always seeing visions and things. I hated it—and then *I* had to accept Her [Kali] too!

—Sister Nivedita, *The Master as I Saw Him*, 1910

◆　◆　◆

MARGARET NOBLE recorded this exchange with Vivekananda in 1899, almost twenty years after his first encounter with Ramakrishna. Although possibly embellished, the conversation nevertheless captures something of their connection. Ramakrishna was a guru who never wanted to be treated as a guru, a "brain-sick baby," who somehow managed to "hold" the more sophisticated and intellectual Vivekananda. For years, the younger man resisted his teachings, ridiculing him in ways that no other disciple dared.

Even the hagiographies admit that their embrace was often as uncomfortable as it was close—Ramakrishna pursuing his disciple and weeping during his absences, Vivekananda wondering why he could not resist the older man's entreaties. It was so powerful because, although a skeptical jnani (a wisdom-seeker), Vivekananda knew that in his inner nature he was a bhakta (a religious devotee). Ramakrishna was the opposite; he lived as a bhakta, but was a jnani inside, showing great intellectual acuity despite his lack of formal education. They both shared a yearning for "God intoxication." Sometimes, after Ramakrishna's death, it was claimed that Vivekananda castigated his guru-brothers when they seemed to indulge in excessive emotion. But in the West, he tried to teach its "sweet" and humanizing lessons to the "dry" and "materialistic" Protestants he encountered.[1] I hope to capture this double-sidedness both in Vivekananda's personality and in his theology.

There are those who argue that Vivekananda reshaped Ramakrishna's legacy so thoroughly that he fabricated something new, that Hindu Universalism was a creation that Ramakrishna would not have recognized.[2] The result is a rather clichéd account—the childlike, illiterate visionary—God's incarnation on earth—with the muscular, energetic, and rationalist representative of a new and reformist generation. Such views suggest another rich seam of legend-making, that Vivekananda would be St. Paul to Ramakrishna's Jesus, an association that Vivekananda later almost reinforced when he traveled in the Anglosphere. Like St. Paul who also at first resisted his master's teaching, Vivekananda kept the man-god at the heart of his work while reshaping his message.[3]

Such interpretations undervalue the emotional and spiritual transformation that Ramakrishna wrought and misjudge Vivekananda's evolution. Neither man was systematic, but this characterization is too polarized to grasp shading and ambiguity. In this telling, Ramakrishna was feminine and Vivekananda masculine; Ramakrishna was a Shakta (Kali worshipper), a Vaishnava, and a Tantric, above all interested in the Puranas (mothological tales); in contrast, Vivekananda was a jnani who stressed the ancient wisdom of the Upanishads and the ethical flights of the Bhagavad Gita. Vivekananda is often regarded as the creator of a Hindu cultural nationalism that prioritized the "biceps and the Gita"; and yet Ramakrishna unequivocally stated that "the Gita is the essence of all scriptures" and suggested that all *sannyasins* (renouncers) should possess a "pocket Gita," though he did not believe that sacred texts were the only path to spiritual knowledge.[4] Such oppositions deform their inner lives and spirituality.

Certainly, Ramakrishna stayed mostly on the banks of the Hooghly (where at Dakshineswar he encountered spiritual seekers of many kinds), whereas Vivekananda traveled to the four corners of India and then around the world; Ramakrishna engaged in spiritual trials that partook of different Hindu strands; Vivekananda instead emphasized Advaita even though he reembraced Kali worship, sometimes extravagantly, when he returned to India in 1897. Vivekananda's universal mission, as well as his cosmopolitan experience, meant that he could synthesize ideas of service, Karma yoga, and anticolonial assertion in a way that Ramakrishna never could. At the same time, Vivekananda never tired of reminding all and sundry that he was "no Ramakrishna," that he would never attain the mystical heights or saintliness of his master.

*   *   *

Gupta maintains that Ramakrishna apparently detected the young man's promise immediately, saying that "I noticed that he did not have body consciousness."[5] He realized that, unlike his companions, Vivekananda "was not concerned about his appearance," and this untidiness hinted at his detachment: "How is it possible," Ramakrishna wondered, "that such a great spiritual aspirant can live in Calcutta, home to such materialistic people?"[6] Ramakrishna was so excited by Vivekananda's arrival at the end of 1881 that he could not live without him.[7] Vivekananda later reported ruefully, "And so he went on raving and weeping. The next moment he stood before me with folded palms and showing me the regard due to a god." He thought Ramakrishna was mad, but he came back nonetheless, and asked the question central to his spiritual preoccupations: "Have you seen God?" to which Ramakrishna replied, "God can be seen and spoken to, just as I'm seeing you and speaking to you." He continued: "For wife, children, money, and property people grieve and shed jugs of tears—but who weeps for the vision of God?

And yet, if anyone really wants to see God and calls upon him, God will certainly reveal Himself to that person."[8]

Ramakrishna claimed to have looked at the face of Mother Kali and offered Vivekananda the vision of "beholding" that the young man craved.[9] Despite the growing emotionalism of Brahmo worship, "seeing" God in this immediate fashion had been largely proscribed by the disallowing of images. These objects, so much a part of household and temple worship, were useless for addressing a deity that was without form. Vivekananda had sought to deepen his spiritual awareness by practicing *brahmacharya* (celibacy), vegetarianism, devotional singing, and meditation. Somehow it was not enough—he needed a teacher. Although he described Ramakrishna as a "monomaniac," a term from nineteenth-century European alienism, the prospect of finally beholding God was irresistible. And so he returned to Dakshineswar in January; Saradananda tells the famous tale—often repeated—of how Ramakrishna placed his foot on Vivekananda's chest, and the world began to move: "My eyes were wide open . . . and I saw that everything in the room, including the walls themselves, was rapidly whirling round me and receding. At the same time, it seemed to me that my consciousness of self, together with the entire universe, was about to vanish into a vast, all-devouring void. This destruction of my self-consciousness seemed to me the same thing as death. Terrified, I felt death right before me, very close. Unable to control myself, I cried out loudly: 'Ah, what are you doing to me? Don't you know I have parents at home?'"[10]

Vivekananda thus experienced the "all-devouring void," the whirling of walls around him, that Ramakrishna had alluded to when speaking of his own desire to "gobble up" Kali Ma. Vivekananda feared for his sense of self. The story's logic suggests how Ramakrishna was also acting like Kali, who placed her foot on Shiva and repeated the familiar gesture of her dominion. Vivekananda's exclamation, "Don't you know I have parents at home?" signaled his attachment to family and resistance to the rigors of the spiritual path. To break the spell, Ramakrishna touched him again on the chest, acknowledging his fear, "All right, let it stop now . . . It will happen in its own good time."[11] Raised in rationalism and critical thought, Vivekananda apparently wondered whether he had been hypnotized, but then questioned whether his strong mind was susceptible to such influence.

Afterward, Ramakrishna fed Vivekananda with his own hand, as he had done during the first visit, a touch that "created a good deal of anxiety" in the young man.[12] Ramakrishna was behaving like a god or guru feeding prasad (a sacred offering) to his disciple, a ritual gesture that pointed the way toward Vivekananda's spiritual vocation. But both the gesture and the relationship also conjured Ramakrishna as mother and Vivekananda as child. Was he honoring Vivekananda as a baby, inviting him to join him in divine play? As with all such play, it was a make-believe drama of two grown men that showed the fusion, and confusion, of the maternal and the erotic, of terror and pleasure.

The image of the foot was vital, for both its holiness and potential for desecration were everywhere in Indian culture. Feet are often dirty and shoes are not permitted in temples or in homes. Throwing footwear is an insult; the haughty and the meek came to take the dust of Ramakrishna's feet; the young touch the feet of their elders; disciples massage their master's feet; and wives, their husband's. Kali triumphantly places her foot on Shiva; the gods' feet are often termed lotus feet, and the Buddha's are said to have left their imprint in relics.[13] As in many of these stories, what was base was also sublime according to its place within the symbolic hierarchy.

Although disturbed by his experience, Vivekananda could not stay away. Walking in the garden with Ramakrishna near the banks of the Hooghly, he was "completely overwhelmed by that powerful touch" and fell into unconsciousness.[14] Ramakrishna, it was thought, had probed beyond Narendra's current incarnation, and learned the secrets of past lives and with it the knowledge that, in Vivekananda, he had encountered a spiritual sage. He recounted a vision of seven venerable *rishis*—the ancient poets from the Vedas, the seers, and sages of the world today—in a state of ecstasy. A beautiful child tried to pull one rishi from his superconscious state. A fragment of the rishi's body descended to the world. Vivekananda, Ramakrishna proclaimed, was "that rishi."[15] In this dream, a part of Vivekananda had to be brought down to earth to illuminate it.[16]

Ramakrishna would be beside himself when Vivekananda was away: "After Narenda left I felt a constant and agonizing desire to see him. At times the pain was so excruciating that I felt as if my heart was being squeezed like a wet towel. When I could no longer control myself, I would run to the pine grove on the northern side of the garden . . . and cry at the top of my voice: 'O my child, come to me! I can't live without seeing you!'"[17]

A religious vocabulary for this abject longing existed in the songs of Radha-Krishna, which described the yearning for reunion.[18] But Ramakrishna provided his own vivid imagery of the wrung-out towel, depleted, and compressed. In contrast to the analogy of the kitten who trusts its mother cat to hold it gently, Ramakrishna is crumpled. The description is so striking because Ramakrishna—normally able to detach mentally and enter samadhi in an instant—is a slave to his emotions. He is dispossessed, his pining little different from the longing he felt for Kali during the earlier days of his mystical trials.

Ramakrishna called Vivekananda "Narayana" and hence regarded Vivekananda as the "Guru of the Universe." He was Purusha, the Cosmic Man sacrificed by the god that created all life, and which represented Consciousness. Certainly, he maintained that "Narayana Himself is present in all living things" (and felt this love for his disciples), but he had a special regard for Vivekananda, as Gupta related in March 1885, "What love! He is mad for Narendra, weeps for Narayan."[19] Although Vivekananda was said to be embarrassed by both the passion and the praises, he accepted the adulation. Ramakrishna's willingness to weep like a vulnerable child suggested that mortal life was impossible without the "pure" one whom he longed to teach.

* * *

Hindu worship emphasizes the importance of the beholding that fixes the devotee's gaze, but the connection between the two men was more than visual. It was multisensory and linked to the theory of *rasas,* a word that evokes "taste" or "essence" (literally, "sap" or "juice"), and which underpins Indian aesthetic theory. They summon the exalted moods that the audience witnesses; indeed, it is hard not to compare this sense of performance to the mystical trials that Ramakrishna undertook.[20] However, the notion of performance—with its theatrical resonance—suggests that the performer carries an inner understanding of the illusion and is party to the artistic deception; it would, thus, be misleading to equate divine play with performance.

There is bawdiness, teasing, and unrefined behavior in the *Kathamrita,* but little prurience, even though physicality is key—Ramakrishna as easily composed beautiful parables as told stories about defecation.[21] Indeed, Dakshineswar was a sensual cornucopia, where the body was endlessly implicated, and where the senses all seemed heightened. Ramakrishna created an extraordinary world of male physicality, often leading his disciples in a rough-and-tumble of ecstatic dancing and wrestling. Movement as worship—inarticulate, but powerful—often overwhelmed them. Ramakrishna tasted rock candy to express some earthly equivalent to the sweetness of devotion and fed his disciples with sweets of all kinds, so that they, too, might experience bhakti. But the senses were not always pleasurable. They also visited the cremation grounds to smell the burning corpses and inhale the stink that Kali so loved. Such terrifying journeys were as important in bonding them as were the pleasures.

The *Kathamrita* also often refers to music, especially Vivekananda's singing and his ability to play various instruments. Music in India is a sacred art, and Vivekananda was apparently well trained, even editing a little book on music.[22] The resounding repetition of "om" is essential to the inwardness required for meditation, whereas the shared chanting of the stories (known as *kirtans*) became a dialogue between the lead singer and the audience. These songs were part of the Bhakti movement that reached its height between the fifteenth and seventeenth centuries, and Keshub Chunder Sen attached his novel spirituality to its rhythmic piety.[23] As mentioned, one account of Ramakrishna's first encounter with Vivekananda occurred when he heard the young man sing.

In the *Kathamrita,* Ramakrishna watches Vivekananda tune the strings of a *tanpura,* a long-necked string instrument with the rounded belly, which drones harmonically behind the soloist's voice. The young man prepares the drums, while they discuss different hymns, the dialogue underlining the difference between a jnani and a bhakta.

> *Narendra:* "There is no regular beat or rhythm in the kirtan songs. That's why they're so popular. People love them."
>
> *Sri Ramakrishna:* "What are you saying! There is such feeling of compassion in them—that's why people like them."[24]

Ramakrishna goes into a trance when Vivekananda sings about Vishnu: "Thakur [the Lord] is standing motionless, his eyes unmoving. It is difficult to say whether or not he is breathing."[25] When Vivekananda sang "bliss like embodied nectar," Ramakrishna fell into "deep *Samadhi,*" diving "deep into the ocean of beauty—the All-blissful Mother."[26] Throughout his mystical moods as servant, lover, mother, and child, Ramakrishna had insisted on music to promote this intimate worship. Unlike the formlessness of Advaita, Ramakrishna's bhakti required the relational, which music heightened.

Moreover, the devotional songs were embedded in an earlier, Bengali legacy that the "son of Ramprasad" sought to resurrect. Ramprasad had combined the passionate wildness of Baul [folkloric] songs with the classical repertoire of *ragas* (melodies) and kirtan songs. Sung in Bengali, they evoked the intimacy of everyday language.[27] Vivekananda's voice plunged the mystic into the supernatural, the altered state of consciousness brought on by its sound. For both, this aesthetic dimension, with its musical rhythms, was essential to their rapture.

Words, of course, were also important. In Saradananda's *Sri Ramakrishna and His Divine Play*, Vivekananda resists while Ramakrishna is almost overeager to win him over. Vivekananda's hesitation, far from undermining their relationship, revealed how, in Vivekananda's words, "a true guru teaches a highly qualified disciple without disturbing his spiritual attitude, and how the guru consequently occupies a place of love and respect in the heart of that disciple,"[28]

No doubt, Ramakrishna devoted loving effort to Vivekananda's spiritual apprenticeship, but the interaction was multilayered: The *Kathamrita* shows Ramakrishna to be alternately teasing, exasperated, willing to learn, and deeply hurt, depending on the subject and situation. Sometimes Ramakrishna was all gentleness. When, for example, Vivekananda rejected the idea of avataras, Ramakrishna moved closer and remarked, "Do you feel that your dignity has been wounded? So be it. . . . we feel for you."[29] He could be almost brusque: "As long as there is reasoning, one cannot attain God. You were reasoning. I didn't like it." Ramakrishna concluded, "The nearer you come to God, the less you reason"; then he stroked Vivekananda gently and added, "Hari Om, Hari Om, Hari Om," addressing him as a god.[30] The touch was meant to take away the harshness of the reproach.

In this case, Ramakrishna dismissed his disciple's arguments, but at other times, he respected Vivekananda's intellect. When Vivekananda took aim at both the Hindu sacred texts and the Christian Bible, Ramakrishna marveled at his questioning whether the Bhagavad Gita contained the words of Krishna. But when he thought about it, Ramakrishna reasserted the priority of experience over sacred texts, and even agreed with Vivekananda.[31]

Vivekananda posed questions that no other disciple dared ask. Perhaps, he implied, Ramakrishna's visions were mere hallucinations? Ramakrishna was so disturbed by this "sharp argumentation" that he apparently went to Kali to ask whether he was right. She responded, "Why do you listen to Narendra? He will accept the truth before long."[32] The account, however, veils Ramakrishna's doubt, which Gupta recorded: "'Mother, what is this? Is it all false? Narendra said so.' The Divine Mother then showed me Consciousness, Indivisible Consciousness, and said, 'If your visions are illusions, why do they tally with facts?' Then I said to Narendra, 'Rascal, you are robbing me of my faith! Don't come here again.'"[33]

Of course, Vivekananda *did* return, in the summer of 1882, and later accepted that his great learning was worth little. In the *Kathamrita,* he spoke of Scottish philosopher Sir William Hamilton, who had argued that contradictions were not the product of reason, but rather an attempt to apply reason beyond its proper domain. Vivekananda congratulated Ramakrishna for this intuitive understanding, again suggesting that Hindu traditions readily confirmed Western thought:

> *Narendra [quoting a song]:* What need for reason; drive me mad, Mother.
>
> *To M[ahendranath Gupta]:* See, I have read in Hamilton. He wrote, "A learned ignorance is the end of philosophy and the beginning of religion."
>
> *Sri Ramakrishna (to M.):* What does that mean?
>
> *Narendra:* After completing the study of philosophy, one becomes a learned fool, . . . Then starts religion.
>
> *Sri Ramakrishna:* "Thank you, Thank you!" (Laughter.)[34]

Nonetheless, Vivekananda struggled for years before he accepted both Kali worship (more about this follows) and nondualism. Schooled in Brahmoism, he conceived of an omniscient, formless God in a dualistic way, as how could the created soul "think of itself as the Creator?" He continued, "is there no greater sin than this? I am God; you are God, and everything that is born and dies is God—what could be more absurd?"[35] Although he would come to advocate Advaitic nondualism, Vivekananda first spurned it as much as he had done Kali worship.

But Ramakrishna changed him: "I was aghast to realize that there really was nothing whatsoever in the entire universe but God. . . . I sat to eat, and saw that everything—the plate, the food, my mother who was serving it, and I myself—everything was God and nothing but God."[36] To test the notion, he claimed later, he would "strike [his head] against the iron railings' in Calcutta's Cornwallis Square, "to see if they were real or only a dream."[37] The idea intoxicated him, and he subsequently sought to convey this spiritual insight to his Western disciples.

But Vivekananda's character did not change. For those who disliked him, he remained spoiled, arrogant, rude; for those who did not, he continued to be vigorous, confident, and unflinching in the face of the world's opinion. Ramakrishna elevated him above the other disciples; he called him "eternally perfect," "perfect in meditation" and, as suggested, Narayana.[38] The *Divine Play*—written after Vivekananda had eaten food and drink that defied orthodoxy while abroad—deemed him never polluted by food that was forbidden to the other disciples.[39] Here was another retrospective example of Vivekananda's sanctification that countered orthodox objection. When he claimed to have consumed such prohibited food in an Indian hotel, Ramakrishna explained that "if a man keeps his mind on God, eating pork and beef is equivalent to eating the purest simple, *havishyanna* [sacred food offerings] made of boiled vegetables."[40] The *Divine Play* describes how the two of them shared a pipe, enjoying a "vice" that was no longer transgressive by virtue of their mutual purity and powers.[41] Ramakrishna explained: "What I see is that I'm this body (*his own body*) and that body (*Narendra's body*) also. It's true—I see no difference. If you lay a stock on the surface of the Ganges, the water seems to be divided into two parts; but it's really all one; there is no division. The same thing is true here."[42]

With this gesture, Ramakrishna insisted that they were one in a way that that recalled something of his sacralized relationship to Sarada.

RAMAKRISHNA AND THE DISCIPLES

His father's death in February 1884, when Vivekananda was twenty-one, created a schism in his life, for he discovered that he was an indebted pauper rather than an heir. His first reaction, apparently, was to proclaim his atheism and pretend that he was now "mixing with people of bad character, and visiting houses of ill repute."[43] He was unemployed and old acquaintances ignored him. It is claimed that this state of semistarvation led him to rare and momentous spiritual experience: "Then I suddenly felt that Providence was lifting up screen after screen in my mind and that all the problems that had been tormenting me—where is the harmony between God's justice and His mercy, why does evil exist within a benign creation—all were resolved. I was beside myself with joy."[44]

His social dislocation drew him closer to Ramakrishna, but he was unable to separate completely from his family and their needs, nor was he above asking Ramakrishna for help with their financial problems. Ramakrishna is said to have refused to approach Kali, only assuring his disciple that she would guarantee their survival. Vivekananda went to the temple himself to ask for help, but even on the third visit, he could not ask for such a "trifling." This word is surprising, as few would suggest that the impoverishment of a beloved family was trifling, especially in the Bengali world of dutiful kinship. Saradananda, from whom we have this story, suggests that Vivekananda was on the way to "detachment," by putting Kali's expectations above family needs. His continued efforts to protect his mother's interests, however, suggest this was never completely the case.[45]

He would become the world's exponent of the formlessness of Advaita, but symbols and images remained as part of his spirituality. He no longer disdained them, as his Brahmoism had taught, but thereafter defended Hinduism against charges of idolatry. Kali afforded him refuge in times of disturbance and crisis. As Margaret Noble explained, he admitted that he had hated Kali precisely because she reminded him of the "debased" Hinduism that he had foresworn in his youth. Now she sustained him.[46]

The more skeptical considered that joining a brotherhood of monks had more to do with poverty than spirituality. But Vivekananda took temporary positions when he could, apparently teaching for a time at his old school and working for an attorney.[47] Dismal worldly prospects are not enough to explain his spiritual turn. Although trailing around Calcutta in search of work was life-altering, Vivekananda claimed he stayed with Ramakrishna because of his guru's unconditional love: "The Master made me his slave by his love for me."[48] Slavery and liberation were two sides of the same coin, integral to renunciation. Indeed, while waiting for Vivekananda, it was Ramakrishna who had seemed to be the "slave." Vivekananda remembered especially the last days after Ramakrishna was diagnosed with throat cancer in 1885: "I always think of him as my child. You know he always depended on me, as the strongest of the whole lot, and at the very end—when he was nearly at the last. He put his arms about my shoulders and said, 'This is a hero!'"[49]

Again, the word suggests Vivekananda's later "heroic" persona. But here, the model for such "heroism" is ordinary parental obligation; it inverts the usual vision of the guru-disciple relationship. No doubt this would have been precisely what Ramakrishna wanted—it maintained his childlike status and left Vivekananda deeply committed. It also reinforced Ramakrishna's lesson—that children, in their innocence, have a hold on their parents. Like the dream of the child bringing the rishi to earth, Ramakrishna pulled Vivekananda back to the world.

The other disciples also felt that Ramakrishna's love had been life-changing in its seemingly endless affection and concern. As Vivekananda testified again: "We saw how often Sri Ramakrishna would encourage people who we thought were worthless and change the whole course of their lives! His method of teaching was phenomenal."[50]

Witnessing and experiencing such transformations created links among the disciples that lasted decades, despite later feuds and moments of anger. These lateral connections were almost as important as the vertical links between master and disciples.[51] They had grown up in joint families, and so the brotherhood they created was necessarily shaped by these "familial selves."[52] One must try and imagine the sprawling many-branched joint families in late-Victorian Bengal, generally of well-to-do or upper-caste background. Anthropologists repeatedly have suggested how Indians combine love, obligation, care, connectedness, and hierarchy in ways that differ strongly from the "individualized selves" of Europe and America.[53] The dichotomy may be overdrawn—and may even contain a kernel of lurking orientalism—but the adult separation so prized in the West, especially among men, may not be the goal of much Indian householder society. Perhaps this was even truer where relationships of sons to mothers remained strong after marriage.

These complicated networks were duplicated in the social relations among the educated Calcutta middle class which came from the same schools and leisure circles, and from Brahmoist ranks. Those not attracted to the sprouting religious reform movements had family with links to neighborhood temples and family gods, charities, and gurus. Many knew one another and had an almost uncanny ability to recognize social distinctions. Each disciple had a story of lineage, family, caste, and often spiritual inheritance that was reshaped by Ramakrishna's influence.

For example, Shivananda was the son of a prosperous lawyer and well-known Tantrika and had family connections to Dakshineswar before he met Ramakrishna. His father had counseled Rani Rashmoni, the temple's founder, and tended Ramakrishna's mysterious sensations of burning. Shivananda had learned about religious philanthropy from his father, who was famous for his support of holy men and penniless students, only reluctantly limiting these activities when his income diminished. By coming to Ramakrishna, therefore, he both continued this family tradition and turned it on its head. From the outset, Shivananda viewed Ramakrishna less as a man-god than as his mother; he abandoned the Brahmo promise never to bow before idols when he accompanied Ramakrishna to Kali and prostrated himself. Like Vivekananda, and with the same intensity, everything in his inner life was thrown into confusion: "I often felt inclined to cry in the presence of the Master. One night I wept profusely in front of the Kali temple. . . . The Master was anxious at my absence and when I went to him he said, 'God favours those who weep for Him. Tears thus shed wash away the sins of former births'. Another day I was meditating . . . when the Master came near. No sooner had he cast his glance at me than I burst into tears. . . . The Master congratulated me . . . and said it was the outcome of divine emotion. . . . He could arouse the latent spiritual powers of a devotee at a mere glance."[54]

This story differs from Vivekananda's argumentative encounters but reveals a similar emotional intensity. Ramakrishna provides no psychological explanation for the release of what seems like deep grief, only a "washing away" of bad deeds from past lives. There was no shame associated with crying, no fear of vulnerability, merely a recognition that such emotion should be welcomed. This, of course, was the essence of Ramakrishna's relational teaching, a connection with his disciples that, in Shivananda's case, mirrored much of his relationship with Kali. Ramakrishna congratulated the young acolyte for having the courage to experience "divine emotion" and stayed to soften the physical agony. He seemed here to be the "good mother," present, supportive, and uncritical in allowing Shivananda to experience difficult emotions without interference.

Other stories describe how Ramakrishna tailored his teaching to each disciple. Although he was the oldest among them, he rarely used discipline, but rather cocooned them in a rare maternal attentiveness. He taught the orthodox and rule-bound to expand their capacity for fun, spiritual adventure, and drama, as he instilled a theology of childishness. And in their joint lives, as wandering renouncers and later as monks, they remained sensitive to their brothers, creating what one might call a collective "soul-scape" of varied possibilities and tendencies.[55] Ramakrishna put it better—if indeed they were his words—when he said, "Our attitude towards the Lord must be . . . made up of many instruments. It is a feast of many dishes."[56] These were metaphors for the infinite variety of spiritual tones and flavors. For example, Akhandananda was devoted to Shiva. With Ramakrishna by his side, he began to see Shiva no longer as an immobile image, but as a "body . . . living and breathing." Ramakrishna pointed to the temple image and showed how "Shiva [was], full of life and consciousness."[57]

The impoverished, illiterate shepherd, Swami Adbhutananda, whom Vivekananda later nicknamed "Plato," exemplified how spiritual wisdom could come without education. One of his brothers is purported to have said that "Many of us had to go through the muddy waters of intellectual knowledge before we attained God, but Latu [another nickname] jumped over them like Hanuman," the nubile monkey god.[58] Ramakrishna's theology of service inspired Adbhutananda, especially his description of a maidservant who works in her "rich master's house [and] looks after her master's young children, saying to them, 'my Ram,' 'my Hari,' yet in her heart of hearts she knows that they are not hers."[59] All parents, it is implied, are nothing but servants.

To become sannyasins, they needed to escape contact with their kin, unleashing familial dramas that had a transformative effect on their inner lives. The laments of wives and mothers form a plaintive backdrop to the spiritual freedom they sought; it is hard not to wonder about the emotional plight of women who "lost" husbands and sons. Stepping aside from the pain and needs of loved ones was regarded as a supreme test, requiring a turn from personal love to the search for "God knowledge." The pull and push of family love and control were ever-present, in which familial calculation may have played a role. Shivananda's parents, for example, needed to marry off his sister Nirada to avoid indigence, but for the union to take place, he, in turn, needed to accept a bride from that same household.[60] His problem only disappeared when his wife died three years later. Saradananda's father reportedly wanted his son to be guided by the family pandit and Tantrika scholar, rather than by Ramakrishna, and was horrified when he dropped out of the elite St. Xavier's College—and lost his prospects of an illustrious householder life—to tend to his dying guru.[61] After Ramakrishna's death,

Saradananda's father kept him in solitary confinement, until a younger brother left a door unlocked—the later author of the *Divine Play* thus is said to have only escaped when his father's absorption in a legal document enabled him to sneak away.[62] There were other examples; after much prayer, Brahmananda even relinquished his wife so that she would not interfere with his spiritual search.[63] And after his father begged, threatened, and cajoled, Ramakrishnananda is said to have exclaimed: "The world and home are to me, like a place infested with tigers."[64]

Such reported remarks seemed categorical and represent the paradox that the renouncer's splitting away from family and society was essential for the body's release of the soul.[65] Sondra Hausner argues that this "fission" was the necessary step for the spiritual liberation that the renouncer sought through wandering and pilgrimage. And yet, the rupture was rarely complete, especially if families came to accept their son's choice. Despite the pain and outrage, both parents and children lived in a world that admired "true" renunciation (despite agreement that this was rare), and which possessed complex institutional structures that supported the lives of sannyasins.

At first, however, the group had no formal grounding. Despite Ramakrishna's attention to detail in his teaching, he failed to organize any formal initiation. When he was dying, a householder disciple—Gopal Chandra Ghosh, later Swami Advaitananda—brought ocher cloths and rosaries for the disciples.[66] Ramakrishna handed them out, but with only a short ceremony, the details of which go unspecified. Even though one account says that the cloth was "preserved as a blessing from their Guru" and was not even worn, this is considered the first initiation.[67] Afterward, the disciples were sent to purge their pride with begging. Vivekananda needed years to build a stronger organization and establish more conventional forms of initiation.

TO RAMAKRISHNA'S END

In 1885–1886, Vivekananda took on more responsibilities for the group and tried to help his family. He filed a lawsuit against the relatives who he believed were dispossessing his mother after his father's death, a legal dispute that, in various forms, lasted for the rest of his life; he prepared for more examinations, and even gave up a job as a teacher that the *Divine Play* insists could have become permanent.[68] He thus lived a double life, still pursuing householder duties while also accepting what seemed his spiritual destiny. When Ramakrishna fell ill, this balancing act became less sustainable. The disciples took him to doctors in Calcutta, then to Shyampukur in June, and in December to the Cossipore Garden House outside the city, put at their disposal by a devotee.

During this period, crowds came in greater numbers to see Ramakrishna. Saradananda described his illness almost as an apotheosis, the ailing guru as a vessel for suffering that redeemed the sins of others: "[Ramakrishna] noticed some wounds on the back of his throat and was wondering how those wounds came to be, when the Divine Mother explained it to him: 'People who had committed various sins had become pure by touching his body and causing those wounds.'"[69] He believed his cancer resulted from his youthful spiritual trials, but did not ask Kali to relieve his illnesses, and feared no separation from his "useless" body. The disciples sought to keep these demanding would-be acolytes at bay.

At this terrible time, it is asserted that Vivekananda learned the most difficult spiritual exercises from his guru, and experienced *nirvikalpa samadhi*, a state of consciousness when the phenomenal world disappeared and self and nonself were united.[70] Mention of this final "gift" showed how, even when in mortal danger, Ramakrishna sought to transfer understanding, to help his acolyte toward "absolute consciousness." Little by little, Ramakrishna wasted away, and died on August 16, 1886.

* * *

Vivekananda's unexpected adherence to Ramakrishna makes sense only in relation to his youthful Brahmo convictions. He had rejected—in an almost visceral way—Vaishnava and Shakta devotion, and especially Tantra. Brahmoism had also questioned many of the customs regulating touch and distance, as well as purity and defilement by holding meetings with women and proposing intercaste marriage. At first, Brahmoism had appeared immensely liberating, opening a brave new world of rational iconoclasm, and casting off all the niggling "dos and don'ts" of Hindu obligation and instruction.[71] When he first entered Ramakrishna's circle, Vivekananda mocked Ramakrishna for his Kali-love and rejected Advaita Vedanta as equally nonsensical. But because of the young man's ardent desire to "see God," Ramakrishna wore down the younger man's resistance. Brahmoism, it seemed, had veiled the supernatural, and made it less apparent. And so, with a certain loathing, Vivekananda reentered this world, this time without the narrow conventions and endless rules. Ramakrishna's genius lay in the sensual and emotional experientialism that emphasized the existential qualities of divine play, urging those inclined to excessive purity to undertake a more expansive spirituality. Vivekananda's remarks, which began this chapter, suggest how embracing Kali tenderly and loving that "brain-sick baby" forever transformed him. Although the path was strewn with obstacles and objections, his sometimes uneasy incorporation of what he had so despised was a profound and enduring relief, a spiritual reconciliation of the highest order, and essential to his love of India.

4

VIVEKANANDA

AND HIS TRAVELS

It is always hard to see the purpose in wilderness wanderings until after they are over.

—John Bunyan, *Pilgrim's Progress,* 1678

◆　◆　◆

WHEN RAMAKRISHNA DIED, he left his disciples grief-stricken and without a map to navigate the world without him. They gathered in an ascetic monastic community and created strong lateral links borne out of mutual devotion, study, and pilgrimage.[1] While they sought to sustain Ramakrishna's legacy, this inheritance was open to myriad interpretations. Nonetheless, his loss made possible novel forms of thinking, travel, and adventures.

At this juncture, Vivekananda was little more than first among equals and, after an early consolidation of the group, he went wandering instead of establishing his primacy. This process transformed his vision of India as both a "sacred land" and the "mother of spirituality." He traveled intermittently between 1888 and 1893, internalizing India's landscape of mountains, temples, rivers, and sacred crossroads, across its length and breadth from the "abode of the Gods" in the Himalayas to the shrine of Devi Kanya Kumari at its southernmost tip.[2] He focused on sites of Hindu discipline, penance, and devotion, but also visited Muslim, Jain, and Buddhist locales. He also was said to have lived with Dalits in Central India and to have studied "such obscure questions as the caste-customs of Malabar."[3] He learned from Sikh gurus in the

Punjab, Jain masters in Gujarat, the scholar Pramadadas Mitra in Varanasi, and Pandit Narayan Das in Khetri. He remained eminently Bengali while also becoming more consciously Indian, seeking out various experiences and speaking about the country from firsthand observation. His vision of universalism, like the many dishes of Sarada Devi's kitchen, was expressed in his learning different religious idioms, scholarly traditions, and devotional styles. The experience certainly pulled him away from the universalist claims of the Western enlightenment.[4]

He journeyed first as a renouncer-scholar on a spiritual quest, begging for food, often ill, and at times near to death, during which his fellows were essential to his survival. Even in these uncertain early years, his sense of purpose gradually emerges through the sources about those times, which are more varied than for the years with Ramakrishna. Although letters remain relatively sparse, there are more reminiscences and scattered reports from those who came across him.[5] During and after 1890, however, he began to deepen his relations with Indian princes, engage with skeptical pandits (scholars), cultivate a middle-class public in Madras (now Chennai), and integrate politics into his spirituality. Vivekananda became more independent, abandoning the robes of the sannyasin (ascetic) for an orange jacket and a turban, the latter a present from the Raja of Khetri.[6]

When Vivekananda traveled to the West, he met unfamiliarity and hardship. However, such trials were insignificant in comparison to earlier ordeals when he observed other religious paths and entered different states of consciousness. In this period, he also developed his capacity for encounter, emotional engagement, and willingness to debate and persuade. As early as 1889, he wrote, "Many a man of wisdom, of piety, many a Sadhu (holy man) and Pundit have I met in so many places." Also, "I know not what sort of soul affinity there is between us," as he considered whether they were significant to his quest.[7] Although only thirty-two when he first left Indian shores, he possessed an unusual fund of human experience, which suggests perhaps why he dared go at all.

BARANAGAR AND THE TRIALS

OF PILGRIMAGE

With the help of a householder donation in September 1886, Vivekananda founded a monastery in a dilapidated house on the edge of Calcutta, between

Dakshineswar and Baranagar. The "haunted" house, as it was known, cost "eleven rupees a month for rent and tax," while the Brahmin cook earned a meager six rupees.[8] For Vivekananda, the early days there were full of care and distress; as Gupta explained, "the brothers of the Math live like mother-less children and wait for you to come . . . they have nothing to eat."[9]

He was now responsible for maintaining the fellowship and spiritual pas-sion that Ramakrishna had generated. The *Kathamrita* records how he re-peated Ramakrishna's injunctions against "lust and greed" and urged them not to return to their families. Ramakrishnananda's father came to them to beg for just that.[10]

Vivekananda proposed a visit to Antpur, the ancestral home of Premananda, who Ramakrishna had loved for his purity and boyish beauty. While there, they "resolved to renounce the world and become monks." As they sat by the fire and prayed into the morning hours, they performed the Viraja Homa ritual. This Hindu sacrifice ceremony is said to come from Vedic times and is designed to release the new monk from physical and mental distress before initiation into sannyasa.[11] This moment remains central to the Math's history, as Vivekananda "related to them the story of Jesus and appealed to them to imitate Christ's life and work, to realize God and deny themselves even as Christ has done, for the redemption of the world."[12] This was a remarkable and highly unusual evocation at this critical moment. The ceremony is considered the second initiation, after the first when Ramakrishna had distributed the ocher robes in 1886 and then ordered his disciples to go a-begging.[13]

But Ramakrishna had not given secret mantras, and the occasion in Antpur at the very end of 1886 was perhaps still more unconventional; despite the im-provised sacrificial fire, it was merely a promise among themselves and involved none of the orthodox rites. Reference to Christ, rather than to Hindu deities, in-dicated how Vivekananda continued to emphasize Ramakrishna's belief in the many paths to the divine. The story is even stranger as it seems they did not re-alize that it was Christmas Eve.[14] Such details show again the striking course of these men, and how they remained both inside and outside the world of Hindu monasticism.

Renouncing society was deliberately complicated, a way perhaps of re-flecting the infinite strata of family, caste, and spiritual communities that typi-fied householder life.[15] Perhaps the need for organization was so great because of renouncers' rootless existence that led them to travel to remote parts of the subcontinent. The stereotype of such people, with their unkempt hair, naked-

4.1. The "Haunted House," Baranagar

4.2. The monks at Baranagar, 1887. Vivekananda is wearing a turban.

ness, and ash-smeared bodies, sums up the solitary madness associated with Hindu "otherness." But few (including Vivekananda and his brothers) were alone for long. Rather, they constantly kept tabs on one another and lived together on well-traveled byways.[16] Sometimes, they would branch off in pairs and trios, and then meet up at another pilgrimage center.[17] They needed community, and in 1891, Vivekananda and five others created a "miniature Baranagore" in Meerut for a few months to recover their health.[18]

Their network is said to owe much to Adi Shankara, the eighth-century philosopher and theologian who is often credited with founding the Dasanami tradition of Hindu monasticism. He elaborated the doctrine of Advaita Vedanta, the nondualist creed that Vivekananda would later reinterpret. At this ceremony, the undisclosed mantras were passed from guru to monk and then to brother-monks. In this way, complicated lineages were created, where caste distinctions were meant to be irrelevant.

The Hindu saint Tota Puri had initiated Ramakrishna into the nondualistic Puri order, so rendering him qualified to do the same with his own followers.[19] Swami Abhedananda is said to have later secured these "formal rituals for the *viraja homa* ceremony" while on a pilgrimage to a sanctuary in the Barabar Hills.[20] Vivekananda now transmitted what Ramakrishna had refused or neglected to pass on, and performed a third initiation ceremony around a massive fire in January 1887 in front of Ramakrishna's slippers, a physical link to their guru. Abhedananda recorded that he sanctified the fire, "while reading out the mantras and poured oblations."[21]

However, this matter-of-fact report gives only a limited sense of such ceremonies, during which men stand virtually naked with shaven heads, chanting in Sanskrit with the senior monk presiding. As Sondra Hausner suggests, they become like newborns, the break with their first family now mirrored by incorporation into another. These scenes often take place at night around the fire to the sounds of bells and conch shells.[22] Several took their religious names at this juncture, with Vivekananda called Vividishananda, "bliss of the desire of knowledge." There were other times when he also called himself Satchidananda, or "he who possesses the bliss of true consciousness." Only after 1893, and before he ventured to the West, did he become Vivekananda, a title that referred to the idea of *viveka* (discernment), a quality that he would always prize. This Sanskrit word is about the ability to distinguish between the real and the unreal, between the self and the nonself, between what endures and what is evanescent.[23]

The monastery that Vivekananda created was hardly a site of organized worship in the way Westerners would recognize; the disciples devoted themselves to meditation, study, and singing, but their spirituality remained individualized and spontaneous, retaining a strong playful element. In the *Kathamrita*, Gupta recounted dips in the Ganges, walking to the ghats (bathing platforms), and dancing and singing together when the urge took them. Vivekananda's brother Mahendranath claimed that they continued to read the Bible, and favored the story of Nicodemus, the Pharisee who visited Jesus and insisted that his colleagues only judge Jesus after giving him a fair hearing.[24] There was none of the time discipline associated with Western medieval orders, the seven canonical hours that punctuate day and night. Sometimes they meditated under a tree while others went to the cremation grounds to worship Kali.[25] They retained such orthodox elements as *arati,* lighting wicks or camphor in the evening and waving them in a rhythmic fashion, as they had with Ramakrishna.[26] They also began singing the hymn "Jai Shiva Omkara," a song of praise to the Great Destroyer, during the evening ceremonies.

Gupta repeats Saradananda's assertion in *Sri Ramakrishna and His Divine Play* that they had begun calling themselves "Shiva demons," suggesting a growing spiritual association with Kali's consort, but not Shaivite dogmatism. They became noted for the privations they practiced, when "for months they lived on boiled leaves of the *bimba* creeper, salt, and rice."[27] They wore only loincloths and slept on straw mats. Ramakrishnananda created a shrine room where the avatara's relics were preserved in a pot and Ramakrishna was worshipped.[28] These austerities and prayers strengthened the mood of exaltation following the blow of their guru's death, but the emphasis on Ramakrishna as a man-god—and the worship of relics—would later involve Vivekananda in disputes with his brother-monks.

These details emphasize how little Vivekananda innovated at this juncture, and how misguided it is to rely on later polarities to explain the shift from Ramakrishna's inspiration.[29] Ecstasy and asceticism remained important in equal measure. Indeed, Vivekananda led the disciples in enthusiastic trials, especially fasting, but it is not clear when he introduced the study of "thought of the world outside" claimed by the order. He was said to have "instructed them in western and eastern philosophy, comparative religion, theology, history, sociology, literature, art, and science."[30] He apparently urged them to read books outside their tradition and discussed problems of religion and philosophy.

We do not know what books he used, but this teaching undoubtedly honed his own skills in comparative analysis, especially regarding Western religion and ideas. When he went abroad, he taught in a similar way but inverted the process, starting with Christian thought and Western science before analyzing Indian traditions.

Many wanted to go wandering. They did not need textual support to justify or prompt this searching, but both the Upanishads and the Puranas refer to such disciplines. For example, the Aruneya Upanishad from the first century BCE described relinquishing everything except the sannyasin's cloth and begging bowl to practice samadhi; the Narada-Parivrajaka Upanishad (3–56 to 3–59), counsels the monk to travel alone; still others prescribe constant travel as the way for the sadhu to find God.[31] The texts focus even more on *tapas* (austerity, meditation, or even pious works depending on the context); bhakti (religious devotion); and *jinjasi* (the quest for spiritual wisdom). Other, less authoritative texts, however, idealize the hermit's life; the Mahabharata, for example, mentions it often and describes the pitilessness of such disciplines.[32]

Few renouncers, however, lived this experience so strictly. While wandering was an important means of cutting off from family and caste, the longing for family often remained. It is said that Akhandananda cried alone on top of a haystack, mourning the loss of sisters and aunts while he traveled with Vivekananda.[33] They often went in pairs or as a threesome: when Vivekananda went in 1886 to Bodh Gaya, the site of the Buddha's enlightenment, he hopped on a train with two other monks, traveling only with "loincloth, clothes and blanket each," and suffering from the cold, food, and lack of funds.[34] The brotherly intimacy that Ramakrishna had fostered was part of the "purest" mystical quest.[35]

Not everyone approved. A fellow pilgrim apparently mocked Shivananda for helping "a brother disciple in need," prompting the response that Vivekananda believed brotherly love was more sacred than visiting temples.[36] Vivekananda went to help Abhedananda when he fell ill in the Himalayan foothills. This justification of "attachment" may have been a starting point for later visions of service. Vivekananda explained to Pramadadas Mitra, a noted Sanskrit scholar: "Well, you may smile, Sir to see me weaving all this web of Maya—and that is no doubt the fact. But then there is the chain of iron, and there is the chain of gold. Much good comes of the latter; and it drops off by itself when all the good is reaped. The sons of my Master are indeed the great objects of my service, and here alone I feel I have some duty left for me. . . ."[37]

Vivekananda himself was looked after by Akhandananda, who was familiar with the Himalayas; Sarada Devi, Ramakrishna's widow, apparently instructed him to care for Vivekananda and make sure he had enough to eat.[38] When Vivekananda sent all the other disciples away, Akhandananda found a way to stay close by; and, although Vivekananda claimed to be irritated by his presence, he also valued him and recognized the depth and sincerity of his care.[39]

The traveling was filled with bliss and pain, the joy of visiting sites that had welcomed thousands of others, and the difficulties of rootlessness. They sought to disregard the body to attain transcendental states of pure consciousness.[40] The Sanskrit scholar Abhedananda heard the passionate "call of the forest" and later "endured all sorts of privation and hardship."[41] Shivananda recalled how he bathed in well water, had only one cloth to cover himself, and slept under trees, but was so aflame with the "spirit of renunciation" that he forgot about his body.[42] Akhandananda had bathed in the Ganges four times a day and practiced holding his breath by weighing himself down with stones to stay under water.[43] The body was an obstacle to union with Brahman, but this merger was possible only through prolonged physical training. Meditation required deep concentration on the breath, harnessing the energy housed at the base of the spine and demanding enormous discipline to marshal the states of consciousness that released the soul from the body. They were thus confronted with an existential paradox, as the maya of the body competed with the transcendence they sought.

It is a cliché that the Cartesian dualism of occidental thought somehow hampers spiritual searching, while "Eastern wisdom" possesses a holism that properly incorporates the body.[44] Ascetics in both traditions possess "embodied dualisms," and both regard the soul or spirit as distinct from the mind, even if what happens to the soul after death is very different; the trials and sacrifices of the sadhus focused as much on the body as those of medieval mystics, and both sought release from its "snares."[45] The nonduality of Advaita Vedanta sought to link the divine within individuals to the formless universal, in much the same way that Ramakrishna's salt doll melted into the infinite ocean. The "subtle body" (atman) or the "soul" (loosely translated) is divested of physical burdens, a rupture which is essential to unity, and is mirrored in the process of breaking family ties, casting off property, and abandoning caste during the renouncer ceremony.[46]

Despite their best efforts, however, the body inevitably harassed them: hunger, cold, and illness were hard to ignore. Saradananda had such bad dysentery that he had to return to Baranagar to be tended.[47] Akhandananda had bronchitis and needed to be nursed.[48] Turiyananda went without food for so long that he was once reduced to eating grass.[49] Shivananda needed a break so badly he went to the Badrinath Temple, a Vaishnava shrine far north of Hrishikesh, where the local authorities helped him live in comfort: "[T]he local Deputy Collector wrote a letter to the temple authorities directing that every possible facility be made available to me. Excellent arrangements for my food and other requirements have been made . . . Only very influential people, or rich people like princes and princesses, who can spend huge sums, can get such hospitality."[50]

Another letter described a cantonment with a full Gurkha regiment and his relief that he had "plain cooked food every day." And he admitted, somewhat shamefacedly, that he also got "delicacies in spite of protests." He said that he did not "like to wander about aimlessly. It only tortures the body . . . Certainly life has a purpose and is not to be wasted like that."[51] He even gave up such travel for a while, because he wrote six months later to Balaram Basu, a householder disciple of Ramakrishna:[52] "Don't you think you have reached the point when you should call it quits? What good will it do you to ruin your health? If you come back and stay with us . . . , it will give us more pleasure than we can say . . ."[53]

Shivananda acknowledged that ignoring bodily needs was essential to transcendent release but commented that meditation was nearly impossible when distracted by weariness and illness. Still, even he at times delighted in the freedom of such treks. At the end of 1891, while meditating at Baranagar, he was overtaken by the urge to visit Rameswaram, a temple with a high tomb and a large Shiva lingam, built on an island off the tip of India's southern peninsula: "The urge was so strong that if I had been a bird with wings, I would have flown to that place."[54]

Vivekananda, who traveled for so many years in India and around the globe, knew that this life required a rare discipline and was not for layabouts. Akhandananda told how they had come across "a Sadhu seated in meditation, covered with a cloth from head to foot," who was "snoring loudly" rather than doing spiritual exercises. Vivekananda believed it would be better if the man "put his shoulder to a plough."[55] When he later evolved a vision of active service through Karma yoga, he envisaged society's revitalization through a massive infusion of *rajas* (energy) that this renouncer so noisily lacked.

These early travels were vital to everything Vivekananda did subsequently, but documentation remain sparse. When he went on pilgrimage, he seemed at first glance—and especially before 1890–1891—to be living "the time-honoured practice" of paying a visit to, and making tapas (spiritual austerities) at, the sacred shrines in the four corners of the "sacred land," claiming the hospitality of Indian householders along the way.[56] Hindus understood this tradition in relation to an elaborate sacred geography. Whereas Judaism, Christianity, and Islam focus on Jerusalem or Mecca, India is transected by the four "abodes of the gods," where Vishnu can be found in Badrinath, near Tibet; Rama, in Rameswaram in the far south; Krishna, on the far west in Dvaraka; and Jagannath, in Puri on the Bay of Bengal.

Diana Eck has shown how this sacred geography is both imagined and tangible—human beings need do little more than discover the gods who inhabit the landscape.[57] Pilgrimage sites possess a common mythology that reappears almost endlessly in the incarnations of the gods and goddesses embedded everywhere in the landscape.

These places were holy *tirthas*, a word that encompassed physical *and* spiritual intersection. Literally, it means "sacred bathing place" and is often translated as "ford," and thus as a way across the river of the cycle of existence (*samsara*).[58] Going to such sites involved toil and asceticism, but the aim was always enlightenment. The tirthas were first listed in the Mahabharata and reappear in the many sacred texts, with the journeying integral to achieving such virtues as "truth, charity, patience, self-control, celibacy, and wisdom." Deemed to be the true waters of purification, "[t]he one who always bathes in earthly *tirthas* as well as the *tirthas* of the heart goes to the supreme goal."[59]

Tirthas thus heightened spiritual possibility; they were the locations where the avataras descended to earth and where pilgrims' prayers ascended to the gods. The tirtha was a "doorway between heaven and earth" or between "this shore" and the "far shore."[60] Vivekananda later offered his own interpretation: "[W]hat is there to wonder at special influences attaching to particular places? There are places where He manifests Himself specially, either spontaneously or through the earnest longing of pure souls, and the ordinary man, if he visits those places with eagerness, attains his end quite easily."[61]

Shiva's wild habitation on the top of Mount Kailash is the most notable example; his passion for Sati is remembered in the way he carries her through the universe in a grief-stricken state, strewing the fifty-one pieces of her body across the subcontinent, her breasts at Tara Tarini and her *yoni* [womb / genitals], at the Kamakhya Temple in Assam. While these celestial objects fall to earth, others are self-manifesting, like the sacred footprints of mythical heroes, the imprints of the Buddha, or the fossilized shells (Vishnu shaligrams) that Ramakrishna's father had discovered before his birth.[62]

Ramakrishna's disciples gave some sense of the mind-altering possibilities of such sites. In the Panchavati, the "garden of the five banyan trees," where Sita and Rama lived in exile in northwest Maharashtra, Brahmananda reportedly "lived continuously in Nirvikalpa Samadhi (the highest state of concentration), for six days and nights."[63] The tirtha thus offered auspicious surroundings for such a strenuous spiritual trial, where he would have died had not a brother-monk kept them both alive with begged food.

Vivekananda entered this world through legend, parable, and myth, while investing his travels with his own yearnings. He alludes briefly to lesser tirthas, mentioning how he "should stay in [Allahabad] during the month of Mâgha [Jan–Feb] keeping the Kalpa vow"; or describing how he was "agog" to go to Varanasi, a light-filled tirtha on the Ganges known for its beauty and antiquity, where Shankara was claimed as an incarnation of Shiva.[64] Those lucky enough to die there break the cycle of reincarnation, never to return to the world of maya.

For Vivekananda, as for his brother-monks, the Himalayas were also evocative: "As peak after peak of this Father of Mountains began to appear before my sight, all those propensities . . . that had been going on in my brain for years seemed to quiet down and mind reverted to that one eternal theme which the Himalayas always teaches . . . renunciation."[65]

In the West, he recalled this "elevation" in a letter from Switzerland to Christine Greenstidel, one of his disciples: "It is a miniature Himalayas, and has the same effect of raising the mind up to the Self and driving away all earthly feelings and ties . . ."[66]

And yet, for all that he remained wedded to pilgrimage, he believed people were the greatest tirthas: "But know it for certain that there is no greater *Tirtha* than the body of man. Nowhere else is the *Atman* so manifest as here."[67]

He emphasized this view when he wrote about Pavhari Baba, a Brahmin sannyasin known as the "air-eating" saint, so called because he ate virtually nothing and lived in an underground cave in Ghazipur, once not emerging for five years. Vivekananda wrote that Pavhari Baba chose a cave because it was where "the temperature is even, and where sounds do not disturb the mind," a perfect place for contemplation and the ultimate tirtha between the bowels of the earth and its surface.[68] When they met in early February 1890, Vivekananda talked to him through a closed door and never saw him.[69] Later, he noted that the saint's humility was such that he only spoke of himself in the third person, but "then fire comes out as the talking goes on."[70]

Accounts describe a moment of temptation, even for Vivekananda, who seemed inclined to stay and learn more.[71] He was still there a month later and had plans to move into a "gentleman's bungalow" in the grounds and with hopes that Akhandananda would join him. His guru-brothers feared the holy man's influence and wondered whether Vivekananda would "go astray," but in a letter of July 6, he announced he was done there: "I am longing for a flight to the Himalayas. This time I shall not go to Pavhari Baba or any other saint—they divert one from his highest purpose. Straight up!"[72] Thereafter, he would rely on himself and on "high places," both geographically and spiritually.

These encounters illustrate how far he had traveled from Brahmo "rationalism," as no one could be further from the Bengali-educated elite than an "air-eating saint." Moreover, Pavhari's example remained an inspiration, an object lesson on the "power of the Mind" and the "religion of love." Vivekananda was back in India in 1898 when Pavhari Baba was said to have burned himself to death, his body the final sacrifice. When asked whether Pavhari Baba had acted wrongly, Vivekananda merely replied, "He was too great a man for me to judge. He knew what he was doing."[73]

◆   ◆   ◆

Vivekananda took with him Hindu lore, tradition, and sacred texts when he first journeyed in 1889, but also unusually a copy of Thomas à Kempis's *The Imitation of Christ*, parts of which he translated into Bengali in 1889. Written in Latin between 1418 and 1427, *The Imitation* advised aspirants to withdraw from the world and to look within for spiritual growth.[74] Immensely influential within Christianity, it appealed to Vivekananda because, like Ramakrishna, Thomas took issue with excessive displays of outward ritual and intellectual prowess, concentrating instead on surrender to God's will and pleasure in his love:[75] "Each letter of the book is marked deep with the heart's blood of the great soul who had renounced all for his love of Christ." He concluded that "all wise men think alike."[76] *Imitation* was one of the volumes that Vivekananda discussed with his brother-monks at Baranagar, a volume that inspired "so much of awe and reverence. . . . towards its author."[77]

However, he also contrasted Thomas's work with the "luxurious, insolent, despotic, barouche-and-brougham-driving Christians of the Protestant" sects that sought to missionize India and impose foreign spiritual traditions.[78] If Ramakrishna condemned the impositions of the British, he had no steely edge, literary reference, or translations from English to Bengali to accompany his disapproval. In contrast, Vivekananda had been educated in a Christian school, and had learned Gospel themes, and now used this training to underscore the hypocrisy of his teachers. His tone shows how the spiritual was often linked to social criticism, to a vision of freedom that went beyond spiritual liberation alone.

The remark about the "barouche-and-brougham" Christians also highlighted the jarring nature of the British presence, and the fast-moving changes they had brought. Despite the ancient history of pilgrimage routes crisscrossing a Hindu sacred land, pilgrimage was not an unchanging project. Vivekananda's experience was shaped by the British train system, new routes of connection superimposed—through both maps and metal tracks—on older commercial and sacred links. Much time and energy has gone into working out his itinerary, fixing who hosted him, what he ate, said, and thought. How he traveled has been equally studied.[79] He tried to walk, especially in the early days, but often no more than for thirty-mile stretches, cursed as he was by lumbago and various illnesses.[80]

For example, he was on foot when he traveled from Agra to Vrindavan (around thirty-one miles), taking in two cities that could not have been more different. The first was over 124 miles south of Delhi where he saw the Taj Mahal and the other architectural wonders of Mughal India; he then journeyed on to Vrindavan, one of the holiest of Vaishnava sites with its magnificent temples devoted to Radha-Krishna. He learned more about Islam when he visited Ayodha and Lucknow, travels which acquainted him with North India and the mix of Hindu and Islamic culture that shaped its identity.

Often, however, he went by train, and so the trips were shaped not by endless walking, but by steam, technology, and Victorian architecture. Some stations—such as the newly completed Victoria Station in Bombay (now Mumbai)—were grandiose, dominating symbols; others, more basic stops,

4.3. Victoria Terminus (Chhatrapati Shivaji Terminus), Bombay. Photograph, constructed between 1878 and 1888.

but the new network allowed him to travel on a scale and at a speed earlier generations of pilgrims could never have envisaged. Before the railway was built, traveling from the Himalayas to the southernmost tip of the subcontinent by land would have taken years. He therefore saw the countryside in a relatively novel fashion, as darting images through the windows, different from the horizon of slowly changing scenery attained on foot. He recruited his first disciple not at a monastery, shrine, or meeting, but on the platform of Hathras railway station, sixty-two miles to the southeast of Delhi.[81] This man, an assistant stationmaster called Sharat Gupta, later Sadananda, heard Vivekananda talk and left everything to go with him.

Vivekananda hesitated to take on a disciple because he was wary of attachment. Like Ramakrishna's other followers, he needed company and care but also searched for "dispassion," opposing impulses that were hard to reconcile. To demonstrate the conflict, Sadananda later dramatized their experience and recounted how Vivekananda suddenly walked off alone: "[A]fter three hours he returned [and] asked for food. Hadn't eaten. 'You haven't taken your food?' Gupta said. 'How could I have eaten alone?' Swami Vivekananda said, '. . . you have become the shackles of my feet. I left you, but eventually decided to return for your welfare. You are dumb, I wasn't sure that you'd do without me.'"[82]

When Vivekananda claimed, not so convincingly, that he had only come back for Sadananda's sake, their shared laughter suggested neither believed his words.

Like his brother-monks, Vivekananda faced physical hardships. Sadananda cleaned his filthy body, cracked feet, and dirty hair after one difficult foray.[83] Retrospective testimony suggests he used spices to alleviate pain and quell hunger: "He liked chillies, pepper, and such other pungent things. When I asked for the reason one day, he said 'During his wandering a monk has to take all kinds of food, and drink water from all sorts of places; that tells upon the health. To counteract their bad effect, many monks become addicted to hemp and other intoxicants. For the same reason I have taken to chili.'"[84]

G. S. Bhate, whose family hosted Vivekananda when he was only twelve, was shocked when the monk asked for "a betel nut, pan and tobacco for chewing."[85] Betel nut contains arecoline, which stimulates alertness and stamina and can even promote euphoria. Vivekananda liked tobacco, a habit that later got him into trouble with Westerners. When in Lucknow, he shared a pipe with a man of low status, a story interpreted to show his indifference to caste; the more cynical suspect he simply wanted a smoke.[86]

These years were hard. At Bodh Gaya in 1886, he had digestive problems. He had high fever for weeks at the beginning of 1889 and complained about the water in Deogarh. In 1890, malaria (or perhaps diphtheria) laid him low for three months in Hrishikesh, where he was so ill that his pulse stopped and his brothers feared for his life.[87] He was still emaciated and weak when he took refuge in Meerut.[88]

He set out again in January 1891, traveling under a false name, though it is unclear whether he remained anonymous. When Vivekananda had first met Sadananda in 1888, the latter claimed that Vivekananda had expressed doubt about his spiritual capacity.[89] However, by 1891, another monk, Saradananda, believed that Vivekananda achieved this transformation because he again realized nirvikalpa samadhi at the perilous moment near death. In its aftermath, Saradananda said, Vivekananda was open to greater activism, as he set aside the dangerous path of visionary asceticism.[90]

Again, hagiographical anecdotes of this kind reflect the spiritual meanings attributed to shifts in Vivekananda's quest. Certainly, the little surviving correspondence, although still concerned with spiritual searching, also suggests someone less keen to impress with erudition, and more able to articulate the amalgam he was mixing.[91] Vivekananda combined the sacred with the practical—a vision that he would later express in his "Practical Vedanta," when he argued against the "fictitious differentiation between religion and the life of the world."[92] By 1891, he seemed more self-assured and less inclined to test his body; he continued to go by train and lived with well-do-do admirers.

The photos of him with shaven head and wooden staff were taken probably in Hyderabad and Madras.[93] The latter was posed in front of a fake landscape (a painting), common enough when outdoor exposures were difficult.[94] Was this an attempt to manipulate his image, or an effort to memorialize, in the best way that technology could offer, his extensive wanderings? There was probably something of both in this image, but certainly he explored different costumes and later created an impressive vision for Westerners.[95] But image-making was not, perhaps, his only concern—the different costumes may well have signified self-exploration. Even as late as 1898, he saw himself as a sadhu again when on pilgrimage in India.[96]

Because of these travels, Vivekananda had a growing sense of India, with his own Bengali identity increasingly integrated into a greater awareness of territoriality and secular power.[97] It is not clear whether he wandered in search of this national understanding, or that it came upon him as he did so.[98] Jung Hyun Kim has shown how he was "most ardently supported" by the "Rajas of Mysore, Limbdi, Ramnad and Khetri, and the Dewan of Junagadh."[99] Except for Mysore (now Karnataka), these were subordinate kingdoms within the Raj, but he hoped they might engage in a pan-Indian reform. They disappointed him in this aim, though the Raja of Khetri (Ajit Singh), in Rajasthan, and the Dewan of Junagadh (Haridas Viharidas Desai), in Gujarat, became personal patrons. Singh encouraged Vivekananda to go to America and welcomed him on his return to India in 1897; Desai defended him against personal attacks while in the West.[100]

Vivekananda also associated with Raja Bhaskara Sethupathi, of Ramnad in the south, who later feted him as a returning hero in 1897. He prized this connection because the Estate of Ramnad included the holy island city of Rameswaram with its massive Ramanathaswamy Temple, famous for its sculpted pillars, water tanks, and magnificently decorated corridors—the

4.4. Vivekananda as mendicant

4.5. Ajit Singh, Raja of Khetri

site that Shivananda had dreamed of visiting. The temple was on Pamban Island, where Rama was said to have built a bridge to Lanka to escape his pursuers, and where a genuine bridge of limestone shoals marks a former land connection between the subcontinent and the smaller country. It was also one of the key spiritual sites of southern India, and hence important to his vision of national identity that connected it to northern sites in the Himalayas and their foothills.

Raja Bhaskara sought to legitimize his meager authority within a powerful Raj as the "lord of the bridge" protecting this ancient trust.[101] But

4.6. Rameswaran Temple

such men were also aware of the wider world. Shankar Pandurang Pandit, a Vedic scholar who administered a minor princedom, reportedly told Vivekananda, "Few will appreciate you here. You ought to go to the West where people will understand your worth."[102] When he went to Mysore, Vivekananda was the guest of the dewan before meeting the prince, Chamarajendra Wodeyar X, who introduced him to other princes. Manibhai Jashbhai of Baroda (Vadodara), a major princely state, also offered hospitality.[103] Raja Dinakara Sethupathi, the brother of the Raja of Ramnad, also connected him to local political and cultural elites. Through this network, Vivekananda became a public intellectual in southern India.

He gained spiritual insights, it seemed, even in this worldly milieu. In August 1891, accounts describe how he had a moving encounter with a girl, one of the so-called nautch dancers who had performed in the eighteenth century for Mughals, nawabs, and lesser princes, but now for Indian notables and British Raj officials; these young women were also often forced into sex work. The Maharaja of Khetri apparently "prevailed upon [Vivekananda] to come, and the girl then sang the song of Surdas of Mathura, the sixteenth-century poet, which reproached the arrogance of virtue and reminded him that God saw no difference between sinners and saints."[104] Vivekananda apparently said to the girl, "Mother, I am guilty. I was about to show you disrespect by refusing to come to this room. But your song awakened my consciousness."[105] This story, often repeated, testified to his spiritualization of women who received at his hands the dignity and respect that mothers were owed, even when they were disdained by others. Such interactions testify to the lack of clerical sanctimony that made him so distinctive in the West and were so important to his theology and to man-making.

These details were important for an emerging public persona that rejected both reformism and revivalism, and any "outmoded orthodoxy still advocated by fanatical leaders and the misguided rationalism of the westernized reformers."[106] In contrast to other Hindu reformers, Vivekananda accepted the princes' moral failings and was willing to work with their Muslim officials. He behaved similarly when he visited the Jain temple of Dilwar, or shared food with Muslims in Kashmir.[107] When such behavior scandalized Hindus, he responded that "as a sannyasin belonging to the highest order of paramahamsas," he was "above all rules of caste."[108] He referred here to Ramakrishna, who held the honorific of paramahamsa, "supreme swan," to indicate a soul able to float gracefully above maya in the cosmic ocean, its body equally sacred. He used this justification again when he associated with Christians in the West.

As Vivekananda traveled, both the subcontinent's vastness and its many religious traditions impressed him. Interestingly, at this stage he rarely used the term "Motherland," though he did much more often after his return in 1897, when it resonated with the growing national feeling of his audiences.[109] But at this stage, he reflected mostly on unity and diversity, on the many permutations of Hindu spirituality, and on his rejection of biological race theory. Like so many people in the nineteenth century, he could confusingly mix ideas of nation, race, and language, but in his reflections on "Aryans" and "Tamilians," he insisted that such designations were little more than philological categories that denoted antiquity, both essential to Indian greatness.[110]

He also engaged with questions of political sovereignty, honoring the rajas in their position, but not fearful of using his spiritual authority to criticize them.[111] They were a countervailing force to British power, but he understood that they were weak and disunited, even if rich. Although he was grateful for their rapturous welcome in 1897, they were of little practical help: as will be seen, most of the funds for his larger works—even the trip to America—came from elsewhere.

His self-vision had also evolved. Renunciation remained central, but he would later deemphasize the austerities that he had so admired when he prefaced *The Imitation of Christ*.[112] He claimed to have forged the link between the sacred, the social, and the political during one of the culminating moments of his travels, in December 1892. He went to Cape Comorin, at the southernmost tip of India at the very end of the north–south axis known as the *char dham*, the pilgrimage trek from Kashmir to Kanyakumari, where he arrived and meditated on Devi Kanya Kumari, the maiden goddess, Parvati.[113] This site sits at the majestic intersection of the Bay of Bengal, the Arabian Sea, and the Indian Ocean. Widely known as Shree Bala Bhadra, the goddess is an adolescent girl on the cusp of womanhood and marriage. Her temple sits on one of the fifty-two Shakti Pithas, the place where Sati's right shoulder and spine fell to earth. He had visions, some of which he never discussed, that shaped the rest of his life.

Of all Vivekananda's pilgrimage experiences, this has attracted the most comment. It is claimed that at this tirtha of seas and continents, he wondered whether India's religion was indeed its greatest weakness. As he stood at the very end of the subcontinent, however, he decided that Indian spirituality was not the cause of cultural decadence and national decline, but the greatest source of its potential power. It is said that he confided this revelation to Alasinga Perumal, a disciple in Madras, and elaborated on it eighteen months later in March 1894, when he wrote to Ramakrishnananda from America that when[114]

> sitting in Mother Kumari's temple, sitting on the last bit of Indian rock—I hit upon a plan. We are so many *Sannyasins* wandering about, and teaching the people metaphysics—it is all madness. Did not our Gurudeva [Ramakrishna] use to say, "An empty stomach is no good for religion"? That those poor people are leading the life of brutes is simply due to ignorance. We have for all ages been sucking their blood and trampling them underfoot ... Suppose some disinterested Sannyasins, bent on doing good to others, go from village to village, disseminating education and seeking in various ways to better the condition of all down to the Chandâla [Dalits deemed polluted for handling the dead], through oral teaching, and by means of maps, cameras, globes, and such other accessories—can't that bring forth good in time? All these plans I cannot write out in this short letter.[115]

4.7. Cape Comorin, with the Vivekananda Rock Memorial in the middle

Here was another aspect of the sannyasin's vocation—a pilgrimage to India's village heartland, since he understood that the "poor were too poor to come to school": "[T]hey will gain nothing by reading poetry and all that sort of thing. We, as a nation, have lost our individuality. . . . We have to give back to the nation its lost individuality and raise the masses. The Hindu, the Mohammedan, the Christian, all have trampled them underfoot. Again the force to raise them must come from inside, that is, from the orthodox Hindus. In every country the evils exist not with, but against, religion. Religion therefore is not to blame, but men."[116]

With these words, Vivekananda may well have been trying to deflect the conventional charge that Hinduism was responsible for the condition of the Chandala, the lowest of the Dalits. The last line might even suggest that he was arguing against Marx, insisting that religion was hardly the "opiate of the people," but rather its galvanizing force. But there is no evidence that he was aware at this juncture of Marxist theory, though he spoke often of atheism and agnosticism as a discouraging trend. He wrote from Chicago in early 1894 under the influence of American progressivism and with an as yet relatively untarnished view of the country's democracy, especially where education was concerned. Although written to a disciple back home, it has an American flavor, with its focus on individuality and strong missionary sense. And yet, his teaching on individuality was almost always joined to its relationship to wholeness, and his view that one religion should never triumph over another. As will be seen, it was a way of forcing respect from Christians, who sought to rob Hinduism and India of what he called its "own law of growth."[117] This would be accomplished not by reformist Hindus nor the pandits of yore, but by those able to appreciate Pavhari Baba and, of course, Ramakrishna, while dispelling the prejudices and the "don't-touchism" of certain orthodox currents.[118]

He put these ideas into practice in Madras in 1892. The brother of the Raja of Ramnad had connected him to the "Mylapore clique," associated with the Triplicane Literary Society. S. Subramania Iyer was a Madras High Court judge active in local politics and another supporter—along with the princes—of Vivekananda's trip to the West.[119] This new constituency, away from his native Calcutta, was a sign of the innovations he sought away from his Bengali homeland; Madras was also a link to the "Hindu heartland," a city which also owed its growth to the East India Company. As a mosaic of connected villages with temples associated with the Tamil countryside and poet saints, Madras also had its White Town and Black Town and, as in Calcutta, new suburbs housing British officialdom. Madras was even more heterogeneous than Calcutta, with Muslims, Europeans, and North Indian neighborhoods, some of which contained the Bengalis who often hosted him.

Vivekananda became associated with Triplicane and the Vaishnava Parthasarthy Temple, famous as one of the oldest buildings in the city. The temple's towers and pillars exploded with elaborate and tangled carvings, its architecture an enduring model for South Indian worship. In the nineteenth century, Muslims flocked to the duty-free bazaar, which offered attractive conditions for commerce. The shrine meant that the neighborhood retained its temple-town ambience in the late nineteenth century, when this Hindu quarter had become an important economic, political, and especially intellectual center.[120]

Vivekananda would later praise the spiritual heritage of southern India, especially the "epoch-making" teachers that created the distinctive schools of Hindu philosophy, such as Shankara, who was central to his Advaitic inspiration.[121] He also referred to the southern origins of the Alwars, Tamil saints who revitalized religion between the fifth and ninth centuries, and their regional poetry as a medium for Vaishnava devotion since the eighth

4.8. Parthasarathy Temple, Madras. Photograph, 1858.

century. He repeatedly celebrated these different traditions to impress his audiences with India's spiritual greatness.[122]

Alasinga Perumal lived in Triplicane. With his nephews, he was the host to an array of guests, not only Vivekananda but also Gandhi, Bipin Chandra Pal, and Bal Gangadhar Tilak, the latter two famous for their role during the first campaign of Indian nationalism—Swadeshi.[123] Alasinga also lived near his uncle, who had been invited to the World Parliament of Religions in Chicago but was unwilling to cross the oceans because of his orthodoxy.[124] Alasinga, himself, was an ardent Vaishnava, teacher, and journalist, whose friends questioned Vivekananda about literary, scientific, historical, and metaphysical issues. This web of acquaintance put him at the center of Madras's cultural life.[125]

Memoirists who encountered Vivekananda in Madras spoke of his charismatic personality, conversational gifts, and ability to dispel religious doubt.[126] He was viewed as a prodigy, able to discourse on Homer and Shakespeare as well as on Indian saint and poets—a versatility that later impressed Western audiences.[127] He resisted his Madras audiences' tendency to sneer at the Vedic seers and challenged them to test the "science of the Rishis" to determine its value.[128] His relationship with Alasinga, moreover, spawned more concrete dreams, such as a training school for young preachers and other educational initiatives.[129] Madras, not Calcutta, provided the first lay nucleus of support for Vivekananda's emerging view of national revitalization.

Vivekananda was thus a novel figure, who believed that even the lowest castes should receive a Sanskrit education, and who had no objection to sea voyages. He was also beginning to present himself differently. One memoir of 1892 described how his resonant voice and distinguished carriage made the author think of a maharaja.[130] G. S. Bhate wrote that "though he wore clothes bearing the familiar colour of the Sannyasin's garments, he appeared to be dressed differently from [...] Sannyasins."[131] He was already wearing the turban the Raja of Khetri had given him as a gift in 1891, a princely accessory that heightened his air of majesty, and a tailored coat; wearing stitched clothes may have been an attempt to suggest a worldly and manly sophistication instead of the more conventional flowing robes of a wandering holy man.[132]

Vivekananda developed a radically altered conception of the sannyasin. If in earlier days, he had lived among Dalits and Muslims, in Madras, he circulated often among other middle-class Bengalis who now lived in the city, finding hospitality from pandits, officials, teachers, journalists, and reformers. Before his trip to America, he had certainly reflected deeply on the plight of the Indian masses, but Ramakrishna had repeatedly warned against do-goodism and its spiritual perils. He had famously told his disciples, "You must always remember, in whatever you do, that the aim of human life is to attain God, not to build hospitals and dispensaries."[133] Such activities lured aspirants away from a more difficult transcendental search. But Vivekananda may have already wanted to unite spiritual detachment with helping the needy—to find a way to work for the poor without tainting the undertaking with "name and fame." This sentiment explains the letter to his guru-brothers in 1894 that spirituality was impossible for "empty stomach[s]."[134] Only in the late 1890s would he be able to put his plans into practice when confronted by plague and famine and prompted by the innovations of his guru-brothers on the ground.[135]

Although he sought transcendence and at times ached for solitude, he had now charted his path, one different to that of Ramakrishna. When a follower had asked Ramakrishna whether a sadhu should travel to holy places, the guru had replied, "Why should he, if he feels calm and peaceful in one fixed place?"[136] Ramakrishna's spiritual audacity lay in his bodily sacrifice to create his mystical vision, but he also knew he was handing over to a young man who was defined by his inability to stay in one place. Vivekananda, too, had sacrificed his body; his pilgrimages had both enhanced his spiritual progress and led him to reflect about the relationship between service and transcendence. He had also begun to entwine his wandering with forms of social and political advocacy, though he often insisted that the latter was none of his business.[137] His youth had taught him to value some Western ideas, but not to idealize them; time with Ramakrishna had persuaded him of the continued worth of Hindu spirituality; and his wanderings forced him to reckon with the India's vastness and the role that religion could play in its "resurrection."

PART TWO

THE WEST

5

THE WORLD'S PARLIAMENT
OF RELIGIONS

It is forbidden to decry other sects; the true believer gives honour to whatever in them is worthy of honour.

—Emperor Ashoka, *Fourteen Edicts*, c. 250–60 BCE

❖ ❖ ❖

EVEN CONSIDERING THE IDEA of going to Chicago would have been impossible without Vivekananda's many Indian advisers and backers. According to Alasinga Perumal's biographer, it was the young devotee from Madras who convinced him to go, but the dewans of Junagadh, Porbandar, and the King of Mysore also seem to have suggested the venture.[1] Some accounts give the credit to the flattery of Shankar Pandurang Pandit, or the advice of Sankaracharya of Puri.[2] Madras High Court judge Subrahmania Iyer, a theosophist and the founder of an organization to facilitate enlightenment, also supported the journey "for the propagation of Indian culture."[3]

Members of a subscription committee in Madras collected contributions to fund the trip. Some say that Vivekananda sent the 500 rupees to the poor, though others suggest he used the money to escape the heat in Bangalore (now Bengalaru) and Ootacamund.[4] It was not clear exactly why Vivekananda hesitated, whether it was the distance and the expense that concerned him; despite his protestations, he may also have feared Western spiritual contamination.[5]

And not everyone was keen: the Maharaja of Ramnad, for example, was not supportive initially.[6]

Vivekananda is said to have dreamed of Ramakrishna walking into an ocean, beckoning him to follow. He sought Sarada Devi's opinion and she responded that she had had a similar dream.[7] He asked again, just to be sure, and she told him he should go because it would "do good for humanity."[8] This response seems to have made up his mind.

Here was early evidence of how he went to Sarada Devi for her counsel and prescience. Indeed, her advice may even have been the deciding factor in his agreeing to go. With time, he relied on her more consistently and consolidated the devotion to her through his own reverence.[9] He took his place in a holy lineage, always *under* the aegis of someone holier than himself, a subordination that demonstrated humility but also cast him as an agent of loftier powers. The exchange—in which successive dreams were invoked and signs of divine patronage given—was a powerful aspect of his spiritual life, which, however, he downplayed in Chicago.

Sarada Devi's approval launched a new campaign, with Alasinga going door-to-door a second time to raise money; shoes (too small) were purchased. The Raja of Khetri insisted that Vivekananda visit to bless the birth of his long-awaited son and, in return, gave him "suitable clothes," which in fact were highly unsuitable for the very different climate of Chicago.[10] Supporters raised 4,000 rupees (around $1,300)—1,500 from the King of Mysore, while the Raja of Ramnad (now in favor of the plan), Manmatha Bhattacharya, and Subrahmania Iyer each gave 500.[11] Alasinga and his friends collected the rest, and outfitted him with European-style attire, printed visiting cards, and bought him a watch. The last gift was important—abroad, Vivekananda would need to keep to a more rigorous schedule than was his wont. He detested this requirement, and throughout his stay railed against the Western tyranny of living by the clock.

These purchases were the material manifestations of the shift in worlds that Vivekananda undertook; he would be a stranger in a strange land, with pinched feet, uncomfortable clothes, nudged and nagged by a timepiece in a country where few had even heard of a sannyasin. He left Bombay on May 31, 1893, and traveled via Colombo, Malaysia, Hong Kong, China, and finally Japan. Like many South Asians, he was mightily impressed by the resurgence of the last country. The Japanese at Chicago's World's Parliament of Religions and World's Columbian Exposition would give him more reasons to reflect upon questions of national and spiritual pride.

These details suggest the magnitude of what he and his wider entourage had undertaken. They had before them a young man full of promise, but they must have wondered whether he was up for the task. No doubt, many of them fretted about the polluting effects of overseas voyages; and yet somehow, they had agreed that the risk was worthwhile.

* * *

Twenty-eight million people, almost a third of America's entire population, visited Chicago in the six months of the Columbian Exposition.[12] Built on over a thousand acres, and encompassing the shorefront of Lake Michigan, Jackson Park, the Midway Plaisance, and Washington Park, the fair was held (albeit almost a year late) to celebrate the 400th anniversary of Christopher Columbus's discovery of America.[13] The White City, so named for the electric streetlights that lit the stuccoed buildings at night, had a fairyland feel, with its new canals, the original Ferris Wheel, and countless exhibitions. Financed by the city's business elite, the fair included enormous displays of foodstuffs, machinery, and commercial products housed in the Agricultural Building, Horticultural Building, Electricity Building, Machinery Hall, and the Manufactures and Liberal Arts Building. This display of technology and abundance was matched by attempts to encompass the architectural heights of Western civilization, with the Romanesque, neo-Gothic, and neoclassical all on show. The United States was personified in a massive beaux arts statue that, with the canals, conjured up a bit of both Paris and Venice.[14] This extravaganza was thus decidedly secular and capitalist, privileging technological achievement but also emphasizing the civilizational aspirations of a burgeoning Great Power.[15]

The message was idealistic but involved inevitable political calculations when allocating space for different pavilions. Vivekananda saw and understood these well. Forty-six nations contributed national pavilions, but the only Asian country to have an edifice on Wooded Isle (located at the center of the fairground) was Japan. Under the direction of the pan-Asianist art historian Okakura Kakuzo (1862–1913), later involved with Vivekananda and especially Margaret Noble, the Japanese filled the interior of the Ho-o-Den

5.1. View toward the Administration Building, Chicago World's Columbian Exposition, 1893

5.2. Interior of the Japanese Pavilion at the Chicago World's Columbian Exposition

(Phoenix Palace), with ancient objects and contemporary artefacts, shining lacquer, intricate tapestries, and musical instruments. The Ho-o-Den was widely visited and greatly admired, the restrained beauty of the design and craftsmanship attesting to Japanese cultural sophistication. The palace was part of Japanese national assertion and was linked to a desire to renegotiate unfair treaties with Western powers, an issue that would emerge during the Parliament.[16] The Ho-o-Den made the point that Japanese civilization had reached high refinement long before Columbus set sail.[17]

However, most of the "exotic" exhibitions—mock African villages, a Bedouin encampment, and dancing Samoans—were consigned to the Midway Plaisance, beyond the Court of Honor and Jackson Park. In addition, China was virtually absent; the government boycotted the fair because of the Chinese Exclusion Act of 1882, which was preventing Chinese laborers from entering the United States.[18]

But what of the Indian subcontinent? Ceylon had a large space with an array of exhibits, but conflicts within the British administration complicated Indian participation. Although the Royal Commission was in favor of a pavilion, the government of India was not until June 1892.[19] Instead, the US government and "the patronage of Indian princes" made possible an East Indian Pavilion reminiscent of the Taj Mahal, where men in "picturesque attire" provided tea; a Hindu juggler performed; and textiles, sculptures, "relics and curios" were on sale.[20] At least it was near the entrance of the White City, rather than cast into the exhibition's margins, and had English-speaking attendants who presumably could talk to visitors.[21]

Even among Americans, the Columbian Exposition was a spectacle; for some, it was a "heavenly city"; for others, a "fancyland palace" that juxtaposed the sacred and the profane. The Parliament, in contrast, focused on the sacred to demonstrate American spiritual aspirations and the country's commitment to a largely Protestant spiritual renewal and attempt at some form of ecumenicism.[22] Technology and wealth were integral to the self-image of US prowess, but so was a vision of the republic as a New Jerusalem.

Traveling to Chicago had already changed Vivekananda's perspective. He voyaged on imperial sea networks and experienced the "transport revolution" by going first class from Bombay to Kobe on the SS *Peninsular* (P&O), a new ship launched only in 1888. We know, from an almost contemporaneous memoir of Mark Twain about a similar ship, that Vivekananda would have been introduced to formal dining, deck promenades, and commodious cabins.[23] In India,

5.3. Exterior of the East Indian Pavilion at the Chicago World's Columbian Exposition

he had used the burgeoning British rail network, but oceanic voyages were entirely novel. On the advice of female supporters, he would thereafter take them whenever possible to strengthen his health.[24] On the confined space of a ship, Englishmen were less likely to avoid or condescend to Indians. The *Peninsular* was small by modern standards, with only 170 passengers in first class. Above all, such voyages permitted a sense of escape, leisure, and the possibility of an elegant transition from one part of the globe to another.[25]

However, when Vivekananda boarded the Canadian Pacific liner the SS *Empress of India* for the voyage from Japan to Vancouver, he was more concerned with the frightful cold and his lack of warm clothing than he was with relaxation and civility. From Vancouver, he went to Chicago at the end of July 1893 and learned that though the fair had been running for three months, the Parliament was not due to open until September 11. Moreover, he would not be allowed to attend without credentials. He also found out that, unlike in India where he would be given alms as a sannyasin, in America, his vocation meant nothing.

Vivekananda's first experience of the city and the fair thus had nothing to do with his reason for being there. He related to Alasinga that when he arrived from Vancouver, he spent twelve days with an unnamed lady of high society. He remarked on the Exposition's magnificence and agreed that it was a "tremendous affair," but was stunned by the exorbitant prices. He had a letter of introduction to a director of the fair and his wife, who took Vivekananda around the exhibitions, but he knew enough about foreign money to realize that he was running out of it quickly. However, on the train from Vancouver he had met an "old Lady," Kate Sanborn, who had offered hospitality and contacts in Massachusetts should he need help. For Vivekananda's devotees, this chance meeting, which led to so many others, was providential.

He arrived at her house on August 18, after three days of wandering in Boston, and Sanborn took him in and introduced him to John Henry Wright, a Persian-born son of medical missionaries, who had become an important scholar of classical philology. Wright was at Harvard and invited the young Indian to spend a few days with him. He introduced Vivekananda to the Parliament's chairman, and even bought his train ticket back to Chicago when he discovered the monk's impecunious state. The connection was Vivekananda's first of several to Harvard men, and the only one that created a lasting friendship. Wright wrote that "Here is a man who is more learned than all our learned professors put together," and Vivekananda remained grateful to Wright for trusting him even though he had come without credentials.[26]

As will be seen, his three weeks in New England were crucial for creating his first female network in America, and learning the art of speaking to an educated, Protestant public, a skill that he would deploy at the Parliament.[27] Mary-Louise Burke, an early historian of Vivekananda's westward journey, has recounted that when he returned to Chicago on September 8, he had lost the address of his hosts. The famous story claims that he spent the night in a box (or a boxcar, depending on the account) and emerged the next morning, "dark-skinned, unshaven, wearing what must have been by now a very rumpled orange robe and strange-looking-turban."[28] As he wandered aimlessly, the American ladies in the neighborhood apparently did not find him an inviting sight. He was said to have walked for two and a half miles from the station, and to have sat down wearily, probably on the curb, on Dearborn Street. There, he was approached by the kindly Mrs. Belle Hale. She asked whether he was a delegate, and then took him in, gave him breakfast, and delivered him to the Parliament's headquarters. Thereafter, he spent much time with the Hales and came to regard their two daughters, Mary and Harriet, as well as their

5.4. Vivekananda meets Mrs. Hale in Chicago after sleeping in a box. Kantha embroidery. Museum of the Ramakrishnan Mission Institute of Culture, Golpark, Calcutta.

cousins, Isabelle and Harriet McKindley, as his sisters. A year after the Parliament, he described these foreign women to his guru-brothers: "The two daughters are blondes, that is, have golden hair, while the two nieces are brunettes, that is, of dark hair. They know all sorts of occupations. The nieces are not so rich, they conduct a kindergarten school; but the daughters do not earn. Many girls of this country earn their living. Nobody depends upon others. . . . The daughters call me brother; and I address their mother as mother. All my things are at their place; and they look after them."[29] He became particularly close to Mary and was to write some of his most moving and frank letters to this American "sibling." From this time on, the Hale household became his home in Chicago, with Mrs. Hale a constant support.

*   *   *

When the Asian delegates criticized Western materialism, the stupendous bustle of the Columbian Exposition confirmed their view that spiritual re-

5.5. The Hale sisters (*left to right*): Harriet McKindley, Mary Hale, Isabelle McKindley, Harriet Hale

flection was not a priority. And yet, they formed this opinion too quickly. Charles Bonney, a Chicago judge, orator, and lawyer, was also keen on "Intellectual and Moral Exposition" and stated that "the crowning glory of the World's Fair of 1893 should not be the exhibit . . . of the material triumphs. . . . [b]ut something higher and nobler . . . demanded by the enlightened and progressive spirit of the present age."[30] This statement expressed Bonney's fear that American spiritual values would be lost among the capitalist display, one of the key reasons that he supported the Parliament. Bonney wanted instead to promote the "progressive spirit," encapsulated in the World's Congress Auxiliary, a parallel organization that emerged in 1891 under his presidency. It presented twenty separate conferences that ranged from Women's Progress, through Social and Economic Science, to Sunday Rest. The program, which needed six months to run its course between May 1 and October 30, was attended by approximately 700,000 people.[31]

The Parliament had several aims, even though the Christian leaders emphasized different aspects of its mission. Bonney had at first wanted a Christian ecumenical conference, as he had taught Bible to Baptists and Episcopalians and knew well the diverging paths of various Christian denominations.[32] He later suggested that Swedenborgianism, his own faith, had attracted him to ecumenicism and furthered his belief in the Parliament.

Emanuel Swedenborg appears often in this book and was important to the American spiritual and intellectual scene—William James's father, Henry James Sr. was a Swedenborgian, while ministers, psychics, and mesmerists often claimed an affiliation to the early eighteenth-century Lutheran pastor and scientist. He was famous for his visions and angels, confusing his contemporaries by "conflat[ing] heaven and earth, spirit and matter, and energy and form," and maintaining that communication existed between different physical and spiritual realms. Swedenborg's immense influence on American popular religion may explain something about Bonney's spiritual position. In midcentury, the so-called Poughkeepsie Seer, Andrew Jackson Davis, had mixed Swedenborgian philosophy and mysticism with popular science and practical healing, which had been disseminated through spiritualism, mesmerism, dream visions, and radical utopianism.[33] His appeal rested on an inclusive vision of an imagined fraternity of loving energy, the so-called influx. He emphasized the rush of the divine in the "life of everyone, whether man, spirit or angel . . . diffused . . . through universal heaven, and even through hell."[34] Swedenborg also believed that the dead, although composed of "spiritual matter," had bodies, which may explain why many nineteenth-century spiritualists believed dead children grew into adulthood.[35] Emerson saw Swedenborgian holism as rejecting a focus on transgression and repentance, in favor of harmony and recalibration.[36]

Bonney held that all men received a "universal influx from God" into their souls, a view he incorporated into the Parliament when he stated that all nations had "some Religion" and that all people received this influx.[37] His approach therefore already conceived of other traditions without the stigma of heresy and eternal damnation. He also, however, had caveats: "Human brotherhood," rather than "unity," was his aim, a stance reinforced by the provision that the "impregnable foundation of Theism" be upheld.[38] Such views should have put Buddhism outside the fold, but it did not. Buddhist delegates appeared at the Parliament, and Buddhism was discussed, often positively, as a "world religion."[39]

The rest of the provisions sought to discover truths in all religions, their application to the problems of contemporary society, and the possibility of more "friendly fellowship in the hope of securing permanent international peace."[40] For the organizers, the aim was to show that religion could unite rather than divide, although this apparent universalism ignored the reality of great power rivalry and the role of Christian mission in underpinning imperialism. Indeed, the world's fair was called the Columbian Exposition, a title that memorialized Christian conquest. But the American organizers believed that their own anticolonial past made them different to their European imperial counterparts. They sent out "ten thousand letters and forty thousand documents" and reassured the "representatives of the non-Christian faiths" of a sincere and courteous welcome.[41]

In 1891, word had gone out to "prominent people" around the globe. American theosophist Henry Steel Olcott first read of the Parliament in the *Madras Mail,* and suggested to Anagarika Dharmapala, a young Sri Lankan who lived much of his life in India, that he attend as the representative of Theravada Buddhism.[42] Many feared that orthodox Hindus would not cross the oceans, but in the end the Indian delegation was large and diverse.[43] The organizers also sought to prove their inclusiveness with speakers such as the Reverend Augusta G. Chapin, chairwoman of the Woman's Committee, who highlighted women's importance to American religious life and their struggle for greater political rights. Women, Chapin averred, had been too timid to offer their views in the past, but she delighted in the range of papers they now delivered on religious topics.[44] Black Americans, however, were still absent except for an African Methodist Episcopalian, Bishop Benjamin Arnett, who announced, "I am to represent on the one side the Africans in Africa, and on the other side the Africans in America. I am also, by the chairman, announced to give color to this vast Parliament of Religions."[45]

Arnett was a token, a very self-aware one, but he also recognized that other men of color were in attendance: "Now, I think it is very well colored myself and, if I have any eyes, I think the color is in the majority this time, anyhow."[46] His perception was inaccurate, but it signaled that he identified with the delegates from South and East Asia who appeared in silks, turbans, and flowing white robes, even if they did not identify with him.

The presence of women, Asians, and a single Black American reflected Bonney's vision. There was no conversation with Mormons (who embarrassed with polygamy) or with Muslims (except for one American convert).[47] But the bonhomie also veiled the Parliament's limits, which were articulated primarily by the Reverend John Henry Barrows, a Presbyterian from Yale Divinity School who later became president of Oberlin College. Although also a "progressive" Christian, Barrows sought to restrain the Japanese when he felt they were speaking out of turn, and criticized Vivekananda when he condemned missionary behavior in India. Barrows was keener than Bonney to insist on Christianity's superiority. Bonney did not believe that all "religions were of equal merit," but did profess that "each system of religion stands by itself in its own perfect integrity uncompromised, in any degree by its relation to any other."[48] Barrows, in contrast, wrote that "Christianity is to supplant all other religions because it contains the truth in them and much else besides . . . Though light has no fellowship with darkness, light does have fellowship with twilight . . . those who have the full light of the cross should bear brotherly hearts towards all who grope in a dimmer illumination."[49]

Rather than promoting pluralism, this approach advanced a vision of American Protestant Modernism as the superior product of a more advanced civilization. The divergence may have reflected the difference between the Swedenborgian Bonney and the Presbyterian Barrows, and their respective views of Christianity. It may also explain why Bonney encouraged women activists in 1894 to continue the Parliament's work (by inviting Vivekananda and others) at the spiritual encampment of Green Acre, Maine, while Barrows went to India in 1897 to argue on Vivekananda's home turf that Christianity was *the* world religion.[50] "Protestant Modernism," therefore, was hardly a bloc.

At the Parliament, Barrows seemed more worried by the prospect of criticism from other Christians than by disruptions from non-Christians. The Presbyterian Church, for example, had at first disapproved of the Parliament, only voting, far from unanimously, to take part in 1892.[51] There were bitter letters condemning Barrows for "playing fast and loose with the truth and coquetting with false religions" and for "unconsciously planning treason against Christ."[52] But the Catholic Archbishop of Chicago did join the Planning Committee, along with one rabbi, and fourteen other Protestants. James Gibbons, the second Roman Catholic cardinal in the United States, also made an appearance, remarking that "our blessed Redeemer came upon this earth to break down the wall of partition that separates race from race and people and from people."[53] Such thoughts expressed tolerance for the unenlightened.

The Archbishop of Canterbury, however, refused to attend; instead, it was left to the Reverend Alfred Williams Momerie of London to assert that a "very large number of the English clergy, and a still larger number of English laity, are in sympathy with your congress."[54] But Momerie was of Broad Church views, and had given up his professorship of logic and mental philosophy and cut his links to King's College London in 1891 because of his lack of orthodoxy. Momerie gave intellectual luster to the gathering, but Barrows longed for more conventional approval. He had to find it elsewhere when he defensively "appeal[ed] to the representatives of the non-Christian faiths' to ask them if Christianity suffers ... from having called this Parliament of Religions?"[55]

If Catholics and Protestants were present but somewhat divided, Jews seemed solidly behind the endeavor. Barrows thought their participation testified to the "spiritual freedom of the United States of America," that "these friends, some of whom are willing to call themselves Old Testament Christians, as I am willing to call myself a New Testament Jew, have zealously and powerfully co-operated in the work."[56]

Barrows pointed to a continuous Judeo-Christian tradition that incorporated the "people of the Book" and contrasted their acceptance in the United States to their intermittent persecution elsewhere. But there was a darker side to this embrace, for it separated Jews and Christians from Muslims, and hence excluded this other world monotheism from the enlightened camp. Barrows expressed "little surprise" when the Sultan of Turkey sent no representatives, and vocally condemned what he denounced as the persecution of Greeks and Armenians.[57]

No one from the Islamic world was present, only Christian ministers who spoke about Islam and a paper on comparative religious literature, which had been written by a Muslim in Paris.[58] An American, Alexander Russell Webb, was Islam's sole representative. Raised as a Presbyterian and influenced by the Islam of India, especially the missionary Ahamadis, he insisted that polygamy was inherently un-Islamic, and that Westerners misunderstood Muhammed. He maintained that the "higher-class of believers" were indifferent to the world and focused instead on universal ethical truths. Islam was mentioned often during the Parliament, but condemned for taking the road to "fatalism," despite the overlap in conceptions of God's sovereignty and predestination.[59] Occasionally, a speaker would compliment Islam for prohibiting alcohol and gambling, while others acknowledged its ultimate vision of a merciful God, but more continued to insist that it was a religion of the "fire and sword."[60] Webb's defensive remarks about polygamy suggest how in the American imagination Islam remained a religion of harems.

If Islam was a contested monotheism, the lack of a personal God among the Japanese and many from the subcontinent remained a key objection to their theology. But they fought back. Japanese speakers, such as Kozaki Hiromichi, the president of Doshisha University, explained how missionary Christianity engendered resentment among Buddhists and Shintoists, who viewed it as foreign incursion; he also condemned Protestant sectarianism, insisting that Christianity in Japan should be indigenized with a self-governing congregation. The interpreter acknowledged that Commodore Perry, the American naval commander who had forced commercial treaties on Japan, had awoken the nation "from its slumber." But he wanted the world to know that Japan was a center of spiritual wisdom, not just a producer of coveted "teapots and teacups," "pictures and fans."[61]

The Japanese Buddhist Hirai Kinzo also rebuked the West for its "foreign devastation under the disguise of religion."[62] Linking a critique of Christianity to an indictment of the unfavorable 1858 trading treaty, he, too, insisted that the Japanese were not "idolaters" or "heathen," that Christians used such slanders to "trample upon the rights and advantages of a non-Christian nation."[63] Hirai took a different view of Barrows's vaunted American "openness" by objecting to the bar against Japanese entry into Pacific Coast universities and trade unions.[64] We can only imagine the effect such forthrightness had on Vivekananda. Only a few weeks earlier, he had seen Japan for the first time and had been enchanted by the "picturesque" tidiness in Nagasaki, and "the short-statured, fair-skinned, quaintly-dressed Japs, their movements, attitudes, gestures."[65] He noted the beauty and the uniformity of the society, as well as the burgeoning industrial and naval might. The encounter was both elevating (a new Asian superpower was emerging that could compete with the West) and humiliating (for India had not made the same progress).

Vivekananda's impressions had overwhelmed him, and he reacted by scolding his Madras disciples to emphasize the distance they still had to travel in comparison. He told them to hide their "faces in shame" and called them a "race of dotards, who spent hundreds of years.... discussing the touchableness or untouchableness of this food or.... promenading the seashores with books in [their] hands—repeating undigested stray bits of European brainwork, and the whole soul bent upon getting a thirty-rupee clerkship ..."[66] He implored them to come out of their "narrow holes and have a look abroad ... to see how nations are on the march," and called for sacrifice, especially for the poor and downtrodden, and acknowledged that the English "had been the instrument" of breaking a "crystallised civilisation" to force India, and especially her young men, to change.[67] Both Hirai and Vivekananda regarded imperial assaults not as victimization alone, but also as opportunities for re-creation.

And yet Vivekananda took a different tack from Hirai. India had no in-dependent army, navy, or industrial base with which to challenge Britain. So, its delegates stressed their spiritual superiority, even over the Japanese. When in Japan, Vivekananda had written to Alasinga that "especially to the Japanese, India is still the dreamland of everything high and good," adding that "in every [Japanese] temple there are some Sanskrit Mantras written in Old Bengali characters."[68] India was the home of a holy language, which only a few Japanese priests had mastered.[69] Despite poverty and subjuga-tion, India had a unique gift to offer the world. When he thought of India as the "Mother of spirituality," he thought not only of the West, but of other Asian countries as well.

Also, even more than the Japanese, the men of the subcontinent pro-claimed the richness of their spiritual heritage, and the delegates included Buddhists, Jains, theosophists, the most orthodox of Brahmins, Brahmos, and of course Vivekananda. At the Parliament, they hid their divisions to stand together. Christians, and especially missionaries, were the common enemy, traducing eastern religions as "those barren, vague, meaningless ab-stractions in which men babble nothing under the name of the infinite."[70]

Even when they expressed sympathy for Hinduism, Christian views were laced with condescension. One commentator wrote that "while between God and the worshipper there is the most direct affinity," he added that "there exists no bond of sympathy . . . no quickening power being exercised on the human will. . . ." and concluded that Hindus, unlike Christians, did not have "the requirements of conscience . . . of personal responsibility . . . to love one's neighbour as one's self."[71] This cliché about the Hindu "love of pure spirit" was a time-honored orientalist trope that Hegel had popularized in his *The Philosophy of History* (1857).[72] It argued that Indians preferred "dream" to reality, and in the process, escaped dilemmas of conscience and honor. Indian religions produced devoted seekers, but could not mold "char-acter," and that Hinduism was too "transcendent" to form correct moral re-flexes. These criticisms partially explain, perhaps, why Vivekananda recast Hinduism as a "man-making" religion.[73]

The South Asians countered such arguments by pointing to the Colum-bian Exposition's materialist grandiosity and underscoring the hypocrisy of preaching love while plundering and conquering. They condemned the philosophical misunderstandings (willful or not) of Hinduism that the missionaries perpetuated and emphasized the sophistication of ethical systems that they claimed could hold up to any in the West, focusing especially on *ahimsa* (nonviolence).

Twenty Indians took part, according to Barrows's record, and the first to speak was Anagarika Dharmapala, the Buddhist from Sri Lanka, a notable figure in the Calcutta intellectual scene, who dreamed of re-creating Ashoka's Buddhist empire in the subcontinent.[74] At this juncture, he was better known than Vivekananda and had forged international connections through his father's business empire, theosophy, and as a collaborator of Sir Edwin Arnold, the author of *The Light of Asia* (1879).[75] Arnold's biography of the Buddha had sold in the hundreds of thousands, and Dharmapala's association with Arnold meant that he also had a Western audience. The epic poem—with its harmonious stanzas that reminded readers of Tennyson—humanized the Buddha for Westerners and crystallized a growing interest in comparative religion that contributed to the Victorian "Crisis of Faith." Relativism resulted almost ineluctably from comparison, and the friendship between Arnold and Dharmapala suggested a growing inclination to see Buddhism as an "enlightened" creed.[76] Their struggle to wrest Bodh Gaya, the site of the Buddha's enlightenment in Bihar, from the Hindu chief priest of the temple who supervised it, juxtaposed the "degeneration" of majority Hinduism with the purity of Buddhist contemplation.[77]

Although not successful, the well-publicized campaign (Arnold had also been editor of the London *Daily Telegraph* from 1873 to 1888) boosted Western awareness of the importance of Bodh Gaya to Buddhism. More generally, parallels were made between Christ and Christianity, the Buddha and Buddhism, with the ethics of compassion deemed important in both.[78] At the Parliament, Dharmapala became the "Eastern Christ" and was admired for his gentle demeanor and longish hair, despite the veiled fierceness of his growing Buddhist nationalism. He praised third-century Buddhist emperor Ashoka as the founding father of the earliest systems of social ethics and contrasted his peaceful reign with the turbulent history of early Christianity.[79]

If Barrows saw Christianity as the pinnacle of evolutionary development, Dharmapala argued the same for Buddhism. He also claimed that Buddhism underpinned science by using evocative evolutionary metaphors of development, and interconnectedness.[80] He mocked English clergymen, whom he called "muddle-headed prelates," and claimed that Christianity was obscurantist, a tactic also important to Vivekananda when disparaging the idea of the literal truth of biblical creationism. Dharmapala also displayed his scientific credentials when he complimented social organicist Herbert Spencer as well as scientific controversalist and iconoclast John Tyndall.[81] Such polemicizing, of course, ignored the growing importance of liberal theology in "advanced" Protestant circles, which sought to admit modern science and especially evolutionary thinking into its arena.[82]

Dharmapala found coming to the West both stimulating and distasteful. It was not merely the materialism, though this shocked so many; he was even more revolted by the brutality, especially against animals. When he was trying to decide whether to attend the Parliament, his diary records his horror of American carnivorousness and the industrial scale of animal slaughter; he had mused that Chicago was "the slaughterhouse of Christendom."[83] An orthodox Brahmin, Narasimha Chaira of Madras, expressed similar views when he added, "so long as Christians, by tacit silence make people believe that the eating of animal food is a necessary preparatory course to be gone through before baptism, so long then will you find you have a stumbling-block in the way of the evangelization of India."[84]

The Jain Virchand Gandhi had to brave the condemnation of his community when he traveled abroad and then labored hard to adhere to prohibitions against meat-eating. He weaved vegetarianism into his explanations of the cyclic dynamic of creation and destruction at the heart of many Indian religions, and the importance of ahimsa as an ethical principle. Vivekananda, who was already considering the significance of meat-eating for a revived India, disagreed, but kept his thoughts to himself, and privately admired the Jain's steadfastness.

A lesser-known but important member of the delegation was the Gujarati novelist and social reformer Manilal Dvivedi, one of the first systematizers and translators of the work of Shankara, the ninth-century Advaitist central to Vivekananda's thought. In 1892, Vivekananda had visited Dvivedi, and much of his speech on Hinduism at the Parliament drew on these exchanges and perhaps also on Dvivedi's volumes *Raja-Yoga* (1885) and *Monism or Advaitism?* (1889).[85] Dvivedi argued that "the absolute implied the relative, as light implies darkness, the positive implies the negative." He insisted that the "idea of original sin [was] foreign to Hinduism," that the "origin of evil" was not found in "disobedience to the Divine Father."[86] Instead, spiritual growth resulted in a self-realization of inner divinity. These were the abiding lessons that Vivekananda would repeatedly teach while in the West.

5.6. Union Stock Yard & Transit Co., Chicago

5.7. Virchand Gandhi, Dharmapala (*slightly behind*) and Vivekananda, Chicago, 1893

Other Indian speakers, such as Gyanendranath Chakravarti, preached the-osophy because they valued its religious universalism.[87] In the West, its claims were frequently ridiculed because of the fraudulent practices, esotericism, and occultism of its advocates.[88] But in South Asia, it gained adherents as a move-ment dedicated to creating a "Universal Brotherhood of Humanity without distinction of race, creed, sex, caste or colour."[89] Dharmapala, for example, retained links to theosophy, even though he disagreed with key Western prac-titioners, and had traveled to the Parliament with Annie Besant, who would become the president of the Indian National Congress in 1917.[90] Both its uni-versalism and the egalitarianism proved elusive, but the aspirations at least were appealing.[91] Helen Blavatsky and Colonel Olcott, despite their early fasci-nation with traditions of Western hermeticism, neo-Platonism, and Egyptian esotericism, saw enough potential in "Eastern religions" to shift their head-quarters from New York to Adyar in 1882; this move suggests that they, too, were exploring India as the "Mother of Spirituality."[92]

Some, like the Narasimha Chaira, were unafraid to berate Christianity. He announced, "I belong to that class of my countrymen who believe in having a

5.8. Helen Blavatsky and Henry Steel Olcott

little more bread to eat and a little less of the much-admired Western civilization."[93] He was appalled by Hindu conversions and saw them as primarily an
attempt to escape caste.[94] He also rejected the reforms that enthused the Brahmos:
"Eating with lower castes is a nauseating process to us; we cannot do it if we try."[95]
Vivekananda would have strongly opposed Narasimha Chaira's don't-touchism,
but heartily agreed with the critique of Western hypocrisy and the need for a
"little more bread."

♦ ♦ ♦

This array of beliefs suggests the many channels through which the various
spiritual tendencies of the subcontinent flowed. And yet, except for the outspoken Brahmin, the Indians recast their spirituality to communicate with
Westerners. Hinduism is supposed to have 330 million gods, but virtually
none of them was mentioned at the podium.[96] In contrast to Buddhism,
which could be encapsulated through its founding figure and ethical code,
"Hinduism" encompassed so many different systems of beliefs, practices, and
values that it was hard to define or present as a unified religion.[97] The
Buddha could be likened to Christ, and Buddhism's morality to the Sermon
on the Mount, but Hinduism had no single God, sacred text, or origin point,
hence the simile of the banyan tree so often used to describe the many
branches that emerge from its massive trunk.[98]

Moreover, the notion of *dharma*—the innumerable understandings of
"merit," "duty," and even "devotion"—was so complex and variable that it
bewildered observers who searched for Western equivalents. The word encompassed and implied both the rules and prescriptions that defined social
and community life, as well as caste; aspects of obligation; as well as the
highest universal ethics and dispassion that focused on agency, choice, and
freedom.[99] The men at the Parliament largely focused on the last, on what
they conceived of as the soteriological aspects—the prospect of liberation—
of Hinduism to convey its spiritual flights. Vivekananda would tackle
dharma, while often avoiding the term, later in his Western mission.[100]

In his speech of welcome made at the opening session on September 11, Vivekananda differed from the other Indians by doing more than explaining or
condemning. Hailing his "sisters and brothers of America"—itself an interesting reversal of the usual form—he set a tone of fellowship, burying an implied criticism in generosity. For example, he thanked the Parliament in the

"name of the oldest order of monks in the world," in the "name of the millions of religions" and in the "name of millions and millions of Hindu people."

He focused on the antiquity of India's religious traditions and on India as the fructifying genitor of spirituality. India, he maintained, was also the author of tolerance, a point he drove home by declaring himself as "belong[ing] to a religion which has taught the world. . . . universal acceptance." Like Ramakrishna, he asserted that he "accept[ed] all religions as true," citing India as the home for religious refugees the world over.[101] And, in a fashion that would become characteristic, he translated 4:11 of the Bhagavad Gita in this way: "'*Whosoever comes to Me, through whatsoever form, I reach him; all men are struggling through paths which in the end lead to me.*'"[102]

He ended by declaring the need to resist "sectarianism, bigotry, and its horrible descendant, fanaticism."[103] This rendering of the Sanskrit has become almost a cliché, and it is perhaps so often repeated because of Vivekananda. He referred to "different paths" without discussing aspects of Indian religion that might disgust, annoy, or perplex his western audience. At the end, he repeated the point inherent in the quotation from the Baghavad Gita, taking the challenge to Christianity to the most fundamental level of the different sacred texts.[104] The quotation contrasted the capacious universality of Hinduism with the emphasis on sectarian exclusivity in the Gospel of John (John 14:6), which states that "no one comes to the Father except though me."

Four days later, he adopted a different style by teaching through parable—a technique familiar to any Christian. Whereas Ramakrishna had used rustic simplicity and raw humor, Vivekananda resorted to more contemporary and "scientific" references. He described a frog living in his little well, growing "sleek and fat," cleansing water in a way that "would do credit to our modern bacteriologists" by eating the "worms and bacilli." This frog was perfectly happy until a frog from the sea jumped into his well and insisted that the sea was much bigger and better than the well. The first frog disliked the bombast and wanted to evict the "sea-frog" from his home. The moral was simple: "'I am a Hindu. I am sitting in my own little well and thinking that the whole world is my little well. The Christian sits in his little well and thinks the whole world is his well. The Mohammedan sits in his little well and thinks that is the whole world.'"[105]

Only on September 19 did Vivekananda seek to "educate" his listeners about Hinduism. He had the knack of preempting the questions of his audience and undermining their stereotypes. He knew Hinduism contained many strands that included the "high spiritual flights of the Vedanta philosophy" and "the low ideas of idolatry"; aspects of the "agnosticism of the Buddhists, and the atheism of the Jains." He asked, therefore, what was the "common centre to which all these widely diverging radii converge?" He maintained that the religion of the Vedas was a revelation that had no "beginning or end." He knew, too, that this idea was puzzling for Bible readers, and he accepted that an endless book sounded "ludicrous." But he explained it as an "accumulated treasury of spiritual laws," a precious store that would be added to and rearranged forever. Those who offered new types of treasure were rishis, the men and women (he made a point of mentioning the latter) who would continue to discover them in new ages, and in new cycles. The "Vedas teach us that creation is without beginning or end," a conclusion that physics now supported through thermodynamics. He described how "the sum total of cosmic energy is always the same. Worlds are created and destroyed in a never-ending cycle, and hence a Brâhmin boy repeats every day: 'The sun and the moon, the Lord created like the suns and moons of previous cycles.'"[106]

Vivekananda added that this process had its parallel in the self-realization of individuals. The "I" of which we were conscious was nothing more than a body, a "combination of material substances," but the soul (atman) was imperishable, and its endurance stemmed from the endless cycles. A God outside his own creation was impossible, for God would then only express "the cruel fiat of an all-powerful-being." In this way, he suggested that karma was kinder to human frailty than the punishments of Judeo-Christianity. Misery or happiness depended on past lives, potentially brought back to consciousness by certain techniques. Indeed, Vivekananda explained that "consciousness is only the surface of the mental ocean, and within its depths are stored up all our experiences."[107] That his contemporaries William James or Sigmund Freud might have made such remarks suggests again why his audience gave him a hearing. Here was a set of ideas that could be readily translated into spiritualist language and views about the nature of the "unconscious," however differently arrived at.

He continued that the "whole object of [the Hindu system] . . . is . . . to become divine, to reach God and see God, and this reaching God, seeing God, becoming perfect, constitutes the religion of the Hindus." The result of the search—if it can be completed—is "bliss infinite." The goal is to cast off "this miserable little prison-individuality" and "to gain this infinite universal individuality" instead.[108] This kind of liberation left conventional American notions of "freedom" and "happiness" far behind, and he hoped through this exposition to overcome the prejudice that Hindus were spiritually debased.

He concluded, therefore, that the worship of form, embodied in the many goddesses and gods who filled the Hindu pantheon, was not polytheism; rather, "if one stands by and listens, one will find the worshippers applying all the attributes of God, including omnipresence, to the images." Although such devotion might not reach the heights of spiritual perfection that he had just outlined, he did not think it should be discarded. On the contrary, if "external worship. . . . is the lowest stage," then we have valuable spiritual childhoods. Like Ramakrishna, he argued that different types of spirituality were not mutually exclusive and defended such practices by comparing them to the symbols, rituals, saints, and relics that many Christians prized and refused to abandon. He asked, "Why does a Christian go to church? Why is the cross holy? . . . Why are there so many images in the Catholic Church? Why are there so many images in the minds of Protestants when they pray?"[109] As he pondered the spiritual constitution of humanity, he sounded a bit like the evolutionary anthropologists of the era: "all . . . religions, from the lowest fetishism to highest absolutism, [represent the] many attempts of the human soul to . . . realize the infinite. . . ."[110]

This heady message summarized much of his later teaching. He sought to cast aside the Christian preoccupation with truth and error, and to tie instead spiritual realization to perseverance. He acknowledged that reverses were unavoidable, but the aim was to "recognize divinity in every man and woman, and whose whole scope, whose whole force, will be created in aiding humanity to realize its own true, divine nature." American ideas of "self-realization" could easily fit into such an approach.

One of the most famous remarks of the entire speech—remembered by those in the audience and then reproduced in newspapers—concerned sin: "The Hindu refuses to call you sinners. Ye are the Children of God, the sharers of immortal bliss, holy and perfect beings. Ye divinities on earth—sinners! It is a sin to call a man so; it is a standing libel on human nature."[111] This line of attack on the very concept of "original sin" would become a powerful weapon in his arsenal.

Vivekananda thus used his cultural breadth to compare Christianity and Vedanta by placing them side by side. Although he was an exotic foreigner, he was oddly reassuring: he focused on the process of becoming, rather than the endpoint of redemption, and thereby softened (especially) Protestant metaphysical doubt. Indian thought, he suggested, was inherently tolerant in understanding the desire for different paths to the Divine. To demonstrate its uniqueness, he played with the dual, but related, notions of timelessness and historical specificity. The Vedas' antiquity demonstrated a civilizational pedigree that the Christianity could never claim. Indian rulers—by providing refuge to victimized Zoroastrians or Jews after the Roman destruction of the Second Temple—responded with tolerance when the persecuted knocked at their door.[112] In this instance, however, India's lesson of tolerance was exemplified by the fate of Jews and Parsis, while the growing tension between Muslims and Hindus in India was not mentioned.[113]

Speaking at the Parliament was an immense honor for Vivekananda. He confided to Alasinga that before he rose to the podium, he was almost overwhelmed: "I who never spoke in public in my life to speak at this august assemblage!!"[114] But as he described the lineup of delegates from India, he bragged a bit about how his spontaneous remarks somehow surpassed the prepared speeches of others. He wrote of the "deafening applause of the two minutes that followed" and how he was now "known to the whole of America."[115] He was also proud that he had "succeeded in society," stating that he was a guest at many of "the handsomest houses in the city."[116] Such remarks suggest how he was courted, and perhaps at first how susceptible he was to American blandishments. There is no doubt, too, that he was touched by American curiosity and frankness, However, it did not take long for him to see that Barrows's real purpose was to "prov[e]the superiority of the Christian religion over other forms of faith." Vivekananda understood the intent, but he was not discouraged; he wrote later: "the philosophic religion of Hinduism was able to maintain its position notwithstanding."[117]

Even at the Parliament, he had moments of exasperation and explained that, "day after day," the delegates from non-Christian nations had been told "in a patronizing way that [they] ought to accept Christianity." He concluded, when speaking of England, that Christianity wins its prosperity by "cutting the throats" of its fellow men and described India's poverty where "300,000,000 men and women liv[e] on an average of little more than 50 cents a month."[118] Christian missionaries, he contended, only fed Muslims or Hindus on condition that they convert to Christianity.[119] He countered that India had "more than religion enough; what they want is bread, but they are given a stone." [120] His words were a virtual quotation from Matthew 7:9: "Or what man is there of you, whom if your son asks for bread, will give him a stone?" What could be a stronger rebuke to the withholding of food in India? This last address was interspersed with applause from the audience, and an appeal to America to help the poor in India.

Evidence of his anger peppers personal reminiscences and reports in magazines, outbursts that contradicted his description as a "mild Hindu": "You trample on us and treat us like the dust beneath your feet . . . You scorn our religion—in many points like yours, only better, because more humane."[121] And he made the contrast clear when he spoke on September 26, 1893, on "Buddhism: the Fulfilment of Hinduism," and said that there was only partnership and connection, not competition between the two creeds: "the philosophy of the Brahmins" was linked to the "heart of the Buddhist."[122] Even if there was some window dressing in these remarks, they were meant to reproach Christians for their internecine quarrels. They also led to the central message of his final intervention: "The Christian is not to become a Hindu or a Buddhist, nor a Hindu or a Buddhist to become a Christian. But each must assimilate the spirit of the others and yet preserve his individuality and grow according to his own law of growth." He also warned, "[I]f anyone dreams of the exclusive survival of his own religion and the destruction of the other, I pity him from the bottom of my heart."[123]

When Barrows published his proceedings of the Parliament, however, he brushed aside this last remark and commented, "Swami Vivekananda was always heard with interest by the Parliament, but very little approval was shown to some of the sentiments expressed in his closing address."[124] Perhaps of all the words Vivekananda spoke, these most troubled those who advanced Protestant Christianity—besides validating all religions, it was concise, respectful but insistent on a pluralism that Barrows, for example, could never endorse.

There is much we still do not know about the Parliament or about Vivekananda's contributions. There are tidbits about his entrée into the burgeoning world of American university life, when he met faculty from Northwestern, lectured in Evanston, and then, a year later, at the University of Chicago chapel.[125] He also socialized in Chicago homes and at more formal occasions: Dharmapala's diary, for example, contains disapproving remarks about Vivekananda's enthusiasm for champagne.[126] Even though Dharmapala received more column inches in reports, photographs show that the newcomer had made an impression, finding himself often at the center of events and his South Asian contemporaries. The newspapers spoke of his handsome and imposing presence, as well as his command of English.[127] After the Parliament closed, he built on his reputation and on the contacts, eventually easily eclipsing Dharmapala in his fame and influence.

6

WOMEN EAST AND WEST

The best thermometer to the progress of a nation is its treatment of its women.

—Swami Vivekananda, "Women of the East" lecture, 1893

◆ ◆ ◆

VIVEKANANDA HAD LEARNED a great deal about America after interacting with women at homes, in churches, and at meeting halls in New England between leaving Chicago on July 30, 1893, and returning in September. From the very beginning, women played a central role in explaining American society, Christianity, and more. His approach to them—and theirs to him—was both life-enhancing and life-transforming. It was also novel and disruptive, since he could not help but compare these foreign creatures to the Indian women he knew and loved (including his mother and sisters). He had come from Calcutta where the situation of women had been at the center of both reformist and orthodox concern. For him, however, women's status was more than an abstraction, as he agonized over the travails of his female kin. His early Brahmoism propelled him towards reform, but he feared British cultural impositions. Moreover, his entry into Ramakrishna's world at Dakshineswar demanded a renewed appreciation of Indian traditions and practices, of Mother-worship, both of Kali, the Holy Mother (Sarada Devi), as well as the women who surrounded her, considerations central to his developing theology.

Somehow Vivekananda had to put together the world of Western activism and avant-garde spirituality with Hindu visions of wifehood, motherhood, and female sainthood; in doing so, he recognized the significance of the worldwide "feminization of religion" to his project. This term has been applied mostly in contexts to describe shifts in devotional practice, theology, and activism in Christianity. Understanding the Protestantism and Catholicism of this period, for example, is difficult without accounting for the explosion of female service in the reformist and missionary fields, both at home and in the colonies, as well as the devotional centrality of Marianism within Catholicism.[1]

Vivekananda recognized that links among women as well as female symbolism were essential to Vedanta as an international project. Without the help of his American and British female acolytes, he would never have been able to implant his ideas, press for non-Western cultural forms of the universal, and open new spiritual horizons. From the beginning, Sarada Devi was vital to everything he did, and she exemplified his hopes for the future when she broke Brahmanical taboos to welcome the foreign women as her friends. Western Vedanta, with its temples, yoga, and meditation, are unimaginable without the energy, resources, and commitment of Western women, while Hindu nationalism, with Kali and Mother-worship, is equally unthinkable without the cult of maternalism that matched Vivekananda's man-making enterprise.

◆ ◆ ◆

From the outset, women found him attractive, as a novelty, personality, and teacher; he took comfort in their welcome, was briefly infatuated by their qualities, then more critical, and finally wary of any effort to direct or exploit him. However, without these sometimes fraught but productive links, his message might never have been heard.

As mentioned, his initial contact was Kate Sanborn, his companion on the train from Vancouver. Sanborn invited him to stay knowing that Vivekananda was bound for Chicago and hardly expected him to take up the invitation, nor was she overjoyed when he appeared on her doorstop in Metcalf, Massachusetts, strapped for funds and in need of care. But she need not have worried. He was grateful to be in America rather than in England. He told Mary Tappan Wright, a noted novelist and wife of Harvard professor

John Henry Wright, that the British conquerors "stank" in the not-so-distant past (400 years prior), and then insisted that, even in the late 1800s, "they are barely emerging from barbarism."[2] But he conversed easily with Sanborn, who, like him, knew about "Shakespeare or Longfellow or Tennyson, Darwin, Müller, Tyndall."[3] She was part of a high-minded, interconnected but factionalized New England world noted for its intellectual and religious fashions. She was impressed by him, but he was less dazzled by her. Unlike Calcutta, which was cosmopolitan in everything and especially in religion, he was now in the "land of Christians, and any other influence than that is almost zero."[4] Nor was he naive about his hostess: "I have an advantage in living with her, in saving . . . my expenditure of £1 per day, and she has the advantage . . . showing them a curio from India!"[5]

His dignity was hurt, but while he was fighting against "starvation, cold, hooting in the streets on account of [his] quaint dress," he realized that "this must be borne."[6] It was August, but he was accustomed to the steaming heat of Calcutta and could not get warm. Breezy Meadows, the name of Sanborn's home, was a good resting place, a house she had lovingly restored, as she had humorously recounted in her *Adopting an Abandoned Farm* (1891).[7] Although rural in ambience, it was on the train line to Boston, an upper-middle-class example of the "back-to-the-land" movement.

Vivekananda now entered a very particular elite. Sanborn, then fifty-three, was of impeccable New England stock—her father was professor of Latin and English literature at Dartmouth; her mother, a grandniece of Secretary of State Daniel Webster. She, herself, was a prolific journalist and author, had taught at Smith College, and had voyaged as far as Alaska on lecture tours, having a love of travel that matched Vivekananda's. Her house lay in a landscape of small towns, high-spired white churches, and hamlets, depopulated by the westward trek in the 1880s but now reinvigorated with country and vacation homes. She was devoted to women's education, complaining in *The Wit of Women* (1885) that members of her sex "do not find it politic to cultivate or express their wit. No man likes to have his story capped by a better . . . from a lady's lips."[8] She deployed humor in her writing to make her points and gain attention—hence her book, *Educated Dogs of To-day* (1916).

Humor is relevant to this story, for one of Vivekananda's greatest attractions was his sometimes cutting, but more often teasing, sense of fun, one of the most important "childlike" legacies of Ramakrishna. Vivekananda was certainly a contrast to dour New England clergy when he "came in a long saffron robe that caused universal amazement."[9] Sanborn recalled a dozen women gathered around him in her house, and even became quite giddy herself: "My overstrained mind began to wobble . . . , with eyes aching from a prolonged stare, my mouth positively ajar, like a rustic at a muster; and as he talked . . . in glowing rhapsody, I suddenly saw myself as an extremely mature American Desdemona, listening intently to the marvelous eloquence of my Bengalese Othello."[10]

In India, he had spoken with men about ideas and social schemes, but in the United States, he was likelier to exchange views with women, who were different from both Indian women and British memsahibs. Nor was his impression of American women's singularity entirely mistaken. We perhaps too readily elide American and British middle- and upper-middle-class women in their joint Protestantism, reformism, and missionary fervor. But there were deeper reasons for their greater openness to him and his ideas.

First, in Massachusetts, and especially Boston, they retained a proud anticolonial heritage in which republican virtue had triumphed over "British tyranny." His remarks about the British thus did not automatically arouse rebuke. The New Englanders also had never encountered an Indian, even if they had numerous fantasies of the "Orient"; they were therefore unlike the British, who felt they "knew" South Asians as travelers or through acquaintance with Indian dignitaries, servants, or members of the Indian diaspora.[11] Moreover, in Britain, the Church of England reigned supreme, despite many dissenting minorities; in New England, however, Vivekananda was thrust into the mixed world of revivalist and orthodox American Protestantism. When, for example, Mary Tappan Wright whisked him off to her cottage at Annisquam, northeast of Boston, she explained how the atmosphere in church when he spoke was like a Protestant "revival"; she admitted that she had "not felt so wrought up for a long time." Indeed, she became almost hysterical: "I retired to my corner and laughed until I cried": she was more accustomed to giving money to convert the heathen to Christianity, not to save them from it.[12]

As news of his eloquence spread, Vivekananda spoke at the Methodist Wesley Church and the Unitarian East Church in Salem, this time invited by another author, Kate Tannatt Woods. He described India's poverty, but also learned about different denominations, Christian ceremonies, and preaching. He rehearsed the arguments he would make at the Parliament when he asked "what they thought of when they prayed."[13] The answers helped him compare Christian images of the cross and statues of Indian gods; both forms of worship, he argued, entailed a process of visualization (darshan) that had nothing to do with "idol-worship," a point he later raised in Chicago.

If the Methodists were noted for their emotional devotions, "democratic congregationalism" and "missionary ambition," Unitarians, in contrast, denied the Trinity and were powerful critics of the mainstream church in New England, ultimately making important inroads into Harvard theology.[14] They charged the Congregationalists with failing to use reason in understanding the Bible and discovering meaning in scripture that did not exist.[15] They had been stalwart abolitionists and had given up proselytizing in India under Ram Mohun Roy's influence.[16]

From midcentury, the Pentecostalists, Jehovah's Witnesses, and Nazarenes also appeared on the American scene, though there is no evidence that Vivekananda encountered them. But many of his acquaintances had experimented with Christian Science, spiritualism, and theosophy, "new religions" that suggested a penchant for spiritual experimentation.[17] The Salvation Army and settlement houses developed as part of the Social Gospel movement, which regarded Jesus as a social and ethical reformer; Vivekananda certainly engaged with such trends, while Margaret Noble would stay for a time at the famous Hull House in Chicago.[18] He understood that such religious effervescence provided opportunities for Vedanta: "I am not going to leave this country without throwing one more apple of discord into this already roaring, fighting, mad whirlpool of American religion."[19]

Finally, he felt that their education helped in explaining his ideas. Although many obstacles remained to attaining parity, these New England women were well educated, as Kate Sanborn's example suggests. The Seven Sisters colleges—again mostly in New England, founded between 1837 and 1889, confirmed Vivekananda's astonished observation that "Schools and colleges are full of women."[20] Oberlin, opened in the 1830s, and later headed by no other than John Henry Barrows, was the oldest coeducational college in America. Alongside its many liberal arts institutions, New England also pioneered adult-education experiments, such as the Cambridge Conferences in Concord and the Chautauquas that cropped up across rural America, where women were important participants.[21] As will be seen, Green Acre, where Vivekananda first taught yoga, resembled a Chautauqua and was founded by two great supporters, Sarah Farmer and Sara Bull.[22] Moreover, he arrived when young American scholars returning from Germany instituted a research culture alongside the liberal arts colleges, especially at Clark and the University of Chicago (begun in 1887 and 1890, respectively). Harvard also experienced this shift, where Wright taught and men like William James and Josiah Royce became international intellectuals and important to Vivekananda's story; women again were central to this network, as he met such men through his female friends.

*   *   *

Vivekananda acknowledged the value of these women's social standing and knowledge, writing to Alasinga that, on their advice, he was going to buy a long black coat in Boston, reserving the "red robe and turban" for lectures, as he could no longer bear "people gather[ing] in the streets" to look at him. He recognized that "they are the rulers here, and I must have their sympathy."[23] At this juncture, he hoped these "mothers" might give money for his work in India, but he also increasingly understood that they, not the men, were central to American spiritual politics and social reform.

They were also enthusiastic about him. When he left and went to Chicago, women flocked to him, so much so that their response sometimes became a way for American men to dismiss him. One journalist at the Parliament claimed they attended to see "the popular Hindu Monk, who looks so much like McCullough's Othello. . . . Ladies, ladies everywhere filled the great auditorium."[24] Journalists also noted how both the "votaries of fashion" as much as the more sober "mothers of Israel" (leading churchwomen) sought him out. A sort of celebrity hysteria took over, so that "he was followed by a crowd wherever he went. In going in and coming out of the building, he was daily beset by hundreds of women who almost fought with each other for a chance to get near him and shake his hand." Initially gracious about the fuss, Vivekananda rapidly became fed up and "made his entries and exits at times when there were no crowds of women in the vestibule and corridors."[25]

He was unused to such attention, a bit shy, but also determined to put it all to good use. After some months in Chicago, he, like some of the other "Orientals," traveled through the Midwest to lecture. He went to Madison, Minneapolis, Des Moines, St. Louis, Detroit, Memphis, and other places, and spoke repeatedly in Unitarian and Congregational churches, where he began to fine-tune his rhetorical style for this new audience.

If he harangued Indians back home for don't-touchism, in the United States, Vivekananda trained his fire on Christianity, which he described as a "shopkeeper religion," a term he inherited from Ramakrishna. He criticized what he saw as the bargaining tone of Western prayer: "They were always begging of God—'Oh God, give me this and give me that; Oh, God, do this and do that.'"[26] The Hindu, in contrast, just loved God, and believed in giving to him. In Des Moines, he denounced Indian converts to Christianity for their whining prayers.[27] However, he exaggerated when he insisted that Hindus in their *pujas* (devotion rituals) did not also ask for favors of the gods.[28] They, too, hoped for better fortune for themselves, family, and friends and were angered at gods who did not keep their "side of the bargain." But he made no mention of this popular Hinduism, and referred instead to Ramakrishna, who never asked Kali to cure his throat cancer.

Surprisingly, Vivekananda was applauded, with the audiences almost egging him on. Did he touch a chord that resonated with their disenchantment with both materialism and Christianity? Certainly, alienation was a persistent theme for the women who responded to his teaching, and yet women, as much as the men, could not help but participate in the new consumer culture that blurred the boundaries between need and desire.[29] Raised on a Puritan diet of sacrifice, prayer, and obedience, they were now encouraged to enjoy God's abundance through American capitalism.[30] For Vivekananda, however, the fault lay not with female consumers but with men so devoted to money-making that they had unduly commercialized Christianity.

He may have referred here to religious currents that eddied out from the so-called Businessmen's Revival in Boston, which explicitly endorsed Christian prayer as a kind of transaction.[31] Vivekananda later encountered these ideas in diluted form in New Thought, where "positive thinking" was linked to the "gospel of success." He also contrasted grasping men with warm and welcoming women: "Your [women] are the grandest women in the world. Your men I do not like; they are all for money; they think of nothing but dollars. But your women—Lord bless them! They have been so kind to me."[32]

Such remarks were part of his intermittent essentializing of the East as spiritual and the West as material; here, however, he excused American women from his blanket condemnation. Indeed, while in the United States, he inverted Ramakrishna's view that women would "ruin" Indian men with their material demands, instead arguing that the male population should take the blame for the country's spiritual desiccation. This inverted vision was central to his global plans.

VIVEKANANDA'S ALLURE

With time, Westerners, especially women, reckoned with a new physical presence, novel personal style, and different ideas about the divine, views perhaps embellished in reminiscences. Vivekananda's allure often centered on their response to his "exotic beauty."[33] Constance Towne recalled, "I thought him as handsome as a god of classic sculpture. He was dark of skin, of course, and had large eyes which gave one the impression of 'midnight blue.' He seemed larger than most of his race; he had a head heaped with short black curls."[34]

His spirituality was expressed through an attentive gaze, meditative absorption, and dignified carriage: Ida Ansell observed, "His eyes were always turned skyward, never down. Someone said of him that he never saw anything lower than a telegraph pole."[35] Edward Sturdy, a Canadian theosophist living in England, pointed to Vivekananda's "bodily strength, virility and also vitality and splendour."[36]

Vivekananda seemed a powerful man yet retained his boyish charm. Matrons thought he was unworldly and worried that "in spite of his great spirituality and this brilliance of mind," he "might be put in a false or uncomfortable position." When they cautioned him, they were surprised by his response: "you dear American mother of mine, don't be afraid for me. It is true I often sleep under a banyan tree with a bowl of rice given me by a kindly peasant, but it is equally true that I also am sometimes the guest in the palace of a great Maharaja and a slave girl is appointed to wave a peacock feather fan over me all night long! I am used to temptation, and you need not fear for me!"[37]

His refusal to conform, however, could cause embarrassment. Sarah Ellen Waldo, a distant relative of Ralph Waldo Emerson, remembered: "It required no little courage to walk up Broadway beside that flaming coat. As the Swami strode along in lordly indifference, with me just behind, half out of breath, every eye was turned upon us . . ."[38]

They were especially attracted to his mysterious eyes: the "glowing eyes," "heavy, dark, liquid eyes, like the 'thick clustering bees.'"[39] Others suggested that his eyes expressed his strength, "the eyes so full of flashing light, and the whole

6.1a, b, and c. Vivekananda in three different garbs

emanation of power, are beyond description."[40] They spoke of his enchanting presence, the turn of his head and the beauty of his hair. A California devotee, Mrs. Alice M. Hansbrough, remarked that his hair was so beautiful, and it set off his features so well, that "we would not let him cut it again."[41] Other women commented on the quality of its blackness, the fact that it seemed never to turn gray. One even asked whether Indian hair stayed black for life, so fascinated was she by its rich cast. Such orientalist fantasies also extended to his way of speaking. Mrs. Hansbrough remarked that his voice was the "most musical voice [she had] ever heard," a deep "baritone," a "resonant," "powerful" voice that enveloped the listener.[42] A famous French opera singer, Emma Calvé, said, "He possesses a voice like a cello, with low vibrations that one cannot forget."[43]

Although only about five feet eight inches tall, he gave the impression of physical substance. Kate Sanborn spoke of him as a "magnificent specimen of manhood" and increased his height to "six feet two," a vision that photographs from the World Parliament later encouraged. Since then, some have said his poses were reminiscent of Napoleon's masculine resolve, a stereotype that has lately been questioned.[44] But even if Vivekananda was not inclined to copy France's conquering hero, Christina Greenstidel nevertheless saw him as a "forceful virile figure" that stepped onto the platform in Detroit, so unlike the "emaciated, ascetic type which is generally associated with spirituality in the West."[45] She referred no doubt to Catholic saints and desiccated pastors, but the stereotype could equally apply to the ascetic yogis and sadhus of the subcontinent. Vivekananda's fleshy, exotic flamboyance countered both Western *and* Eastern visions of embodied spirituality, and, for her, testified to his uniqueness. Moreover, the virility they admired was off-limits because he was a monk, a masculinity of self-restraint that reinforced his moral power and may have made him less dangerous.[46] The emotional boundaries, however, often remained blurred.

They therefore sought to define Vivekananda's "charisma," the term Max Weber employed to denote a rare ability to arouse faith in an otherwise disenchanted world. Weber focused on the "psychological satisfaction" that followers experienced in "knowing" that an abstract set of ideas, principles, and sentiments was embodied in a magnetic individual who could engender faith. In Vivekananda's case, the "force" was spiritual, even if Weber had focused on its political dimensions. Beyond it were the ideas, which affected listeners in surprising ways, almost turning their world upside down. It again underscored the "enchantment" that Weber argued had been lost in most modern interactions.[47]

An example was Martha Brown Fincke, whose parents had been missionaries in India.[48] She had been brought up "in the strictest Protestant Christian orthodoxy" and her horrified parents had despaired when one of her friends who had gone to Vassar College was "rumored to have 'lost her faith.'"[49] She met Vivekananda at Smith College after the Parliament, where he debated with the "College president, the head of the philosophy department, and several other professors, the ministers of the Northampton churches, and a well-known author." The panel "dealt mainly with Christianity and why it was the only true religion," but nevertheless, Vivekananda effectively resisted his adversaries with "more apposite" stanzas from Wordsworth and ideas from British philosophers. Suddenly, Fincke found herself identifying not with her own world, but the "black-coaled and somewhat austere gentleman," and that she was "exult[ing] in the air of freedom that blew through the room."

Fincke claimed that Vivekananda represented "freedom" and "personified [a] Power," which armed her against the "father she adored." Her father apparently badgered her with letters mocking Vivekananda, until she mentioned the latter no more. But Vivekananda's presence remained a bone of contention between them. When a "pretty little Guernsey calf was added to the family livestock," she called it "Veda," and when it died a few months later, her father "said its name had killed it."

She remembered a crucial conversation with Vivekananda about the blood of Christ. Like many South Asians, he was disquieted by Christianity's focus on God's Son bloodied and broken on the Cross, and she realized that she, too, had always detested the hymn, "There is a fountain filled with blood, drawn from Emmanuel's veins. . . . And sinners, plunged beneath that flood, lose all their guilty stains." She claimed that her free-thinking self emerged from this brief exchange. She did not want to be engulfed in a pool of bodily fluids—even of divine power and holiness—or to think of herself either as a sinner or as stained. This account provides, albeit retrospectively, a rare narrative of Vivekananda's impact, which combined generational resistance, Christian religious doubt, and intellectual conviction.

Fincke was an example of the women Vivekananda praised when he wrote to Indian friends: "They are the goddess Lakshmi [Vishnu's wife] in beauty and . . . Saraswati [goddess of learning and wisdom] in talents and accomplishments," outstripping American men in culture.[50] He was astounded that their freedom had not interfered with their morality: "I have seen thousands of women here whose hearts are as pure and stainless as snow"; and he contrasted, with sadness, their lives to those of Indian women who could not be "safely allowed to walk in the streets!"[51] He had feared women's emancipation would become license, that there would be "unwomanly women smashing under their feet all the peace and happiness of home-life in their mad liberty-dance."[52] Instead, he encountered only hospitality, loyalty, and a broadmindedness that did not negate spirituality. But he also betrayed his disquiet at "unwomanly" behavior, particularly in domestic settings, while reveling in American women's enlightenment and spiritual passion. He concluded that perhaps India was degenerate because it mistreated women: "Do you know who is the real 'Shakti-worshipper'? It is he who knows that God is the omnipresent force in the universe and sees in women the manifestation of that Force. Many men here look upon their women in this light. Manu [the ancient Hindu lawgiver] . . . has said that gods bless those families where women are happy and well treated. Here men treat their women as well as can be desired, and hence they are so prosperous, so learned, so free and so energetic. But why is it that we are slavish, miserable, and dead? The answer is obvious."[53]

He told his "Chicago Mother," Mrs. Hale, "I am shrewd enough to know that in every country in general, and America in particular, 'she' is the real operator at the nose string."[54] The image was striking—a woman leading the Holy Cow, the source of nourishment and the symbol of beneficence. He accepted India's belief in matriarchal power and had refused to leave the country without Sarada Devi's permission and proof of his mother's well-being.[55] However, American women also had their own spiritual power and could exercise it beyond the domestic sphere in ways that might help him in his mission.

In the summer of 1894, he observed American freedoms and reflected that the young people, especially the women, were "quite free and happy."[56] They even wore "scientific dress," a reference to the early patterns of home dressmaking, which no longer required several fittings.[57] For the first time, he spent extended periods in mixed-sex company outside the family and saw that summer pastimes did not compromise virtue: he enjoyed the company of a "lady from Detroit—very cultured and with beautiful black eyes and long hair" who promised to take him to an island out at sea.[58] He noted that the "people are healthy, young, sincere."[59] When a sudden storm uprooted their tents at night and drenched them to the bone, they uncomplainingly put them back up. He found them brave and practical.

He also loved that he was accepted: "I am, as it were, a woman amongst women."[60] Like his guru, he refused to be captured by manhood alone. If Ramakrishna had lived and played among village women in India, so did Vivekananda pursue something of the kind in America, reporting that he was "now closely associated with them in all their affairs."[61] He knew of their marriage prospects and love affairs and pitied those who needed to strategize to find husbands—so unlike India where these delicate matters were arranged by parents. Here again, his identity was fluid. He enjoyed being an "honorary woman," despite his later reputation as a zealous man-maker. Rather than trying to kill off the "inner feminine"—the courtly, cooking, sensitive, even musical aspects of his Bengali self—he celebrated it while in America.[62] Indeed, one might argue that Vivekananda's charisma rested on how his "manly" embodiment and intellect also embraced a femininity that he never abandoned. In this way, he retained important aspects of Ramakrishna's persona and beliefs that many have felt he jettisoned.

* * *

While impressed with these women, he also found fault. In the summer of 1894, he compared his carefree pleasures with their emotional aridity: "I had nice yachting, nice sea bathing, and am enjoying myself like a duck."[63] But his hosts were a "dry sort of people . . . they do not understand 'Madhava,' the Sweet One."[64] It is hard to know what to make of these observations. Vivekananda may have found it difficult to converse with women who were intellectually earnest. He was shocked that "even girls talk dry metaphysics!!! . . . Nobody here understands 'my Beloved.'" There was no tradition of Radha-Krishna to inspire them, just scripture and emotional constraint. "Religion to these people," he continued, "is reason and horribly stony at that."[65] He spoke more generally here, and included men in his condemnation, referring to forms of Protestantism that, in his view, lacked passion, ritual, and color.

He suggested that this New England "dryness" was embodied in a straitlaced, armored, and brittle physicality. When he went to Magnolia, Massachusetts, he observed that the "women do not give up their coat of

7585.   BATHING BEACH, MAGNOLIA, MASS.

6.2. The beach at Magnolia, near Gloucester, Massachusetts. Postcard, c. 1900.

mail even while bathing [swimming] . . . that is how these mailclad [*sic*] she-warriors of America have got the superiority over men." He joked about them, but at times also regretted their "hardness," especially when referring to their corsets. He concluded that the mailclad [*sic*] ones of this country are 'armadillas' . . ." and concluded that they were too body conscious: "Just as we always dwell in the soul, so they take care of the body, and there is no end to the cleaning and embellishing of it. One who failed to do this has no place in society."[66]

Vivekananda admitted his difficulty in adapting to Western bodily practices and did not like wearing shoes indoors or going "to the toilet. . . . so circumspectly."[67] Later, he would instruct his female disciples not to criticize Indian customs and required Margaret Noble to eat with her hand and to go barefoot. He knew from personal experience how important such standards were to the exercise of social power. Some of his worst quarrels with his Western associates would focus on his refusal to conform to their ideals of asceticism, both Western and Indian.[68]

With time, he recognized that Americans were not always so brave or fine either. In Baltimore, small hotels would not "take in a black man," and he had to go to a larger one, which "knew the difference between a Negro and a foreigner."[69] In San Francisco, a Mrs. Hansbrough noted how her respectability shielded him from harassment in the street. When one American woman insisted that Boston was more civilized than Calcutta, he quoted the Bible and said that "he had been a stranger in a strange land" but had been obliged "to run [into] a dark passage, just before the mob in full pursuit swept past." He concluded with irony that "Massachusetts is a very civilized place!"[70] This mixture of public vulnerability and private welcome powerfully shaped his impressions of the United States.

WOMEN IN INDIA

On June 28, 1897, Josiah John Goodwin, who acted as Vivekananda's stenographer for a time in India, reported that he had remarked that "If I have to come back again as a woman I must & will come as an American woman."[71] Such comments reveal his recognition that American women's prospects were very different than those of their Bengali counterparts. As Tanika Sakar has shown, many Hindu women could not inherit property from their father, had no definite claims on their husband's estate, often holding only usufruct rights until their sons came of age. Frequently given away in marriage when only children, they were sent away from their mother and extended families, and then lived within their husband's households. Women spent their early years knowing they must depart, and often uncertain of their class and caste status.[72] Above all, they often became mothers when they, themselves, were little more than children.[73] They were not always powerless, however. Wealthy women had servants poorer and even less secure than they, often of a lower caste; while mothers-in-law could inflict woes upon their sons' new brides, especially before the young women, themselves, became a mother (especially of sons), and hence achieved the same maternal status.

Women's emancipation had been a central concern of Bengali reformers, but their ardor for change cooled in the decades after the Indian Mutiny in 1857, when British repression, high-handedness, and economic exploitation increased. The Great Famine of the 1870s, press and cultural repression, as well as rural rebellion and urban immiseration, all prioritized British pockets over Indian needs. The Ilbert Bill (1883), which initially allowed high-level Indian magistrates to judge the British, caused such a furor that a new measure required that white people be tried with 50 percent

European jurors.[74] The anguish of lean times and poverty stalked even high-caste Indians, as the tales of family ruin which surrounded Vivekananda and Ramakrishna's other disciples in the 1880s demonstrate.

Vivekananda therefore came of age when many educated Bengalis were reassessing British intentions and, in turn, seeking to revalidate Indian "tradition." They pivoted to what has been called "indigenism," infused by ethnic and religious nationalism, a reaction against British pretensions of cultural superiority and especially critiques of Indian family arrangements. The commentary reified an upper-caste and monolithic view of Hindu family relations; it excluded many caste rules as well as ethnic and regional variations, leading even those subordinate in the hierarchy to hanker after upper-caste respectability.[75] In reality, however, there was no single, primordial family structure, no one view of women's role in families in the way that the term "indigenism" suggests. When the Crown exerted greater power over public law as well as notions of citizenship and rights, Hindu and Muslim leaders often responded by pressing for tighter rein over private law and domestic arrangements. Gender, therefore, became central to legal, political, and cultural debate.

A large literature expressed nostalgia for some mythological "Hindu household"—and the saintly Hindu wife and mother—where the British could not rule. English judges, often with their own conservative views of women's place in society, regarded such matters as outside their purview.[76] Hindu pundits confirmed scriptural precepts, and such novelists as Bankim Chandra Chattopadhyay even glorified *sati* as a moment of sacrificial inspiration.[77] Pious pamphlets and journalism praised child marriage as a refuge from the polluting effects of the Raj, which obliged Indian men to toil in offices and shops.

Vivekananda had his own views on these subjects. As a young Brahmo, he knew of Keshub Chunder Sen's great blunder, the 1879 arranged marriage of his twelve-year-old daughter Suniti Devi to the Maharaja of Cooch Behar. Sen had campaigned for the "Brahmo Marriage Act" of 1872, which proscribed marriage for girls under age fourteen, but nevertheless married his own, underage child to a Hindu prince. He never recovered from a decision that erstwhile admirers found both reactionary and hypocritical.[78] Certainly, he was a traditionalist in his own marriage and his Brahmo biographer, Mazoomdar, described how Sen had his wife "represented as a primitive Aryan devotee," with Sen as her "god."[79] Mazoomdar suggested that Sen's opposition

to "female reform" bordered on intolerance and was reinforced by an instinctive sense of nationality.[80]

Vivekananda, however, retained the earlier Brahmo position that young
girls should not wed and wrote in 1894 to a Madras friend, "you will have to
stop this shameful business of marrying off nine-year-old girls."[81] A year
later, he told his guru-brother Saradananda not to associate with people
who supported child marriage, concluding, "I am sorry, . . . I cannot have
any partnership with such doings as getting husbands for babies."[82] In 1898,
he exclaimed, "Somehow, the parents must dispose of a girl in marriage, if
she is nine or ten years of age! And what a rejoicing of the whole family if a
child is born to her at the age of thirteen!"[83] He was disgusted by the selfish
feelings that made families want male children to perform the rites for the
dead.[84] He even invoked a eugenic argument with a touch of British political
economy (reasoning he generally eschewed) to express his dismay: "it may
be argued that early marriage leads to premature child-bearing, which accounts for most of our women dying early; their progeny also, being of low
vitality, go to swell the ranks of our country's beggars!"[85]

But he seems never to have set out these feelings publicly. Nor did he use
the notion of "consent," which took account of women's subjectivity, to argue
against child marriage.[86] And yet, he was different from the more orthodox
who concentrated on ideas of puberty—and hence biology—to suggest that
girls were ready for sexual relations. In 1891 (when Vivekananda was traveling and intermittently returning to Baranagar), a ten-year old-girl named
Phulmani was raped to death by her twenty-nine-year-old husband. Because
she was of legal age and deemed "pubescent," the man went unpunished; orthodox Hindus were horrified but defended her husband to protect "traditional" values against British hegemony.[87] He never named Phulmani, but
Vivekananda seemed to know the debate, and in 1896, raged: "A girl of eight
is married to a man of thirty, and the parents are jubilant over it. . . . And if
anyone protests against it, the plea is put forward, 'Our religion is being
overturned.'"[88] This was a dig against the worst of orthodoxy, and a refusal
to blame the Mughals, as others were wont to do, for never legislating against
the custom.

His ideas on child marriage were therefore clear, but his views on
mothers and widows were more in line with reactive cultural currents.
Mothers, he believed, were the heart of Hindu civilization and he prized
them as a reserve army in protecting the "Hindu way of life": "In the west

woman is the wife; in the east she is the mother. The Hindoos worship the idea of mother, and even the monks are required to touch the earth with their foreheads before their mothers."[89] He explained to Westerners that "the highest of all feminine types in India is mother, higher than wife."[90] And he remarked in early 1900: "[J]ust as the mother's own daughter married and went out, so her son married and brought in another daughter, and she has to fall in line under the government of the queen of queens, of his mother . . . Who is she, then, that would try to ride over my head and govern my mother? She has to wait till her womanhood is fulfilled; and the one thing that fulfils womanhood, that is womanliness in woman, is motherhood."[91] The link between mother and child, and especially that between mother and son, therefore surpassed all others: "One who does not worship his mother can never truly rise."[92]

Vivekananda did not consider how such vaunted bonds might further female subordination by reproducing the exclusionary intimacy of the mother-son relationship. In glorifying the matriarchal ideal, he also veiled or ignored important domestic alliances among women. He did not acknowledge the new political and feminist sisterhoods developing within emerging Indian nationalism. This debate was wide-ranging, with elite Bengali families expressing hope for the recalibration of Indian "domesticity" increasingly based on mutual consent rather than "patriarchy" alone.[93] Nor did he know, it seemed, the more radical critique made by feminist writer Tarabai Shinde against caste and patriarchy, which had appeared as early as 1882.[94] However, he did correspond with Sarala Ghosal, Tagore's niece, who was active in promoting women's education, a concern that he advanced explicitly when he invited Margaret Noble to India.[95]

The Mother cult that Vivekananda evoked was integral to his cultural nationalism and may have drawn in part on Bankim Chandra Chattopadhyay's wildly popular Bengali novel *Anandamath* (*The Sacred Brotherhood*, 1882). This volume recounts the patriotic resistance of an eighteenth-century Hindu sannyasin force that revolts against a despotic nawab, a Muslim client installed by the East India Company, who attempts to destroy the Hindus' "honor, faith, caste, and women."[96] Vivekananda never names the novel, but may have embraced aspects of Bankim's language of Hindu strength when envisaging his Ramakrishna Math and Mission as a sannyasin army.[97] The book was in some ways an outlier (regarding Muslims) in Bankim's otherwise liberal corpus, but was central to the creation of a "new and supreme deity within the Hindu pantheon—the motherland—the goddess who demanded protection from her sons."[98] This was certainly a worship which Vivekananda understood: "She it is whose shadow is life and death. She is the pleasure in all pleasure. She is the misery in all misery. If life comes, it is the Mother; if death comes, it is the Mother. If heaven comes, She is. If hell comes, there is the Mother; plunge in."[99]

Here, he spoke as much about Kali as about human mothers. At moments, he also referred to the "motherland," but almost exclusively with other Indians, and especially on his return tour in 1897.[100] Interestingly, he also used this term when writing to Muslim friends, such as Mohammed Sarfaraz Husain of Naini Tal, whose help he courted in 1898: "I am firmly persuaded that without the help of practical Islam, theories of Vedantism, however fine and wonderful they may be, are entirely valueless to the vast mass of mankind."[101] In his view, the notion of the "motherland" provided an emotional rationale for opposing British oppression, whether the Indian was Hindu or Muslim.[102]

These words seemed more than an exercise in cultivating the Muslim poet. On visits to Punjab, he met leaders of the Arya Samaj, who had sought to prove the radical, egalitarian aspects of Hinduism by converting lower castes, an aim jeopardized by their often aggressive tactics. Vivekananda sought to bring peace between this Hindu reformist group and the Muslim community.[103] This is not to suggest that he did not make negative remarks about Islam—especially regarding the violence of earlier conquest—but he included Muslims within the greater Indian "brotherhood." His ideas about Muslims hovered between affectionate respect and grumbling disenchantment, but he regarded such fluctuations of feeling as inevitable, since both Muslims and Hindus were all sons of the same "Mother."[104]

The abstractions of nascent nationalism were matched by an awareness of the plight of women, especially in his own family. His mother was an only child with doting parents, who did not have to compete with a brother for education, money, or regard.[105] She was known for her beauty, singing voice, and memory, all traits which she passed on to Vivekananda.[106] Like her husband, she enjoyed literature and was said to have spoken English (albeit slowly) with Margaret Noble when they met.[107] She cared about her daughters' education, and one of Vivekananda's elder sisters, Jogendrabala, learned English from Kamini Shil, the principal of Bethune College, the first ladies' college in Bengal, and had an Englishwoman as a private tutor.[108]

6.3. Bhuvaneshwari Devi

She even won a prize for her fluent English, while the younger sisters went to Rambagan Mission School. The family thus reflected progressive ideas concerning women's education, while he was personally accustomed to intelligent, educated women.

Moreover, his female kin also knew sorrow and hardship. When Vivekananda was on pilgrimage in the Himalayas, Jogendrabala, in her twenties, committed suicide in the home of her in-laws where, it was speculated, she had been unhappy.[109] Three of his own siblings had died in infancy; moreover, his mother experienced poverty after her husband's death and faced legal battles to get compensation for the loss of her home.[110] Although Vivekananda grew up amid relatively "advanced" views, he also knew that Indian domestic arrangements had devastated his female relatives. His brother Mahendranath recalled Vivekananda's grief upon being informed of his sister's death by telegram. It was doubly hard for Vivekananda to receive such dreadful news, as he felt it impossible to retain the detachment of a sannyasin. Years later, he recalled the pain he had experienced to one of his American mothers, Sara Bull: "My mistakes have been great, but every one of them was from too much love. How I hate love! Would I never have any Bhakti! . . . I went years ago to the Himalayas, never to come back; and my sister committed suicide, the news reached me there, and that weak heart flung me off from that prospect of peace! It is the weak heart that has driven me out of India to seek some help for those I love. . . ."[111]

Here, he was concerned not to pantheonize women, uplift India's poor, or to bring Indian spirituality to the West, but simply to "seek some help for those [he] love[d]." His mission connected to the impulses of his "weak heart," especially when he thought of his mother. Worry overcame him in 1893 when, during a stay in Madras with Manmatha Babu (Manmatha Nath Bhattacharya), he dreamed his mother had died, and he refused to leave for America until he had news. Manmatha Babu not only sent a telegram to Calcutta, but also consulted a fortune-teller to reassure him.[112]

As a monk, he should have given up his family feeling, but he could not. In 1898, he wrote to his old patron, the Raja of Khetri, in despairing terms: "I have one great sin rankling always in my breast, and that is to do service to the world, I have sadly neglected my mother. . . . she has become awfully worn-out with grief. Now my last desire is to . . . serve my mother . . . I want to live with my mother and get my younger brother married to prevent extinction of the family. . . . She lives now in a hovel . . . I have exposed myself to your Highness, and no one else shall know of it. I am tired, heartsick and dying."[113]

His sister's death and his mother's plight are, therefore, of more than passing interest; above all, they suggest the pressure of trying to encompass an abiding love for female intimates with the rigid gender expectations of an emerging cultural nationalism. He wanted to improve the lot of women, but he feared the effects of foreign interference and rapid reform. He was devoted to the women in his family but upheld the mother-son bond, a vision of masculine protection that he readily transferred to the "motherland."

◆   ◆   ◆

If he hated the marriage of "babies," Vivekananda was much more ambivalent about widow remarriage. Widows had been given the right to remarry in 1856 after a campaign undertaken by the educationalist, social reformer, and scholar of Sanskrit Ishwar Chandra Vidyasagar, who claimed that no evidence existed in sacred texts to forbid second marriages; this was seconded by the Hindu philosopher, teacher, and leader Swami Dayananda Saraswati of the Arya Samaj, who wanted to outlaw the marriage of girls until age sixteen. Dayananda Saraswati even suggested the creation of temporary unions of widowers and widows for the birth of sons but insisted that "neither the widow nor the widower" should contract a second marriage, thus applying the same regulations to both sexes in high-caste families.[114]

However, by the 1860s, few widows even tried to buck the tide of what Tanika Sarkar calls Hindu "common sense," which continued to perceive widows as still "belonging" to, and indivisible from, their dead husband. This view of women implied a lack of personhood.[115] Widows in India included toddlers and young girls whose husband's death prevented them from experiencing sexual love or having children. Male relatives often saw these "pure" young women as objects of romantic adventure, so that widows were more likely to commit infanticide and become prostitutes if they bore unwanted children.[116]

For Vivekananda and many other Bengalis, however, widow remarriage was "the greatest degradation," entailing guilt and spiritual desolation, shaming widows with a suggestion of unbecoming lustfulness.[117] Vivekananda saw widowhood as a spiritual vocation, suggesting that they were somehow like Christian nuns. They shaved their heads, wore no jewelry, and refrained from food deemed to stoke sexual desire. Like sannyasins, they practiced austerities and fasted twice a month, and were said to undertake such penances willingly. Vivekananda, therefore, sought to elevate their status by spiritualizing it, but he risked justifying a punitive regimen.[118]

Such views embroiled him in disputes with the vocal American followers of Pandita Ramabai, a Christian convert and widow who was dedicated to the "uplift" of Indian women.[119] She had arrived in America in 1886 and, with the help of a Unitarian minister, had organized the influential Ramabai Circle in Boston; by 1888, there were seventy-five groups of this kind in the United States.[120] Ramabai was a serious Sanskritist of Brahmin origin, who had given public lectures in Calcutta and founded the Arya Women's Society that was devoted to women's education and ending child marriage. Linked to Brahmoism, she left for Britain to become a physician but ultimately joined the Anglican sisters in Wantage, not far from Oxford, in 1883.[121]

6.4. Pandita Ramabai

Ramabai thus preceded Vivekananda and was later a thorn in his side. Perhaps she appeared as Ram Mohun Roy's successor in internationalizing the debate over women's treatment in India, which had begun over *sati*.[122] Vivekananda disliked the idea that Ramabai's allies were often American upper-class women and disapproved of British missionaries who claimed to protect "native" women from indigenous patriarchies. He defied Western stereotypes of Indian mothers as either heartless or victimized: "Women in India do not throw their children in the rivers to be devoured by crocodiles," he reportedly told the North Shore Club in Lynn, Massachusetts: "Widows are not burned on the funeral pyre of their husband unless it is a voluntary act of self immolation."[123] This pronouncement underscored his difficulty; here he suggested that consent justified the sacrifice, a view of human agency that Indian freedom fighters, Gandhi among them, would later endorse.[124] But could widows' "consent" be real if they fled the flames only to have their relatives, fearful of dishonor, tie them to the pyre?[125]

Ramabai's arguments shadowed Vivekananda from his earliest days in America, with her followers' objections undermining his argument about the superiority of Indian spirituality. Moreover, she seemed authoritative when she warned her audiences not to be "charmed" by the "grand structures of oriental philosophy," and insisted that Hindu men "oppress widows and trample the poor under their heels."[126] She highlighted the contradictions within Hindu sacred texts, which, in her view, only agreed that women "were bad, very bad, worse than demons."[127] And she explained how, after her family had all died from famine, she had married a Bengali Shudra (a person of low caste) and had lost all status.

Vivekananda defended Hinduism against Ramabai activists at the Brooklyn Ethical Association in early 1895.[128] He admitted in 1900 that widowhood was "a hardship to many," but compared the regimen to that of students who were also obliged to avoid meat, fish, or wine. He concluded unapologetically that India was "a nation of monks—always making penance, and we like it."[129] In this way, he endorsed the power of expiatory exercises but failed to address the specific plight of widows, and the way, for many, such austerities lasted decades.[130]

But more often, he changed the subject, as he did in 1894: "the fate of a nation does not depend upon the number of husbands their widows get, but upon the *condition of the masses*." As he contemplated a program of man-making while speaking in America, he wondered whether the Indian "masses" could become "occidental.... in [a] spirit of equality, freedom, work, and energy," while remaining Hindu in religion.[131] He thus focused more on poor men than on widows, insisting that the latter's plight was an upper-caste concern alone. Admirers remembered how he "declare[d] ... himself sternly against all interference against the scriptural ... injunctions in regard to ... marriage" while also insisting that low castes and women receive a Sanskrit education.[132] This paradox rested on his belief that women's education, when joined to man-making, would permit Hindu society to develop with neither British impositions nor top-down, Westernized solutions. Old hierarchies might persist, but in an altered form, as Indians reorganized their own society on their own terms. The question of widow remarriage was thus delayed, and the plight of the Indian (male) masses prioritized.

He told his brothers in India that "there is no distinction of sex in the soul," and even fantasized about "thousands of men and ... thousands of women who will spread like wildfire from the Himalayas to Cape Comorin" to remake India.[133] The nationalist Bal Gangadhar Tilak later confirmed that

Vivekananda wanted the "women in the Maharashtra" (the western peninsular region in India) not to be confined by "the *purdah* system" and hoped
that "widows of the higher classes" might "devote their lives to the spread
of spirituality and religion alone like the old *yogis* of the Buddhist period."[134]
He thereby advocated that undefended widows should act as solitary sannyasins, a view which envisaged their spiritual vocation in national renewal,
a position that again set aside the question of remarriage.

WOMEN AND SPIRITUALITY IN INDIA:
GOPALER MA AND SARADA DEVI

In line with these views, he furthered the cults surrounding the "mothers" who
would enhance the movement's spiritual aura. Vivekananda knew Gopaler
Ma, and the stories surrounding her. Born Aghoremani Devi in 1822 to a
Brahmin family and married at age nine, she was widowed at fourteen years
old, and devoted to Baby Krishna; after selling her property, she lived in tiny
quarters in the garden of a Krishna temple on the Ganges, rising at two a.m.,
and meditating, needing no more than a few rupees to survive.

In *Sri Ramakrishna and His Divine Play,* Saradananda tells how she first met
Ramakrishna in 1884 as part of her spiritual quest; rather than talking about
God, however, he demanded some "sweet coconut balls" and "a hodge-podge
curry with pumpkin leaves."[135] She visited for months, but all Ramakrishna did
was ask for food. She was so disappointed that she vowed never to return to
Dakshineswar, but somehow kept on doing so. According to this story, the talk
of food prepared her for the visions that soon overwhelmed her.

In the spring of 1885, Ramakrishna appeared at three in the morning.
When she tried to touch his hand, he disappeared to be replaced by the infant deity—"a large baby, ten months"—who immediately asked for butter.
She would have believed he was the actual "butter thief" and explained that
she was too poor to have what he desired.[136] He screamed for food until she
found some dry coconut balls; he prevented her from performing "the repetition of the mantra," sitting on her lap, pulling her rosary, and crawling
around the room.[137] Overcome by Gopal's insistence, she ran to Dakshineswar with the child in her arms, marveling at the baby's "two tiny, rosy
feet dangling over [her] bosom."[138] When she arrived in Ramakrishna's

6.5. Gopaler Ma

room, he entered ecstasy and sat on her lap like a child, tears pouring down her cheeks as she fed him with cream, butter, and sweets.[139]

Witnesses were said to be astonished to see Ramakrishna touch a woman while in samadhi. When he got up, she remained "in rapture, [and] began dancing around the room," as the "luminous boy" went into her arms and then back into Ramakrishna's body.[140]

The ecstasies continued for only two months, during which Gopaler Ma is said to have experienced the pleasures and pressures of a baby's incessant demands, especially those of food and feeding. She had become the mother to the avatara Krishna in his child-god form. This account of her visions suggested that true spirituality did not come from austerities, but from the endless nurturing and emotional suppleness that motherhood required: "If God is worshipped with devotion, what is the need for asceticism? . . ."[141] She stopped rejecting spoons that had been used by others or demanding that the fireplace be purified endlessly; instead, she began to emulate the mischievous side of Ramakrishna's spirituality.

Even more important to Vivekananda than Gopaler Ma was Sarada Devi. Her story perhaps exemplified Vivekananda's ideal of saintly widowhood. Despite the spiritual marriage to Ramakrishna, her future was uncertain when he died in 1886. Toward the end, she had tended him and cooked his meals, inhabiting a tiny room in the Shyampukur house and praying for his recovery.[142] She risked shame by living with men, rising at three a.m. to go to the bathroom before they arose. If at Cossipore she could again move freely, she was still consigned to a small room, cooking the food prescribed by the doctor.[143] But even before Ramakrishna died, she was said to have had visions: when she spoke of a girlish Kali, her head contorted to the side from a sore throat. Sarada concluded that the "Divine Mother [Kali] and Sri Ramakrishna were one and the same."[144]

If she remained Ramakrishna's Shakti, she was not, however, compliant. After he died, she refused to throw away her marriage bangles as was customary, while her neighbors criticized her for not shaving her head, wearing a red-bordered sari (widows were meant to wear only white), and keeping her jewelry.[145] One of Ramakrishna's disciples, the mischievous Hazra, may have tried to assault her, a story that suggests how unprotected she was.[146] Until well-to-do householders came to her aid, she was so poor that she could not always afford salt and had no permanent home—it was not until 1909 that she had her own modest house.

But stories of hardship were matched by others of growing spiritual authority. Between August 1886 and August 1887, for example, she went on pilgrimages to Vaidyanath Dham, to Varanasi, Ayodha, and Vrindavan, visited holy men and attracted new companions; she even traveled by train like Vivekananda. In a peculiar way the death of their husbands could "free" Brahmin widows from their marital cloisters and put them on the open road with pilgrims and mingling crowds.

However, 1889–1890 was a turning point. With the help of Ramakrishna's devotees, she fed the poor and performed funeral rites; she even employed a maid who went to market (it was disreputable for a Brahmin woman to shop in public). She landed in Ghusuri in May 1890, and in July, Vivekananda and Akhanananda visited her before their joint pilgrimage to the Himalayas.

They wanted her blessing, and Vivekananda continued to want it for the rest of his life. When she returned to her village in October, devotees flocked to her for instruction. Increasingly she cooked, fed, and advised.[147]

Although a Brahmin widow, Sarada experienced both opprobrium and life-enhancing travel as well as mystical experiences, ultimately attaining a unique authority. The cynical might suggest that she had mastered the art of being a saint from Ramakrishna; or imply that her mysticism saved her from obscurity and probable starvation. But such views obscure her spiritual intelligence and unique subjectivity. Part of the reason for this misapprehension lies in early accounts, which discerned nothing exceptional about her.[148] Nonetheless, her personality emerges, even in hagiography. She returned repeatedly to Dakshineswar, despite Ramakrishna's lack of interest in her fate, and braved an encounter alone with robbers, who ultimately escorted her to Dakshineswar because of her courtesy to them.[149] When Hazra attacked her, she was said to have slapped him and held his tongue to make him stop. She associated also with "impure" women and continued to do so despite Ramakrishna's disapproval.[150] Sarada asserted herself in later years both by bestowing sannyasa on men and by tussling with unworthy would-be disciples.[151] As time went on, devotion to her blossomed.

Perhaps Vivekananda saw Sarada as a mother figure reminiscent of his own mother, even if less educated. She was not like Kali, and it is difficult to imagine Sarada Devi as the erotic and violent denizen of the cremation grounds. As Holy Mother, she remained a pure vessel, endlessly nurturing, unsullied by sex, childbirth, or lactation, and elevated after her early years of renunciation when she even worshipped herself in acknowledgment of Ramakrishna's belief in her supernatural qualities. She was, however, also savvy and strong. She became more powerful still after Vivekananda's death, especially for the sound advice she offered to supplicants. We have a sense of her growing commitment to Vivekananda and his to her. Not only did she give permission for him to go to the West, she also reportedly became, in his words, the person "who is always guiding and inspiring my intellect in this world, she is my all-auspicious Mother. She is my goal–whether I succeed or fail."[152]

Sarada believed herself to be Ramakrishna's legatee, but she fulfilled her role through a combination of orthodoxy and unconventionality. She remained veiled, obscure even to Vivekananda, yet refused to dress like a widow. In this regard, she was not so different to her husband's favorite disciple, who wore an orange jacket, but donned an unfamiliar turban as a sannyasin when he met disciples in Madras. These qualities made her Vivekananda's perfect support—she remained in seclusion but was willing to break Brahmin taboos by eating food with the foreign women whom he brought to her door. Although he refused to fight for Hindu widows, his most profound spiritual connection after his guru's death was with a widow. He did this, perhaps, because she seemed to embody the impossible: Sarada bucked tradition and still manifested the special qualities of ascetic women in India, in which "motherhood [had] to do with intimacy, food, scolding and compassionate love."[153] Orthodoxy and liberation (*mukti*) seemed to live in her without apparent conflict.

If from a twenty-first-century perspective we find their alliance anchored in a troubling female self-abnegation, Vivekananda envisaged Sarada's Holy Motherhood as central to the larger Indian "fraternity" and as a bulwark against westernization. Despite her evident devotion to Vivekananda, we have no firsthand evidence of how Sarada regarded her idealized role in this collaboration.

◆   ◆   ◆

By going to America, Vivekananda's appreciation of women's talents and possibilities increased, even though he balked sometimes when he needed them to navigate this new society. He admired Western women's virtue and education, while also finding them unyielding. They were nevertheless essential in an experimental journey to acquire help from a Western avant-garde. He relied on their collaboration to internationalize a view of India not as decayed and archaic, but spiritually elevated. In the process, he revealed astonishing "feminine" capacities for engagement and nurture. In India, however, he was often different. As a brilliant and favored male child, he furthered the cult of motherhood (Sarada Devi's, Gopaler Ma's, and Kali's) and underpinned a view of man-making that was sometimes unyielding in a different way. He always perceived himself as a jnani, a "wisdom-seeker" with the melting heart of a bhakti. Even while in the West, he often displayed the "masculine" qualities of rational skepticism that had irked Ramakrishna. Nowhere was this more important than in the exhilarating battleground where magic, science, healing, and consciousness were discussed. Here he challenged the stereotypes of Western orientalism and rejected Western views of the distinction between science and religion.

7

MAGIC, SCIENCE,
TRANSCENDENCE

Science without religion is lame, religion without science is blind.
—Albert Einstein, 1940

◆ ◆ ◆

VIVEKANANDA OFTEN HAD TO ASSURE his audiences in the United States that he could not perform magic, walk on coals, or sleep on beds of nails: "Swami Vivekananda was questioned concerning the truthfulness of the marvelous stories of the performance of wonderful feats of conjuring, levitation, suspended animation, and the like in India. [He] said, 'We do not believe in miracles at all . . .'"[1] The *Evening News* on February 17, 1894, asked him to "work a miracle in proof of [his] religion," but he had to explain that he was "no miracle worker," that the "pure Hindu religion" was not based on such things.[2] To earn money, he briefly went on the lecture circuit, but the company that organized the tour billed him as "One of the Giants of the Platform" and "An Orator by Divine Right; A Model Representative of his Race; A Perfect Master of the English Language; the Sensation of the World's Fair Parliament."[3] In this prospectus, he sounded more like a circus act than a monk, and he thereafter resisted attempts to commercialize or trivialize his message.

The expectations demonstrate how India was regarded as the birthplace of occultism. Travelers to the subcontinent reported on snake charmers and magicians who performed rope tricks by ascending an unattached cord hanging in the air. Similarly, Bram Stoker's *Dracula* (1897) described the "vampire able to slip out of a locked tomb with the powers of India's wonder-workers."[4] Indian performers continued to reinforce these impressions by making money with magic shows in such places as Paris and London.

Vivekananda fought against these notions by emphasizing a spirituality that embraced science, while also refusing to separate science from religion. In his view, science was not a disruptive Enlightenment legacy that broke the link between authority and knowledge, nor did it presage the "death of God."[5] Rather, he quickly grasped that "modern" science had become a rhetorical cudgel both to beat orthodox Christians at home and to ridicule the colonized (and their beliefs) abroad. He thus realized that the West's missionary impulses were jointly rooted in Christianity *and* science. Assuredly, science offered new normative models for knowledge that he yearned to further; and he believed that if the British unlocked their monopoly, Indians would contribute massively to this domain.[6] Vivekananda welcomed scientific discoveries and believed they would enhance the spiritual and cosmological truths he held dear.[7] He therefore campaigned against *Christian* obscurantism by focusing on the "superstitions" of the Judeo-Christian conception of an all-powerful and punitive God as well as biblical creationism. In contrast, he argued that the rishis, yogis, and the Buddha had long ago understood the mechanisms of evolution and had always promoted rationalism, saying in 1897 that "it seems to us . . . that the conclusions of modern science are the very conclusions the Vedanta reached ages ago only in modern science they are written in the language of matter."[8]

He joined many other Indians in claiming precedence in analyzing the natural world and the cosmos, while insisting that past achievements be linked to "modern" science and India's present and future. This belief was central to the view that India was different to the West because Vedanta did not require "disenchantment."[9] Rather, the "death of God" that Enlightenment rationality seemed to presage suggested the incomplete nature of Christianity that had often rejected scientific understandings.

He also argued that Western science remained value-laden and permeated by metaphor, and that often even reputable scientists engaged in metaphysics.[10] In a lecture in London, he remarked: "if a man quotes a Moses or a Buddha or a Christ, he is laughed at; but let him give the name of a Huxley, a Tyndall, or a Darwin, and it is swallowed without salt. 'Huxley has said it,' that is enough for many. We are free from superstitions indeed! That was a religious superstition, and this a scientific superstition."[11]

He understood that science could be as polemical as religion, while emphasizing his appreciation of it. At the same time, he inserted himself into Western debates about spiritualism, Christian Science, and theosophy. Like Hindu Universalism, these beliefs challenged the boundaries between science and religion, but Vivekananda sought to show Vedanta's superiority to all of them. He also tried to separate himself from the occult, while making important incursions into this arena.

RAMAKRISHNA, THE OCCULT, AND SCIENCE

Understanding Vivekananda's views takes us back to India, and to Ramakrishna, who believed that often great yogis were empowered with *siddhis*— mastery over the forces of nature gained through special training. It was traditionally held that they could change size; travel in light and retrieve objects from emptiness; grant wishes, and walk on fire (and other feats); as well as control the actions of others.[12] Ramakrishna, however, asserted that such feats did not bring spiritual fulfilment.[13] In making these arguments, he reiterated the orthodox Indic position that spiritual achievements brought magical powers, but the truly advanced rarely resorted to them.

In *Sri Ramakrishna and His Divine Play*, Saradananda recounts how he knew what was hidden in the minds of others but "never divulged this. . . . to display his divine power," preferring instead to learn about the devotee and tailor his teaching to the individual.[14] Similar accounts of these powers abound in the *Kathamrita*, with his touch generating physical laughter, tears, meditative concentration, and ecstatic shouts. Disciples reported feeling a "mysterious substance or force creeping upward within [the] body," while others saw "a light that [they] had never seen before."[15] Such reactions were not presented as magical manipulation, however, but rather as progress toward illumination spurred by yogic penetration.

When he was dying of throat cancer, Ramakrishna's disciples implored him to cure himself. He responded that he had not preached the eternal nature of the soul to surrender now to the body's needs.[16] Once again, the reply suggested that he did indeed have such powers, but he insisted he was too unconcerned with his physicality (and with maya) to use them.

That said, Ramakrishna did allow himself to be treated by noted physician Mahendralal Sircar, saying: "As long as you have a body, you have to take care of it."[17] The head of the Indian Association for the Cultivation of Science (IACS) in 1876, Sircar championed science and saw British expertise as proof of a superiority that he hoped Indians would emulate.[18] He disapproved of Ramakrishna's past Tantrism, just as he condemned idol worship and polytheism; he maintained that science was essential to man-making and self-reliance, qualities that Ramakrishna never sought to cultivate, but which Vivekananda embraced. It is not clear where Sircar and Vivekananda first met, but the latter is cited in the *Kathamrita* as one of the participants in Sircar's conversations with Ramakrishna.[19] Gupta's account is silent about what Vivekananda made of the exchanges between the two giants of the Calcutta intellectual and spiritual landscape, but he had long realized that "science"—a term that encompassed a range of meanings and possibilities—would be central to his mission.

◆　◆　◆

As we know, Vivekananda laid claim to powers while also dismissing their importance. At age fifteen, he had experienced ecstasy when "bathed in white radiance" in Raipur in the Central Provinces and recalled how an aura of illumination appeared between his eyebrows before sleeping.[20] Only later did he realize that not everyone fell asleep in this way. He also sometimes felt that he had had a conversation before and believed he had envisaged who he would meet *in this life* even before he was born.[21] When his guru-brothers were together in Baranagar, one told of how he found Vivekananda's body illuminated by a Batuk Bhairav, the terrifying boy form of Shiva, often evoked to ward off evil; Vivekananda is said to have told him they had protected him since early childhood.[22] He also induced deep meditation in a brother-monk with a touch "like an electrical shock." Ramakrishna, Saradananda tells us, criticized this act as an arrogant injection of Vivekananda's own "attitude of mind" into another.[23] When he went abroad, Vivekananda equally disapproved of "operators"—both Christian Scientists and hypnotists—who interfered with individual spiritual development, a view that may have sprung from this episode.[24]

He tended to limit such discussions to Indian audiences. After his return in 1897, he reportedly told Sharat Chandra Chakravarti, a Bengali householder disciple, about Ramakrishna's legacy to him: "before the Lord [Ramakrishna] left his body he called me aside alone one day. . . . he looked steadily at me and fell into a state of trance. Then I really began to experience that subtle emanation like an electric shock was entering my body! Gradually I also lost external consciousness and became inert. For some time, I remained like this, unaware of anything. . . . When external consciousness came back, . . . the Lord said affectionately, 'Today, I've given you everything I possess, and have become a beggar! With this power you will do a lot of work for the world and then return.'"[25]

This account emphasized Vivekananda's yogic lineage, but also made him an inheritor of Ramakrishna's abilities, and here he used the "modern" vocabulary of electricity to describe his spiritual power. But he was unimpressed by the psychic, telepathic phenomena in the West, perhaps believing that these "adepts" were simply incapable of the mystical heights that such Indian masters as Ramakrishna had achieved.

As with the finest psychical researchers of the era—including William James—Vivekananda believed that the first port of call for curious phenomena were natural explanations.[26] However, the meaning of "natural" or "scientific" remained elastic for both. This suggests why sometimes his views seemed changeable, and why now—and even in his own time—they seem to betray occult influences.

THEOSOPHY

If he merely steered clear of spiritualism, Vivekananda was contemptuous of theosophy, which he knew from India and its founders Helen Blavatsky and Colonel Henry Steel Olcott. Blavatsky was the daughter of a Russian aristocrat who had married young and unhappily and was an omnivorous reader, polyglot, and traveler who claimed to have visited Tibet and to have met Buddhist mahatmas there.[27] She was raised in Eastern Orthodox Christianity and spent much time in Saratov (Tblisi), and Erivan, which had Muslim and even Buddhist (Kalmyk) populations. She was hence not "Western" in the same way as her Anglo-American and many European collaborators.[28] Olcott was an American Presbyterian who had been a soldier, journalist, and lawyer, and had even served on the commission to investigate Lincoln's assassination.[29] The two had met observing the spiritualist performances of William and Horatio Eddy in 1874 at a farm in Chittenden, Vermont, where the brothers claimed to have performed ectoplasmic materializations and communicated with spirits.

Olcott and Blavatsky founded the Theosophical Society in New York in 1875, and two years later, the latter published *Isis Unveiled,* a work combining hermeticism and neo-Platonism.[30] Their decision to travel to South Asia in 1879 meant that, in addition to Western esotericism, theosophy increasingly exhibited traces of Indian thought and religion.[31] When they arrived in India, they met Dayananda Saraswati, the head of the Arya Samaj, outside Bombay.[32] Saraswati championed new Vedic schools, and saw himself as the proselytizer of *sanatana dharma,* the "eternal way." The Arya Samaj, like the Brahmo Samaj, opposed idol worship and endorsed monotheism, but otherwise sought to inculcate a rigorous and unadorned Hinduism to save a new generation from secularism and British education.[33]

The theosophists' approach to Saraswati typified their ignorance of the Indian spiritual landscape. Hostile to missionizing themselves, they assumed they would be automatic allies of colonized peoples wanting to thwart Christian incursions. However, Saraswati wanted to rejuvenate an orthodox, "purified" Hinduism, whereas both Blavatsky and Olcott sought to westernize so-called Eastern wisdom and uncover the universal affiliations among various creeds.[34] Saraswati also steered clear of their occult interests. So, Blavatsky and Olcott moved on to Sri Lanka, where they patronized Dharmapala and took lay Buddhist vows. While there, Olcott produced a widely used "Buddhist Catechism" even though local monks disputed his understanding of "nirvana."[35] He dreamed of uniting all Buddhist sects by stripping Buddhism of its "superstitious" accretions—particularly relic worship—to create a "rationalist" Buddhism more palatable to his own Protestant and Enlightenment tastes. And yet, his vision of Buddhism also incorporated clairvoyance, faith cures, and spiritualism, aspects of American alternative spirituality that he promoted during his healing sessions.[36] He regarded these occurrences not as miracles, but as "naturalized," scientific phenomena.

Blavatsky and Olcott believed that science and religion could be united, and wanted a fashionable idealism to supersede the narrow positivism of the previous generation.[37] Like more highbrow philosophers in the Anglosphere, they sought to reinstate religious emotion, to regard the world's materiality as springing from divine thought and / or spiritual principles, and thus as essential to moral development.[38] The theosophists were the least disciplined members of an amorphous tendency that sought "a place for religion in a world of scientific facts."[39] They attacked Christianity particularly for its dogmatism, and both they and South Asian critics judged it as obscurantist, above all for its opposition to evolution.[40]

They argued that there was one "Absolute," one "Reality," causeless, timeless and indescribable, in which states of matter and consciousness become manifest, and "the appearance and disappearance of Worlds is like a regular tidal ebb of flux and reflux." Both theosophy and Hinduism generally sidestepped Darwin's mechanism of natural selection for emphasizing struggle and chance. "Karma," an Indian concept that theosophists borrowed, meant that the soul evolved according to the rules of "cause and effect" with individual souls (*monads*) fundamentally identical to the "Universal Over-soul" in much the same way that sparks were part of a greater fire. The term "monad" probably derived from Leibniz's *Monadology* (1714) and resonated with their idea that the supernatural coordinated the infinite perspectives of the universe, from the simplest to the most complex. According to Blavatsky, the monads evolved—as did the greater whole—in a process informed by intelligence and purpose. Laws of periodicity and cyclicity shaped events in both invisible and visible worlds.

By stressing karma, theosophists also embraced aspects of reincarnation (even if they interwove it with progressive evolution) and the idea that death was the beginning of rebirth. Blavatsky also argued that unfeeling matter ultimately becomes the thinking subject from which human consciousness emerges. The reductionism of neuroscience, which focused on the physical brain, failed to grasp the reality of this "superconsciousness." Vivekananda would have agreed with Blavatsky that biological forces "intermingle with, and often merge into, those forces that we have named intellectual and moral."[41] He even accepted that "behind such strange names as Indian Theosophy, and Esoteric Buddhism, . . . there was something real, something worth knowing."[42]

He also recognized that Blavatsky and Olcott were attempting to synthesize science and religion.[43] But as few Indians had ever been drawn to the reductive positivism that these Westerners now rejected, he was annoyed that theosophy claimed novelty in this arena, while also condemning its homogenization of

Eastern religions. Moreover, he was irked by an eclecticism that haughtily cherry-picked from the "East" without deeper understanding.

Although theosophists preached the "brotherhood of man" and religious universalism, he may also have known that they did not practice these ideals. Blavatsky had insisted she had superseded spiritualism by contacting not the ordinary dead but the *mahatmas*, the teachers of occult wisdom who lived in elevated planes. For many, they were composite images of Indian gurus and symbols of less hierarchical relationships. However, even in the astral domain, Blavatsky's mahatma, Koot Hoomi, complained about the quality of his writing paper and seemed suspiciously like the stereotype of a native clerk, the Bengali *babu* who fussed and fretted about nonessentials.[44] Moreover, by making herself the (admittedly feminist) vessel of the mahatmas' messages, she became the European mediator of a decontextualized Indian philosophy.

Vivekananda knew that Blavatsky was controversial. In 1884, her erstwhile disciples, the Coulombs, accused her of fraud, charging her with forging letters from her mahatmas and using secret doors to fake their supernatural comings and goings. Richard Hodgson of the London Society for Psychical Research traveled to Adyar to examine these accusations.[45] He sided with her friends, and his report in 1885 undermined her reputation in the West, even if theosophy remained popular in India.

Moreover, the duo set themselves up as spiritual masters exploiting Indian *chelas* (trainee adepts), who surrendered their inheritance and families to follow them.[46] Damodar Mavalankar, the son of a wealthy Maharashtra Brahmin family, gave up property, caste, and wife to follow Blavatsky. To restore her reputation after the fraud accusation, he journeyed to the Himalayas in 1885 to find the abode of the masters and prove her honesty. Sickly, frail, and coughing up blood, he went as far as the Tibetan border, where he took off his clothes and froze to death.[47] Despite the controversies and even this harrowing outcome, Blavatsky and Olcott continued to create what has been called a "great white brotherhood [with] little dark helpers," a hierarchy that would plague theosophy for decades.[48]

Vivekananda wanted nothing to do with them. In undated notes, he denounced "[t]his Indian grafting of American Spiritualism—with only a few Sanskrit words taking the place of spiritualistic jargon—Mahâtmâ missiles taking the place of ghostly raps and taps, and Mahatmic inspiration that of obsession with ghosts."[49] He wanted Indians to trust their own traditions, rather than think they had a "need of [the] dead ghosts of Russians and Americans."[50]

He was disgusted, too, by the presumptuous creation of Blavatsky's mahatmas, when he had his own "real" one in Ramakrishna. As will be seen, he ultimately internationalized Ramakrishna's reputation though his collaboration with Max Müller.[51] Hindu spirituality, Vivekananda insisted, had "no need nor desire to import religion from the West. Sufficient has been the degradation of importing almost everything else."[52] Theosophy was just another imperialist imposition, made worse by intellectual flimsiness and orientalism.

In 1895, he scolded his beloved Alasinga—the disciple who had begged funds for Vivekananda's voyage—for advertising a lecture on theosophy in the *Brahmavadin*, a Vedantin publication in Madras, as "people of sound mind" were repelled by such ideas.[53] He also wrote, though did not publish, a paper arguing that theosophy had rendered Indian thought risible by connecting it to "Charlatanry, and mango-growing fakirism."[54] He accused Alasinga of trying to "get more subscribers in England by advertising Annie Besant," the British feminist and politician who headed the movement after Blavatsky died in 1891.[55] He even threatened to stop associating with the *Brahmavadin* if Alasinga put a foot wrong again.

There was also a history of personal antipathy, which began when Vivekananda refused to join the Theosophical Society, resisting Olcott who had already invited Dharmapala and others to represent the organization in Chicago.[56] At that stage, he was irritated by Olcott's patronizing tone, but was not yet categorically opposed. As late as 1894, he had told Alasinga not to "quarrel" with theosophy, and even said that they were "our pioneers," deserving thanks for presenting Hinduism to the American public: "we must sympathize and . . . conquer all by your love!"[57] But he did not want Alasinga to reveal the letter's contents, because he had advised his followers to side with William Quan Judge, an American who broke away from Olcott and Besant in 1895, taking most of the American section with him. The same year, he even expressed his gratitude that the theosophists liked him and hoped he would be able to help them to Vedanta, "for they are all mumbling half realised truths."[58]

A few months later, however, Vivekananda was writing in outrage to Alasinga: "The Theosophical magazines [are] saying that they, the Theosophists, prepared the way to my success! Indeed! Pure Nonsense!"[59] Jung

Hyun Kim argues that this battle was waged to neutralize the theosophists' influence in Adyar, near Madras, where they had set up their international headquarters, and perhaps to distance them from the literati and intellectuals of Triplicane. By the new year, Vivekananda was stung by criticism in India in Christian and theosophical publications and begged Alasinga not to send any more.[60] In October 1895, his acolytes were horrified that Judge—as part of his effort to take over the American section—had also forged documents ostensibly sent to Blavatsky by the mahatmas. Each was as bad as the other and Vivekananda did not want to be tainted by "such ludicrous revelations."[61] By 1897, his rejection of theosophy was complete and personal: he acknowledged Besant as a friend of India but recalled that Olcott had refused to help him when he decided not to join their society.[62]

Thus, Vivekananda was never willing to be the "dark helper" to the "White brotherhood," and refused to moderate his criticism even when his patroness and friend Sara Bull asked him. In early 1897, he wrote: "Acceptance, love, toleration for everything sincere and honest—but never for hypocrisy."[63] By the time he was in California in 1899, theosophy was an object of fun: when a female theosophist who had come to his lectures phoned to ask for his help because she was having trouble with her "elementals"—spirits in different "planes"—Vivekananda refused: "we are just preparing dinner. You come over here. Bring the 'elementals' and we will fry them for dinner!"[64]

Theosophy is one of the most paradoxical movements of the fin de siècle. Esoteric and elitist (and never with a strong institutional base), it nonetheless gripped the imagination of a wide circle of both admirers and detractors. Dharmapala, for example, retained a long affiliation to it, despite his own heated quarrels with Olcott, and admitted to learning Buddhist texts through theosophical translations in English.[65] Gandhi read the Gita and Vivekananda's *Raja Yoga* with theosophists in London; and Nehru's English tutor, Ferdinand T. Brooks, was a theosophist, while Nehru himself was inducted into the Theosophical Society by no other than Annie Besant at the age of thirteen.[66] It is not clear whether Indians loved Annie Besant more for her advocacy of Home Rule or for esteeming Hindu philosophy. There is no doubt, however, that theosophy enabled some Western-educated Indians to take pride in their own traditions. Even if they only savored its dishes for a short time, theosophy nourished a small part of their spiritual and intellectual constitutions.

CHRISTIAN SCIENCE

Christian Science was a more challenging opponent than theosophy, despite, in Vivekananda's view, falling far short of the insights of Vedanta. Strangely, he considered it troublesome because he respected it more; its very name made explicit the connection between science and religion that he himself sought to forge. Almost all his close American associates had experimented with it before becoming his acolytes. He even admitted to his Chicago "sister," Mary Hale, herself keen on Christian Science, that he had "tried [it] for insomnia and really found it worked very well."[67]

In the United States, he noted that Christian Scientists "formed the most influential party, . . . figuring everywhere," and even called them "Vedantins." In late 1894, however, he qualified this remark by saying that he merely meant that "they had picked up a few doctrines of the Advaita and grafted them upon the Bible." At least, he concluded, "they all admire me highly."[68] The statement was not mere vanity, and his characterization of Christian Science was astute—Mary Baker Eddy, the founder of the movement, had a little familiarity with Vedantin ideas, although her deepest inspiration remained biblical. Like Vivekananda with his Hindu Universalism, she always sought to separate Christian Science from other mind-cure therapies, such as mesmerism and, hypnotism, even if her followers often resisted what they saw as her doctrinaire approach.[69]

Eddy's life exemplifies how an American woman of modest beginnings and unsystematic education could create a thriving religious movement. Christian Science helps map out the spiritual landscape Vivekananda encountered and the porous boundaries among Evangelical Protestantism, Christian Science, and "mind-cure" into which he inserted Vedanta.

* ❖ *

Disputes remain about exact dating, but certainly from the 1870s, American evangelists had reacted against the subversive currents of biblical criticism and liberal Protestantism. They opposed the "academicizing" of scripture and reaffirmed the gift of healing that often accompanied a rejection of Calvinism (broadly interpreted). They dismissed the idea that miracles had ended with Jesus and his apostles; and rejected the common view of the "doctrine of afflicted Providence" contained within Protestant martyrologies of Cotton Mather, Jonathan Edwards, and John Wesley, which held that suffering brought "glory to God." Nineteenth-century Evangelicals wondered instead whether virtuous resignation was nothing more than a "cowardly skepticism" that denied God's sovereignty.[70] Ideas of faith healing were central to celebrating God's benevolent, parental nature.

These trends were also part of a wider critique of orthodox (allopathic) medicine, which targeted especially opium and calomel—mercury chloride, a highly toxic white powder that was a powerful purgative and used to treat venereal disease. "Christian physiology" and new medical therapeutics often overlapped.[71] Others founded hydrotherapeutic institutes and health farms, the most famous being the Battle Creek Sanitarium, managed by the Seventh-Day Adventist John Harvey Kellogg, who believed in the imminent Second Coming of Christ.[72] With its hydrotherapy, nutritional regimens, and exercise, he pioneered a holistic approach to healing. Vivekananda's Chicago "siblings," the Hale sisters, went to the sanitarium for their health, and he also tried Battle Creek diets for his digestion.[73] The treatments were conducted sometimes with prayers so that the Great Physician might bestow his grace. The embrace of God's love may have separated illness and "sin," but Protestant moralism focused yet more fixedly on "bad habits." As will be seen, such attitudes were crucial later in separating Vivekananda from disciples who disapproved of his "transgressions"—his "overeating" and especially smoking, which many Christian Scientists deemed offenses against God.

Mary Baker Eddy came from Lynn and Swampscott, the very same places that Vivekananda would visit twenty years later. She also emphasized divine love over spiritual austerity, rejecting her father's belief in the Last Judgment and eternal damnation.[74] The first edition of *Science and Health* (1875)—a work that went into more than 406 editions, after which she stopped counting—appeared after he had tried to cure her digestion by instructing her to consume only bread, water, and vegetables, a regimen that some later historians suggest may have indicated an eating disorder.[75] She had also experienced years of grief and the loss of her son to relatives when she could not support him. Her invalidism, which lasted until she developed Christian Science, led her through the gamut of American therapies, which included homeopathy, orthodox medicine, and electrical treatments.

None of these worked, but her invalidism certainly fostered a rare experimentation.[76] In 1853, she married again, but divorced after discovering her husband's infidelity, becoming a patient of the magnetic healer Phineas Parkhurst

Quimby. A pioneer of the American mind-cure movement, he emphasized the healing power of positive emotions and beliefs, ideas important later to William James in defending a truly American, "practical" "religion of healthy-mindedness."[77] Quimby believed in magnetic fluids and even magnetized water treatments, but also argued that "beliefs and expectations" were central to illness or health.[78] He underscored the role of the patient's "mind" in conjunction with an external operator's authority, to promote healing.[79]

Between 1862 and 1865, Eddy's health improved, and the pair began to collaborate, but were distressed by their inability to assure lasting remissions. Eddy ultimately rejected both mesmerism and hypnosis on the grounds that the suggestibility of the subject was a form of deception (a view with which Vivekananda would concur). In 1866, a few weeks after Quimby's death, Eddy fell on ice in Swampscott and injured her spine, but maintained that after reading Matthew 9:2, the story of Jesus's cure of a man with palsy, she got up, dressed, and walked unaided across the room. The "miracle" led her to biblical exegesis, especially to Old Testament figures who had also experienced God's "science"; she used the word to denote "revelation, explanation, discovery, inspiration," or all of them at once.[80] Again, "science" clearly had many connotations.

She retrospectively created a linear vision of Christian Science's development that omitted her continued links to spiritualism.[81] But she was denounced for stealing Quimby's ideas as early as 1883, as he, too, had used the term "Christian Science" and been inspired by the gospel miracles.[82] She insisted on her originality and argued for a subtle distinction between "mind" and what she called "Mind," or the Divine Mind, which was the Deity's. For her, this was not mere semantics; the human mind, she said, was the source of the disease, riven by error and immorality, and convinced of the materiality of the world. In conventional Christian teaching, the Kingdom of God was in the future, but Eddy believed that this spiritualized realm existed now, even if confined mentalities veiled its presence. She believed that humanity's suffering, which seemed so overpowering, was nothing more than "waking dream-shadows," a description strikingly like the maya of Vedanta. The illusion of egos inhabiting separate bodies dissolved in a greater reality that was Spirit. Christian Science meant entering this "real" world. Whereas the orthodox clergy preached human finitude, mortality, and sinfulness, Eddy, in contrast, believed that Jesus's resurrection had taken away these limits like the stone that "rolled way from his tomb." To her, resurrection had nothing metaphorical about it—it was literal truth, the "Science" that under-pinned her belief.

After the publication of *Science and Health* in 1875, she set about organizing a church and married one of her first converts. Thereafter, she mobilized fol-lowers, established publications, preached, and healed. In 1881, she founded and taught at the Massachusetts Metaphysical College in Boston, where she developed a vision of God as "Father-Mother." This parental conception of the Almighty was known among Evangelical Protestant ministers but dif-fered in stressing God's feminine aspects.[83] In this regard, Mary Baker Eddy joined liberal theologians who also began to think of God as Mother, ideas that may have made Vivekananda's vision of the Divine Mother less foreign to his new audience.[84]

Indeed, she may have come across some notion of Hindu ideas through American transcendentalism. Ralph Waldo Emerson is credited with this infusion of Eastern thought, but as early as the 1720s, Cotton Mather had cor-responded with Danish missionaries in Madras, while Benjamin Franklin had investigated Confucianism.[85] Emerson had inherited these interests and later read the Bhagavad Gita and an essay by Colebrooke on the Vedas.[86] In 1841, Emerson wrote "The Over-soul," in which he expressed the nonbiblical view that all souls—and hence all humanity—were united.[87] After reading more Indian works, he came to believe that the "material universe is an ema-nation of divine power" and that human beings needed to unite with this "Over-soul." He also contended that the material world was an illusion, which hides the "Oneness" that so shaped Eddy's spirituality. He addition-ally endorsed ideas of the transmigration of souls, the notion that that they found new bodies to inhabit over time.[88]

Emerson's wide impact reveals the often unattributed reverberations of orientalism on middle-class Americans.[89] Philip Goldberg has suggested that in Emerson's later writings, it is nearly impossible to separate out "Indian mo-nism" from "Western idealism, the Hindu atman [soul]" from the Western "self," "oriental mysticism" from "Neo-Platonism."[90] Vivekananda knew that his audiences translated Indian spirituality into more familiar terms and he did the same thing, but in reverse, as when he cast Christian Scientists as "Vedantins." But he camouflaged the similarity when he "essentialized" Eastern wisdom to set it off as superior. This bifurcated characterization dis-guised the global connections, while reifying the oppositions.

If Mary Baker Eddy absorbed some of this ambient transcendentalism, she was also connected to Hinduism through Amos Bronson Alcott, who advocated a new "Bible of Mankind" that included Eastern texts.[91] Such religious universalism was common in this milieu, and between 1886 and 1891, *Science and Health* even included a quotation from the Bhagavad Gita.[92] This insertion may have been the work of James Henry Wiggin, a Unitarian minister turned agnostic who edited Eddy's sometimes disjointed prose. Eddy excised the references in 1891 when the two fell out, and Wiggin later scoffed that "there is nothing really to understand in 'Science and Health'; except that *God is all* and yet there is no God in matter!"[93] Such formulations, however facile they may have seemed to him, made Vivekananda's efforts to explain something of Vedanta much easier.

Eddy later condemned currents of religious universalism that emerged in the wake of the Parliament. She had alienated potential allies by rejecting their version of "science"—spiritualism, hypnotism, "mind-cure," homeopathy, and hygiene—because Christ had not had recourse to them. She now rejected Eastern religions and insisted that Christian Science rested on the Gospels alone. When asked whether Christian Science was like Buddhism, she replied, "Christian Science destroys such a tendency," and maintained that her beliefs did not "tend toward Buddhism or any other 'ism.'"[94] Hinduism was equally dismissed as "heathenish," despite any truths that the Gita might contain. She thus retained a belief in Christianity's superiority and contended—despite all evidence to the contrary—that the Bible had been her only true inspiration.

◆ ◆ ◆

Vivekananda had recognized the attraction of Christian Science a year after his arrival in the States when he noted that Eddy's followers were "spreading by leaps and bounds and causing heart-burn to the orthodox."[95] Ministers lamented how committed parishioners—many of them women—had deserted their pews, enlivened by doctrines focused on love and healing rather than predestination and resignation. If Eddy repudiated any association with Vedanta, Vivekananda returned the favor by privately ridiculing Christian Science—though it is not clear how much he knew about her views. In writing to his guru-brothers, he compared it to the Kartabhaja sect, a stream of esoteric Bengali Vaishnavism that called God "Karta": this sect was led by lower-caste headmen who, he charged, exploited the poor with "miracle-making" during annual fairs.[96] Echoing Ramakrishna's earlier pronouncements about bargaining with God, Vivekananda now applied similar arguments to forms of Protestantism. He suggested that Christian Science was a "shopkeeper's religion," and that it placed prayer and physical healing in too close a relation—hence the comparison. Certainly, much of Christian Science's success *did* rest on "miracle working," though certainly not on monetary exchange. Despite Eddy's growing emphasis on prayer and contemplation, she was also a healer and her early ministry rested on the seemingly innumerable testimonies of cure.[97]

In more temperate moments, Vivekananda compared Christian Science not to the Kartabhajas, but to "the Brahmo Samaj which spread in Calcutta for a certain time and then died out." He concluded, "It has done its work—viz social reform. Its religion was not worth a cent, and so it must die out."[98] He believed that Eddy had debased Christ and Christianity by promoting miracles, and when he thought of "miracle making," he thought of what was dangerous in the "occult" in both the East and West: "The great strength of Christ is not in His miracles or His healing. . . . Fools can heal others, devils can heal others. I have seen horrible demoniacal men do wonderful miracles. . . . I have known fools and diabolical men tell the past, present, and future. I have seen fools heal at a glance, by the will, the most horrible diseases."[99]

But he retained a certain respect for Christian Science: "The whole struggle of life is not to obey. That is why I sympathise with Christian Scientists, for they teach the liberty of man and the divinity of the soul."[100] And yet, the gulf between Vivekananda and Mary Baker Eddy was immense. She was steadfastly Christian, often dogmatic, a fabulously successful church-builder, who believed her *Science and Health* was almost like a second Bible, and hence a gateway to real scripture. The volume was revised repeatedly, but the new editions (the final one in 1910) aimed to create a final, new incontrovertible text after decades of changes and augmentations. Nothing could be further than Vivekananda's view of the Vedas. His teaching was flexible, hence his insistence that he had not come to America to convert, as the missionaries forced Indians to become Christians. As will be seen, he briefly flirted with creating new rites for a Western "church," but rejected the idea.[101]

EVOLUTION

No late-nineteenth-century thinker, either in India or in the West, could be taken seriously by a thoughtful audience without tackling evolution, and

Vivekananda was an ardent participant in this worldwide discussion. Vivekananda knew that evolution fed into Western debates over bodily morality, political theory, and cosmology, concerns that also preoccupied India's educated elites, many who believed that engaging in Western science would ultimately prove their intellectual parity with Europeans and also encourage national self-reliance.[102] However, subscribing to evolution was not the same as endorsing natural selection, as Darwin's theory was only one among many evolutionary ideas.

Darwin had argued that within any given population of species, those better adapted to the environment would survive—that even smaller traits that favored the production of progeny might promote "natural selection." Two aspects of Darwin's theory especially discomfited orthodox Christians. Its randomness belied the biblical narrative of creation and, more worrying still, it presented destruction as integral to "progress," with maladapted species doomed to extinction. When applied in the imperial domain (let alone among warring European nations), Darwinism suggested that the "unfit" were bound to disappear or be dominated by the "more fit."[103]

Even within the Western scientific community, many biologists rejected the randomness of Darwin's theory, and wondered how such remarkable organs—for example, the human eye—could manifest without directional change. They argued instead for progressive evolution, or "progressionism" (called orthogenesis), a topic of intense debate among scientists.[104] How much Vivekananda knew of such specialist discussions is unclear, but he used the metaphor of crystal formation when he suggested that there was an immanence to chemical constructions that only God understood, an argument that some scientists also deployed.[105]

Men like Vivekananda thought of themselves as evolutionists and turned to philologists in Britain, France, and Germany who maintained that evolution had been presaged by the work of "Vedic and Puranic scholars."[106] Some, like him, argued that karma and reincarnation provided a pathway toward understanding a directional evolution, that "Christ-man," "Buddha-man," and the "Free" of the yogis had been "perfect men" who had "gone beyond the laws of nature" through repeated births and deaths, successive incarnations already evident in the "cell of the [lowest] protoplasm."[107] Vivekananda also rejected the idea that something could be made from nothing. He said, "Hindu . . . ideas of the origin of the world are governed by the doctrine of *sat-karya-vada* [the doctrine of existent effect], with creation only possible from something else."[108] Rather than an ex nihilo creation, Hindus believed in periodic cycles (*yugas*), with several creation stories appearing in various Sanskrit texts.

Mostly, however, he contrasted the evolution that occurred in nature with that of the imperishable soul and its inevitable "manifestation" when properly cultivated.[109] Once, while visiting the Zoological Garden in Alipur, Vivekananda acknowledged somewhat reluctantly that Darwin might account for gradual change among animals but could not "yet admit that it is the final conclusion about the causes of evolution."[110] He insisted instead that "the moment the obstacles to the evolution and manifestation of nature are completely removed, the Soul manifests Itself perfectly.... [A] greater manifestation of the Soul takes place through education and culture, through concentration and meditation, and above all through sacrifice."[111]

As for many English-educated Bengalis, including scientists, this kind of evolutionary thinking kept intact the theological and ethical cosmos.[112] Vivekananda condemned the "horrible idea of competition," which, he believed, was "neither the cause nor the effect, simply a thing on the way, not necessary to evolution at all."[113] He thus rejected the biological arguments coming to underpin imperialism and believed that British dominion had put stumbling blocks in the way of Indians. For these reasons, he used evolutionary arguments to sustain both his anticolonialism and his national project for India.[114]

He also saw that evolution, if improperly applied, could promote a logic of annihilation. For example, he condemned Americans "who say that all criminals ought to be exterminated and that that is the only way in which criminality can be eliminated from society."[115] Here, he took a swipe at the New World legatees of Cesare Lombroso and his notion of the "born criminal," adding in another context that "the attempt to remove evil from the world by killing a thousand evil-doers, only adds to the evil in the world."[116] Vivekananda thus resisted any "predictive" form of life science that claimed to know when people would transgress, and realized that criminality and resistance to British rule in India might be confused; we do not know whether he knew that fingerprinting—first developed in 1858 and born out of the attempt to identify criminals through physical traits—was piloted in his native Bengal.[117]

Struggle, Vivekananda believed, was a human creation, not inherent in natural law. When a fire strikes a theater, he explained, "only a few escape" in the crush. But, "[i]f all had gone out slowly, not one would have been hurt. That is the case in life. The doors are open for us, and we can all get out without the competition and struggle; and yet we struggle. The struggle we create through our own ignorance, through impatience; we are in too great a hurry."[118]

Like Gandhi after him, Vivekananda saw impatience as an aggression that impeded rather than enabled a "higher manifestation."[119] Such pronouncements were heartfelt, as he himself was prone to irascibility, restlessness, and impetuosity. To understand evolution, he turned to Patanjali, the Hindu sage who authored the Yoga sutras: "The change of one species into another is attained by the infilling of nature. The basic idea is that we are changing from one species to another, and that man is the highest species." Patanjali explains this "infilling of nature" by the simile of peasants irrigating fields.[120]

This simple metaphor meant "taking away the obstacles" and allowing "divinity [to] manifest itself." Once again, he saw this "manifestation" as internally driven, only shaped by environment insofar as it enabled what was already there to emerge. For him, "each soul [was] the sum total of the universal experiences already coiled up there."[121] And it confirmed his vision of the causality implicit in karma, in which individuals inherited (acquired) characteristics to allow spiritual evolution through rebirth.[122] He accepted continuity between the animal and the human planes to show his full-throated support for evolution, in contrast to Christians who were appalled by the idea that "man should come up from an animal." But because of karma and reincarnation, Vivekananda maintained that "if we have a soul, so have they, and if they have none, neither have we."[123]

But these remarks obscured other aspects of orthodox thinking, in which successive origins of the world somehow contained the same animals and "the same four classes of mankind, [castes] and so on."[124] Thus, Vivekananda could envisage the immensity of geological time by comparing it to successive epochs (yugas), even though dinosaur extinction and other paleontological finds weakened notions of the fixity of species. Vivekananda ignored these considerations, in the same way that many Western evolutionists also disregarded what their spiritual beliefs opposed.[125]

Vivekananda believed that even if "competitions and struggles and evils. . . . did not exist, still man would go on and evolve as God, because it is the very nature of that God to come out and manifest Himself." When he spoke of the "infilling of nature," he talked not about creation or adaptation, but rather about removing barriers toward God's manifestation in humanity.[126] He also stepped away from the cyclical Hindu view in which animals may become gods; and gods, animals. Instead, he envisaged more purpose and progress: "To my mind this seems very hopeful, instead of the horrible idea of competition."[127]

As he had done at the Parliament, he understated the downward possibility. His keen-eyed guru-brothers noticed this unorthodox view and deleted it later from his corpus.[128] Instead, he focused on the God-within, imprisoned but keen to break out: "So in man there is the potential god, kept in by the locks and bars of ignorance. When knowledge breaks these bars, the god becomes manifest." Here again, he suggested that the atman required only proper "irrigation" for the seed of divinity to emerge. He often spoke of "involution," which today implies a shrinkage, a kind of curling in on itself (such as the shrinkage of an organ).[129] In his evolutionary thought, however, it denoted what was present in its incipient, germinal form: "The whole of the tree is present in the seed, its cause. The whole of the human being is present in that one protoplasm."[130] Once again, karmic reasoning was key in this analysis.

He seems to have been influenced by Ernst Haeckel, and the German's zoologist's argument that "ontogeny" recapitulated "phylogeny," insisting that the various stages of in utero development of the infant "recapitulated" the successive stages of remote evolutionary ancestors.[131] Haeckel's controversial embryo drawings depicted stages that run from fish and salamanders through hogs, calves, rabbits, and the human baby.

Now discarded, these ideas were powerful, the equivalence between human development and evolution seeming to encapsulate a fundamental unity. For Vivekananda in 1895, such thinking provided yet another bridge between science and Vedanta: "On the physical side, the embryo goes from the amoeba to man in the womb. These are the teachings of modern science. Vedanta goes further and tells us that we not only have to live the life of all past humanity, but also the future life of all humanity."[132]

* * *

The late nineteenth-century saw how new spiritual movements either endorsed occult power (as did the theosophists) or denied its value (such as

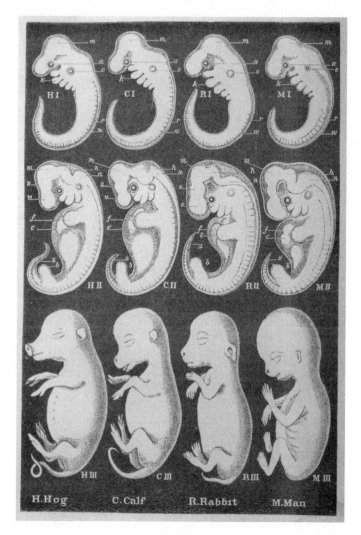

7.1. Haeckel's development of the embryo

Vivekananda and the Christian Scientists). Vivekananda was unsurprisingly insulted when he was compared to a magician or miracle worker, and instead sought to prove that Indian spirituality had a natural affinity to modern science. He believed that occult power existed but tended to discuss seriously such phenomena only in India, where they would not be used to beat both him and his homeland as somehow credulous and degenerate.

Vivekananda questioned many of the verities of orientalism, Christian theology, and even science, and insisted that his intervention was a crucial spiritual *and* political restatement of the value of Indian thought. He found himself in what he saw as a provincial world among people who believed, wrongly in his view, that they alone possessed civilized knowledge and that their society heralded "modernity" in all its facets. He quickly recognized the spiritual crisis among Americans who came to hear him, especially those disturbed by the inroads made by biblical criticism and fears associated with scientific reductionism. He positioned himself, therefore, both as the representative of an enlightened ancient culture and as the future of a universal spiritual tendency. For those willing to listen, "modernity" took on a more complex and relative meaning.

In the summer following the Parliament, he went with some of New England's most avant-garde intellectuals, religious figures, spiritual luminaries, eccentrics, and vacationers to participate in the universalist and humanitarian dreams of Sarah Farmer and Sara Bull at Green Acre, Maine. His American odyssey now plunged him into a world of spiritual and therapeutic adventure. He was interested in their pastimes and healing journeys, offered his first lessons in yoga, and enjoyed himself. It was through such interactions—where emotions, practices and ideas met—that he felt his way toward an understanding of how to make a "Vedanta in the West."

8

GREEN ACRE, WILLIAM JAMES,
AND RAJA YOGA

At bottom the whole concern of both morality and religion is with the manner of our acceptance of the universe. Do we accept it only in part and grudgingly, or heartily and altogether?

—William James, *The Varieties of Religious Experience* (1902)

When Meditation is mastered, the mind is unwavering like the flame of a lamp in a windless place.

—Bhagavad Gita, 6:30

*　◆　*

IN THE SUMMER OF 1894, Vivekananda visited Green Acre, Maine. A photograph recording the occasion shows him with his turban in the middle of a group of respectable Americans who had gathered in search of spiritual enlightenment. He was center stage and impossible to miss. At this summer retreat, he came across a broad cross-section of people concerned with New Thought, a term that emerged toward the end of the century to encompass the amorphous beliefs and religious groupings that focused on mind-cure and positive thinking. Many were also interested in comparative religion and especially Eastern philosophy, concerns that enabled Vivekananda to insert his emerging vision of yoga into the American scene. He taught Sanskrit chanting and meditation under what became known as "Swami's Pine" and lived in the

8.1. Vivekananda at Green Acre, 1894

tent city where men and women cohabited in ways he had not before imagined possible.[1] The link with nature revived him, and he again took up his sannyasin habits, sleeping on the ground and meditating under a "tree in the forest."[2]

His experience at Green Acre helped Vivekananda translate Indian metaphysical concepts into the language of science and also recast Western notions of the occult. Through these overlapping realms, he shifted the nature of yoga, spurred on by his devotees' desire to achieve harmony and healing by concentrating on meditation's spiritual dimensions, while also moderating their search for cures and miracles. In the process, he redesigned the ancient lessons of Patanjali on the theory and practice of yoga so that the magical power of the yogis was underplayed in the text. Rethinking and remaking Vedantic ideas had begun in India, but now he went further still by observing and imbibing the beliefs of the Green Acre–ites so that he might reach them.

Green Acre brought together many uniquely American and international trends into one arena. Enterprising women invited non-Westerners and enabled Vivekananda to witness a microcosm of "alternative" American spiritual culture. He took full advantage of the opportunity and later built on this experience in Britain when he visited Max Müller, already a hero to many Indians for creating a new orientalist canon from which his American acolytes took inspiration. The concerns of the Green Acre–ites with religious experience, healing, and comparative religion were part of an equally important dialogue with Harvard intellectuals. Vivekananda was integral to these transnational collaborations, which meant that Vedanta became part of Western debates over philosophical pragmatism and idealism.

＊　＊　＊

The brainchild of Sarah Farmer, and created with the help of Sara Bull, Green Acre showed Vivekananda what American women could accomplish. He regarded Farmer as special, and Bull became his Dhira Mata, or "Mother of Steady Wisdom," a financial supporter and adviser. Although he went only once, preferring instead to encamp in Thousand Island the following summer, Green Acre was crucial for what he learned and for what he taught. Bull chose to follow Vivekananda, but after 1900, Farmer picked the head of Baha'i whom she would meet in Palestine, but their mutual passion for "Eastern wisdom" suggests the ability of "oriental" teachers to attract notable followers.[3] These relationships with Asian teachers enabled them to separate conclusively from what they rejected in their childhood Christianity and to cement their commitment to "religious universalism."[4] Green Acre became a focal point for this form of globalism, which embraced not only Eastern spiritualities, but also healing therapies.

The World Parliament and its afterlife made Green Acre possible. Farmer had already been dreaming of an annual event when she went to Chicago to help her father, Moses Gerrish Farmer, exhibit his inventions—especially the incandescent lightbulb and an electric trolley—that he had never commercialized.[5] The father and daughter duo epitomized the tension between the Columbian Exposition and the Parliament: the practical (and potentially commercial) and the spiritual were linked in ways that remained unresolved. Indeed, Moses Farmer's reluctance to profit from his inventions was transmitted to his daughter, who also could not reconcile spirituality and money. In any event, the triumph they envisaged did not come about; Moses was already seriously ill when he arrived in Chicago and died before the fair even opened.

8.2. Sarah Farmer and followers

For Sarah Farmer, this loss was catastrophic, not least because she had hoped that her father's inventions would finance her envisaged educational project. Grief-stricken, she was whisked away by friends and only returned to Chicago in October, when the Parliament had finished, where she met some of the representatives of Eastern religions, who later came to Green Acre. She also met Sara Bull, the daughter of wealthy suffragist Susan Amelia Thorp, whom Farmer asked for funds, as well as for her blessing, to support the new undertaking.[6]

Farmer's vision was partially fashioned by her early Unitarianism, a denomination that repeatedly crops up in this story. Ram Mohun Roy had had contacts with Unitarians in Britain, and they seem to have spread his thoughts to their American counterparts.[7] When Vivekananda toured America after the Parliament, he spoke in Unitarian churches, and encountered its diluted presence in transcendentalism and certainly at Green Acre. Although tracing its origins to Central Europe, Unitarianism was especially important in New England, where it influenced Christian congregations as well as aspects of Harvard theology. Its example shows how, especially in New England, "orthodox" or "establishment" institutions were fertilized by more widespread religious developments. Unitarians were distinctive in denying the Trinity, while seeing Christ's moral teachings as essential for an exemplary life. Unlike many Christians, they rejected original sin as well as predestination and hellfire, views that discomfited many of Vivekananda's acolytes. Nor did they believe that non-Christians were doomed for possessing different beliefs.

Like other Unitarians, Farmer did not believe in inherent human depravity; hence Green Acre focused on Christian virtue, and an emphasis on increasing goodness in the world. Unitarianism emphasized "self-culture" and the capacity to exercise conscience over scripture. "Culture" in this sense also implied the sowing of a seed which would germinate if not thwarted by spiritual dearth. This idea, however, was in tension with an equally strong focus on husbandry and ideas of spiritual perfection almost ubiquitous in American Protestantism. Farmer wanted to "sweeten the soul," to enhance self-realizing tendencies with many utopian educational and communal projects, for which New England was famous.[8] Transcendentalism had sprung from Unitarianism, and Vivekananda sought to pour notions of Advaitic unity into this self-divinizing vessel.[9] His view of "involution" as a seed ready to burst forth into a tree was readily transposed onto a discussion of the soul, which also needed proper tending to manifest itself. Vivekananda may have refined his ideas of involution at Green Acre, where Sara Farmer's ethos was widely shared.

In a later pamphlet, Farmer described aspirations which ranged from scientific farming and self-sufficiency to investigating the "purest ideals" of global religions.[10] She not only invited Vivekananda and Dharmapala, but also Booker T. Washington and W. E. B. Du Bois, thus providing a platform for both Eastern gurus and Black intellectuals. She may have sensed some relationship between imperialism and slavery or perceived herself as following in the abolitionism of her mother, Hannah Shipleigh, although the loss of Farmer's papers in a fire means that we will never know for sure. From the outset, Green Acre also continued the Parliament's work through the Monsalvat School for the Study of Comparative Religion, managed by Lewis G. Janes, the head of the Brooklyn Ethical Association and another of Vivekananda's allies.[11] The school taught the tenets of all religions and questioned Christian dogmatism.

For the people at Green Acre who championed this approach, comparative religion was about education and understanding, not about conversion.

Farmer refused to charge fees and personally underwrote the expenses of the speakers and their families; consequently, she was drained both emotionally and financially when the yearly events came to an end. Her idealism later exasperated Janes, who thought that she should adopt a modicum of professionalism.[12] There was also a simmering conflict between the school's focus on comparative religion and Farmer's interest in mysticism and spiritual healing.[13] The heady optimism of the Parliament masked differences that emerged more clearly in later years.

SARA BULL

Sara Chapman Bull was much richer and even better connected than Sarah Farmer; she also had a summer residence in Green Acre, where she seems to have moderated Farmer's enthusiasms. She was a midwestern heiress, and the widow of the (much older) Norwegian Ole Bull (1810–1880), one of the most famous violinists of the nineteenth century. They married in 1870 when she was twenty, and she managed his business affairs and accompanied him on the piano. He later bought an island in Norway named Lysøen and constructed a fantasy villa where he gave private concerts.[14]

Throughout the Bulls' lives, politics, culture, and religion intermingled. When she wanted to memorialize her husband as a founding figure of Norwegian culture, she and Margaret Noble connected India's subjugation under the British to that of "small nations" like Norway; she was also delighted when Norway broke from Sweden in 1905.[15] Such "anticolonial" thinking was integral to this unlikely milieu. By joining forces with her, Vivekananda, moreover, expanded the network he had begun with Sanborn. Bull's brother, for example, married the youngest daughter of Henry Wadsworth Longfellow, an alliance that moved the family into the prestigious center of an interconnected Yankee world.[16] At Green Acre, she oversaw the concerts and brought great sopranos, such as Emma Calvé, into Vivekananda's orbit; Calvé later claimed that his spiritual instruction saved her from depression.[17] Another musician, the singer Emma Thursby, was Bull's close friend, involved with the Columbian Exposition, active at Green Acre, and a keen promoter of Vivekananda's lectures.

8.3. Sara Chapman Bull

8.4. Lysøen

Bull's correspondence reveals the extent of her acquaintance, and something of her spiritual trajectory. Like Vivekananda's other close associates, she was disillusioned with her Christian upbringing, and attracted to spiritualism after Ole's death in 1880. She probably knew of Olcott's book *People from the Other World* (1875), which chronicled the Eddy brothers' séances and contained illustrations of the "turbaned men in loincloths smoking water-pipes," stereotypes that Vivekananda battled.[18] She had probably also read, or knew of, Irving Babbitt's lyrical translations of the *Dhammapada*, a widely read collection of the Buddha's aphorisms as love-filled as any of the gospels: "For hatred does not cease by hatred here below; hatred ceases by love; this is an eternal law."[19] Buddhism penetrated America through such translations and especially through Edwin Arnold's *The Light of Asia*.[20]

Her course hints at the possibilities in this "alternative" West and suggests why Vivekananda inspired her. Like Farmer, Mary Baker Eddy, and many others, Sara Bull also experimented with spiritualism when, after the horrendous losses of the Civil War, many Americans were attracted by the possibility of contacting dead sons. When her husband died, she turned to spiritualism to communicate with him, and was gratified when the poetess and author Celia Thaxter said she had made contact.[21] Bull spent much of 1883–1884 traveling, combining séances with music, and attending meetings on women's rights and education; she even became part of a circle of psychics under the leadership of Minot Judson Savage, a Unitarian minister and medium, dedicated to human potential and world peace.[22]

Bull's and Farmer's turn to spiritualism emerged as much from bereavement as the earlier wave in the 1840s and 1850s, and should not be seen as a retreat from the public sphere into "narrow" self-realization.[23] In the spirit world, babies grew up and matured, and grieving mothers could contact infants who had become adults; spiritualism was also linked to abolitionism and women's rights.[24] When Sara Bull experimented with it, currents of racial "uplift" and feminism remained important, even if the politics focused more on an inchoate agenda of religious universalism, world peace, and often anti-imperialism. It was also linked to new forms of healing experience exemplified by Christian Science.

For Sara Bull, the international dimension existed even before the Parliament. Celia Thaxter had introduced her to Mohini Mohan Chatterji, a Calcutta lawyer and scholar who, like Vivekananda, had come under the sway of the Brahmo Samaj and became part of the Bengal Theosophical Society in 1882. Sent by Blavatsky as one of her chelas (disciples), Mohini traveled to London and Ireland. For Bull, his published lectures on the Bhagavad Gita (which also entranced William Butler Yeats) were a revelation.[25] As with many Westerners, the Gita unlocked India's spiritual treasures while acting as a new kind of "gospel" for those moving away from Protestantism.[26] Mohini's edition linked Indian thought to Christianity through commentaries, notes, and citations, his erudition creating a comparative manual to underpin universal religion: "God is infinite in attributes and yet devoid of attributes [Job 11:7, Rom. 11:33, 34]. This is the God the Bhagavad Gita proclaims; the God whom the Scriptures of all nations proclaim;—the God who is the true and only Self in all creatures. [John 1:1–9]."[27]

The instruction transformed Sara Bull, who reengaged with Christianity and acquired an unaccustomed spiritual serenity. She advised a friend struggling with grief to "study the life and teachings of Christ without reserve—it has been the great joy of my life the past year and I owe this to Mr. Mohini. The study of other systems has brought me to my own.'[28] Her contact with Mohini suggests that, even before Vivekananda, Indian teachers gave lessons in Vedanta in "advanced" circles without trying to convert. Moreover, she put forward a view that studying other religious traditions confirmed rather than undermined faith by revealing the "same" God everywhere. Important Western thinkers, from Romain Rolland through Thomas Merton, would claim that Indian thought ultimately re-enhanced their Christian understanding.[29] In this sense, therefore, India was already becoming a "guru to the world."

The encounter with Mohini seems to have led Bull to discard spiritualism. In 1887, she corresponded with Richard Hodgson from the American Society for Psychical Research, who had been informed that at the "time of [her] hus-band's funeral" she had heard music—a psychic event that Hodgson sought to investigate.[30] But she refused to illuminate him and told him instead how she now believed such experiences were harmful. She had moved on to mind-cure, and advised friends to gain mental discipline so that the "law of heredity may be overcome, and tendencies of mind or body regulated."[31] Spiritualism, an early acquaintance with Vedanta, and mind-cure help explain her passion for Green Acre and "prepared" her for Vivekananda.

GREEN ACRE AND NEW THOUGHT

Farmer envisaged Green Acre as a temporary summer tent city not far from a permanent lodging (Green Acre Inn, which she built) with her own home, Bittersweet, as part of the settlement. In many ways it was like a Chautauqua, the popular adult education communities of the 1880s, in emphasizing moral improvement and reformism, but was more expansive in focusing on spiritual exchange and world peace.[32]

Charles Bonney sent a message of congratulations for the opening celebrations, thus linking the Parliament to the new undertaking. He concentrated on the "Golden Rule," and the "earnest desire to know the Truth," and made no mention of any one religion. However, he introduced a discordant note when he referred to "the fierce conflict between Capital and Labour" and the dangers of leaving "Government" to still "political strife," words that suggest he saw spirituality as a countercurrent to class conflict.[33] It was a rare admission; at the Parliament, it had only been the Asian delegates who had insisted that spirituality and politics were intertwined. Addressed to this elite (if not necessarily wealthy) group of genteel spiritual seekers, such remarks vaguely acknowledged contemporary social tensions.

Bull also spoke at this ceremony on July 3, 1894, and stressed the universal "message that had been brought to the world by prophet after prophet," a foretaste, perhaps, of Farmer's later engagement with Baha'i.[34] An enormous white banner with the word "Peace" inscribed on it was raised above the American flag to show that universalism was more important than particularism, or even patriotism.[35] The ambience was infused by an unusual openness. Green Acre was also gently eccentric. People remembered going berry-picking in lush, wild lanes; taking dew-drop walks in the early morning, an invigorating course suggested by the hydrotherapist Sebastian Kneipp; and attending Dharmapala's candlelit processions, made more mysteriously spiritual by his sonorous chants.[36]

People, as much as the ideas and practices, were essential to Green Acre's unique atmosphere and the place of women in it. While Vivekananda astounded with his scarlet robe and orange turban, Sarah Farmer often wore gray with a hint of lavender, very like a Quaker, and finished off the ensemble with a touch of white lace around her throat. An intensified air of discretion, modesty, and vivid femininity were all illuminated by an "inner light."[37] She also did powerful mothering, even if in surrogacy, and as a virgin. She had turned down offers of marriage several times and remained celibate; and may have adopted two boys only to give them up to a cousin when Green Acre became too demanding. This ideal of "spiritual mothering," often divorced from "real" mothering, was central to this milieu; it was also a role taken up by many of Vivekananda's most intimate collaborators.[38]

Farmer was called "Motherheart" and revered as a living, breathing example of the "divine feminine."[39] As one admirer explained: "On the mirror of my soul was reflected, Greenacre [sic], Miss Farmer, the last of her race. The sun with its glory no longer was on me. The flowers with their perfume were carried from sight, and the walls of the room were falling before me, replaced by Miss Farmer transfigured with light. On a knoll by the river she was standing alone, with the white flag of Peace, and garments all sheer. With Love, Faith, was beckoning e'er beckoning on."[40]

Such testimony suggests the value placed on a woman with unusual personal qualities. Orientalism, comparative religion, popular science, and social uplift were all factors in the story, but none was as important as the often-quirky search for connection and "rapport," in which religion, science, and healing all mixed. Sarah Farmer seemed to understand this yearning, and in her personal attentions and calls for harmony, she embodied it like no one else.

*   *   *

Classes took place in tents, but also in the forest, and hence in nature. Along with the "Swami's Pine" where yoga was taught, there was also the Emerson tree, later the "Persian Pine," and the "Bodhi Tree," where Hinduism, transcendentalism, Baha'i, and Buddhism could all be had.[41] Reverence for nature linked their studies to the transcendental legacy. Vivekananda's old friend Frank Sanborn, Kate's cousin, had perceptively characterized American transcendentalism as a "certain inward tendency of high Calvinism and its counterpart Quakerism" and saw it as indigenous to America rather than derivative of English romanticism.[42] Sanborn knew Thoreau inside and out, and was apparently present when the hermit "enshrined" the "forty-four books dealing with India and its scriptures back in 1855" in his bookcase.[43] For Sanborn, Vivekananda *was* "India" as much as a link to Thoreau, who in *Walden* had described bathing his "intellect in the stupendous and cosmogonal philosophy of the Bhagvat-Geeta [sic]."[44] He compared the hermit of Walden with one who sits "on the Ganges reading the Vedas, or dwell[s] at the root of a tree with his crust and water jug."[45] Now, Vivekananda was with them, sitting under his own tree, seemingly offering them the same wisdom lessons.

In addition to transcendentalism, Green Acre was shaped by Swedenborgianism, as Bonney's message suggests. Sara Bull had joined the psychic circle with Minot Savage, who had also imbibed Swedenborgian ideas, while many at Green Acre knew of Andrew Jackson Davis, the "Poughkeepsie Seer," and his interest in Swedenborg's "illuminations."[46] Jackson stressed different orders of creation—vegetable, animal, human, and spiritual: "the essential person is actually still alive. . . . we are not people because of our bodies but because of our spirits. . . . We can see, then that when we die we simply move from one world to another."[47] He continued, "The deepest communication between our body and our spirit is with our breathing and heartbeat: thought connects with our breathing and affection, and attribution of love, with our heart."[48]

Such explicit reference to the "breath" and the "deepest communication between our body and our spirit" would be key to Vivekananda's exposition of *prana* (literally "vital principle," but often translated as "breath"), which was central to Raja yoga, and yoga generally. As early as February 1894, only five months after the Parliament, the *Detroit Free Press* had associated the swami with the Lutheran mystic.[49] The newspaper described the heaving crowd in the city's Unitarian Church when the "Hindu philosopher and priest" concluded his lectures on the "Divinity of Man": "Swedenborg seemed like a European successor of an early Hindoo priest, clothing in modern garb an ancient conviction . . . [that] every individual has in himself perfection."[50]

Swedenborgian preoccupations often pervaded the therapies Vivekananda encountered at Green Acre, in concentrating on the relationship between microcosm (individual) and macrocosm (nature); these ideas were also integral to transcendentalism, theosophy, and later Advaitic currents that were often difficult to disentangle. Horatio W. Dresser, to name only one who crossed Vivekananda's path, belonged to the Metaphysical Club in Boston, and was a Swedenborgian minister of a New England church. He argued that "there is an influx of spiritual life into the human soul, and that our spiritual life is conditioned by our response to this inflowing of power from heavenly sources."[51] Dresser believed that the "Divine inflow" prepared the aspirant for the spiritual and physical healing necessary to create a larger "harmony."[52]

Ralph Waldo Trine, so named to emphasize the link with Emerson, and well known within New Thought circles, was also within Farmer's orbit. Trine invited Vivekananda to the Procopeia Club in Boston at the very beginning of 1896, now superintended by Sara Bull, Sarah Farmer, Kate Tannatt Woods (the novelist he had met when he first came to Massachusetts), Trine, and the art historian Ernest Fenollosa, all of whom Vivekananda now knew.[53] The following year, Trine published his most famous work, *In Tune with the Infinite,* a favorite of Queen Victoria and a volume that Henry Ford credited as vital to his success. The "self-trust" and "self-knowledge" Trine advocated were key to American entrepreneurial culture, with Trine's work incorporating Swedenborgianism and the wider current of positive thinking. Trine argued that a "golden thread runs through every religion in the world," a "divine flow," both Swedenborgian ideas that also combined with notions of the Over-soul and Advaita.[54] In this volume, he wrote, *"the central fact in human life, in your life and mine, is the coming into a conscious, vital realization of our oneness with this Infinite Life."*[55] Vivekananda had explained in 1896 that the "aim of Raja Yoga" was "the realisation of our absolute oneness with the Divine."[56] Such words made it difficult on occasion to see where Vivekananda ended and Trine began.[57]

If some mutual influence existed, Vivekananda doubted many of the therapies on offer at Green Acre: he was playful with Mary Hale, his Chicago "sister": "How are you going on with your Christian Science lessons? I hope you will go to Greenacr [*sic*]. There you will find quite a number of them and also the Spiritualists, table turnings, psalmists, astrologers, etc., etc. You will get all the 'cures' and all the 'isms' presided over by Miss Farmer."[58] He was a bit harsher about Henry Wood, another important figure in New Thought, as a "mental healer of metaphysico-chemico-physico-religiosio what not" and made fun of "the Editor . . . of the Universal Truth . . . [who] is conducting religious services and holding classes to heal all manner of diseases and very soon I expect them to be giving eyes to the blind and the like!"[59] He also had wearied of traveling with William Juvenal Colville, an English spiritualist and author of fantasy novels, who had been engaged by the same lecture bureau that had taken on Vivekananda.[60] A California devotee quoted Vivekananda as saying: "'If you think X is hard to live with, you should have travelled with Colville.'"[61] Colville was so full of little illnesses that he had a nurse accompany him. Nor could Vivekananda resist, while at Green Acre, making fun of his old traveling companion, who tried to speak during a thunderstorm: "Yesterday there was a tremendous cyclone, which gave a good 'treatment' to the tents. The big tent under which they had the lectures had developed so much spirituality, under the 'treatment,' that it entirely disappeared from mortal gaze, and about two hundred chairs were dancing about the grounds under spiritual ecstasy! . . . You will be astounded."[62]

Given these skeptical views it is remarkable that Vivekananda was also so tolerant. As has been noted, he used Christian Science in 1894 to treat his insomnia, and was well acquainted with homeopathy from Calcutta, where it had been so thoroughly Indianized that many Indians did not realize its foreign origins.[63] Used by Brahmo physicians who associated it with middle-class improvement, it was Vivekananda's first recourse when he was ill in 1889.[64]

He knew, too, of mesmerism, since the British had brought it to Calcutta in the 1840s, and had tried magnetic healing at the end of 1899, but decided that any improvement was due to exercise and the Californian climate rather than the "healing woman who skin[ned] [him] every time she treat[ed] [him]."[65] In a satire he wrote in Bengali, he described a learned ascetic countryman, Gurguré Krishnavayal Bhattacharya, who was "omniscient about the flow of electric magnetic currents all over the human body, from the hair-tuft to its furthest nook and corner."[66] He dismissed magnetism's more outlandish claims, but used its metaphors in *Raja Yoga* (1896), which described "fluid" and "vibrations."[67] Osteopathy was invented by Andrew Taylor Still, a one-time magnetic healer and spiritualist, who was convinced that disease could be remedied by a correctly adjusted body.[68] Still does not seem to have been part of Green Acre, but another disciple hoped Vivekananda would try it. He was not interested: "What is this osteopathy, anyway? They cut off a rib or two to cure me?" He thought his bones would be better left to nature, where they were "destined to make corals in the Ganga."[69] He resisted the treatment, therefore, with this jest, which probably invoked Shakespeare's *Tempest*—"Full fathom five thy father lies / Of his bones are corals made." A month later, he tried osteopathy in New York and would later say that it did not do him much good.[70]

WILLIAM JAMES AND MAX MÜLLER

While at Green Acre, Vivekananda objected to the way that his audience believed that God was "either a terror or a healing power, vibration and so forth."[71]

He made clear his dislike of fire-and-brimstone Protestantism as much as the many currents in New Thought, albeit with his characteristic wit. But while observing and criticizing, he was also constructing, hoping to reorient his listeners to Vedantic concepts. He understood that they often did not distinguish between "Nature," "God," "Mind," and "Spirit," and recognized their desire for "harmonization," "revitalization," and "regeneration."[72]

So, while he resisted their emphasis on cure, he reached out to them by deploying traces of New Thought in *Raja Yoga*, the outline of which he created under the Green Acre pines. Emma Thursby's notes of these sessions show how he adopted popular science idioms when instructing pupils to concentrate their "nerve energies" into the "spinal column" until they touch "the centre of the brain." Other references, especially to the guru, however, were less familiar.

Vivekananda insisted that the guru was nothing more than the higher self, and therefore domination had no role in spiritual guidance—a claim not always accepted or understood. He sought to explain the value of concentration: "meditation is a sort of prayer and prayer is meditation." He remarked, also, that yoga entailed realizing that "our present consciousness is only a little bit of an infinite sea of mind" that should not constrain us: "the word Yoga is the root of which our word yoke is a derivation—meaning 'to join'—and Yoga means 'joining ourselves with God'—joining me with my real Self."[73] This was the essence of his teaching.[74] It ended with an English rendering of a Sanskrit chant: "I am Existence absolute."

Raja Yoga was an elaborated version of these lessons, one where the language of science, and especially the psychology (and emerging philosophy) of William James, was prominent. James was Vivekananda's interlocutor and acquaintance, who also frequented Green Acre and traveled in the same circles. Sara Bull held philosophical soirées in her magnificent Cambridge home on Brattle Street, where she invited not only James and Vivekananda but also Josiah Royce, another professor at Harvard.

Jamesian pragmatism is now so prevalent that we forget its profound impact. Rather than focusing on whether religious mysticism and supernatural communion was "real," it provided an intellectually feasible means of justifying belief for its psychological and social value.[75] James's *The Will to Believe* (1897) and the more famous *Varieties of Religious Experience* (1902) privileged belief, faith, and inner experience over theology, dogma, and institutions. His pragmatism was also linked to the university's golden age of

Sanskrit, when fascination with Eastern religion and its sacred texts peaked as a high-brow reflection of the wider enchantment with Indian thought that Vivekananda helped develop.[76] Although James did not learn Sanskrit, he knew about Eastern philosophies, which figured in his lectures and writings. Royce had studied the Rig Veda, ancient Vedic hymns, in the original Sanskrit, and knew the Bhagavad Gita. Unlike James, he was an "Idealist," a man who believed in the "absolute mind" and in the "infinite unity of consciousness," terms that reflected his interest in Eastern religions and especially in Advaita Vedanta.[77] Indeed, he opposed what he saw as instrumental in Jamesian pragmatism, a debate that was integral to their friendship and diverging philosophies.

That both men attended when Vivekananda lectured shows their interest in his ideas as well as Sara Bull's influence. James and Vivekananda were said to have had a tête-à-tête after a reception and supper organized at her home in late March 1896; James then invited Vivekananda to dinner.[78] Bull made sure that copies of Vivekananda's lectures both at Harvard and at her home were printed and circulated to local bookshops, and she hoped that James or Royce would preface *Raja Yoga*. She believed that a Harvard philosopher's imprimatur would enhance its intellectual credentials, but James dallied. Vivekananda cared less than Bull for James's endorsement. He was in a hurry, and simply wrote to her in May 1896, "Why do you not write something plain and decisive? Life is short and time is flying."[79]

However, pressure of work was not the only reason for James's reluctance. He was also ambivalent about Vivekananda's ideas, even though he remained interested. James later asked Margaret Noble to send on certain works and had wanted to give Vivekananda a copy of his *The Principles of Psychology* (1890).[80] But when he wrote *Pragmatism: A New Name for Some Old Ways of Thinking* (1907) almost a decade later, he characterized Advaita Vedanta rather negatively as a world-denying mysticism: "This separation between man and man, man and woman, man and child, nation from nation, earth from moon, moon from sun, this separation between atom and atom is the cause really of all the misery, and the Vedanta says this separation does not exist, it is not real. It is merely apparent, on the surface. In the heart of things there is Unity still."[81]

James thought Vivekananda's "monist absolutism" was emotionally reassuring but intellectually suspect. But even if he personally was not convinced, James accepted that Hinduism had a "high pragmatic value" in imparting "a perfect sumptuosity of security" and recognized the allure of a creed that claimed to unite "all sentient life."[82]

James's earlier ideas on the subject were hardly as adamantine as this later reflection suggests. Although famous for his pragmatic rationalism and emerging "radical empiricism," he had been as concerned as Vivekananda with the "unconscious depths of human personality." His work encouraged Americans "to view self-exploration as spiritually significant and religious experience as psychologically profound," strengthening the tradition of American religious searching and furthering the study of altered states of consciousness.[83] He hoped such phenomena would now be accepted as bona fide evidence in a larger enquiry into the "sciences of mind" analyzed in *The Varieties of Religious Experience*.

James thus paid attention to the unconscious mind's upper reaches—through telepathy, clairvoyance, religious experience, or trance states. His interest stemmed perhaps from past emotional difficulties, in particular his own "suicidal neurasthenia" and the accompanying loss of faith he had shared with other psychical investigators, such as Frederick Myers and Henry Sidgwick, cofounders of the London-based Society for Psychical Research.[84] Henry James Sr. had been a Swedenborgian minister, and his son William knew well ideas surrounding "divine influx," mystical creativity, and human-divine correspondences.[85] Indeed, he may even have wanted to ground Swedenborgianism in a positive science of "mind"; spiritualism thus enabled all these sons of clergymen to explore immortality without a Christian heaven, thus providing an alternative to neuroscientific reductionism that did not entail the abandonment of experimentalism.

Despite hating organizations, James therefore took on the presidency of the American Society for Psychical Research and spent years debunking frauds. He played an indirect role in exposing Madame Blavatsky and a famous Italian medium, Eusapia Palladino. Indeed, his skepticism enabled him to champion a third way (the "*tertium quid*") between an experimental psychology that equated brain and mind and a spiritualist philosophical position that presupposed a "soul" that organized consciousness. He characterized the study of psychology as a struggle between what he called the "tough-minded" and the "tender-minded": the first was "Empiricist, Sensationalistic, Materialistic, Pessimistic, Irreligious, Fatalistic, Pluralistic [and] Skeptical"; the second was "rationalistic, intellectualistic, idealistic, Optimistic, Religious, Free-Willist, Monistic [and Dogmatical]."[86] The first included laboratory investigators, the second, spiritualists and such men as Vivekananda. The first valued facts above all else; the second, "principles."[87]

No doubt, this appreciation was hardly as dichotomized as James proposed, but it was a powerful shorthand for encapsulating late-nineteenth-century philosophical tendencies. To counter such perceived oppositions, he developed a "pragmatic" position to include subjectivity within the realm of scientific fact-finding and analysis. His psychical research began in the late 1860s and continued for over forty years, and ranged from studying the planchette (a small board on wheels used for automatic writing), through investigating séances, to heading the American Society for Psychical Research.[88] James was fascinated by Leonora Piper, a Boston spiritualist, an exception among a flock of fraudulent mediums.[89] His engagement with her revealed his own "will to believe" that unveiled the "dramatic potential of human nature."[90] Piper became a subject also for Minot Judson Savage, Richard Hodgson, and G. Stanley Hall, the American founder of child psychology, among others, and was as important in creating "psychical research" as the men who studied her.

At this time, James confided that he did believe in some "unity" that Vivekananda might well have endorsed: "there is a continuum of cosmic consciousness, against which our individuality builds but accidental fences, and into which our several minds plunge as into a mother-sea or reservoir."[91] The "accidental fences" he referred to sounded very like the planks of wood that Ramakrishna had said marked the elusive boundaries between "self" and "God." Moreover, in talking about the "mother-sea of consciousness," or the cosmic "reservoir," James used similar watery metaphors of dissolution and connection.[92]

He almost certainly adopted these "oceanic" metaphors through his secondhand knowledge of Ramakrishna. James had read Max Müller, who wrote on Vivekananda's guru and edited a volume of the mystic's sayings.[93] James knew Müller not just as a great Sanskritist, but also as the editor of a fifty-volume *Sacred Books of the East* (even if Müller himself had never once set foot on Indian soil). Müller was equally well known to Indians and his Oxford home was constantly visited by members of the Hindu diaspora.[94]

Vivekananda, as one of these admirers, was jubilant in 1894 when he read Müller's *Three Lectures on the Vedanta Philosophy* and wrote to the Hale sisters in 1895 that Müller "must see the whole truth in the long run."[95] When he met Müller in Oxford in 1896, he told Mary Hale that Müller was "a saint—a Vedantist through and through. . . . He has been a devoted admirer of my own Master for years . . . and has written . . . on my Master in the *Nineteenth Century*."[96] For him, Müller was the "Vedantist of Vedantists. He has, indeed, caught the real soul of the melody of the Vedanta, . . . the one principle of which all religions are only applications. And what was Ramakrishna Paramahamsa? The practical demonstration of this ancient principle, the embodiment of India that is past, and a foreshadowing of the India that is to be, the bearer of spiritual light unto nations. . . . Is it a wonder that this Western sage does study and appreciate every new star in the firmament of Indian thought, before even the Indians themselves realise its magnitude?"[97]

Remarks of this kind suggest that Müller's stellar reputation among Indians may indeed owe a great deal to Vivekananda. Müller's article "A Real Mahatman" had already targeted Blavatsky's "inventions" and contrasted her fictional "mahatmas" with the "true" mystic and avatara, Ramakrishna. A man of enduring Christian faith with Pietist leanings, Müller feared that the West was losing its sense of the infinite that Ramakrishna's mysticism exemplified. Although Müller was an unparalleled scholar, and Vivekananda a jnani, neither regarded the knowledge of sacred texts as equal to experience and belief—hence their joint admiration for Ramakrishna.[98]

Together, Vivekananda and Müller "explained" Ramakrishna to the non-Indian world in an 1896 publication. For Vivekananda, Müller's contribution on Ramakrishna was a godsend.[99] If he had considered James a "very nice man" after meeting him at Sara Bull's house, he viewed Müller as unassailable, the Oxford academic who exemplified imperial learning.[100] He wanted Vedanta to benefit from this power: "This British Empire with all its drawbacks is the greatest machine that ever existed for the dissemination of ideas. I mean to put my ideas in the centre of this machine, and they will spread all over the world."[101] He likened Müller to the "sages of ancient India" in his portrait of the man and exalted him as saintlike. Müller was "neither the philologist nor the scholar," but a "soul . . . realising Its oneness with the Brahman. . . . Indeed his heartbeats have caught the rhythm of the Upanishads."[102]

They jointly refashioned Ramakrishna to separate Vedanta from modern theosophy, with Vivekananda supplying Müller with notes and readings about Ramakrishna that appeared in *Ramakrishna: His Life and Sayings* (1898). Müller's little book again condemned the theosophists for sullying the notion of the "Mahatman," as well as the word "theosophy," which, for him, meant the mystical intuition that many creeds shared.[103] Müller instead presented Ramakrishna as the embodiment of "pure" Hinduism, despite his devotion to Kali and his frequent dualism. Was *Ramakrishna: His Life and Sayings* a strategic misconstrual to link the mystic to the cerebral philosophy of Advaita to foster global awareness? It is more likely that both regarded Ramakrishna's simplicity and saintliness as exemplifying this philosophy, "teaching the unity of humanity and divinity" integral to the "Hindu Mind." Both then glorified Ramakrishna because his saintliness embodied bhakti's "religion of the heart" that, in Ramakrishna's case, had also led to the confirmation of Advaitic "cerebralism."[104]

Müller freely translated Ramakrishna's aphorisms and parables, often retaining their homespun quality, and especially the water metaphors. Saying 158, for example, reiterated the story of the salt doll, "represent[ing] the man who merges his self in the Universal and All-pervading Self and becomes one with it."[105] Saying 279 described the "plank of wood . . . stretched across a current of water," and the misplaced belief that the barrier had divided the water in two. Müller's Ramakrishna urged believers to "dive deep into the ocean of the Eternal-Intelligent-Bliss," a world James evoked in the "Mother sea of consciousness."[106]

James cited Müller's book in *The Varieties of Religious Experience* and credited Vivekananda in the same volume.[107] We know, too, that James had read *Raja Yoga* and the "The Real and the Apparent Man," a lecture first given in New York in mid-February 1896.[108] Vivekananda wrote, "Look at the waves in the sea. Not one wave is really different from the sea, but what makes the wave apparently different? Name and form, the form of the wave and the name which we give to it, 'wave.' That is what makes it different from the sea."[109]

Reading excerpts of Vivekananda reinforced what he had learned from Müller's little book on Ramakrishna. In *Varieties,* James also quoted Vivekananda to explain Advaita as the "nearest of the near, my own self, the reality of my own life, my body and my soul.—I am Thee and Thou art Me. That is your own nature. Assert it, manifest."[110]

That James continued to ponder these questions is evident in his letters in 1899 to William Sloan Kennedy, an American author and journalist, who asked James how this undifferentiated vision could account for individuality in the afterlife. Americans repeatedly feared that the self would be subsumed by the "mother sea," a form of words that James repeated exactly in another letter. They dreaded extinction, a body and ego without boundaries.[111] James's uncharacteristically wordy response suggests his own confusion and ambivalence: "the 'mother-sea' need not be monistically or 'transcendental-absolutely' determined. Provided your consciousness, here organically determined, be a filtrate from an already existing larger consciousness, I am quite willing that the latter should be individualistic in form. One would simply revert then to one's own lower wider self, which would meantime have become enriched by the memories of one's earthly career. Of course the brain process works on the filter as well as on the filtrate; and may leave memory marks there as the stubs are left in check books."[112]

James aimed again at a path between "cerebralism," with its reductionist physicalism, and the "monistic transcendental idealism" that he believed Vivekananda represented. He reiterated this to James Ward, the author of *Naturalism and Agnosticism* (1899): "the individual's consciousness may survive the brain, for in the Mother Sea the scars of cerebral operations may remain as records of the transaction, like stubs in a check book, and form the basis of an eternally remembered account. I should have said more explicitly that there is no objection to considering the Mother Sea in as individualistic a form as you like."[113]

As Krister Dylan Knapp suggests, James strikingly mixes the metaphor of the "mother sea" with the transactional notion of a checkbook with its stubs, reflections that perhaps reveal the conflict between "tender-minded" and "tough-minded" impulses, and the philosopher's desire to encompass them.[114] They also hint at Vivekananda's own difficulties translating the message of Vedanta to a new generation of Westerners, even to minds as supple and searching as William James's.

RAJA YOGA

Vivekananda also sought the "authentic" in psychical research and wished to contain it within a deeper truth. Thus, he recognized the positive aspects of Christian Science, dismissed theosophy as nonsense, and maintained that Western psychical science was taking (infantile) steps toward a deeper transcendence.[115] If James criticized Advaita for wallowing in a "sumptuosity of security," Vivekananda might have retorted that if he was a "Monist," he was hardly "dogmatical." Like James's, his teachings exemplified flexibility, religious universalism, and a focus on "self-realization" that was anything but rigid.[116] Christianity, he thought, was far more dogmatic. Nor did he believe that Vedanta was about spiritual "security," as he had always argued that the world's beauty could only be grasped through ugliness, and the realization that the two were interconnected. He became exasperated with devotees who wanted him to teach people to be "good"; he held such notions as "sin" to be Christian in the worst sense. Like the cycle of destruction and rebirth that Kali encompassed, spiritual knowledge encompassed both "evil" and "good," offering a "panorama of beauty and sublimity" that was integrated rather than one-sided.[117] Vivekananda's vision of Hinduism rejected a Christian vision of eternal damnation because it cordoned off evil rather than encompassing it.

Both James and Vivekananda agreed on the need for a "science of religion" that highlighted subjective experience. Vivekananda wrote: "It is not much use to talk about religion until one has felt it."[118] There was nothing intrinsically Western about such an emphasis, however, even if Vivekananda had borrowed from James's *The Principles of Psychology* (1890) when writing that "[s]urface Scientists, unable to explain the various extraordinary mental phenomena, strive to ignore their very existence."[119] James advocated "looking into our minds and reporting what we there discover," a practice Vivekananda championed when he enjoined people to understand the psyche's workings by "observing the facts that are going on within" during meditation. In the study and art of acquiring these "higher perceptions," Vivekananda felt he could speak from personal experience. In characterizing them, he switched back and forth between materialist science and Hindu traditions of nondualism. He remarked that one exists as many, that "there is no difference between the sun and you, [. . .] between the table and me," with nonduality experienced through "super consciousness."[120]

The term "Raja yoga" refers to the union of the practitioner with the "higher self" as much as the method of attaining this merger through discipline and practice. The technique focuses on "mind" and "mental force," though, as will be seen, Vivekananda also linked it to the marshalling of the "vital force," known as *pranayama*. "Raja," of course, referred to a prince or a king, to express the majestic power that comes with this form of concentration.[121]

In the West, *Raja Yoga* (1896) remains Vivekananda's best-known work, and for many became *the* term for the practice of yoga itself. It acknowledges the difficulty of attaining mental discipline when faced with constant changes in both mind and body, unavoidable processes of creation and destruction. Mental focus was also aligned to breathing; or the disharmony that might stimulate healing; or the transformation in which individuals constantly regulated and rebalanced the three *gunas* (*tamas, rajas,* and *sattva*). Tamasic (dark) qualities caused disorder, chaos, and negativity; rajas created passion, activism, dynamism, and often self-centeredness; and sattva reposed in harmony, goodness, purity, and, as a consequence, calmness.[122] Vivekananda, therefore, sought to convey wider Hindu notions of balance— older, and in his view, more valuable than the Christian physiology and harmonialism he had encountered in Green Acre.

To write *Raja Yoga,* he used the *Kurma Purana,* the *Samkhya Karika,* and two works on hatha yoga that came from the theosophical orbit and put Patanjali sutras in loose translations with commentaries at the end of the text.[123] Patanjali was associated with Samkhya philosophy, a dualist vision of self and God that Vivekananda had rejected with Advaita, an inclusion that suggested contradictory elements in the work. He knew they came from a different philosophical school to his own but maintained that both focused on the "self's liberation from material constraint."[124] For Patanjali, meditation focused the individual on God so that the self could be freed from Universal Matter. In contrast, Vivekananda used Patanjali to move yogic concentration away from the Deity (or personal God) to the Vedantic notion of the Universal Self, incorporated in the idea of the unity of self and nonself.[125]

Was Vivekananda then merely another influential system-maker who brought yoga to a wider audience? This would have been a substantial achievement, but *Raja Yoga* represented more. Rather than a guru transmitting technique and spirituality to a disciple (which he continued to do), the book prepared the novice to use "mind" to "observe mind," while also insisting on the similarities between the "science" of yoga and contemporary psychology. With Patanjali, he also repurposed an ancient Indian text for a modern audience. Indeed, Patanjali had been virtually lost until British orientalist Henry Thomas Colebrooke rediscovered it in the early nineteenth century. Only a few of the aphorisms focused on the eight components of yoga: the observance of ethical rules, virtuous habits, correct postures, breathing control, drawing in awareness, concentration (or introspective focus), profound abstract meditation, and finally, samadhi. These aspects now dominate contemporary practice, but they were a small part of a work otherwise devoted to philosophy, much of which remained obscure.[126]

The theosophists also prized Patanjali: its third chapter emphasized such magical phenomena as the ability to levitate and to enter people's bodies—which Colebrooke and Müller had condemned as deceitful and subversive.[127] Vivekananda avoided the more extravagant descriptions, while nodding to the extraordinary powers some yogis—after much training and perseverance—might realize.[128] Once again, he concluded that "when the Yogi has seen all these wonderful powers, and rejected them, he reaches the goal." He concluded that they were no "better than dreams."[129]

By including his translation of Patanjali in *Raja Yoga* while also commenting on the sutras, Vivekananda placed the ancient scholar at the center of a revised canon, so that today it has become the "bible" of contemporary yoga, despite its unintelligibility and only brief excursion into the now-vaunted "eight-fold path." Vivekananda reappropriated him, taking back these aphorisms from the orientalists and especially from the theosophists. The work also reintroduced the notion of prana (breath) that Blavatsky had taken in *The Secret Doctrine* as early as 1885. He introduced the term "psychic prana," which sought to encompass the breath and the psyche in some combination. He taught how to focus prana to control the senses; to concentrate; and, finally, to meditate, to fix the mind to reach full absorption [samadhi] and ultimately superconsciousness.[130]

Vivekananda used ideas from Green Acre when he spoke of the harmonious distribution of the prana that recalled mesmeric fluid and healing.[131] He also expounded with brio on the quality of *akasha*, the Sanskrit term for "ether," which was "omnipresent, all-penetrating existence. Everything that has form, everything that is the result of combination, is evolved out of . . . Akasha. It is the Akasha that becomes the air, that becomes the liquids, that becomes the solids; it is the Akasha that becomes the sun, the earth, the moon, the stars, the comets; it is the Akasha that becomes the human body, the animal body, the plants, . . . everything that exists . . . ; it is so subtle that it is beyond all ordinary perception . . ."[132]

Ether, in the nineteenth century, was seen as the medium for electromagnetic waves (for example X-rays) and was regarded as a kind of "subtle fluid" that could contain heat, electricity, and chemical activity. Even the great Russian scientist Dmitri Mendeleev worked assiduously to prove the reality of such ether, but abandoned the concept after many failed experiments.[133] However, belief in "ether" had a long afterlife. Vivekananda demonstrated his familiarity with these ideas by citing Newton, Jean Bernard Foucault, and the pioneer in electromagnetism, Wilhelm Eduard Weber, in an anonymous piece in the *New York Medical Times* in 1895.[134] The term migrated regularly across the boundaries of respectable science, into theosophy, and back into Vivekananda's Advaita, despite its Aristotelian and mesmeric overtones. He described meditation by using a vocabulary of electrical connection: "When the mind has been trained to remain fixed on a certain internal or external location, there comes to it the power of flowing in an unbroken current. . . . towards that point."[135] He also deployed metaphors of light refraction and vibration: "The powers of the mind are like rays of light dissipated; when they are concentrated, they illumine."[136]

Such terminology showed Vivekananda straying into occult arenas, but he was hardly alone: Max Müller, for example, also had studied aspects of the Western hermetical tradition to gauge their value.[137] When in Paris in 1900, Vivekananda lodged for a time with Henri Antoine Jules-Bois, a well-known occultist, whom he described as a "French savant."[138] The Frenchman's book *Le Satanisme et la magie* (1895) discussed exorcism, love potions, and even vampirism along with reflections on modern science. Vivekananda traveled with Jules-Bois to Brittany and enjoyed his conversations, even if there is no evidence that his traveling companion had any influence on him.[139]

Vivekananda not only had to position his yogic teaching in the West, but also in India, where it, too, was undergoing transformation, integral to a deeper resistance to the British and especially Christian ideas of bodily control and discipline. Like many other yoga manuals in India, *Raja Yoga* did not insist on the presence of a guru. These other publications prescribed breathing exercises as vital, to be deployed when buying an elephant or a camel or closing a business deal."[140] Vivekananda rejected such transactional use and warned against "getting powers." However, the means to discover this religious experience were simple: "The key lies in daily meditation."[141] He directed his listeners to find a firm seat and assume the right posture, but only to achieve realms of higher consciousness.

Devotees in the West recalled how his lessons were anything but "esoteric," and how he sought to demystify his practices. One of his closest associates described a disciple's conversation: "'I see a light.' He said, 'Good, keep on,' 'O no, it is more like a glow at the heart.' And he said . . . 'Good, keep on.' That is all he ever taught me."[142] Nor did he direct: "You may meditate on whatever you like, but I shall meditate on the heart of a lion. That gives strength."[143]

He advised meditation simply as part of a daily routine: "The monkey mind [a term which described mental chattering], . . . the silence of the Inner Self, the necessity of practice, the study of the teaching which teaches liberation of the self," is how another devotee described the swami's lessons.[144]

However, in reproducing Patanjali and the sutras in his text, Vivekananda undermined the connection between Hindu yogis and Sufi Muslims who had long practiced many of the same meditative and magical arts. Even though Patanjali was torn away from its moorings in Indian dualist thought, Vivekananda reconnected it to Sanskritic tradition and linked it to a primordial Hindu past. In this way, it separated "Hindu" and "Sufi" mysticism from each another.[145]

The impulse to embed Yoga in Hinduism was integral to the larger project of making India the "guru to the world," to lay out a form of teaching that the "superconscious . . . mind" gathered "spiritual fact," and that Indians were particularly capable of paying special attention to "this side of religion."[146] Keshub Chunder Sen had similarly claimed exceptional powers for the "Hindu Mind" and the "yoga faculty," which, in his view, "enable[d] [Indians] to annihilate space and time."[147]

If he endorsed this essentialist view of spiritual power, Vivekananda was wary of hatha yoga because he believed it dealt "entirely with the physical body" and thus with the achievement of physical effects.[148] He inherited this skepticism from Ramakrishna, who had criticized a hatha yoga for excessive rituals of purification and for focusing on the body, rather than on God.[149] Vivekananda also disapproved of hypnotherapy and Christian Science in *Raja Yoga* for parallel reasons: they emphasized "cure" unduly and thus might disturb the individual's spiritual progress.

In *Raja Yoga*, Vivekananda speaks of the primal energy located at the base of the spine that is awakened by deep meditation.[150] The great yogis of India unleashed this primal energy to master "the whole universe" and "to control the whole of Prana."[151] The highest energy stored in the brain was the *ojas*: the more ojas a person possessed, "the more powerful he is, the more intellectual, the more spiritually strong." Everyone could increase their ojas: "the Yogis say that that part of the human energy, which is expressed as sex energy, in sexual thought, when checked and controlled, easily becomes changed into Ojas."[152] Celibacy could be achieved by anyone and, with it, the first steps toward unleashing new spiritual possibilities.

He thus regarded his own sexual continence as key to his capacities and spiritual achievements. A California devotee remembered that Vivekananda said how at Camp Taylor in the Sierras that "In my first speech in this country, in Chicago, I addressed that audience as 'Sisters and Brothers of America,' and you know that they all rose to their feet. You may wonder what made them do this . . . Let me tell you that I did have a power and this is it—never once in my life did I allow myself to have even one sexual thought. I trained my mind, my thinking, and the powers that man usually uses along that line I put into a higher channel, and it developed a force so strong that nothing could resist it."[153]

This exaltation of brahmacharya (celibacy) was important to Vivekananda's vision of his personal power and to venerated Indian traditions of bodily control.[154]

Women, however, did not possess "seminal energy." How were they to release their *kundalini* (divine female energy)? As will be seen, Margaret Noble would do so with celibacy and with a devotion to Kali and militancy.[155] Although he did not believe that marriage was an unworthy state, Vivekananda regarded it as an "austerity,'" requiring deep sacrifice: "In heaven there is no marrying or giving in marriage; why not begin at once and have none here?"[156] True "geniuses" he argued, "clear out the deck for battle. No encumbrance— no marriage, no children, no undue attachment to do anything except the one idea, and live and die for that."[157] Certainly, he had chosen this path for himself, and his closest female Western disciples followed him. When Indians remarked, like Ramakrishna, that "women are bondage and a snare to men," Vivekananda countered that through celibacy women might reach meditative heights and become "teachers and preachers of the Math."[158]

His Western followers barely noticed the militant, anticolonial undertone concerning yogic concentration. When visiting the dungeon cells (*cachots*) of Mont Saint-Michel in Normandy, Vivekananda reportedly muttered under "his breath, 'What a wonderful place for meditation!'"[159] These *oubliettes* (where miscreants and political prisoners were supposedly stored away and forgotten) symbolized despotism. He certainly had not missed the parallel with British oppression. Vivekananda's vision of Raja yoga, in controlling the prana and hence "vital energy," reinforced Indian resistance to tyranny, now reinforced by psycho-physiology. This showed how the deepest renunciation could also encompass the highest "activism," a paradox that he would reinforce when speaking of *seva* (service) and "practical Vedanta." Moreover, while he had counseled Americans against doing meditation with the aim of "getting powers," Vivekananda understood that yoga should embody a different kind of power—not miraculous or magical—but one invested in mental strength, "character" and "bodily composure."[160] The radical activist Aurobindo Ghose saw Vivekananda in a vision while incarcerated awaiting trial for terrorism in 1908 and proceeded to promote a version of this revolutionary asceticism among his fellow prisoners.[161] While meditating for long hours, Aurobindo believed that he and his comrades were "born like Krishna in the prison-house," where they engaged in resisting the Raj's tyranny as a form of divine play. By emphasizing self-control, moral strength, and physical prowess, yoga would take its place as a counter to British claims to hegemony over "feeble" Indians.[162]

*   *   *

Despite the landmark nature of *Raja Yoga* and its democratizing impulse both in America and in India, Vivekananda knew the importance of the guru-disciple relationship. After the 1894 summer in Green Acre, he went to New York and decided to teach anyone interested, defying Sara Bull, who preferred him to concentrate on the "right people." By the following summer, he escaped with a small group to Thousand Island and hoped there to form the first American sannyasins. He intended to establish a network of workers in the New World—as he hoped would materialize in his homeland—under his guidance.

9

FEMALE DEVOTEES AND THE
LABORS OF THE GURU

He who is rooted in oneness
realizes that I am
in every being; wherever
he goes, he remains in me.

—Krishna in the Bhagavad Gita, Chapter 6, verse 30

How bold one gets when one is sure of being loved.

—Sigmund Freud, June 22, 1882, to Martha Bernays, his fiancée

◆　◆　◆

THOUSAND ISLAND is a forested region between New York and Canada, with 1,800 islands strewn across the Saint Lawrence River. One of the bigger islands, Wellesley, is nine miles long and two miles wide and is renowned for its gingerbread cottages, wooden porches with rocking chairs, lighthouses, baronial-style castles, and bridges that link the United States with its northern neighbor.

Vivekananda initiated his first American sannyasins in this paradise of birds and grasses, small pleasure crafts, and grandiose yachts in 1895, the summer after Green Acre, when Mary Elizabeth "Libbie" Dutcher invited a group to her cottage. In this faraway place, both civilized and remote, they created together something novel as they adapted the relationship between guru and disciple to

9.1. Boldt Castle, Heart Island, New York

9.2. Dutcher House, Wellesley Island, New York

the New World. The experiment was only partially successful, for not all stayed within the fold, but they nonetheless forged an enduring model.

Until Thousand Island, Vivekananda's stay in America had been divided into two parts. On Sara Bull's suggestion, he had at first mixed with the "right people" in Boston, Cambridge, and New York, but he changed course by living and teaching in humble lodgings in Manhattan sometime after 1894.[1] The following summer, he escaped first to a friend's fishing camp in New Hampshire before making his way to Thousand Island, writing to Bull, "I go into the forest alone and read my Gita and am quite happy . . . I will meditate by the hour there and be all alone by myself. The very idea is ennobling."[2] He had resumed aspects of his sannyasin's life, arriving in a landscape with none of India's ancient, layered associations, a seemingly virgin spiritual territory (he felt Native Americans had not left a great mark on the continent), except for the Methodist settlement, with its white church spire, on one side of Wellesley Island.[3]

He used his stay to try out his own ideas, far away from the experimental hubbub of Green Acre. He had grasped that the spiritual seekers were preoccupied with the nature of "rapport," fascinated by the rival claims of science and religion, and searching for new philosophies and healing possibilities. William James, Mary Baker Eddy, and, as will be seen, even Sigmund Freud, all worked within a common context in which the relational and its therapeutic prospects were explored. Vivekananda was part of this larger context but differed in uniting the Western vogue for self-realization and healing with anti-imperialism. This last was the final link in a chain of discernment and deeper understanding of yoga in this period, which Westerners today have abandoned or no longer even perceive.

He underscored the value of Eastern wisdom by criticizing concepts of Protestant "duty" and its politics of uplift; he constantly reminded his acolytes of the harm that such ideas did both to the unfolding "self" and to the poor and dominated. In becoming their guru, moreover, he showed how relations of spiritual tutelage could be easily inverted, with a dark-faced Indian, rather than a white missionary or healer, taking charge of their transfiguration.

THOUSAND ISLAND AND CHRISTINE

Christine Greenstidel first heard Vivekananda in Detroit in a Unitarian church on a cold February night in 1894, but she only met him in person when she traveled to Thousand Island. She was overwhelmed by his presence and her conviction that she had "known that mind before," recalling that he had "caught and concentrated the sun's rays" with his scarlet robe and orange turban.[4]

She believed her early spirituality was indelibly marked by her family's loyalty to Jan Hus (also known as John Huss), a fourteenth-century Czech theologian, church reformer, and predecessor to Luther, who was burned at the stake for his beliefs: "Yes, I have the nature of a fanatic. After all, I am a descendent of a follower of John Huss. My family . . . lived for eight hundred years . . . in a tight little group in a village near Nuremberg, only my father went to America with me his oldest daughter, a mere child. I was the oldest of seven and had to be the mother for them all—yes, and the father too in a few years."[5]

Christine thus saw herself as a stoical outsider with a venerable spiritual pedigree now grounded in Lutheranism. She had lost her father at age seventeen and became the effective head of a family of younger sisters and a widowed mother. She worked as a schoolteacher and led a penurious, downtrodden existence, becoming one of the first Christian Scientists in Detroit.[6] Vivekananda's devotion slowly pried her away from her depressive tendencies and family duties until she arrived in India in 1902.

Years later, she reflected on the oddness of the group of twelve which gathered at Thousand Island. First, there was the hostess, Libbie Dutcher, who had invited everyone to the arts and crafts–style cottage built in the 1880s on Wellesley.[7] Libbie was a Methodist who came from what was known as upstate New York's "'Burned-Over District"—so named because of the religious fervor that "burned" the region in the 1830s. Its social experimentation and early feminism were evident in the remnants of the Methodist Church on the island.[8] An artist sympathetic to impressionism, she had encouraged her pupils in Rochester, her winter home, to draw from life, even though such study was still disreputable for women. She thus joined the others in having a nonconformist streak.

Stella Campbell was an actress, whose behavior prompted Christine to wonder whether she were looking for "another play [to] bring back her lost youth."[9] But Vivekananda saw her as another "Baby," "free from art and guile," who would in time resemble Baby Krishna. He was right—far from being an attention-seeker, Stella "went to live on a small island in Orchard Lake [near Detroit]" and built a "tiny one-roomed house and lived alone"

9.3. Libbie Dutcher in her studio

for thirty years.[10] She was not the only "Baby." There was also Mary Caroline Funke, Christine's friend, who met "his moods," rather than asking that he tend hers. Mary admitted that "I know he thinks I am a fool, but I don't care as long as it amuses him."[11] She felt he needed her love, and she did everything to supply it.

Christine explained that if Vivekananda appreciated the "Babies," he hoped for more from the "fanatics," especially from Marie Louise Davitt, soon to be Swami Abhayananda. She cut a rather dramatic figure: "A tall, angular woman, about fifty years of age, so masculine in appearance that one looked twice before one could tell whether she was a man or a woman. The short, wiry hair, in the days before bobbed hair was in vogue, the masculine features, the large bones, the heavy voice and the robe, not unlike that worn by men in India, made one doubtful. Her path was the highest, she announced, that of philosophy—*jnana*." She had been the spokesman for ultraradical groups and had learning and some degree of eloquence: "'I have magnetism of the platform,' she used to say."[12]

Mary-Louise later preached on her own authority, causing Margaret Noble spiritual heartburn in the process.[13] Was Vivekananda at first undisturbed by her appearance because Ramakrishna had long ago claimed that he did know whether he was a man or a woman? Vivekananda may even have been attracted to her "mannish" qualities and her claims to the jnana path, rather unusual among the women who tended to undertake Bhakti or Karma yoga.

The other "fanatic" was Leon Landsberg, Russian Jewish by birth, but American by citizenship. Vivekananda had been in search of a male intellectual and spiritual companion and shared the apartment on 54 West Thirty-Third Street in New York with him. Christine claimed that Landsberg had all the "great qualities of his race—emotion, imagination, a passion for learning, and a worship for genius." She knew, too, that Vivekananda relied on Landsberg's "knowledge of Europe, its philosophies, its languages, its culture."[14] When, for example, he needed a translation of the work of Paul Deussen, the great German Indologist, Landsberg provided it.

Christine was also aware that Landsberg had helped Vivekananda create his teaching center. Even though the Waldorf Astoria was at the end of the street, the neighborhood was not grand, and their more respectable friends feared it would frighten away potential devotees. But the audience happily "sat on chairs . . . on tables, on washstands, on the stairs." According to Landsberg, even the "millionaires were glad to sit on the floor, literally at [Vivekananda's] feet."[15] The two men ate "rice and lentils or barley" but were happy, especially Vivekananda, who felt that he was "more a Sannyasin now than he ever was in America."[16] By the end of April, Vivekananda had an audience of 130 for his Jnana yoga class, and announced to Sara Bull that he now planned to "manufacture a few 'Yogis'" in Thousand Island, where he would be spared Green Acre's "curiosity-seekers."[17] Landsberg was delighted.[18]

Sarah Waldo, another distant relative of Emerson, was also there and summarized the swami's lessons in what would become *Inspired Talks*. She had a gift for articulate compression—indeed, these talks, so important to interested novices, were perhaps as much her creation as Vivekananda's.

Respectable and reserved, she was devoted to the swami. Finally, there was also a benign physician and a younger man (among others), but these men did not later become important disciples, so far as we know.

Christine described his impact on individual hearers. She believed Dutcher once left the group for a few days because she was upset by Vivekananda's dismissal of notions of "duty." We do not know whether Christine's impression was correct (Dutcher left no memoir), but he wrote in *Karma Yoga* (1896), "this idea of duty is the midday summer sun which scorches the innermost soul of mankind. Look at those poor slaves to duty! Duty leaves them no time to say prayers, no time to bathe. Duty is ever on them. They go out and work. Duty is on them! They come home and think of the work for the next day. Duty is on them! It is living a slave's life, at last dropping down in the street and dying in harness, like a horse."[19]

Vivekananda wanted instead to unfetter the soul, a search for freedom that appealed to the worn-out Christine.[20] Although he criticized Christian notions of duty, he was more reticent about talking about dharma, its Indian parallel (though not equivalent).[21] Commentators also often translated the word "dharma" (from the Sanskrit root *dhṛ*—"to hold") as both "nature" and "law," which set the order of beings and substances.[22] In South Asian languages, it is also a conventional translation of "religion," which is used to gather information for government censuses. But "dharma," in essence "right living," was much more, and involved manifold prescriptions about how husbands, wives, ascetics, and even courtesans should behave, and insisted on a complex of interlocking obligations to do with caste, embracing them all in a web of ethical and spiritual significance.[23] It was, and remains, central to Indian society and culture.

As will be seen, when Vivekananda discussed the moral imperatives of Karma yoga, he tended to set aside these rules and obligations, since they did not apply in the West, concentrating instead on the Bhagavad Gita and the highest flights of Hindu ethical theory. He celebrated disinterestedness and the bravery that detachment made possible, a "higher duty," very far from the joyless fulfillment of "duty" that he associated with Christian obligation.[24] He pressed his acolytes to dismiss fears of punishment and find instead a new self-possession that would emerge with "detachment."

At Thousand Island, Christine believed she first glimpsed how to escape "duty": spiritual transformation, she wrote, "is not difficult if one's devotion to the *guru* was great enough, for then, like the snake, one dropped the old and put on the new."[25] She also realized that her love for her guru was paradoxical, for such feeling required a kind of submission. Christine, like those who balked at William James's formulation of the "Mother Sea of Consciousness," feared the loss of agency and individuality. Once again, Vivekananda's teaching of Advaita brought them back to discomfiting contradictions inherent in the merging of self and nonself. He knew the paradox well and spoke often about the dangers of "personal love" blocking spiritual transformation. In one lesson at Thousand Island, he explained that "The real Guru . . . is the channel through which the spiritual current flows to us. . . . Too much faith in personality has a tendency to produce weakness and idolatry, but intense love for the Guru makes rapid growth possible, he connects us with the internal Guru. Adore your Guru if there be real truth in him; that Guru-bhakti [devotion to the teacher] will quickly lead you to the highest."[26]

He argued elsewhere that "the one thing necessary is to be stripped of our vanities . . . and to surrender ourselves completely to the guidance of our Guru."[27] The problem was, of course, how to judge whether "real truth" existed in the teacher.

He sought to convey the mystery of Advaitic opposites—the intimate relationship between surrender and self-sovereignty that he had himself experienced with Ramakrishna. And yet, he understood the need to create different Vedantic contexts by judging what different cultures would absorb or reject. One of his Indian acquaintances from the past, A. Srinivas Pai, explained: "He spoke of . . . Shri Ramakrishna's apparently mad actions undertaken with a view to killing the 'self' in him, the significance of which many—especially in Europe and America—could not understand. With reference to ordinary American audiences he said, 'If I had spoken of these acts to them, they would have thrown me and my *guru* into the nearest ditch.'"[28]

Instead, Vivekananda offered them everything he thought feasible—a strategy that some in India would later condemn. If "friends" were left their opinions, conventionalities, and above all, privacy, this was not so for disciples: "He deliberately attacked foibles, prejudices, valuations—in fact everything that went to make up the personal self."[29] He destroyed naïveté and enthusiasms, forcing the disciple to understand that "[b]oth good and evil are in 'maya,'" and that freedom comes with liberation from both: "Worship the terrible even as now you worship the good. Then get beyond both"—

this was his essential teaching.[30] Of all his Western disciples, Margaret Noble, more than any other, would imbibe this teaching most painfully. For the disciples at Thousand Island, brought up to believe that God and the Devil were separate, and God the more powerful, such a metaphysical shift was nigh impossible.

Vivekananda tried to make them experience the paradox during day-to-day lessons. Christine recounted how he "hammered" some disciples with the "the severest asceticism . . . with regard to diet, habits, even clothing and conversation"; with others, who were intent on self-denial, and in whom "good had become a bondage," he advocated greater expansiveness.[31] In all cases, he sought to uncover "weaknesses which might have been hidden for a lifetime in ordinary intercourse."[32] Like Ramakrishna, he concentrated on each person individually.

Furthermore, they were meant to live "without servants, each doing a share of the work." Christine was used to such tasks, and at first found "the result . . . amusing," until it "threatened to become 'disastrous'" because "[n]early all of them were unaccustomed to housework and found it un-congenial."[33] For these genteel folk, spirituality and manual labor did not mix well, and their decision to hire a servant suggests that they did not delve into the moral and social contradictions of their incapacity. Christine even acknowledged that they might be repeating history: "Some of us who had been reading the story of Brook Farm felt that we saw it reenacted before our eyes. No wonder Emerson refused to join that community of transcenden-talists."[34] Brook Farm, a utopian community of the 1840s, ultimately found-ered because nonlaboring families found agricultural toil not to their taste. Vivekananda, born and bred in a household with servants, may well have ac-cepted these inequalities more easily than Americans nurtured on demo-cratic and utopian ideals. Willing, even eager, to cook, he was in this regard different from both the men and the many women who were his disciples. However, he did not like to do the dishes afterward, and this would later cause tensions.

If the trials of domesticity strained them, Vivekananda's questioning of everything they believed was more onerous still, especially when he of-fended their notions of decorum, important to a group that was "conven-tional and proper to the point of prudishness." Christine explained that "in the days when men did not smoke before ladies," he "would approach, and blow the cigarette smoke deliberately into one's face."[35] One can only wonder how Vivekananda felt; in India, such a contemptuous gesture toward a high-caste woman, let alone an imperious British memsahib, would have been even more unthinkable than it was in the United States. Such transgressions may have added an extra frisson by turning colonialism on its head. He revealed an insouciance, even a superciliousness that the British regularly showed toward Indians. Did he seek to convey a spiritual lesson that was meant to revolt them? Whatever lay behind the deed, it shows that he was adjusting himself—and his teaching—to new conditions.

If Christine found the smoke disconcerting, he also attacked Western notions of chivalry. Until Thousand Island, she believed that "[a]ll fine men reverence womanhood, the higher the type, the greater the reverence." But Vivekananda instead insisted that they "climb up and slide down the rocks without an extended arm to help." He explained that he would have assisted them had they been old or infirm, but to do so for the sake of "chivalry" was to bow to "sex," a code of helplessness that men imposed on women. Rather than attracting men through "lady-like behaviour," he urged them to be robust. He had seen their strength in operation, and he hoped that by ridding the world of chivalry, he would make them believe in their power. Christine concluded, "Strange as it may seem, with these words came a new idea of what true reverence for womanhood means."[36]

He also began to mention Kali and worshipped God as Mother; and he dared to initiate women into sannyasa in America, for he saw in them only the "sexless Self." In this regard, he was following in the footsteps of Ramakrishna, but recruited women in a way his guru would have found unimaginable. When Christine arrived in India, she would learn more of his reverence for women, especially for Sarada Devi.[37] She never doubted the notions of female purity that the devotion to Sarada reinforced, ideas that Margaret Noble would question once Vivekananda died.[38] And yet Christine, Margaret Noble, Sara Bull, and others were all enraptured by the idea of the Divine Feminine, a vision of God so different from the patriarchal God of their childhood.

Vivekananda continually insisted that they stand on their own two feet. Here again was the paradox: how could they know their own views if he was always criticizing and directing? And yet again, Christine realized that he had a mode of questioning, a "Yes?" that urged the devotee to go off and think again. Only at the third time might he "point out the error" and suggest that "our Western mode of Thought" had narrowed their vision.[39] He let his devotees choose, saying simply, "It is not for you."[40] In this way, there was no dogma, only the trust that underlay the bond between guru and disciple, which permitted the mutual exploration of spiritual possibilities.

That trust, however, was not easily achieved. One time, he asked them whether they would jump out of the window for him, explaining that he needed "that quality for his work" to succeed. He told the story of Guru Nanak, the fifteenth-century founder of Sikhism. Guru Nanak asked who was willing to pass the "supreme test...who would trust him even unto death." As recounted by Christine, "One came forward. He took him into his tent and in a few minutes the great leader came out, his sword dripping with blood. Again he put their faith in him to the test, and again one went into the tent with him and did not come out again. This was repeated until five had gone into the tent not to return. Then he threw open the tent-flap, and they saw their companions unharmed in the tent, and with them a goat which the Guru had killed. Is it to be wondered at that with disciples whose devotion was unto death it was possible for Guru Nanak to accomplish the great work he did?"[41]

It is not clear why Vivekananda repeated this tale. He recognized, perhaps, its powerful unconscious associations for his disciples with the deepest sacrificial mysteries of the Old Testament, when Jehovah asked Abraham to kill his beloved Isaac. In any case, it provided another fierce example of the devotion and sacrifice the connection demanded.

At Thousand Island, Vivekananda sought to show that he was worthy of such loyalty; those, such as Waldo, who accepted this bond wrote that the "tie [to the guru] was so important" that it outranked "that of parent and child, or even husband and wife.'[42] To her, he was a "spiritual father," but to others he was a "mother in patience and gentleness."[43] For all the criticism and sternness, Christine believed that he tried to make people "feel great." Although he sought to correct "faults and weaknesses," he sought the "Divine Self in others. Little faults can drop away, but *That* remains and shines forth." He valued strength: "the greatest sin is to think yourself weak," and so he favored manliness in men and the equivalent in women, even though he could not find a word to describe this quality.[44] He seemed to know better than they did what they needed: "each has an individual path which is known to the guru."[45] Mary Funke remembered his saying, "'The *guru* is like a crystal. He reflects perfectly the consciousness of all who come to him. He thus understands how and in what way to help.' He means by this that a *guru* must be able to see what each person needs and he must meet them on their own plane of consciousness."[46]

He took the analogy even further, when he gave them each a small crystal ball (perhaps suggesting the far-seeing qualities he associated with yogis), inscribed with their names. Their praise revealed their regard for him: he was "like a loving mother, warn[ing] him of dangers, explain[ing] experiences that otherwise might alarm or dismay." He was the "Guardian of the Threshold," the door into new spiritual climes, the one who gives the mantra, the spiritual word or phrase that quiets the mind and body.[47] The guru had to be endlessly strong, and (in a phrase easily understandable to Christians) had to "take on the sins and tribulations of their disciples and let the disciples go on their way rejoicing and free."[48]

If Vivekananda played down Ramakrishna's mystical trances and tantric devotions, he was not above referring to his powers to impress them. Once in a while, Christine claimed he fulfilled their expectations: "[H]e added rather shyly, 'I have a power which I seldom use—the power of reading the mind. If you will permit me, I should like to read your mind, as I wish to initiate you with the others tomorrow.' We assented joyfully. Evidently he was satisfied with the result of the reading, for the next day, together with several others, he gave us a *mantra* and made us his disciples."[49]

He told them they would make spiritual progress and said that one among them—presumably, Christine—would be connected to India. Even minor events were foretold, "all of which have come to pass."[50] There were dreams too, and he talked about Kanheri, outside Bombay, where 109 caves hewn out of rock had once been the cells of Buddhist monks. He had visited their massive assembly and devotion halls and believed that he had once lived there in a previous life. When he spoke in this way, Christine felt his spell; certainly, these stories confirmed an expectation of the exotic—and what Christian doubters would have called the "enticements" of Vivekananda's spirituality and personality.

At Thousand Island, initiation occurred in a way that his Indian guru-brothers would hardly have recognized. Whereas in Antpur, they had reportedly stood in the darkness around a fire on Christmas Eve; here, Vivekananda merely gathered his disciples at dawn before a "small altar fire" decorated with beautiful flowers, the "earnest words of the Teacher alone mark[ing] it as different from our daily lessons."[51] Stripped of the rich and improvised ritualism of his Bengali homeland, he provided a fitting simplicity for the Protestant American context.

◆ ◆ ◆

Along with the storytelling, sternness, attention, care, and laughter, there was more formal instruction. As they were all Christians except Landsberg, Vivekananda began with the Gospels, and during the first lesson he quoted the Book of John: "In the beginning was the Word, and the Word was with God, and the Word Was God." This typified his comparative approach in which he used Christian texts to explicate Hindu meaning. The Word had two manifestations, the Absolute and its incarnation: "The absolute cannot be known: we cannot know the Father, only the Son. We can only see the Absolute through the 'tint of humanity,' through Christ."[52] He explained that, first, "Christ as Incarnation was no different from Krishna, Buddha or Ramakrishna"; and second, that our spirituality was constrained by how these beings "assume our form and our limitations for a time in order to teach us," but who disappear, leaving us to connect with the supernatural in our own way. For Vivekananda, the "Trinitarian Christ" was elevated beyond the seeker and hence separate, whereas the Unitarian Christ was merely a "moral man," deprived of all supernatural qualities, and hence of only limited interest.

In seeking release from maya, he used Ramakrishna's metaphors, asking them to "look at the 'ocean' and not at the 'wave,'" again subsuming the individual within a greater whole: "There is only one Power, whether manifesting as evil or good. God and the devil are the same river with the water flowing in opposite directions."[53] Evil was necessary to stop homogeneity and he compared the world to a bucket, with cork particles floating in water, buoyant in their irrepressibility: "There is no possibility of ever having pleasure without pain, good without evil; for living itself is just the lost equilibrium. What we want is freedom, not life, nor pleasure, nor good."[54] Creation was not anything new, but the restoration of equilibrium—notions that radically collided with Christian ideas of a creating, omnipotent, and separate God.

By emphasizing equilibrium, he suggested that greater movement did not necessarily bring greater change, an implicit critique of American "busyness" and its spiritual desiccation. He also used the competing influences of his earlier life in Bengal as an example: "There was a great contrast between Keshab Chandra Sen and Shri Ramakrishna. The second never recognized any sin or misery in the world, no evil to fight against. The first was a great ethical reformer, leader, and founder of the Brahmo-Samaj. After twelve years the quiet prophet of Dakshineswar had worked a revolution not only in India, but in the world. . . ."[55]

Vivekananda here offered a rare insight into his own guru-Bhakti. These words suggest that he believed that Ramakrishna's path was both deeper and more expansive than Keshub Sen's. Vivekananda advocated spiritual illumination above all else, and disinterested work as one of the paths to this goal. He wanted his disciples, as he told them at Thousand Island, to "be like a lily," staying in one place and blooming, so that the bees would come without being courted. And yet, he had not always followed his own advice. While in America, he worked dizzyingly hard, and constantly feared that so much movement would bring him back to maya with its disillusionment and false demands.

As an imperial subject, moreover, he was ambivalent about reform. He knew well the self-interest and cruelty that such intervention could entail—hospitals that ripped women from their homes, and sanitary measures that destroyed villages and neighborhoods. In the "Inspired Talks," he underscored an ethical relativism that shunned the dangers of moral judgment and criticized imperialism for deploying it. At Thousand Island, he wanted his followers to accept that their vision of "uplift" could be subjugating, even coercive. He insisted that the "quiet prophet of Dakshineswar" was more effective than Sen precisely because no organization, plan, or action was required—Ramakrishna's example was enough to galvanize the world. By refusing to say a "harsh word against anyone," by engaging in what was only "beautifully tolerant, Ramakrishna made everyone believe that he belonged to them."[56]

If Vivekananda believed Ramakrishna's path was superior to that of Sen's, the tension between reformism and otherworldliness remained powerful, as did the conflict between institution building and transcendence.[57] He rejected the social conservatism of Hindu orthodoxy and its don't-touchism, but also resisted a reformism that might entail a contaminating alliance with the colonial state.[58] Later he would remark about his own Bengali compatriots: "our educated Babus want the British to hand over the government to them to manage! It makes me laugh and cry as well."[59] Hence in India he preached more activism (Karma yoga), engagement, and strength but always by "asking nothing, and not consciously doing anything."[60]

How such views resonated with his American listeners is unclear. He admired their activism, absorbed aspects of their enthusiasms, but he was always on guard against superficiality and self-righteousness. He disliked any hint that those helped were the passive recipients of Christian charity. Sarah Waldo may well have thought of Emerson, who had always worried about an overemphasis on the social and the secular, the worldly and the humanitarian, despite his stalwart abolitionism.[61] Thoreau had gone further, perhaps, by expressing an almost "transcendent disdain" for the things of this world, echoing themes of "detachment" that Vivekananda might have appreciated.[62]

Vivekananda showed similar sensibilities when he denounced denunciation, which he regarded as nothing more than ambition; he also believed that "violent attempts at reform always end by retarding reform," evincing a conservatism with a small c that implicitly expressed his horror at the cultural attack and social disruption unleashed on India.[63]

But it would be wrong to reduce his theology to politics. Repeatedly, he discoursed on love, but one detached from lust, sexuality, and "desire for reciprocity," offering a recipe for attaining that "wholeness" through the love he had encountered in Ramakrishna.[64] He spoke of *tapas* (penitence), which, like a burn, was necessary to heat the higher nature and realize the power of Shakti.[65] In his view, the mother's power was a higher idea than the father's because it accorded with a primordial "baby-knowledge," borne out of the infant's understanding that "its mother [was] all powerful" and "able to do anything."[66] Like a baby who believed in the mother's power, so a true devotee understood that "Knowledge of God is independent of moral duties." Love of mother and mother's love, he concluded, were not grounded in good deeds. Since he believed that "neither reasoning nor books can show us God," he advocated meditation so that the devotee understood that the body did not house the self.[67] This experiential theology divinized the self (or atman) as the only holy book to be deciphered, so relativizing Protestant reliance on scripture: "Control the mind, cut off the senses, then you are a Yogi; . . . Get rid of the fundamental superstition that we are obliged to act through the body . . . [G]et the Upanishads out of your own Self. You are the greatest book that ever was or ever will be, the infinite depository of all that is. Until the inner teacher opens, all outside teaching is in vain. It must lead to the opening of the book of the heart to have any value."[68]

Thus, although the Gospel of John helped to begin their instruction, he prioritized meditation. Like Christine's snake that sheds its skin, loving the guru and meditating involved growth, breaking through an old covering. This process created a neediness and desire that subjected the disciple to the emotional discipline of criticism and correction, but also constant attention and love. Such love was powerfully securing but also potentially explosive—not always did the trust endure.

JOSEPHINE MACLEOD

Margaret Noble recounted that Vivekananda had once told her, "I am never mistaken in my estimate of a woman. That power of my Guru is passing over to me and I know at a glance."[69] The remark displayed the self-regard of a man who believed himself in touch with higher powers; but it was also odd coming from someone who had spent his youth almost always around other men, had directed a bevy of male disciples and monks in Baranagar, and later became famous as the "virile" incarnation of the "warrior monk."[70] And yet, he knew women well from early familial experience, and felt he drew his knowledge of them from these early relationships. Remarkable and unusual women surrounded him, who were rare in rejecting the Christian and racial premises of imperialism as early as the 1890s. By adopting a Vedantin framework, they asked questions that few contemporaries dared even formulate. With time, Vivekananda regretted that more important Western men had not joined the movement, but he still valued the women around him.

Christine became an incomparable teacher in India; Sara Bull, a poised patroness; and Margaret Noble, a fiery radical and revolutionary, but Josephine MacLeod was none of these. She was a socialite, known for her grand airs among the poorer women who housed Vivekananda in California in 1899 and 1900, and for her designer clothes. The great pacifist and intellectual Romain Rolland later sneered at her "feminine dilettantism" because of her imperfect French and incessant talk.[71] And yet, this assessment (especially considering he was monoglot himself) entirely misjudged her capabilities.

9.4. Josephine MacLeod in older age

Like Margaret Noble—but without the revolutionary edge—Josephine created networks in Paris and Tokyo, Calcutta, and London, as well as New York and California. Like Vivekananda, she traveled almost relentlessly, and they both shared the strain of chronic constitutional weakness that depleted them.[72]

She depended on her sister, Betty Leggett, whose husband supported her. Frank was a wealthy wholesale grocer and had introduced them to Vivekananda after he met the swami in late 1895. In the days of mutual affection, Vivekananda nicknamed him "Frankincense" and went to his wedding to Betty in Paris.[73] This second marriage was a love match, and Vivekananda an important emotional and spiritual presence, visiting their upstate New York house, Ridgely Manor, on three occasions.

9.5. Ridgely Park, c. 1900

We know of Josephine's family history from her niece, Frances, who married David Margesson—later a member of Churchill's War Cabinet and a viscount.[74] Frances's access to this exalted British milieu (after all, she was the daughter of a wholesale grocer) suggests the social distance the MacLeod sisters had traveled, and how they were responsible for Vivekananda's ideas penetrating even this aristocratic citadel.[75]

Josephine's early life had been filled with loss and disruption. Her mother died when she was only twelve, and she remembered how her father prayed constantly, especially for money that was often short. The family was Calvinist, and Frank Leggett maintained that both sisters had a sense of "chosenness" that intensified when Josephine met Vivekananda. She carried herself as, and believed herself to be, part of the "elect" (although a "true" Calvinist would not have dared to present herself so), though how she translated her early Protestant formation into neo-Vedanta remains uncertain.

From one of Sara Bull's letters, we know that she read Emerson and believed that the sage of Concord prepared her for Vivekananda.[76] Josephine, however, did not refer to any specific texts—no remarks about the Over-soul, nothing about which aspects of transcendentalism struck her. Like Bull, she had met Mohini Mohun Chatterji and read his translation of the Bhagavad Gita, and so we know that their thoughts ran in similar directions before their acquaintance through Vivekananda.[77] Josephine was close to Dora Roethlesberger, a well-known psychic; and she, Dora, and Margaret Noble never abandoned their interest in psychic phenomena, despite Vivekananda's warnings.[78] Josephine knew something of Buddhism, and her biographer suggests she may have read Arnold's *The Light of Asia*.[79] At moments, she seems to have regarded both Prince Gautama and the Bengali Swami as incarnations of the "eastern Christ."[80] She and Betty had read the Gita before meeting Vivekananda, and Josephine later claimed that she had memorized it.[81] They had also investigated Christian Science under the instruction of a Miss Andrews in New York.[82] Josephine never completely abandoned it and seemed to have grafted her preoccupation with "mind" onto her interpretation of Vedanta. Similarly, she valued osteopathy as a harmonizing therapy, and was the devotee who suggested that Vivekananda try it.

She was able to travel so widely because she never married, even though this kept her dependent on her brother-in-law's generosity. She and her sister at times resembled characters from a Henry James novel—they preferred life in London, Paris, and the Riviera, ultimately leaving Leggett alone to brood in Ridgely Park about the foreign lifestyle he was financing. The two sisters left a home that felt foreign and went to foreign climes to feel at home. They also devised an unusual division of labor. Betty tried to become a European hostess, a vocation so consuming that Josephine took on the task of raising her children, Hollister and Alberta, from a first marriage, and Frances from the second. She organized their lives, packed their trunks, chose the boarding schools for the older children, and hired the nanny for the younger, who often accompanied them. A family where the mother had died provided a "sister-companion," named Florence, for Frances.[83] Florence's father was apparently amenable to this arrangement and, after seven years, his daughter returned to him.[84]

The MacLeod sisters thus mixed their past economic insecurity with spiritual certainty and blended it with a certain moneyed self-regard. And, for all their assorted weaknesses and strengths, Vedanta would never have emerged in the way it did without them. Josephine was not personally rich (and saved madly, so that she could donate funds), but she traveled in high social and intellectual circles. This perhaps was why she seemed more friend than disciple, although the distinction in her case was exaggerated. She never sought to become a *brahmacharini* (a celibate female novice) like Margaret

Noble, but she did vow herself to celibacy, while appreciating how she differed from her friend: "I *haven't any* Renunciation, but I've freedom. Freedom to see and help India to grow—that's my job and how I love it."[85] Despite economic dependence, she felt free, and believed that a formal vocation would have inhibited her "real" self. She admired "fiery idealists" like Noble but felt she could best help from the sidelines.[86] Even she experienced the lash of Vivekananda's tongue like other disciples, but he never sought to mold her. He said that she had come to him "fully developed."[87]

At times, Vivekananda would call her his "good luck" or his "good star." One day, he wrote that "there cannot be any work in London because you are not here."[88] The remark suggests her ability to put people together and capacity to stand back and watch the connections spark. Although at times brisk, mostly Josephine was esteemed for her tact. Vivekananda admired the "strength in that little body," and her "power to suffer."[89] Although his own body was hardly "little," he may have identified with her "power of suffering," since he, too, experienced unrelenting pain for years.

Sara Bull was a mother figure, organizer, and financier of many of his projects: in jocular moments, Vivekananda called her his "sacred cow." She was loved as a "mother," and laid claim to the authority of one when trying to impose the "right kind of people" on him. In contrast, Josephine was a facilitator, using her social skills and networks to widen his circle. Patrick Geddes and Romain Rolland came into Vivekananda's circle through her.[90] When she went to Japan, she connected Vivekananda with the art historian and cultural critic Okakura Kakuzo. Vivekananda was too ill to travel to Japan, so the Japanese went to India, where he collaborated with Margaret Noble. Josephine enticed Vivekananda to go and investigate the spiritual possibilities in what she whimsically dubbed "Kali-fornia."[91] Vivekananda, intrigued by theater since his youth, was happy to meet actress Sarah Bernhardt and soprano Emma Calvé.[92] First a connection of Sara's, Calvé became a lifelong friend, traveling through south-central and southern Europe as well as Egypt in 1900 with Josephine and Vivekananda.[93]

Josephine also buoyed up Vivekananda when he was discouraged, ran out of clean clothes, or needed a cook to host a dinner party in India.[94] And, she found a magnetic healer, Mrs. Melton, who removed a corroded needle plaguing her sister's leg and who unsuccessfully treated Vivekananda.[95]

Despite Josephine's independence, her love for Vivekananda was as passionate as any of his followers'. Because of him, she believed that she was "utterly secure in [her] grasp on the ultimate": "It is the Truth I saw in Swamiji that has set me free!"[96] It is hard not to caricature her as the skinny spinster aunt, the semi-invalid, or the itinerant *salonnière*. But she was more than these stereotypes allow—raising her sister's children, and traveling the world, often when ill, both for her own pleasure, but above all, to spread Vivekananda's teachings. As the "spinster aunt," she was the most dependent, but strangely she was also the most autonomous of Vivekananda's "disciples."

Ramakrishna and Vivekananda were groundbreaking gurus. The former resisted the formal initiation of disciples, while having the inspirational qualities traditionally associated with the role. For Ramakrishna, and for Vivekananda after him, familiar forms of address suggested that hierarchies were erased, but no doubt remained about their spiritual authority. Both men encouraged "play"—as much as instruction—within their entourage. Josephine was not a disciple, as she was never formally "dedicated," but her relationship to Vivekananda suggests the innovative gray zone that they together created.

FASCINATION AND RAPPORT

Despite his doubts about American men, Vivekananda craved male disciples, but he found himself relying on Western women. They were often fascinated by him. When he touched trees, for example, he explained that sometimes he had an "intuition of [their] conversation"; he told how Ramakrishna would return in two hundred years' time with "his own people."[97] With others, such as artist Maud Stumm, he would simply "fascinate" with his honesty and daring. She remembered one evening after dinner, some matrons with their daughters were momentarily shocked when he spoke about "the space that makes attraction felt" between men and women.[98] Nothing was off-limits, and yet his talk left them feeling uplifted rather than tainted.

Occasionally a healing rapport derived from this fascination. Mrs. Hansbrough, a Californian disciple, recalled how he left behind his pipe on the mantelpiece before he left Pasadena in 1900. Her sister, Carrie Wyckoff, had been ill with an unspecified but painful nervous ailment when she heard his voice, "'Is it so hard, Madam?' For some reason she rubbed the pipe across her forehead; the suffering left, and a feeling of well-being came over her."[99]

Although not a Catholic, she treated the pipe like a relic and apparently kept it forever. Josephine MacLeod regarded his gifts as sacred objects and was glad to have Vivekananda's ring, which he gave to her on impulse.[100]

She also had her own "reliquary" (the word both she and Margaret Noble used) that she wore around her neck after 1904. She had been given a large sapphire by a wealthy Indian as token of her love of the country, and some years later, René Lalique, the French jeweler, made her the ornament to celebrate her love of France. Famous, as Margaret Noble expressed it, for his ability to "think in symbols," Lalique created a "cosmic heart, containing two angels of pale blue glass with wings of ivory, kneeling on a cloud of crystal on either side of a gleaming sapphire which they held in their hands."[101] Behind the jewel, a locket contained strands of Vivekananda's hair. Both Carrie and Josephine, therefore, wanted to possess something that had either touched Vivekananda's body or been a part of him.

The women often felt that the personal and the impersonal could not be easily separated. In India devotion was typified by darshan, and the devotion to Vivekananda among these women suggests a "darshanic" element when they spoke of his beauty.[102] In India, so much of what had passed between Ramakrishna and Vivekananda had focused on the young man's voice, on music's capacity for nonverbal communion. But in the West, there was no *tanpura* (Indian drum), no conch shells or bells, none of the familiar tones and harmonies that had electrified devotions during the evening arati at Dakshineswar. In contrast, Vivekananda largely refrained from singing in the West, even though his speaking voice was, as mentioned, a topic of conversation.[103] We know he chanted at Green Acre, sometimes before his lectures in London's drawing rooms, but mostly he kept this side to himself. On rare occasions, however, associates might overhear him. Mrs. Roxie Blodgett remembered how "he would come in for his morning plunge in the bath. Soon his deep, rich voice would be heard in the something resembling a solemn chant [sic]. Though Sanskrit [was] an unknown tongue to me, I yet caught the spirit of it all, and these early morning devotions are among my sweetest recollections of the great Hindu."[104]

If, as Christine's testimony suggests, the gallant niceties of the late-Victorian era were abandoned, Vivekananda realized the need for physical distance and sought to reorient guru-Bhakti for his female disciples. If today Indian gurus who travel to America are seen as potentially preying upon their female devotees, Mrs. Lyon, a grandmother of an acquaintance, feared the seduction would come from the other direction: "Swamiji was such a dynamic and attractive personality that many women were quite swept away and made every effort by flattery to gain his interest."[105]

But he did not abandon touch entirely. Margaret Noble recounted how in November 1900, after a moment of despair, when weakened by chronic illness and disappointed by his progress in America, Vivekananda called her to him and exploded, begging her to go out into the world to "fight for him." After he had calmed down, he invited both Noble and Mrs. Bull into his presence, took "two pieces of cotton clothing of *gerua* [ocher] colour" and, shutting the door, "he arranged the cloth as a skirt and *chudder* [shawl] round [Mrs. Bull's] waist—then he called her a *Sannyasini* and putting one hand on her head and one on mine he said, 'I give you all that Ramakrishna P. gave to me. What came to us from a Woman I give to you two women. Do what you can with it. . . . Women's hands will be the best anyway to hold what came from a Woman—from Mother.'"[106]

Repeatedly, Vivekananda, who urged meat eating, muscularity, and activism among his male followers in India, underscored the centrality of feminine power with these women; they responded to a vision that offered them both spiritual and personal strength. He showed the importance of such rituals of transmission at the very end of his life with Margaret Noble. This time, however, he borrowed from Christianity. As Josephine MacLeod recounted: "Sister Nivedita always ate with her fingers, a la Hindu [*sic*]; and after she had eaten, Swami poured water over her hands. She said, very much the disciple, 'I cannot bear you to do this.' He answered, 'Jesus Christ washed the feet of his disciples,' Sister Nivedita had it on the tip of her tongue to say, 'But that was the last time they ever met.' It was the last time she ever saw him."[107]

Noble was often discomfited by the intensity of the connection and struggled both to contain and to explain it: "I think perhaps the whole of one's nature comes out in that relationship—the bad as well as the good—and no one else matters very much. Probably this is always so with the Guru . . . I am willing to admit after all that one's love for Swami is sadly 'personal'—if you will let me claim that it is at the same time in some ways the most *impersonal* thing of which one is anyway capable."[108]

She recognized that the love for the "real" human being opened the disciple to self-knowledge as well as the possibility of something greater. She realized, too, that the heart of the process was relational, a spirituality of rapport linked to Indian notions of bhakti, but also, for her, inseparable at times from "personal" love.

Such relationships were challenging for both sides. Once, in a disarming and revealing letter to Noble, Vivekananda wrote: "I see persons giving me almost the whole of their love," and he understood that he could not give the "whole of [his] in return" lest he induce "jealousy and quarrels." He admitted, therefore, that the guru-disciple relationship was not equal, but also acknowledged the need to guard against becoming instrumental: "I do not mean that one should be a brute, making use of the devotion of others for his own ends, and laughing in his sleeve meanwhile." He knew that he had to open himself up to being hurt, as he was "intensely personal in [his] love" but also needed to "pluck out" such feelings, lest they take him into the "bondage" of attachment.[109] As will be seen, he *was* hurt when English disciples later abandoned him.

❖　❖　❖

Comparing the guru-disciple relationship to psychoanalytic transference and countertransference might help us understand these intense relationships. The similarities and differences are hard to avoid because these "therapies" emerged almost simultaneously in the West—*Raja Yoga* appeared in 1896; and Freud's *Studies on Hysteria* in 1895. Although Vivekananda, William James, and Freud held differing views of religion and mystical experience, they all worked within a global context that emphasized a shifting view of the self that was based on their investigations of rapport and its relationship to new sciences of mind. Freud encountered "transference" when he observed hypnosis in Jean-Martin Charcot's Parisian clinic and in Nancy, where Hippolyte Bernheim treated all kinds of ailments with hypnotherapy.[110] Freud thus experienced "mind-cure" without the Christian underlay that typified the search for rapport that Quimby and Eddy had identified. In contrast to the Americans, Charcot was virulently anticlerical; and Bernheim was of Jewish origin. Both sought to establish hypnosis in a secular arena, Charcot especially seeking to dissociate it from religious experience.

Freud was fascinated by the way subjects surrendered their will during suggestive therapy. But he was a poor hypnotist, unable to achieve the dramatic results of his French contemporaries. Unconvinced by the technique, he proceeded to develop therapeutic methods without hypnosis.[111] He surrounded the client with constraints and boundaries when developing the "talking cure," which entailed the subject's "contracting the disease of love."[112] He treated bourgeois, largely Jewish, paying clients—women very different from the impoverished patients of Charcot's public hospitals or the well-heeled Christian spiritual seekers who flocked to Vivekananda. Freud, like Charcot, wanted to avoid the "illusion" that was religion.[113] Tellingly, he also feared too much "sight," and so the analyst hid away, so that the subject could concentrate on her own thoughts and fantasies, with the analyst's voice invisible behind a supine patient. In psychoanalysis, the visual was dangerous, as practitioners might reveal boredom, affection, annoyance, and disgust, thereby distracting the client from her own feelings and imaginings.

Thus, the analytical hour was to be only about the client, the transaction sealed by payment. Despite these conditions, Freud understood, and indeed hoped, that the client's sovereignty was only partially maintained by the "contract"; he emphasized the process of confiding, explaining, free-associating, and fantasizing, which would catalyze a "transference" that forced regressions which might prove therapeutic when analyzed.[114] Another part of the contract was not to promise too much—Freudian psychoanalysis did not offer miracles, but only an "ordinary unhappiness."

In contrast, Vivekananda refused all payment—hence, there was none of the contractual arrangements of Freud's consultations—and thus resisted "liberal" notions of the transacting "self." He also did not try to minimize the process's impact by denying visual access to the devotee. Instead, he encouraged an exchange that was friendly, permitting the disciples to comfort him with the gaiety of their personalities and solicitude—something which Freud would have rejected. Having experienced himself the heady spiritual passion of guru-bhakti and observed it among his brother-monks, Vivekananda revered the emotional journey that spiritual experience entailed and applauded its transformative power. Had he thought about it, he might have said that Freud's transference, like Darwin's evolutionary theory, was a pale reflection of Hindu wisdom, which had long developed a protected place for emotional release and psychological creativity. Rather than regulated, professional treatment, the relationship "worked" because the guru became more than family. As Waldo put it: "Every one of the students there, received initiation, the Swami assuming towards them the position of *guru*, or spiritual father, as is done in India, where the tie uniting *guru* and disciple is the closest one known, outranking that of parent and child, or even husband and wife."[115]

If, like Freud, Vivekananda had no faith in "miraculous display," he wanted more than "ordinary unhappiness." He sought the bliss of detachment and engagement without erotic desire for any return. His remained a metaphysical quest for union with the divine, while Freud's atheism dismissed such hopes as illusion. There was no parallel between Freud's view of the "dynamic unconscious" and Vivekananda's vision of "superconsciousness," grasped through Advaita and the techniques of yoga. The former sought to excavate the unconscious layers, whereas the latter hoped to soar above consciousness in the search for unity.[116] But despite the many and important differences, both connections were based on rapport, with a similar scope for disharmony, misunderstanding, cultural confusion, and disappointment. Vivekananda and his disciples experienced the delights of transformation but also, as will be seen, the lows of loss and incomprehension.

10

THE PAINS AND PLEASURES
OF LOVE IN AMERICA

We are never so defenseless against suffering as when we love.
—Sigmund Freud, *Civilization and Its Discontents* (1930)

⋄ ◆ ⋄

VIVEKANANDA'S EARLIEST FOLLOWERS were entranced by a guru who offered both the innocent love of a baby and the affectionate attention of a parent. But they also had to contend with parental disapproval and scolding. They strained to understand how such chastisement could be a sign of his affection and care, but they accepted his spiritual authority and readily attended him—in this regard, the gender roles of women in India and in the United States shared much.

Vivekananda and his prospective male disciples abroad, however, lacked any agreed notions of male intimacy. If Western conventions for male friendship often expressly veiled emotion, in India the opposite was the case, where male connection may be as close as that often ascribed to female "best friends." Male friends in India walk arm in arm and hold hands, public contact unthinkable in late nineteenth-century Protestant America. Not yet householders, they share their belongings and negate caste and other forms of hierarchy in their intimacy.[1]

In Vivekananda's monkish milieu, Ramakrishna's disciples furthered these bonds through dancing, singing, and even wrestling, with such physical play regarded as following in Krishna's footsteps.[2] Once they became sannyasins, novices often served older monks and furthered the spiritual trials of their brothers. Indian male householders, too, befriended the monks, and often supported their communities.[3] None of these traditions existed for Vivekananda's male associates in the United States, who sometimes worried that he might lead "their women" astray or create a cult.

THE GURU AS BABY-MOTHER

When Vivekananda explained the dangers of personal love to Margaret Noble in October 1897, he suggested that the "the best leader . . . is one who 'leads like the baby.'" The baby, he said, is "the king of the household. At least to my thinking, that is the secret. . . ."[4] The sentiment owed much to Ramakrishna; the baby's gift is to be the neediest, the most precious, the most fragile. A baby's unworldliness was its greatest spiritual offering, as Ramakrishna's mischievous and demanding baby Krishna revealed when Gopaler Ma fondled and tended him.

In his work on the "wisdom path" (*Jnana Yoga*, 1899), Vivekananda explained that when a baby witnesses a thief taking a "bag of gold on the table," it remains blissfully unconcerned because "the baby has no thief inside and sees no thief outside."[5] This innocence, he insisted, was the real "individuality" that "will never change; and that is the God within us."[6] When describing the actress Stella Campbell at Thousand Island as "Baby," and referring to the Hale sisters as "the Babies," he thus celebrated their artlessness.

The child psychoanalyst Donald Winnicott elaborated on why the baby was the "king of the household" and suggested that mothers adapted to the physical and emotional needs of the infant, engaging in a loving struggle to foster its development.[7] He maintained that their attentions and sacrifices were crucial to providing the foundations of love and the "object relations" that shape human connection. Winnicott would not have used Vivekananda's spiritualizing and essentializing terminology, but understood what Vivekananda sought to convey in 1895: "In women, the mother-nature is much developed. They worship God as the child. They ask nothing and will do anything."[8]

What Winnicott theorized, Vivekananda practiced by periodically emulating his guru and becoming the "baby" who was incapable of giving anything more than his unpredictable and helpless presence; baby worshippers were, for Vivekananda, "true bhaktas" because there was no "place for begging or bargaining." If the guru could be a baby, God also manifested babylike qualities, as the example of baby Krishna showed; asking anything in return was pointless, even sacrilegious.[9] Roxie Blodgett, who tended Vivekananda in Southern California, noted how "the child side of Swamiji's character . . . was a constant appeal to the Mother quality in all good women."[10]

Baby worship—the baby Jesus and baby Krishna—was thus an important bridge between Christians and Hindus.[11] Vivekananda explained that in India, women saw themselves as Krishna's mother and he knew that Christian women adored the Christ Child and often identified with the Virgin, even if this feeling was more explicit in Catholicism than in Protestantism.[12] Images of the Infant Jesus abound in Catholicism, from Jesus's birth through the ubiquitous paintings of the Madonna and Child, to the many depictions of Christ's prodigious youth in the Infancy Gospels of the Apocrypha. Calvinists in theory abhorred such images and stories, and also downplayed the Virgin, but Protestants still celebrated the Nativity.[13] The worship of domesticity, and above all, children were central to American and British Protestantism, and girls were encouraged to "baby" their dolls. If anything, Victorian toy culture reinforced the gender divide, with girls playing doll games, and boys at toy soldiers.[14]

Many female devotees "babied" Vivekananda. Sara Ellen Waldo traveled for hours in a jogging horsecar to care for him and was pleased when he cooked for her; he said he "found genuine rest and relaxation in the freedom and quiet of Miss Waldo's simple home." There he "invented new dishes or tried experiments with Western provisions and ran back and forth from one room to the other like a child at play."[15] Josephine MacLeod loved the combination of holiness and childlike absorption when, after a talk on Jesus, he "seemed to radiate a white light from head to foot." On the way home, she did not want to interrupt his "great thoughts," but was delighted to learn that, despite the halo "over his head," he was in fact pondering "the best way to complete a recipe for mulligatawny soup."[16] They admired his "learning of a university president" or "dignity of an archbishop," but loved the "child side" when the "prophet and sage would disappear."[17] Maud Stumm, who gave Vivekananda drawing lessons, loved to watch him "lying at full length on the green couch in the hall, sound asleep like a tired child."

Sometimes, he would get up after a meal to smoke or think, but be lured back to the table by ice cream: "he would sink into his place with a smile of expectancy and pure delight seldom seen on the face of anybody over sixteen."[18]

Mrs. Blodgett, a Californian disciple, happily gave over the top floor of her little house to him. While he cooked for them sometimes (they remembered his sitting on the floor, grinding spices), she in turn lived to feed him. She "seldom went to hear him lecture, saying her duty was to give [him] delicious meals."[19] At her home, the swami walked around in an untidy dressing gown, relaxed in the garden, joked, and conversed during long breakfasts. The photographs of California suggest the pleasures of picnics, lectures, meals in Chinatown, and retreats in the Sierra Madre.

The child emerged also in Vivekananda's humor, sometimes gently targeting imperialism and racism. For example, he said he loved chocolate ice cream, because he "too was chocolate." But he also inverted the jest when he told the story of the "missionary to the cannibal islands" who asked what his predecessor had been like and was told he had been delicious. He mocked singing in Congregational churches as a "bottle-breaking business" and sang the "Missionary Hymn": "In vain with lavish kindness / The gifts of God are strown / The heathen in their blindness / Bow down to wood and stone"— adding at the end that "I am the heathen they came to save."[20] He told the jokes with his usual boyish charm, but they also had a definite edge.

He also targeted Americans' lack of spiritual depth; when a woman asked whether he was a Buddhist, pronouncing the word like "bud," he answered, "wickedly but with a grave face. 'No Madam, I am a florist.'"[21] He recounted how a man and wife who lived next door to his New York apartment made their living as spiritualists. When they argued, the wife consulted Vivekananda: "'Is it fair for him to treat me like this,' she asked, 'when I make all the ghosts?'"[22] To them, his spirituality was both irreverent and profound, and they never forgot how he made them giggle. His humor therefore allowed him to transgress social rules, to laugh at ignorance, and to force his listeners to question their preconceptions. Above all, it cleared an easy path to friendship.

His intermittently childlike relationship to these "mothers'" was very different than Ramakrishna's displays with Gopaler Ma, for example. Revealing childlike pleasure in drawing, cooking, and eating ice cream suggests how easily Vivekananda became a "baby" in a way in which his Western companions would approve; almost certainly, he also retrieved aspects of his

10.1. Vivekananda in Pasadena, California

own very middle-class and urban Bengali childhood. As will be seen, how-ever, when he returned to India in 1897, and went on pilgrimage with female Western associates, his "childlike" mysticism centered on a kind of Kali devotion that could be as disconcerting and overpowering (to them) as was that of Vivekananda's guru.[23]

THE "SICK BABY"

The maternal effect was reinforced by recurring illness, an unending reality that necessarily affected his relationships. When he arrived in

California, Josephine MacLeod put him under the care of Mrs. Melton, the magnetic healer, and wrote optimistically that Vivekananda was "quiet like a child—goes daily to Mrs. Melton, walks 2 or 3 miles, scarcely talks a word."[24] The treatments involved some kind of friction of the skin that raised "red patches" on Vivekananda's chest.[25] Mrs. Melton was famous for her results, and Josephine was so persuaded by her prowess, she advised the magnetizer to travel east and to enlarge her practice in Europe, where she treated an elite clientele in Paris during the 1900 Exposition Universelle.[26] Vivekananda was less convinced but recognized Josephine's need to try and help him. Sometimes he hoped that such treatments might work, as when he asked Christine, should he not be able to go to Kellogg's Sanitarium, whether she might nevertheless bring the special food to him.[27] He also asked Sara Bull to send his terra-cotta cashmere coat should a trip to frigid Detroit be necessary.[28]

His habitual stoicism, especially when it was mixed with philosophy, worried them. He wrote to Margaret Noble from New York in 1899, "On the whole I don't think there is any cause for anxiety about my body. This sort of nervous body is just the instrument to play great music at times [and] at times to moan in darkness."[29] He sought to gain strength from illness and wrote again in February 1900 from Los Angeles: "Well—but I am strong now, Margo, stronger than ever I was mentally. I was mentally getting a sort of ironing over my heart."[30] To Mary Hale, he wrote in March 1899 that he was on a "merry-go-round" with his body which, contrary to his search for detachment, kept on trying to "convince him for months that it too much exists."[31] Other times, he acknowledged the horrible dyspepsia and flatulence, the diagnosis of Bright's disease (acute or chronic nephritis). Once, from India in June 1901, he reported to Josephine that he had to retire to a sanitarium in Shillong because of "fever, asthma, increase in albumen"; his "body [had] swelled to almost twice its normal size."[32] Later, diabetes impaired his eyesight.[33] Because healing was such a concern of his milieu, his own ill health constantly tormented his female devotees.

When Vivekananda called a woman "baby," he recognized the intimacy of bhakti, even if it was a form of address that he never used with Western men. No doubt, too, such exchanges defused sexual tension, and made possible the inversion of the maternal-child bonds within his entourage. Above all, the jokes and lack of constraint expressed a joie de vivre that was entirely his own, which meant it was much harder to "orientalize" him. Deploying humor with Western references so deftly was a rare ability allowing him to live in a foreign culture without losing his sense of self. Through these connections, he may have even created a persona that fleetingly defied the stereotypes of both cultures and societies that could not help but affect their interactions.

THE SCOLDING MOTHER

Ramakrishna once called Vivekananda a "blackguard" for traducing Kali as a false goddess, and even told him never to return. Vivekananda merely filled the hubble-bubble with tobacco for his guru, who said: "Do you know that if a person who is intimate is rebuked, he does not protest?"[34] On another occasion, Vivekananda chastised Swami Premananda so severely that the latter went and hid on the roof. While in America, he scolded Alasinga Perumal by letter for his connections to the theosophists.[35] Although it often pained them, they seemed to have generally accepted such reprimands. He explained in *Jnana Yoga* that the path towards detachment meant finding a way to "not feel" harsh words: "that is how we are all trying to conquer" through attuning the self to the Absolute.[36]

But for some American devotees, his rebukes were difficult to endure, and seemed at times abusive. Vivekananda sensed this when writing whimsically to Mary Hale in February 1895: "My scolding letter I deplore, and beg forgiveness o'er and o'er."[37] In America, where a culture of gurus and disciples did not exist, he sensed that he might devastate the Western "ego." Thirty years later, the best-selling memoirist Paramahamsa Yogananda (born as Mukunda Lal Ghosh but different from Ramakrishna's disciple of the same religious name), explained how his own guru had relentlessly "corrected" his failings, but had instructed him not to use "blunt assaults on the ego" in the West.[38] Yogananda concluded, "I refuse to state the amount of truth I later came to find in Master's words!"[39]

Do such generalizations merely reinforce clichés about the "individualist" West in contrast to the "selfless" East? There is no definitive answer. It is certainly true, however, that Vivekananda's female acolytes hated the scolding. Mrs. Hansbrough recounted: "He was constantly finding fault and sometimes could be very rough. 'Mother brings me fools to work with!' ... This was a favourite word in his vocabulary of scolding. And though he himself said, 'I never apologize,' he would nevertheless come after the scolding . . . and say in a voice so gentle and with a manner so cool that butter and honey would not melt in his mouth, 'What are you doing?' It was clear that he was seeking to make amends for the scolding. He used to say, 'The people I love most, I scold most,' and I remember thinking he was making a poor kind of apology!"[40]

When he could not stop himself, she would say, "if you're not through, just keep right on." She admitted that she "would often get angry and sometimes walk out of the room," even if she claimed not to be hurt. She admitted, though, that he also gave credit for work well done.[41]

Even Josephine MacLeod did not always escape. When she arrived in India in 1898, she observed the Vaishnava markings on the face of Alasinga, signs of devotion she did not then understand.

She remarked to Vivekananda that she thought it a pity he wore such markings, and this instantly prompted a stern response from Vivekananda, who scolded: "'Hands off! What have you ever done?'"[42] He told her of Perumal's sacrifices for his family and his constant labor in Madras. He later regretted his harshness; Margaret Noble wrote to reassure Josephine in June 1899 that "he said he had made you shed torrents of tears many a time by the outrageous things he had said to you. Had I not yet found out that where he loved most he scolded most?"[43]

Others came in for similar treatment: "One day when he found Miss Waldo in tears, he asked her for the reason. Waldo replied, 'I try my utmost Swami, but I seem unable to please you. Even when others annoy you, you scold me for it.' 'See Ellen,' he said, 'I do not know those people well enough to scold them. Since I cannot rebuke them, I come to you. I consider you my own; whom can I scold if I cannot scold my own?'"[44]

Vivekananda considered Waldo to be family and tried to explain that criticism indicated loving attachment. Here again was the paradox—he was meant not to engage in "loving attachment," but its strength unleashed his disapproval. Even the pluckiest among them quavered before it. Was he unconsciously projecting the intimacy of "mother's discipline" in imitating Kali, who allowed her children to play in her lap, but also unleashed her wrath? Kali differed from the Divine Feminine in Christianity precisely because she represented the negative as powerfully as the positive.

Certainly, Vivekananda grew up in a family culture very different to that of these British and American women. In India, children often slept with

10.2. Alasinga Perumal

their mothers or ayahs until they were four years old, whereas Western girls were separated from their mother earlier. Moreover, in Protestant America, floods of passion were stifled; and in much of this milieu, surrogates—especially nannies—took on many of the roles of biological mothers. Did he believe that their spiritual "dryness" came from these upbringings? He never said so explicitly, but he hoped they might experience the sweetness of bhakti through his maternal care. They loved the devotion, but rejected the harshness, which they felt was undeserved. They may well have tasted the sharpness of Indian maternal idioms of intimate authority, but this did not make it easier.[45] As will be seen, it almost broke Nivedita when she first came to India.

MALE DISCIPLES

If female acolytes loved the playfulness, male devotees were more skeptical of his boyishness and regretted the presence of so many women around him. Frances Leggett, Josephine's niece, described Vivekananda's impact on the household in Ridgely between August 27 and November 6, 1899: "the atmosphere was now redolent with . . . the dynamism of Vivekananda's personality, the scope of his ideals. It was heady stuff. . . . The ground is parched, the seed falls, and then comes the rain of grace . . ." She conceded that it all became too much for her father.[46] Despite his wealth, Frank Leggett later refused to contribute to Vivekananda's activities in America and feared that the swami had unwittingly stoked "hysteria" among the women of his circle. Betty wrote to Frank explaining that he should blame human nature, not Vivekananda, for such exaggerated feelings.[47]

Frank was not the only man who complained about the women in Vivekananda's entourage. Another was Leon Landsberg, whom Vivekananda met at a Theosophical Society meeting in New York in May 1894.[48] As has been seen, Landsberg went to Thousand Island, and Vivekananda did not find either his "fanaticism" or threadbare appearance off-putting. He only worried that others would, and so urged Landsberg to accept Sara Bull's gift of a new coat, assuring him that he could dress as he pleased when he had his own followers.[49] Vivekananda enjoyed directing so unique a personality; for his part, Landsberg liked that Vivekananda was not an impersonal "Yankee tutor" and reveled in the lifelong and intimate possibilities of the guru-disciple relationship. He had no idea in these early days that Vivekananda's habits would come to irritate him.

However, early signs existed of Landsberg's "fanatical" turn of mind. When he lectured at the Theosophical Society in New York, there was a woman in the audience wearing a scarlet blouse, and whenever Landsberg mentioned the Devil, he pointed at her with "great emphasis."[50] Whereas Vivekananda was charismatic, Landsberg was often peevish and awkward. In the spring of 1895, after commenting on how his behavior was misinterpreted, Landsberg told Sara Bull that he opened "the secret chambers of [his] heart" to her and was in search of sympathy: "I stand alone in the world. Father and mother are long dead. No wife or child that makes life worth living and spurs me to restless action!"[51]

Landsberg even referred to his need to "escape. . . . prejudice and bad experience," a reference to anti-Semitism, emotions which he now channeled into his relationship with Vivekananda: "when I met the Swami and realized the greatness of his soul, all the love of which my heart was capable, and which was only waiting for an opportunity to escape its prison built up by prejudice and bad experience, blazed forth all its interiority . . . , and focused in his person. He became to me the object of divine worship . . . I became his servant, his slave, his shadow . . ."[52]

At first glance, this response appeared to make him ideally suited to discipleship. Vivekananda had explained the dangers of even the "faintest shadow of Ahamkâra [egotism]" in the search for transcendence, and had insisted that "the one thing necessary is to be stripped of our vanities—the sense that we possess any spiritual wisdom—and to surrender ourselves completely to the guidance of our Guru."[53] Instead, Landsberg revealed a "misplaced love of personality" that Vivekananda himself had warned against when he struggled to explain that the guru was merely an aspect of divine guidance.

Landsberg accepted all in theory but absorbed little in practice. He was infuriated that women might displace him and insisted that he was far better than the "President, Vice president, Secretary and all the rats' tails of trustees and committees."[54] He and Vivekananda seemed to have had arguments, and certainly Landsberg talked about "little 'family brawls.'"[55] He also disliked Vivekananda's love of cooking. Cooking was creative, but also a quotidian process of transformation, central to Vivekananda's maternal relationship to his disciples. He bragged to his Bengali friends about his culinary prowess: "Last night I made a dish. It was such a delicious mixture of saffron, lavender, mace, nutmeg, cubebs [a java pepper with a tang of allspice], cinnamon, cloves, cardamom, cream, lime juice, onions, raisins, almonds, pepper, and rice. . . ."[56] He adored spices, but also loved sweetness, as the ingredients to this recipe suggest. In California, he taught his disciples to make rock candy, which he boiled and boiled to ensure its purity.[57] For him, it symbolized the sweetness vital to his spiritual lessons.

With Landsberg, Vivekananda had resumed vegetarianism and was happy to eat simply after the dinner parties and receptions. But Landsberg could not appreciate how cooking could be in some sense sacred, not least because Vivekananda was also a messy cook and Landsberg hated having to clean up after him: "I regarded it as unworthy of men of spiritual aspirations to waste the greatest part of their time with thinking and speaking of eating, preparing and cooking the food, and washing dishes, while the frugal meals required by a Yogi could be had quicker and cheaper in any restaurant.... I only wonder that this 'doing our own cooking' suggested by some evil demon, did not land me in the lunatic asylum."[58]

The fight ended their living arrangements: in mid-April 1895, Landsberg complained that Vivekananda had "left without telling me even goodbye." This was another abandonment on top of all that Landsberg had already experienced; the friendship also seemed to have become almost dangerous to Vivekananda. He wrote to Josephine MacLeod in June 1895 and recounted how he stayed with a Dr. Guernsey, who would "watch and cure" his many ailments: "Doctor Guernsey ... was feeling my pulse, when suddenly Landsberg (whom they had forbidden the house) got in.... Dr. Guernsey burst out laughing and declared he would have paid that man for coming just then ... The pulse before was so regular, but ... at the sight of Landsberg it almost stopped from emotion."[59]

Freud would have called this reaction a negative "counter-transference"; Vivekananda understood it as a sadhana (spiritual trial) that required an effort at detachment. He did not lash out at Landsberg, and simply said "a few kind words" to him and went upstairs.[60] He even invited him to Thousand Island for the summer.

But the chasm between them had more to it than food and untidiness. For Landsberg, asceticism implied not only eating simply, but also waging war on the needs of the body, a view of renunciation that Vivekananda now sought to shift. Landsberg considered a meal of "soup, macaroni and apple sauce" to be extravagant.[61] For his part, Vivekananda knew well the cost of asceticism, and had paid heavily for it during his wandering years. Ramakrishna had been matchless in asceticism when necessary but believed that the "bit of 'I-ness' that remained" after divine connection was there "for enjoyment."[62] And so, Vivekananda refused to conform to the image of a disheveled, hollow-cheeked monk or sadhu that Landsberg wanted. Ida Ansell in California remembered how he later remarked: "[s]piritual people are not fanatical or severe. They are not long-faced and thin." Rather, he insisted, "They are fat, like me."[63]

Sara Bull helped keep Landsberg within the fold, underlining how Vivekananda was not singlehandedly creating a movement, but rather depended always on the women around him. She suggested that Landsberg be less defensive: "if you will not permit yourself to think others are opposed to you because of race or religion, you will carry with you the calm love of God and man that the Swami has taught us all."[64] But taking such advice was often beyond him. Nor was it clear that there was no anti-Semitism where everyone else came from a Christian background. Who knows whether he remained so poor—he called himself a tramp—to avoid accusations of being a "grasping Jew"?[65] By the end of August, he had given away everything he owned and had wandered to Detroit to begin preaching.[66]

The differences between Vivekananda and Landsberg are striking. Although sometimes mistaken for a Black American, Vivekananda was much less sensitive about his origins than Landsberg, his confidence buoyed by an elite education, adoring family, and Ramakrishna's love. Moreover, Vivekananda insisted on Hinduism's spiritual value, even superiority. Landsberg, in contrast, had to contend with Christianity's views of Judaism's inferiority, and the Protestant conviction that the New Testament had superseded the Old. In this instance, Vivekananda's self-assurance was intensified by his sense of difference, while Landsberg's was diminished.

Landsberg moved his affections from Vivekananda to Bull and claimed that, with her support, he again believed in the Divinity of Man and in women's spiritual possibilities. He made her "the subject of his Yoga meditations," and commissioned his first disciple, another Jewish man, to draw a picture of Ramakrishna, which he sent as a "gift of love."[67] He quoted from many religious texts, among them the Talmud, and offered to make her either a "seal (signet) or an amulet," from a New York "Hebrew engraver who understands the Hebrew letters."[68] He sought to provide her with spiritual comfort when he borrowed from Jewish idioms and ritual to ground his universalism: "Imagine that I am sitting now at your side and repeat that Hebrew benediction. I recommend you to God who will watch and guard you and make you a vessel of glory." It is not certain which Hebrew prayer he meant, but it seems to echo the Priestly Blessing, one of the oldest in the Jewish liturgy and also employed in Christian rites: "May the Lord bless and guard you—May the Lord make his face shine unto you and be gracious to you." (Numbers 6:23–67).[69]

Landsberg had returned to the "simple short precept [he] used to say during [his] childhood morning and evenings in [his] prayers."[70] The "She'ma Yisrael" proclaimed that "Thou shall love the Lord, Thy God, with all thy heart and all thy soul, and all thy might" as the surest way to attain the highest goal. He only distinguished between a search for salvation—which he no longer believed in—and the Advaitic conviction that he "was always in God" and that the surest route to liberation was through loving Him "for His own sake." Thus, through the thick fog of self-recrimination, accusation, and self-pity, Landsberg found a pride in his origins. He seems here to have taken Vivekananda's advice: rather than becoming a "better Methodist," he became—at least for a short time—a "better Jew."

But the gulf between him and the other disciples nevertheless deepened. He expressed annoyance with the "committee of petticoats" who, in his view, got in his way.[71] Although he claimed to be liberated from his habitual misogyny after his connection with Bull, Landsberg was unhappy with the apparent "feminization" of Vivekananda's enterprise. Sarah Waldo now transcribed Vivekananda's lectures that Landsberg had not been rapid enough to complete.[72] Later, it would be Josiah John Goodwin—a qualified stenographer with whom there was no friction—who took on this task of recording Vivekananda's words in English, and who accused Landsberg of preaching ideas that Vivekananda would have rejected.[73]

Things went from bad to worse. Without a monastery or brother-monks, Landsberg lived in want and insecurity, taking bits of money from Bull and Vivekananda.[74] In India, sannyasins begged and preached, slept in the open air, and made pilgrimage where they were supported, if not always respected. They lived without knowing what the future would bring, an exercise in worldly detachment integral to their vocation. Landsberg had no model for such a way of life, and nor did the society in which he lived. It is unclear whether he thought he should receive a stipend, like a priest, minister, or rabbi.[75] If this was his hope, he never said so. In the end, he wrote to Sara Bull to explain that he had been reduced to bartending; she refused further help because she felt that he had broken his vow of purity "of life and deed" by serving such poison.[76] Landsberg sought reconciliation later, but the closeness never returned.

Others besides Landsberg would find Vivekananda's lack of asceticism troubling, especially if he fell short of their idea of an Indian holy man. As will be seen, such views would disappoint and frustrate him, as he sought to deflect such judgments to create different priorities for Hindu Universalism.

11

THE PAINS AND PLEASURES OF
LOVE IN GREAT BRITAIN

Dignity . . . is about being oneself with all the multiplicities, systems and contradictions of one's way of being, doing and knowing. It is about being true to one's Self.

—Ziauddin Sardar, Foreword to Frantz Fanon, *Black Skin, White Masks*, 2008

✦ ✦ ✦

VIVEKANANDA WAS ABLE TO ACCEPT philosophically that some of his relationships did not produce results, but he was disinclined to take criticism of his spiritual "unworthiness" from Westerners. As an Indian monk, he believed he was entitled to criticize don't-touchism and democratize Advaita without Westerners trying to impose their view of Hindu orthodoxy on him. These disputes were not sidelines to more important philosophical and theological issues, but rather went to the heart of debates about what Vedanta was. They displayed, yet again, the role of orientalist clichés in bringing to the fore the relationship of the body to spirituality, of race and gender, and hence the impact of imperialism on love and friendship.

Britain ended up being less congenial than America, but he nevertheless found some of his most devoted disciples there, people who ultimately followed him and founded new ventures in India. At the same time, he had to fend off those Britons who felt they could decree what was "best" in Hinduism. He stayed in England between August and December in 1895 and returned in October 1896 before embarking for India again in December (and then briefly returning in the summer of 1899). During these sojourns, he met Edward Sturdy and the Seviers, while also encountering his new and inimitable "daughter," Margaret Noble.

EDWARD TORONTO STURDY

Vivekananda's relationship with Edward Toronto Sturdy (1860–1957), like his link to Landsberg, also began with enthusiasm, but was less dramatically followed by disillusionment and finally estrangement. Whereas Landsberg and Vivekananda were both outsiders and foreigners (it is likely Landsberg spoke English with an accent), the connection with Sturdy was heavy with colonial associations. Sturdy was Canadian but lived in England and was wealthy from his property business. Moreover, unlike Landsberg, whose intellectual and spiritual roots were in central and eastern Europe, Sturdy had already encountered some of Ramakrishna's disciples in India. Vivekananda's guru-brother Shivananda had met him in Almora in 1893 and had been impressed by his asceticism: "He is very quiet, and his habits and manners are exactly like a Brahmin's. He only eats food cooked by a Brahmin. He eats one meal a day, and he eats it at 1:00 P.M. The meal consists of Khichuri [rice and lentils], mung dal, and rice cooked together. That is all he eats in twenty-four hours. The quantity of food he eats is also small, barely three hundred and seventy-five grams. He sleeps for four hours a day. The quality of *sattva* [calmness] is dominant in him. He also has a strong urge to attain self-knowledge."[1]

In cultivating Sturdy even before he arrived in London in August 1895, Vivekananda knew that he had been in Mme. Blavatsky's inner circle, was acquainted with Annie Besant, and had only recently broken with the Theosophical Society. Vivekananda wanted to distance Advaita Vedanta from theosophy without alienating a potential recruit, and wrote, "only the Advaita philosophy can save mankind, whether in East or West, from 'devil worship' and kindred superstitions, giving . . . strength to the very nature of man. India herself requires this, quite as much or even more than the West."[2] He also made clear in this letter from New York in April 1895 that, while "some truth underlies the mass of mystical thought which has burst upon

11.1. Edward Sturdy's fireplace at Norburton House, with a Sanskrit inscription, "There is no higher law than truth."

the Western world of late," he suspected its motives. He sought to cultivate Sturdy by telling him that "mystics as a class are not very favorable to me. . . ."[3] Vivekananda thus stressed wisdom-seeking, rather than Ramakrishna's mystical inheritance, perhaps judging that Sturdy wanted an "authenticity" based on "enlightenment" (which Vivekananda seemed to embody) and his "rationalist" preaching of Advaita.

In his letters, Vivekananda discoursed on Ramanuja's theory of the soul, and explained how this medieval sage had preached Vishistadvaita (qualified nonduality), an understanding different from his own. Their discussion led into his study of Schopenhauer, whom he repeatedly acknowledged for his appreciation of Indian thought. However, he also argued that any philosophy based on "will," and the suggestion of insatiability, had to be erroneous. Vivekananda rejected Schopenhauer's implication that will and atman could ever be the same, arguing that the former could be "transcended through self-denial and asceticism."[4] Will belonged to "Mind" while atman was beyond time, space, and cause. He also believed that the preoccupation with will as a state of constant striving "play[ed] into the hands of the Darwinists."[5]

Vivekananda thus agreed with Shivananda that Sturdy's nature was "Brahmanical"; that he possessed both a philosophical mind and spiritual refinement. He was reassured by Sturdy's willingness to immerse himself in Indian culture and society, and was impressed, rather than put off, that he had had a Brahmin cook. In London in September 1895, Vivekananda rejoiced that Sturdy's life was "full of India. He has been years there—mixing with the Sannyasins, eating their food, etc., etc.; so you see I am very happy. I found already several retired Generals from India; they were very civil and polite to me."[6]

His reference to the military men suggests that he may even have hoped to gain them as disciples. He also esteemed Sturdy's wife, who "was surely an angel"—a view which did not last long.[7] He had expected prejudice, but discovered that, unlike the Americans who "identify every black man with the negro, [. . .] nobody even stares at me in the street."[8] Vivekananda knew that the relationship between colonialism and race in Britain was complex, but he was relieved not to be categorized as part of an "underclass," as he had been sometimes in the United States. These concerns reveal his continuing concern with respectability, despite his abhorrence of the way Black Americans were treated.

Vivekananda's English associates in London and in Reading (where Sturdy lived) impressed him by their "standard of education and civilisation" that he contrasted with his American audiences.[9] He found Sturdy to be both energetic and persevering and was gratified that he knew some Sanskrit and wanted to learn more. Together, they translated a "little book on Bhakti" while Vivekananda also lectured and taught classes.[10] Sturdy listened when Vivekananda expatiated on his plans; although he claimed "no aptitude for organizing" and that "it nearly breaks [him] to pieces," Vivekananda also prospected for opportunities.[11] On one occasion, he wrote excitedly about meeting two Englishmen, one an engineer and the other in the grain trade, who made him think that a Western "church" of Vedanta might be created. They were "fine, intelligent and educated men" who had given up their own church or were in the process of doing so, and who desperately wanted to "know the rituals" of his creed. For all that he had focused on Advaita, Vivekananda admitted that their request "opened [his] eyes": "The world in general must have some form. In fact, in the ordinary sense religion is philosophy concretised through rituals and symbols. It is absolutely necessary to form some ritual and have a Church. . . . We will fix something grand, from birth to death of a man. A mere loose system of philosophy gets no hold on mankind."[12]

Vivekananda never went far with this idea but understood that Christians naturally "want to form a congregation."[13] In India, there were pujas (acts of worship) and temples linked to caste, sect, and family. However, such devotions were alien to Western practice and thus a nonstarter in Europe. At the same time, he was wary of factionalism, and had witnessed splits in both Protestantism and the Brahmo Samaj. He did not create such a church, but Swami Trigunatita did build the first Hindu temple in the West (called Old Temple, to be completed in San Francisco in 1906), which suggests that aspects of this idea had an important afterlife.[14]

He was also grateful for Sturdy's material help: "being a rich man, . . . [Sturdy] bore the major part of the expenses of lecturing in big halls."[15] Another supporter was Henrietta Müller, a vocal feminist also active in theosophy who had introduced the two. She was the daughter of a successful furniture maker who had grown up in Chile and was an unmarried heiress. Like Annie Besant, who adopted two Indian Brahmin boys, she took in and educated a young disciple of Vivekananda's, Akshay Kumar Ghosh.[16] She later offered money for the land on which the Belur monastery was built.[17]

By the end of December 1895, after he had returned to New York, Vivekananda was still writing warmly to Sturdy, explaining that his "health [was] breaking down under constant work," so that he could not return right away as he had hoped. He was "so unused to these Western methods, especially the keeping of time."[18] Vivekananda praised Sturdy's classes, saying how much he regretted his absence, and saluted Sturdy as his "Blessed and Beloved."[19] Perhaps alluding both to Landsberg and to the problems of American commercialism, he added: "My great want here is a strong man like you, possessing intellect, and ability, and love. In this nation of universal education, all seem to melt down into a mediocrity, and the few able are weighed down by the eternal money-making."[20]

Sturdy was left with a great deal to do that was difficult to sustain without Vivekananda's energizing presence. Moreover, irritation may have grown as distance and time increased. There were spats over the publication of *Raja Yoga* in Britain, which revealed Sturdy and Vivekananda's annoyance with Sara Bull as she waited for a preface from William James that never arrived.[21] The erudite Swami Abhedananda, one of Vivekananda's guru-brothers, arrived in London in September 1897 when Vivekananda was already back in India, but there was no fit between Abhedananda and the English, and Sturdy sent him on to New York.[22] When he arrived there, he began to reorganize the Vedanta Society and irritated Vivekananda's most loyal disciples, including Josephine MacLeod and Sara Bull.[23] Vivekananda refused to intervene, wary of entangling himself in organizations that he now believed should be "autonomic, independent groups."[24]

Vivekananda felt overburdened and Sturdy felt neglected. Did the latter think of Abhedananda as only a second-rate Vivekananda? None of this is clear, but the relationship broke down and the reasons later given were deeply wounding and personal. In the middle of August 1899, Vivekananda went to America to stay with the Leggetts in the Catskills, writing only that "Sturdy seems to have got disgusted with the work; he does not see any asceticism in us from India."[25] Little by little, the reasons for the Sturdy's disenchantment leaked out. Vivekananda wrote on September 14 to Frank Leggett, Betty's husband, that "[Another friend of Henrietta Müller] is of the opinion that no spiritual person ought to be ill. It also seems to her now that my smoking is sinful etc., etc. That was Miss Müller's reason for leaving me, my illness."[26]

Clearly, both the criticism and the desertion hurt him, and he could not understand either. Was the objection to smoking part of the "Christian physiology" pervasive on both sides of the Atlantic?[27] His habit was frowned upon as a lack of holiness. These issues caused trouble in India as well: while there, Vivekananda had been "driven out of a private temple by the owners for eating with Europeans."[28] He concluded that he could not "satisfy everyone," and expressed his dismay when he wrote in September 1899: "When I first came to America, they ill-treated me if I had not trousers on. Next I was forced to wear cuffs and collars, else they would not touch me etc., etc. They thought me awfully funny if I did not eat what they offered etc., etc. . . ."[29]

Back in India, he encountered equally strong expectations about dress: "the moment I landed they made me shave my head and wear 'Kaupin' [loin cloth], with the result that I got diabetes etc."[30] He admitted to a rare sense of victimhood even if he accepted such harsh treatment as part of his karma.

However, hurt turned into disappointment two months later; he remembered no luxuries with his English hosts, just "boiled cabbage and boiled rice and boiled lentils three times a day, with your wife's curses for sauce all the time." He did not remember receiving any cigars as presents, just living "as a thief, shaking through fear all the time, and working every day for you." His brother Mahendranath had joined him in London, and Miss Müller had driven his sibling away, even though he was ill; when living with her, Vivekananda had eaten nothing but "fruits and nuts." He mentioned that he had "had to work almost day and night and cook the meals oft-times for five or six, and most nights with a bite of bread and butter." If Sturdy maintained Vivekananda was not a true sannyasin, Vivekananda felt like a poorly treated brown servant. Mrs Sturdy, once an "angel," was now his antagonist, who, when giving him a night's lodging, had "criticis[ed] the black savage—so dirty and smoking all over the house."[31]

His brother's presence in London indicates that Vivekananda remained connected to family. Mahendranath, in turn, eulogized Vivekananda in a 1937 Bengali memoir, in which he discussed their life with Henrietta Müller (who dressed, apparently, in men's clothing). Josiah John Goodwin and Saradananda are part of the cast of characters, as are the Sturdys. It describes the intermittent tension in 63 St George Road in Elephant and Castle (South London), where Müller is painted as a vegetarian with a "peevish" disposition.[32] The Indians would sneak into the kitchen to make fiery curries, while Mahendranath denounced Sturdy's stinginess, especially when purchasing tobacco for Vivekananda.[33] Although the text was written decades after the events, it confirms many of Vivekananda's impressions, albeit in different words.

By 1899, Vivekananda saw Sturdy as imperious and condescending, and Sturdy thought of him as intemperate and inappropriate. Although Vivekananda generally praised the English for their interest in Indian culture, Sturdy's rejection reminded him of imperial realities. In contrast to his American hosts who were warm, welcoming, and generous, the English (and the Canadians) were cold and tightfisted.

Margaret Noble intervened, as did Josephine MacLeod, both angry at this treatment. Sturdy responded that others in London had also condemned Vivekananda's "sybaritic life," and that even Max Müller disapproved. Sturdy's injection of Müller into the dispute implied that Vivekananda had hurt his own cause. How, Sturdy asked, could a cigar-smoking itinerant who loved to eat too much compete with the "Vedantist of Vedantists?"[34]

Sturdy also implied that Müller knew more than Vivekananda; and he, Sturdy, knew more than Josephine. He had been studying Vedanta for seventeen years and believed that Vivekananda only partially realized its ideals. He expressed an orientalism in which the English (or in his case, near-English) claimed a deeper knowledge of "authentic" Hinduism than did Indians such as Vivekananda. In the same way, but with some masculine superiority as well, Sturdy told Josephine that he knew Vivekananda better than she did: "You must not compare your 'glimpses of Swami's real nature' with what I know of him," an insinuation that suggested other vices lurked behind the ones he had already mentioned. Sturdy conceded that Vivekananda was perhaps still a "great man-teacher," but for his part he was not looking "so much for a teacher as the embodiment of what was taught," and in his opinion Vivekananda fell short of his ideal of an Indian holy man.[35]

Vivekananda had had to cope with orthodox Hindu detractors, and also with Christian missionaries who did not see the holiness they desired.[36] Amid all the eulogies, especially after the World Parliament and then his whirlwind return to India in early 1897, he was impugned for "cross[ing] the ocean and eat[ing] un-Hindu food"; luxuriating in expensive hotels and for having eaten "Chicago's famed luxury pork, thereby renouncing vegetarianism."[37] From the outset, he had been hampered by his lack of a formal invitation to the Parliament as well as other credentials, facts that Protap Chunder Mozoomdar of the Brahmo Samaj (who had also spoken at the World Parliament) had used intermittently to undermine his reputation. In 1894, Vivekananda had written to friends in India for references to prove his bona fides to Professor Wright at Harvard, who had paid for his train fare to the Parliament.[38] Some Vaishnavas also rejected his claim to represent Hinduism anywhere—in India or abroad—because he was not a Brahmin.[39] When he returned to India, he responded by tracing a connection between a branch of his Kayastha caste and the warrior Kshatriyas to prove his worthiness (and fighting spirit).[40]

There were many reasons that they may have cast these aspersions. Some, perhaps, were jealous of his success; others angered by his transgressive campaign against don't-touchism; and still others resistant to the creation of "Practical Vedanta" that undermined aspects of Advaitic orthodoxy. When people attacked his vision of purity, he emphasized his sexual continence, and the way his body would and did rebel against any kind of moral pollution.[41] But Sturdy rejected Vivekananda's decision to live by his own monkish standards. He even compared Vivekananda to Mme. Blavatsky, saying that he shared her "leonine temperament, large heartedness and good comradeship." They both, he continued, had a "certain bursting out into passion and indignation which entirely died away as quickly." Unlike her, Vivekananda was not a fraud, and his "word is always straight and his acts too," but both were excessive, and had "constant ill health from the same organs, the same lack of control in eating and smoking. The same devotion in disciples."[42] Sturdy acknowledged, therefore, that both were deeply loved, not just as incarnations of the Eternal Teacher, but also for their human selves. However, both had brought their illness on themselves. How, the British Canadian suggested, could such people be worthy of the spiritual mission in their charge?

We can only imagine what it meant to Vivekananda to be compared to Mme. Blavatsky, considering how he detested theosophy and its orientalism.[43] Later Vivekananda wrote to Sturdy: "There need be no bitterness . . . as I don't think I ever posed for anything but what I am. Nor is it ever possible for me to do so, as an hour's contact is enough to make everybody see through my smoking, bad temper, etc. 'Every meeting must have a separation'—this is the nature of things. . . . I hope you will have no bitterness. It is Karma that brings us together, and Karma separates."[44]

He concluded that he had perhaps been insensitive to Sturdy's shy nature and accepted that his host would have found it difficult to "work with people who were so different from [Sturdy's] ideal."[45] Had he known, Vivekananda averred, he would have saved Sturdy "a good deal of mental trouble."[46] He was honest, not ironic, in saying as much. But he stood firm in repudiating Sturdy's puritanism and the judgment it spawned as much as he took issue with orthodox Indians who criticized his eating habits.[47]

These seemingly trivial conflicts addressed questions central to the relationship of the body to spirituality. Vivekananda had strong views on this subject. The niggardly, insipid fare of Mrs. Sturdy's kitchen, served up with ill-humor and rudeness, could not have been further from the fragrant, Bengali delicacies that included sharp, spicy, and sweet elements, which he later served with such pleasure to his followers in Southern California. When he had written to Sturdy in the halcyon days of friendship in early 1896, he had remarked on the textures and flavors that he would bring to the spiritual table: "I want to give them dry, hard reason, softened in the sweetest syrup of love and made spicy with intense work, and cooked in the kitchen of Yoga, so that even a baby can digest it."[48]

He knew that vegetarianism was crucial for many, but wrote in "Food and Cooking" that "the nations who take the animal food are always, as a rule, notably brave, heroic, and thoughtful," and he wanted to implant these traits in Indians.[49] Food was thus intimately related to India's rebirth, and he urged carnivorousness so Indians could resist the British, despite the spiritual sacrifice. He was also suspicious of Western "faddism." Unlike Gandhi, whose first political involvement in London focused on vegetarian activism with like-minded Englishmen, Vivekananda rejected such ideas.[50] In California, he asked Lucy Beckham and George Roorbach, vegetarians in the Bay Area, to provide him with "'proper food' . . . I must have meat. I cannot live on potatoes and asparagus with the work I am doing!" They obliged him, despite their preferences.[51]

THE SEVIERS

Charlotte and Henry Sevier were also acquainted with India, though in a very different way to Sturdy. Henry had served in the Indian Army for five years, and then returned to London, where the couple was captivated by Vivekananda's lectures in June 1896. Once again, it was the woman who seems to have led the way. Both came from wealthy families—she, the daughter of a successful lawyer and property owner in Cheltenham; he, from a landowning family in Gloucestershire. Henrietta Müller had introduced them and they all traveled together to Switzerland, where Vivekananda was entranced by the mountain scenery and especially the glaciers. During the trip, the idea of the Seviers' setting up an Indian monastery was discussed, to the point that Vivekananda wrote to one Lala Badri Sah to ask him to look for a suitable site near Almora.[52] He thought of this project because the Swiss landscape was "a miniature Himalayas and has the same effect of raising the mind up to the Self—and driving away all earthly feelings and ties."[53] Back in London, the Seviers rented him a flat, at 14 Greycoat Gardens in Westminster, a "black hole" that enabled him to separate from Henrietta Müller and exist independently with Abhedananda (now in London temporarily) and stenographer Josiah John Goodwin.[54] The Seviers offered him everything they possessed, although he urged them to keep a portion for the future.

His view of them was also important in relation to his Indian compatriots, as he compared the energy of his Western recruits with his ineffectual Indian followers. He told Alasinga Perumal in March 1896, for example, that the new female sannyasins and other "white faces [would] have more influence in India than the Hindus" because the Hindus were "dead." He castigated India's elites, insisting that the "only hope of India is from the masses."[55] A year later, he wrote to Sarala Ghosal, Tagore's niece and the editor of the Bengali newspaper *Bharat*, that India needed the Westerners because in India, there was "no appreciation of merit . . . no financial strength, and what is most lamentable of all, there is not a bit of practicality."[56] Of course, in the West he inverted this strategy, and harangued his disciples for their excessive preoccupation with money, materialism, and punctuality. And yet, with the Seviers, he felt he had a couple who exemplified his "practical" ideal.

The pair went to India in 1897, scouted out British hill stations, but ultimately rejected Almora. Henry Sevier preferred isolation to tea parties in town, and they fixed on an old tea plantation called Mayavati, 6,400 feet up and fifty miles to the east in the Champawat district of Uttarakhand, a little over five and half miles from the town of Lohaghat, where the mountain people worshipped the Divine Mother. Vivekananda hoped that, far from a train station, his dream of an Advaitic sanctuary would materialize. He told a group in San Francisco that in Mayavati there would be no "Christs and Buddhas and Shivas," that the people would "cast off their kindergartens of religions and shall make vivid and powerful the true religion."[57] That he chose English people to fulfil this vision is significant. The Seviers—now in their fifties—undertook a massive renovation project with the monks who came to help them and employed mountain villagers as laborers.

This outpost was different from the other institutions of the Ramakrishna Math and Mission, as it was kept away from "all superstitions and weakening contaminations." He had protested vehemently against what he saw as the Western misinterpretation of the worship of Indian gods and was not iconoclastic in India. But in Mayavati, if not elsewhere, he rejoiced in disciples who shared his yearnings for a worship room without "form." He later discovered a shrine with a photograph of Ramakrishna surrounded by flowers, incense, and offerings; ultimately the shrine was dismantled.[58]

11.2. Mayavati Ashrama, Uttarakhand

Mayavati thus embodied Vivekananda's most cherished spiritual ideas, and became the place where the *Prabuddha Bharata*, the order's monthly journal, was published. The couple renovated with an elegant simplicity, and Charlotte also established a charitable dispensary to tend the villagers, which underpinned the dream of outreach and activism.[59] Vivekananda wrote to Margaret Noble, "the Seviers are the only English people who do not hate the natives, Sturdy not excepted. Mr. and Mrs. Sevier are the only persons who *did* not come to patronize us. . . ." an extraordinary compliment for people who may not have been fluent in Hindi.[60] They also recruited new workers to send out people to train and educate others. Nonetheless, Mayavati became a sanctuary for men—women did not join its ranks, despite Charlotte's stewardship and Christine and Nivedita's later visits. Nor were householders except the Seviers part of the enterprise—it seems that only a few physicians stayed and worked there without being initiated.

Vivekananda recognized the enormous achievements of his Western disciples and, despite his split from Sturdy, especially valued the British. But sometimes they assumed a knowingness that could easily be transformed into a supposition of superiority. When Vivekananda told Margaret Noble that the Seviers were the only English he knew who did not hate the natives, he expressed his view of colonial hierarchies. Interestingly, he did not include her in this assessment. He had never sought to "Hinduize" the Seviers, but when writing to Margaret Noble, he now thought of her as one of his own.

MARGARET NOBLE

And yet, Margaret Noble had not been an easy or ready recruit.

Born in 1867 in provincial Dungannon in Northern Ireland, she was the granddaughter of a Protestant Irish nationalist, John Noble, whose anti-British stance emerged from resistance to the pro-English Church of Ireland.[61] Did her Irishness mean that she more readily understood India's plight and its subjugation? Certainly, when she wrote about the famine-stricken villages of Barisal in 1906, she may have had Irish history in mind.[62] Later, she demonstrated a love for Celtic culture and encouraged her brother to engage in Irish politics. But when she first arrived in India, she shocked Vivekananda with her British patriotism and firm conviction that Britain was a force for good in the world.

Her father, Samuel, became a Wesleyan minister in Manchester, leaving Margaret in the care of her grandmother in Ireland. She thus only came to know her parents, and a younger sister, when she was four. She admitted to Josephine MacLeod that she had found her mother's disapprobation difficult, and recognized its enduring impact on her: "I think the sense of being disapproved of, or of deserving to be disapproved of is wrought so deep into every fibre with me, that I always act with a sense of protest even in the most private things, a feeling of justifying myself by force against some unseen judge. Perhaps without this I would have had too great a force of self-confidence, but if I had had a child of my own, I would have tried to obviate it, by creating a first impression of being loved and smiled upon!!"[63]

11.3. Dungannon. photograph, nineteenth century

Her relationship with her father was easier; she admired his vocation as a teacher and spiritual advisor to the rural poor in Devon. He died in 1877, however, and the loss was formative: "I have often wondered what my own life would have been, had the awful blow of my father's death not been dealt me at its start. That made me a sannyasin."[64] The remark about becoming a "renouncer" suggests her inner homelessness. She understood that her passion for Vivekananda assuaged this childhood blow, telling Sara Bull in 1899: "A few minutes ago, no an hour ago, I felt so hopeless about India and the world, . . . Now I am like a giant refreshed with wine . . . for Swami is at home and once more I have a father—the thing I lost when I was 10."[65]

When her father died, she and her sister went to Halifax College, a boarding school for the children of ministers with a strict religious regime but scope for intellectual and artistic endeavor. She took advantage of the opportunities and, when eighteen, passed her final examination to teach in 1884.[66] She taught first at Keswick, then Rugby, where she instructed orphan girls, before spending three years (between 1886 and 1889) at a school with miners' children at Wrexham.[67]

She began to write articles in local newspapers, where she protested the plight of the poor and the fate of women.[68] Rarely read or considered, these early works—as much as her later productions in India—show a curious mixture of convention and unorthodoxy, sentimentality and learning, emotion and intellect. For example, for a Christmas edition she spoke of the Christ Child and a "little black lamb," who gazed sweetly on the "mother's love treasure on her lap."[69] Alongside the pathos, however, she also referred to pre-Christian Yuletide in "northern lands" and to the Buddha and Socrates, indicating her interest in different spiritual and intellectual traditions. She wrote a strange short story about "Janet Nuttal, Herbalist," an old woman with psychic gifts and healing pretensions, a tale which acknowledged both the power and danger of occultism.[70] She would remain wary and fascinated by these "forces" for her entire life.

When she went down a mine in Wrexham, she wrote of the tropical forests and surging seas that had created the coal, shale, and slate. The visit made her dream of a mining college teaching mechanics, geology, and physics, interests in engineering and science that became central to her nationalist politics.[71] She also ventured into the poorest districts of Wrexham, differentiating between the "neat woman with tidy children" of the respectable working man and the "thriftlessness and improvidence" of households with unemployed husbands.[72] She transferred her engagement with the working class in Britain to their counterparts in Calcutta, but in India entirely abandoned this form of purse-lipped morality.

Noble also wrote revealingly on women and their rights. She argued for a new kind of beauty, opposing restrictive clothing and the addictions of fashion in favor of "health": "The Natural, the Free, the Proportionate, these are the Beautiful," a kind of mantra that would guide her Swadeshi activism after 1905.[73] She wanted women to be educated, but her feminism remained familial. After Wrexham, she feared male pauperism and saw women's labor as focused on child-rearing, housekeeping, and renunciation. Although her views on gender shifted wildly in private, she would maintain an almost doctrinaire adherence to an idealized notion of the Hindu family in public.

While in Wrexham, she had been targeted for helping the "undeserving" poor, an episode that seems to have heralded a move to Wimbledon. There, after training with a Dutch colleague, Madame de Leeuw, she created a new, progressive school in 1894, based on pedagogy that focused on play and experiential learning, which, as will be seen, were vital to her Hindu spirituality and early Calcutta activism.[74]

When she arrived in London in 1891, she was twenty-four, supporting her mother, and still unmarried—her fiancé, a young engineer, had died, and a second fiancé had apparently left her for another woman. She traveled in the higher circles of intellectual London and associated with the New Ireland movement.[75] She is said to have known George Bernard Shaw and William Butler Yeats and had connections with anarchist theorist Prince Alexander Kropotkin.[76] This blending of science, politics, and spirituality would all be channeled in her Indian experience.

She met Vivekananda through Lady Isabel Margesson, later a vociferous suffragist, who invited Noble to hear Vivekananda talk. The introduction had come through contacts at the Sesame Club, a group interested in progressive educational reform. Noble remarked that her first meeting with Vivekananda—on a cold Sunday afternoon in November 1895—was underwhelming, despite the "crimson robe and girdle." She thought he had said nothing new to the dozen people in the room, though a few remarks stuck in her mind. He objected to the word "faith" and insisted instead on "realization"; and contrasted the Eastern idea of the freedom of the soul with the "Western conception of service of humanity."[77] Vivekananda again proved disruptive: in India he emphasized service in a society that urged spiritual withdrawal, but in the "busy" and "'distracted" West, he worried about the dangers of "do-goodism." He chanted in Sanskrit and had the curious habit of invoking Shiva at regular intervals, quirks that made an impression.

Her feeling that the lecture was uninspiring stemmed from a mixture of spiritual weariness and repressed hope.[78] The London audience had deserted conventional Christianity, and reacted coldly because they feared disappointment.[79] Noble acknowledged that "Christianity had once meant to [her] the realisation of God as the Father," but she "had long mourned . . . the loss of faith in this symbolism."[80] She admitted later that for seven years, she had been unable to reject Christianity but no longer believed: "I shunned going to Church and yet sometimes my longing to bring restfulness to my spirit impelled me to rush into Church . . . But no peace, no rest was there for my troubled soul all eager to know the truth."[81]

Like Vivekananda's other key disciples, she turned to spiritualism—and would do so intermittently—even though she occasionally denounced it as "religious drug-taking."[82] She, too, was interested in Christian Science and believed that it had "made a bridge to . . . Vedanta as I cannot imagine anything else doing."[83] Only later, when she went to America in 1899, did she denounce "positive thinking" as incapable of confronting the spiritual consequences of aggression, violence, and catastrophe. By this stage, she was already a public devotee of Kali.

She later claimed she was struck by the "dignity" and "strangeness" of Vivekananda's morality and lack of dogma as she listened in Lady Margesson's drawing room.[84] As she attended other lectures between April and December in 1896 (with Josephine MacLeod, now beside her in London), she became intrigued by the notion of maya, the world of the senses and the "torturous, erroneous and self-contradictory character of that knowledge."[85] Indian religion aimed to break out of this "bondage"' to attain mukti (freedom). She learned slowly that this release was only possible through renunciation. For her, the lesson was simple. Renunciation, rather than Christian sacrifice, meant "mastery," and hence a form of power.[86] She learned, too, that "the body comes and goes" but that the atman, freely translated here as "soul," was immortal and reincarnated.[87] She concluded that her spiritual apprenticeship was "not so much an intellectual exposition" as a life of new and lofty emotions—or as they would be called in India—"realisations."[88] Vivekananda also provocatively suggested that society might not exist at all, that it was transient and contingent, unlike the "Infinite." This idea powerfully subverted Enlightenment social contract theory and underscored a critique of utilitarianism.

While still in London in 1896, Vivekananda wrote to Margaret Noble: "I am sure, you have the making in you of a world-mover . . ."[89] In *Raja Yoga* (1896), he had spoken of Christ and Mohammed in such terms—and now applied the same words to describe her. Such praise was irresistible, especially when he wrote again from India at the end of July 1897. He told her he wanted "a real lioness to work for the Indians, women especially" because India was not yet capable of producing "great women." He told her that he required her fiery Celtic blood as much as her "purity, immense love, determination." Although he celebrated India while in the West, he now warned her of his country's "misery, the superstition, and the slavery." and the "mass of half-naked men and women with quaint ideas of caste and isolation, shunning the white skin through fear or hatred."

He also cautioned her that British people would spurn her and consider her a crank, that she would be lonely (he was wrong in this prediction). By trying to deter her, he tantalized her all the more. He ended with remarks that, for her at least, presaged the defining difficulty of their relationship. He promised he would stand by her "unto death" whether she stayed in India or not, whether she gave up Vedanta or not: once "[t]he tusks of the elephant come out, . . . they never go back." He, of course, was the elephant, ready to defend her loyally and forever. But in virtually the next sentence he insisted: "you must stand on your own feet." Like many of his Western disciples, she had difficulty apprehending how these two visions fitted together.[90]

When she sailed in January 1898, she was thirty-one, and she had known Vivekananda on and off for two years. She had studied the Gita in London, worked with Sturdy (it was why she felt qualified later to censure his criticism of Vivekananda in 1899), and raised money for famine relief. She was a mature woman and was no more a Western innocent than he was an Eastern seducer. Rather, she was a professional, well-respected, and, for her time, widely experienced woman, who embarked for Calcutta only after serious reflection.

PART THREE

INDIA

AND THE

WORLD

12

VIVEKANANDA RETURNS

True happiness, we are told, consists in getting out of one's self; but the point is not only to get out—you must stay out; and to stay out you must have some absorbing errand.

—Henry James, *Roderick Hudson* (1875)

◆ ◆ ◆

VIVEKANANDA WAS HARDLY a different man in India, but the emphases of his speeches and the rhythm of his work changed. When he returned in early 1897, the pace was just as, if not more, frenetic, but he now addressed larger audiences and built institutions in ways unimaginable in the West. While abroad, he had focused on a spirituality of mildness and contemplation (especially for male hearers) and encouraged women toward robustness and "freedom." In India, however, he used the term "man-making" more frequently. As will be seen, this term meant many things—a rethinking of the monastic vocation as much as a rallying cry to householders of different ranks to join in a program of self-reliance and national rejuvenation.

Above all, Vivekananda focused on service (seva), and on an unusual and innovative theological pairing of "Karma yoga" and Advaita Vedanta. As will be seen, this combination—which can still arouse indignation—also appeared to tear him away from Ramakrishna, who feared that worldliness might lurk behind a veil of altruism, contaminating such philanthropy with self-interest. In contrast, Vivekananda linked what he called "practical Vedanta" in the world to a novel vision of spiritual realization. Above all, he sought to find a way to "do good" without do-goodism, remarking in *Karma Yoga* (1896) that "this world was not made that you or I should come and help it."[1] Rather, service done with detachment was the means toward spiritual perfection. Seva—in its many different forms—became central to the ethos of Vivekananda's Ramakrishna Mission, but also to the Indian freedom struggle.

THE SACRED MOTHERLAND

Vivekananda's tour of India began on January 15, 1897, and finally ended in December. As he traveled on trains, in carriages, and on foot from Sri Lanka to the Himalayas, he delighted his compatriots by the way he had somehow forced Westerners to take Indian religion seriously. Newspapers reported eagerly on what became a national event, albeit one concerned with Hindu themes. It was accomplished in three blocks, beginning in Sri Lanka, the south and Madras; then around Calcutta and Belur (he arrived at his hometown by ship); and ending in the northwest. It seemed almost to reiterate his perambulations of the subcontinent when a young monk, albeit more focused on India's vertical tangent than on its east–west axis; by going to so many places, he sought to encompass the "sacred territory" that composed the "Motherland."

And yet, it was different; his earlier tour had concentrated on his spiritual search and creating a network for Hindu revitalization. Now, his travel was about dissemination and coalition building, and a celebration of Indian resurgence exemplified by his reception in the West.[2] Often, he aimed his remarks at young men with English education who, from the newspaper accounts, often dominated the crowds.

In Colombo, he emphasized India's special spiritual vocation: "Eastern wisdom: If there is one word in the English language to represent the gift of India to the world, if there is one word in the English language to express the effect which the literature of India produces upon mankind, it is this one word, 'fascination.'"[3]

He thus embraced in India the orientalist stereotypes of fascination even though, in the West, he had focused mostly on rationality and devotion. He credited India with cultivating the "spiritual food" that the West needed to stop its own self-destruction—a theme that Gandhi would develop: "the

12.1. Vivekananda in Calcutta, 1897

whole of Western civilisation will crumble to pieces in the next fifty years if there is no spiritual foundation. It is hopeless and perfectly useless to attempt to govern mankind with the sword."[4] He also argued that "constitutional government, freedom, liberty, and parliaments—are but jokes," making short shrift of Western liberalism.[5] This critique was important—it was a condemnation of Indian reformism that believed in the ameliorative power of the state, and was matched by an equally strong critique of "society"—its customs and hierarchies—when he denounced conservative don't-touchism and Brahmin exclusions of Shudras (low-caste Hindus).[6]

India had endured, he reminded them, while other civilizations had perished, through renunciation, and he continued by denouncing British arrogance that focused on social evolution: "they talk a great deal of . . . the survival of the fittest, and they think that it is the strength of the muscles which is the fittest to survive."[7] In another instance, he stated that the sadhu laughed at physical death, because he knew he was the "Infinite, the Omnipresent, the Omniscient."[8] Here, weakness was strength, and it was this power that Vivekananda sought to cultivate. He also reveled in the tale of

Alexander the Great, the representative of Western Aryanism, "standing on the bank of the Indus, talking to one of our Sannyasins in the forest."[9] It is important to recognize, therefore, that here and elsewhere he sneered at the "muscle-making" stereotype that now defines him and deplored the pseudoscience that insisted physical prowess ensured "true" strength.

He made a parallel argument in 1897 about wealth: "In the West, they are trying to solve the problem how much a man can possess, and we are trying here to solve the problem on how little a man can live."[10] Again, like Gandhi, he suggested that material accumulation was a kind of violence, linked ineluctably to sensuality, low desires, and of course, the acquisitiveness exemplified by empire. If he reiterated these criticisms of the West, he relied on the diversity of Hindu traditions to uphold his vision of the "sacred Motherland" and reinforce this notion of tolerance within its boundaries. He spoke of Advaita but emphasized that he was not inclined to be dogmatic. So, at the Victoria Hall in Madras, he stressed the heights of his preferred "way," while also acknowledging the power of the Indian religion of gods and goddesses: "It has become a trite saying that idolatry is wrong. . . . I once thought so, and to pay the penalty of that I had to learn my lesson sitting at the feet of a man who realised everything through idols; I allude to Ramakrishna Paramahamsa."[11]

Vivekananda also spoke about caste and dared to say that the British Empire's internationalism had "come to the rescue of India" by "throwing open the doors of life to everyone, by destroying the exclusive privileges of caste."[12] He declared that Brahmins should no longer have special spiritual prerogatives, and mocked those who said, "If the Shudra [low caste] hears the Vedas, fill his ears with molten lead, and if he remembers a line, cut his tongue out."[13] This position echoed his familiar critique of "priest craft."

But he did not believe that the Brahmins should be obliterated; instead, he focused on uplift from below, not destruction from above, and on non-Western social organization: "Competition—cruel, cold, heartless—is the law of Europe. Our law is caste—the breaking of competition, checking its forces, mitigating its cruelties, smoothing the passages of the human soul through this mystery of life."[14] Such statements both turned the tables on the conquerors and sought to change Indian social structures without destroying them. His Madras audience roared in such approval that Vivekananda was forced to stop speaking and leave the stage.

Vivekananda's views on caste, and his unapologetic insistence on its value, are not easily reduced and must be understood in a changing context. The

British regarded Indians in terms of caste and religion, "scientizing" these categories through sociology and statistics, especially through the census. Such investigations undoubtedly contributed to a growing sense of religious and caste identity, with Hindus starting to worry about being "swamped" by Muslims; and castes pleading for better designations and / or promoting especially lower castes through new histories and traditions.[15] He was almost certainly aware in the 1880s, for example, that Bengali Kayasthas, his own sub-caste, were struggling to be considered "twice-born" and hence considered part of upper-caste society. Moreover, he never tired of naming the "great men" that the Kayasthas had produced to show their value.[16]

In speaking of caste, as he did to the roaring crowds in Madras, Vivekananda responded to this novel awareness and seemed to share it. He wanted "sub-castes" to multiply and saw their effusion as a sign of creative social and religious life, as well as anti-colonialism. He maintained that the British had brought a degrading homogenization by creating a mass of "coolies" and undifferentiated "natives."[17] He did not believe that such divisions should be concretized, however. Yet again, he constantly referred to history, citing examples of people changing caste—usually upward—to indicate spiritual achievement. He awaited the day when people who had left the Hindu fold would "gain their own castes. . . . And new people will make theirs." And he cited the great "Ramanuja and Chaitanya of Bengal"—as well as "all great Vaishnava Teachers"—who had been so creative in this domain.[18] His vision of caste was not only about lineage (though as has been seen, he *did* speak about his own lineage to prove its caste worthiness), but about community- and self- (re-)creation. It was for this reason that he wanted to open Vedanta even to the Chandalas, the most abject of society, so that they, too, would learn self-esteem. Moreover, he insisted that caste intermarriage and interdining had been a part of ancient Hindu civilization—another important weapon in his arsenal against don't-touchism, but also a Brahmoist legacy.

Vivekananda was aware that his position caused offense, but he persisted in a vision of a democratizing, dynamic society that remained unapologetically hierarchized. He famously remarked that "the present want of India is the Kshatriya force," and hence the martial spirit ready to resist subjugation. When making such statements, he underscored a militant but undoubtedly high-caste ethos.[19] Rather than excoriating caste as imposing not only inequality but even cruelty and violence (especially against Dalits), his trip to the West had convinced him of its universality. Moreover, like many others, he saw caste as important for soteriological reasons, as a spur to the disciplined process that enabled self-realization.[20] It was also important in making possible social harmony, and hence dharma, central to a vision of Hinduism that was decidedly antistatist. The maintenance of these hierarchies—such as his preference for Advaita over the worship of images—suggests just how important caste remained in his formulation. For these reasons, he has been accused of fostering a complacency about caste inequities—a critique that follows Vivekananda's monks when they argue today for "spiritual" solutions to social problems.

There was another side to his ideas on caste that was even more unconventional. As his remarks before the Madras crowds suggest, he also contended that caste was "socialistic," by which he meant it expressed a deep-rooted collective mentality that Western individualism could never fathom.[21] He expressed his own practical belief in "collectivism" to Mary Hale: "I am a socialist not because I think it is a perfect system, but half a loaf is better than no bread."[22] While in India in March 1899, he even sketched out a dynamic historical sociology of caste by suggesting that "the Brahmin, Kshatriya, Vaishya [merchant caste], and Shudra" would govern "in succession," with the Shudras ultimately achieving "absolute supremacy in every society." He acknowledged as well the role of "Socialism, Anarchism [and] Nihilism" in creating a "vanguard" that would promote social revolution. If, while in Cape Comorin, he seemed little concerned with Marxist theory, something like it now appeared to emerge in his four-stage theory of social development.[23] As Shamita Basu has suggested, Kshatriya rule resembled the "feudal-royal" stage, while the conflict between monarchy and priestly power suggested debates over authority between church and state. The rise of the "Vaishyas" represented the growing importance of capital, while the Shudras were the working class. Indeed, he saw the Shudras as the inheritors of the next stage of world history.

Vivekananda did not regard "Shudrahood" as inherently good or evil, only inevitable, and believed it was the sannyasin's role to alleviate the poor's hatred of one another and educate them for the future, as their ignorance was integral to their oppression. In this instance, at least, he set aside a vision of Western progress often associated with evolutionary thinking and saw no progression, citing both the failings and strengths of each caste.[24] It is interesting that he believed that the Shudras *did* hate one another, but he does not explain why. Nonetheless, in this instance, he did not want them to adopt upper-caste values or sensibilities (as he did when he invoked the Kshatriya force), but maintained instead that they should become themselves in the fullest sense. It was for this reason that he spoke of "Shudrahood." This important qualification showed the aspect of his Universalism that continued to encompass difference. These views of caste, therefore, advocated diversity and dynamism, but certainly retained hierarchy.

On this tour, he sought to boost Hindu self-esteem by speaking in English about Brahman, not God, and agreed with his host in Kumbakonam, who said that Hinduism intrinsically "harmonise[d] with the aspirations of the age," because of Vedanta's "wonderful rationalism" that sought a link to contemporary science.[25] And yet Vivekananda also asserted that "[h]ere have been the Aryan, the Dravidian, the Tartar, the Turk, the Mogul, the European—all the nations of the world, as it were, pouring their blood into this land. Of languages the most wonderful conglomeration is here; of manners and customs there is more difference between two Indian races than between the European and the Eastern races."[26]

How was unity in such diversity to be achieved? Was there a primacy to Hinduism? Was he implying that respectful tolerance was only a Hindu notion, and that other religions needed to find their place within this larger structure? It is certainly true that the idea of cultural and "racial" mixing did not frighten him. Indeed, he used history to point to the difference between different religious groupings—including Muslims—but did not advocate segregation.[27] None of these ambiguities, however, was resolved in his speech, which instead simply celebrated Indian heterogeneity in the same way that he championed an explosion of "castes" as indicative of burgeoning religious and social life. Vivekananda was forthright in recognizing that language and race in an ethnic and historical sense could *not* bring Indians together; nor could any exclusive vision of religion. Instead, the emphasis on the unquestionably *Hindu* vision of Advaitic unity permitted all creeds and spiritual inclinations to find shelter under its capacious umbrella.[28] This is what I think he meant when he extolled "sacred tradition, our religion" as the "one common ground."[29]

When speaking, Vivekananda buoyed up or scolded depending on his audience in a way not dissimilar to how he treated disciples. For example, he did not blame the English alone for India's degradation, but rather upbraided his compatriots for not uplifting the poor and downtrodden. He rarely criticized the "masses," instead viewing them as both undifferentiated and cruelly exploited. When abroad, he had been dismayed by "muscular Christianity," Darwinism, racism, and imperialism, trends that, for him, were tied to a dangerous from of masculinity. He had been wary of Western body consciousness and wondered whether it had sapped Western men of their spiritual force. He also viewed American materialism as masculine, hence his derogatory references to a Christianity that bargained with God for favors. Once back home, however, he tended to exalt man-making and often—although not always—extolled more rigid notions of gender differ-ence. His American disciple Alice Hansbrough, in California, remembered how he boasted in private: "I teach meat-eating throughout the 25 lengths and breadth of India in the hope that we can build a militant spirit."[30] When he first came home, he had warned his hearers in Colombo of overvaluing physical force, but then changed his tune, famously adding that "you will understand the Gita better with your biceps, your muscles, a little stronger. You will understand the mighty genius and the mighty strength of Krishna better with a little of strong blood in you. You will understand the Upani-shads better and the glory of the Atman when your body stands firm upon your feet, and you feel yourselves as men."[31]

Vivekananda did not mention the symbol of the sword (which later figured in Swadeshi after his death), but he alluded to "blood"—the fluid of strength iron—and the Bhagavad Gita, which described Arjuna's struggle on the bat-tlefield. Although he and Martha Brown Fincke, the free-thinking under-graduate at Smith, had both been revulsed by the idea of "sacred blood," he now spoke of "strong blood" to celebrate manly vitality.[32] In other instances, he *did* also focus on Kshatryias, the warrior caste, and martial prowess—ideas that Margaret Noble would later develop in a rather different direction. He re-marked that "The present want of India is the Kshatriya force."[33] But he would specify later what he meant by a "martial spirit"—it was not "self-assertion but self-sacrifice," the conviction that ultimate freedom came from prioritizing the nonself. "One must be ready to advance and lay down one's life at the word of command, before he can command the hearts and lives of others."[34] Militancy, meat, and blood *were* crucial to the masculinity he preached, but only if under-girded by the ethical imperatives of the Bhagavad Gita.

In his lecture "The Future of India," he compared Indian men to women to shock them out of "effeminacy," saying, "Ladies, excuse me, but through centuries of slavery, we have become like a nation of women. . . . Women . . . in European countries . . . make tremendous declarations of women's power and so on; then they quarrel, and some man comes and rules them all. All over the world they still require some man to rule them. We are like them. Women we are."[35]

Was this a thinly veiled allegory of the Indo-British relationship, with Indian men squabbling "like women," who therefore required the masculine handling of the British? Here, he conceded all the negative stereotypes of femininity (many of which he had rejected while in America) and compared Indian men to European women, who talked big but had little real power, and who required masculine authority.[36] But there was hope: historical patterns could be changed, and effeminate men could become virile.

For Vivekananda, this whirlwind tour was strange and exciting, but ultimately depleting. From Darjeeling, he wrote to Mary Hale how, in Ramnad, "a monument forty feet high is being built on the spot where he landed," and that his return had been one "huge procession—crowds of people, illuminations, addresses."[37] In another letter, he recounted that "the whole country here rose . . . to receive me. Hundreds of thousands of persons, shouting and cheering at every place, Rajas drawing my carriage, arches all over the streets of the capitals with blazing mottoes etc.!!!"[38] From the Alambazar Math in Calcutta, he told Sara Bull that he had "not a moment to die. . . . what with processions and tomtomings and various other methods of reception all over the country."[39]

He was not entirely joking, however, when he suggested that he *had* almost died: his "health broke completely down."[40] As early as late January, he told Mary Hale, "I am on the very height of my destiny, yet the mind turns to the days we had in Chicago, of rest, of peace, and love."[41] Here again was an allusion to the need for a spiritual retreat from the hurly-burly of speaking, debating, and appearing before crowds. In fact, the pressure was so great that he cut the trip short because the exertion and heat, he believed, had brought on diabetes.[42] He wrote another letter to Mary Hale at the end of April to explain that he was in Darjeeling to tend his health and eat meat (no starches), complaining that he could no longer have even sugar in his coffee.[43]

SEVA (SERVICE)

No aspect of Vivekananda's mission has caused more heated discussion than his advocacy of seva.[44] For some, this promotion of social virtue and "practical Vedanta" was a brave and necessary innovation; for others it was a "betrayal" of Ramakrishna, since the mystic had warned his disciples to remain focused on attaining "God Knowledge" rather than the "name and fame" that came with philanthropy.[45] Orthodox Advaitists also found Vivekananda's "synthesis" troubling. Although they accepted the unity among all beings, they believed it operated on a deeper level, and thus did not object when Dalits were prevented from entering temples; in doing so, they preserved mundane distinctions and the social conservatism that went with them. Brahmins had believed that because Dalits had nothing to renounce, this higher path was closed to them.[46] Vivekananda's insistence that Advaita could and should be democratized therefore had radical elements.

Many asked whether there was not a fundamental mismatch between the Advaita philosophy, which sees the world as maya, and Vivekananda's command to work incessantly in the here and now. How could service matter in a temporal realm that was mere illusion? How indeed, could one attain the necessary detachment for uniting with the Absolute if social engagement were prioritized?

These debates are linked to whether Vivekananda fostered these ideas from within Hindu theology and custom, or whether they were a foreign import. Some insist that it had to have come from the Germans, especially from Paul Deussen, an acquaintance whom he had met at Kiel.[47] If it was not from the Germans, perhaps he refashioned it from Brahmoism, a view which suggests that it had been deeply influenced by Western thought.[48] Certainly, notions of "charity" as a *religious duty* were integral to Judaism, Islam, and Christianity, but not to Hinduism, even though Indians had their own traditions of pious giving, which Margaret Noble would explore in her works on Indian domestic life.[49] Householder society had long depended on supporting sprawling family connections, the poor, and sannyasins through almsgiving, practical obligations matched by virtues of patience, compassion, and integrity; other public responsibilities of social welfare were part of *raj-dharma* (the ruler's prerogatives and obligations).[50] In both Christian and Hindu societies, practices of selfless giving were valued, though the motives which underlay such apparent "altruism" also had important critics, such as Ramakrishna.

New welfare organizations in the 1860s, such as the Red Cross, Red Crescent, and Prevention of Cruelty to Children increasingly moved away from an ethos of charity to one based on service, much of which focused on health, education, and youth. These pioneering groups, however, tended to congregate in Christian and Islamic societies.[51] When Vivekananda proclaimed his own, Hindu ethos of service, he remained ambivalent about "charity": On the one hand, in 1897, he gratefully acknowledged Queen Victoria in "inspiring the English to unique acts of charity by contribut[ing] herself to the cause of famine relief."[52] On the other, as late as 1900, he reiterated Ramakrishna's view that all charity—be it Hindu or Christian—might promote evil and vain impulses: "Charity is not fundamental. It is really helping on the misery of the world, not eradicating it. One looks for name and fame and covers his efforts to obtain them with the enamel of charity and good works. He is working for himself under the pretext of working for others. Every so-called charity is an encouragement of the very evil it claims to operate against."[53]

Instead, Vivekananda translated his ideals of service through a prism of Indian spiritual and ethical life, which he had developed prior to his departure to the West. The skeptical might suggest that he merely sought to "invent tradition," to create a Hindu past that justified this altered program. Vivekananda, however, looked to history because he doubted both the practical efficacy and spiritual value of charity. Instead, he extolled bhakti saints, such as Chaitanya, who embraced Dalits, and his talks are peppered with references to him.[54] Vivekananda concluded that uplift—especially among the most dispossessed—*was* indeed native to India. Repeatedly he returned to the "Old Masters" and included in this category Shankara, Ramanuja, Chaitanya, and even Kabir Das, an Indian mystic who began life as a Muslim, but was educated by a Hindu bhakti teacher, Ramananda.[55]

Vivekananda asserted that, despite interruptions to this tradition and many missteps, contemporary India offered a new opportunity to make seva and universal uplift central to Hindu sensibilities. When he spoke of Chaitanya, he evoked bhakti, but when he used the term "militant spirit," he may have harkened back to the armed sannyasins of the seventeenth and eighteenth centuries who resisted Muslim and British authority in the north and east of India.[56] But he did not seek a return to some idealized precolonial past; rather, he was intent on the new synthesis of "practical" activism.

His journey along the road to seva was long. Vivekananda knew from personal experience about service when he had sought to preserve the health and well-being of his guru-brothers, though as a young man even he regarded such responsibilities as distractions from his transcendental search. Indeed, in urging his fellow disciples to tend each other in the late 1880s, he was already developing a special ethic, unconcerned with critics who accused them of caring too much for this life and "weaving a web of maya."[57] As he gathered them in the garden of Meerut to teach them "world thought," he may have been unconsciously preparing them (or himself, or both) for service in India and abroad. When he spoke at the Mylapore Society in Madras, he had begun to create a special blend of spiritual, social, and political ideas from which aspects of his service ethic may have emerged. In 1891–1892, for example, he spoke about the Hindu monkey god Hanuman, whose steadfastness to Rama had fascinated him even as a child.[58] Certainly, in designating sannyasins as workers obliged to serve, he diverged from tradition in creating a form of renunciation that was both contemplative *and* active.

Although he later insisted that he was a "severe advaitist," a jnani, who had gained insight through wisdom and intellectual power, he believed that nothing—and especially not Karma yoga—was possible without the heart of a bhakti.[59] The unreasoning devotion of his guru remained greater than anything that reason could provide.[60] In insisting on this unorthodox link, he often alluded to his own experience, and especially the inspiration of Ramakrishna's love. In 1890, when wandering, he wrote to Pramadadas Mitra: "Never during his life did he refuse a single prayer of mine; millions of offences has he forgiven me; such great love even my parents never had for me. There is no poetry, no exaggeration in all this. It is the bare truth and every disciple of his knows it. In times of great danger, great temptation, I wept in extreme agony with the prayer, 'O God, do save me,' but no response came from anybody; but this wonderful saint, or Avatara, or anything else he may be, came to know of all my affliction through his powers of insight into human hearts and lifted it off."[61]

This remark strikingly recalled passages from Swami Saradananda's *Sri Ramakrishna and His Divine Play* and Mahendranath Gupta's *Sri Ramakrishna Kathamrita,* which described a connection that Vivekananda admitted was life-changing. There is little doubt that he felt Ramakrishna not only "saved him," but also recognized his inner divinity.

Throughout his life, Vivekananda sought to link the ethics of compassion to the "severity" of Advaita. In his writings, he returned often to the examples of Ramakrishna, Jesus, Chaitanya, and the Buddha, all avataras.[62] He expressed a special regard for the Buddha (if not for Buddhism) and wrote to Akhandananda, his old wandering companion, of his desire to bring together "the bright sun of intellectuality joined with the heart of Buddha." He concluded, moreover, that "this union will give us the highest philosophy."[63] The Buddha, moreover, had exemplified this selflessness when, rather than seeking his own spiritual liberation, he constantly returned as a bodhisattva to help suffering humanity. By speaking so often about bhakti, Vivekananda may have felt that he kept Ramakrishna's teaching alive within his new formulation. He embroidered on this theme at the World Parliament, when he said, "Hinduism cannot live without Buddhism, nor Buddhism without Hinduism." He called Buddhism the "fulfilment of Hinduism," thereby claiming Buddhism's compassionate inspirations, while veiling the "borrowing"; indeed, he often insisted that this great missionary religion had been absorbed by the "mother that gave it birth."[64]

Moreover, although Ramakrishna did not prioritize Advaita above other spiritual paths, he acknowledged its power in his love for Vivekananda when he called him (and the other disciples) "Narayana."[65] With such terms of endearment, Ramakrishna expressed not only his love for them, but his belief in their divinity. Also, his ready recourse to oceanic metaphors expressed an Advaitic sensibility that was in harmony with the yogic disciplines of Tota Puri, though he expressed no explicit intellectual debt.[66]

Given these lessons, Vivekananda came to believe that the sought-after union between the soul and the absolute was about human solidarity and connectedness. Before the World Parliament, he wrote to Alasinga Perumal that "every being is only your own self multiplied," in much the same way that God in souls was linked to the Absolute. He thus elaborated a psychology of fellow feeling and insisted on "sympathi[zing] with the poor, the miserable, the sinner."[67] This letter already tied such ideas to action, by asserting the need for practical application built on love and compassion.

Julius Lipner argues that the eighth-century jnani and Advaitist Adi Shankara had shunned bhakti because it affirmed distinction by requiring "a devotee and an object of devotion"; it also mandated that devotees perform sacrifice and worship, which Shankara viewed as tainted by worldly concerns, such as family and caste.[68] But even the ancient philosopher had acknowledged that bhakti could hasten individuals to Oneness by lightening the burden of accrued "bad" karma. "Selfless action," as prescribed in the Bhagavad Gita, described such behavior, and its protean inspiration transformed the social and political consciousness of nineteenth-century Indian intellectuals and activists.[69]

Vivekananda also turned to the Gita in *Karma Yoga*—we meet Krishna, now incarnated as a human charioteer, who has descended into the world to advise Arjuna, a warrior. The knight is about to engage in a fratricidal struggle and Krishna urges Arjuna to kill his relations without fear or hesitation.[70] Arjuna understandably pauses before the horror of killing those he loves and the upending of the chivalric order that their deaths would entail. Rather than condoling with Arjuna, however, Krishna told him that true dharma required detached engagement: "Arjuna became a coward . . . ; his 'love' made him forget his duty towards his country and king. That is why Shri Krishna told him that he was a hypocrite: 'Thou talkest like a wise man, but thy actions betray thee to be a coward; therefore stand up and fight!'"[71]

Vivekananda recognized that a Western audience might find the Gita's injunctions almost counterintuitive, and so he tried to explain the unfamiliar ethical reasoning.[72] Krishna's advice, he suggested, demanded an almost inhuman embrace of principle, an overwhelming moral steeliness—even more shocking and self-sacrificing in a culture that prioritized family connection and lineage almost above all else; in such cases, even a "hollow victory" was more righteous than a refusal to take up arms. True ethics thus involved cruel choices.

In writing of the Gita, Vivekananda criticized Christian "duty" as both a form of slavery (as he had done in Thousand Island) and as a crucible of sanctimony; he believed that duty was inseparable from a vision of a personal God who directed and chastised. Only with Advaita, he argued, could men and women be truly free, for an impersonal God (Brahman) had no role in human lives. As Amiya Sen has suggested, Vivekananda implied that ethics had no "independent foundation" but were rather part of the "realisation of the Universal Self"—a vision of radical freedom—from both society and a personal God—that his Western audiences in particular found difficult to comprehend. There was, however, a possible instrumentality in this argument—that doing for others was inescapably doing for oneself: the problem of selfishness lurked, but it was an issue that Vivekananda evaded.[73]

Important also to this synthesis, if rarely discussed, was Vivekananda's Hinduization of "character." the word he used to describe the firmness and persevering impulses in personality.[74] Despite its Western and very nineteenth-century associations, however, he viewed the idea of character through a karmic lens, the ineluctable law of cause and effect that attracted "all the powers of the universe." He concluded that, out of such a whirling "current," the human being "fashions the mighty stream of tendency called character and throws it outwards. As he has the power of drawing in anything, so has he the power of throwing it out."[75]

This view of character was central to his vision of man-making and mandated that the individual resist evil: "let him work, let him fight, let him strike straight from the shoulder. Then only, when he has gained the power to resist, will non-resistance be a virtue."[76] Vivekananda wrote these words in *Karma Yoga,* but they may very well have described his self-vision. Once again, he underscored the unity of opposites in his reasoning.

He thus required "work for work's sake," and the "unselfishness" that would bring about new "manifestation[s] of power," especially for sannyasins. In *Karma Yoga,* he vaunted self-control as an inner strength that enabled "intensest activity, and in the midst of the intensest activity [to] find the silence and solitude of the desert."[77] Because they have no stake in society, renouncers could dwell unselfishly in the world. They were indifferent to society's norms, which enabled them to be heedless of consequences, to recognize that individuals should not labor for name and fame—hence his view that he remained true to Ramakrishna's legacy.[78] Here again, he rebelled against utilitarianism, a position which explains why he has recently been reinterpreted not as the inventor of Hindu nationalism, but as a key figure in the creation of the radical "modern political" in India.[79]

Vivekananda instead advanced "practical Vedanta," so that Indian culture would not succumb to what he saw as the cruel pressures of imperialism. In acknowledging the technological, organizational, and economic power of Western civilization, he seemed to concede the need to absorb cultural influences that were not Indian, but felt adaptation to the new worldly reality was necessary. Ramakrishna had understood the dangers as well when he feared the spiritual death of his disciples if they worked for the British and imbibed their traits. Vivekananda shifted this understanding onto a new terrain by enjoining his monks (and his compatriots more broadly) to slave for other Indians instead, especially the "poor," both to (re)gain a sense of self and become one with the Absolute. Confronted by the horrors of both famine and plague, there was little wonder that he thought about "practicality." And yet, as will be seen, remnants of the desire to regain "spiritual babyhood" remained strong.

"PRACTICAL VEDANTA"

"Practical Vedanta" was tied to Vivekananda's dislike of excessive ritual and don't-touchism. Even before his trip to America, he had tussled with his guru-brother Ramakrishnananda, who had set aside a special room at Baranagar to worship Ramakrishna's relics and his slippers, objects that linked the divine presence to his human incarnation.[80] Ramakrishnananda furiously grabbed Vivekananda by the hair and threw him from the room.[81] The others were astonished by the anger that overtook the ordinarily peaceable Brahmin mathematician. So was Vivekananda; he did not interfere again—but the incident shows the difficulty in converting his fellows to his ideas.

When in America, he merely restated his position: "just throw your ceremonials overboard and worship the Living God, the Man-God—every being that wears a human form—God in His universal as well as individual aspect." He wrote in despair: "Today you have your bell, tomorrow you add a horn, and follow suit with a chowry the day after; or you introduce a cot today, and tomorrow you have its legs silver-mounted, and people help themselves to a rice-porridge, and you spin out two thousand cock-and-bull stories—in short, nothing but external ceremonials . . ."[82]

He even linked this love of ritual to the "slavery" of colonialism: "Those whose heads have a tendency to be troubled day and night over such questions . . . simply deserve the name of wretches, and it is owing to that sort of notion that we are the outcasts of Fortune, kicked and spurned at, while the people of the West are masters of the whole world. . . . There is an ocean of difference between idleness and renunciation. . . ."[83]

After the scolding, he urged: "Spread ideas—go from village to village, from door to door—then only there will be real work. Otherwise, lying complacently on the bed and ringing the bell now and then is a sort of disease, pure and simple . . ."[84] Vivekananda complimented his guru-brother Akhandananda for his work in Rajputana, where the monk had upbraided the prince for not improving the lot of his "poor tenants [who] lived in dingy huts, with scarcely any access to air and light, . . . and how like leeches the rich sucked them dry to satisfy their own love of luxury."[85] Furthermore,

No good will come of sitting idle and having princely dishes, and saying "Ramakrishna, O Lord!"[86] . . . . You must give your body, mind, and speech to "the welfare of the world." You have read—. . . "look upon your mother as God, look upon your father as God"—but I say—"the poor, the illiterate, the ignorant, the afflicted—let these be your God." Know that service to these alone is the highest religion.

He assured Akhandananda that service to the poor would purify him through sacrifice: "If people object to the kind of food you take, give it up immediately. It is preferable to live on grass for the sake of doing good to others." There was heroism in this work, and Akhandananda indeed worked heroically, becoming, as will be seen, the "famine swami" for his tireless efforts.

In "Practical Vedanta," Vivekananda furthered these ideas via lectures delivered in London just before his return to India at the end of 1896.[87] The timing and location are important, as he mentioned the famine in the midst of recent efforts to alleviate the suffering. In 1896, £1.7 million had been collected as Arthur Conan Doyle did readings, theaters produced plays about famine, and Indian elites joined in rescue activism.[88] In these lectures, Vivekananda urged Indians to adopt "practicality," but also suggested how the British cruelly subjugated his compatriots.[89]

He argued that "Vedanta philosophy is not the outcome of meditation in the 'forests only,'" now almost a motto for Ramakrishna monks, and yet radical at the time.[90] He wanted them to forfeit the hermitage for the schoolroom and hospital, and honored the "busy man." He thus sought to link the stillness of meditation with the roar of temporal life. Like so many other Indian national theorists of the time, he returned yet again to Arjuna's quandary in the Gita and the need for detachment: "in every page. . . . [there] is intense activity, but in the midst of it, eternal calmness . . . Inactivity, as we understand it in the sense of passivity, certainly cannot be the goal."[91] In fact, he maintained that the greater the detachment, the better the work.

In Britain, Vivekananda opposed the stereotype of indolent Indians without enough character to deal with real-life problems. Instead, he proclaimed the universal message of Advaita, the famous "Thou art That" that made all human beings divine. While he gloried in the goal, he presented a psychology of imperfection, rather than a theology of sin. Again, in contrast to many Protestant views, he argued that error rather than fault prevented the spiritual seeker from progressing fearlessly. "Practical Vedanta" was a manual of self-belief and self-acceptance, and he illustrated the point by speaking of his own "errors": "I myself may not be a very strict vegetarian, but I understand the ideal. When I eat meat I know it is wrong. Even if I am bound to eat it under certain circumstances, I know it is cruel."[92]

He reapplied himself to embracing the "brotherhood of all souls." If Christian critics accused him of moral laxity, he riposted that good and evil were relative, as were heaven and hell; Hinduism was tolerant because it rejected Christian rigidity (and with it such conceptions as "duty"). Here, he again seemed to essentialize Hinduism almost as an aspect of anticolonialism, strengthening his attack on what he saw as self-righteous monotheism. To believe oneself divine was not to preach immorality, but rather to help the world to the "ideal" that our human selves—attached to maya—found difficult to attain.

These ideas fed into another key precept—the need not to show contempt for others. Was he speaking here of the British attitude toward Indians, or high-castes' disdain for those below them? Perhaps both. Above all, he wanted Indians (and his Western acolytes) to feel strong. When teaching meditation to his women devotees, he said that he concentrated on the heart of a lion because such thoughts gave courage. In London, he reiterated that "the remedy for weakness is not brooding over weakness, but thinking of strength," poignant remarks given the waning of his own physical strength.[93]

He concluded with a surprising statement: "From my childhood everyone around me taught weakness; I have been told ever since I was born that I was a weak thing. It is very difficult for me now to realise my own strength."[94] Stories of his childhood and schooling do not support this view, but we must take Vivekananda at his word. Clever, talented, accomplished, even arrogant, he had also felt undone by the poverty that his father's death had caused. But the weakness he described went deeper still—it also resulted from an English, Christian education, and from living with foreign domination. For Vivekananda, "Practical Vedanta" was about throwing off that power in one's inner life. Seva was one way to reach this goal. As he had explained to Alasinga in 1893, universal love was based on the love of oneself, and on self-forgiveness, as when he admitted his "fault" when eating meat.

And yet, Vivekananda and his brother-monks did not always possess the humility that Karma yoga required. As upper-caste men, they felt their position within Hindu society. As sannyasins, they were now without caste, and yet they embodied the physical and cultural signs of the caste of their birth, and, in India, their social position was instantly visible. Even Akhandananda, the "famine swami," admitted that in his earlier days of wandering, he could not eat food served by a Goan Christian, who filled him with "repulsion." Hindu Brahmins regarded such Christians as opportunists, who had converted to escape poverty. His host gravely remarked, "'I see you have not yet been able to cast off caste prejudice.'"[95] Akhandananda admitted his failing but still fled to a Brahman household where he could eat his meals without discomfort.[96]

Vivekananda was sincere when he said, "Alas! Nobody thinks of the poor of this land," but he possessed views that both upper-middle-class Westerners and upper-caste Hindus shared.[97] He thought the poor "unworldly," and he wanted his monks to "open their eyes."[98] Around the same time, he wrote a letter to the Maharaja of Mysore, which is striking both for its anti-Westernism, and for how it spoke of the Indian "masses": "our poor Hindu people are infinitely more moral than any Westerners. In religion they practice here either hypocrisy or fanaticism. . . . The poor in the West are devils; compared to them ours are angels, and it is therefore so much easier to raise our poor."[99]

Vivekananda reckoned the Hindu masses needed education to develop "their lost individuality," a remark that reflected his wish to inculcate self-belief, but also betrayed his view of their current state. He was concerned for their fate, but cast the assistance as a process of spiritual enlightenment that he would direct: "I love the poor, the ignorant, the downtrodden, I feel for them—the Lord knows how much. . . . I do not care a fig for human approbation or criticism. I think of most of them as ignorant, noisy children—they have not penetrated into the inner nature of sympathy, into the spirit which is all love."[100] He thus mixed an inchoate process of social and spiritual mobilization with a dream of religious benevolence and uplift. He also revealed that, like the British who regarded all the "natives" as undifferentiated, he, at times, similarly saw "the poor" as uniform.

Such remarks suggest how central ideas of childhood and childishness remained in his thought on "practical Vedanta" and seva. Ramakrishna's unworldliness must be contrasted to a deeper ignorance that allowed no mystical intuitions to penetrate the consciousness of these downtrodden and noisy children. And yet, the model of child-likeness remained potent and ever in the background: in the first lecture on "Practical Vedanta," he mentioned "children" and the "child" seven times, and almost always positively for their intuitive understanding of the nature of divine Unity. For Vivekananda, Ramakrishna's legacy remained, albeit in a different, more veiled form: "intellect is necessary" to avoid "crude errors," he asserted, "but ... do not try to build anything upon it ... the real help is feeling love."[101] Practical Vedanta was, certainly, about taking on certain aspects of Western organization, but it also retained Ramakrishna's anti-intellectualism and experientialism. Amid the cerebralism of Advaita and the ethical activism of Karma yoga, the ethos of bhakti powerfully endured.

Vivekananda's ideas on service had matured by the time he returned to India. When he spoke at the Rameswaram Temple on his tour from Colombo to Almora, he sought, as ever, to detach the worship of Shiva from the god-image to the worship of all people, to enhance the relationship between social solidarity and spirituality: "He who sees Shiva in the poor, in the weak, and in the diseased, really worships Shiva; and if he sees Shiva only in the image, his worship is but preliminary. He who has served and helped one poor man seeing Shiva in him, without thinking of his caste, or creed, or race, or anything, with him Shiva is more pleased than with the man who sees Him only in temples."[102] Without this sense of connection, how could any country rise? "I see clear as daylight that there is the one Brahman in all, in them and in me— one Shakti dwells in all."[103] Such remarks—repeated often in various contexts— were central to his Universalism.

Although he wanted to uplift the poor for their own sakes, their condition also deeply offended his national pride. In an interview with one of the order's publications, *Prabuddha Bharata*, in September 1898, he called for "national efficiency," the term later popularized during the Boer War when Britain sought to combat its own fear of racial decline and degeneration.[104] He asked, "Can you adduce any reason why India should lie in the ebb-tide of the Aryan nations? Is she inferior in intellect? Is she inferior in dexterity? Can you look at her art, at her mathematics, at her philosophy, and answer 'yes'? All that is needed is that she should ... wake up from her age-long sleep to take her true rank in the hierarchy of nations."[105]

These words imply a relatively rare preoccupation with Western rankings of national (even racial) strength and value.[106] Were such statements part of a larger fear of "retarded" development tied to evolutionary theory? Or was he responding to a colonial ethnography that harped on Indian "backwardness"?[107] When he spoke in this way, such notions were inextricable from his loftier spiritual project of service. They showed, moreover, how difficult it was for him to remain detached, how his love for the Motherland led him, willy-nilly, to reflect on national rivalries and assert India's civilizational value, rather than on the universalism that undergirded Advaita.

THE MATH AND MISSION

At the end of April 1897, Vivekananda felt better, and, in early May, he began to organize a permanent Math and Mission to give his ideas concrete form. The monastery's history can be linked to its locations and buildings—the first at the Cossipore House where Ramakrishna died; the second in the dilapidated dwelling at Baranagar where the monks first gathered (1886–1892?); the third in Alambazar (February 1892–February 1898), half a mile north of Dakshineswar Temple; and finally at Belur Math.[108] The Belur plot was purchased in early 1898 and dedicated in December of that year, and the main Math building was ready for habitation in January 1899. Henrietta Müller, who Vivekananda had found so difficult as traveling companion and disciple, bought the land for 39,200 rupees; Sara Bull gave another large sum for new buildings.[109] When Bull, Nivedita, and Josephine MacLeod came to India, they would stay in a little cottage not too far away. The community shifted to Belur on January 2, 1899, a year and a half after its formal foundation. Vivekananda's relationships to women were thus central to his fund-raising capacity and show how he used British and American money to create this new foundation based on the revised teachings of his guru.

It is difficult to provide an exact timeline for the innovations that Vivekananda instituted, but the changes were incremental. In Baranagar, they had begged for food and, when they went to Alambazar, many continued to wander as sannyasins, with Ramakrishnananda remaining always in place. In 1895, however, Vivekananda began to outline regulations for reading, classes, meditation, and hymn singing; and in 1896, to forbid the monks "to huddle together in a room and chat the whole day away, with any number of outsiders coming and joining in the hubbub."[110] After his return, he instituted what he called the "Belur Math Rules" in Alambazar, guidelines that he also instituted in Madras to foster greater discipline and cooperation. They were scolded as in the past, but now their worship, theological preferences, and bodily rhythms were more dramatically reshaped.

Although Ramakrishna had chosen Vivekananda to lead, he had also recognized five other "Eternal Companions'" or "divine attendants of the Lord'"[111] Like courtiers to the avatara, they were meant to be reborn continuously to instruct the world and had a keen sense of their spiritual pedigree. His "reforms," therefore, unsettled some informal hierarchies established in Ramakrishna's time, while his demands and inspiration began to alter their activities and expectations.

They argued, for example, about Ramakrishna's place in the community. Some believed that Vivekananda had been ungratefully reticent about Ramakrishna in the West; they grumbled that he might have become a Calcutta barrister or have married a rich American woman had it not been for Ramakrishna.[112] Others, such as Yogananda, one of Ramakrishna's "divine attendants," feared losing the spiritual intimacy that meditation on the avatara permitted. Vivekananda countered by arguing that Ramakrishna's universality would be undermined by a focus on his image and relics.

Vivekananda had always disliked sects and his contact with Protestantism abroad had made him even warier.[113] He had sporadically referred more positively to Catholicism, which he considered to be "religious in the highest sense" and was not averse to Catholic ceremony—"all those lights, incense, candles, and the robes of the priests" that reminded him of the "lower" levels of Hindu worship.[114] But he also worried about the dangers of "priest craft" and symbolism: "one sect has one particular form of ritual and thinks that that is holy, while the rituals of another sect are simply arrant superstition. If one sect worships a peculiar sort of symbol, another sect says, "'Oh, it is horrible!'"[115]

He feared similar confrontations in India between the worshippers of one avatara and another, one god and another, hence his endorsement of the formless universalism of Advaita, now increasingly evident in seva. To instill this ethos, Vivekananda hoped that observing good rules, correct habit, discipline, and character would ready the brothers for this shift. Swami Premananda, who had always been one of Ramakrishna's favorites and a "divine attendant," was at first disturbed by Vivekananda's attempts to initiate new routines, but soon became the manager of the Math, enjoining his fellow monks to accept the rigorous new schedule and to execute even the simplest tasks in the spirit of Karma yoga.[116]

Vivekananda even introduced François Delsarte's "natural movement." Delsarte was a voice coach, singer, and orator, whose exercise system was integral to the Western physical culture movement of the late nineteenth century.[117] Vivekananda may have learned the techniques from Sarah Bernhardt, who had been Delsarte's pupil, or more likely her colleague, the soprano Emma Calvé. His "Practical Vedanta" lectures, however, had described Delsarte's exercises as inferior to pranayama, which was "practised to get mastery" over spiritual energy, in which the breath was only an outward manifestation; in contrast, Delsarte's exercises merely controlled the breath and strengthened the lungs.[118] Physical prowess was not the same as enlightenment, which was why he had focused on meditation (and not hatha yoga) to deal with spiritual weakness in the West. Why then did this inferior Western technique appear in the monks' daily schedule? Perhaps he brought these new disciplines to enhance bodily control, while also imposing mandatory training with dumbbells. He clearly desired that his monks would have the physical endurance to sustain the seva he now envisaged.

He also imposed sanctions, making the monks beg for food if they did not rise early enough in the mornings and go about their work.[119] For some, these corrections simply did not work, and compliance took years, especially as Vivekananda adopted a flexible approach. For example, Vijnanananda accused him of straying from Ramakrishna's teachings by working with women while abroad and reminded him that the Master had wanted them not even to look at a woman's picture, an injunction that he, himself, had followed to the letter.[120] Vivekananda's views were different, but rather than expelling him, he accepted that Vijnanananda could best serve the order by meditating deeply on Ramakrishna. Swami Adbhutananda, also known as Latu, the illiterate orphan mentioned earlier, regarded Vivekananda's innovations as an unacceptable deviation from Ramakrishna's teachings. He objected to the bell that heralded the new routines and disturbed his meditation, refused the dumbbells, and rejected Vivekananda's call to become a trustee of the Math, fearful of worldly entanglement. In a moment of exasperation, Vivekananda asked him to leave, and then thought better of it. Both he and Ramakrishna had esteemed Latu and realized his importance in proving that the poorest and least educated could reach spiritual heights. Of all the monks in Vivekananda's charge, Latu resisted most effectively.[121]

But for every "failure," Vivekananda inspired and impelled others to undertake life-changing shifts. For example, he persuaded Abhedananda to become an apostle in the West. Known for his erudition and for belief that

Christ had prepared his mission first in India, Abhedananda first collaborated with Sturdy, but later headed the Vedanta Society in New York.[122] Saradananda, who had been educated at St. Xavier's College in Calcutta, now shared his knowledge of St. Paul and Sanskrit, went to the West for a time and later, as secretary of the Math and Mission until 1927, organized and raised money.[123] Swami Trigunatitananda established the *Udbodhan*, a Bengali magazine for householders in 1899; when a disciple suggested that it seemed wrong that "that Sannyasins in ochre robes should go from door to door" like common salesmen, Vivekananda riposted that he should "[l]earn from them how to work. Here, for instance, Trigunatita has given up his spiritual practices, his meditation and everything, to carry out my orders. . . . Is this a matter of small sacrifice? What an amount of love for me is at the back of this spirit of work . . . Have you householders such determination?"[124]

Shivananda, who had met Sturdy on his travels in 1893, went to Sri Lanka to teach Vedanta, translated Vivekananda's Chicago lectures into Hindi, and started another branch of the movement in Varanasi. He was president of the order from 1922 until his death in 1934.[125] Even Ramakrishnananda, who had exploded when Vivekananda had criticized his worship of Ramakrishna's relics, began the Sri Ramakrishna Math in Madras and became an important figure in the city; Vivekananda obliged the reserved Turiyananda to come west with him despite the latter's preference for asceticism and contemplation.[126] He headed the Vedanta Society in San Francisco, founded by Vivekananda in April 1900. Turiyananda also led Shanti Ashrama, 168 acres of land in the San Antonio Valley given by a wealthy donor. After Turiyananda left, Trigunatita further developed this first American yogic "retreat" (the original Meditation Cabin remains) and raised funds for the Old Temple in San Francisco.[127] In India, even Vijnanananda began in 1910 to dispense medicines, despite knowing little about disease, chanting Ramakrishna's name while giving away homeopathic remedies.[128] The later date suggests that Vivekananda's teachings may have taken on new meaning after the Swadeshi campaign and the growing power of the Ramakrishna Mission, but we cannot know for certain.

Although these initiatives took time to bear fruit, they show Vivekananda simultaneously "nationalizing" and "internationalizing" the Vedanta movement. On the one hand, his triumphal tour reinforced a geographical vison of the sacred Motherland, repeatedly emphasized through contact with

Madras, the southern capital of the movement. On the other, he uprooted men bound to Ramakrishna, Dakshineswar, and Belur and sent them away, disrupting the link between place and their early mysticism, which their pilgrimages had only reinforced. He also unknowingly laid the spiritual and institutional foundations in America and elsewhere for the Indian diaspora to find Hindu Universalism outside of the subcontinent, both in urban temples and centers, but also in topography far removed from Indian associations.[129]

He did, however, fail to establish a house of female nuns. When, in 1895, brother-monks wanted to exclude women on certain days during the festivities that honored Ramakrishna, he resisted, and even defended the rights of "public women" (sex workers) to find solace in the veneration of their guru.[130] In 1896, he wrote that Ramakrishna, as a man who had dressed as a woman, had been women's champion, and that a women's Math should be created that was not under male "dictation."[131] Back in India, when men argued the case, he insisted on its worthiness.[132] The British, too, did their best to suppress the project, vetoing land deals that might have made it possible. Margaret Noble and Christine Greenstidel, from the beginning, had created a sisterly community in Bagbazar, a north Calcutta neighborhood. Nonetheless, the convent only officially opened in 1954. The first head of the Sri Sarada Math, Bharatiprana, had nursed Sarada Devi in her final illness; she therefore provided a link to the founding generation.[133]

FAMINE

Today, Indians remember the Raj as a period of recurrent famine, and rightly so; between 1860 and 1901, some twelve to thirty million people died of starvation or of illnesses related to famine.[134] There was the Orissa (now Odisha) famine of 1866–1867 in the Madras Presidency, Hyderabad, and Mysore (now a region in Karnataka); the so-called Great Famine of 1876–1878 that forced millions into indenture in tropical zones of the British Empire; and the famine of 1896–1897, which extended beyond these dates and which concerns us here. More fearful of encouraging pauperism than feeding the starving, the government responded inadequately. Only once, during the Bengal famine of 1874, did the British alleviate the distress, but regarded the cost as disproportionate.

Preceded by a drought in Madras, the British worsened hunger by continuing to export grain, a ruinous policy that continued through the Second World War. On his return, Vivekananda thus experienced the extent of British violence in seeing this mass starvation, though he did not know yet that it would generate experiments of seva central to the mission.[135] He understood something of hunger's gnawing pangs after his father's death and during his wandering years.[136] But the famine of the late 1890s was of a different order—widespread and inexorable. British clerics on the ground estimated that "quite sixty millions of people, or more than one fifth of the entire population" were affected.[137] Between 1899 and 1900, photographs from hard-hit areas, such as Rajputana, revealed horrific images of skeletal corpses. One British witness in Deccan in March 1900 reported on the "family parties on tramp," parched with thirst, "their eyes hollow with hunger."[138] British testimonies spoke of orphaned children and women being eaten by scavenging animals, the cruelty of Indian middlemen raising the price of cheap grain, circumstances made worse by cholera and the smell of burning dead bodies. The government in London realized that a full-fledged scandal was in the making.

Voluntary activism—both Christian/European and Indian—had expanded massively since the famines of the 1860s and 1870s. The former claimed a humanitarian, missionary mantle, while the Indian associations were fired by political ideas that often embraced recent shifts in religious outlook, as they created their own ethic of service, vision of character, and forms of association.

In the year of Vivekananda's return, thousands of more prosperous and educated Indians raised funds for hard-hit areas.[139] Official reports note missionaries annoyed by the presence of "wealthy natives" on the famine committees and feared that they would mistreat Christian "natives." There was, however, evidence of Indian solidarity across caste, class, and region, as well as town and country, and mutual efforts of Hindus and Muslims to feed the hungry.[140] The growing network was part of a wave of voluntarism that would turn into a tide during Swadeshi.[141]

The Ramakrishna monks therefore had to insert themselves into an already diverse relief landscape. Christian missionaries sometimes profited from the desperation—the London Missionary Society at Kadapa in Andhra Pradesh built and reconstructed scores of churches, schools, teachers' houses, and latrines with labor hired in exchange for food.[142] They opened orphanages and schools for Hindu and Muslim children who had been abandoned or lost parents. American missionaries set up teacher-training schools, feeding corn (an unaccustomed staple for Indians) to new recruits and organizing their evangelical instruction.[143] The Ramakrishna monks had also to compete with Indian Christians, such as Pandita Ramabai, who had established a school for widows in Poona (now Pune), well funded by Christians abroad; by 1900, she had assembled 2,000 women and children in "Mukti," a settlement that both government and missionary officials praised.[144]

In the rush to serve, Lala Lajpat Rai, later a vocal freedom fighter, encouraged the Arya Samaj to create the Hindu Orphan Relief Movement, which, by 1900, looked after 1,700 children, no doubt founded to combat the Christian "theft" of Hindu children.[145] The Arya Samaj preached patriotism and, like Vivekananda, wanted to convert the alms given to Brahmin priests into more "worthy" and coordinated service.[146] The Buddhist Maha Bodhi Society—headquartered in Calcutta and headed by Dharmapala—as well as the Brahmo Samaj—also had funds and activists, and both groups were present on the ground when Akhandananda, Vivekananda's old pilgrimage partner and guru-brother, began his work. Indian theosophists also created their own networks, increasingly including people from lower-middle-class backgrounds, and even some women.[147]

One of the Mission's pioneers was Swami Trigunatitananda, who went in 1897 to Birole in Dinajpur district (today in northern Bangladesh) to serve eighty-four villages, sitting on bushels of rice to guard them from thieves, and distributing the grain without regard for caste or creed.[148] On January 28, 1898, the *Indian Mirror* reported on B. N. Bonham-Carter, the British official who characterized Trigunatitananda's efforts as an example of "a beginning of self-help in the right line," but finished his address by lecturing the Indians on the self-governing traditions of British trade unions and athletic clubs.[149]

When Trigunatitananda responded, he diplomatically did not blame the British for food shortages, but rather condemned the "vain Zemindars [*sic*], Rajas or Maharajahs . . . of the land" for their profligacy and cruelty.[150] But his loyalties were clear—he focused on labor, the "only real thing that produces wealth" and compared the American worker to his Indian counterpart, insisting that the first was valued; the second, despised. He warned through historical examples—from ancient Rome to the Indian Mutiny—to prove that rebellion would ensue if the aristocrats (and the British) did not learn their lesson.[151]

Swami Akhandananda wrote a memoir, *From Holy Wanderings to Service of God in Man,* which disclosed the inner turmoil that this novel course had produced. As a youth, he had been scrupulous in asceticism, eating only once a day and bathing four times a day, but Ramakrishna urged him to explore a more expansive spirituality.[152] As has been seen, even before his famine activism he still refrained from taking food from a Christian Goan.

Akhandananda's encounter with the famine, however, changed him. He described starving families and recounted how he tended an old woman, Gaya Vaishnavi, who, brought low by an attack of diarrhea, believed that he had been her son in former births; he insisted that he was her son *now,* "in this very life."[153] Described in this way, the encounter became a sadhana (spiritual trial) that offered the self-realizing possibilities that Vivekananda praised. He suggested, too, that the change surprised those who encountered him. One pandit, in explaining who Akhandananda was, apparently remarked, "he is a genuine Sannyasin. . . . But the peculiarity with him is that . . . [his] principal aim in life is to remove distress."[154] Somehow, these activities were regarded as an important break with the past.

Akhandananda's commitment deepened as he traveled in West Bengal, living among the inhabitants of Berhampore, chanting the "Chandi" (a hymn to Durga), teaching the proper intonations for prayers, and talking about the Bhagavad Gita. He was enchanted by the local singing and dancing and, like a good ethnographer, wrote down the lyrics that spoke of drought and want of food. But when the famine arrived, both Premananda and Ramakrishnananda begged him to return to the Math. "You are but a mendicant Sannyasin. It is not possible for you to provide food for thousands of mouths."[155] Even Vivekananda asked him to come home, but Akhandananda cited a vision that steadied his resolve: Calcutta's palaces were no longer made of bricks, but of human skulls, the brick dust now made of human flesh and blood. The skulls laughed at him and told him not to return where death awaited him. Instead, he should remain in the "holy abode of Sita," in villages of thatched cottages. Sita, of course, was the loyal and self-sacrificing wife of Rama, but in this instance the word also denoted "sita" or cultivated land, now strangely transformed into a bucolic paradise.[156]

When a Maha Bodhi Society representative offered to help, Akhandananda used the order's money to buy rice and, as the crowds grew, his guru-brothers, as well as Vivekananda, changed their tune. Brahmananda wrote letters about the work, while Suddhananda acted as Akhandananda's private secretary. Difficulty arose when they turned to fund-raising and publicity, and asked Akhandananda to do the same. They explained that "the Brahmos sen[t] weekly reports of their work . . . and appeal[ed] for money . . ."[157]

Akhandananda tried to obey this request for a report on his activities, but instead wept. He claimed that Ramakrishna appeared in a vision to make him even more miserable: "the Master appeared before my mind's eye and said, 'Whom do you want? Me or the public? You need give a report of your work to the press—not for Me but for the public . . . Now choose either Me or your public.' As I heard these words of the Master in my heart, tears overpowered me."[158]

He had been willing—even eager—to undertake seva as a mendicant monk, but Akhandananda, his dramatic memoir claimed, resisted getting "name or fame." When he finally delivered his account, Vivekananda wrote in June 1897: "Accept a hundred thousand embraces and blessings from me. Work, work, work—I care for nothing else. Work, work, work, even unto death! . . . It is the heart, the heart that conquers, not the brain. Books and learning, Yoga and meditation and illumination—all are but dust compared with love. It is love that gives you the supernatural powers, love that gives you Bhakti, love that gives illumination, and love, again, that leads to emancipation."[159]

In June and July in 1897, Vivekananda recorded the progress of famine relief, the need for strict accounting (and hence the necessity of engaging in money matters), and the training of young men to prepare them for the field.[160] At the end of September, he wrote from Kashmir that by working near "different famine-centres," the monks were "influencing the lower classes more and more." He was grateful that "nearly all the Hindus" approved and proud that his workers made "no distinction. . . . between the different religions of India" when offering relief.[161] Vivekananda urged householders to send food to the poor and to use only the ubiquitous tulsi leaves and water as offerings to the gods.[162] He sought to make service the primary sacrifice, rather than promoting austerities, while also condemning the Indian predilection to build monuments and temples as panaceas for misdeeds. In his view, they smacked of the vainglory he and Ramakrishna despised. These edifices were examples of traditional India's wasteful charity that he, along with Hindus and many Muslims (including those of orthodox temperament), increasingly criticized. This was one of the ways in which he remained true to his guru while changing direction.

Vivekananda suggested that the ascetic trials of their Baranagar days were insufficient to "know God." He had criticized Western acolytes for their relentless busyness and urged them to meditate, but when he came home, he began Delsarte exercises and dumbbell workouts.[163] He accepted Latu's rebellion and Vijnanananda's reproaches, but he did not abandon the schedule or his larger institutional project. There were religious classes for the public, "question-answer sessions for monastics," an emphasis on guiding the novices and creating an increasingly dynamic organization.[164]

While Vivekananda scolded his brothers and pushed them to do what he had done—preach, talk, change their bodily rhythms, and travel abroad—he also confessed to Josephine MacLeod in the spring of 1900 that he was utterly depleted: "After all, Joe, I am only the boy who used to listen with rapt wonderment to the wonderful words of Ramakrishna under the Banyan at Dakshineswar. That is my true nature; works and activities, doing good and so forth are all superimpositions. Now I again hear his voice; the same old voice thrilling my soul. Bonds are breaking—love dying, work becoming tasteless—the glamour is off life. Only the voice of the Master calling— . . . I come, my beloved Lord, I come."[165]

Before he left for his second trip abroad in June 1899 (when Sturdy deserted him, and California unexpectedly beckoned), he addressed the junior sannyasins of the Math. If he was sometimes indulgent with his guru-brothers, he showed no doubts with new recruits. This is the Vivekananda of legend, the muscle-building, man-making warrior monk of renunciation, both for the poor and for the nation. Again, very much like Gandhi, he explained that renunciation was the "*love of Death*."[166] This prescription was not about romantic melancholy, but life as a "sacrifice for the whole world." Here, he prioritized a form of activism linked to the "ideal" that the Mission now set itself. It should serve "millions of brothers rather than aggrandize this little self": "So we must not lower our ideal, neither are we to lose sight of practicality. We must avoid the two extremes. In our country, the old idea is to sit in a cave and meditate and die. One must learn sooner or later that one cannot get salvation if one does not try to seek the salvation of his brothers.

You must try to combine in your life immense idealism with immense practicality."[167]

In this exhortation, he summed up what he meant by Karma yoga. He aimed to make rishis, sages who nourished their minds but recognized the limits of book-learning and even of meditation. "You must stand on your own feet. You must have this new method—the method of man-making."

However, he still retained something of the fluid notions of male and female at the heart of Ramakrishna's spiritual idealism: "The true *man* is he who is strong as strength itself and yet possesses a woman's heart." Central to this man-making was obedience: "If your superiors order you to throw yourself into a river and catch a crocodile, you must first obey and then reason with him [*sic*]." This type of yogi put sacrifice before rationality: to give up one's life without a thought was to be the freest of all. He also emphasized an almost military loyalty to the order that squashed the temptation of sects and schism. And yet, there remained that impossible paradox: 'You must be as free as the air, and as obedient as this plant and the dog."[168]

13

THE CLINCH

The patient must learn to live, to live with his split, his conflict, his ambivalence, which no therapy can take away, for if it could, it would take with it the actual spring of life.

　　　　　—Otto Rank, *Will Therapy* (1929; trans. 1936)

Ambivalence—having mixed feelings, entertaining contradiction, living with fluctuation—is a widened embrace.

　　　　　—Charles D'Ambrosio, *Loitering* (2016)

◆　◆　◆

WHEN RAMAKRISHNA selected Vivekananda and gathered the other guru-brothers, he sought to transmit something of the experiential theology he valued after years of visions and spiritual trials. But unlike Ramakrishna, Vivekananda had no need to seek out "sons" when he returned in 1897; they were already abundant in the guru-brothers and the novices of the new Math and Mission. When he asked for Margaret Noble's help, however, he *explicitly* sought a Western "daughter" to extend this legacy.

Vivekananda's life cannot be fully understood without her. Of course, she is also important on her own terms—and deserves her own account—hence, the investigation here of both her passion for her guru and attempt to attain her own liberation. Nonetheless, her journey must be examined within the context of Vivekananda's aspirations, for he spoke openly about how she was, for him, his "Besant in the making," an Englishwoman of intellect, character, and drive, who he hoped would broadcast India's worth to the world. As has been seen, he chose a "Celtic lioness," the daughter of a Protestant minister and a woman who had earned her living as a progressive teacher and occasional journalist. He also chose someone with political commitments that were inseparable from her spiritual aspirations.[1]

Nivedita's devotion to her adopted homeland, and her rejection of empire, were thus crucial to Vivekananda's project of dispatching orientalist clichés of Indian degeneracy and barbarism. She perhaps replaced them with other, inverted clichés, but asserted them as a Westerner who now inhabited the world she depicted. In partnership, moreover, Nivedita and Vivekananda were bold, embracing what had been the most "heathenish" aspects of Hinduism. When she wrote *Kali the Mother* (1900), she set out a dynamic and indomitable vision of the Mother Goddess that undermined mythologies of Indian passivity. She thus heralded a return of Ramakrishna's "primitive" Kali-love and made it important to early Indian nationalism.

Vivekananda and Margaret Noble also pioneered a pattern of interaction that seemed to invert more usual colonial relations. By living in the Calcutta slums as a Hinduized Westerner, she worked to alleviate the famine and plague, and in the process, came to reject her own people.[2] She had already given up her London life and income to exist on a small allowance from Sara Bull. By accepting Indian customs and values at this juncture, she was a living rebuke to the flimsiness of British claims to civilizational superiority. Her devotion, moreover, to an Indian "great man" prefigured a future that recognized Indians not as the people of a subjugated nation, but as worldmakers of spiritual and political freedom. Finally, by bringing her to his side, Vivekananda connected the women's worlds of the East and West. He had a long connection with a female saint in Sarada Devi, the Holy Mother, but Nivedita became someone Sarada could never be—teacher, public figure, authoress, and political activist. As friends and allies, moreover, Sarada and Margaret Noble paved the way for women around the globe to sustain his Hindu Universalism.

◆　◆　◆

Margaret Noble's life was unusual even before she met Vivekananda, but it became exceptional after she decided to "Hinduize" herself. The path was perilous, and never complete; it also resulted in a psychological bond that

13.1. Nivedita on a street sign, Kolkata, 2019

might be called a "clinch": a tight intellectual, spiritual, and—for her in the early years, at least—personal connection that was as uncomfortable as it was close. She intermittently found their connection fraught, as she went through various forms of attachment that, in her own reckoning, exposed the pains of childhood.

Sometimes her closeness to him occluded perspective, so that at moments she seemed to perceive fragments of Vivekananda as part of herself. At turns, she became desolate, lovelorn, and angry, unable to separate the "personal" love that overwhelmed her and the "universal" love that he insisted upon. In some of the hardest moments, he asked her to wipe clean the slate of her personality, to create the "Hindu woman" of his wishes. She lived with a passion that was at turns both painful and joyful, an experience that led to her being at times exhausting in her demands and in her responses. And yet, she persisted in this unfamiliar form of spiritual apprenticeship, hoping it would bring the self-realization she craved.

These feelings often heightened the imbalance in their relationship. She focused intensely on Vivekananda but, though he cared deeply for her, he coped more easily. When wounded by disciples and friends, he would erupt painfully, but turned both to humor and to karma to withstand the blows.

Both he and Margaret Noble were able to let go of wrongs; she, however, was inclined to obsess over her feelings and regrets, whereas he was not.

The imbalance was reinforced by circumstance and culture. When he first returned to India in 1897, his field of operation was vast, as he toured and lectured, constructed the Math, encouraged the relief operations, gave interviews, established Mayavati, and much more. In contrast, she needed to adapt quickly to Calcutta, a beginning that intensified her vulnerability. Certainly, these early years there were full of pleasure and learning, but she operated on a smaller scale to him. Nor could she always hide her ambivalence toward aspects of Indian life. At moments, she felt reborn; at other times, near death, as she tried to dispose of one identity and assume another. This was the cycle of renewal and destruction that Kali encompassed, and that Nivedita experienced both in the recesses of her psyche and among the sick and dying in Calcutta.

LIFE AND DEATH IN ALMORA

Margaret Noble arrived in Calcutta on January 28, 1898. At the beginning, she stayed with Josephine MacLeod and Sara Bull, who welcomed her to their cozy cottage on the banks of the Ganges. Here, they created an interior arranged so that Indians could recline on cushions, while Europeans could sit on chairs, a composite domesticity that Vivekananda admired: "You will find that little house of Dhira Mata [Sara Bull] like heaven, for it is all love, from beginning to end."[3] He attended to the women's needs both for their sakes, but also because Bull provided the money to begin building the monastery.[4] He also gave the three private lessons, which Noble, a professional teacher, described as a paragon of pedagogy: "he knew that the first material of a new consciousness must be a succession of vivid, but isolated experiences, poured out without proper sequence, so as to provoke the mind of the learner to work for its own conception of order and relation. At any rate, whether he knew it or not, this was the canon of educational science that he unconsciously fulfilled."[5]

Vivekananda, however, was both more attentive and more severe with her than with the other women, who were older and had a different status. Sara Bull was a "Mother," adviser, and patroness; Josephine was the inimitable friend. Noble now had to confront a swami sometimes very different from the one she had known in London, a man who became at moments the enraptured bhakta rather than the eloquent jnani. She watched him in procession with his fellow monks, who "with drums, cymbal, and gongs," was "completely carried away . . . intoxicated with love."[6] In seeing the mesmerized dancers, she realized that her habitual studiousness had given her almost no sense of Indian devotionalism. At the end of March, Vivekananda initiated her, marking her head with ashes and renaming her the "Dedicated." Thus she became Sister Nivedita (and will remain so from now on), a brahmacharini (celibate female probationer), her status lower than the sannyasins he had initiated in Thousand Island. Yet rather than the sannyasins' dawn induction with flowers and a small altar fire, at Nivedita's initiation, Vivekananda was said to have sung devotional songs and to have plucked his tanpura. Like a Shaivite yogi, he "put on a wig, the plaited tresses of which reached to his knees," wore bone ornaments in his ears, and covered his chest with ashes and beads. With cymbals striking in time with the music, he sang ecstatic incantations.[7] Thus attired, he enacted Shiva's wildness in her honor.

This tale—again written retrospectively and impossible to verify—suggests that on his return, Vivekananda reanimated those aspects of himself that had "died" abroad, returning to Indian music, and singing so that the bhakta within could once again take flight. Akhandananda remembered Vivekananda rapturously intoning the devotional songs of the Bengali poet Nilakantha Das.[8] Nivedita experienced a parallel process, but in the opposite direction. She had prepared for her Indian trip through knowledge, rationalism, and activism, but now she underwent a turbulent emotional reordering and awakening. Her early time in India taught her to think about the cycle of life and death—both in her immediate world where plague struck and famine stalked—but above all, in her inner life, where she observed many cherished loyalties die and new inclinations emerge.

Vivekananda first attacked her patriotism. In a letter to her friend Nell, she had said, "I [am] the most loyal Englishwoman that ever breathed in this country (I could not have suspected the depth of my own loyalty till I got here)."[9] When Vivekananda asked her to which nationality she belonged, she replied that she had a "passion of loyalty and worship" for the British flag, a strong belief in Britain's service to India. She dreamed of making "England and India love one another" and even argued that England had "in many ways well and faithfully served" the subcontinent.[10] Perhaps understandably at this stage, she could not "bear England to do the mean thing."[11] She castigated British missionaries for "stirring up . . . attacks on the King [her nickname for Vivekananda]." He railed at her, told her that such patriotism was a "sin," unable to hide his disgust with such national sentiments.

Not surprisingly, becoming a new person was difficult, as Nivedita wrote in June 1898: "I cannot yet throw any of my past experience of human life and human relationships overboard."[12] She simply could not forget her previous existence and habits within six months of her arrival. Vivekananda proceeded with what she quaintly called "her going-to-school," when he told her to remove the imperialist lens through which she viewed Indian society.[13] "I had been little prepared for that constant rebuke and attack upon all my cherished prepossessions which was now my lot."[14] This new discipline had begun when she, Josephine, and Sara journeyed to Almora, an epic trip worthy of the greatest fantasies of Raj travel, with coolies, baggage trains, tents, and Kashmiri houseboats. She was proud that they were intrepid enough to withstand the "horrid insults" that "three white women travelling with the Swami and other 'natives'" elicited from the British.[15]

She took in the unfamiliar magnificence of the Himalayan cedars and unaccustomed wildflowers (she was enthralled by botany throughout her life) and admired the cooks who produced sumptuous meals in the open air. Amid the beauty, however, she felt so hurt by his "instruction" that afterward she would weep in the arms of the American women. They protested against Vivekananda's harshness toward her; he seemed to want to kill off those aspects of her character that reminded him of British arrogance, and her vaguely professorial air and parochial judgments clearly irritated him.

Was his treatment of her worse than the discipline other gurus mete out to inculcate self-abnegation? It is not clear. However, scolding a British woman of independent nature and intellectual power certainly inverted the usual colonial relationship. The intimacy of his scolding alternated with the loneliness his coldness induced. Moreover, at this juncture at least, Vivekananda did not permit the exploratory give-and-take that Ramakrishna had allowed him. He did not instruct her himself, recruiting instead the young Swami Swarupananda to teach her Bengali and Indian customs. Swarupananda taught her the sayings of Ramakrishna; and together they studied the Gita again, but this time in its Indian setting. He understood that Vivekananda was giving Nivedita a hard lesson in detachment. Above

13.2. The four travelers: Josephine MacLeod, Sara Bull, Vivekananda, and Sister Nivedita (*left to right*)

all, he took her into the forest to meditate under a tree to regain psychic equilibrium. Here was a new bodily discipline, simple and yet central to her new spirituality: "I don't know if you ever got so far as to sit in the Buddha-attitude for meditation. I never took that seriously in England, but here in India one does it quite naturally. . . . And it is quite worthwhile. . . . Meditation simply means concentration—absolute concentration of the mind on the given point . . ." [16] But such calm was only intermittent, and it is not clear how persistent Nivedita was about meditation, either then or later.

Despite the difficulty of the journey, Vivekananda took her on a special pilgrimage to the Himalayas, leaving the other two women behind. Already ill with diabetes, he struggled to reach Amarnath Cave, 13,000 feet up, as they labored through the treacherous mountain paths with other pilgrims, the chanting intensifying the closer they came to the shrine. In the cave was the ice lingam, one of the holiest places in India's sacred geography, the place where Shiva had explained the secret of life and eternity to his consort Parvati. Shiva lingams were the abstract representations of the great god, a

13.3. The route to Amarnath, 1920

13.4. The ice lingam

key symbol in many shrines all over India, but also manifest in nature as in this faraway cave. The lingam grows and ebbs with the changing seasons and is accessible for only a few short weeks in summer.

For Vivekananda, the trip was a holy pilgrimage, but for her, it was about communion with him as much as with Shiva. She told her friend Nell that "he was anxious to dedicate me to Shiva," and she hoped for both a spiritual experience and a greater connection to her guru. Vivekananda felt it was a "wonderfully solemn moment" and believed that Shiva granted him the power to die when he wished—the so-called gift of Amar. Indeed, he felt the presence of Shiva "visible before him" and was entranced by the "purity and whiteness of the ice-pillar."[17]

For Nivedita, the occasion was a miserable disappointment. She wrote, "it is such a terrible pain to come face to face with something which is all *inwardness* to someone you worship, and for yourself to be able to get little further than externals." She felt excluded from a cardinal moment in Vivekananda's spiritual life and regretted a "lost chance that can never never come again." We can only imagine how out of her depth she felt in the high mountains and dark cave with a man who seemed a stranger to her in his spiritual self-absorption. In fact, she became demanding and blurted out her need: "You see I told him that if he would not put more reality in the word Master he would have to remember that we were nothing more to each other than an ordinary man and woman, and so I snubbed him and shut myself up in a hard shell."[18]

Her statement inadvertently revealed the "personal" love she tried so hard and so often to suppress. His acceptance of her pain made her feel even worse because he did not respond with anger, but rather sought to console her by "only caring for [her] little comforts."

She also recognized that what had happened was part of the "inevitable suffering that comes of the different national habits," a cultural explanation that veiled a deeper emotional difference: "My Irish nature expresses everything, the Hindu never dreams of expression, and Swami is so utterly shy of priestliness, whereas I am always craving . . . it."[19] The memory of Amarnath stayed with her as one of privilege and humiliation. She had gone there with Vivekananda, but the outcome had been neither spiritual nor personally fulfilling in the way she had hoped.[20] She concluded that the failure was hers alone and defended him against reproach. She was perhaps unduly harsh on herself, as journeying together in this way was unusual. Whatever the mu-

tual misperceptions, he explained, as in other moments when he felt un-
equal to the spiritual or emotional task, that he was "no Ramakrishna"; he
assured her, however, that someday she would experience the pilgrimage's
beneficial effects. Two years after this suffering, she admitted that he had
been correct: "[H]ow curious is this mystery of pain. . . . And it was that
state at Amaranth—the place whose name I cannot write without tears, so
keen is it to the day!—that made me really love Siva!"[21]

After their return, they continued their stay on their houseboats and
Nivedita was amazed by the transformation in him. He seemed to regress to
childhood, singing the songs of Ramprasad, the poet who had inspired Ramakrishna. Vivekananda became obsessed with Kali and felt her presence so
forcefully that he wrote a poem in her honor. In it, he meditated on her infinite darkness (the "pitchy sky"), power for destruction ("wrenching trees by
the roots"), and love of madness (like the "souls of a million lunatics").[22]

This lyrical, if black, meditation suggested he could not release his mind
from pain, nor did he attempt to; rather, he set off on another pilgrimage to
Khir Bhawani, a temple constructed over a sacred spring and famous as the
shrine to the Mother in Kashmir. On returning, he again abandoned himself
to a childlike state, wanting nothing more than to sit in the lap of Kali. Here
again, he surrendered to the maternal embrace, discarding any pretense to
masculine activism. Nivedita was thus excluded a second time. At first, she
was impressed by the "mingled solemnity and exhilaration of his presence,"
but she and the other Western women quickly became so worried that they
called a doctor.[23] She was disappointed that "to him at the moment 'doing
good' seems horrible," that his "patriotism [was] a mistake."[24] She was dismayed when he described himself as unworthy to teach anyone anything, and
shocked when he told her that "Swamiji is dead and gone."[25] In speaking of
himself as "Swamiji," he referred to his vocation as a spiritual teacher and as
a renouncer, the suffix "ji" denoting respect. He therefore seemed at that
moment to want to throw away the persona of educator or master. She concluded that "nothing would surprise one less than his taking the vow of silence and withdrawing forever."[26]

Nivedita never completely grasped the side of Vivekananda that sought
to articulate a "nonself," to reject the hyperactivity that had so often been
his fate, and which would be adopted by the nationalist radicals that she
later admired.[27] If she realized that he must have had "*awful* experiences
spiritually and physically" when he had been away, she also felt that monkish

13.5. On the houseboat

13.6. Khir Bhawani Temple, c. 1880s

withdrawal "in his case . . . would not be strength, but self indulgence [sic]."[28] Rather than concluding that he was on a path to spiritual liberation, she was impatient, and perhaps a little angry. She explained her reaction when she wrote in a letter: "Yesterday, he made me catch my breath and call *him* 'God.'"[29]

Vivekananda's experiences at Amarnath and at Khir Bhawani have been interpreted as his relinquishing a political mission. I would nuance this appraisal. Certainly, they were also a profound response to the frenetic activities of the previous year—the touring, organizing, and supporting the new program of famine relief and service. By renewing his bonds with Kali and "sitting in her lap," Vivekananda seems have been also renewing his relationship to Ramakrishna and his earlier mystical apprenticeship. This process was ambivalent and ongoing, as he sought to reconcile the ecstatic spirituality of his guru with his own intellectual prowess and rationalism. Nor did Nivedita comprehend that this reemerging nonself was integral to Vivekananda's insistence on detachment as the only state in which a sannyasin *might* intervene effectively in the world. By pursing the infantile self that Kali's divinity made so small, he was rebalancing his inner world, reclaiming unworldliness and its spiritual power so as to reenter the fray.[30]

There is no doubt, however, that this transformation in Vivekananda's demeanor frightened the women—hence, the call to the physician—and Nivedita was alarmed by his inner struggle. She was shocked and uncomprehending when he wanted her to call him "God" and saw his surrender to Kali as inertia rather than as victorious renunciation. She was, moreover, put out, as she had traveled more than halfway around the world to undertake a life of service, only to fear that he might be abandoning it. Even before the journey, she had chafed at her inactivity, eager to begin work. She hoped that he would soon rise "above this mood and become a great spring of healing and knowledge to the world."

And yet he seemed locked in mystical foreboding, as when he spoke instead of Kali's divine play: "Mother is flying kites," he said, "in the marketplace of the world, in a hundred thousand. She cuts the strings of one or two. / We are children playing in the dust, blinded by the glitter of dust in our eyes."[31]

Bengalis would have known that these were the beginning of a song by Ramprasad, the eighteenth-century Kali worshipper who so powerfully shaped Ramakrishna's devotion. Whether Nivedita knew the connection was unclear, but she seemed to realize that the kite-flying game was important. Commonly, Hindus fly kites after Dussehra, which celebrates the victory of Rama over Ravana, the demon king of Lanka. During these moments of postmonsoon winds, householders ascend to their rooftops to fly kites. They make glue from glass fragments and paste and rub it into the kite strings. The object of the game is to cut the string of an opponent and make it crash to the ground.[32] Through such analogies, Nivedita may well have begun to understand what Vivekananda meant when he spoke of the goddess's whimsical cruelty in breaking the strings of these toys. Many would fall ultimately to the ground, while only a few would soar to the heavens, but such flimsy playthings were incapable of commanding their own destiny. Such themes became central to her book *Kali the Mother*.

His mystical observations on Kali thus became important to her spiritual education and made a deep impact, allowing her to transmute this legacy of Ramakrishna's into the spirituality and politics of early nationalism.

LIFE AND DEATH IN BAGBAZAR

Nivedita's time in India involved a shift in her deepest sense of self and involved both guilt and annoyance with her family. She had left London, giving her Wimbledon school over to her sister, but all was not well back home. Her sister wrote to say that "she had broken down with strain and worry." How was she to marry without help? Nivedita immediately thought of going back, and she reflected that it was "very conceited for [her] to think [she] was very necessary to GOD anyway?" However, in the next sentence, she wrote that this would "be like tearing the heart out of [her body]."[33] She wanted to burn her family's letters "unread," and acknowledged she would "never be happy until some catastrophe swept them all unawares into another world."[34] Such thoughts plagued her most either when she was happiest or when she worried that she might "vindicat[e] heathenism" and break her mother's heart.[35]

If she fantasized about being free of family, she also missed her friends. When Josephine MacLeod wrote to discuss their meeting at the Exposition Universelle in 1900—which Nivedita thought was "as much a concern of mine as the other side of the moon"—she was brought unexpectedly to tears when her friends bought her a pair of gloves.[36] But her new life was exciting, and she loved it. Early letters reveal her glee over a tea party where she could show off her "big lion," another reference to Vivekananda, to notables from the Brahmo Samaj.[37] The list included Rabindranath Tagore, scientist Jagadish Chandra Bose, members of the Roy family, Mohini Chatterjee who had first introduced Sara Bull to Vedanta, and Sarola Ghosal, Tagore's niece and one of the first Indian women university graduates. On another occasion, she reveled in Tagore's magnificent drawing room—like a "royal nest of European taste and intellect of the first water"—when invited to meet a maharaja.[38]

She began to know Calcutta better. Initially, she returned from her stay in northern India "with insular rigidity," asking to become the guest of Sarada Devi, not realizing her insistence created social embarrassment. Her hostess glided over the faux-pas and the discomfort Nivedita's presence would cause her "kindred in their distant village." Nivedita admitted that she imagined "caste to be only a foolish personal prejudice—which must yield to knowledge."[39] She did not realize that cultural differences would make renting a house and finding a servant difficult. When her maid and cook did arrive, Nivedita was shocked that the old woman had felt obliged to bathe before reboiling and reserving the hot water for Nivedita's teapot.[40]

Her prose retained an orientalism that focused on the seeming timelessness of the culture she observed—"What a beautiful old world it was in which I spent those [early months]"—but her carapace of ignorant superiority began to crack.[41] She soon looked beyond the missionary stereotypes of a debased and superstitious culture: "Eating and bathing—with us chiefly selfish operations—are here sacramental acts, guarded at all points by social honour and the passion of purity." The local people would glance worshipfully at the Ganges or bow to a bo tree or tulsi plant. She had been warned against the "constant ablutions, endless prostrations, unmeaning caste-restrictions," but the ritualism of daily life now became both comforting and uplifting.[42]

She was fascinated by Sarada Devi: "fancy worshipping a man as she worshipped her Husband and never giving Him even a glimpse of your face to make sure that He sometimes thought of you again! This is a deep self-abnegation."[43] Sarada's purity was so legendary that "men came up to the Zenana [women's quarters] to worship her." At the early stages of their relationship, Nivedita continued to have moments of condescension—or at least incomprehension. While she acknowledged that Sarada was perfect "in

13.7. Sarada Devi and Nivedita

feeling," she concluded that in "*thought,* outside the range of practical experience, these ladies have no range."[44]

With time she recognized that Sarada Devi's judgment might be better
than her own. Vivekananda worshipped her as the "incarnation of Bagala [a
great wisdom goddess] in the guise of Saraswati [the goddess of wisdom and

learning]."[45] After his return to India, Vivekananda had purified himself with Ganges water before going to see her again, fearful that his "spirituality had been diminished by associating with all kinds of people."[46] Sarada Devi's household and women attendants provided an example of the intimate relationship between Indian domesticity, maternalism, and spirituality. And Nivedita was touched. If she had hoped that Vivekananda would be her father—and described him as such at times in her letters—in Sarada, she felt at moments that she had found a mother. She wrote to her sister, May: "She is the very soul of sweetness—*so* gentle and loving and as merry as a girl. . . . And she is so tender—'my daughter' she calls me."[47]

In Britain, Nivedita's "real" family languished without her as she created a new Indian one. Through these women, she learned about the *zenana*, a sacred inner household, and its relationship to the outer rhythms of the *para* (neighborhood). She mentioned how the people in Bagbazar had begun to call her "Sister," a less formal title that she preferred to the earlier address as "Mother." In Bagbazar, she absorbed the rhythms of urban Calcutta, a world that sociologist and urban planner Patrick Geddes would later help her interpret when he transformed her thinking about Indian cities and landscape in general.

Although uneducated, Sarada became a model: "Her whole experience is of theocratic civilisation. Yet she rises to the height of every situation."[48] Sarada would expel novices if she sensed a lack of seriousness but was playful and "full of music" with her intimates.[49] Whereas Nivedita applied her analytical intelligence to all problems, Sarada was wise, and had the "strength and certainty of some high and arduous form of scholarship."[50] She also spoke of Sarada's "winsomeness," a quality that recalled Ramakrishna and another trait that Nivedita lacked. Nivedita appreciated talents she did not possess but remained in an awkward position. Sarada Devi was perhaps the person that Vivekananda considered the "ideal Hindu woman," but he had sought out Nivedita as a "Celtic lioness" who could lecture in public. It was unclear how much of a "Hindu woman" she was meant to be, for surely, she had not come to India to emulate Sarada Devi.

Nonetheless, in March 1899, Vivekananda seems to have asked her to seclude herself for a time. She agreed, and only Sadananda, Vivekananda's disciple from the Hathras train station, entered her quarters, although she was touched that English people, contrary to Vivekananda's expectations, sought her out.[51] In the end, she understood "the danger of gossip in this country," that she needed to guard her reputation and adopt Hindu customs.[52] Perhaps also Vivekananda did not want people to misinterpret his actions; by living close to Sarada and being welcomed into the household of a saint, Nivedita was partially protected; otherwise, in Bagbazar, the strange phenomenon of a white, single woman who was not a missionary was bound to lead to talk. It is not clear how long she observed these rules and in what way, but her acceptance that she needed to heed them even temporarily suggests that she was beginning to adapt to local customs.

LIVING AND DYING: THE PLAGUE

Events contributed to Nivedita's dissociation from a British identity. One of the most important of these was something she first mentions on May 22, 1898.[53] The misery the famine had caused had so weakened the population that bubonic plague broke out in Calcutta at the end of April 1898, and, with it, panic and violence. For the British and for many Indian elites, it seemed as if the "coolies" had taken over India's capital. The *Englishman* described a riot and denounced the "mob of bundmashes and goondas" who were "virtually in possession. . . . of Calcutta, and its suburbs," as a massive strike by carriage and wagon workers succeeded in bringing parts of Calcutta to a standstill.[54]

The fear and turbulence were heightened by the government's response. Rumors flew that the British intended to do away with 200,000 poor Calcuttans, while sparing the well-to-do, who were to be isolated at home, or were to leave the city.[55] It was "rumoured that they had colluded with the authorities" so that they could flee, "leaving the People to their fate."[56] The poor feared inoculation, and were terrified of quarantine, isolation camps, restrictions on travel, and the suppression of Indian medical practices.[57] The British were also cruelly insensitive in touching patients who regarded such contact as polluting.[58] Political leaders condemned the "tyrannical" expedients—women pulled from their homes, military house searches, and the examination of corpses prior to cremation.[59] Many of the measures seemed almost frenzied, rather than scientifically justified.[60] By the time Nivedita began her work in May 1898, British impositions frightened Indians so much that they hid away and denied illness, a consequence that inadvertently encouraged the spread of the disease. In the end, they allowed Indian medical practitioners to renew their treatments and made vaccination optional. Nivedita had a close view of the plague when she nursed a boy of twelve or fourteen, and she explained to Josephine MacLeod that "it was not repulsive in any way. I stole some of the love that he meant that last day for his mother. In delirium once he seized my hand. . . . And often he looked at me and smiled—and at the end—when he had begun in a paroxysm of delirium to say 'Haribol.' [Chant the name of the Lord] Hari!' I stood it up and stood repeating it and he with a look of relief and soothing, lay quietly back and gradually died—so that those words were the last in the poor child's consciousness."[61]

Vivekananda, however, was having none of this. When she went to see him, "[h]e was frankly insulting—with a sort of playful tone in it." Although he emphasized renunciation and self-sacrifice, he thought her "do-goodism" colluded with evil British policies. What good was standing beside one dying child when the whole neighborhood was in peril? He was willing "after all this battle" for her house to be turned into a woman's hospital, but he knew that there were already many hospitals in Calcutta: the problem was that so few were willing to go to them.[62]

Nivedita abandoned the nursing; instead, she and Sadananda instituted sanitation measures (which seemed to combine sweeping and disinfecting) in the immediate neighborhood. He became known as the "Scavenger Swami," a title that connected him to Dalits: "in the early morning Sadananda like a hero superintends his gang of scavengers." Almost a year from the first outbreak, she mentioned in April 1899 how the disease had made its way to the next street.[63] Amid the growing horror, her passion for sanitation, hygiene, and health first displayed in Wrexham was given a new direction.

But she hardly touted the sanitation gospel of the British, but rather looked to Indian models, and, in the *Indian Mirror,* she criticized the British refusal to create a "Woman's Hospital that could take into account the customs of the country"; she wanted the creation of a corps of visiting nurses in each district but knew she could not magic such a group into existence. Nivedita prescribed "old treatment," by which she meant "disinfectants."[64] She was appalled that Calcutta had a municipal staff of only 1,200 "scavengers" and begged young male students of the city to risk their lives as volunteers.[65]

She sought to save lives, and when Mr. Bright, the chairman of the Plague Commission, came to Bagbazar to view their efforts, she reportedly told him "that we did not know he would care . . . We wanted to help people, not make a fuss."[66] More than any other event, the plague brought her closer to becoming an Indian. Having witnessed the toxic mixture of incompetence and coercion the British had unleashed, she no longer expected much from her compatriots.

Above all, Nivedita began to make fun of herself. "What is an infinitely higher proof of self-sacrifice and obedience on my part . . . than the delightful excitement of risking Plague. . . . ?"[67] She had begun to sound a bit like Vivekananda. When the plague had broken out in early 1898, he had written to Josephine Macleod that he was going back to his native city: "I am determined to make myself a sacrifice; and that I am sure is a 'Darn sight better way to Nirvana' than pouring oblations to all that ever twinkled."[68] Here he mocked ritualism (he was speaking of the consecrated fire ritual) and declared himself ready for action. On April 22, 1899, he appeared at the Classic Theatre, and complimented a Brahmo lady and another from a zenana for being willing to risk their health in this way. He cited their presence (without naming them) to the young students, to dare them to join the cleaning operation that would go from "bustee" to "bustee" (from slum to slum) to slow the plague's course.[69] He also issued a Plague Manifesto in May 1898, giving assurances that the British would not force vaccination on them; that Nivedita's hospital (at this stage it still seemed in the offing) would pay "full respect to religion, caste and the modesty (Purdah) of women"; and that the "servants" at the Math would be there to help.[70]

Throughout her years in Calcutta, Nivedita spoke repeatedly of Sadananda with his disinfectants, directing the neighbors in sanitation that was now routine—for Nivedita, this was proof that "self-reliance" worked. Even if she came to embrace the "Terrible," she was never inured to the horror of plague. After the Partition of Bengal in 1905, she wrote: "Sadananda is away at Bhagalpur, doing plague work. Plague has been so bad there that monkeys and bats have dropped dead from the trees with it."[71] The scourge never seemed to end; it is said to have peaked between 1903 and 1907.[72]

From the beginning of Nivedita's Indian sojourn, then, plague was an omnipresent reminder of death and dying, and the new spirituality she was trying to understand. Hinduism did not just worship "goodness" or "ease and pleasure." For both Vivekananda and Nivedita, Kali urged devotees to "banish fear and weakness," to show a courage that was the opposite of passivity, and which she would later explicitly call "aggressive."[73] It also demanded a spirituality that "recognise[d] the Mother as instinctively in evil, terror, sorrow, and annihilation, as in that which makes for sweetness and joy."[74] The true test was in becoming "one with the terrible." She tried to paraphrase some of Vivekananda's deepest and most difficult lessons when she dismissed the "underlying egoism of worship that is devoted to the kind God, to Providence, the consoling Divinity, without a heart for God in the earthquake, or God in a volcano."[75]

In her book on Kali, published in 1900, she might have added plague to the list of calamities. Vivekananda always emphasized that love of God remained steadfast even when horror and death abounded. Nivedita may well have begun to have a deep, and experiential, sense of his meaning during a catastrophe that fell within Kali's domain. Finding a way of encompassing it spiritually was as important to her as the measures that she and Sadananda took in Bagbazar, or the plague missions that became part of the order's most important social endeavors.

◆　◆　◆

As the plague raged in early 1899 in Bagbazar, Nivedita was thinking and writing about Kali under her guru's direction. Vivekananda had been reticent about Kali in America and Europe because of stereotypes of Indian "primitivism." As late as 1898, Lucy Guinness, a devotee of Ramabai, was still quoting William Caine's *Picturesque India* (1890) to shock English-speaking readers: "In earlier days human sacrifice was often [Kali's] only propitiation; and as late as 1866, during the terrible famine, human heads decked with flowers were found before her altar. . . . Her secret cult is too repulsive for description."[76]

Vivekananda vetted Nivedita's text, but she gave the talk on Kali at the Calcutta Albert Hall on February 13, 1899, a year after her arrival in India.[77] Vivekananda thus chose a respectable, educated British lady to champion Kali, and Nivedita appealed to her audience by admitting that she, too, had held the same erroneous prejudices about the goddess.[78]

Her attraction to Kali stemmed from the way the goddess swept away the conventions of "gentlehood" in favor of something rawer, what she called the "*greatness of fact*"—the recognition that life and death were undeniably connected. Kali was more than the queen of the cosmos or the fount of love and protection; Kali was the universe in flux, where "the right hand

[is] uplifted in blessing, *while* [her emphasis] the left destroys."[79] Kali, it seemed, was a supernatural symbol of her own very human crisis, as part of her "self" died, and a new one struggled to emerge. To her audience, Nivedita reinforced a message of the popular and gendered nature of Kali-love: "Religion is for the heart of the people. To refine it is to emasculate it."[80] Despite the cruelty of life, there was always a promise of renewal: "It is always on the bosom of dead Divinity that the blissful Mother dances Her dance celestial." Nivedita reveled in this toughness. She spoke of Kali's placing her foot on Shiva and awakening him with her explosive force.[81] Later, she wrote that Shiva was like "the knight [who] waits for the sight of his own lady, powerless without the inspiration of her touch."[82] Perhaps, too, she thought of herself as the sleeping knight who had required Vivekananda to become strong.

Unlike the missionaries, who dismissed the "cult" as the epitome of Indian superstition, she insisted that Indians were the least idolatrous of people. Kali was both a "primitive" form of worship—with the blood sacrifices that she rejected—and the most sublime, capable of unifying opposing cosmic forces. But in harnessing the cruelty and violence of Kali, she diverged substantially from the many other nationalist writers of the era, especially those in Europe. In her native country, for example, the likes of Sinn Féin adopted the image of Mother Ireland who, in the words of the poet Eavan Boland, was "invoked, addressed, remembered, loved, regretted, and, most importantly, died for. She was a mother or a virgin. . . ."[83] Here, there was no hint of the erotic, violent, and bloodthirsty aspects that Kali embodied and Nivedita now honored.

Nivedita understood that Kali was important because she was inherently "polysemic": for each worshipper, Kali would signify something different. For all that Kali was Terror, she was also the mother, who played, comforted, and defended her offspring. Symbols were never static, but rather were "like the fire in opals," leaping and dancing with light.[84] She accepted that, by conventional standards, Kali was ugly, but that Shiva thought her beautiful when she awoke him with her touch.

Nivedita's earliest public pronouncements on Kali mixed gender, spirituality, and nationalism with martial connotations. The nucleus of the later notion of "aggressive Hinduism" was already present. She insisted that the "great glory of this Mother-worship lies in its bestowal of *Manhood*," and gave models of the masculinity she revered. She extolled Pratap Singh, the sixteenth-century Rajput king who had single-handedly fought off the Mughals; Shivaji Maharaj, a seventeenth-century warrior king; and the present-day Sikhs, their daggers ready for battle. The first two heroes would reappear as important symbols during Swadeshi. Nivedita also mentioned the Bengalis, her audience, who had nurtured the Kali cult and who now needed to resume the devotion.[85] Within a few years, Kali worship would become central to the young generation of Swadeshi activists in Bengal, who both claimed Kali's power and sought to protect their "Mother" from British dominance.[86]

The lecture was controversial and annoyed some Brahmos, but the hall was crammed and both Vivekananda and Nivedita were "greatly pleased."[87] She had chanted Vivekananda's poem, emphasizing the goddess's darkness, and hence the need to reflect on the "Terrible." There was no doubt, however, that her acceptance of this worship derived from her experiences in Bagbazar. Shortly after the lecture, she recorded the "most pathetic death of a young girl in the mud hut just opposite."[88] Nivedita had done her best to comfort the keening mother by saying that the girl was with Kali; and she was comforted in turn for being "just one with them at such a moment, no bar and no difference in ideals or faith or anywhere."[89] Nivedita sat with the family and "sang the names of Kali and Sri Ramakrishna softly for an hour or more"; and when she told Vivekananda of her experience, he reportedly responded, "'That was why Ramakrishna Paramahamsa came into the world to teach . . . that we were to talk to everybody in his own language.'"[90] She even felt pity for Christian missionaries who, even at such moments, continued to impose their alien spirituality. Kali worship was thus important both as religious knowledge and as politics, but also as a bridge to the people around her.

She also lectured at Kalighat, the seat of Kali worship in Calcutta, where baby goats are sacrificed and the offering cooked and distributed. She reported that Vivekananda believed that the occasion was "the greatest blow that could be struck against exclusiveness," an allusion to the different audience she would face.[91] She expected to be fearful but told Josephine that it had not been "so formidable at all. The men's faces were almost refined" and the crowd had not frightened her.[92]

She recounted that, on the day of the lecture, Vivekananda told her that "every bit of that place is holy. Every drop of it. I could lick it all up out of reverence."[93] Whether these were his words remains uncertain—the language has something of Nivedita's cadences—but he entirely supported her in this endeavor. Vivekananda, she explained, now embraced aspects of Hindu sacrificialism, as when he mixed his own blood with blossoms, staining them before laying them at the goddess' feet: "The sacrifice of animals only goes on till the devotee is strong enough to offer himself instead—and then ... he draws his own blood and buries the feet of the Mother in flowers dipped in it. This is how Swami worships now—and to me it explains and justifies the whole."[94]

Her view of Kali worship as a "bestowal of Manhood" was certainly different from Ramakrishna's, whose adoration of Kali depended on the fluidity of such categories, despite the gender "types" that peopled his creation. There was, moreover, nothing of the martial or manly in Ramakrishna's mysticism, which instead had emphasized childhood. Nivedita's interpretation instead relied on a more rigid vision of difference, despite how she and Vivekananda both explored the "feminine" and "masculine" qualities within themselves. They all agreed nonetheless that Kali-love brought a courage that came from facing the harshest trials of "divine play." For Ramakrishna, such understanding was the foundation stone of his mysticism; for Nivedita, such views might also entail a "manly" sacrifice for the nation that was increasingly associated with a primordial mother.

14

EDUCATION, "DIVINE PLAY,"

AND THE NATION

[T]o learn a thing in life and through doing is much more developing,
cultivating, and strengthening, than to learn it merely through the
verbal communication of ideas.

—Friedrich Froebel, *Die Menschenereziehung* (1826)

The first principle of true teaching is that nothing can be taught.

—Sri Aurobindo, *A System of National Education* (1921)

◆   ◆   ◆

IN THE YEAR OF HER ARRIVAL, Nivedita went on pilgrimage, lived in
Bagbazar, fought the plague, adjusted to her new milieu, and finally established her school. She was also keen not to offend Hindu sensibilities and to
fulfil her role as a bramacharini (celibate probationer) linked to the Mission.
She thus lived among the poor and frequented Sarada Devi. But, as Vivekananda's "star turn," she had access to Bengali high society and its leading
cultural figures, while remaining closely associated with the British world.
Few were better placed to observe and encompass the spiritual and political
at once.

And yet this unusual position also left her ill-defined, a reality illustrated
by her costume. At first glance, she could have passed as a Christian missionary or nun, but her garb was of her own making, a badge of uniqueness

14.1. Nivedita in her self-designed habit

rather than institutional belonging. Although an ardent disciple of Vive-kananda, she remained adrift, embracing new Western influences during her 1899–1900 trip. Vivekananda was not hostile to novelty, but he *was* wary of Europeans imposing their schemes on Indians and warned her against too great a susceptibility to Western fashions.

She was thus a pioneer in becoming her "own woman," but also bewildered by being betwixt and between that entailed tremendous uncertainty. She was British but had come to despise her compatriots. She had a magpie-like curiosity and was passionate about ideas—which sometimes meant she dissipated her energies. Moreover, she was preoccupied with universals and idealism—the nature of love and freedom (both personal and political); masculinity and femininity; and the power of aggression.[1] In her search for almost existential independence, she was, perhaps, far ahead of her time; in other ways, however, she was conservative, especially concerning the role of women, and in her own inability to detach herself from the authority of "great men." Men continued to see themselves as world movers and to regard her as a helpmate; she sometimes acquiesced in this vision of the relationship and was unsure about her own contributions to the new syntheses she helped to create. Indeed, part of her lack of definition came from her inability to separate from them, while also regarding them as the embodiment of the ideals she sought to attain. And yet, she was extraordinary: in the day-to-day, she was a practical educator, amanuensis, lecturer, radical, and above all, thinker and author, living many of these roles simultaneously.

No matter how painful and disorientating at times, she was Vivekananda's true disciple. If he has been credited with creating "Vedanta for the West" while also remaking it for India, she continued in this vein. Vivekananda had bequeathed a flexible framework that she reshaped for a younger generation by linking it to the newest trends in art, science, the environment (cityscapes and topography), and politics. When Vivekananda was weakening, she showed—through her writings and international contacts—Hindu Universalism's capacity to become part of the next generation of avant-garde Western speculation and important to the battle for Swadeshi that Vivekananda would not live to see.

EDUCATION

Nivedita's greatest area of expertise was education, using ideas and techniques based on notions of experiential play and "object lessons" through which she first understood Vedanta. She took inspiration from Swiss Enlightenment educationalist Johann Pestalozzi, who urged "learning by head, hand, and heart." More important still was Friedrich Froebel, the early-nineteenth-century founder of the German kindergarten movement, who had encouraged children to play.[2]

He used a series of so-called gifts—play objects, such as blocks and cubes, tablets, rings, and sticks—to lead children to higher levels of capability and understanding, while also fostering singing, dancing, theatricals, and contact with nature.

This pedagogy revolutionized Noble's thinking and practice. Before even traveling to India, she stated that her aim was to "develop faculty rather

14.2. Examples of Froebel's gifts

than impart knowledge."[3] She believed that *"Knowing comes by Doing"* [her emphasis] and disdained abstraction in favor of concrete example and experience.[4] In line with Froebel's ethos, she maintained that both the classroom and nature provided myriad "object lessons"—a term first invented by Pestalozzi and which she described as "the heart of the New Education School."[5]

In 1894, her Ruskin School (named after art critic and social thinker John Ruskin) trained other teachers and pioneered methods of free play. She connected with Ebenezer Cooke, her beloved "Cookie," who introduced art lessons and encouraged her interest in painting and art criticism.[6] One anecdote relates how Vivekananda had visited the school in 1895–1896 (the date is uncertain) and was so moved that he was said to weep.[7] Both she and his guru emphasized experience and "play," albeit of different kinds, in their work.

She also built these insights into her understanding of Hindu theology and Kali-love. At Christmas 1898—her first in India—Nivedita wrote a fairy tale for Frances Leggett, the new baby of Josephine MacLeod's sister Betty and her husband, Francis Leggett. "The Story of Kali" described early play with the mother:

> Baby, darling, what is the very first thing you remember? Is it not lying on mother's lap, and looking up into her eyes, and laughing?
>
> Did you ever play hide and seek with mother? Mother's eyes shut, and baby was not. She opened them, and there was baby! Then baby's eyes shut, and where was mother? But they opened again, and—oh! . . . .
>
> Then, all our lives long, baby darling, we try to catch the Great Mother peeping. . . . [8]

As a teacher of small children, Nivedita focused on peek-a-boo, the game that is essential to laughter and the development of what is called "object permanence." When a baby closes its eyes, the object vanishes, but when it opens them again, the mother (or the playmate) is still there. Such play is apparently universal and rests on the view that "it is a joy to be hidden and disaster not to be found."[9] The game relies on trust, on knowing that the other person will be there. Few things are worse than the fear of abandonment. Nivedita knew the feeling well, as she explained in the fairy tale:

> Sometimes God is like that too. We get so frightened because those eyes will not open. We want to stop the game. We don't like it. We feel alone, and far away and lost. Then we cry out. It has grown quite dark, and still the Mother's eyes are shut . . .
>
> But the eyes are not shut, really. We think so, because it is dark all round. Just at the moment when you cried out, the beautiful eyes of the Mother opened and looked at Her child like two deep wells of

love. . . . But Kali is always there, always loving, and always ready to play with Her child.[10]

The story describes the double-edged experience of exploring and doubting, the uncertainty at the core of human interaction. She sought to bind her teaching to her deepest personal concerns, and forebodings. She explained soon after to Josephine how pedagogy had been "a good training to understanding the Hindu-Idea."[11] Her discipleship both exaggerated her fears of loss and instructed her on the importance of self-reliance. She came to believe also that even in the most undirected play, there was always a pattern, even if undiscerned at first.[12] In her mind—and certainly in Vivekananda's—play and education were often indistinguishable, for the "play of birds and of kittens is, as we know, simply a schooling."[13]

Discipleship was also about learning and, at Almora, Vivekananda had explained in one of his lessons to the three women how such insights applied to understanding the sacred. Vivekananda had described the Crucifixion, for example, as a lesson in divine play, once again using his skill as a cultural translator: "You know we have a theory that the Universe is God's manifestation of Himself, just for fun, that the Incarnations came and lived here, 'just for fun.' Play, it was all play. Why was Christ crucified? It was mere play. And so of life."[14]

What, after all, could be more outrageous than calling Christ's passion "mere play"? But he chose this example as the ultimate object lesson to demonstrate the greatest cruelty that the Divine deployed to teach detachment. Ramakrishna's trials were holy precisely because they encompassed horrible pain and unfettered bliss within this divine "game."

Nivedita hoped she had learned more about this ego-less state in Calcutta during her "transformation." In Bagbazar, she washed her hands with lemon and powdered lentils, and ate with her fingers like a Hindu; she mentions that she had even learned to go barefoot. In Bagbazar, she had bowed to the ground before Sarada Devi.[15] And later, a female colleague at the school noted how she was "intoxicated with the nectar of love for India" to the point that "people went so far as to call her mad."[16] If Vivekananda praised this "selflessness," others thought her zeal excessive.

Vivekananda tried to instruct her on the relative boundary between freedom and "unfreedom," and she later explained that experiencing submission during discipleship *had* ultimately produced a detached "self," which could be active in the world. But at moments, she was not so sure. As both a teacher and disciple, she wondered how childish play could be likened to the more harrowing forms of divine play. The first was about self-discovery; the second could induce terror. Ramakrishna exemplified how these two opposing tendencies could be united, how a visionary could "sit in the lap of Kali" at one moment and fantasize about "eating up" the Mother in the next. Still, Kali could cruelly test devotees. Nivedita suggested at times that she knew that childhood was often "unfreedom," where a mother of erratic black moods exacted and punished. During her discipleship, she wanted love, but realized she needed to accept disapproval. But at this stage the latter paralyzed her, and this tension simmered underneath the surface of her relationship with Vivekananda.

◆ ◆ ◆

As she watched and learned more about the poor girls who were her pupils in Bagbazar, Nivedita realized that her own methods also applied in Calcutta. She turned to Ramakrishna—who had taken a "clod [of earth], a precious stone, and a piece of gold as being of equal worth," and threw them all in the Ganges.[17] "Even he could not leap at once to same sightedness about wealth, but he had to practise it in the concrete, and change earth and gold from hand to hand and finally cast them both away seeing no difference between them. It was this *practice* that made his realisation so dynamic and powerful . . ."[18]

Concrete understanding, not abstract thought, was essential to grasping this spiritual insight. Nivedita later explained that a baby cannot understand the idea of two but can experience it by pointing to two eyes and two cheeks. Rather than Froebel's gifts—far too expensive—she proposed for her school "rag balls of the bazaar" for play, and seeds to learn to count and divide.[19] She believed that clay, readily available, was vital because "every illiterate builder can model. All ladies are used to make beautiful clay plates."[20] In her bedroom, she displayed the clay sculptures and dolls that her charges produced. Very quickly, she sought to reanimate Indian handicrafts—later central to her political activism: "The right course is not [to] introduce a foreign process, but to take home-art, and develop it along its own lines, carrying it to greater ends, by growth from within."[21] Indian girls were to learn how to draw by making *alpana,* the decorative motifs used in Hindu religious rites. Even ink was unnecessary—ground rice dissolved in water created beautiful intricacy.[22]

She thus joined in an emerging transnational trend—from Okakura's lacquer work to Matisse's obsession with textiles and William Morris's with artisanship—that praised handicrafts as equal to fine art. Anticolonial theorists and activists endorsed such products as central to Asian aesthetic traditions, insights that show how Nivedita moved from pedagogy through aesthetics to politics.

Despite her dedication, however, she told Vivekananda that her school was a "waste of time" only a year after it had begun.[23] While in the Himalayas, she realized that she had just 800 rupees for the entire year. She had dreamed of charging a rupee a month and hoped for 100 pupils but had to cut the fees to compete with the missionaries.[24] But more than money discouraged her, for "when a girl grows exquisite, she marries, and I can do no more for her."[25] Although she made this observation in private, she remained impatient with Indian mores. She therefore devised a project for a home for widows and girls, and hoped that an impending trip to Europe and America would enable her to raise the money for it. She may well have modeled this scheme on Ramabai's successful venture in Poona; she wanted to create Hindu "EDUCATIONAL MISSIONARIES," whose work she would supervise.[26] In the end, this plan went nowhere, but the original school continued. After 1902, it was managed by Sister Christine, who introduced new activities among women in the neighborhood.

THE TRIP WEST

On June 29, 1899, Nivedita left India with Vivekananda and Turiyananda for England, enjoying five weeks with the swami aboard ship. There had been endless discussion about the decorum of this arrangement. She laughed that Vivekananda could be so "worldly-wise" as to worry about her reputation, but the trip undoubtedly rekindled her imaginings. He reminded her repeatedly that she was "Kali's child in some special sense," but she wanted to be more than a mere "child." She wrote to Josephine MacLeod: "I never try to tell him what I hold to be the truth—what I see now like daylight—'Not child at all—but Shiva—Consort and Spouse!'"[27] The word "consort" may have conjured associations of Sarada Devi, who had been Ramakrishna's Shakti, indivisible from him in holiness and spirituality. Perhaps she thought of a royal spouse; for Nivedita, Vivekananda was the "King," now and after his death. Prince Albert was widely known as Queen Victoria's "consort," a title central to their partnership. Once again, there was gender play in Nivedita's thoughts and feelings, for, if I am right, she was Shiva, and he, Kali, in this description. She reported that Vivekananda explicitly asked her to remain a "man" until he could find worthy men:

> "The men are not yet here to whom all this must be handed over. You must keep the responsibility yet a little while." Oh how he wants great strong men for disciples!
>
> "Give me men! Give me men!" He has said over and over again. "You know I have never wanted money or power or anything but persons. Them I *must* have."[28]

She was happy to remain an honorary man and accepted that he saw her sex as a demerit in his search for greater influence. Whatever she meant by being his consort, she admitted that she was once again experiencing "personal love" and she did not hide her feelings from Josephine: "instead of growing less, I have grown infinitely *more* personal in my love. I am not sure but his least whim is worth the whole [...] When one turns to him in thought the heart grows free. Blessed be God for making it possible to love like this ..."[29]

A cauldron of longing still burned within her despite the discipline of her earlier "going-to-school," but she never again wrote about him in this way after the trip ended. Without her knowing it, this interregnum of closeness began a period greater emotional and geographical distance. They arrived in Britain on July 31, 1899, and the tranquility vanished the moment they disembarked. Although she was relieved—and delighted—that her family in London recognized his value, they arrived during the blighted summer of 1899 to find that Sturdy, and Miss Müller had all deserted him, and that finding male disciples of quality remained elusive.[30] The work in London was over before it had begun, and Vivekananda and Turiyananda boarded ship again on August 16 to go to America for another year, much of it spent in California.

◆　◆　◆

Nivedita stayed in Britain for her sister's wedding, and only arrived at Ridgely Park, the home of Frank and Betty Leggett, on September 20. She was to return to the West twice more, in 1907, and then in 1910, although not always enthusiastically. Indeed, she remarked in 1905 during the early days of Swadeshi, "if a good fairy could give me the wish of my heart, I suppose I should hear that I was never to leave India."[31] But she did look forward to seeing family and friends during the 1899 voyage. It also led her to new intellectual and political mentors and, for a time, away from Vivekananda.

She found Vivekananda in Upstate New York, where his moods went up and down and when, in her words, he sometimes seemed like a "caged lion."[32] He wanted to get out and cause a stir, but instead needed to rely on her, calling Nivedita his Kshatriya (warrior) and asking her to go and "fight for him."[33] The outbursts may have been due to his uneven health, and in teaching Nivedita at this time, he emphasized *Titikshâ,*" the virtue of endurance without lament.[34] Perhaps he was reminding himself of this quality as much as instructing her when he spoke about the fortitude of a "monk whose fingers were rotting away with leprosy and who stooped gently to replace the maggot that fell from the remaining joint."[35] Ultimately, he blessed both her and Sara Bull in early November, realizing that they were his truest Western followers.[36]

They left the East Coast, and Nivedita went to Chicago in November. Her trip was designed both to raise money and to provide a counterpoint to Ramabai's view of Indian women, but it additionally enlarged her educational horizons, helped her form new contacts, and enabled her to lecture on her own. In many ways, she seemed to reenact Vivekananda's own journey in the other direction, encountering America for the first time as a foreign Anglo-Saxon, and a Hinduized Scots-Irish woman to boot. She also went to Chicago to enlist Vivekananda's "sister," Mary Hale, but this connection went awry; on the surface, they disagreed over Nivedita's improvised nun's costume, which neither Mary nor Olea Vaughan (Sara Bull's daughter) could abide, but the deeper division focused on what she saw as Nivedita's blind devotion. Mary wanted her to be "simply an English woman."[37] She implied that Nivedita's costume was "wrong" and that she could never be like Vivekananda, who embodied "Indianness" (even if the scarlet robe and orange turban were invented). Moreover, she had counseled Vivekananda when he had made "mistakes," implying that Nivedita should now take her advice as well.[38] Nivedita responded that she was "only a disciple—and to [her] Swami made no mistakes."[39] Mary was family, a sister; she merely an inferior. She did not want to relinquish a costume that symbolized her discipleship but also the inner transformation it represented.

Perhaps there was some false humility in this. Nivedita saw her submission as spiritually superior to Mary's equality; it was the first of several emotional triangles in which she became enmeshed, some productive, others less pleasant. Her view of discipleship affronted the American's vision of individuality: Mary believed that Nivedita had surrendered too much. On the other hand, Nivedita disliked Mary's continued attraction to the "platitudes of X'tn [Christian] Science," and believed her own embrace of Kali's darkness made her stronger than Mary Hale, who chose to walk on the sunny side of spirituality with "positive thinking."[40] Although miserable at losing Mary Hale's patronage—she refused to support Nivedita's endeavors—Nivedita struck out on her own.[41]

At this juncture, her "surrender" to Vivekananda seemed total, and yet she was already moving unconsciously toward greater independence, a process begun by her recognition that she could not depend on Vivekananda's intimates in the way she had hoped. Once in Chicago, she settled into Hull House whose founder, Jane Addams, like Nivedita, had decided to bring education and culture to the poor. Addams was becoming nationally famous as social worker, sociologist, suffragist, and pacifist, a woman who lived and campaigned alongside her impoverished, immigrant neighbors. She was a famous reformer who seconded Theodore Roosevelt's nomination at the Progressive Party Convention in 1912. She was admired especially for her work with mothers and in child development, public sanitation, and later for world peace.[42] Nivedita never mentions John Dewey, the premier educational reformer and philosopher of the era, but she may well have imbibed some of his ideas at Hull House, as he had worked alongside Addams in Chicago; much of his work would have aligned with her own "experientialist" pedagogy. Nivedita had already tried her hand at public speaking and writing, but perhaps Addams's example intensified her ambitions. Although the pair would disagree about pacifism—and Nivedita would turn her hand to "man-making" instead of "woman-making"—Hull House was an important inspiration.

Living in a female-run institution showed Nivedita's investment in forms of international feminism that Vivekananda could not enter. Perhaps surprisingly to us, she saw no contradiction—or failed to express any—between this new world and her equally strong attachment to Hindu theocratic culture. Hull House delighted her, and she felt that she could be herself there: "When I have been *free* everything has gone well."[43] While elsewhere in America there was "the constant worship of the self-made or self-to-be-made man," at Hull House, the "whole interest is in the life and ideas."[44] She connected to the neighborhood's immigrants when she went to see a play in Yiddish. She did not mind spending a whole dollar on it since it was "so replete with the life of a whole people."[45] At this juncture, there is no sense of the anti-Semitism that would later erupt in her correspondence.

But her lecture tour was far less successful than she had hoped. Nivedita was not particularly adept at raising money, while her own dependence was amplified by traveling. In India, Sara Bull supported her, with the Leggetts providing funds for her travel, lodging, and board.[46] She tried to get perpetual subscriptions of a dollar a year, but it was hard going. She aimed to raise $3,000 to create and run a "special Pratt Institute," a school of arts and crafts, industrial design, and architecture.[47] Again, her words show how she was inspired by the cutting-edge educational institutions. Established in 1887 in Brooklyn, Pratt had opened its doors to men and women, rich and poor, producing the architects, dressmakers, and furniture makers for the burgeoning American economy. But this innovative model also showed how far Nivedita was from achieving her dreams. She received some orders for a few "Hindu brass utensils and some embroideries!!!," but she had hardly opened a new market for Indian products. She became angry when audiences took her time and energy but then failed to donate.[48] When a sum of $5,000 arrived, it was through Vivekananda; and the final total of nearly $7,000, though a tidy amount, was hardly enough for her grandiose plans.[49]

Nivedita put her heart and soul into these talks, which included addresses on Indian women, Mother-worship, and on the ancient arts of the subcontinent. She endured attacks from the Ramabai women and began to understand Vivekananda's displeasure when he experienced ignorance or casual racism, such as when she heard remarks "about giving babies to crocodiles." When they insisted that she teach a "higher way" to Indian couples by enjoining them to eat together, she responded that, as an Englishwoman, she did not impose on Americans, so she did not dare advise Indians either.[50] She defended non-Western cultural forms, prizing Hindu notions of family hierarchy rather than companionate marriage, a stance that often disturbed her listeners.[51]

When she heard that the British were taking Boer prisoners in South Africa in December 1899, she sided with the Boers. Linking anti-imperialism to Vedanta, she wrote that she wanted "thrones [to] totter and nations [to] change their places."[52] Her often middle-class and middle-brow female audience always applauded the anticolonialism, but they may have been less enthusiastic about extinguishing Anglo-Saxon hegemony just as America was preparing to inherit it. But she did try to cultivate her audience when she argued that "it was the duty of America to assume the responsibility of spreading the Anglo-Saxon type of Civilisation over the world"; and extolled "Humanity and Freedom and American ideals."[53] Perhaps for obvious reasons, Vivekananda had never made such proclamations. Was Nivedita sincere or merely strategic when she made such remarks? What is certainly true is that the flattery was followed by thunderous reception, but very little money. If she was being instrumental, it simply did not produce results.

PATRICK GEDDES AND ANNA MORTON

Nivedita went further down her independent path when she met Patrick Geddes and his wife, Anna Morton, in New York in early March 1900. In Anna, she found a true friend; and in Geddes, a man as concerned as she with human and environmental interaction. He was a mold-breaker, a town planner, social theorist, and visual thinker whose aesthetic sensibility appealed to her own love of design. He was also a botanist, biologist, and sociologist who, as much as Spencer a generation before, wanted to produce a "living theory of society."[54] Indeed, Nivedita was so fascinated by the Scotsman that she admitted being "glad that [she had] found [her] own place in the world before [she] met him."[55]

Such statements revealed her difficulty. As a celibate woman with a serious spiritual vocation, she fell outside the known "types" of Western social intercourse. She was not a Catholic or Anglican nun, nor had she opted to be the family spinster and aunt like Josephine. On another level, she was all these things (even if not Catholic), and yet her collaborations with men brought her into unusually close contact with them; she was an intellectual enabler, but also needed them to further her own projects. Because this position enhanced her ideas and offered personal connection, she delighted in this indeterminacy but was frustrated by uncertain boundaries. She was

14.3. Patrick Geddes

open about her attraction to Geddes but neutralized any danger by be-friending his wife. The two women celebrated Geddes together, as she cele-brated Vivekananda with Josephine MacLeod.[56]

When she first met Geddes, she exclaimed: "he is a light—beautiful and lovable—but with the most lovable kind of Westernness and *most* Western kind of loveableness—the air of the patient investigator." He had none of the "godlike solemnity of the East and of the church that becomes itself the In-carnation, and says, 'I AM the Life.'"[57] Despite her love for Vivekananda, his towering presence may have discomfited her at times. Nor did Geddes pos-sess the Christian self-righteousness that she had long left behind.

With Geddes, Nivedita returned to the European intellectual world at its most pioneering and thoughtful. His interests momentarily cut her adrift from her Indian preoccupations, but also prepared her to adapt Vedanta to the next generation of "alternative" Western culture. She had spent her early childhood in Northern Ireland, whereas Geddes had grown up in the fire-and-brimstone Calvinism of the Scottish Free Kirk. Both had Celtic connections, and when he worked in France at the Roscoff Marine Station, he was intrigued by Brittany's "primitive" remains.

He was profoundly influenced by Frédéric Le Play, the Catholic social thinker, whose emphasis on "Place, Work, [and] Family" inspired the socially conservative aspects of his work, while also predisposing him (and Nivedita) toward forms of anarchism that spurned centralist, top-down intervention.[58] They both admired the arts and crafts gospel of William Morris. An episode of blindness in Mexico had transformed him, deepening Geddes's belief in Emersonian self-cultivation and experiential learning. Thus, he understood Nivedita's pedagogy, the "child's desire of seeing, touching, handling, smelling, tasting and hearing."[59] Equally, as an urbanist, he knew the importance of monuments and museums in collective and national memory, work so important to Nivedita and her later involvement with Indian artists.

In the Outlook Tower constructed in 1892, Geddes had pioneered new observational techniques with a camera obscura that looked down upon Edinburgh and the interplay of its inhabitants. There was a curious link between the microscopy he had done earlier on tiny organisms and the new interactional perspectives that he observed from above; in both, different viewpoints and magnifications shifted perception. When he met Nivedita, Geddes was already well known for his work in Edinburgh that had adjusted city planning to the habits and customs of the affected population.[60] He had purchased slum tenements, converted them into single dwellings, and begun the process of "conservative surgery" that made him famous.

Nivedita warmed to Geddes because she wanted to retain "Indianness" by proposing similar projects for Indian cities. She believed that the politics of place and space were central to opposing imperialism; and she did not want European models, derived from Roman monumentalism, to be imposed on Indians. She believed that Indian cites, like their medieval European counterparts, were naturally designed for sociability and community as well as spirituality and festival.[61] She also shared Geddes's lifelong passions for botany and hygiene, and lyrically described plans for a garden in Bagbazar with sunflowers, nasturtiums, snapdragons, petunias, and sweet

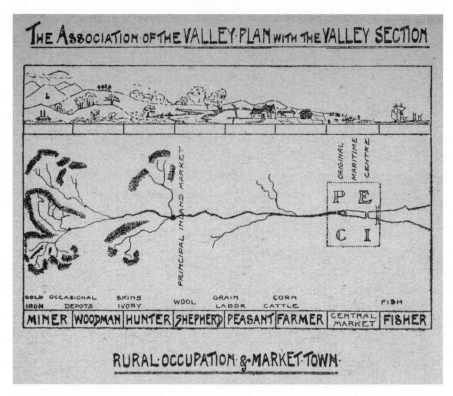

14.4. Geddes's Valley Plan, from Victor Brandford and Patrick Geddes, *The Making of the Future: The Coming Polity*, 1919

peas.[62] Her words suggested a lingering nostalgia for these Devon blooms over native Indian species but underscored her "hygienic" desire to beautify Indian cities.[63]

She explained to Vivekananda that the Scotsman was "more [of a] psychologist than a sociologist" because he understood that landscape shaped individual selves as much as nations.[64] He had been formed, he believed, by the Tay Valley, and when he later taught in India, he felt that the Ganges had the same impact on Indians.[65] He also focused on how "the lake river or seaside" creates "fisher folk" and boat crews, leaving women behind to develop their own occupations, enabling different "types of life" with their own ideals. Geddes thus offered an environmental perspective on cultural difference and the sexual division of labor, again perspectives that shifted Nivedita's intellectual outlook.[66] This "idealism" was grounded in what they both felt was a sociology embedded in experience. Here, the idealism suggested the very opposite, that ideals were determined by material realities. She may have been attracted to Geddes's work because its emphasis on "unity" echoed Vivekananda's vision of Advaita, which also sought to bring together abstract ideals with "practicality."

Out of these concerns, Geddes and Nivedita focused on the specificity and "integrity of myth systems," while recognizing "their links and similarities across cultures." For Geddes, this understanding emerged from evolution, the idea that heredity produced both "the tendency to persist and the tendency to diverge," a view that underpinned his social philosophy.[67] Given Vivekananda's perspective on the relation between unity and diversity, Geddes's evolutionary thinking must have been music to Nivedita's ears.

Myths, she believed, were central to national revival, and with Geddes's inspiration, Indian epics became as important to Nivedita's anti-imperialism as her later engagement with Indian art. She had met Geddes after her stay in Chicago, where she had told Indian stories to schoolchildren.[68] When Longmans, the publisher of *Karma Yoga*, asked her to write a text for American schools, she dreamed that these tales would find their place alongside Grimm's fairy tales and Greek mythology. Because of the tortuous publication negotiations, *Cradle Tales of Hinduism* did not come out until 1907 (and were more popular in Britain than in America); still, they introduced in accessible English a mythology that extolled masculine heroism and female sacrifice—important to the man-making enterprise that she perceived as vital to reinforcing and inspiring Indian "national character." Children's stories—and the playful imaginings of early development—was central to Indian nationalism.

The mark of their collaboration also appeared in *The Web of Indian Life* (1904), which focused on the intricacies of family, ritual, and environment.[69] Moreover, by focusing on women, it brought kinship, female labor, domesticity, and spirituality together in an original way. The apparent conservatism—bound to neighborhoods and small-scale urban locales—aligned well with Le Play's sociology and anarchist social arrangements that both she and Geddes admired.[70]

Of all her writings, *The Web of Indian Life* caused the greatest stir. Those who liked it praised her love and sympathy for her subject.[71] The *Detroit Free Press* called it a "revelation. . . . It is being regarded as an epoch-making book. For in it the inner life of the Indian woman, the life below the surface, the ideals the mainsprings of action . . . are set forth."[72] The

Chicago Daily Tribune also reviewed the work positively.[73] But just as readily, the book was condemned for "misunderstanding and misstatement,"[74] for the rose-tinted view of a society that missionaries called depraved. As the *Church Times* put it: "It is the suppression of the other side of the picture that we deprecate in the interest, not only of the truth, but of the cause of Indian women themselves, whose lot will never be improved if this sort of sentimental idealism about them is allowed. . . ."[75]

The reviewer argued that Indians might reach the heights she described, but only if Indian men were radically transformed. Nivedita might have privately agreed with this, but certainly not with the conclusion that "only Christianity can effect that transformation."[76] The tone of the *Church Times*'s review was hardly surprising, but the *New York Times* responded similarly, albeit with less heat but more sarcasm.[77] The coverage—and the range of views—suggest that her work on Indian women was an important if controversial counter-narrative to Ramabai's.

◆ ◆ ◆

Nivedita had already shown signs of greater independence when in 1900 she refused to alter *Kali the Mother* to meet Vivekananda's criticisms, even if she never told him so directly. She informed Josephine Macleod: "If Swami *orders* me to cut it out, I shall: if he does not, . . . it will stay in." She was "sorry that . . . [she] seem[ed] so obstinate," and she was "not . . . at all sure" that she was "wise or right in this decision." She was, however, "decided," although she added, "If HE will write something for me, I shall be glad to insert that instead."[78] With such words, she accepted her subordinate position vis-à-vis her guru, but made sure that Vivekananda understood what was at stake for her by going to Josephine to ask for her friend's advocacy.

Nivedita sought out Geddes again in Paris during the Exposition Universelle. She agreed to act as his assistant, but realized quickly that, while his "companionship and thought [were] . . . a priceless gift," she could not be the "voice . . . his thought and heart require."[79] She concluded that "I *cannot* be a reporter—it is not that I will not; it is that I cannot."[80] She decided to "ceas[e] to be an ear, and to becom[e] also a thought."[81] This remark was a jest of sorts, for Geddes was the master of "Thinking machines," and she hence insisted that she, too, deserved to move from the realm of the senses (hearing) to that of the "mind."

After this experience, she told Josephine, "you have been right about the greatness of the freedom Swami gives. Freedom to be oneself and to express Him in one's own way is the height of divine and human giving."[82] She was angered when Geddes decided to add James Mavor, a Scottish Canadian economist, to the collaboration, and felt that they ganged up on her "to pass severer criticisms on [her] 'flamboyance.'"[83] This would not be last time that she felt belittled, especially as a writer. They wanted her help but would not consider her an equal. So, she did virtually nothing on Geddes's book, and he, glumly and wrongly, decided she "had succumbed to the joys of the Exposition and given him up."[84]

After her time in Paris, she vacationed with Sara Bull at Perros-Guirec in Brittany. After the congestion and heat of Bagbazar and the frenzy of the French capital, she was transplanted to a land that enveloped her senses in wind-sculpted pink granite and emerald seas, glinting light, and freshening winds. She was quickly restored by the rare holiday: "After a week of walking, eating and sleeping I am like a giant refreshed with wine." She stayed in Lannion, famous for its half-timbered houses, frescoed chapels, and stone-paved roads, and her thoughts, now infused by Geddes's as much as her own, focused on her "Celtic cousins," the "simple peasant-life" of the Bretons. She believed that Brittany had changed little since "the Guises ruled, and the Medicis came" and enjoyed the landscape of "stone calvaries and sad Christs and simple, honest working folk."[85] She idealized yet again and did not appreciate how the tourist economy—of which she was a part—had already irrevocably changed Breton society. Instead, she let the monuments feed her imagination, now rendered "scientific" through her study of geography and culture.

However, she felt crushed when Vivekananda disapproved of her new enthusiasm for Geddes and believed he was even jealous. He retorted: "You must know. . . . I am born without jealousy, without avarice, without desire to rule—whatever other vices I am born with . . . Only I do believe the Western people have the peculiarity of trying to force upon others whatever seems good to them, forgetting that what is good for you may not be good for others. As such, I am afraid you might try to force upon others whatever turn your mind might take in contact with new friends."[86]

It is not clear what offended Vivekananda about Geddes's ideas, for, on the face of it, the two men had much in common.[87] He would have approved of Geddes's desire to retain "Indianness," though what that was remained highly contentious.[88] But as the letter explained, he worried about Western impositions and had long criticized Indian reformers who had assimilated too much from the West. Did he think that she was slipping back into British arrogance? If there was a "personal" dimension to his warning, he never accepted it.

Moreover, he may even have judged correctly. In writing to Anna Morton, Nivedita enthused: "Not one lecture can I give without blessing the methods of observation that Mr. Geddes has put into my hands. If a Young India rises, to bring about a national rebirth, we shall owe it more to him than either he or we shall ever wholly know."[89] These words, although designed to flatter, suggest how she regarded Geddes as *the* inspiration for "Young India," not the Indians themselves. Vivekananda rejected such presumption, especially from a British person, even though he remained frustrated by Indians who remained unready to sacrifice for their country.

On August 29, 1900, Nivedita wrote to explain to Josephine that she felt truly thrust aside, as someone he no longer relied upon: "Swami has cut me off by a well-deserved stroke—and you stand to be all in all."[90] When in *The Master as I Saw Him* (1910), she recounted their September 1900 parting, she wrote that it had "crossed his mind that old ties were perilous to a foreign allegiance," and that somehow he had "seen so many betrayals" that he was "ready for a new desertion."[91] Perhaps she sensed that he feared she would no longer be his standard bearer: "There is a peculiar sect of Mohammedans who are reported to be so fanatical that they take each newborn babe and expose it, saying, 'If God made thee, perish! If Ali made thee, live!' Now this, which they say to the child, I say, but in the opposite sense, to you tonight: 'Go forth into the world and there, if I made you, be destroyed! If Mother made you, live'!"[92]

She was now on her own, her fate utterly in Kali's hands. But that was not the end of the farewell, nor was the severance total. She claimed that he appeared early the next morning, his "hands uplifted," having sent her off with a poem called "A Benediction."[93] She explains how she drew away from him in a "peasant market cart," as they lost sight of each other in the dawn light of an August morning.[94] Then followed a year of relative distance that ended without overt articulation (it was said that Sarada Devi called her back to Calcutta), when she returned to India in February 1902 with Sara Bull and Romesh Chunder Dutt.

Vivekananda was perhaps remarkable in letting her go—despite their mutual distress. He recognized that something had come undone, and that a different connection needed to emerge. Although he had hoped that she was his "Besant in the making," he stepped aside at this juncture and recognized her need to find her own path, even if he did so in a manner that left her feeling cast aside. In the end, however, the change in their relationship enabled her to stock up on new ideas and collaborations in the West. By bringing so many disciplines and ideas into play, Geddes modeled the very mold-breaking that she hoped to undertake herself.

JAGADISH BOSE

In April 1899, just as plague hit the city and Nivedita began relief efforts, she turned to Jagadish Chandra Bose's troubles with the British administration. A physicist and biophysicist, Bose is one of the greats of Indian science, famous for his work on radio waves. In her inimitable way, she connected the callous attitudes of the British to the plague-stricken population with their maltreatment of the great Indian scientist; both in her view were deplorable.

Although feted in 1895 by the Royal Institution while in England, Bose's career in India had been obstructed both by the lack of a proper laboratory and by "insults and slights."[95] Nivedita was sickened by the "cruelty the cruelty the cruelty [sic] and the meanness of a conquering people."[96] She asked Sara Bull why "this great soul [should] be tortured to death. And by nothings—unmanlinesses [sic]—deliberate slights, and difficulties made without necessity."[97] She admitted toward the end of the letter, "I *hate* [her italics] my own people. . . . They are poltroons."[98] A few days before, she had written to Josephine MacLeod, "Do you remember how I told Swami that I could never fire on the English flag? I could no more identify myself with that now than I could fly. I see that England's course is not yet run here—but I LONG with all my heart for the day when it shall be."[99]

Nivedita made no further efforts to make India and England "love one another," her aim when she first arrived in Calcutta. When she was in London in the autumn of 1900—after her American tour—she continued to lobby for Indian science.[100] She told Bose how she clashed with Sir George Birdwood when asking him to consider a postgraduate university scheme for Indians funded by Indian steel magnate Jamsetji Nusserwanji Tata. When she explained the dangers of repressing "native" scientific talent, Birdwood trotted out hated stereotypes: "the people of India will never rise against

14.5. Jagadish Chandra Bose at the Royal Institution, 1897

us. They are all vegetarians."[101] He added, moreover, that in the "interests of SCIENCE," the British needed to exclude Indians who were natural metaphysicians but incapable of exact science.[102] When the discussion became heated, Birdwood suggested that she was "disloyal."[103]

Bose had to contend with such clichés throughout his career.[104] Ironically, Vivekananda, in praising Indian spirituality, had indeed argued for Indians' skill in metaphysics, but did not feel that this capacity ruled out scientific talent. But the argument again underscored the difficulty of promoting Vedanta as inherently both spiritual and scientific. Birdwood's disparagement, however, revealed the hollowness of imperial claims: the British presence in India was legitimated as a project in uplift and "rationalization," but denied Indians the normative knowledge and techniques to achieve these very goals.[105]

By mid-November 1900, Nivedita had thrown herself into another collaboration with Bose, in which "whole days pass in Science and in translating and talking India."[106] The following month, she was nursing him in London after an operation, with Vivekananda returning to Calcutta alone after his stay in California. The forty-two-year-old Bose quickly became her "Bairn," the child she never had. She resolved to promote him as the man who could exemplify Indian science *and* metaphysics. In her view, creative science—real science—was inseparable from Vedanta, a conviction that Jagadish Chandra Bose sometimes endorsed.

She craved a "nationalist" science and attempted to explain its political import when she wrote to Josephine years later from Clapham, London, in the spring of 1909: "About Dr. Bose's Laboratory—one must not talk of it. Here is nothing that would so quickly bring down the wrath of the government, as any whisper of such an undertaking. I am engaged in no politics. But SCIENCE *is politics,* in the eyes of the Gov. . . ."[107]

Rabindranath Tagore also thought that Bose's work was vital and believed that his scientific theories supported Tagore's own universalism while augmenting India's scientific reputation.[108] Nivedita was also pleased that Bose forged a connection with Geddes, who finally took up a post in India in 1915. The Scotsman loved Bose's work on plant "sentience" and linked biophysics to his vision of "cooperative evolution."[109] For him, Bose's plant studies proved the importance of garden cities, because plants sustained human interaction. But while Geddes loved Bose's work, it is not clear what the physicist or Vivekananda would have made of Geddes's belief in "neurasthenia" among the Indian poor and the need to combat it with gardens. They may have regarded such schemes as echoing older, not to say Malthusian, assumptions about native degeneracy.[110] These many views reveal how everyone saw Bose's work as essential to their own projects. Geddes wrote a volume on Bose's life and work in 1920, publicizing "Vedantic" science for English-speaking readers.[111]

Bose had demonstrated his experimental prowess with homemade instruments employing gunpowder and a bell before British officialdom in the Kolkata Town Hall. He used a homemade "coherer," an apparatus he did not seek to patent because he had no interest in making money. Instead, Guglielmo Marconi, who Bose had met in London in 1896, was celebrated for similar work in wireless telegraphy. Bose did all this with limited funds and constant struggles with officialdom.[112]

Born in Eastern Bengal and educated in a village school (unlike Vivekananda and other Calcutta luminaries), Bose arrived in St. Xavier's and was taught by a French Jesuit, Father Lafon. Like Vivekananda, Bose was a Kayastha, became a Brahmo, and had an orthodox mother. However, Bose chose science rather than religion and, with time, helped craft a professional identity for Indian scientists by demanding that the government pay the same to all teachers, Indian or European.

Nivedita, for her part, tried to help him institutionally, intellectually, and spiritually, because British "race-prejudice" outraged her; and because she hoped that Bose's work on the apparent similarities between muscular and metal fatigue would become central to the creation of Vedantic science.[113] In August 1900, he presented his arguments to the International Congress of Physics, held in France, saying that "there is no discontinuity between the living and the non-living."[114] He later remarked at the end of his Royal Institution lecture-demonstration in May 1901 that "It was when I came on this mute witness of life and saw an all-pervading beauty that binds together all things—it was then that for the first time I understood the message proclaimed on the banks of the Ganges thirty centuries ago—'they who behold the One, in all the changing manifoldness of the universe, unto them belongs eternal truth, unto none else, unto none else.'"[115]

Such statements caused as much of a stir as did his painstaking results. Geddes described Bose's interaction with Sir Michael Foster, a veteran Cambridge physiologist, who asked why the Indian showed him a graph with the "curve of muscle response" to electrical stimulation, something he already knew about. Delighted, Bose replied, "Pardon me; it is the response of metallic tin."[116] Foster was so astonished that he apparently "hurried Bose to make a new communication to the Royal Society" on May 10, 1901. For Nivedita and Sara Bull, who were both present, his appearance was a triumph. He concluded that there was no rigid demarcation between "where the physical ends" and "where the physiological begins," and that "such absolute barriers do not exist."[117] He argued that where electrical response existed, "life is said to be; where it is not found, we are in the presence of death, or else of that which has never lived."[118]

Whether Bose considered himself—or should be properly considered—a scientific "mystic" remains contentious, but Nivedita was not concerned with such matters. For her, Bose's science was nationalist, and hence political (though she said the opposite), because he had acknowledged the power of Vedanta in his scientific worldview.[119] Bose's subsequent book, *Response in the Living and Non-Living* (1902), was a product of their collaboration the previous year. The epigraph began with the quotation from the Rig Veda, "The real is one: wise men call it variously."[120] Whether it was she who pressed for this introduction is not clear.

Nivedita discussed Bose's work in October in the *Review of Reviews,* a monthly dedicated to news in the global Anglosphere; she asserted that "irritability" was a characteristic of both "life" and "non-life" and sought to draw analogies between muscles and metals in their reaction to fatigue, asserting that "even metals respond precisely in the same way as human beings!" She concluded that "the gulf that yawned between vital and non-vital had been bridged" and argued that Bose's scientific insights were "in some special sense the contribution of his whole race." Remove the modern methods and scientific language, she argued, and even the "simple ryot [cultivator]" and the "grain-seller in the Bazar" would understand this oneness.[121] The mythology, folklore, spirituality, and science of India, she argued, permeated the consciousness of the "people."

Some suggest that she wrote much of his work for him.[122] Certainly, her own account implies that she contributed a great deal to his later *Plant Response as a Means of Physiological Investigation* (1905): "I want you to understand the appalling white heat of thought in which the Bairn now is. He gave me 4 sheets of notes in a rush last Sunday, and tomorrow I expect to begin to work them into papers."[123]

When *Plant Response* came out, she was delighted that *Nature* gave it a long and serious review. The author admired the novelty of Bose's instrumentation but believed that plant physiologists would be mystified because the book did "not start from any place in the existing corpus of knowledge."[124] Its originality made it difficult to evaluate, but in the end, his objections focused on what he considered Bose's "Don Quixote"–like qualities. Outside of biophysics and physiology, however, Westerners praised Bose's poetic and cosmological daring, and he was to receive plaudits from Romain Rolland, Albert Einstein, George Bernard Shaw, and Henri Bergson (who embraced Bose's vision of natural continuities).[125] Nivedita also reported on a more unambiguously positive review in the *Boston Evening Transcript,* which spoke about Sanskrit terminology, which was said to have caused much pride in India.[126]

The collaboration, which brought Advaita into the center of Bose's work, had taken both in new directions. Bose was a Brahmo and connected to Mohini Chatterji, the "guru" who had instructed Sara Bull in Boston before she met Vivekananda. Ashis Nandy has offered a retrospective analysis of Bose's family history—and the tension caused by different beliefs that his mother and father held—to explain the appeal of metaphysical ideas that emphasized unity.[127] The more obvious stimulus, however, may have come from his wife, Abala, who for example, apparently urged him to examine the feminine principle (that is, the Mother-Goddess).

But Bose did not embrace such views easily or entirely. For example, in 1899, Nivedita reported that he told her he had been horrified by her submission to what he viewed as orthodox Hindu prejudice regarding women and that her "narrowness hurt him unbearably." He was also disgusted that Ramakrishna should be regarded as an avatara.[128] He explained: "'A man cast in a narrow mould—a man who held woman to be something half fiend—so that when He saw one He had a fit'!!!!!! Between a gasp and a smile I said I could not accept the narrative. I confessed that I too worshipped blindly—but pointed out that we none of us, least of all Swami wanted him to worship too.'"[129]

But toward the end of 1900, Nivedita felt he was turning to Advaita, and that she had been responsible for bringing the Bhagavad Gita back into his consciousness. She felt his pride in his Indianness increase: "it has been good to hear Dr. Bose talk unguardedly for hours together—giving story after story of the tremendous renunciations of the Indian past."[130] She believed Vivekananda's ideas were taking root, and that his adoption of the "oneness of all" would save him "from errors that other men of science walk into blindfold."[131]

She thus actively sought to shift Bose onto new paths. In return, she tried to "lov[e] all religions equally" by thinking and worshipping like a Brahmo—another illustration of her experientialism.[132] She found Brahmoism unappealing, however, because it reminded her of Protestantism, but she persisted, hoping it would lead her to serve "S.R.K. Himself [Sri Ramakrishna]."[133] But she simply could not commune with a tradition that held no place for pageantry, storytelling, and Kali worship, all so important to her national ideas—despite her Advaitic framework.

During these heady times, Nivedita sometimes thought of Vivekananda and worried: "I do not think *he* could understand or approve—and to be disapproved of by him is still the uttermost depth to me."[134] This concern was perpetual, but, from her time with Geddes, she carried on exploring. Perhaps as a devotee of Kali, she accepted that creation required destruction, that her desire to break out of past confines entailed unavoidable moments of regret. She continued to long for India, but she was also enjoying herself, writing for William Thomas Stead's *Review of Reviews,* and traveling to Norway to help Sara Bull with commemorations for her husband, the violinist Ole Bull. May 1901 was a special and freeing time when she vacationed with Dutt and the Boses in Scandinavia and began to write *The Web.* There, she broke all her self-imposed dietary rules and indulged in mutton, fish, and eggs. She even slept out of doors to become more robust, preparing herself for her return to India. Like the stay in Brittany, the holiday rejuvenated her. She wrote that she now saw "some value in the soul of R. N. Tagore [Rabindranath Tagore]," the man whose eroticism and sensuality Vivekananda had condemned.[135] She thought that "all that the King has said about Tagore" was probably true, but now believed there was more to understand.[136] Diverging from her guru filled her with a pleasurable sense of autonomy:

> To my great horror, Freedom has meant something to me, for my life has come to include many elements that Swami would not have put there. They are all for him—and he will not hold me less his child than before. . . . .
>
> You must not think from all this that I cherish any idea of going out to tea with Brahmos when I get back . . . I belong to my work—to the women—and to the girls. . . . And I belong to *Hinduism* more than I ever did. But I see the *political* need so clearly too! That is all I mean—and to that I must be true. I believe now that I have something to do for grown-up India and for Indian men.[137]

Talking about freedom in this way was unusual, for it was not about renunciation but rather about physical relaxation and strength, as well as forms of "forbidden" spiritual experimentation that she feared, but did not know, would make Vivekananda object. The Boer War had made politics more urgent; she now believed everything that was "noble in Britain" was dead.[138] She wanted "nothing to do with Xtians or government-agencies, as long as the government is Foreign. That which is Indian for India, I touch the feet of, however stupid and futile."[139] She attacked the British mission-aries and their view of Indian women in her "Lambs among Wolves" and published this polemic in the prestigious *Westminster Review*.[140] She even acknowledged her extreme feelings, her desire to harm. But she believed that harm done by Indians was better than altruism from the British. She had, in fact, begun to appreciate her own aggressive feelings.

Nivedita felt that within twenty years, more British people would condemn imperialism and call for its end, while in India, the national struggle would become still more radical. She sought the "passion of the multitude, the *longing* for death" that Kali inspired.[141] She took from Vivekananda the belief in "national man making" that, she believed, went "to the root of the matter," but insisted that she was going further: "About India, you will think it too much if I say that I feel as if I had something now that *no one* ever had before."[142]

She feared that Josephine MacLeod might think her "dangerous."[143] After all, both she and Sara Bull were women who associated with the interna-tional great and the good. Nivedita worried that Josephine might require a leap of faith to accept her new political radicalism, though she was wrong to doubt her old friend.

She had written from Norway in July 1901, and then two months passed before she wrote again, this time from an Anglican retreat run by Sisters of Bethany in England. Nivedita admired the beautiful "reserve and self-restraint" of the nuns and hoped someday to "establish such an engine of in-tensest force and dedicate it to the Freedom of Man."[144] She wanted to cap-ture "the marvellous round of brooding love" encapsulated in the four and a half hours of daily public prayer and private devotions. She was equally im-pressed with the convent's "efficiency," a word now creeping more often into her writings. In this case, "practical" work, displayed through cleanliness and order began to make her think how spirituality and activism could—and should—go together.

Occasionally, an underlying tension between the friends emerged, when, for example, Nivedita wrote that Josephine's Muslim friend was wrong to say that India "requir[ed] foreign rule."[145] Such thoughts were fatuous, she asserted, given the degradation caused by the British. She defended herself against any suggestion she was forgetting the primacy of Vivekananda's teaching. But she also knew that she was changing: "Do you think I do not know that the great message of my sweet Father is unique? That I could never forget, but beyond that I do not understand. For all this last year I have been going through experiences that lie far outside his course for me. I have held so hard to Sri Ramakrishna the while that if at any point I have been wrong, I can only count it His fault, not mine . . ." [146]

She wanted to forge a synthesis of politics and spirituality, "to write another little book like Kali, and call it Freedom, and though it will be religious and political, the whole of politics will be implied in it." [147] She never did write it, but the search for freedom—personal, spiritual, and political—underpinned all her preoccupations. [148] Her relationship with Vivekananda had encompassed, often uneasily, open-endedness and self-mastery, freedom and subjection, spontaneity and discipline. She had tried to explain to Mary Hale that freedom was not a lack of authority, but the ability to choose one's own authority. After her voyage to Europe, she did so with greater self-assertiveness. For all that Geddes inspired her, she refused to be his "reporter." She accepted her guru's right to change the wording of her book on Kali but would only alter it if ordered to do so. She took umbrage when Vivekananda questioned her friendships and, despite her sorrow over being cut off, focused on her evolving political mission. She even warned Josephine that she would no longer accept any implication that foreign rule in India was acceptable. She had learned the creed of "man-making" from Vivekananda and now wanted to further it in political action. She applauded Josephine for her "impersonal love," and now sought to translate that into an "engine" powering the "Freedom of Man." The psychological and spiritual journey of discipleship had intensified her radicalism.

15

FEMININITY, THE NATIONAL IDEA, AND POLITICS

The Motherland is our only mother. Our Motherland is higher
than heaven. Mother India is our mother. We have no other mother.
We have no father, no brother, no sister, no wife, no children, no home,
no hearth—all we have is the Mother.

—Bankim Chandra Chattopadhyay, *Anandamath* (1882)

Neither the colourless vagueness of cosmopolitanism, nor the fierce
self-idolatry of nation-worship, is the goal of human history.

—Rabindranath Tagore, *Nationalism* (1917)

⋄　◆　⋄

RAMAKRISHNA AND VIVEKANANDA refused narrow confines and encompassing identities while remaining deeply anchored in India and its many Hindu
spiritualities. Nivedita, however, found mooring herself more difficult, and she
remained awash in India with Western and Christian perspectives. She appears
somewhat bewildering at times because she defies contemporary notions of social or political coherence. She has a kaleidoscopic quality—she was a tireless
worker for what contemporaries called Swadeshi, the campaign for national independence that boycotted foreign goods; a Western reformer with elitist tastes;
a reactionary traditionalist; a progressive feminist and mold-breaker. That she
inhabited all these positions suggests how her inner world was in constant

motion, both stimulated and buffeted by different environments, new ideas, and feelings of inner homelessness. The last decade of her life was tumultuous.

She returned to India in February 1902, and over the next few years developed political networks for her activism. She elaborated the doctrine of aggressive Hinduism and launched herself into Swadeshi, which fused her interests in education, handicrafts, civic festivals, and symbolism. In public pronouncements she celebrated the "warrior" cult, while also agitating for women's education and elevating ideas of motherhood among intimates and in public. In private, however, she articulated ideas on masculinity and femininity, shifted and refined her political views, and reshaped her vision of the relationship of sexuality to spirituality. She again undertook another important collaboration, this time with the Japanese aesthete and pan-Asian ideologue Okakura Kakuzo, influential for Indians who looked to Japan's example to counter their subjugation.

THE DEATH OF VIVEKANANDA

Although his strength had been failing even before she met him, Vivekananda's decline accelerated with the onset of diabetes after the first part of his Indian tour in 1897. That spring, he told Christine Greenstidel that the "disease. . . . must carry me off," though he lasted longer than the two years he anticipated.[1] Little by little, he told his close American women friends: "my hair is turning grey in bundles, and my face is getting wrinkled up all over."[2] He took up horseback riding and thought it helped his liver complaint but abandoned this new pastime when the sun inflamed his eyes. He became almost fascinated by the extra "adipose tissue" developing around his abdomen.[3] His own sickness, and that of the country during the famine, were often juxtaposed in his letters. When he wrote to Brahmananda on July 13, at one moment he spoke of feeling "suffocated while getting up or sitting down" and the next urging his colleagues "to go to a separate place[s]" because people were starving in so many localities.[4]

He suffered from asthma, dyspepsia, and nervous prostration, and wondered whether his nerves brought on his breathlessness.[5] When he returned to the West in 1899, he spoke of his "nervous body," and wrote to Brahmananda of his need to disappear, begging his brother-monk not to let anyone write to him.[6] He told Nivedita in May that news of the plague overwhelmed him; although he had long lectured her to see God in the Terrible and to re-main spiritually detached, such fortitude now eluded him. In California, he enjoyed the climate, followed Mrs. Melton's cure, and took exercise, but to little avail. On June 9, 1900, he mentioned that he had also been diagnosed with Bright's disease, and in August 1901—still nearly a year before he died—he was so ill that he wrote a farewell letter from Belur to Mary Hale: "I now do nothing, except trying to eat and sleep and nurse my body the rest of the time. Good-bye, dear Mary."[7]

The years of wandering and his ferocious schedule had long weakened his health. In America, he had been dubbed the "cyclonic monk," a title that sug-gested the stormy energy that surrounded him and which defied stereotypes of neurasthenic Indians. He often paused for respite, but afterward only redoubled his efforts. Indeed, the monks of the Ramakrishna Order were bid to follow in his footsteps—hence their reputation for unceasing service. But he was also aware of the physical dangers of distress, evidenced by his reference to his "ner-vous body." For years, he had been plagued by insomnia, and he did not doubt that his "nerves" may have contributed to his dyspepsia. There is evidence of much internal duress—bouts of disappointment, moments of high blood pressure (when dealing with Landsberg, for example), and the hurt caused by "abandonments" (such as Sturdy's). Also, his return to India engendered new tensions, especially the disputes with his old guru-brothers. And, throughout his adult years, he continued the legal battle over his mother's property. As his 1898 communion with Kali suggests, he was also beset by uncertainty about his path, especially when he told Nivedita that "Swamiji was dead."

At the end of June 1902, just before he died, Nivedita recounted two meet-ings during which the Math's future was discussed. Around the same time, Vivekananda also settled the legal dispute with his uncle, resolving a problem that had consumed him since 1884.[8] On July 2, he blessed Nivedita and washed her hands, embarrassing her with his gesture. We are told that his last day seemed ordinary; he went to the shrine at Belur, meditated, and then asked his disciples to arrange a puja (worship ceremony) for Kali. He conducted a class in Sanskrit and went home in the late afternoon to meditate. By this time, he felt suffocated, and lay down to chant the name of Ramakrishna. In the eve-ning, he fell asleep and then entered *mahasamadhi,* the final state of concen-tration when one intentionally leaves the body. His attendant noticed that blood came out of his nostrils and mouth, and his body went cold. According to Hindu tradition, yogis are relieved of the spirit through their head, and so the end seemed fitting. He died aged thirty-nine.

This soft passing was a counterpoint to Vivekananda's otherwise eventful life. The end was virtually solitary, the death itself silent, seemingly painless, and portrayed as consummately spiritual. On the last day, there were no final instructions to his monks, no lamentation, just the daily routine of spiritual contemplation, devotion, and seva accomplished through teaching. Even though they knew of Vivekananda's enfeebled state, the many mourners were distressed to find such a towering figure gone, with Nivedita particularly facing practical dilemmas and unresolved feelings.

◆ ◆ ◆

Early in the morning of July 5, Nivedita went to the Math, and reportedly fanned Vivekananda's body until two a.m. the following day.[9] She wrote to Josephine Macleod about "how ideally great the last scene" had been, "how even enemies catch breath and worship."[10] In stating that he had "put the body down as a worn-out garment at the end of an evening meditation!"[11] Nivedita was referencing the Bhagavad Gita (2:22): "As a person sheds worn-out garments and wears new ones, likewise, at the time of death, the soul casts off its worn-out body and enters a new one." Josephine was also bereft; shortly before the end, she had been so upset by Vivekananda's uneven temper that she had considered "cutting the connection for ever."[12] Nivedita had reassured her that his words "mean[t] less than nothing" and were the result of illness.[13] After the cremation, Nivedita caught a bit of charred cloth floating in the air and saved it for her friend—an object that, in addition to the Lalique "jewel," Josephine cherished.[14]

Despite Nivedita's growing independence, Vivekananda's death was a turning point.[15] Only a month later, his acts just before he died took on a biblical tone. "He insisted on. . . . fanning me while I ate, washing my hands, and so on. I said—'Swami, I hate you to do this. I should do it for You.' Then he laughed in his daring way—'But Jesus washed the feet of His disciples.'"[16] By July 19, she had publicly detached herself from the order, telling Brahmananda that "painful as is the occasion I can but acquiesce in any measures that are necessary to my complete freedom."[17] She wrote that "her work shall henceforth be regarded as free, and entirely independent of [the Mission's] sanction or authority," for she had decided to concentrate on politics, a course that Vivekananda had not endorsed.[18]

She also wanted to dispel rumors that she was angling to take over the Math and condemned the "deplorable" assumption that "the Hindu people require European leaders for their religious life."[19] But she promised to "reverence daily at the feet of the ashes of Sri Ramakrishna and my own beloved Guru." Ever after, she signed her public statements "Nivedita of Ramakrishna Vivekananda."[20] She remained faithful to the order, but occasionally worried that perhaps it might sever contact with her.[21] It never did.

Nivedita was the only woman seated on the dais at the "monster public meeting of Indian gentlemen" at the Kolkata Town Hall "for the purpose of erecting a suitable memorial."[22] At this juncture, she determined to combine devotion to him with "social doctrines or something à La Geddes [. . .]—no National Congress and no Government."[23] She thus hoped to instruct beyond the factions of mainstream politics. She lectured on "The Hindu Mind in Modern Science"; the "Duties of a Hindu"; and the "Unity of India," topics that showed her discipleship to Vivekananda and collaboration with Bose.[24]

Her feelings are difficult to disentangle, but they help clarify what now galvanized her. Much more than his followers in America and Britain, Nivedita's spiritual search and sojourn among the poor of Calcutta had demanded, and produced, great psychic transformation. Vivekananda had started her Indian adventure, and his loss compounded her dislocation. At times she acknowledged that she felt closer to him now than when he was alive. She remembered her earlier sense of abandonment: "As for me—that anguish in Brittany has made me strong now."[25] She told Sara Bull: "Don't you remember the night in Brittany before I left for England—when I told you how I was going out into the unknown—to Sri RK [Ramakrishna] and Mother—away from the 'Father' who had become so beloved?"[26]

She could not dissociate the heartbreak of his death with a renewed sense of autonomy. By August, she expressed her distaste for the path of "[w]oman-making" he had mapped out for her.[27] She wrote: "But the great stream of the Oriental woman's life flows on—who am I that I should seek in any way to change it? Suppose even that I could add my impress to 10 to 12 girls—would it be so much gain? . . . Only I think my task is to awake a nation, not to influence a few women."[28]

Such views were shot through with contradictions and frustration. Her own spiritual apprenticeship had been a process of self-realization that had begun by his enjoining her to become a "Hindu woman," a path that had taken her to political radicalism. She had earlier acknowledged that teaching orphan girls had proven disappointing because they were often married off young. When in America, she was impressed by the feminism of Hull House that was activist and public-spirited. She was anticolonial and acknowledged that Western feminism might not suit Indian conditions, but there is no evidence that she engaged with Indian feminists, who now also combatted certain aspects of Hindu family arrangements and customs.[29] Her questioning whether she had any right to change them suggests that, at this moment, she accepted the orientalist stereotype of unmoving tradition, especially for women.[30]

Certainly, Nivedita's desire to "awake a nation" reveals how, at times, she wanted to inhabit the "manhood" that she hoped to promote. In one striking letter to Josephine MacLeod, she wrote: "Do you know I am growing more and more sure that I am a man in disguise. I don't seem to be a woman at all! What do you think?"[31]

She saw her femininity as merely a "disguise"—and this she now wanted to cast aside. It is not surprising, perhaps, that given the fears for her young Indian charges, she wanted no part of the lives of "Oriental" women: "A man has come and shown me how—but this is only giving edge to my sword."[32] Vivekananda, was of course, the man who had pointed the way, but at that moment she thought herself more clear-sighted about politics than he: "already I saw these things—and believed that I saw them more clearly than He had ever done."[33] She believed that he was an inadequate theorist of radical nationalism and said later in print: "as Shri Ramakrishna, in fact without knowing any books, had been a living epitome of the Vedanta, so was Vivekananda of the national life. But of the theory of this he was unconscious."[34] Contrasting intuitive, saintly men with a female rational system-maker inverted the normal stereotypes, and nominated her as the legatee of a *political* tradition that she felt uniquely qualified to elaborate on.

In August 1902, Nivedita became very ill, and the monks tended her.[35] Whereas earlier she had just asserted her priority over Vivekananda in nationalist thought, she now identified so strongly with him that she told Josephine, "My little Bairn [Bose] is divine . . . but where the country is concerned—*I am the Guru*."[36] She added that the scientist sometimes talked "nonsense."[37] Such remarks suggest the sense of fusion that she had sometimes felt about Vivekananda. She exclaimed, the "future is all the King, the

King."[38] She wrote that Vivekananda "shall be the whole of my Religion and my Patriotism too."[39]

Her claims were given some public acknowledgment when she lectured in Bombay on September 26 and the loyal Sadananda, who had worked with her against plague, transferred "his service as body-guard to [her] *just* as he gave it to Swami."[40] Later, when young Indian nationalists were insufficiently reverent, she thrust them aside. She wrote of a possible recruit that "I find that he has been rather misunderstanding my attitude, and taking what I wrote to him, as from an equal, whom he could set right; whereas I thought of my words as those of the Guru. I have not *said* this, but have left him to infer that I would ask more reverence."[41]

She also appreciated newspaper accounts of the applause at the Gaiety Theatre after she rejected "the statement someone had made of her being a 'foreigner' and requested that she should be considered one of them."[42]

Public lecturing (it seems mostly in English) helped her feel she was stepping into Vivekananda's shoes. She spoke at Nagpur, Wardha, Amaravati; met the radical intellectual and activist Aurobindo Ghose; and traveled to Ahmedabad. By December, she had undertaken another tour in South India, reaching Madras and connecting with Swami Ramakrishnananda, now head of the order's efforts in the south. Like her guru, she also experienced hollowness and desiccation: "Ever since he went, I have felt the utter impossibility of being personal in my love for anyone."[43] She worried that she would become a "machine," but she kept moving and lecturing with Sadananda at her side.

Even a full year after Vivekananda's death, before another round of political activism, she asked Josephine whether "it is true that you saw Swamiji blessing me and the things I do?" Not for the first time, Nivedita desired a "supernatural message" to reassure her; she found some solace in a dream about Vivekananda in early 1904. "It was his last illness. Suddenly He seemed to remember us all in a personal way. He said something gentle and loving, and then 'And you need not keep so quiet, Margot!' He said, 'Come to the door in a carriage next time, and let it be a *wicked* carriage!' You know how silly a dream is. But I understand that the expression was only a mask for the fact that I had remembered Swamiji's personal *love*. He would not mind noise. He would like so much to know that one was there!"[44]

The dream may have recalled his affection and acceptance of her "noisy," revolutionary "wicked" self. Even at the height of Swadeshi in 1906, she still feared that Vivekananda would have disapproved of her "overwhelming need to choose [her] own path and assert [herself]." She asked, "But oh! Am I betraying a trust?"[45] She wanted to be independent, but in 1907, told Josephine that all she really needed was "a fireside, with its home-circle . . . —and a great man very [sic] very occasionally."[46]

OKAKURA KAKUZO

And so, Nivedita engaged in another collaboration with another "great man," Okakura Kakuzo, who had designed the Japanese Phoenix Pavilion at the World Parliament of Religions. In working with him, she accepted Vivekananda's view—stated as early as 1893—that Japan could become Europe's challenger. She was thus central to a larger anticolonial upsurge that focused on Asia. When the Japanese triumphed easily over the Russians in the war of 1904–1905, the victory was met with barely disguised glee by men as diverse as Tagore and Gandhi in India, Liang Qichao and Sun Yat-sen in China, and Jamal al-Din al-Afghani in the Muslim world.[47] Nivedita and Josephine, who had met Okakura in Japan, sought to further links between India and Japan, intent on a synthesis between "Eastern" nations.[48]

Okakura, like Vivekananda, had the gift of "fascination." He dressed as a samurai, despite only a very loose connection to the warrior nobility; rode a horse while wearing the uniform of the Tokyo Fine Arts School; and sometimes outfitted himself in a fisherman's costume or in a hooded kimono. Even more than Vivekananda, he seemed intent on self-fashioning, epitomizing both "tradition" and "modernity."[49] Famous for his exquisite taste, he was a pioneering art historian and museum curator. *The Book of Tea* (1906), still widely read today, aestheticized Japanese culture and romanticized its social order.

Okakura spoke English as fluently as Vivekananda and had also had a Christian missionary and Buddhist education, a background that facilitated communication with Nivedita.[50] He became a director of the Tokyo School of Fine Arts at age twenty-seven, a curator at the Imperial Museum, and in 1897, established the Nihon Bijutsuin (Fine Arts Academy), which promoted a New Asian art to resist Europeanization. This last move was necessity as much as radicalism, as he had been pushed out of the museum for drinking too much and having an affair with the wife of his former superior.[51] He

15.1. Okakura Kakuzo, c. 1905

went to India to study the origins of Buddhist art. He contributed to the Bengali art world, but was also inspired by India, joining his knowledge of classical Chinese painting principles to Indian doctrines.[52] Later, he moved to Boston, where he and Ernest Fenollosa established the Asian art collection at the Museum of Fine Arts.[53]

Once Okakura arrived, Nivedita's letters were full of his nicknames—the "Rhinoceros," the "Chieftain," and "Nigu"—endearments that suggested his importance to her. She loved working with him, even when she was skeptical of his views, remarking that he "almost convinced her that sovereigns have not always and everywhere been vulgar and rich and self-indulgent." Had he been a woman or a child, she believed the friendship might have been "exquisite," but she understood that it might undermine her reputation: "the sad fact stands out before me that I have met one person in this whole world with whom I could have worked literally hand in glove—and if only that person had had the good sense to come into this world a woman or I a man, we might have done great things. As it is, Farewell! We are swept apart and must be."[54]

When her introduction to his *The Ideals of the East* came out in in 1903, she described him as the "William Morris of his country," and praised the Nihon Bijutsuin for its "lacquer and metalwork, bronze casting, and porcelain" as much as for its painting and sculpture.[55] Both were passionate about handicraft and their collaboration prepared her to further its significance during Swadeshi.[56]

Her connection in London to economic historian Romesh Chunder Dutt also primed her for Okakura.[57] She considered Dutt her godfather, and learned about the "social conditions . . . of imperialism and its system of exploitation."[58] He traced how the British extracted raw materials from India, while turning the subcontinent into a market for British industrial goods, especially textiles.[59] The result was India's immiseration, a conclusion that reinforced her belief in the need for technical and scientific education, despite her seeming emphasis on aesthetics, handicrafts, and Hindu culture. "Orientalism" may have led her to support high-grade handicrafts for their beauty (after all, she, like Josephine, loved the artistry of Lalique), but it did not cancel out the engineering interests that had begun in Wrexham.

Okakura's pan-Asianism engendered new thinking about historical alternatives to global Europeanization. In early December 1903, Nivedita visited the caves of Ellora and Ajanta, temples and monuments hewn out of the rocks of Northern India and containing, especially in Ajanta, ancient monuments and paintings that exemplified India's magnificent Buddhist heritage.[60] Okakura had challenged her views, inherited from Vivekananda, that Buddhism was not a "defined and formulated creed but part of the 'vast synthesis known as Hinduism'" that was responsible for "*Indianising* the Mongolian mind."[61]

She praised Okakura for providing another lineage for Indian art, which he believed derived from China, not ancient Greece.[62] Rather as Vivekananda had "provincialized" Christianity as a reflection of the greater truths of Hinduism, so did Nivedita present European culture as a whole "as a mere outpost of Ancient Asia."[63] She described Japan as "a great mountain ravine, through which India pours her intellectual torrents."[64] Again, she followed Vivekananda, who had commended the Japanese for combining art and "absolute cleanliness," with spiritual subservience to India as a "holy land."[65]

Okakura wrote famously in *Ideals of the East*: "Asia is One." He characterized the continent as a fusion of the "*communism* of Confucius, and the Indian with its individualism of the Vedas."[66] Together, they had created an Asian essentialism that challenged Western values and illusions of supremacy. But the book showed that he was more concerned with ethno-racial types and their formative influence on Japanese development than on Asian union. He compared the "past glory in the mouldy walls of Ajanta, the tortured sculptures of Ellora" with the pristine appearance of a Japan able to resist "corrupting" innovation and enhance traditional beauty.[67] Japan *was* Asia, "the beach where each successive wave of Eastern Thought" had left its imprint on "national consciousness."[68]

Nivedita mostly endorsed Okakura's criticisms of Europe, but she did not mention his remarks on an inert and decadent India. By August 1902, a new pamphlet, *The Awakening of Asia*, had been drafted, writing so extreme that she feared it would "be enough to send us all to prison. He is a reckless child."[69] She did not elaborate further; elements of this work appeared in his *The Awakening of Japan* (1904), and the handwritten manuscript seems to have been uncovered in 1938.[70] She also publicly attacked Japan's annexation of Korea as imperialism, a sentiment that many others shared.[71]

She also sensed that Okakura might pose a danger to her personally, as he seems to have made a sexual approach at the very end of July 1902. She wrote to Josephine about an unspecified "misunderstanding" and was relieved when he returned to a more impersonal address.[72] Josephine offended her by suggesting that Nivedita had acted improperly by nursing Okakura through an illness in his room at night. But the accusation prompted her to think about how both women had foolishly "tortured" themselves over questions of purity. Sexuality itself, Nivedita concluded, was not innately wrong, only distracting, a new load to carry: "it is not in itself any more impure than seeing and hearing and tasting."[73] This view was different from that of Vivekananda, who had regarded sexuality as both impure *and* distracting; she now contended that married love was not inferior—celibacy was for spiritual and political reasons. She also came to fear that Okakura's charms might entail the cruel seduction of unwary women: "one should not extend an intimacy worthy only of Swamiji unless one KNOWS that it will be understood and used as he understood and acted."[74] This statement suggests how much she valued the guru-disciple relationship that she and Vivekananda had created. She honored the "REAL" Okakura but rejected the man who, she feared, might be a cad.[75] She never saw him again.

FEMININITY AND CATHOLICISM

Nivedita often referred to Catholicism when thinking about Hinduism, as Vivekananda had sometimes referred to Indian religious "sects" to grasp Western spiritual trends. Although the daughter of a Protestant minister, her attraction to Catholicism ran deep, as she had confessed after the pilgrimage to Amarnath.[76] Her upbringing suggested that, without Vivekananda's intervention, she might ultimately have converted, as had other notable Protestant Europeans of her generation.[77]

However, she chose Indian religion because she felt it compatible with science in a way that Catholicism was not, writing to Josephine: "You know I love Catholicism—in spite of my worship of Science. When I was quite young—growing out of childhood—I thought, and I think, I still think, that the only passion I would ever know would be the passion for Truth. And the conflict between that and medievalism made the anguish of life [sic]. But Swamiji took all the pain out of it—and lo, it is a new world."[78]

As will be seen, by "medievalism," she meant the panoply of its late-Victorian associations, from its social organicism to aesthetic delights and Catholic spiritual mysteries. She honored several Catholic saints who helped her understand the Hindu pantheon and celebrated the Madonna.

These provided models for heroic femininity, but in contrast also highlighted her own "imperfections." When she had dreamed of being "noisy," she was probably comparing herself to Christine Greenstidel, Vivekananda's acolyte of Thousand Island who had finally arrived in India in April 1902, shortly before his death. Nivedita alternated between praise and condescension as she used the "quiet" that surrounded Christine to reflect on issues of femininity, discipleship, and political action: "She is the Eastern Woman and the Nun, without seeming to love it as an ideal, or even to think of it— . . . and I am nothing but an impulsive publicity seeking fool. . . . She yields to her own instincts, because they always lead her right. In me, sweetness wars against strength, and strength against sweetness."[79]

She envied Christine (whom she worried Vivekananda sometimes seemed to prefer) and saw her as "curiously like an Indian Woman." Nivedita was annoyed that men admired such "passivity," faithfulness, and simplicity, when she held such "feminine" qualities in vague contempt.[80] Christine was also maddeningly effective, with her fluency in Bengali (which Nivedita never managed) and her ability to teach married women and widows: "You know it is absolutely the first time in history that married ladies left their houses in this way, and she has any number [of students] from 20 up to 60."[81] Nivedita increasingly relied on Christine to innovate and persevere at the school.

Thankfully for Nivedita's self-confidence, her own strengths were accentuated by the contrasts: "I like her best as my little sister, leaning on one a little, and this, owing to ill-health and loneliness, comes a good deal."[82] Unlike the reserved Christine who had "little power to make new worlds for herself," Nivedita wanted "bigger things, for which [she had] the force and fire."[83] Such self-justifications helped her define the nun-warrior-guru role to which she aspired. Given these self-perceptions, it is not surprising that she found lifelong inspiration in Joan of Arc, who brought together the bravery of knighthood, androgyny, and visionary spirituality—all important to her intimate and public reflections.[84] She also signed letters to her confidante Josephine as "Your childe." Perhaps here she was alluding to *Childe Harold's Pilgrimage,* Byron's poem about a restless young romantic who roams the world. It could also have denoted a youth of noble birth destined for knighthood, a reference to androgyny, chivalry, and warriorhood. Both references sought to capture the idea of youthful masculinity in various guises.[85]

None of these roles, however, were as important as motherhood.[86] Both women were mothers in surrogacy only; Josephine in charge of her sister's children, while Nivedita fantasized of a similar role when waiting for Abala Bose, the wife of her "Bairn," to give birth: "Is it not wonderful? I feel too as if the presence of a child would add a great mystic significance to all I love . . . doubtless it will be a consecrated babe."[87] Aged thirty-three when she wrote this letter, she may barely have been able to repress her own desire for a baby.

When Abala's baby died, Nivedita expressed sadness that no baptism had been performed, but also asserted that the soul "knows no birth and death—but is always grown up—and radiant and strong."[88] She insisted that the "little one" was with Abala still, and that Abala "had achieved greater motherhood in her "grand sacrament of sorrow."[89] We do not know whether Abala found these views comforting, but they pervaded Nivedita's view of Indian motherhood. In *The Web of Indian Life* (1904) she explained that mother-worship in Bengal was rooted in the way "every child is a nurseling for its first two years of life."[90] Thus "consciousness and even thought" emerged from a living memory of the maternal presence that to Westerners was only "vague imagination."[91] Sons turned first to mothers for advice, and the primary connection was the mother-son bond; moreover, maternal counsel was often based on instinctive, unlettered wisdom that, like Sarada's, was eminently practical. She believed Indian civilization was grounded in a pervasive maternal influence that made the Hindu household a "cloister," where the mother was a Madonna who performed the "sacraments."[92] All these ideas fed into her vision of Mother India and expressed her Catholic-Hindu idealizations. She was part of a kind of "sisterhood" in Bagbazar, where she, Christine, Gopaler Ma, and Sarada Devi lived near one another, with the school for married women attached. She also exalted Gopaler Ma: "She is ill—dying probably—diabetes has appeared— and we are to have her. I feel thrilled and the words of Elizabeth redound in my ears—'Whence is this to me—that the Mother of my Lord should visit me?' For I believe that in Gopaler Ma is sainthood as great as that of a Paramahamsa."[93]

In 1906, Nivedita is captured sitting in attendance as a woman fans the aged Sarada.[94] She realized that Sarada's spiritual inspiration as Holy Mother was as powerful—if not more so—than her own concrete engagement. Young nationalists of all stripes who had been imprisoned offered their respects to her, causing Nivedita to say: "'the day foretold by S.R.K. [Sri Ramakrishna] when you would have too many children, is almost here—for the country is yours!' She answered, 'I am seeing it.'"[95]

In December 1910, when in America caring for a dying Sara Bull, Nivedita sought comfort by going to church and there had darshan of Sarada Devi: "All the people there were thinking of Mary, the Mother of Jesus, and suddenly I thought of you. Your dear face, and your loving look, and your white sari and your bracelets . . . It is a golden radiance, full of play. . . ."[96]

Such experiences in a Christian sanctuary expressed Ramakrishna's religious universalism, but also exposed the inner spiritual translation that pervaded Nivedita's psyche and politics. Its consequences—both negative and positive—were various and could be far reaching.

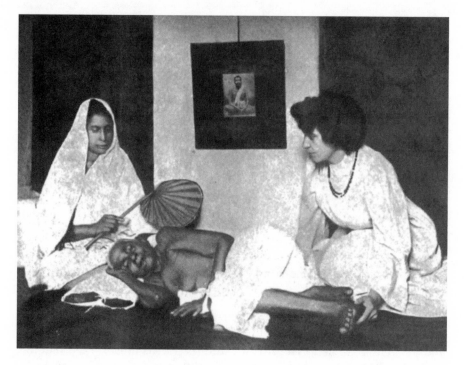

15.2. Nivedita with Gopaler Ma, as she lay dying, with a photograph of Ramakrishna on the wall

THE PARTITION OF BENGAL AND SWADESHI

When Nivedita came to India in 1898, mass mobilization against British rule seemed a long way off. But within a few years, plans to split Bengal in two caused an explosion of protest. After two years of various proposals, the viceroy, Lord Curzon, carried out the Partition in 1905, an ostensibly administrative reorganization that was in fact designed to curb growing nationalist agitation. He sought to quell a province with a large population of almost eighty million, one which had enormous cultural and political clout, as well as having the Raj's capital. The proposal to separate the more Hindu west from the more Muslim east—essentially creating modern Indian Bengal and what became later Bangladesh—provoked immediate protests as an attack on Bengali's cultural identity, language, and ultimately, India's nationhood. The result was a series of interlocked campaigns, including mass demonstrations, unrest in rural regions, and Swadeshi, the indigenous movement to boycott British products. It also entailed a wave of "terrorist" attacks against the British, especially after 1907. These events, taken together, were part of what has been dubbed the "Bengali Revolution."

This movement contributed to a global convergence of nationalist and revolutionary sentiment intent on resisting European expansion. If the Russo-Japanese War had destabilized the balance of power, the 1905 revolution in Russia (and the continued ascent of revolutionary socialism) intensified the turbulence. Emerging pan-Islamism heralded further turmoil in Indonesia and parts of the Middle East (and later in India).[97] Finally, the Boer War had demonstrated both British ruthlessness and weakness, while domestic opposition to the war revealed how the imperial project was far from monolithic. Anarchists in Europe, such as Georges Sorel, created an apocalyptic vision of the "general strike" invested with a mythology of redemption; and endorsed the radical freedom of the individual, a warrior cult, and, at times, strident nationalism when associating with right-wing theorists.[98] Indian nationalists shared many of these ideas, but there was little imitation in these grander world patterns. As will be seen, the radical upsurge in Bengal contributed uniquely to the surge.

The ferment began as early as December 1903, when the first draft of the Partition plan was presented, followed by petitions asking Curzon to reconsider the Universities Act. This legislation limited both the number of Indian recruits and what they could study (especially restricting access to science and technology, a cause dear to Nivedita). At this stage, dissent focused on the middle classes and Curzon believed wrongly that when the act went through, opposition to Partition would fade; he also believed that Muslim elites would respond positively to British reassurances. The revolt also crystallized resentment against the intermittent cruelty of British rule. In 1903, Tagore's niece Sarala Ghosal organized a fund for the family of a poor laborer who had been kicked to death by an Englishman.[99] Moreover, the movement overflowed into other parts of India, with Bal Gangadhar Tilak in Maharashtra important in turning Bombay into another radical hotspot.[100]

Politicians and activists debated how much to accept British guarantees that liberal constitutionalism would ensure reform and self-government, while radicals argued that the imperial government had become irrelevant by persistently foiling any real progress. Liberal activist Gopal Krishna Gokhale, a friend of Nivedita's, hoped that ensuring British cooperation would speed reform (the so-called mendicant position), while the more radical, such as Tilak, Bipin Chandra Pal, and Aurobindo Ghose advocated a massive boycott of both British goods and the administration.[101]

In this struggle, religious symbols, ideals, and practices provided what Shruti Kapila sees as the "foundational concepts" of modern Indian politics.[102] Rather than the product of "false consciousness" or "backwardness," these ideas had deep cultural and theological resonance, which explains their broad appeal. Leading Hindu radicals had differing emphases, but all were deeply afflicted by the moral crisis generated by imperial subjugation.[103] In this regard, Vivekananda's concern with Karma yoga fitted into a wider focus on the Gita's imperatives, on forms of "right action" prescribed in dharma, and thus impatience with Gokhale's "mendicancy."[104] They engaged with ethical precepts that valorized a radical sovereignty of the individual detached from what they regarded as the emasculating effects of British tutelage. In this vision, each person had the capacity for courage and sacrifice. Indeed, for Gandhi later, this forfeiture of one's bodily self—the only "possession" that one could rightfully give—exemplified the power of agency in the cause of "truth."[105] In turning to the "yoga" of boycott, dharma, Swadeshi and swaraj, Indian nationalists showed their originality, but also its Hindu valence.

Nivedita favored Aurobindo's commitment to "Swaraj, Swadeshi, Boycott and National Education," the slogan that split the famous Indian National Congress meeting of 1906 while her previously warm connection to Gokhale cooled.[106] She continued to emphasize handicrafts (especially for Indian women in textile), and in 1906, wrote excitedly to Josephine MacLeod asking for the "run of American factories" so that Indians could produce "glass—pottery, soap, brushes—candles—plumbing—wool manufacture—tanning—metalwork."[107] As Vivekananda's disciple, she endorsed the trend for self-help, or "constructive swadeshi," based on education, work, and service, efforts which both the Congress and various *samaj* groups extended. She also supported striking students rusticated for their activities, and lined up with Tagore's campaign for the Bengali language to have a larger place than English in schools, though there was less agreement between Muslims and Hindus about the exact content of "proper" Bengali.[108]

Nivedita, along with her colleagues, believed that Hindu-Muslim unity was central to any attempt at successful boycott and constructive development. Nor at the outset did these ideas seem farfetched when, on September 23, 1905, Hindu and Muslim students walked together and Brahmin pandits embraced Muslims. Muslim activists, such as Ismail Hossain Siraji and Maniruzzaman Islamabadi, joined the early "swadeshi-wallahs" in criticizing Partition.[109] And mass prayers among Muslims took place in My-mensingh (December 1904), Barisal (now Barishal), and Serampore (August 1905) to criticize British high-handedness.[110] Although they venerated the distant holy places in Arabia, most Muslims readily acknowledged their ties to their Bengal and to India.

Nivedita was inspired by these possibilities and as early as 1903 wrote: "The whole task now is to give the word 'Nationality' to India—in all its breadth and meaning. . . . Hindu and Mohammedan must become one in it, with a passionate admiration of each other."[111]

When, in 1904, *The Web of Indian Life* was published and Partition plans already announced, she wrote a cliché-ridden chapter on Islam in which she admired its "practical" aspects that prioritized a tolerant polity. For Nivedita, Islam had its origins in the "shifting constancy of the desert sands," where the Prophet exemplified an "Asiatic" theology, in which compassion and mercy dwelled alongside "ethical passion."[112] But she also admired Islam's civilizational contributions to India: "No one can stand and face the ruins behind the Qutab Minar [a famous minaret] at Delhi, no one can realise . . . the beauty of Persian poetry, without understanding that Arab, Slav, Afghan, and Mogul came to India as the emissaries of a culture different . . . from, but not less imposing than, that of the people of the soil."[113]

She thus recognized the value of the Mughals' military past and reveled in the unmatched splendor and beauty of Muslim architecture and gardens (Muslims brought roses to India); she praised Muslims in India who refused to eat meat and had forms of God-devotion that equaled those of Hindu bhaktas (here again, the ideal was a Hindu one). She also lectured on "Islam in Asia" at the Corinthian Theatre under the patronage of the Calcutta Madrasa.[114]

Her relationship to Islam at this juncture, however, was not limited to high culture and "civilization." In 1906, she went to Barisal to investigate the plight of the largely Muslim population in East Bengal for the *Review of Reviews*. She extolled the Hindu schoolteacher Ashwini Kumar Dutta, who had joined local Muslim notables in important relief work, which Vivekananda may have inspired.[115] It is not clear if she came under his auspices. Ashwini Kumar Dutta recognized the importance of regional/national celebrations with which the local Muslim population might identify, and even suggested the revival of Satya Pir (which had fused Islam with local religions)—all ideas that focused on his belief in the need for rural regeneration.[116] When visiting the region, Nivedita did not talk about "forced" Muslim conversion, but instead argued that the local population had turned to Islam's "message of democracy and brotherly love" in the hope of "real emancipation."[117] She, too, focused on the cultural similarities between Hindus and Muslims, writing of the widows in white saris and how the community still appreciated the Hindu epics, despite their dedication to the Quran. Again, such remarks focused on fraternity, of people linked by culture and "blood," even if she again emphasized the spiritual link to Hinduism as *the* indication of the population's worthiness.

One thing is certain, however: she sought to convey the enormity of the tragedy she was witnessing: "I have never experienced anything that enables me to imagine what it means, to be one, of what is officially declared to be eleven hundred thousand persons all in the same district, who have not had a sufficient meal for months."[118]

Finally, she was eminently "practical," looking at how to store food during times of scarcity; observing that the cost of rice in devastated Mymensingh was twice that of Calcutta; and analyzing the dangerous consequences of the overproduction of jute, which took land that could otherwise be used to grow food. She showed a passionate interest in the lives of the "fisher-folk" and peasants (part of Geddes's legacy, now reinforced by "practical Vedanta" and her work in economic history with Romesh Chunder Dutt). Although there were still moments of idealization (she likened the poor to Homer's peasants), for the most part she wrote simply and clear-sightedly:

> There seems to be no vital connection between the farmer-fold of country places, and the business and professional people of our twentieth century cities.
>
> But in India the presence of a foreign bureaucracy adds immensely to an evil characteristic of the modern epoch.[119]

At times so elitist in her tastes and social views, especially regarding Islam's contribution to Indian civilization, in this instance she revealed her human and political engagement with the Muslim rural poor and the "peasant question" more generally, a stance rather rare within her circle. These aspects of her early Swadeshi activism have been little recognized.

◈ ◈ ◈

And yet, despite her journalistic foray into Barisal, Nivedita remained within a largely urban, revolutionary milieu preoccupied with Hindu concerns and symbolism and increasingly with a notion of heroic militancy.[120] She therefore reengaged with Calcutta colleagues who, despite a stated interest in Hindu-Muslim solidarity, almost reflexively aligned nationality with Hinduism. The Mission's periodicals and the radical *Bande Mataram* reshaped Ramakrishna's visionary mysticism around this growing nationalism.[121] Aurobindo Ghose quoted Vivekananda: "the first gods you have to worship are your fellow countrymen," while radical journals, such as the *Bala Bharata,* drew equally on Vivekananda.[122] Charles Freer Andrews, an Anglican priest later so important to Gandhi, wrote privately on March 1, 1908: "There is a rapid Hinduising of 'national' ideas going on among the younger men . . . The religious element becomes mingled with the political. The key to a great deal of what is happening is contained in a sentence in recent Oxford Mission Report: . . . 'Young Bengal is looking now to the ideals of Ramakrishna and Swami Vivekananda.' . . . Our students are all reading cheap prints of the latter's works."[123]

It is hard to gauge the exact nature and extent of this "Hinduization"; the degree of personal religiosity within the volunteer associations and physical training societies varied with individuals, but there was no doubt that Vivekananda's teachings of the 1890s now seemed to be reactivated, enhancing national pride and sparking Hindu resurgence during Swadeshi.[124]

If between 1898 and 1900 Nivedita had spoken of Kali as the dynamic underpinning of the Hindu cosmos and of its nationalism, during Swadeshi she focused increasingly on masculine heroism. She exalted the idea of the "Kshatriya force," and joined other activists, such as Sarala Ghosal who, in April 1903, chose the sixteenth-century Pratapaditya as her national hero. Like Vivekananda, Pratapaditya came from the Kayastha caste and was a landowner, becoming a Hindu king of an enlarged Bengal; while Tagore wrote in honor of Shivaji, a seventeenth-century Maratha hero. Both struggled against the Mughals as foreign invaders, but Pratapaditya had extorted money from his Muslim tenants, whereas Shivaji was a model Kshatriya (warrior caste) famous for his piety (but also had had Muslim allies). Luminaries of the Swadeshi elite, such as Tagore, Lokmanya Tilak, Bipin Chandra Pal, and Vivekananda's brother Bhupendranath Datta, all admired Shivaji, but they were also all Hindus. Nivedita had championed him too.[125] These historical figures suggest how difficult it was to find unifying symbols that could encompass Muslim sensibilities, and the Shivaji festivals continued during Swadeshi with flamboyance.[126]

The search for symbolism also reflected the competing influences of her inner life. Vivekananda had transformed the English notion of character by "Hinduizing" it, and Nivedita continued in this task by focusing on the ideals of the warrior caste to shift Brahmin prerogatives.[127] She wrote, "instead of a progressive Brahmanising of all castes, we have deliberately to turn about and Kshatriy-ize everyone, including the Brahmins."[128] She wanted to democratize Kshatryia values, but, even more perhaps than Vivekananda, did not question its high-caste ethos, a view that Aurobindo shared. She set out these arguments in *Aggressive Hinduism* (1905), in which she advocated "activity" over "passivity," "Hindu character, rather than Hindu custom."[129] She called India's sons "to a battle-field on which the bugles of retreat shall never more be heard," and urged Indians to be willing to die, using the example of Kalki, the tenth avatar of Vishnu, who rode on a white horse with a blazing sword, the harbinger of the end of Time before the Satya Yuga (the Age of Truth).[130]

She associated with the Anushilan Samiti, the conglomeration of local youth organizations and gymnasiums. When Aurobindo Ghose organized a central revolutionary council in 1903, she was one of the founding members, even if its effectiveness has been questioned.[131] She provided radical young men surrounding Barindra Kumar Ghose, Aurobindo's militant brother, with revolutionary and anarchist texts, hence enabling them also to feel a connection to men like Kropotkin.[132] She wrote admiringly to Aurobindo Ghose, who had introduced oaths on Kali's sword and the Gita when training a new generation of "masculine" fighters with sword and *lathis* (wooden sticks), even if these rites were often more like body- and bond-building exercises than preparation for combat.[133]

Like others, she turned to the Gita and the famous scene of Arjuna trying to decide whether to engage in fratricidal combat. She explained that the true knight, as Arjuna's example proved, "alone has freedom from self-interest," by forgoing "an advantage to pursue the right course."[134] For her, Arjuna's struggle exemplified "divine play" in its open-endedness and self-mastery, freedom and subjection, spontaneity, and discipline. Such sacrifice defined the Indian knight, a spiritual being who—like the Christian medieval knight who inspired her privately—"alone has true courtesy."[135]

If in her personal life spirituality was inflected by Catholicism, her vision of the Gita owed much to notions of Western chivalry, and, it seems, the British public school. Although surprising for a teacher who had taught in working-class Wrexham, she compared Western chivalry—"disciplined cooperation . . . on the cricket field and in the football team"—to Indian models; and welcomed a schooling which honored "reserve and privacy," "courtesies and restraints," as well as "daring and personal pride." Horrified by British "brutality and unscrupulousness," she nevertheless advocated that this "masculine" upbringing become part of Indian man-making, but without the cruelty.[136] She claimed to have repudiated her Englishness but could not entirely dispose of its models.

Nivedita also turned for inspiration to Western medievalism and an idealized form of Christian society, which explains the sometimes curious ideas that buffeted her during this time. She asked Josephine about the Sherborne pageant when the sleepy town of 6,000 inhabitants in Dorset celebrated its 1,200th anniversary. Over several days in 1905, a cast of 900 people in medieval costume performed for an audience of 30,000. The spectacle had a hint of Oberammergau's passion play, or of a Wagnerian *Gesamtkunstwerk*.[137]

15.3. Sherborne pageant, 1905: The Death of Ethelbald

In 1907, she pushed for a civic pageant of Indian history to celebrate "All India day—Oct. 16th."[138] The Indians, she believed, were made for this kind of national drama, for they had elaborate worship ceremonies and processions from time immemorial.[139] She glorified the Kathaks, the traveling bards who took "nature, or the crafts, or family life" as the subject of epics.[140] In India, as in medieval Europe, work and domesticity were linked to Saints' Days, feasts, and fasts, a cycle of spirituality that Indian communities also celebrated. In her view, "the whole of Hinduism is one long sanctification of the common life. . . ."[141] Her ideas thus projected onto India a nineteenth-century vision of British chivalry, knighthood, and masculinity—which saw India as connected to an earlier and less alienated world that Europe had abandoned with the Renaissance and Reformation.

• • •

Swadeshi's early élan based on unity soon evaporated. Hindu leaders quickly turned to their own traditions for political symbols and drew strength from the "nationalist" faith. Aurobindo and Tilak, keen to edge the British out of India as quickly as possible, emphasized a vision of sanatana dharma, the classical Hindu faith, as necessary for India's rescue from subjugation.[142] Bipin Chandra Pal, the so-called high priest of Swadeshi, believed that India must encompass Muslim aspirations and minority concerns, but still believed that the nation's "bedrock" should be Hindu.[143] In fact, he advocated a "composite nationalism," which promoted self-help and development within different communities. Nivedita was hardly alone, therefore, in praising intercommunal solidarity while turning to Hindu symbolism and religious concepts.

For them (and for Vivekananda, Aurobindo, Tilak, and Gandhi), European secularism was anathema. Vivekananda, had he lived, would have endorsed Ashwini Kumar Dutta's activism among the Muslim population, even if he would have promoted such service as operating within the embrace of Advaita. Gandhi later cultivated religious "neighborliness" and was devastated when postwar Partition broke India apart. Muslim views were as variable and changeable as Hindu ones. Even when Muslims supported partition, they continued to feel both Bengali and Indian with only a minority (often conservative and orthodox) rejecting localism. Certainly, Muslims disliked what they saw as cavalier Hindu rhetoric about Muslim "invaders" (even though some Hindus now claimed that Mughal rule had been better than its British counterpart); raged against the way Muslim communities received fewer resources; and sought to break the hold of Vidyasagar's Sanskritized Bengali by retaining many Arabic, Persian, and Urdu phrases and vocabulary.[144] Men in government service thought Partition would further careers, while others hoped that a program of Muslim self-reliance and education especially might be achieved more easily after Partition. Still others turned to federalism. Peasants rioted in April 1907, with the British blaming Swadeshi for the high prices that this mostly Muslim constituency could ill afford, another attempt to "divide and rule" as much, perhaps, as an expression of Hindu dominance among the zamindars. What exactly sparked the riots remains uncertain; although efforts were made to understand its causes, there was no concerted campaign to cope with rural misery and the religious tensions which exacerbated it.[145]

There were important consequences to Nivedita's sojourn among the famine-stricken in East Bengal. When she returned in November 1906, she fell ill with malaria, had "brain fever," weariness, and had months of taking quinine and other medicines. This period of ill-health caused another, important shift in her psyche, and moved her away from "public work," which she no longer felt able to undertake. Whether her illness prevented her from mentioning the riots in East Bengal is not clear, but they do not appear in her letters, and were perhaps indicative of her decision not to reengage. For a time, she lived quietly in Dum Dum, not far from Calcutta, but was relatively secluded. Instead, she devoted herself to collecting material for *The Master As I Saw Him* and composed the *Cradle Tales of Hinduism* for Longman when she returned to Bagbazar.

She returned to journalism, but her aesthetic interests were what now focused her attention as she pivoted from Hindu man-making to Hindu ideals of femininity. Her art-historical thinking remained strongly influenced by Okakura and Ernest Binfield Havell, the founder of the Indian Society of Oriental Art, and their mutual interest in the frescoes on the cave walls of ancient Buddhist sites, about which she had written to friends as early as 1903.[146]

"Ajanta," she wrote, "[was] another Florence of another Italy and Italy of a large and different thought," utterly new and world-changing.[147] Unlike the derivative realism of recent generations of Indian artists, these murals were untouched by the West, and Nivedita admired their "purity" as an inspiration for Indian national art and the "Bengal School."[148]

15.4. Bodhisattva of Compassion. Wall painting in Ajanta, Cave 1,
5th century CE

The ancient frescoes suggested perspective without imposing it, a flattened technique perfect for "spiritual" rather than "realistic" representation. But during Swadeshi, she was equally, if not more, focused on French mural painter Pierre Puvis de Chavannes, whose works thrilled her because they broke down the barriers between classicism and modernism, and modernism and symbolism. [149] Geddes again was probably a mediating influence in this

15.5. Abanindranath Tagore, *Bharat Mata*, painting, 1905

passion, as he had had strong associations with Scottish symbolists also deeply influenced by Puvis.[150] She begged for images of the staircase of the Boston Public Library, which she now regarded as the "grandest modern civic building in the world," with a greater intensity of higher ideals built into it than any other.[151] She adored the gracefully robed figures representing the "muses of inspiration" as well as the other murals celebrating poetry, philosophy, and science.

With Swadeshi, she focused on the famous painting by Abanindranath Tagore, *Bharat Mata*, depicting Mother India. This image—still one of the most famous in India today—portrayed an "Asiatically-conceived figure with its four arms" among lotuses with the "white radiance of a halo." In her limbs—"the symbol of the divine multiplications of power"—she gives faith, learning, clothing, and food to her millions of children, and hence again in her graceful garb personified the ideals Nivedita valued. She wrote: she is the "Spirit of the motherland, giver of all good, yet eternally virgin . . . is she not after all, our very own, heart of our heart, at once mother and daughter of the Indian land?"[152]

She praised a maternal vision that could not be further from Kali's sword-wielding aggression and eroticism. This image celebrated the virginal giver "as she appears to the eyes of Her children."[153] Mother India is "perfect," a "virtuous woman," divine in her body, mind, and capacity for love, a transcendent, idealized image that, for Nivedita, may have recalled the young Virgin Mary.[154] Such characterizations of the "Mother Goddess," so evocative for Hindus, were none the less much more difficult for Indian Muslims and Christians; neither could worship such an image easily (the Muslims especially so), and yet, the intoning of Bankim Chandra Chatterjee's hymn in praise of Mother India would increasingly become proof of patriotic conviction.[155]

Such images fitted more easily than did Kali into contemporaneous, global visions of nationalism that saw womanhood as nurturing and fructifying. However, Nivedita highlighted the female counterpart to that of the Kshatriyas who sacrificed for divine union, an ideal even more august than dying on the battlefield. She described Nandalal Bose's *Sati,* where a woman in a widow's white sari was "set on the moment of triumph, yet without the slightest consciousness of her own glory."[156] As she kneels before the fire, Nivedita insisted, the mind of the woman about to perform sati set on "union," and an ideal of feminine courage, detachment, and hence divine play.

Her commentary also suggested how far Nivedita was willing to go in idealizing Hindu sacrifice, an aestheticization that saw only peace and prayer, not the contorted face, suffocation, and bubbling skin of women's bodies. Indeed, the fire's light is a holy radiance. This beautification contrasted sharply with the "practical" way she had characterized the famine crisis in Barisal, with its analysis of food storage, price increase, and the social paralysis that ensued from starvation. Nor was she alone: Rabindranath Tagore also lauded the courage of the "foremothers of Bengal" who had sacrificed themselves on funeral pyres. If Tagore later disowned such idealized femi-

15.6. Nandalal Bose, *Sati,* gold wash and tempera on paper, 1907

cide, Nivedita never did. She implied here that women mounted the pyre as consenting agents and may well have found inspiration yet again in the model of Joan of Arc.

Also, she explicitly looked to idealist trends in French art because the French, like the Indians, needed to "remake the homeland," this time after German defeat and domestic political strife.[157] She referred explicitly to Pierre Puvis de Chavannes's *Sainte Geneviève veillant sur Paris* (Saint Gene-vieve Overlooking Paris), the patron saint of the city scanning the horizon for invasion from the Huns.

15.7. Pierre Puvis de Chavannes, *Ste. Genevieve Overlooking Paris*, 1898

The mural decorated the Paris Panthéon, the secular church of France, and displayed the civic and historical mural paintings that she dreamed of for India; for Nivedita, Ste. Geneviève was almost "oriental"; she explained that that the "elderly saint wears a veil" much like the women of an "eastern household," concluding that Ste. Geneviève had "the face and figure of . . . some Hindu widow."[158] The rosebush reminded her of the tulsi plant associated with Krishna; the lantern, the darkly illuminated interiors of Bagbazar; the terraces, outdoor rooms, and rooftops of Calcutta.

Such views were grounded in a vision of the "Hindu Household" or the "Eastern Home" as cultural bulwarks against imperial domination.[159] In *The Web of Indian Life* (1904) and *Studies from an Eastern Home* (1913), she lovingly described each ceremonial detail, insisting that the domestic sphere underscored the quotidian beauty of Indian life. She wrote of the sacred tulsi tree, ritual bathing, and gestures of hospitality, arguing that this spiritual enchantment was made possible by women's self-abnegation. Moreover, because beauty and spirituality were linked, she described the saris and veils, the silks shot through with many colors, and the radiant whiteness of the widow's weeds, the lines on pieces of cloth reminding her of the brushstrokes of a "great master, defining and emphasizing the whole."[160] This commonplace but striking beauty was integral to her Swadeshi nationalism.

As has been seen, Nivedita seems to have had a brief time in (semi-)seclusion after her arrival in Bagbazar, while also coming to know this world through her connection to Sarada Devi. She celebrated and valued it in these publications, but her idealizations tended to lock away women in a cultural nationalism almost as restrictive as the zenanas that hid them. When she explained what Swadeshi meant to her, she spoke of a softened notion of caste as essential to Hindu dignity, but revised the vision of dharma to encompass an ethical / ascetic struggle against "temptations of self-indulgence, of comfort, and of individual selfishness."[161] In the West, cooperation occurred for self-interest; but in India, she claimed, self-sacrifice was inherent in Hindu understandings of society—remarks which recalled her admiration for the Kshatriya ethos.[162] During Swadeshi, she transformed dharma into a form of "National Righteousness." She knew that dharma had links to caste obligation, but endeavored to soar above it, encompassing all ranks of society by pressing, especially, for historical murals and pageants, which mythologized the Hindu past.[163] Finally, she designed a national flag with a yellow *vajra,* the thunderbolt of the ancient Hindu god Indra, on a scarlet background, choosing this symbol perhaps because Vivekananda had called himself a thunderbolt.[164] She suggested, however, that it was appropriate for India precisely because it had had "cosmopolitan associations" in ancient Greece and Rome; while also being famous "amongst the Aryan races."[165] For her, the Buddha had properly spiritualized the thunderbolt and was depicted with this symbol of might and light.[166] She hoped that Muslims would not be offended by the design because it did not contain a human figure, but did not alter the Aryan associations.[167]

Given this abundance of symbolism, which often appeared Hindu and upper caste, it is perhaps not surprising that Muslims and ultimately lower castes, tribal cultures, and women would express doubts about a "natural fraternity."[168]

*   *   *

In August 1907, Nivedita left Calcutta until July 18, 1909. She went away in the midst of political upheaval; despite her public call for the greatest sacrifice, she herself had decided to become less self-sacrificing: "I see that when one struggles too hard one shuts out light from all about one." She wanted to put in less effort and to do more growing.[169] She had decided to do no more public work because she had had "to pay too heavily in the sacrifice of the private."[170] She responded to Josephine's letters to "shake it off"—a reference to her illness—by trying to do so, but ended by remarking: "We are never passive—and I am beginning to think that all great things come in passive moments."[171] In June 1907, before her trip abroad, she sensed her mortality, and predicted—correctly—that she would die in 1911.[172] She wanted also to see her elderly mother and to accompany the Boses on a tour to disseminate his work and raise money for herself and Christine. Once abroad, she decided to stay longer. She also kept writing.

Moreover, she sensed that events were slipping from her grasp. The Japanese showed no solidarity with Indian manufacturers and crafts people.[173] Curzon's successor, Lord Minto, was overseeing a "mental and moral Armageddon," a disappointment made worse because of Nivedita's friendship with his wife.[174] She denounced Bipin Chandra Pal as a "coward" and a traitor, though she did not explain why.[175] All around her, she saw men without sufficient "character" and was appalled by police repression, amazed that, even as a European, she could no longer hold an opinion.[176]

Her letters praising "passivity" (especially since they came not too long after *Aggressive Hinduism*) reveal feelings that recalled Vivekananda's experience after his pilgrimage to Amarnath, when he wanted nothing more than to sit in the lap of Kali. Perhaps here she had an inkling of the search for the "nonself" that Vivekananda had undergone after Khir Bhawani. But she did not withdraw entirely. Writing from Britain in early February 1908, she expressed her views on the Surat Split, the 1907 Congress meeting in the city in the Bombay Presidency, which broke the body into the "Extremists" and "Moderates." She condemned its rowdyism (chairs and shoes were thrown) and disavowed these political labels as unhelpful and needlessly divisive.[177] She could not persuade her associates to unite, and perhaps too readily glossed over their differences.

She was not in India when on April 29, 1908, Sahid Khudiram Bose and Prafulla Chaki tried to kill Douglas Kingsford, an English judge notorious for severely sentencing nationalists. In a poorly conceived attack, the assassins missed their target and instead killed two Englishwomen. The two young Indians were swiftly tried and executed (Khudiram was only eighteen), but another trial, known as the Alipore Bomb Case, involved Aurobindo Ghose and went on for almost a year. Despite mountains of evidence, the Crown could not prove his involvement; it ultimately focused on the testimony of Naren Goswami, who was in turn assassinated in prison by Aurobindo's fellow captives. The trial was a sensation in both India and Britain, giving these men an important political platform. It was during his time in preventative incarceration that Aurobindo heard "constantly the voice of Vivekananda speaking to [him] for a fortnight in the jail in [his] solitary meditation and felt his presence."[178] This connection underpinned the patriotic and spiritual lineage that Aurobindo was creating.

After her time abroad, she returned in disguise to Calcutta, believing she was in danger from the British, but never had any real trouble with the authorities. Unlike Tagore, she applauded Vivekananda's brother Bhupendranath when he defended the terrorists.[179] She proposed to write a history of Aurobindo's trial, but never did. She recognized that times had changed. When in 1907, Lady Minto, the wife of the viceroy, had tried to visit her, Nivedita had refused on principle. By early March 1910, however, she had no such qualms, and happily went on a trip to Dakshineswar with the vicereine.[180]

* * *

How do we assess Nivedita's role and impact on Swadeshi and the national movement more generally? Her departure after Swadeshi reached its zenith in 1907 suggests that she will not be remembered for hands-on activism. When she died in 1911, a moderate, Rash Behari Ghose, acknowledged her possible "unwholesome influence on the rising generation," but also insisted that "India's budding national life . . . [was] in no small measure due to the teaching of Sister Nivedita."[181] If this was a myth, it circulated almost immediately after her death. Other admirers included Gokhale and Surendranath Banerjee, also moderates. Nagendranath Gupta, who had met her in Srinagar in 1898, appreciated her work and even admitted to liking her, but niggling doubts remained. He could not comprehend a woman who was both before her time but also "odd." Gupta wrote, "One Anglo-Indian paper has called her love for India 'a craze' and that is how other people will call it, for how many of them can fathom the depth of her nature or the passion that burned in her as a holy flame? To the shallow critic and the casual observer she was only a crank—gifted beyond doubt but only a crank."[182]

Nivedita's "oddness" derived perhaps from her unusual mixture of radical nationalism and cosmopolitanism. Nor was Gupta the only one to be confused. She was accused both of leading the young astray with radical ideas and of being a "reactionary," a characterization that was understandable given that, through Geddes, she had inherited Le Play's conservative familialism—hence the ideal of the Hindu household.

She combined a range of ideas and practical work during her Indian career that was both exemplary and sometimes original, albeit also inconsistent and occasionally troubling. Aurobindo later denied the story that she had arranged his escape to Pondicherry, but admitted that she had been "a friend and a comrade in the political field" and admired her *Kali the Mother*.[183] Her energetic nationalism had inspired him and other activists with its ideal of cosmic maternity, a vision that was paired with her advocacy of an aggressive Hinduism.[184] Admirers congratulated her for finding the models for this combative spirit within Hindu culture itself.[185] She was also important to the shaping of Pan-Asianism, her commitment to true partnership much more genuine than Okakura's. Her passion for handicraft was, moreover, equaled by her love of science and technology. Nivedita was unusual in seeing the possibilities of both for India and urged their coordination, and in this way would have disagreed with Gandhi. The constant translation she undertook between cultures—so challenging for her inner peace—was precisely what made her writings on art, politics, and science striking. Finally, she was able to explain to Westerners, as few else could, the more radical ideas of Indian nationalists.

Although Aurobindo considered her a Westerner to the core with nothing of the Hindu "outlook," he admitted she had a singular "power of penetrating by an intense sympathy into the ways of life of the people around her."[186] She displayed this quality in her observations in Barisal during the famine, but the illness that resulted also turned her forever away from "public work." She may well have been overwhelmed.

Because she was British, her love for India implied that the subcontinent was not backward or degenerate, merely oppressed and brutally exploited—she insisted that the British, not the Indians, were the cause of India's woes. Indeed, from the moment of the plague in Calcutta in 1898 and 1899, she refused to put any blame on Indians for their plight.[187] Her work in the "filthiest bustis (slums), full of moral and material filth" was deemed heroic because she was not a Christian missionary, but someone "who had thoroughly surpassed her English personality."[188] Even if this was not true (as her focus on medievalism suggests), she had understood that Europeans "must work under black men," and she was quoted with appreciation when, in October 1902, she insisted that "India should remain India."[189] At this point, some Indians were gratified to receive such approbation from an educated British woman and were galvanized by her admiration of Indian traditions and civilization.

Although she never liked Bipin Chandra Pal, he esteemed her. In 1918, he suggested that she and her guru were a "beautiful picture of Vivekananda in Nivedita, and Nivedita in Vivekananda; The Master in the Disciple and the Disciple in the Master;—the Two thus Made One."[190] He reveled in a form of fusion that made an Indian the leader and the Westerner a follower. Significantly, his remarks came at just the moment when the myth of European invincibility had been well and truly shattered.

However, Bipin Chandra Pal's depiction of their relationship was far too harmonious; it occludes those aspects of their intimacy that were unreconciled, incomplete, and, for Nivedita at least, dangerously fragmented. When both Vivekananda and Nivedita thought of Shiva's Shakti, they thought of Kali; sometimes she overpowered her husband, while at others, he sought to soothe and contain her. Sometimes Nivedita saw herself as Kali; at others, as Shiva. But certainly, Kali remained mysterious—she is Shiva's potency but also transcends him by dancing on his prostrate form. Because Shiva's name looks like a lifeless husk when the *i* is removed from the Devanagari script, there is a popular saying that Shiva without Shakti is merely *shava*—a corpse. At this juncture at least, the Anglo-British connection that Vivekananda and Nivedita exemplified could, perhaps, be likened to that of these gods. Depending on the moment of her life course, Nivedita was both hollowed out and liberated by the connection to her beloved guru.[191]

16

MALIGN INFLUENCES AND HARROWING DEATHS

I dread outliving everyone I care for.
—Sister Nivedita, August 16, 1911

The thing that killed her was the Will case.
—Sister Christine Greenstidel, October 1911

✦ ✦ ✦

IN THE LAST TWO YEARS of Nivedita's life, many currents converged in a torrent of loss and disappointment. Her mother died, her closest associates became ill, and Swadeshi subsided in repression and surveillance. This book began with a brief allusion to the "global idealist moment," to intellectual exchange that promised new kinds of internationalism, some decidedly anti-imperialist. During her last years, however, Nivedita seemed at moments to abandon this idealism.

In November 1910, she went to tend her dying patron and friend Sara Bull, and as a result, became involved in events that resembled the sordid contrivances of an Edwardian melodrama. The story swirled around a sickroom, a contested will, betrayal of an employer by long-trusted servants, and even accusations of murder. But this final episode was about more than money and family dysfunction; it was also linked to a host of invisible fears. Nivedita invoked Jewish conspiracy to explain the persistence of both capitalism and imperialism, while others saw her as a "Yogi priestess" intent on murder for gain. Bull herself felt her illness was the result of "malign influence," and refused to see her real daughter, Olea, as she feared Olea's friend Abbie Shapleigh was manipulating her with evil thoughts.

Certainly, the "invisible forces" each invoked were different, and yet it is striking that both women turned to such explanations. This was also true of Bull's daughter Olea, who maintained that Hinduism had turned her mother away from her. The concatenation of these fears—which saw global conspiracy and foreign obtrusion in the most cherished familial ties—were as integral to the pre-WWI climate as the twenty years of idealism that had created "Vedanta in the West." They were the shadow that stalked these female pioneers, the darker side of the "global idealist moment" that had animated their life work.

◆   ◆   ◆

When Nivedita returned to India in July 1909, her adopted country entranced her anew. She wrote to her friend Mrs. Ratcliffe that the "dirt, the (far from fragrant) smells, the Maharatta women in the costumes I had always imagined so ungraceful—I assure you, there was NO discrimination in my joy that morning!"[1] She loved India as much as before, but was devastated by Swadeshi's aftermath—the growth of political repression, poverty and ill-health (especially smallpox and beriberi).[2] Young nationalists still bowed low to Sarada Devi, while Nivedita worked on the *Karmayogin*, the newspaper handed over to her by Aurobindo.[3] She also had a new "son," Vivekananda's brother Bhupendranath, while retaining links to the activists she admired.

None of the excitement of her Indian life, however, could veil her growing preoccupation with Jews. As early as 1905, she had commented on Jewish world organization, and wondered whether such people as Landsberg, and a Mme. Wallerstein (with whom she was collaborating) were fate's way of spreading Vivekananda's message: "But what does it mean—this circle round Swamiji, of one race? Landsberg, you remember, also belonged to it. Is it the Birth of Christianity being repeated? . . . Do they at first reject and almost insult, and afterwards assimilate and suffer for a truth?"[4]

She elaborated when she wrote to a British churchman, Dr. Cheyne: "And the Jew merely a distributor, as to this day—and organiser of ideas then, perhaps, as now of finance, but always one who ran up and down the world—then in a caravan across deserts, now in long-distance trains across Europe—scattering his view of the Universe."[5]

She thus esteemed their ability to disseminate new creeds but feared their influence. She accused Lord Curzon, the hated ex-viceroy, of promoting the British expedition to Tibet at the behest of his wife, operating for the "Jew Mining Syndicate."[6] This unpopular colonial expedition involved the death of thousands of Tibetans and ended with the Anglo-Tibetan Convention of Lhasa in 1904, which sought a large indemnity that the Tibetans could not pay. Mary Curzon, Nivedita maintained, had forced her husband to manufacture this invasion so that rich Jews might become richer.[7] The accusation, moreover, was based on a misplaced assumption. Lady Curzon was the heiress of American Levi Leiter, a dry-goods entrepreneur, but he was not Jewish. Rather, he was of Amish, Lutheran, and Swiss-German descent. By 1909, therefore, Nivedita's anti-Semitism revealed reckless conspiratorial thinking.

She did not limit her views to the rich, but also targeted Henry Salomon Leon Polak who, with his wife, Millie, was one of Gandhi's earliest South African collaborators. Polak visited Nivedita to connect with Indian nationalists in 1909, but she misunderstood the message about Gandhi's *satyagraha* ("truth force") that Polak tried to convey: "I have just had a visit from Mr. Polak—the handsome young Jew who represents the Transvaal Indians here. I loathe the kid glove manners of these people—who announce that they will use only 'moral force,' and thereby defeat their own intention of getting access to it. . . . Moral force! How I wish they had some!"[8]

She wrote in this vein mostly to Samuel Kerkham Ratcliffe, an English journalist and lecturer, and an important contributor to the *Statesman,* the English-language newspaper that he had to quit over his support for Indian nationalism. For her, therefore, anti-imperialism and anticapitalism could be easily attached to anti-Semitism and revealed the shifting contours of contemporary left- and right-wing politics.

How her anti-Semitism emerged is not clear, for she had praised the Jewish working people in Chicago when staying at Hull House in 1900.[9] Her first anti-Semitic statements (early August 1905) came in the wake of the 800-page report asking that Alfred Dreyfus's conviction be quashed.[10] Dreyfus had been convicted in 1894, transported to Devil's Island on trumped-up charges of treason in 1895, reconvicted in 1899 and pardoned, but not finally exonerated until July 12, 1906. As late as August 1910, she remarked to Ratcliffe, "I am afraid I am not quite sound on Dreyfus. I can see too clearly the position of France!" She then wrote out a simple equation: "Empire = Jewish international net of Finance. Nationality = Anti-Jewish struggle."[11] She was so convinced of their machinations that she wrote, "Zemindars [*sic*] of all countries will soon be Hebrew in blood" and insulted the former prime minister, Lord Rosebery, who had married Hannah de Rothschild, Europe's wealthiest heiress. In her view, Rosebery's daughter and "Lady Curzon's children" would become "coarse middle aged Jewers [*sic*]!" and their presence confirmed again the "equation" between Empire and the Jewish international.[12]

The source of these ideas is equally unclear, for Vivekananda had been more likely to suggest that Jews and Hindus were spiritual brothers who shared civilizational endurance despite persecution. He had written: "What may be that force which causes this afflicted and suffering people, the Hindu, and the Jewish too (the two races from which have originated all the great religions of the world) to survive, when other nations perish? The cause can only be their spiritual force."[13]

Nor were her ideas unduly grounded in biological racialism (at least for the time). The remark about the "Zemindars [*sic*] of all countries" suggested how she drew from an anticapitalist tradition that saw rentiers—no matter what their origin—as inherently Jewish and here suggested that they would ultimately all possess the same "blood." She once referred to Jewish "hooked noses," but focused, above all, on Jewish financial prowess, and contrasted Jews to the "stay-at-homes," the small farmers and the "Nonconformist shopkeepers."[14] Given her own love of travel, her negative view of Jewish "globetrotting"—the "wandering Jew"—is ironic.

Certainly, the resentment that burst into anti-Semitism grew out of bitterness with the fate of Swadeshi and the strength of British repression. "Education in a state, journalism has been crushed. Swadeshi has been shattered. The poverty grows worse and worse. The brave still say that things are better than they were—that to stand face to face with death is life—that 10 years ago was neither life nor death, but only slumber and degradation—that Art is begun and Literature is afoot and a certain courage and unity have come. . . . but oh things are dreadful!!! The poverty makes one ill, to look upon—and it is growing. And is there, after all, any hope? These people are children. It is really sheep against wolves."[15]

But such resentment did not automatically mean that she would turn to anti-Semitism, since many who shared her views on imperialism and capitalism certainly did *not* share these views.[16] There remain imponderables here.

Surely, the loss of her political hopes was linked to grief and existential musings. Her life had been upended in January 1909 by her mother's death from a harrowing cancer. She had done everything she could to mend this difficult relationship, and even later idealized it. When she returned to India, she consoled herself with Vivekananda's teaching on death and, for the first time, read Swedenborg, but had been horrified when Lady Isabel Margesson—her old friend at whose home she had first met Vivekananda—suggested that the "psychic world" would lift her sorrows.[17] Back in Calcutta, she criticized a political ally who had turned to spiritualism, denigrating it as "religious drug taking."[18]

Such remarks obscured her own continuing interest in psychic powers. Nivedita often mentioned the medium Dora Roethlesberger and waited for messages "from the Unseen."[19] She wrote to Dora: "How I envy you, your gift of sight! . . . even now, if you said you saw Sri Ramakrishna leading us by the hand, one could believe it."[20] She had even been susceptible to Cheiro (from "cheiromancy"), William John Warner, an Irish astrologer and occultist, who predicted her death; it turned out he was only a year off.[21] She was ashamed by these "illicit longings!" but acknowledged she could not stop them.[22]

All around her, harbingers of mortality abounded, and she feared the loss of pioneering colleagues. She worried, for example, that Alasinga might have cancer, and grieved that her partner against plague, Swami Sadananda, Vivekananda's first disciple, a "great fine-looking man had become a little bent, shrunken priest!"[23] Frank Leggett also died unexpectedly, a loss that floored his wife, Josephine's sister Betty, who became bedridden with remorse and guilt. "Frankincense" had introduced the sisters to Vivekananda, and Nivedita was mindful of his kindnesses to her.[24] She concluded mournfully about Frank's country estate, "Ridgely will seem to be full of ghosts."[25] The Indian women in Sarada Devi's entourage were also going gray, though the Holy Mother had survived a bout of smallpox.

Nivedita, moreover, was scornful of political action that she felt was pointless. Although she believed that women would and should one day vote, she was appalled that close friends had been drawn into the suffrage campaign back in Britain. In 1909, she was astonished that "dear Kitty Margesson went to prison" (for her activism as a suffragist) and wondered how this "pretty" aristocratic girl would "do her hair" while incarcerated.[26] This jesting observation revealed a deeper fear that both femininity and women's authority would be undermined. After all, her time in the north of England had convinced Nivedita of the necessity of the male breadwinning family. For her, it remained a conflict between rights and duties, between individualism and social cohesion; she worried that the "woman-movement" would ignite "chaos about marriage, such as they have in America"; and so, like Vivekananda, she feared "unwomanly women."[27] To the Ratcliffes, she wrote, "I have a horror of woman's disorder, and the utter unscrupulousness and frivolity of her use of her will, that I could, if I yielded to my feelings, write against her, just as strongly as anyone."[28]

Nivedita was also opposed to women going on "hunger-strike,—and the silly laughter there will be, at the men they have defeated."[29] And so, she ascribed elevated symbolism to feminine self-immolation (sati) in India, but was disgusted by the "courage" of women who were force-fed. She resisted any analogy between suffragists and Indian political prisoners, though she acknowledged that the British used a primitive form of waterboarding (not too different from force-feeding) to elicit confessions.[30] She desired manly heroes rather than helpless victims to exemplify the Indian freedom struggle, and she similarly worried that suffragists, by exposing themselves to such violation, would also lose their moral authority.

•   •   •

Before Vivekananda, Nivedita had been an independent woman, who earned her living and supported her mother. When she came to India, however, she had lost this autonomy, and became Sara Bull's dependent. For the most part, she did not worry about the penny-pinching (and hugely praised the secondhand clothing that came her way). On occasion, however, she could not help but notice Christine's shabbiness, which was even worse than her own.[31] By 1906–1907, she had become poorer, older, and weaker. When, in 1907, she decided to take on no more "public work," Bull's allowance evaporated. Bull wondered whether Nivedita was exploiting her, while Nivedita, in turn, was wounded by the mistrust.[32] She asked Bose to intervene, and when the money still did not come, she resorted to Josephine. It was humiliation piled upon humiliation: "I could not have written to S[aint]. Sara for help. And that, just because she is rich and does so much. To go to her is simply to ask for money—a thing impossible. To go to you, is to *make the need known.* I wonder if you can feel the difference. It is moral, as well as formal. I mean, it goes very deep—this difference."[33]

The money finally came and Sara and Nivedita repaired their relationship by caring jointly for Nivedita's mother in Wimbledon. Nonetheless, their association was never plain sailing. When, for example, Nivedita published her *The Master as I Saw Him* (1910), Sara was troubled that much of it was lifted verbatim from her own diary; she may have felt violated, but in time she magnanimously accepted the situation.[34] That Nivedita did not understand how problematic such "borrowing" might be suggests something of her impetuosity, if not insensitivity.

Despite these ups-and-downs, however, the connection between the women remained strong. Nivedita wrote: "'Poor poor s[aint] Sara! I wd not for anything have her die. How much one loves people, underneath the surface-tossing of the waves."[35] In autumn 1907, she was aghast when Sara needed an operation to remove a tumor (which was benign). When she went back to India in 1909, she wrote perceptively about the grief over her mother's death and the fear that Sara's would follow: "I cannot tell you what a difference mother's death has made to me! I find now that as long as she lived, one felt always young—things seemed stable—life was good to one. Now I see how short it all is. I feel that sweet things only happen once—that everything is drawing to a close. Everyone seems to be saying Good-bye. I am so anxious about S. Sara. As long as one's mother lives, one remains young—you see. When she dies, one is old."[36]

⋆　⋆　⋆

Motherhood was indeed at the heart of the tragedies that would ensue from Sara Bull's life and death. Both Vivekananda and her closest friends knew that Sara suffered painfully from lack of fulfilment as a mother.[37] She was wealthy, accomplished, refined, and intelligent, but had a "difficult" daughter who seemed to give her no end of trouble. Sara admitted to regretting her absences during Olea's childhood, when she had accompanied her husband on his concert tours.[38] Olea's letters reveal no obvious hostility to her mother, but the estrangement became increasingly clear. Bull disliked Olea's first husband, Henry G. Vaughan, but had become reconciled to the marriage when they had a child named Edwina and was desolate when the little girl died. She also felt displaced by Olea's apparent preference for Abbie Shapleigh, a connection that continued, till the end, to disturb the mother-daughter relationship.

These regrets perhaps explain Sara's eagerness to discharge her motherly duties to the new family that she had created with Vivekananda. He was her "son"; and Sara, his Dhira Mata (Mother of Wisdom); Nivedita was the "daughter"—troublesome at times, but loyal and self-sacrificing. The Math and its monks were her other "children." On all of them, Sara bestowed attention, loving support, and important financial aid. She was at the center of an international network, the woman who had introduced Vivekananda and later Nivedita to such luminaries as William James and who had invested time with near-outcasts and "fanatics" like Leon Landsberg. She was powerful by virtue of her resources and generosity, but fragile in requiring love and gratitude.

Did Olea feel crowded out by this bevy of admirers and supporters? We have only others' testimony to suggest that sometimes it might have been an ordeal. Nivedita recounted how once at Ridgely Manor, in October 1899, Vivekananda had spent three and a half hours alone with Olea. According to Nivedita, she came out a "different woman," but we have no idea what Olea felt about such focused attentions. Indeed, Nivedita had made an unsuccessful attempt to connect herself. It is unclear what they wanted to shift, but there are hints that Olea was somehow unsteady—especially in contrast to her upright and committed mother.[39] Certainly, Olea had a history of nervousness, and Sara Bull's correspondence suggests that her daughter's health was far from robust.

The crisis came when Olea began an affair with Ralph Bartlett, a lawyer and childhood friend, while still officially married to Vaughan. At this juncture, Sara "emotionally disowned her daughter" while continuing financial help and legal aid to secure the divorce.[40] High-minded and scrupulous herself, Sara was disappointed. But even in this cauldron of resentment and disapproval, tension lifted when she met Olea's illegitimate daughter, Sylvea, whom she could not resist. All the women who had been close to Vivekananda—including Nivedita—continued generous and affectionate contact with Olea. Nivedita wrote from Sara Bull's house in Eliot, Maine, in early October 1908 of the joy the baby had brought: "Olea is with her mother—both as natural as possible—thanks to the baby. How very pleasant this is! The baby is healthy and good. And the whole thing is like a wonderful revelation. Such a simple thing, to cure all the heart aches."[41] Despite pangs of moral conventionality, Nivedita suspended judgment when love was at stake. But she was wrong to think that the "heartaches" were over, as Sara's illness and the psychic complications that ensued encroached on this moment of reconciliation.

Nivedita returned to India in July 1909, but then went back to America in October 1910; during this time, she kept tabs on Sara's progress. She improved under the ministrations of a Mrs Edith Swanander and her daughter, Swedish friends from the Brooklyn Ethical Association. But she was thin and breathless and, when Mrs. Swanander ventured that perhaps Sara had intestinal trouble, she responded that her illness was the result of "some malign influence" without physical cause. Apparently, she had found solace in a vision of Vivekananda under a blossoming cherry tree and another of her dead granddaughter, Edwina, illuminated in a pink light. Back in Cambridge, she had a meditation room with images of Ramakrishna, Vivekananda, and Edwina, a trio that focused her concentration. At this juncture she instructed her brother and lawyer, Joseph Thorp, to keep Olea at bay. This prohibition—and then the conditions surrounding Olea's later rare visits—no doubt contributed to the enmities that exploded after Sara's death.

As she declined, Thorp summoned the "adopted" daughter Nivedita, rather than the "real" one, to tend his sister. Nivedita readily answered the call, but worried that she might not be up to it: "I *don't* minister to people! I only neglect them."[42] This was not true—she had been devoted to Sadananda— but she preferred servants to tend her intimates.[43] When she arrived, Sara was ill with a wasting condition that the death certificate would later name as "pernicious anemia."[44] Many physicians had described the condition, but it could not be treated effectively until after 1920, and then only with difficulty and without the confirmation of blood tests. She was also apparently getting serum injections daily, but of what is not clear.[45]

Nor was Nivedita straightforward about her reasons for leaving India. She wrote on October 14, 1910, to Mrs. Ratcliffe, that there was another "circumstance . . . on the Indian side, that decided. . . . a prompt move." She hinted that there was a plan afoot that "would have made a fool [of her] conveniently, without giving [her] the chance of dying for a cause," a remark that suggests that political motives may have prompted her flight.[46] She traveled incognito as "Mrs. Theta Margot." A cloak-and-dagger ambience thus pervaded her departure and was later intensified by her request that Josephine destroy her letters.

She arrived in Cambridge, Massachusetts, on November 15 and first stayed with the Longfellows, the in-laws of the Thorps, before lodging with Sara at her home on Brattle Street and sleeping with her by night.[47] She spoke of the prevalence of "diabolist belief among psychics in this 20th century America," suggesting that such ideas may have infected Sara. Nivedita found her "*intensely* difficult" and was glad that Sara did not demand her presence all day.[48] She also administered "medicine and treatments from . . . India," Ayurvedic remedies that she prayed would alleviate her condition.[49] At one moment, she wrote, "the Devil must flee." Two days later—in a letter with pages missing—she wrote, "pray for S. Sara that in *grave danger she may learn to be herself, and discriminate between the Real and the Unreal.*"[50]

We do not know what Nivedita referred to here. At the trial, it was suggested that Sara Bull's fears focused on Abbie Shapleigh, who she thought "could propel killing thoughts over the telephone." Olea lived with Shapleigh, and it may have been that Sara feared her daughter brought these thoughts with her when she visited.[51] If indeed these were Sara's fears, and not just sensational reporting, it was not surprising that Nivedita worried for her friend's sanity. Another of Sara's friends, a Mrs. Briggs, was said to try and counteract this evil influence with her own powers.

By December, however, Sara seemed better, and both she and Nivedita returned to the Swananders in Brooklyn. Sara saw her daughter, but only with Nivedita present; on another occasion, however, she risked an encounter alone, and Nivedita reportedly returned home to find Sara deeply disturbed. A Mrs. Hellyer calmed Nivedita by assuring her that Sara was on the verge of neither death nor insanity, that she had merely been "contaminated" by the unwholesome atmosphere: "I suppose I made a tempest in a teacup about Saint Sara's queer notions and Mrs. Briggs' influence. . . . the whole world is a criss-cross of psychic desires and intentions and we wade knee-deep through it all the time."[52]

She felt she now had more of a grip on the situation and began to wonder whether Sara had unwittingly encouraged this undertow of fear through her habit of "getting a crowd round her."[53] Nivedita seemed almost relieved, therefore, to see Sara less as a victim of possible malignity, and more as an agent in her own difficulties.

Sara's condition caused such upheaval and uncertainty that Nivedita wanted nothing more than to return to India. When the women came back to Cambridge, however, the atmosphere lightened, and she was ashamed that she had been so critical and suspicious. She now sought to take the advice of the level-headed Mrs. Hellyer: "The beloved Mrs. Hellyer said 'Get her to *give* money, while living, and break this bondage!' And that is precisely the direction in which I have been able to put in a stroke or two. That, I think, would be a good thing."[54]

Nivedita naturally wanted independence but may have tormented herself later when the world accused her of diverting Sara's affections and money from her daughter to herself. She may also have been unaware of her resentment at a benefactress who had left her dependent. As fears of the occult and invisible forces once again pervaded the atmosphere, she understood why Vivekananda had preached detachment, and warned that "we do harm where we mean nothing but good."[55]

There is no doubt that the women lived on an emotional roller coaster. Nivedita was once again relieved when, after Christmas, Sara seemed to recover; the two even thought of arranging "a house and a boat" in the French territory of Chandernagor (Chandannagar) in India (and thus away from British surveillance).[56] Nivedita liked the idea of traveling to Switzerland and then on to Chandernagor, where she could return to her writing. The old closeness momentarily returned on New Year's Day when the older woman spoke of her love for Vivekananda, but Nivedita's hopes were dashed after this moment of evanescent brightness.[57] Sara Bull died on January 14, 1911.

* * *

Money now became the key issue. Over the years, Sara had made several wills, and during her life she had donated substantially to Indian causes. By March, it became clear that Olea planned to contest the will. According to a letter from Sara's brother, Joseph Thorp, Olea was not disinherited; in fact the extant will confirms that $500,000, or 80 percent, of the estate was made over to her in trust. Mr. Thorp explained the reasons for these conditions: "Olea's marital relations, her inexperience in dealing with large affairs, and her mother's choice that the estate should be cared for, so that in case Olea left no children who would take it, the property should come back into our family whence it all came."[58] The wording of the will suggests that Sara's motivation was mainly to keep the family fortune from falling into the hands of her daughter's lover.[59]

No doubt from Olea's perspective, these conditions relegated her to a state of permanent minority; there were also the sentimental hurts. In April 1911, it was reported that "not even a keep-sake of her father's [was] left her under these instruments."[60] This was not the case, however; the will specifically leaves the house and its contents to her. At the same time, Olea had an annual income of $4,500 from property and was able to draw up to $3,500 of the principal in any year in case of special circumstance. Mr. Thorp agreed to take away the stipulations of the $3,500 limit, but he refused to get rid of the "trust promise" that would have allowed her full control.[61] It was widely believed, however, and repeatedly reported, that the lion's share of the estate went to followers of Vedanta.[62] For five weeks, between March and June, the subsequent case became national news, its details also reported in the Norwegian press.

As the press coverage became more sensational, Nivedita decided to leave America without telling anyone except the Thorps. Indeed, she left even before the trial began, boarding the *Lusitania* on March 1, apparently disguised as the maid of her friend, Mrs. T. J. Bolker of Beacon Street; much was made of the fact that Thorp had urged her to go.[63] It is not clear how much she knew of the sordid press coverage but the *Boston Traveller,* on May 25, called Vedanta a "cult" and suggested that "Mrs. Bull had been reduced by Nivedita's Hindoo practices that she was incompetent when she made her last will." It was even suggested that Nivedita, now back in Calcutta, had "dictated" the will—hence why she had always been present when Olea had visited. Olea, herself, did not attend the trial because she was ill with tuberculosis, but she wrote: "My poor mother must have been entirely under the control of others, for I feel sure that never . . . would she have consented to sign such a document. . . . I felt so assured of my own dear mother's real love for me."[64]

Olea's lover and lawyer Mr. Bartlett contended that "Oriental magic and mysticism" were behind Sara Bull's illness and death. Nivedita was a "Yogi priestess" who had turned Mrs. Bull away from her motherly duties.[65] It was true that a codicil written a month before her death had given Nivedita

$30,000. Indeed, the *Boston Herald* accused Nivedita of being "the 'chief conspirator' in the band of psychics."[66] Even Olea's claim that Nivedita had taken papers out of the safe was confirmed by Mr. Thorp, though he insisted that they were her own documents.

To those seeking scandal, Sara's meditation room could easily be seen as evidence that she was "under the influence" of Ramakrishna and Vivekananda and, as a practitioner of Bhakti yoga, was somehow engaged in some sexual cult. Nivedita's Ayurvedic tonics seemed like magical potions—one turned red and another brown—and she had even warned a servant to administer the medicine with a glass rather than metal spoon, a suggestion that implied that she knew they were poisonous.[67] The trusted servants—whom Nivedita suggested were in Bartlett's pay—testified to her nefarious doings with these compounds.[68] The case seemed never-ending, and it was made worse by the knowledge that Olea was also ill, living in a tent in Lebanon, Maine, in a final effort to overcome her tuberculosis with fresh air. Olea won the case and was awarded the estate on July 22, 1911, but died the same day.[69]

* * *

When the trial was done, Nivedita wrote on July 4 to Josephine MacLeod, "I am not always strong. I have terrible moments when I face the paper clippings."[70] She wanted no more letters, not even supportive ones, because "each reference [to the trial] is an added pain." She wrote: "I gather that I must be shining in the press in a very undesirable light, because I have received so many chivalrous letters from private acquaintances in America." She admitted that she was "subject to horrible spasms of nervousness, when anything new arrive[d]."[71] On July 20, she wrote again to Ratcliffe: "I have such a queer feeling as if things have come to an end, and there were no future."[72]

A week later, she continued: "Our little world seems silent and deserted now! Of course I can't help feeling like this—so don't take it too seriously—after the two deaths of mother and S. Sara."[73]

Nivedita occupied herself with a tribute to Sara in the *Modern Review* and began again to make plans, explaining how Christine would teach in a Brahmo school for a time, while they thought through the future. She traveled to Darjeeling with the Boses, but fell ill with dysentery. She remarked on Abala Bose's kindness during her illness and felt sorry that they could not play in the snow. She died soon after, on October 13, 1911, despite the attempts by doctors, nurses, and the Boses to restore her to health. Three days later, Christine wrote to Josephine: "The thing that killed her was the Will case. There is no doubt whatever about that. When I begged her to stay here a month or two longer just before she left, she said that she could not bear the solitude, that she must be active and surrounded by people to keep from thinking. So I did not urge it. She looked so ill then that I was very anxious—until the trial ended. After then I thought the danger was over."[74]

* * *

Nivedita's turn to anti-Semitism and Sara Bull's belief in malign forces underscore how, although the belle epoque may be a foreign country—full of surprising phantoms—the period nonetheless has parallels to our own times. Even these high-minded and well-educated women conjured up conspiratorial fantasies and morbid fears that they had previously suppressed.

Nivedita's late burst of anti-Semitism suggests how difficult it is *not* to read history backward and see her remarks as an early manifestation of the hatreds that led to disaster in the twentieth century. She remained tied to a vision of the nation as Hindu, but she could not envisage India's magnificence without Muslims. Contradictory and at times shocking, her views were not informed by our knowledge of their deadly consequences. Judging her retrospectively does little to further historical understanding.

She had passed through a harrowing time; although the Boses reported that she was brave in her last illness, the dysentery and utter nervous depletion meant she died without the detachment and spiritual bliss that attended Vivekananda's final moments. Indeed, the comparison is striking. As early as 1898 after the fateful pilgrimage to Amarnath, he said he "knew" that Shiva would enable him to die when he wished; he expired after teaching a Sanskrit class and left the world of maya in mahasamadhi.

We will never know how he would have reacted had he, too, witnessed the Swadeshi era and its disillusionments; his life was tempestuous, and his temper could be also, but there was a deep meditative dimension to his character. Nivedita's life, in contrast, was stormier, and her disenchantment deeper. Her last two years—when death abounded, repression increased, and distress mounted—left her both drained and anguished. She began to suspect malign influences and was, in turn, accused of unleashing them. By this stage, she had lost much physical strength and even more idealism, circumstances making "discernment" increasingly difficult. "Viveka" in Sanskrit means "discrimination" or "right understanding," a quality that Nivedita's guru valued. It is tragic that this quality seemed to elude her, as it eluded so many who searched in the occult world for the invisible forces of destruction.

CONCLUSION

Life is neither happiness nor sorrow, but infinite significance, using both of these, as its instruments.

—Sister Nivedita, January 6, 1910

◆ ◆ ◆

WRITING AN HISTORICAL account of Vivekananda has posed unusual problems, not the least of which is that, while many Westerners have never heard of him and may wonder why he requires such study, most Indians (and especially Bengalis) may feel that they know the story so well that there is nothing new to learn. This imbalance, however, underscores why it is so important to present him with all his facets and place him securely in his many contexts. In this regard, the tools and aspirations of global history are essential, but they can only ever be secondary to a necessary focus on relations between people, and especially his links to Ramakrishna and Nivedita.

By choosing a guru foreign to his intellectual and social world, and then an unusual female disciple of British origin, Vivekananda expressed an ambition to encompass ideas and experiences beyond his own ken. All three protagonists thus refused to be categorized or pigeonholed. It is striking—and perhaps important—that each became man or woman (at least imaginatively) when they felt so inclined; Ramakrishna was an inspirational guru, but claimed he was nothing more than a knowledge-less child; Vivekananda was a self-professed jnani but saw himself as a bhakta; Nivedita was born British, but lived in India like a Hindu, while often looking to Catholic saints for inspiration. Ramakrishna generally wore no clothes, whereas Vivekananda devised many different costumes, and Nivedita created a "habit" that underscored her discipleship but irritated her Western friends. These intimate musings and external signs were integral to their expansive but contradictory personalities, but also hinted at the tensions in Hindu Universalism, which sought to fuse opposing tendencies.

Vivekananda's close associations with these two figures may have reified his own internal struggles as he stood between childhood and manhood, between the worldly and otherworldly, between East and West. His apprenticeship enabled him to create a new balance, permitting him to undertake a global mission with uncommon self-confidence that was intermittently marred by moments of extreme vulnerability and doubt. Above all, Ramakrishna taught Vivekananda the importance of speaking in a language that his audience could understand—hence his success in communicating to very different kinds of people.

For this reason, Vivekananda's writings provide little joy for the intellectual historian. He was no ordinary system maker, but rather adjusted his remarks for different publics during lectures and conversations. He constantly sought to respond, and unapologetically found the spiritual Absolute in what was relative and the relational, in what could be created between people in the human tirthas (crossing places) that he encountered. Like a good guru with a disciple, he wanted each audience to have individualized attention, alternately persuading, scolding, or instructing depending on what he felt were their temperaments and capacities. Although invested in Hinduism's textual traditions, he was also happy to transform them. His dislike of don't-touchism therefore applied to outmoded practices and prejudices, but also extended to Patanjali's sutras, which he reformulated to create Raja yoga.

Vivekananda innovated in ways that have long been recognized. Certainly, he pulled Advaita Vedanta away from Brahmin elitism in maintaining that such spiritual heights were possible for everyone; and also attached it firmly to Karma yoga and a vision of seva (service) that required a dedicated—and organized—order of monks. But Ramakrishna endured within him and in his teaching. He reshaped his guru's inspirations about the many paths to God and extended them in the service of both universalism and nationalism. Although he underscored Ramakrishna's (spiritually) egalitarian and experiential ethos, he did so by shifting its focus to new forms of seva that, he claimed, originated from Indian precedent rather than Christian models. Indeed, as late as 1900, he evinced his suspicion of Christian "charity" and "altruism" and reasserted his allegiance to his guru's view.

Ramakrishna believed he had become a woman in his mystical search; Vivekananda instead relied on women, such as Sarada Devi and Nivedita, to build a movement, while also valuing their spiritual insights. Sarada's self-abasement meant that she had a degree of spiritual dominion even over Vivekananda, yet it sanctified her in a way that proscribed normal human feelings: we have no way of knowing how she felt about her childless destiny. The "feminization of religion" had placed Western women on a pedestal, but Sarada's spiritualization was even more enveloping. For the Western women, she was both an ideal and a reproach. Nivedita promoted this ideal while seeking to break the mold when exploring her inner aggression and doing work generally reserved for men. In the process, she undeniably underwent psychic contortions that cost her dearly.

For Vivekananda, Kali worship underpinned a vision of maternal sovereignty essential to creating national fraternity, so important in opposing an imperial discourse infused by a vision of feminized Indians. We may sympathize with the political dilemmas he confronted in creating a man-making nationalism that defied such stereotypes but reject such formulations today. In his own spiritual quest, however, he later returned to and then clung to the childlike mysticism of his guru as he explored the dialectic between conquest and surrender that Ramakrishna had taught him and that Kali-worship strengthened.

In considering science, he insisted that Western "disenchantment" would only undermine its progress, again focusing on the unity of knowledge and its ultimate *spiritual* aim—"superconsciousness." Above all, however, he reiterated endlessly that Enlightenment rationality was not the only or ultimate universalism. Indeed, in his constant reiteration of the primacy of the "spiritual," he saw Western "disenchantment" as both incomplete and faulty. Different societies enshrined different visions of the universal, and he believed that Western societies would do well to take a leaf out of India's spiritual book. Even more, by seeking to unite Reason and Unreason—the wisdom of the Upanishads and an ecstatic devotion to Kali—he pursued rational wisdom-seeking but found a place for the intuitive, mysterious, and primordial.

In my view, the desire to remain in touch with the second under-standing of human-supernatural connection explains his embrace of what was deemed "feminine" and "infantile," despite the man-making persona. His Western women followers were particularly attracted to these dimen-sions of his personality. Even if Kali-worship was difficult to understand, women like Nivedita were thrilled by his evocation of the "divine feminine" precisely because it emanated from such a well-educated and otherwise ra-tional man. If, today, this description of Vivekananda seems far from con-temporary popular assumptions, it is vital to understanding who he was and how he was received, especially by his female fin-de-siècle listeners.

* * *

When he went abroad, Vivekananda sought to be recognized as an "enlight-ened" representative of a set of religious ideals very different to the orien-talist view of contemporary Hinduism as degenerate and heathen. He has been credited with "introducing" Vedanta to the West, a commonplace of patriotic and nationalist thought that is perhaps misleading. Rather than bringing the ideas of the subcontinent to the West (these had been in circu-lation in Enlightenment America), he proposed to take back Indian thought for Indians by interrupting the traffic of exotic and circuitous ideas about Hinduism curated by transcendentalism, theosophy, and the various practi-tioners of "New Thought."

With Ramakrishna, he had foregone the rationalism that had sustained him in the battles against the don't-touchism of his heritage, only to reinte-grate those "rationalist" proclivities when battling for his vision of Vedanta both abroad and in India. In the process, he created a global synthesis that refused to condemn the image worship and rituals of his homeland, but which also prioritized the formlessness of Advaita. He wanted thereby to avoid sects and to create a new universalism that focused on uniting self and nonself.

He tempted Nivedita to come to India with the prospect of being a "world mover." He sensed her own huge ambition, her desire to go beyond the ordi-nary, but realized that, like his young self, she was too "cerebral," that her skepticism prevented her from spiritual understanding. In their encounter, the colonial relationship was paramount: when "Hinduizing" her, he had moments of harshness and seemed to want her to *feel* the brutal subordination that was part of Indian life. As she emerged from her "going to school," she at first seemed to accept the process of re-creation. As she lived through the plague and grew disenchanted with many British compatriots in India, she penned perhaps her most important work, the book that recast Kali from being a symbol of Hindu degeneration into an icon of national dynamism.

If Vivekananda recaptured aspects of himself in the West, Nivedita had to recombine her earlier passions with her new "Indian" persona. She abandoned schoolteaching and returned to the journalistic and intellectual work that was her true passion and, despite the tussle over Patrick Geddes's influence, Vivekananda freed her to attach Vedanta to the new Western intellectual trends. For all his conservatism vis-à-vis the social role of women, he understood her desire to be a female groundbreaker. The loosening of bonds proved productive for her and for her male collaborators, especially Jagadish Chandra Bose and Romesh Chunder Dutt. Vivekananda provided a universalist foundation in Advaita, and she showed where new Western ideas fitted onto this structure. Despite the uneven results, her example was important.

•　•　•

There were unexpected parallels between Ramakrishna's disciples in Calcutta and those Vivekananda gathered around him in America. The young Indians came from largely orthodox backgrounds, many of whom had been first enthused and then shaken by Brahmoism. This "brave new world" and their English education created new forms of cultural ambidexterity, but the gains were matched by numerous losses, both in social confidence and in spiritual possibility. Ramakrishna offered the new horizons that helped temper these multiple griefs and integrate their fragmented experiences.

If he created the possibility for Vivekananda (and his guru-brothers) to achieve spiritual relief, Vivekananda did the same for some Western disciples. Many in his Christian audience had been tested by biblical criticism, scientific rationality, and the harshness of Protestant morality, their faith in God's benevolence undermined by the Civil War. People as different as Sara Bull and William James suffered doubts about immortality and were attracted to spiritualism.

Many came from conventional Protestant milieus and remained fearful of the consequences of transgression. Those who had lost their faith worried that new scientific "certainties" left no room for the spiritual yearnings that remained, whereas others who came from less mainstream denominations, such as Unitarianism and Swedenborgianism, were perhaps even more susceptible to Vivekananda's teaching because Vedanta aligned with long-held spiritual ideals. Vivekananda realized his new audience knew little of the humiliation of conquest; he set out to teach them, and did so with intellect and wit, but also reminded them often of the brutalities of their civilization.

He displayed exceptional deftness in sorting through various scientific concepts to attach Westerners to his project of Hindu Universalism. This was not merely an instrumental strategy or a form of "updating"; his passionate interest in science emerged from a desire to add another level of meta-phorical richness to Indian thought, but also to put science's normative power in the hands of Indians deprived by imperialism of scientific and technical education. He was similarly deft in separating out the many dif-ferent strands of Western experimental spirituality. In the early days he was eager to try new possibilities, especially in the realm of therapeutics and health. But his private musings and letters reveal how swiftly he became alienated by the spiritual thinness of much New Thought.

Was he trying to establish Hinduism as a world religion like Christianity? Yes and no. He certainly wanted to elevate a philosophically rigorous the-ology, and to dispel any idea that Hinduism was a nihilist creed, its adher-ents passive in their search for transcendence. However, he also regularly took the diversity of paths that he had learned from Ramakrishna and his guru's hatred of sects as object lessons in the need for universalism—both Indian and global.

He adapted his teaching to the new context, initiating both American women and men into sannyasa, remaking Indian rituals for Western tastes, and began the teaching of Vedanta with quotations from the Chris-tian gospels. During his first trip abroad, he had no conscious plan to center his activities in the United States, as his first positive impressions of Britain suggest. In some sense, however, the *familiarity* between England and India made progress there more difficult. In Britain, an audience that deemed itself more knowing and sophisticated meant that Vivekananda's bona fides were questioned. His credentials in America were also constantly criticized, but his connections to Harvard men and New England society hostesses meant his struggle for recognition was more easily won. Only in California—a new spiritual territory without venerable Christian foundations and Asians who brought their unfamiliar creeds across the Pacific—was he was he able to operate without influential supporters.

We do not know how deliberate he was when he deployed orientalist clichés himself. Clearly, the scarlet robe and orange turban served to attract attention but also to secure regard. Was he aware that, when they admired his "beautiful eyes," they may have conjured the "knowing" and "haunting" eyes of Blavatsky's mahatmas? Did they see him as handsome because they were acquainted with Mohini Mohun Chatterji, who only a few years earlier had broken hearts with his "oriental" good looks? Vivekananda's skill lay in how he managed both to win their help and to avoid being patronized.

He needed to reject the androgyny and childlikeness of India's sadhus in favor of an intellectual mien and spiritual gravitas. At the same time, he could not disown the ecstatic heights that men like Ramakrishna and Pavhari Baba epitomized, nor abandon his own "simplicity" among his intimate circle. He preferred the formlessness of Advaita but defended the Hindu worship of images by comparing it to the way even Protestants visualized Christ on the cross when they prayed. This was a telling riposte that revealed another legacy of his apprenticeship to Ramakrishna—the ability both to explain and to respond at once. But the power of Western stereotypes meant he was always slightly on the defensive.

Such clichés penetrated even the most avant-garde Western "science." For all his philosophical subtlety and focus on experience, James's characterization of Vedanta as a monist creed that lulled its followers into a false "sumptuosity of security" was just another version of the belief that "Eastern" religions were fundamentally passive and nihilistic. Vivekananda wanted to engage with James's *Principles of Psychology,* but only if it was the handmaiden to Vedanta, rather than Vedanta being cast as mere evidence supporting James's own approach. With this in mind, he wrote *Raja Yoga* and thus laid out the ground rules for an enormous lay constituency that would turn to meditation. But in doing so, he dissociated yoga from other mystical beliefs, such as Sufism, and cut it away from its age-old Tantric foundations, visceral and even sanguinary traditions that Ramakrishna had professed with Kali-love. Raja yoga became a global practice, but at the cost of obscuring important elements of its protean nature.

Vivekananda struggled to balance his anger over Western abuses with a deeper belief in sympathetic connection, as shown in his friendships with Josephine and Mary Hale, to whom he admitted his greatest doubts and fears.

As an officer in the British military, Colonel Sevier had been an agent of imperialism, but Vivekananda accepted the Seviers as exemplary practitioners of Advaita. By refusing to condemn their childhood faith or demand the conversion of his Western followers, he set out to exemplify the Hindu "tolerance" that he maintained Western civilization so sorely lacked. This certainly was a strategy designed to show the superiority of Indian religion. But it was also an outgrowth of the immense and genuine affection he felt for his disciples, as well as his gratitude for their help.

◆ ◆ ◆

Vivekananda's new celebrity when he returned home stemmed from his foreign achievements, but he remained above all concerned with India. He was as determined to recraft Vedanta there as he had been set on reshaping views of Hinduism in the West, and his tour of the subcontinent from Sri Lanka to the Himalayas in 1897 symbolized his wish to unify Hinduism as well as the nation. The creation of two major temples—one in Belur and the other in Madras—literally set in stone the desire to unite North and South. But his idea of unity was different from that of the Brahmos; he did not want a reform which stripped away all difference. Rather, he praised local customs and exalted "local heroes," the saints, scholars, and visionaries of different regions, and gave due reverence to various Hindu traditions. He encouraged local spiritual patriotisms as much as a vision of the Hindu Motherland.

Vivekananda saw this immense variety through Ramakrishna's emphasis on a diversity of beliefs and hatred of sects as the key to true universalism—both Indian and global. By implanting his ideas institutionally across the subcontinent, he became an "Indian Father," and not merely another variant of the reforming Bengal intellectual seeking to impose his ideas. But this desire to unify did create an implicit hierarchy, with Advaita and its cerebral conception of the unity of self and nonself as its central belief. The additional emphasis on Karma yoga, seva, and character further highlighted the central tenets of a new framework—he thus became the chief advocate of loving fellow Indians as manifestations of the divine and sought to lay these themes over the range of Hindu belief and practice. Certainly, in the ranking, "higher" and "lower" necessarily emerged and, in the process, much was reordered. This hierarchy could not help but favor one path and tended to see everything else as a lower version of it.[1] And yet, this apparent certainty was always shadowed by another that Ramakrishna had realized "everything through idols." Nonetheless, emphasis on Advaita—on notions of unity and an omnipresent God within—no doubt helped bring together Hindus of many different stripes, from radical activists, through the orthodox and xenophobic, to more temperate progressives.[2]

He remained rooted in a monism that saw everything as needing to be encompassed (even if hierarchized). Reason and experience, male and female, the national and the international, and, above all, self and nonself could never be separated in his mind or in his teaching. But he also saw these polarities as being in constant motion and as integral to the relationship between unity and diversity; this same sense of fluidity and movement underpinned his vision of caste, while, yet again, retaining an inescapable hierarchy.[3]

Although he celebrated India's religious and ethnic heterogeneity, Vivekananda remained largely preoccupied with Hinduism. He once remarked to his Muslim friend, Mohammed Sarfaraz Husain of Naini Tal, that "for our own motherland a junction of the two great systems, Hinduism and Islam—Vedanta brain and Islam body—is the only hope. I see in my mind's eye the future perfect India rising out of this chaos and strife, glorious and invincible, with Vedanta brain and Islam body." He therefore acknowledged the potential for rivalry and combustion between "brothers," but he yearned for a Motherland that embraced both Muslim and Hindu in unity, if not uniformity. Nevertheless, the fervent hope for a religious partnership that he described implied an ordering between "higher" and "lower" and prioritized Hindu ideas: "Advaitism is the last word of religion and thought and the only position from which one can look upon all religions and sects with love."[4]

Just as Vivekananda had reshaped the image of the sannyasin in the West, so he sought to do the same in India, but as part of an explicit program of national rejuvenation, hence his suggestion that his monks should perhaps first meditate in the forest but then must become active in fighting famine and plague. He attempted to find a course between reformist meliorism and reactionary revivalism inspired by a model of compassionate and radical activism. This formulation was highly political. By linking renunciation to activism, he insisted that the contemporary renouncer retain the otherworldly subjectivity of yore but now tackle India's contemporary problems. The sannyasin, by "clearing the deck" of domesticity, was ideally suited to be above interests, to join in life's endless flux, while retaining his inner stillness.[5] Somehow, however, the transcendent and the mundane were no longer meant to oppose each other.[6] We remember Vivekananda for his "Practical Vedanta," and yet this was impossible without his idealism and the global moment to which he contributed so much.

But this new focus caused terrible tensions and doubts. When he returned to India, Adbhutananda (nicknamed Latu and Plato) refused to adhere to the new rules and withdrew into solitude. Even Akhandananda, the "famine swami," was pained by the need to recount his achievements to help the order raise money and expand its operations. It took time for these men to reconcile such needs with their spiritual habits. But one after the other, they ultimately responded, a choice made easier by the violence and incompetence of British rule.

If in the West Vivekananda had to challenge the view that Indians knew nothing "practical," back in India he wished to encourage practicality by looking beyond don't-touchism and redirecting dharma for higher religious and national ideals. As his views evolved, he struggled to find the precise terminology he needed to express his ideas. When Mary Hale asked him in 1895 to define "dharma," he showed how difficult it was to explain. His answer, that it was "religion," obscured its many Hindu associations for Western consumption; in India, however, he could be equally unclear. Sometimes, he seemed to equate dharma with forms of Western "duty" and to condemn it as don't-touchism. This lack of terminological precision was part of the labor of religious comparison across continents, and the search for new ways of thinking.

His views on seva, for example, revealed the many tensions that this novel engagement entailed. Vivekananda coined the term "Daridra Narayan," as the god that resides among the poor, and directed his followers to dedicate their lives to serving the poor. This radical project was crucial in spreading both Karma yoga and forms of spiritual and practical solidarity. For Vivekananda, the violence and shame of British rule lay in famine and poverty: hunger and epidemic were the context in which pre-Swadeshi nationalism was forged. Nonetheless, his vision of seva largely avoided social and economic analysis, as well as questions of caste and minority repression. It was sometimes laced as well with the language of nineteenth-century benevolence, especially when he called the poor "ignorant noisy children," a charge also leveled against Gandhi when he later called Dalits "the Children of God."[7]

Despite the many limitations of his thought, Vivekananda's synthesis was and remains powerful. His work enabled sannyasins to join with middle-class, lower-middle-class, and female lay people who sought both to "uplift" the masses but also to wrest control of "philanthropy" from Christian missionaries. It facilitated the struggle against British rule and underscored the importance of that uplift coming from within individuals and communities, and not through state action. The Gita's lessons along with "practical Vedanta" provided tools to hammer away at both the Indian sense of subjugation and the utilitarian logic that still largely animated the British approach to Indian administration.

In opposing colonial power, Vivekananda resorted to man-making, deploying the body as an instrument to fight against weakness and helplessness. If the body needed meat to fight the British, then meat was necessary; if the warrior needed to fight his own flesh and blood as Krishna enjoined Arjuna to do, then remorse was misplaced, a distraction from the steely detachment necessary for battle. Vivekananda sought to defeat timidity, an emotion he understood all too well as a man brought up in the ranks of the Bengali middle classes. Nor did he underestimate what Indians faced. He understood that they might be dying helplessly from the famines that the British inflicted, but he nevertheless insisted that they should not accept the conquerors' verdict of their bodily or mental inferiority.[8]

This aspect of his program has often overwhelmed his attention to forms of "motherliness"; his love for India and Indian spirituality—on display when battling missionaries and in fighting against famine and plague—has meant that his equally strong emphasis on universalism and localism are sometimes discounted. In the changing currents of Indian politics, he is often portrayed as the polar opposite to Gandhi, although both were very much indebted to the "global idealist moment," especially its "alternative" experimentation; both, too, refashioned ideas of sacrifice, self-reliance, and seva that pervaded their resistance to British rule.

Indeed, it is hard not to be struck with how, in his insistence on sacrifice—and particularly bodily sacrifice—Vivekananda anticipates Gandhi. In the light of contemporary Indian views of the two men, such an assertion may seem farfetched. Both men also deplored "Western civilization," but Vivekananda was impressed by its organization and efficiency as well as its scientific and technical triumphs, achievements that Gandhi could do without. Gandhi abhorred meat eating, delighted in his "puniness," and appeared in public with only a loincloth. The scarlet-robed and stout Vive-kananda, with his love of meat and fondness for tobacco, could hardly have been more different. Gandhi would never have called himself a man-maker, though he did speak often of virility. While Vivekananda's universalism prioritized Advaitic—and hence Hindu—religious concepts as the prerequisite for tolerance and religious diversity, Gandhi tirelessly promoted "neighborli-ness" to counteract tensions among communities, especially with Muslims.

And yet, the similarities between the two men are impossible to avoid. Both emphasized experience and seva as well as ethical, spiritual, and po-litical freedom. Both championed forms of physical courage and moral fearlessness. Both wanted to retain caste in revised form and readily ac-cepted a measure of inequality. They also, however, expressed their power through "motherliness." Vivekananda enjoyed cooking and feeding his dis-ciples, who, in turn, sought his maternal love but feared his scolding. Gandhi was similarly "maternal" in his preoccupation with food, nursing, and spin-ning, while he, too, acted as guru to many of those he lived with in his various ashrams. Both exalted feminine qualities and women but were un-comfortable with (especially female) sexuality and conservative in their view of women's role in society.

Vivekananda's claim to being apolitical—belied at later moments by the order's involvement in protecting radical nationalists—also had important ramifications. After he died, it seemed for a time that much of the excite-ment surrounding his ideas was fading. But Swadeshi renewed it, and the nominally apolitical stance permitted his ideas to gain a diffuse and impor-tant influence. Aurobindo quoted Vivekananda (freely) when he said the "first gods you have to worship are *your own fellow countrymen*," while Charles Freer Andrews noted that "'Ramakrishna Vivekananda' had be-come a rallying cry for activism and pride."[9] Nivedita was equally important in this process, even if her nationalist vision was decidedly stronger than her guru's.

I choose to end with Nivedita, even if is harder to see her as a "world voice" (the words she used to describe Vivekananda), despite her importance for transmitting ideas. Indians widely acknowledge her as an important figure in the early anticolonial struggle, even if few Westerners even know her name. Nivedita's work exemplified the extension of Vivekananda's legacy by attaching Vedanta to a new set of avant-garde Western preoccupations. She and Vivekananda were innovators in another way—perhaps without conscious awareness, they created a type of collaboration in which Western women internationalized an Indian message. Nivedita experienced passionate commitment but also intense insecurity.[10] She explored the entrancing possibilities that new routes to self-expression and political impact offered and showed the possibilities of a global collaboration between cultures and individuals. But she also demonstrated how very difficult it was to be "betwixt and between" in so many different and overlapping worlds.

Chronology

1882–1883	Vivekananda returns repeatedly to Dakshineswar.
1884	Vivekananda passes Bachelor of Arts at Scottish Church College; his father dies on February 25. Ramakrishna learns of Sen's death; meets Gopaler Ma. Sri Sarada Devi comes to live at Dakshineswar and cares for her husband. Nivedita finishes at Halifax College and begins teaching at Keswick in Cumbria.
1885	Ramakrishna is ill with cancer; lives at Shyampukur and is treated by Dr. Sircar. Vivekananda tends Ramakrishna but is also busy with lawsuit and studying for legal examinations.
1886	Vivekananda receives gerua cloth that Ramakrishna distributes among twelve disciples in January; has first experience of nirvikalpa samadhi; visits Bodh Gaya briefly in April; with brother disciples takes up residence at Baranagar. Ramakrishna is at Cossipore house; dies August 15. Nivedita teaches at Rugby.
1886–1888	Vivekananda mostly remains at Baranagar; spends Christmas at Antpur, joins with others to create monastic community; 1887: undertakes scriptural vows. Vivekananda continues to visit Calcutta to conduct lawsuit; travels to Varanasi, Ayodha, Lucknow, Agra, Vrindaban, Hathras, Hrishikesh; returns intermittently to Baranagar.
1889	Vivekananda mostly stays at Baranagar because of ill health; in December, he goes to Vaidyanath, Allahabad, and Ghazipur.
1886–1890	Nivedita teaches in Wrexham (Wales) and later Chester near the Welsh border; she becomes a journalist.
1890	Vivekananda meets Pavhari Baba in January in Gazipur and stays for three months; goes to Varanasi and returns to Baranagar in April; makes Himalayan pilgrimage in July; visits several places and is joined by Saradananda and Kripananda in Almora, where he receives news of his sister's death; visits other pilgrimage cites with brother disciples.
1891	Vivekananda travels in January to Meerut and Delhi alone, then meets other monks in Delhi.
1891–1892	Vivekananda is on pilgrimage alone for virtually two years (February 1891 to March 1893); encounters people of all ranks of life from the poorest to Indian princes. The Madras Subscription Committee is organized for trip to America, spearheaded by Alasinga Perumal. Vivekananda visits the Raja of Khetri in April and tells him of his plans; leaves for Bombay in May. Other monks at Baranagar settle at Alambazar near Dakshineswar temple.
1893	Vivekananda leaves Bombay for Chicago May 31, via Colombo, Malay, Hong Kong, and Japan; lands in Vancouver on July 25, and after train journey arrives in Chicago on July 30; finds World Parliament not yet in session but visits Columbian Exposition; goes to Massachusetts to stay with Kate Sanborn. World's Parliament sessions begin September 11; Vivekananda becomes an important participant.
1894	Vivekananda lectures throughout America. Sister Christine listens to Vivekananda speak in Detroit but does not meet him. Vivekananda lives with Landsberg and teaches in simple quarters in New York; spends

	important summer in Green Acre, where he gives lessons in yoga under the Swami's Pine.
1891–1894	Nivedita learns new teaching methods at Madame de Leeuw's school at Wimbledon.
1894	Nivedita opens her own school at Wimbledon; helps found Sesame Club in London; continues journalism. Vivekananda starts Vedanta Society in New York.
1895	Vivekananda finishes *Karma Yoga* in June; in Thousand Island in June and July teaching disciples, including Sister Christine; offers classes in Karma yoga and Bhakti yoga in New York and resumes lecturing.
1896	Vivekananda leaves America for England in April and stays until July; meets Edward Sturdy and other British devotees, including Mr. and Mrs. Sevier; teaches on Jnana yoga and meets Max Müller in Oxford in May; leaves in July for Switzerland with British friends and goes to Germany, where he meets Paul Deussen in Kiel; returns to England in October and stays there until December 16; lectures on "Practical Vedanta"; takes short journey to Italy, then returns to India.
	Nivedita meets Swami Vivekananda at Lady Isabella Margesson's house in London; hears Vivekananda's lectures between April and December; works with Sturdy in London; helps raise funds for famine relief.
1897	Vivekananda arrives in Colombo on January 15 to a warm welcome; in Pamban on January 26; invited by Raja of Ramnad to Rameswaram and Ramnad; in Madras, received with great enthusiasm on February 6; goes by sea to Calcutta on February 15, then to Budge Budge on February 19, from where he takes a special train to Sealdah in Calcutta; greeted by large crowd at station and returns that evening to Math in Alambazar after seven years; is ill and recuperates in Almora; Ramakrishna Mission is formed on May 1 in Calcutta.
1898	Vivekananda works against plague and accompanies Nivedita, Sara Bull, and Josephine Macleod through Punjab, Lahore, and ultimately Kashmir; Vivekananda's stenographer, J. J. Goodwin, dies; Vivekananda goes to Amarnath with Nivedita and beholds Shiva; pilgrimage to Khir Bhawani in July; composes Kali poem in August; tells Nivedita that he is no longer "Swamiji"; returns to Belur in December, where new Math is being built.
	Nivedita leaves for India in January; meets Gopaler Ma in February; meets Sarada Devi and initiated by Vivekananda in March; plague in Calcutta begins in May; later travels north with Vivekananda, Bull, and MacLeod; at Cave of Amarnath with Vivekananda in August; returns to Calcutta and opens school in November.
1899	Nivedita lectures on Kali and meets Debendranath Tagore with Vivekananda in February; nurses plague victims in March, but then begins sanitation work after Vivekananda's objections; lectures at Kalighat Temple in May; travels with Vivekananda and Turiyananda to Britain in June; returns to Wimbledon with Vivekananda in July; reaches Ridgely Manor in upstate New York in September; completes *Kali the Mother*,

October–November; Vivekananda blesses her and Sara Bull; November-December lectures in America.

1899   Vivekananda is involved in opening Ramakrishna Mission in Belur on January 2; travels to London for a second trip to the West via Naples and Marseilles on July 31; encounters disappointment with some English disciples, especially Sturdy; leaves for New York on August 16 and stays a year in America, setting up Vedantic Centers in California.

1900   Nivedita lectures in America from January to June; tells "Indian Stories" to schoolchildren in January (these later become *Cradle Tales of Hinduism*); meets Patrick Geddes in March; sails to Paris at the end of June and works with Geddes; *Kali the Mother* is published in July; goes on holiday with Jagadish and Abala Bose to Perros-Guirec in Brittany with Sara Bull in August; has a misunderstanding with Vivekananda but ultimately receives his blessing; talks with George Birdwood about Tata Research Institute scheme in November; nurses Bose after surgery in December, offering lodging to the scientist and his wife.

Vivekananda arrives in France on August 1 and stays until October, attending the Congress of History of Religions during the Exposition Universelle; leaves France in October and tours Vienna, Constantinople, Austria, Greece, and Egypt; sails for India and arrives in December, goes to Mayavati after hearing of Captain Sevier's death while he is away.

1901   Vivekananda arrives January 3 in Mayavati and celebrates his thirty-eighth birthday on January 13. He is unhappy with images of Ramakrishna; returns to Belur Math in January; experiences many illnesses; goes on pilgrimage to Dacca and Shillong with mother during summer, but remains ill; Durga Puja celebrated at Math in October; meets Okakura in December.

Nivedita lectures in England and Scotland during February and March; holidays in Norway with Sara Bull and Romesh Chunder Dutt and begins writing *The Web of Indian Life* with his encouragement; urges Bose to write *The Living and the Non-Living* between September and December; continues in her defense of Bose and Indian science; decides to dedicate herself to politics of Indian liberation.

1902   Vivekananda goes to Bodh Gaya and Varanasi with Okakura at the beginning of the year; celebrates Ramakrishna's birthday in February; dies unexpectedly on July 4.

1902   Nivedita travels to India with R. C. Dutt and Mrs. Bull and reaches Madras in early February; begins friendship with E. B. Havell and works with him and Okakura in influencing Indian Art Movement; first meets Okakura in March and helps him rewrite *Ideals of the East;* obtains help with school from Christine, who arrives in April; visits Mayavati with Okakura and others in May; has discussions with Vivekananda in late June; meets with Vivekananda for the last time at Ramakrishna Math in July; receives news of Vivekananda's death on July 5; sends open letter declaring her independence from the Math on July 19; publishes important eulogy of Vivekananda for *The Hindu* on July 27; writes introduction to Okakura's *Ideals of the East* in August; embarks on lecture tour in India in September; conducts lecture tour October 7–18; meets Aurobindo Ghose on October 20, lectures October 26–29, and reviews Bose's book; visits Caves of Ellora in November; becomes suspicious of Okakura in November and deepens her friendship with S. K. Ratcliffe; conducts more lecture tours in December.

1903   Nivedita begins working with radical groups in January; finishes *Web of Indian Life* in September; Gopaler Ma comes to live with her in December; throughout this year writes constantly on Indian topics, and especially nationalism.

1904   Nivedita lectures January–May; in Mayavati May–June with Sister Christine and the Boses, where Jagadish begins *Plant Response*; reviews of *The Web of Indian Life* in June; suggests "Thunderbolt" for India's national flag in December; between July and December Curzon passes "University Act" and limits science education; contacts such organizations as the Anushilan Samiti and donates books to the group led by Barindra Kumar Ghose.

1905   Nivedita designs another national flag in February; campaigns against Curzon and finishes *Aggressive Hinduism* in March; in Darjeeling May–June with the Boses; announcement of Partition of Bengal on July 20; implementation of Partition with "Bengal" and "Eastern Bengal and Assam" in October; persuades Gokhale to support Boycott in December.

1906   Nivedita travels to ancient sites in India in January; government repression increases in April; serial publication of *Master as I Saw Him* and *Notes of Some Wanderings*; Nivedita's close associates die in May and June; Gopaler Ma dies in July; Nivedita travels to Barisal in September and October and describes the famine that occurs in flood-affected East Bengal among a largely Muslim population; is afflicted with serious fever and convalesces in Mussoorie and finally Dum Dum; continues her journalism and works with Jagadish Chandra Bose in November and December.

1907   Nivedita publishes on Indian art and nationality in January; writes without attribution for *Modern Review* on sociology, nationalism, history, and politics; encourages work of Abanindranath Tagore and Nandalal Bose, among others; in July, Bhupendranath Datta (Vivekananda's brother) is arrested; Nivedita leaves Calcutta on August 12; stays with family and meets friends and colleagues in Europe between September and December; publishes *Cradle Tales of Hinduism*.

1908   Nivedita works on articles related to civic life and the National Idea in January; urges unity in February among different groups after Surat Congress; learns of an attempt on the life of lieutenant governor of Bengal and the arrest of such Swadeshi activists as Aurobindo, Bepin Chandra Pal, and Ashwini Kumar Dutta, among others; in America between September and December, where she visits institutions and friends, and makes more political contacts with activists outside of India.

1909   Nivedita's mother dies of cancer; Nivedita arrives in Calcutta in July and writes of nationalists coming to pay respect to Sarada Devi; begins campaign for Bose's laboratory in September. Between September and December, she continues to write on Indian art and visits Ajanta caves.

1910   Nivedita's *The Master as I Saw Him* published in February; Aurobindo is cautioned about imminent arrest and goes to Chandernagore and then to Pondicherry, territories under French rule; Nivedita takes on editorship of *Karma Yogin;* works on papers on national education in March; on pilgrimage with Boses from May to June; produces copious articles, other writing, and reviews in September; is in Darjeeling with the Boses in October when she learns of Sara Bull's illness; travels to America as "Mrs. Theta Margot"; nurses Sara Bull.

1911   Mrs. Bull dies in January, and Nivedita leaves America; Olea attacks Nivedita for receiving money for the school and Bose's laboratory; Nivedita returns to India in April; is at Mayavati between May and June with the Boses; Christine rethinks her career; Bhuvaneswari Devi, Vivekananda's mother, dies in July; Nivedita stays in Darjeeling with the Boses in October and gets dysentery. She prepares her will and dies on October 13.

Dramatis Personae

Ramakrishna's Disciples, and Other Swamis and Guru Brothers

Abhedananda, born as Kali Prasad Chandra—first journeys to England and later became head of the New York Vedanta Society.

Adbhutananda, born as Rakhturam and known as Latu or Plato—one of the first of Ramakrishna's disciples.

Akhandananda, born as Gangadhar Ghatak—the "famine swami," devoted to Vivekananda.

Balaram Basu—prominent householder disciple of Ramakrishna and philanthropist.

Brahmananda, born as Rakhal Chandra Gosh—first president of the Ramakrishna Mission.

Girish Chandra Ghosh—Bengali actor, director, and writer.

Mahendranath Gupta—mystic and author of the Sri Kathamrita.

Pratap Hazra—argumentative disciple of Vivekananda.

Premananda, born as Baburam Ghosh—significant contributor during the early days of the Ramakrishna Mission and subsequently managed Belur Math.

Ramakrishnananda, born as Shashi Bhusan Chakravarty—devoted to the worship of Ramakrishna and responsible for creating a shrine with his relics. Later head of Ramakrishna Mission at Chennai.

Saradananda, born as Sarat Chandra Chakravarty—first secretary of the Math and Mission.

Shivananda, born as Tarak Nath Ghosal—second president of the Ramakrishna Math and Mission.

Swarupananda, born as Ajay Hari Bannerji—first president of Advaita Ashrama, the major publishing press of the Ramakrishna order.

Trigunatitananda, born as Sarada Prasanna Mitra—responsible for beginning work on the first Hindu temple in the West in San Francisco.

Turiyananda, born as Harinath Chattopadhyay—one of the earliest monks to travel to America with Vivekananda.

Yogananda, born as Jogindranath Chowdhury—known to criticize Vivekananda.

Vivekananda's Family

Narendranath Datta—Swami Vivekananda.

Bhupendranath Datta—his brother and eminent sociologist.

Jogendrabala Datta—his sister who committed suicide.

Mahendranath Datta—memoirist and his brother who joined Vivekananda in London.

Vishwanath Datta—his father.

Bhunvaneshwari Devi—his mother.

Indian Women

Bhairavi Brahmani—female ascetic, guru who initiated Ramakrishna into Tantra.

Gopaler Ma—born as Aghoremani Devi; visionary and close associate of Sarada Devi and Margaret Noble.

Rani Rashmoni—widow, philanthropist, and founder of the Dakshineswar Temple with strong personal links to Ramakrishna.

Kamini Shil—principal of Bethune College, the first ladies' college in Bengal.

Gaya Vaishnavi—woman helped by Akhandananda.

American Women

Jane Addams—social philosopher and activist and founder of Hull House.

Roxie Blodgett—Vivekananda's hostess in Southern California.

Sara Bull—one of Vivekananda's most important "mothers"; important adviser and philanthropist.

Stella Campbell—actress who joined Vivekananda at Thousand Island.

Rev. Augusta Jane Chapin—Universalist minister and women's rights' activist.

Cornelia Conger—a girl who met Vivekananda and whose father was a Louisiana sugar planter.

Marie Louise Davitt—initiated as Swami Abhayananda by Vivekananda; of French Canadian origin.

Margaret (Libbie) Dutcher—lent her house in Thousand Island.

Mary Baker Eddy—founder of Christian Science.

Sarah Farmer—organizer of Green Acre, later a key devotee of Baha'i.

Mary Caroline Funke—close friend and associate of Christina Greenstidel; another of Vivekananda's acolytes.

Christine Greenstidel—known as Sister Christine, one of Vivekananda's most stalwart disciples and a teacher.

Alice M. Hansbrough—known as Shanti; recounted life of Vivekananda in California.

Josephine MacLeod—important "friend" of Vivekananda and dedicated associate of the Ramakrishna Math and Mission.

Mrs. Melton—healer who treated Vivekananda in California and others in Europe.

Leonora Piper—medium, famous in spiritualist circles and important for the work of William James.

Kate Sanborn—author, wit, and one of Vivekananda's first hostesses.

Maud Stumm—society painter of Jewish origin.

Celia Thaxter—poet and friend of Sara Bull, also hostess at the Appledore Hotel and famous for her garden.

Emma Cecilia Thursby—American vocalist who sang to audiences in America and in Europe.

Olea Vaughan—daughter of Sara Chapman Bull; well acquainted with Vivekananda.

Sarah Ellen Waldo—disciple who composed Vivekananda's "Inspired Talks."

Kate Tannat Woods—author, editor, and journalist.

Mary Tappan Wright—American novelist and short-story writer, who wrote about academia.

Carrie Mead Wyckoff—also known as Sister Lalita, another Californian disciple; her Hollywood home later became the headquarters of the Vedanta Society of Southern California.

British and European Women

Helena Blavatsky—Russian born spiritualist who cofounded theosophy.

Emma Calvé—French soprano opera star with international career; credited Vivekananda with helping her with depression.

Mrs. Ethel Mary Ashton Jonson—aspiring playwright who wrote under the name of Dorothy Leighton; she was disinclined to support Nivedita's efforts.

Isabel Augusta, Lady Margesson—suffragist and radical campaigner; hosted meeting where Vivekananda met Nivedita.

Mary Caroline Grey, Lady Minto—wife of the viceroy and governor-general of India, friend of Nivedita.

Henrietta Müller—of Chilean-German origin, but active in London; theosophist and feminist, with connections to Vivekananda and the Ramakrishna movement.

Margaret Noble—Sister Nivedita, English educationalist who became Vivekananda's most prominent Western disciple.

Eusapia Palladino—Italian medium, famous for her physical feats as well as spiritual communication; widely known in spiritualist circles in England, France, and Italy.

Indian Spiritual Figures, Reformers, Politicians, and Intellectuals

Pavhari Baba—Hindu ascetic and saint who lived in an underground hermitage.

Surendranath Banerjee—founder of Indian National Association, one of the earliest nationalists; cofounder of the Indian National Congress.

Manmatha Bhattacharya—Mahesh Chandra Nyayratna Bhattacharyya, Sanskrit scholar and educator.

Jagadish Chandra Bose—scientist and author.

Sahid Khudiram Bose—revolutionary who attempted to assassinate Douglas Kingsford; executed when only eighteen.

Prafulla Chaki—revolutionary who attempted to assassinate Douglas Kingsford.

Gyanendranath Chakravarti—Indian theosophist and mathematician at the World Parliament.

Mohini Mohun Chatterji—a theosophist, well known for his commentary on the Bhagavad Gita; known to Josephine MacLeod and Sara Bull before acquaintance with Vivekananda.

Anagarika Dharmapala—Don David Hewavitharana (of Sri Lankan origin but mostly living in Calcutta), "Buddhist Modernist" and important figure in Sinhalese cultural nationalism.

Romesh Chunder Dutt—economic historian, translator of sacred Indian texts, and civil servant.

Ashwini Kumar Dutta—educator and important Swadeshi activist.

Manilal Dvivedi—social thinker and philosopher who wrote in Gujurati; his ideas were important to Vivekananda.

Virchand Gandhi—Jain scholar who lectured widely on Jainism and other religions.

Aurobindo Ghose—known as Sri Aurobindo, Indian philosopher, yogi, poet, and famous nationalist thinker.

Rash Behari Ghose—"moderate" leader in Indian National Congress.

Narendranath Goswami—traitor to other revolutionary prisoners in Alipore Jail; target of assassination.

Subramania Iyer—High Court judge in Madras and important early supporter of Vivekananda.

Manibhai Jashbhai of Baroda—minister (dewan) of Kutch and Baroda.

Damodar Mavalankar—young theosophical disciple of Blavatsky who died during his trek to the Himalayas.

Pramadadas Mitra—orthodox Hindu whose scholarship Vivekananda respected.

Surendra Nath Mitra—prominent householder devotee of Ramakrishna, who donated generously to the Ramakrishna movement.

Protap Chunder Mozoomdar—important figure in Hindu reform movement, prominent in Brahmo Samaj, and critic of Vivekananda.

Bipin Chandra Pal—Indian nationalist and writer; also key to Swadeshi activism.

Pandit Sankar Pandurang—author of historical poetry and literary critic. Famous for erudition and a distinguished translator; encouraged Vivekananda to learn French.

Alasinga Perumal—Vivekananda's beloved disciple in Chennai.

Tota Puri—guru who taught Ramakrishna the disciplines of Advaita Vedanta; also head of monastery in Punjab.

Lala Lajpat Rai—early and important Indian nationalist; ultimately beaten to death by the British in 1928.

Ram Mohun Roy—the "Father of Modern India," famous as reformer, intellectual, and activist; he founded the Brahmo Sabha, the forerunner of the Brahmo Samaj.

Dayananda Saraswati—Indian philosopher and founder of the Arya Samaj; promoted rights for women; famous for belief that the Vedas were the foundational texts of Hinduism and resisted what he saw as priestly corruptions.

Keshub Chunder Sen—Hindu philosopher and reformer, perhaps tempted by Christianity.

Ajit Singh, Raja of Khetri—close friend and disciple of Vivekananda, who gave financial support to Vivekananda's trip to America.

Pratap Singh—sixteenth-century prince, king of Mewar, remembered for his resistance to Mughal empire.

Debendranath Tagore—Hindu thinker and active in the Brahmo Samaj.

Rabindranath Tagore—Nobel Prize–winning author and son of Debendranath.

Abanindranath Tagore—painter, brother of Rabindranath, one of the founders of the Bengal School of Art.

Jamsetji Nusserwanji Tata—industrialist, philanthropist, founder of Tata Group.

Raja Bhaskara Sethupathi Thever of Ramnad—manager of the Rameswaren Temple and financial supporter of Vivekananda.

Bal Gangadhar Tilak—the first leader of the Indian independence movement, feared by the British for stoking unrest.

Ishwar Chandra Vidyasagar—Indian educator and Hindu polymath.

Haridas Viharidas Desai, Dewan of Junagadh—pious and capable administrator, well connected to Vivekananda.

Chamarajendra Wodeyar X—Maharaja of Mysore who instituted a representative assembly.

Paramahansa Yogananda—born Mukundal Lal Ghosh, an Indian monk, who also went to the West in the early twentieth century; important for the spread of Kriya Yoga and the Self-Realization Fellowship; author of best-selling *Autobiography of a Yogi* (1946).

Ramakrishna and Family

Ramakrishna Paramahamsa—born Gadadhar Chattopadhyaya.

Khudiram Chattopadhyaya—his father.

Chandramani Devi—his mother.

Ramkumar—his brother.

Indian Spiritual Figures (Historical)

Chaitanya Mahaprabhu—fifteenth-century Indian saint, whose devotees regard him as an incarnation of Krishna; widely admired in Bengal.

Shivaji Maharaj—seventeenth-century ruler who was later lionized as a proto-nationalist.

Patanjali—thought to be the ancient sage who is the author of the Yoga Sutras.

Pratapaditya—a zamindar and later Maharaja of Jessore who fought against the Mughal empire in the sixteenth-century in Bengal.

Ramanuja—eleventh-century theologian who promoted Vaishnavism so important to the Bhakti movement.

Ramprasad Sen—Hindu Shakta poet and eighteenth-century Bengali saint; his works were central to Ramakrishna's spirituality.

Shankara—the eighth-century philosopher and theologian credited with creating the monastic system with its ten orders; also famous for his importance to the tradition of Advaita Vedanta.

Guru Nanak—the first Sikh guru and spiritual master, also warrior, poet, and philosopher.

Japanese Men

Noguchi Aenshiro—interpreter at World Parliament.

Kozaki Harnichi—president of Doshisha University.

Kinzo Ryuge Hirai—Japanese Buddhist at World Parliament.

Kakuzo Okakura—Japanese scholar, art historian, and ideologue.

British and European Men

Charles Freer Andrews—Christian missionary, educator, and friend and collaborator of Rabindranath Tagore and Mahatma Gandhi.

Edwin Arnold—author of *The Light of Asia* (1879), a widely read account of the Buddha's life.

Hippolyte Bernheim—French physician from Nancy who became known for his hypnotic and suggestive therapies.

Henri Antoine Jules-Bois—French occultist who wrote *Le Satanisme et la magie;* companion of Vivekananda.

Ole Bull—virtuoso violinist and Norwegian romantic nationalist; husband of Sara Chapman Bull.

Jean-Martin Charcot—French neurologist active in the study of hysteria and hypnotism.

Paul Deussen—German Indologist.

Alexander Duff—Church of Scotland missionary in India and the founder of the General Assembly's Institution, the school that Vivekananda mostly attended.

Ernst Johann Eitel—German-born missionary in China and compiler of Cantonese dictionary.

Jean Bernard Léon Foucault—nineteenth-century French physicist who measures the speed of light and whose "pendulum" demonstrated how the earth rotated.

Sigmund Freud—leading Austrian figure in establishing psychoanalysis and creating the "talking cure."

Friedrich Froebel—German student of Pestalozzi known for his work in establishing kindergartens.

Patrick Geddes—sociologist, town planner, and innovative transnational thinker.

Josiah John Goodwin—British stenographer, who recorded Vivekananda's lectures and speeches.

William Hastie—Scottish clergyman and polemicist; one of Vivekananda's teachers.

Ernest Binfield Havell—art historian with keen interests in Indian art, and principal of the Government School of Art in Calcutta.

Richard Hodgson—of Australian origin, but studied and lived in Britain; active in the Society for Psychical Research; investigated Helena Blavatsky's spiritual "communications."

Douglas Kingsford—magistrate notorious for harsh sentences to Indian nationalists.

Sebastian Kneipp—Bavarian priest who advocated naturopathic medicine and hydrotherapy.

Leo Landsberg—also known as Swami Kripananda; troubled disciple of Vivekananda, and one of the initiated at Thousand Island.

Gottfried Wilhelm Leibniz—seventeenth-century German scholar, mathematician, and philosopher.

Frédéric Le Play—French social theorist and sociologist.

Cesare Lombroso—Italian criminal anthropologist.

James Mavor—Scottish Canadian economist; collaborator of Patrick Geddes.

William Miller—missionary, and head of Christian College in Madras.

Alfred Momerie—English cleric with broad Church views; academic theologian.

William Morris—leader of English arts and crafts movement, textile designer, and socialist activist.

Max Müller—German-English philologist and orientalist.

Johann Pestalozzi—eighteenth-century Swiss pedagogue.

Pierre Puvis de Chavannes—innovative French mural artist.

Romain Rolland—Nobel Prize winner and author of books on Ramakrishna, Vivekananda, and Gandhi.

Henry Sevier—British army officer in India who returned with his wife, Charlotte, to found Mayavati, the Himalayan retreat for the Ramakrishna order.

Herbert Spencer—Philosopher, biologist, and sociologist; applied different aspects of evolutionary theory to society and ethics.

William Thomas Stead—controversial investigative journalist; close associate of Nivedita.

Edward Sturdy—Canadian disciple of Vivekananda, living in Britain.

John Tyndall—Irish physicist and scientific popularizer.

James Ward—British idealist philosopher.

Wilhelm Eduard Weber—German physicist who invented the electromagnetic telegraph.

American Men

Amos Bronson Alcott—educationalist and writer; father of Louisa May.

Benjamin Arnett—American bishop, educator, civil rights activist.

Charles C. Bonney—one of the organizers of the World Parliament.

William Juvenal Colville—spiritualist, and Vivekananda's companion during his lecture tour.

Horatio Dresser—New Thought leader and involved with the Metaphysical Club in Boston.

William and Horatio Eddy—brothers and psychics in Chittenden, Vermont.

Ernest Fennollosa—professor of philosophy and political economy in Tokyo; convert to Buddhism and collector of Japanese art; first curator of collection at Museum of Fine Arts in Boston.

James Gibbons—second American Cardinal and labor activist.

Stanley Hall—first president of the American Psychological Association and of Clark University.

William James—philosopher who developed "pragmatism" and functional psychology; one of America's leading intellectuals; brother of novelist Henry James.

William Quan Judge—Irish American mystic, and important theosophist.

John Harvey Kellogg—physician, nutritionist, and health activist, as well as director of the Battle Creek Sanatorium.

William Sloane Kenney—biographer, editor, and critic; correspondent of William James.

Henry Steel Olcott—cofounder with Helena Blavatsky of the Theosophical Society.

Phineas Pankhurst Quimby—mesmerist and mental healer, often regarded as the "founder" of New Thought.

George Roorbach—an American painter living in Alameda, California, when he met Vivekananda.

Josiah Royce—Harvard Idealist philosopher and historian.

Minot Judson Savage—Unitarian minister and medium, who later founded the "New Humanitarianism."

Ralph Waldo Trine—New Thought philosopher and educator.

Alexander Russell Webb—Prominent Anglo-American Muslim convert, writer, and publisher.

James Henry Wiggin—Unitarian minister; editor who worked with Mary Baker Eddy.

Henry Wood—New Thought practitioner; successful businessman and author.

Notes

Introduction

1. "Swami Vivekananda," *Indian Mirror,* January 21, 1897, in *Vivekananda in Indian Newspapers, 1893–1902: Extracts from 22 Newspapers and Periodicals,* ed. with intro. by Sankari Prasad Basu (Calcutta: Dineshchandra Basu, Basu Bhattacharyya, 1969), 124 (hereafter Basu).

2. *Indian Mirror,* January 31, 1897, Basu, 128.

3. *Indian Mirror,* January 31, 1897, Basu, 128.

4. "Swamy Vivekananda at Pamban [From Our Own Correspondent]," *Indian Mirror,* January 30, 1897, Basu, 133–134.

5. "Swami Vivekananda," *Tribune* (Lahore), n.d., 1897, Basu, 150.

6. "Swami Vivekananda's Return to Calcutta," *Indian Mirror,* n.d., 1897, Basu, 148.

7. "Swami Vivekananda in Calcutta," *The Statesman,* n.d., 1897, Basu, 153; and *Indian Mirror,* March 3, 1897, Basu, 168; "The Return of Swami Vivekananda to Calcutta," *Indian Mirror,* March 23, 1897, Basu, 187.

8. Swami Vivekananda, "Responses to Welcome," Addresses at the Parliament of Religions, vol. 1, in *Complete Works of Swami Vivekananda,* 10 vols., https://en.wikisource.org/wiki/The _Complete_Works_of_Swami_Vivekananda (hereafter *CWSV*).

9. "The Universal Appeal of Swami Vivekananda," remarks by Hindol Sengupta and Amish Tripathi, Nehru Centre, London, January 12, 2021.

10. Ajaya Kumar Sahoo, "Hinduism in the Diaspora," *Social Change* 35 (2004): 71–82; Angela Rudert, "Research on Contemporary Indian Gurus: What's New about New Age Gurus?" *Religion Compass* 4, no. 10 (2010): 629–642; and Torkel Brekke, *Makers of Modern Indian Religion in the Late Nineteenth Century* (Oxford: Oxford University Press, 2002), 41–60.

11. See "The Tale of the Two Narendras: Narendra Modi and Swami Vivekananda," *The Statesman,* July 4, 2016; "PM Narendra Modi Invokes Swami Vivekananda, Lord Krishna in International Yoga Day Message," *Business Insider,* June 21, 2020; "PM Modi Compliments the Hindu Group for Compilation on Swami Vivekananda," *The Hindu,* March 20, 2020.

12. Jyotirmaya Sharma, *A Restatement of Religion: Swami Vivekananda and the making of Hindu Nationalism* (New Haven, CT: Yale University Press, 2013), xiv. Peter van der Veer, *Religious Nationalism: Hindus and Muslims in India* (Berkeley: University of California Press, 1994), 136.

13. Prathama Banerjee, *Elementary Aspects of the Political: Histories from the Global South* (Durham, NC: Duke University Press, 2020), 40. For more on Vivekananda's views on caste, see chapter 12.

14. Shamita Basu, *Religious Revivalism as Nationalist Discourse: Swami Vivekananda and New Hinduism in Nineteenth-Century Bengal* (New York: Oxford University Press, 2002), explores this duality.

15. See Catherine Albanese, *A Republic of Mind and Spirit: A Cultural History of American Metaphysical Religion* (New Haven, CT: Yale University Press: 2007), 330–393, especially 353–359 and 366–372. On yoga, see Elizabeth de Michelis, *A History of Modern Yoga* (London: Continuum, 2004), 67–180; Mark Singleton, *Yoga Body: The Origins of Modern Posture Practice* (Oxford: Oxford University Press, 2010), 18–19; Joseph S. Alter, *Yoga in Modern India: The Body between Science and Philosophy* (Princeton: Princeton University Press, 2004), 7, 52, 64; James Mallinson and Mark Singleton, *Roots of Yoga* (Harmondsworth, UK: Penguin, 2017); Stefanie Syman, *The Story of Yoga in America: The Subtle Body* (New York: Farrar, Straus and Giroux, 2010), 37–79.

16. See also the claims in Mira Rakicevic, "27 Meditation Statistics for Your Well-Being in 2022," disturbmenot (blog), January 3, 2021, https://disturbmenot.co/meditation-statistics/, which suggest that 200 to 500 million people worldwide meditate, with other broad claims for improved health from mindfulness through yoga. For *Raja Yoga* (1896), see Chapter 8.

17. Amiya Sen, "Aggressive Hinduism: Ecumenical, Evangelist and Expansive," to be published in *Colonial Hinduism*, Oxford Centre for Hindu Studies, forthcoming, cited with kind permission of the author.

18. See Chapter 4.

19. See Chapters 9 and 10.

20. See Chapter 6.

21. Leela Gandhi, *Affective Communities: Anti-Colonial Thought, Fin-de-Siècle Radicalism and the Politics of Friendship* (Durham, NC: Duke University Press, 2006); and Elleke Boehmer, *Indian Arrivals, 1870–1915: Networks of British Empire* (Oxford: Oxford University Press, 2015).

22. Chris Bayly, "Making Hinduism a Public and a World Religion," 2, unpublished manuscript in possession of the author. Bayly used this notion at the University of Chicago Division of the Humanities on April 8, 2014. This term could certainly be applied to other periods, but I hope it conveys here something of a flexible unity of concerns to which Vivekananda contributed.

23. See Chapter 5.

24. Swami Vivekananda, Sayings and Utterances, no. 82, vol. 5, *CWSV*.

25. Swami Vivekananda, "On the Bounds of Hinduism," *Prabuddha Bharata*, April 1899, Interviews, vol. 5, *CWSV*.

26. See A. Raghuramaraju, *Debating Vivekananda: A Reader* (New Delhi: Oxford University Press, 2014).

27. This tendency endured; see Stephen N. Hay, *Asian Ideas of East and West: Tagore and His Critics in Japan, China, and India* (Cambridge, MA: Harvard University Press, 1970), 14–25, 246–311; and Wilhelm Halbfass, *India and Europe: An Essay in Philosophical Understanding* (New Delhi: Motilal Banarsidass, 1990). For the allure of Eastern Wisdom see my "Vivekananda, Sarah Farmer, and Global Spiritual Transformations in the Fin de Siècle," *Journal of Global History* 14 (2019): 179–198.

28. See the current debate of levels of scale in the field: John-Paul Ghobrial, ed., "Introduction: Seeing the World like a Microhistorian," *Global History and Microhistory* (Oxford: Oxford University Press, 2019).

29. See S. Kapila, "Vishwaguru to Burning Front Pages—Modi's Festival of Democracy Is Taking a Beating," *The Print*, August 31, 2021. Modi speaks about India as the Vishwaguru.

30. See, for an important example, John-Paul Ghobrial, *The Whispers of Cities: Information Flows in Istanbul, London, and Paris* (Oxford: Oxford University Press, 2013), 88–121. For the pioneering

works of "connected history" see Sanjay Subrahmanyam, *The Career and Legend of Vasco da Gama* (Cambridge, UK: Cambridge University Press, 1998); and Sanjay Subrahmanyam, *Three Ways to Be Alien: Travails and Encounters in the Early Modern World* (Waltham, MA: Brandeis University Press, 2011). For a sensitive global biography, see Nadine Willems, *Ishikawa Sanshiro's Geographical Imagination* (Leiden: Leiden University Press, 2020).

31. C. A. Bayly, *Recovering Liberties: Indian Thought in the Age of Liberalism and Empire* (Cambridge: Cambridge University Press, 2011), deploys this term in the introduction, ch. 11, and the conclusion.

32. See, for example, Fruela Fernandez and Jonathan Evans, *The Routledge Handbook of Translation and Politics* (London: Routledge, 2018), especially chapters 1 and 18.

33. I am especially indebted to the work of Sumit Sarkar, *Writing Social History* (New Delhi: Oxford University Press, 1997), especially 282–357, which began to discuss these inner tensions in Vivekananda. See also Partha Chatterjee, *The Nation and Its Fragments*, in *Partha Chatterjee Omnibus*, 37–75 (New Delhi: Oxford University Press, 1999), especially 68–75; and the more revisionist Amiya Sen, especially Sen, "Sri Ramakrishna, the *Kathamrita* and the Calcutta Middle Classes: An Old Problematic Revisited," *Postcolonial Studies* 9, no. 2 (2006): 165–177. See also Narasingha P. Sil, "Vivekananda's Ramakrishna: An Untold Story of Mythmaking and Propaganda" *Numen* 40 (1993): 38–62. I owe important perspectives on Bengali cultural history to the work of Dipesh Chakrabarty, *Provincializing Europe: Postcolonial Thought and Historical Difference*, new ed. (Princeton: Princeton University Press, 2009). An astute exploration of intellectual, religious, and spiritual context is found in Basu, *Religious Revivalism as Nationalist Discourse*.

34. A. Raghuramaraju, "Universal Self, Equality and Hierarchy in Swami Vivekananda," *Indian Economic and Social History Review* 52 (2015): 185–205, confirms Vivekananda's complexity and suggests some of my concerns; Amiya Sen, *Hindu Revivalism in Bengal 1872–1905: Some Essays in Interpretation* (Oxford: Oxford University Press, 1993), 199, also underscores continuities with Ramakrishna. Chaturvedi Badrinath, *Swami Vivekananda, the Living Vedanta* (New Delhi: Penguin, 2009), 339–405; and Ashis Nandy, *The Intimate Enemy: Loss and Recovery of Self* (New Delhi: Oxford University Press, 1983), discuss issues of the "divided self." I disagree with aspects of these interpretations, but they were vital in helping me frame my response. This is also true of Jeffrey Kripal, *Kali's Child: The Mystical and Erotic in the Life and Teachings of Ramakrishna*, 2nd ed. (Chicago: University of Chicago Press, 1998), precisely because it was so controversial (see Chapter 2 for more).

35. Reba Som, *Margot: Sister Nivedita of Vivekananda* (New Delhi: Penguin India, 2017), underscores these pleasures and tensions; other biographies are cited in the text.

36. See Chapter 2.

37. Halbfass, *India and Europe*, 230–242; and see my Chapter 12.

38. Halbfass, *India and Europe*, 378–402.

39. See Banerjee, *Elementary Aspects*, 23–43.

40. See especially Gyan Prakash, *Another Reason: Science and the Imagination of Modern India* (Princeton: Princeton University Press, 1999); Luiza Savary, *Evolution, Race and Public Spheres in India* (New York: Routledge, 2019); the many other works on science will be cited throughout, especially in Chapters 7 and 8.

41. The bibliography is enormous, but was pioneered for India by Bernard S. Cohn, *Colonialism and Its Forms of Knowledge: The British in India* (Princeton: Princeton University Press, 1996).

42. Michel Foucault's work on knowledge and power was central to this trend.

43. Somak Biswas, "Passages through India: Indian Gurus, Western Disciples and the Politics of Indophilia, 1890–1940," (PhD diss, University of Warwick, 2020), 120–155.

1. Earliest Days

1. Sudhir Kakar, *The Inner World: A Psychoanalytic Study of Childhood and Society* (New Delhi: Oxford University Press, 2012), 194.

2. Richard M. Eaton, *India in the Persianate Age: 1000–1765* (Harmondsworth, UK: Penguin, 2019); Thibault d'Hubert, "Persian in the Court of the Village," in *The Persianate World: The Frontiers of a Eurasian Lingua Franca,* ed. Nile Green (Berkeley: University of California Press, 2019), 93–112.

3. Bhupendranath Datta, *Swami Vivekananda, Patriot-Prophet: A Study* (Calcutta: Nababharat Publishers, 1954), 10; Tapan Raychaudhuri, *Europe Reconsidered: Perceptions of the West in Nineteenth Century Bengal,* 2nd ed. (New Delhi: Oxford University Press, 1989), 222–223.

4. Mahendranath Gupta, *Sri Ramakrishna Kathamrita,* 5 vols. (Calcutta: Kathamrita Bhawan, 1902–1932), www.kathamrita.org/kathamrita, 4:314.

5. Swami Vivekananda, "My Plan of Campaign," Lectures from Colombo to Almora, vol. 3, *Complete Works of Swami Vivekananda,* 10 vols, https://en.wikisource.org/wiki/The_Complete_Works_of_Swami_Vivekananda (hereafter *CWSV*). His brother Bhupendranath writes at length about the family's lineage, linking it also to the Kshatriya caste: see Datta, *Swami Vivekananda, Patriot-Prophet,* 72–87.

6. Datta, *Swami Vivekananda, Patriot-Prophet,* 100–102, 106–107; Kakar, *Inner World,* 196.

7. Nikhilananda, *Vivekananda: A Biography* (Calcutta: Advaita Ashrama, 1964), 11.

8. Kakar, *Inner World,* 196; and Nikhilananda, *Vivekananda,* 9.

9. Kakar, *Inner World,* 196

10. Kakar, *Inner World,* 197, claims that Vivekananda was named Vireshwara, but that the name was changed; this is repeated in Sailendra Nath Dhar, *A Comprehensive Biography of Swami Vivekananda* (1975–6) (Chennai: Vivekananda Kendra Prakashan, 2012), 1:15.

11. Swami Vivekananda, *Swami Vivekananda on Himself* (Calcutta: Swami Vivekananda Centenary, 1959), 1.

12. Dhar, *Comprehensive Biography,* 1:15.

13. Jan Gonda, *Visnuism and Sivaism: A Comparison* (London: Bloomsbury, 2016), 3; Diana L. Eck, *Banaras, City of Light* (London: Routledge and Kegan Paul, 1983), 31–32 and 230. The Mahabharata (c. 300 BCE) describes Shiva's uniqueness: "Who else shares half his body with his wife and has been able to subjugate *kama* [lust]"; see Wendy Doniger, *The Hindus: An Alternative History* (Oxford: Oxford University Press, 2010), 393–395; and Wendy Doniger O'Flaherty, *Asceticism and Eroticism in the Mythology of Śiva* (Oxford: Oxford University Press, 1973), 172–209.

14. Swami Saradananda, *Sri Ramakrishna and His Divine Play,* trans. Swami Chetanananda (St. Louis, MO: Vedanta Society of St. Louis, 2003), 764–765 (hereafter *Divine Play*).

15. Nikhilananda, *Vivekananda,* 11. Also, Kakar, *Inner World,* 199–200; perhaps he overinterprets when he suggests that alternating adoration and punishment explains Vivekananda's later periods of elation and depression.

16. Swami Vivekananda, "Shiva in Ecstasy," Writings: Prose and Poems, vol. 8, *CWSV.* The Sanskrit motifs of skulls, matted locks, and the Ganges are common; in Vivekananda's poem; however, the "moon," normally a cooling presence, is also ablaze which suggests that even it is burning when the world is annihilated. I thank Diwakar Acharya of All Souls College, University of Oxford, for this point.

17. Mary Tappan Wright, "Vengeance of History," end of August 1893, http://www.vivekananda.net/ReminiscenesOnSwami/MaryTappanWright.html. Mary Tappan Wright was the wife of Harvard professor John Henry Wright, Vivekananda's friend. Swami Vivekananda, "From the Diary of a Disciple," XXXII, vol. 7, *CWSV.*

18. Mary Tappan Wright, "Vengeance of History."

19. See Chapters 7 and 8.

20. Nikhilananda, *Vivekananda,* 12; Vivekananda, *Vivekananda on Himself,* 4.

21. Nikhilananda, *Vivekananda*, 6. He was considered a *jaathiswar*, a type of person immortalized in Satyajit Ray's film *Sonar Kella* (1974); the film *Jaatishwar* (2014) uses this idea to underpin its romantic plot.

22. Swami Vivekananda, "Karma in Its Effect on Character," Karma-Yoga, vol. 1, *CWSV*.

23. Vivekananda, *Vivekananda on Himself*, 4.

24. Nikhilananda, *Vivekananda*, 3.

25. Nikhilananda, *Vivekananda*, 4. See Joseph S. Alter, *The Wrestler's Body: Identity and Ideology in North India* (Berkeley: University of California Press, 1992); wrestling, especially, was seen as a disciplined vocation, not too different to the discipline required of renouncers; see Chapters 3, 10, 12.

26. Joseph S. Alter, *Yoga in Modern India: The Body between Science and Philosophy* (Princeton: Princeton University Press, 2004), 142–177, takes this story into the history of Hindu nationalism.

27. Rianne Siebenga, "Colonial India's 'Fanatical Fakirs' and Their Popular Representations," *History and Anthropology* 23 (2012): 445–466. These images portray Muslim holy men but apply equally to Hindu renouncers; see Edmund Demaître, *The Yogis of India* (London: G. Bles, 1937), 30.

28. Dhar, *Comprehensive Biography*, 1:1, 34–35.

29. Nikhilananda, *Vivekananda*, 4; and Swami Gambhirananda, *Life of Swami Vivekananda by His Eastern and Western Disciples*, 6th ed. (Calcutta: Sri Gouranga Press Private Ltd., 1960), 17.

30. Maud Stumm, in *Reminiscences of Swami Vivekananda*, 3rd ed. (Calcutta: Advaita Ashrama, 1983), 270–275, https://www.ramakrishnavivekananda.info/reminiscences/263_ms.htm.

31. Quoted in Gambhirananda, *Life of Swami Vivekananda*, 16.

32. *Divine Play*, 760.

33. Nikhilananda, *Vivekananda*, 7.

34. Nikhilananda, *Vivekananda*, 5.

35. Dhar, *Comprehensive Biography*, 1:1, 39.

36. Nikhilananda, *Vivekananda*, 5.

37. *Divine Play*, 831.

38. Swami Vivekananda to Mrs. G. W. Hale, July 1, 1894, Letters–5th Series, XXIII, vol. 9, *CWSV*. For such comparisons more broadly, see Wilhelm Halbfass, *India and Europe: An Essay in Philosophical Understanding* (New Delhi: Motilal Banarsidass, 1990), 308.

39. See Torkel Brekke, *Makers of Modern Indian Religion in the Late Nineteenth Century* (Oxford: Oxford University Press, 2002), 15–28; Cheever MacKenzie Brown, *Hindu Perspectives on Evolution, Darwin, Dharma, and Design* (London: Routledge, 2012), 131–154; Swami Vivekananda, "Vedic Religious Ideals," Lectures and Discourses, vol. 1, *CWSV*.

40. Rudrangshu Mukherjee, "'Forever England': British Life in Old Calcutta," 45–51; Pritha Chowdhury and Joyoti Chaliha, "The Jews of Calcutta," 52–54; Jaya Chaliha and Bunny Gupta, "The Armenians in Calcutta," 54–55, Pradip Sinha, "Calcutta and the Currents of History, 1690–1912," 42–43, in *Calcutta: The Living City*, ed. Sukanta Chaudhuri, vol. 1: *The Past* (New Delhi: Oxford University Press, 1990).

41. See Sumit Sarkar, "Calcutta and the Bengal Renaissance," in *Calcutta: The Living City*, ed. Sukanta Chaudhuri, 1:95–105.

42. See Chapter 6.

43. The present lodge, which I visited in 2018, was built in 1904; its records display Vivekananda's name.

44. He later forged links to Madras but retained deep roots in Bengal. Tagore was Vivekananda's senior by two years; Jagadish Chandra Bose, the biophysicist, was two years younger; Aurobindo Ghose, the nationalist and philosopher, was seven years younger. Their presence at the turn of the century testifies to Calcutta's continued intellectual and political heft.

45. David Kopf, *British Orientalism and the Bengal Renaissance: The Dynamics of Indian Modernisation, 1773–1835* (Berkeley: University of California Press, 1969) remains a classic; see criticism by Sekhar Bandyopadhyay, ed., *Bengal: Rethinking History: Essays in Historiography* (New Delhi: Manohar Publishers, 2001), 26 and 140–151, 163n acknowledges the difficulty of abandoning the expression; and also see Sarkar, "Calcutta and the Bengal Renaissance," 95.

46. Dhar, *Comprehensive Biography*, 1:61–63.

47. Sumit Sarkar, "The City Imagined," in *Writing Social History*, ed. Sarkar (Oxford: Oxford University Press, 1997), 158–185; and Sarkar, "Calcutta and the Bengal Renaissance," 96.

48. Kopf, *British Orientalism and the Bengal Renaissance*, 65–126 and 215–272; and Poromesh Acharya, "Education in Old Calcutta," in *Calcutta: The Living City*, vol. 1: *The Past*, ed. Sukanta Chaudhuri (New Delhi: Oxford University Press, 1990), 85–94.

49. Acharya, "Education in Old Calcutta," 93–94.

50. See Gauri Viswanathan, *Masks of Conquest: Literary Study and British Rule in India*, 2nd ed. (New York: Columbia University Press, 2014), 47–54.

51. For the readings see Viswanathan, *Masks of Conquest*, 54, as well as the more neoclassical (eighteenth-century) works studied at the government schools.

52. Amiya Sen, "Aggressive Hinduism: Ecumenical, Evangelist and Expansive," to be published in *Colonial Hinduism*, Oxford Centre for Hindu Studies, forthcoming, cited with kind permission of the author.

53. Swami Vivekananda, "Inspired Talks," August 1, 1895, vol. 7, *CWSV*.

54. Andrew Sartori, *Bengal in Global Concept History: Culturalism in the Age of Capital* (Chicago: University Press Chicago, 2008), 78.

55. Ethical reasoning: Roy wrote *Tuhfat al-Muwahhidin* (c. 1803–1804) [*A Present to the Believers in One God*], in Persian with an Arabic preface. See Brian Hatcher, *Hinduism before Reform* (Cambridge, MA: Harvard University Press, 2020), 141; Christian missionaries: Brian Hatcher, *Bourgeois Hinduism, or Faith of the Modern Vedantists: Rare Discourses from Early Colonial Bengal* (Oxford: Oxford University Press, 2008), 22

56. Hatcher, *Bourgeois Hinduism*, 24.

57. Hatcher, *Bourgeois Hinduism*, 24.

58. His constitutionalism, however, came from Britain, Latin America, and India. See C. A. Bayly, "Rammohan Roy and the Advent of Constitutional Liberalism in India, 1800–30," *Modern Intellectual History* 4 (2007): 25–41.

59. Andrew Sartori, *Bengal in Global Concept History*, 77.

60. Lynn Zastoupil, *Rammohun Roy and the Making of Victorian Britain* (Basingstoke, UK: Palgrave Macmillan, 2010), 44 and 46; Alan D. Hodder, "Emerson, Rammohan Roy, and the Unitarians," *Studies in the American Renaissance* (1988): 133–148; and Clare Midgley, "Transoceanic Commemoration and Connections between Bengali Brahmos and British and American Unitarians," *Historical Journal* 54 (2011): 773–796. For Vivekananda's remarks on Roy, see Vivekananda, "Inspired Talks."

61. J. Barton Scott, *Spiritual Despots: Modern Hinduism and the Genealogies of Self-Rule* (Chicago: Chicago University Press, 2016), 51–54.

62. The term in Sanskrit is *brahmajnana*; according to Bhupendranath Datta, this distaste for Brahmin priests was a family tradition: Datta, *Swami Vivekananda, Patriot-Prophet*, 139; and Hatcher, *Bourgeois Hinduism*, 24–25; Halbfass, *India and Europe*, 212.

63. Lata Mani, *Contentious Traditions: The Debate on Sati in Colonial India* (Berkeley: University of California Press, 1998), 42–82; "conservatives" argued their case as "rationally" as Roy, basing it on and tradition rather than scripture.

64. Mary Louise Burke, *Swami Vivekananda in the West: New Discoveries, His Prophetic Mission*, 4th ed. (Calcutta: Advaita Ashrama, 1992), 1:3.

65. Tapan Raychaudhuri, "Love in a Colonial Climate: Marriage, Sex and Romance in Nineteenth-Century Bengal," *Modern Asian Studies* 34, no. 2 (2000): 349–378, 350–351.

66. Elizabeth de Michelis, *A History of Modern Yoga* (London: Continuum, 2004), 56; Hatcher, *Bourgeois Hinduism,* 34–48.

67. Sister Nivedita to Sara Bull, February 23, 1898, *Letters of Sister Nivedita,* collected and ed. Sankari Prasad Basu, 2 vols. (Kolkata: Advaita Ashrama, 2017), vol. 1, no. 22.

68. Amiya Sen, *Hindu Revivalism in Bengal 1872–1905: Some Essays in Interpretation* (Oxford: Oxford University Press, 1993), 28; and Hatcher, *Bourgeois Hinduism,* 35–48, for Debendranath's spiritual evolution.

69. Cited in Mackenzie Brown, *Hindu Perspectives,* 96.

70. Vivekananda, *Vivekananda on Himself,* 4.

71. MacKenzie Brown, *Hindu Perspectives,* 94.

72. MacKenzie Brown, *Hindu Perspectives,* 101. Debendranath thought of God more as a "benevolent designer" but regarded this "Supreme Spirit" as a detached witness of human action (96).

73. Debendranath regarded Victor Cousin, the founder of philosophical "eclecticism," as his "guru," and applauded Cousin's attempt to combine aspects of Scottish common-sense philosophy with Idealism; Wilhelm Halbfass, *Tradition and Reflection: Explorations in Indian Thought* (Albany: State University of New York Press, 1991), 570. For Roy and Debendranath, see Sen, *Hindu Revivalism,* 48–52.

74. For Sen's background, see Frans L. Damen, *Crisis and Religious Renewal, Documentary Study of the Emergence of the "New Dispensation" under Keshab Chandra Sen* (Leuven, Belgium: Dept. Oriëntalisktiek, Katholieke Universiteit Leuven, 1983), 46–47 and 50.

75. Partha Chatterjee, "The Nation and Its Fragments," in *The Partha Chatterjee Omnibus,* 37–75 (New Delhi: Oxford University Press, 1999), 38.

76. John Stevens, *Keshab, Bengal's Forgotten Prophet* (New York: Oxford University Press, 2019), 37. For Vivekananda's doubts about Sen, see Chapter 9.

77. Moralism: P. C. Mozoomdar, *The Life and Teachings of Keshub Chunder Sen* (Calcutta: Baptist Mission Press, 1887), 87; his religion: Mackenzie Brown, *Hindu Perspectives,* 94.

78. Datta, *Swami Vivekananda, Patriot-Prophet,* 59; and De Michelis, *A History of Modern Yoga,* 100, say his father urged him to join.

79. Shamita Basu, *Religious Revivalism as Nationalist Discourse: Swami Vivekananda and New Hinduism in Nineteenth Century Bengal* (New York: Oxford University Press, 2002), 22.

80. Stevens, *Keshab: Bengal's Forgotten Prophet,* 29.

81. Chatterjee, "The Nation and Its Fragments," 38.

82. Chatterjee, "The Nation and Its Fragments," 39; and Mozoomdar, *The Life and Teachings of Keshub Chunder Sen* (Calcutta: J. W. Thomas Baptist Mission Press, 1887), 254; and Roy Wilson Organ, *The Hindu Quest for the Perfection of Man* (Athens: Ohio University Press, 1970), 338.

83. Stevens, *Keshab: Bengal's Forgotten Prophet,* 129.

84. Chatterjee, "The Nation and Its Fragments," 37–54, especially 39.

85. Datta, *Swami Vivekananda, Patriot-Prophet,* quoted on 174–175.

86. Datta, *Swami Vivekananda, Patriot-Prophet,* 62.

87. Mozoomdar, *Life and Teachings of Keshub Chunder Sen,* 124.

88. Rabindranath Tagore, "The Religion of My Father," in *Religion and Rabindranath Tagore: Select Discourses, Addresses, and Letters in Translation,* ed. Amiya Sen (New Delhi: Oxford University Press, 2014), 201. Contrary to Rabindranath's view, Sen may well have been building on his father's Shaktism and his mother's Vaishnavism.

89. Manilal Parekh, *Brahmarshi Kesub Chunder Sen* (Calcutta: Oriental Christ House, 1926), 74; his son, Rabindranath said, "It was not at all improbable that my father did not pay due respect to the Paramahamsa," in Tagore, "The Religion of My Father," 200.

90. Gambhirananda, *Life of Swami Vivekananda,* 30.

91. Vivekananda, *Vivekananda on Himself,* 23.

92. Chatterjee, 'The Nation and Its Fragments," 50. Ramakrishna may have acquired his view of Calcutta's spiritual disarray from Sen.

93. Cited in Chatterjee, "The Nation and Its Fragments," 40.

94. Mackenzie Brown, *Hindu Perspectives.* Their views had different emphases, however; see 103–116. Keshub Chunder Sen, *Lectures in India* (London: Cassell, 1901–1904), 1:12–14; see Chapter 9.

95. Damen, *Crisis and Religious Renewal.*

96. Sen, "Aggressive Hinduism."

97. Swami Vivekananda to Mrs. G. W. Hale, September 27, 1894, Letters–5th Series, XXXVII, vol. 9, *CWSV;* and Swami Vivekananda, "Indian Missionary's Mission in London," *The Echo,* London, 1896, Interviews, vol. 5, *CWSV.*

98. They belonged to the *bhadralok,* a term used to describe Bengali "gentlefolk." I have not used this term because, for many Indians, it is associated with an ill-defined elitism.

99. See Chapter 2.

100. This is mentioned in Rajagopal Chattopadhyaya, *Swami Vivekananda in India: A Corrective Biography* (New Delhi: Motilal Banarsidass, 1999), 28; *Divine Play,* 778n2.

101. Varuni Bhatia, *Unforgetting Chaitanya: Vaishnavism and Cultures of Devotion in Colonial Bengal* (New York: Oxford University Press, 2017), 41.

102. Datta, *Swami Vivekananda, Patriot-Prophet,* 173.

103. William Wordsworth, *The Excursion, a Poem* (London: Edward Moxon, 1858), 119.

104. Lisa Hirschfield, "Between Memory and History: Wordsworth's Excursion," *Romanticism on the Net,* no. 16 (1999); for "trance" in the poem, see "Book First: The Wanderer," *The Excursion,* in *The Poetical Works of William Wordsworth,* vol. 5: *The Excursion; The Recluse,* ed. Ernest de Selincourt and Helen Darbishire (Oxford: Oxford University Press, 1959), 1, page 34, line 784. Hastie's letters are published in *Hindu Idolatry and the Enlightened Englishman* (Calcutta: Thacker, Spink and Co.; Edinburgh: David Douglas, 1882).

105. Bankim Chandra Chatterjee, "The Modern St. Paul," *The Statesman,* October 6, 1882, reproduced in *Essays and Letters: Bankim Chandra Chatterjee,* ed. Sajanīkānta Dāsa (Calcutta, 1940), 92; Amiya Sen, *Bankim Chandra Chattopadhya* (New Delhi: Oxford University Press, 2008), 75–92.

106. *Divine Play,* 755.

2. Ramakrishna

1. See Sumit Sarkar, "Kaliyuga, Chakri and Bhakti," *Writing Social History* (New Delhi: Oxford University Press, 1997), especially 290–292.

2. Swami Saradananda, *Sri Ramakrishna and His Divine Play,* trans. Swami Chetanananda (St. Louis, MO: Vedanta Society of St. Louis, 2003), 81–89 (hereafter *Divine Play*).

3. Sarkar, "Kaliyuga, Chakri and Bhakti," *Writing Social History,* 292. *Divine Play* explains how his father refused to testify falsely despite pressure to do so.

4. Partha Chatterjee, "The Nation and Its Fragments: The Nationalist Elite," in *The Partha Chatterjee Omnibus,* 37–75 (New Delhi: Oxford University Press, 1999), 48.

5. All humans are meant to have Vishnu in their heart; see Steven M. Parish, *Moral Knowing in a Hindu Sacred City: An Exploration of Mind, Emotion, and Self* (New York: Columbia University Press, 1994), 41, 83–84.

6. *Divine Play,* 105. A closer translation is "was emanating from the beautiful body of Mahadeva (Shiva)," Swami Saradananda, *Sri Sri Ramakrishna Lilaprasanga,* 2 vols. (1960); Kolkata: Udbodhan, 2021), 1:34, 107 (hereafter *Lilaprasanga*).

7. Shaligrams brought together the subcontinent's "sacred geography" a "naturalized" history and geology. See Pratik Chakrabarti, *Inscriptions of Nature: Geology and the Naturalization of*

Antiquity (Baltimore, MD: Johns Hopkins University Press, 2020), 101–109; Narasingha Sil emphasizes these Vaishnava connections in "Kali's Child and Krishna's Lover: An Anatomy of Ramakrishna's *Caritas Divina*," *Religion* 39 (2009): 289–298.

8. *Divine Play*, 131, speaks of how he memorized epic stories and musical narratives.

9. See John Zubrzycki, *Empire of Enchantment: The Story of Indian Magic* (London: Hurst, 2018), 52, for yogis' extraordinary powers.

10. Romain Rolland, *The Life of Ramakrishna*, trans. E. F. Malcolm-Smith (Mayavati: Advaita Ashrama, 1947), 25, 56, 242, 325, 327.

11. *Divine Play*, 121.

12. *Divine Play*, 121. See the quotation, for example, in Romain Rolland, *Life of Ramakrishna*, 25, which is reiterated in Sudhir Kakar, *The Analyst and the Mystic: Psychoanalytic Reflections on Religion and Mysticism* (New Delhi: Penguin Books, 1991), 10.

13. *Divine Play*, 126.

14. *Divine Play*, 130. This was called a "bhava samadhi," or a state of ecstatic consciousness.

15. Sarkar, "Kaliyuga, Chakri and Bhakti," *Writing Social History*, 292; *Divine Play*, 130.

16. See Edward Dimock and Tony K. Stewart, eds., *Caitanya Caritāmrta of Kṛṣṇadāsa Kavirāja: A Translation and Commentary* (Cambridge, MA: Dept. of Sanskrit and Indian Studies, Harvard University, 1999), 103. Radha-Krishna were the combined natures of the feminine and masculine aspects of God. See John Hawley and Donna Marie Wulff, eds., *The Divine Consort: Radha and the Goddesses of India* (Berkeley: University of California Press, 1982), especially the chapters of Barbara Stoler Miller, "The Divine Duality of Radha and Krishna," 13–26, and Donna Marie Wulf, "A Sanskrit Portrait: Radha in the Plays of Rupa Gosvami," 27–28. See also David Pocock, *Mind, Body, and Wealth: A Study of Belief and Practice in an Indian Village* (Oxford: Basil Blackwell, 1973), which describes grizzled peasants singing of themselves as cowgirls.

17. Swami Vivekananda to Shashi, August 23, 1896, Epistles–2nd Series, CVI, vol. 6, *Complete Works of Swami Vivekananda*, 10 vols., https://en.wikisource.org/wiki/The_Complete_Works _of_Swami_Vivekananda (hereafter *CWSV*); here, he defends female sex workers who come to the Ramakrishna anniversary festival in Dakshineswar.

18. *Divine Play*, 183.

19. Chitra Deb, "The 'Great Houses' of Old Calcutta," in *Calcutta, The Living City*, ed. Sukanta Chaudhuri, vol. 1: *The Past* (New Delhi: Oxford University Press, 1990), 61.

20. The food offering is called *prasad*; *Divine Play*, 186.

21. *Divine Play*, 183; and Elizabeth U. Harding, *Kali: The Black Goddess of Dakshineswar* (Carlsbad, CA: Nicolas-Hays, 1993), 22–23, 30–31.

22. *Divine Play*, 192; *Lilaprasanga* 1:46. The original uses two Sanskritic terms: *ashudraya-jitva* (not to officiate for Sudras) and *apratigrahitva* (to decline or not receive gifts from anyone).

23. Mahendranath Gupta, *Sri Ramakrishna Kathamrita*, 5 vols. (Calcutta: Kathamrita Bhawan, 1902–1932), www.kathamrita.org/kathamrita, 2:4 (hereafter *Kathamrita*).

24. Swami Vivekananda, "My Master," Lectures and Discourses, vol. 4, *CWSV*. See also C. J. Fuller, "Gods, Priests and Purity: On the Relation between Hinduism and the Caste System," *Man* 14, no. 3 (1979): 459–476; David N. Gellner, "Living with Polytropy and Hierarchy: The Anthropology of Hinduism," in S. Coleman and J. Robbins eds., *The Oxford Handbook of the Anthropology of Religion* (Oxford: Oxford University Press, forthcoming 2022).

25. "Story of Rasik," available at the website for the Educational and Cultural Wing of Sri Sarada Math, http://srisaradamathrb.org/story-of-rasik/. The author has visited Sri Sarada Math-Rasik Bhita in Dakshineswar where this story is told.

26. Harding, *Kali: The Black Goddess*, 52.

27. See Rachel Fell McDermott and Jeffrey J. Kripal, eds., *Encountering Kali: In the Margins, at the Centre in the West* (New Delhi: Motilal Banarsidass, 2005).

28. David Kingsley, *Hindu Goddesses: Visions of the Divine Feminine in the Hindu Religious Tradition* (Berkeley: University of California Press, 1988), 95–115; Julius Lipner, *Hindus: Their Religious Beliefs and Practices,* 2nd ed. (London: Routledge and Kegan Paul, 2010), 321, who describes Kali and Shiva as the "energizing" force of the Hindu cosmos.

29. *Divine Play,* 209.

30. *Kathamrita,* 2:3.

31. P. J. Mazumdar, "Shree Ramakrishna Paramahamsa—Timeline," Advaita Vedanta and Yoga Philosophy website, http://www.advaitayoga.org/advaitayogaarticles/ramakrishnaparamahamsa timeline.html. This is the term used to describe what happens to him in 1856: "thrusting aside," *Divine Play* 236.

32. *Divine Play,* 236.

33. *Divine Play,* 236.

34. See Nikhilananda, *Vivekananda: A Biography* (Calcutta: Advaita Ashrama, 1964), 15. The concept of "beholding" is expertly analyzed in Diana Eck, *Darśan: Seeing the Divine Image in India,* 3rd ed. (New York: Columbia University Press, 1999), especially 3–10.

35. Rolland, *Life of Ramakrishna,* 39.

36. *Divine Play,* 212.

37. *Divine Play,* 216.

38. *Divine Play,* 217. He was also following Ramprasad Sen, who was similarly besotted with Shyama, imagining Kali as a sixteen-year-old maiden.

39. "Ramachandra" is the preferred name of the hero of the Ramayana, but to be consistent I have used "Rama" throughout this work.

40. *Divine Play,* 228, recounts that the end of his spine had lengthened "nearly an inch" (232).

41. The International Society for Krishna Consciousness (Ishkon).

42. Lucian Wong and Ferdinando Sardella, eds., *The Legacy of Vaisnavism in Colonial Bengal* (London: Routledge, 2020), 2–3.

43. *Divine Play,* 820.

44. *Kathamrita,* 2:197 and 207.

45. Varuni Bhatia, *Unforgetting Chaitanya: Vaishnavism and Cultures of Devotion in Colonial Bengal* (New York: Oxford University Press, 2017), 1–20; Amiya P. Sen, "Chaitanya Mahaprabhu: A Relook at the Saint and Reformer," Sahapedia, August 20, 2019, https://www.sahapedia .org/chaitanya-mahaprabhu-relook-saint-and-reformer. Sen suggests that this characterization of Chaitanya may be an invention of the nineteenth century, and a controversial one.

46. *Divine Play,* 220; *Lilaprasanga* 1:73: "A very dark-bodied and terrible looking man with blood-shot eyes."

47. *Divine Play,* 248.

48. See Chapter 3.

49. She seems to have been important in teaching trance states; see Michael Comans, "The Question of the Importance of Samādhi in Modern and Classical Advaita Vedānta," *Philosophy East and West* 43, no. 1 (1993): 19–38, 33n3.

50. David Gordon White, *The Alchemical Body: Siddha Traditions in Medieval India* (Chicago: University of Chicago Press, 1997), 1; Walter G. Neevel, "The Transformation of Sri Ramakrishna," in *Hinduism: New Essays in the History of Religions,* ed. Bardwell L. Smith, 53–97 (Leiden: E. J. Brill, 1976), 75–78.

51. Lipner, *Hindus: Their Religious Beliefs and Practices,* 325.

52. *Divine Play,* 263; this English translation does not explain that she was "undressed"; Lilaprasanga 1:116.

53. *Divine Play,* 265. This was considered "right-handed Tantra," in which symbolic thought was deemed sufficient.

54. *Divine Play,* 265.

55. *Divine Play*, 261.

56. *Kathamrita*, 5:314, Gupta partially reproduces Vivekananda's speech against Tantra.

57. Neevel, "Transformation of Sri Ramakrishna," 78.

58. Sarkar, "Kaliyuga, Chakri and Bhakti, *Writing Social History*, 316–317.

59. *Divine Play*, 272; these were the "five standard *bhavas* (moods)" typical of the Gaudiya Vaishnava tradition, which particularly suited him. Sarkar, "Kaliyuga, Chakri and Bhakti," *Writing Social History*, 316–317.

60. Radha "state": Dimock and Stewart, eds., *Caitanya Caritāmrta*, 103; frenzy: Kingsley, *Hindu Goddesses*, 81–94; T. M. Madan, "Hinduism: The Anthropology of a Civilization," in *The Hindu Omnibus*, 283–293 (New Delhi: Oxford University Press, 2003), describes Chaitanya as a "character of demonic passion and Dionysiac frenzy" (283).

61. *Divine Play*, 297; the blood came from the *swadhisthana chakra*, the term used in both the Bengali and English editions and refers to the sacral circle said often to be blocked by fear.

62. *Divine Play*, 301.

63. *Divine Play*, 289.

64. *Kathamrita*, 1:179

65. This is part of an older Vaishnava tradition; see Madan, "The Anthropology of a Civilization," 281–282.

66. *Kathamrita*, 4:6.

67. Neevel, "Transformation of Sri Ramakrishna," esp. 73, emphasizes Ramakrishna's vision of the Deity as feminine.

68. *Divine Play*, 408; *Lilaprasanga*, 1:21. He referred to the "self-aware atman"; the atman is considered sexless, but this is an inference.

69. See Jeffrey Kripal, *Kali's Child* (Chicago: University of Chicago Press, 1998), and the response, Swami Tyagananda and Pravrajika Vrajaprana, *Interpreting Ramakrishna: Kali's Child Revisited* (New Delhi: Motilal Banarsidass, 2010); more specific references will be cited in the text. For a different psychoanalytic vision of Ramakrishna, see Kakar, *The Analyst and the Mystic*.

70. See Michel Foucault, *History of Sexuality*, vol. 1: *An Introduction* (Harmondsworth, UK: Allen Lane, 1979); Birgit Land, Joy Damousi, and Alison Lewis, *A History of the Case Study: Sexology, Psychoanalysis, Literature* (Manchester: Manchester University Press, 2017); Florence Tamagne, *History of Homosexuality in Europe, Berlin, London, Paris, 1919–1939* (New York: Algora, 2004); Vernon A. Rosario, *Science and Homosexualities* (London: Routledge, 1997); Jennifer Terry, *An American Obsession: Science, Medicine, and Homosexuality in Modern Society* (Chicago: University of Chicago Press, 1999); Christopher E. Forth, *Masculinity in the Modern West: Gender, Civilization and the Body* (Basingstoke, UK: Palgrave Macmillan, 2008).

71. See Chapter 8.

72. Bhatia, *Unforgetting Chaitanya*, 41.

73. When Vivekananda arrived in India in 1897, the first civic reception was organized by the Raja of Shovabazar, whose family had earlier been famous for its Vaishnavism. Sen's family had also been involved; see John Stevens, *Keshab, Bengal's Forgotten Prophet* (New York: Oxford University Press, 2019), 27.

74. Bhatia, *Unforgetting Chaitanya*, 26.

75. Bhatia, *Unforgetting Chaitanya*, 43. See also Jeanne Openshaw, "The Radicalism of Tagore and the Bauls of Bengal," *South Asia Research* 17, no. 1 (1997): 20–36.

76. See Varuni Bhatia, "The Afterlife of an *Avatara* in Modern Times," 17–32; and Amiya P. Sen, "Theorising Bengal Vaisnaivsm: Bipin Chandra Pal and New Perspectives on Religious Life and Culture," 33–56; both in *The Legacy of Vaisnavism in Colonial Bengal*, ed. Ferdinando Sardella and Lucian Wong, vol. 1 (London: Routledge, 2019); and Lucian Wong, "Universalising Inclusivism—and

Its Limits: Bhaktivinod and the Experiential Turn," *Journal of South Asian Intellectual History* 1, no. 2 (2018): 221–263.

77. *Kathamrita*, 1:36–37.

78. *Kathamrita*, 1:382.

79. See Edwin F. Bryant, "*Samadhi* in the *Yoga Sutras*," in *Asian Traditions of Meditation*, ed. Halvor Eifring (Honolulu: University of Hawai'i Press, 2016), 48–70.

80. *Divine Play*, 312.

81. *Divine Play*, 312.

82. *Divine Play*, 312.

83. *Kathamrita*, 1:136.

84. *Kathamrita*, 1:318.

85. Shamita Basu, *Religious Revivalism as Nationalist Discourse: Swami Vivekananda and New Hinduism in Nineteenth-Century Bengal* (New York: Oxford University Press, 2002), 77.

86. *Divine Play*, 319.

87. *Divine Play*, 319.

88. *Divine Play*, 357.

89. *Divine Play*, 358.

90. Swapna Banerjee, "Everyday Emotional Practices of Fathers and Children in Late Colonial Bengal India," in *Childhood, Youth and Emotions in Modern History: National, Colonial and Global Perspectives*, ed. Stephanie Olsen (Basingstoke, UK: Palgrave Macmillan, 2015), 139–157.

91. *Kathamrita*, 5:215.

92. *Kathamrita*, 1:87.

93. Brahmo convert: For earlier drafts, see Swami Chetanananda, *Mahendranath Gupta: The Recorder of the Gospel of Sri Ramakrishna* (Kolkata: Advaita Ashrama, 2011), 221–288; subcaste: see Bandyopādhyāÿa, *Śekhara Caste Culture and Hegemony: Social Dominance in Colonial Bengal* (New Delhi: Sage, 2004), 111 (they also resisted widow remarriage) and 148.

94. *Kathamrita*, 1:485.

95. *Kathamrita*, 1:496.

96. Swami Nikhilananda, ed., *The Gospel of Ramakrishna*, with a foreword by Aldous Huxley (New York: Ramakrishna-Vivekananda Center, 1942). Margaret Wilson, the daughter of Woodrow Wilson, prepared the text. Nikhilananda claimed it as a "literal translation" but excised the bawdier elements and reframed the five narratives into one.

97. Sumit Sarkar, "Kaliyuga, Chakri and Bhakti," *Writing Social History*, 286–287.

98. Chatterjee, *The Nation and Its Fragments*, 51–55.

99. Amiya Sen, "Sri Ramakrishna, the *Kathamrita* and the Calcutta Middle Classes: An Old Problematic Revisited," *Postcolonial Studies* 9, no. 2 (2006): 165–177, 172–173, especially.

100. Basu, *Religious Revivalism*, 33.

101. Offerings: *Kathamrita*, 5:17.

102. *Kathamrita*, 1:190.

103. *Kathamrita*, 1:447.

104. *Kathamrita*, 1:447.

105. Sarkar, "Kaliyuga, Chakri and Bhakti," *Writing Social History*, 282–357.

106. "A clerk is jailed": *Kathamrita*, 4: 187; "even when set free": see Sumit Sarkar," Kaliyuga, Chakri and Bhakti," *Writing Social History*, 168. See also Chapter 3 in this volume.

107. *Kathamrita*, 1:37.

108. *Kathamrita*, 1:228.

109. Dipesh Chakrabarty, *Provincializing Europe: Postcolonial Thought and Historical Difference*, new ed. (Princeton: Princeton University Press, 2009), 219–223.

110. Chakrabarty, *Provincializing Europe*, 224.

111. *Kathamrita*, 2:120.

112. *Kathamrita*, 2:117.

113. *Kathamrita*, 1:242.

114. *Kathamrita*, 1:261.

115. *Kathamrita*, 1:92.

116. *Kathamrita*, 1:92.

117. *Kathamrita*, 1:40.

118. *Kathamrita*, 4:54.

119. *Kathamrita*, 1:128.

120. *Kathamrita*, 1:199.

121. *Kathamrita*, 1:277.

122. *Kathamrita*, 2:87.

123. *Kathamrita*, 3:39.

124. *Divine Play*, 29.

125. Swami Chetanananda, *Sri Sarada Devi and Her Divine Play* (St. Louis, MO: Vedanta Society of St. Louis, 2015), 46.

126. Lina Fruzzetti, *The Gift of a Virgin: Women, Marriage, and Ritual in a Bengali Society* (New Brunswick, NJ: Rutgers University Press, 1982).

127. *Her Divine Play*, 60.

128. *Kathamrita*, 2:276.

129. Chetanananda, *Sri Sarada Devi and Her Divine Play*, 62. In Tantric teaching, Kali has ten incarnations.

130. Lipner, *Hindus: Their Religious Beliefs and Practices*, 325.

131. *Her Divine Play*, 65.

132. Swami Gambhirananda, *Holy Mother: Sri Sarada Devi* (Mylapore: Advaita Ashrama, 1955), 51.

133. *Her Divine Play*, 68.

134. Swami Purnatmananda, ed., *Reminiscences of Sri Sarada Devi by Monastics, Devotees and Others*, trans. Maloti Sen Gupta (Kolkata: Advaita Ashrama, 2004), 14; the story is repeated with slight differences in Chetanananda, *Sri Sarada Devi and Her Divine Play*, 60.

135. *Sri Sarada Devi: A Biography in Pictures* (Kolkata: Advaita Ashrama, 2010), 22.

136. *Her Divine Play*, 68.

137. *Sri Sarada Devi: A Biography in Pictures*, 22.

138. The name of the man was Shambu Mallick; Chetanananda, *Sri Sarada Devi and Her Divine Play*, 70.

139. See Chapter 15.

140. *Kathamrita*, 1:73.

141. See Sanjukta Kupta, "The Domestication of a Goddess," 60–79; and Usha Menon and Richard A. Shweder, "Dominating Kali," 80–99; both in McDermott and Kripal, *Encountering Kali*.

142. *Kathamrita*, 1:73.

143. *Kathamrita*, 1:74. Translation altered slightly by Somak Biswas.

144. *Kathamrita*, 1:41, 106; Jyotirmaya Sharma, *A Restatement of Religion: Swami Vivekananda and the Making of Hindu Nationalism* (New Haven, CT: Yale University Press, 2013), 50–58.

145. *Kathamrita*, 3:106–108.

146. *Kathamrita*, 3:280.

147. *Kathamrita*, 2, 237.

148. *Kathamrita*, 2:236–237.

149. *Kathamrita*, 2:249.

150. *Kathamrita*, 2:236.

151. *Kathamrita*, 2:236.

152. *Kathamrita*, 2:237.

153. *Kathamrita*, 1:381.

154. *Kathamrita*, 2:172. Did the doll's house represent the materialism of domesticity, suggested in the description of the British houses mentioned earlier? Was Gupta aware of Ibsen's 1879 play, repeatedly performed across the globe and endlessly reinterpreted, but always focused on Nora's destruction of her "gilded cage"? These are questions that cannot be answered, though the closeness in time frame suggests tantalizing possibilities, especially because of Girish Gosh's theatrical connections.

155. *Kathamrita*, 3:343.

156. *Kathamrita*, 1:225.

157. *Kathamrita*, 3:343.

158. Donald Winnicott, "Ego Distortion in Terms of True and False Self" (1960), in *The Maturational Process and the Facilitating Environment: Studies in the Theory of Emotional Development*, 150–152 (London: Hogarth, 1965; repr. Routledge, 2018); Donald Winnicott, *Playing and Reality* (London: Routledge, 1971), 53–64; Adam Phillips, *Winnicott* (Cambridge, MA: Harvard University Press, 1988), 139, 142–144.

159. Ramakrishna sometimes depicted the "yogi" as "beyond good and '"evil."'" *Kathamrita* 1:208, records this dialogue: Neighbour: "So, there is no sin and no virtue?" Sri Ramakrishna: "They are, and yet are not. If God keeps the ego in you, He also keeps your sense of differentiation and the knowledge of virtuous and sinful acts. However, in a few, God completely erases the sense of I-consciousness. Such people go beyond virtue and vice, good and bad."

160. Chakrabarty, *Provincializing Europe*, 216–217.

161. *Divine Play*, 827; although having long possessed supernatural powers, he was unable even to "keep a wearing-cloth tied around [his] . . . waist!"

3. Ramakrishna and Vivekananda

1. See Chapter 6.

2. See Chapter 12.

3. Shinjini Das, "An Imperial Apostle? St. Paul, Protestant Conversion, and South Asian Christianity," *Historical Journal* 61 (2017): 103–130; Vivekananda referred to the Christian apostle, but never equated himself with St. Paul while abroad.

4. "The biceps and the Gita": Swami Vivekananda, "Vedanta and Its Application to Indian Life," Lectures from Colombo to Almora [1897], vol. 3, *Complete Works of Swami Vivekananda*, 10 vols., https://en.wikisource.org/wiki/The_Complete_Works_of_Swami_Vivekananda (hereafter *CWSV*); Ramakrishna unequivocally stated: Mahendranath Gupta, *Sri Ramakrishna Kathamrita*, 5 vols. (Calcutta: Kathamrita Bhawan, 1902–1932), www.kathamrita.org/kathamrita, 3:301 (hereafter *Kathamrita*).

5. *Kathamrita*, 2:87.

6. Swami Saradananda, *Sri Ramakrishna and His Divine Play*, trans. Swami Chetanananda (St. Louis, MO: Vedanta Society of St. Louis, 2003), 755 (hereafter *Divine Play*).

7. *Divine Play*, 755.

8. *Divine Play*, 758.

9. Here again is the notion of darshan.

10. *Divine Play*, 771.

11. *Divine Play*, 771.

12. *Divine Play*, 773.

13. Analayo, *Buddhapada and the Bodhisattva Path* (Freiburg: Projektverlag, 2017), 27.

14. *Divine Play*, 777.

15. *Divine Play*, 774.

16. Hans Torwesten, *Ramakrishna and Christ or the Paradox of the Incarnation*, trans. John Phillips (Kolkata: Ramakrishna Mission Institute of Culture, 1999), 132. See also Chapter 4 on the parts of Sita's body brought down to earth.

17. *Divine Play*, 756–757; Swami Saradananda, *Sri Sri Ramakrishna Lilaprasanga*, 2 vols. (Kolkata: 2021), 2, 34. (hereafter *Lilaprasanga*). The Bengali does not have the word "child," but the colloquial address suggests affection.

18. This is called *viraha* in Hinduism.

19. "Narayana Himself": Eknath Easwaren, *Thousand Names of Vishnu* (Mumbai: Jaico Publishing House, 2003), 28; "What love!": *Kathamrita*, 1:374.

20. See Michael Benamou and Charles Carmello, eds., *Performance in Postmodern Culture* (Milwaukee: Center for Twentieth Century Studies, University of Wisconsin–Milwaukee, 1977).

21. *Kathamrita*, 1:252.

22. Sailendra Nath Dhar, *A Comprehensive Biography of Swami Vivekananda* (1975–1976) (Chennai: Vivekananda Kendra Prakashan, 2012), 1:57.

23. Partha Chatterjee, *The Nation and Its Fragments*, in *Partha Chatterjee Omnibus*, 37–75 (New Delhi: Oxford University Press, 1999), 39.

24. *Kathamrita*, 4:241.

25. *Kathamrita*, 1:53.

26. *Kathamrita*, 1:178.

27. Rachel Fell McDermott, "Bengali Songs to Kali," in *Religions of India in Practice*, ed. Donald S. Lopez Jr. (Princeton: Princeton University Press, 1995), 55–76; and Rachel Fell McDermott, *Revelry, Rivalry and Longing for the Goddesses of Bengal: The Fortunes of Hindu Festivals* (New York: Columbia University Press, 2011), 41–76. See also Guy L. Beck, "Sacred Music and Hindu Religious Experience: From Ancient Roots to the Modern Classical Tradition," *Religions* 10, no. 2 (2019), 85.

28. *Divine Play*, 784.

29. *Kathamrita*, 2:368.

30. *Kathamrita*, 2:369.

31. *Kathamrita*, 3:302. See May 9, 1885.

32. *Divine Play*, 792.

33. *Kathamrita*, 3:300.

34. *Kathamrita*, 1:182. I thank Somak Biswas for altering the text slightly and for explaining the Bengali word *ga*, which has no English equivalent. It is a familiar term for "near ones" but does not mean "brother" as listed on the website Kathamrita.org.

35. *Divine Play*, 799.

36. *Divine Play*, 802.

37. Swami Vivekananda, *Swami Vivekananda on Himself* (Calcutta: Swami Vivekananda Centenary, 1959), 25.

38. *Divine Play*, 795.

39. *Divine Play*, 796.

40. *Divine Play*, 796.

41. *Divine Play*, 845.

42. *Divine Play*, 844, *Lilaprasanga*, 2:124: "I see—this is me, and that too is me; really I can observe no difference. Like when you put a stick in the Ganges making the water split into two parts—but in truth there is no split, there is only one."

43. *Divine Play*, 840. *Lilaprasanga*, 2:118: "associating with immoral people and visiting prostitute houses."

44. *Divine Play*, 841.

45. See Chapter 14.

46. Sister Nivedita, *The Master as I Saw Him*, in *The Complete Works of Sister Nivedita*, ed. Pravrajika Atmapranam, 2nd ed., 5 vols. (Kolkata: Advaita Ashrama, 2016), 1:121.

47. *Divine Play,* 854.

48. See "Swami on Ramakrishna," Vivekananda.net, https://www.vivekananda.net.

49. "Swami on Ramakrishna."

50. "Swami on Ramakrishna."

51. Juliet Mitchell, *Siblings: Sex and Violence* (Cambridge: Polity Press, 2003), 1–31.

52. See Alan Roland, *In Search of Self in India and Japan: Toward a Cross-Cultural Psychology* (Princeton: Princeton University Press, 1988), esp. 209–241. This is the thrust of much of Sudhir Kakar, *The Inner World: A Psychoanalytic Study of Childhood and Society* (New Delhi: Oxford University Press, 2012).

53. These questions are explored in David Arnold and Stuart Blackburn, *Telling Lives in India: Biography, Autobiography, and Life History* (Bloomington: Indiana University Press, 2004). Chakrabarty speaks of the differing kind of "family romance" in Bengal in Dipesh Chakrabarty, *Provincializing Europe: Postcolonial Thought and Historical Difference,* new ed. (Princeton: Princeton University Press, 2009), esp. 117–139 and 214–236.

54. Swami Gambhirananda, ed., *The Apostles of Shri Ramakrishna* (Calcutta: Advaita Ashram, 1982), 205.

55. For the woes of itinerancy see Chapter 4.

56. Quoted in Swami Chetanananda, *How a Shepherd Boy Became a Saint* (St. Louis, MO: Vedanta Society of St. Louis, 2015), 28.

57. Swami Annadananda, *Swami Akhandananda: An Apostle of Sri Ramakrishna,* trans. Shri Narayan Chandra Bhattacharya (Calcutta: Advaita Ashrama, 1993), 25.

58. Chetanananda, *How a Shepherd Boy,* 13.

59. Chetanananda, *How a Shepherd Boy,* 16–17.

60. Gambhirananda, *The Apostles of Shri Ramakrishna,* 206.

61. Swami Aseshananda, *Glimpses of a Great Soul: A Portrait of Swami Saradananda* (Chennai: Sri Ramakrishna Math, 1982), 17–19.

62. Gambhirananda, *The Apostles of Shri Ramakrishna,* 177.

63. Swami Yatiswarananda and Swami Prabhavananda, *The Eternal Companion: Life and Teachings of Swami Brahmananda,* rev. ed. (Chennai: Sri Ramakrishna Mission, 2016), 25.

64. *Swami Ramakrishnananda, as We Saw Him: Reminiscences of Monastic and Lay Devotees* (Chennai: Sri Ramakrishna Math, 2012), 9.

65. Sondra L. Hausner, *Sadhus: Ascetics in the Hindu Himalayas* (Bloomington: Indiana University Press, 2007), 55–57.

66. Swami Aseshananda, *Glimpses of a Great Soul: A Portrait of Swami Saradananda* (St. Louis: Vedanta Society of St. Louis, 1982), 19; and Swami Chetanananda, *God Lived with Them: Life Stories of Sixteen Monastic Disciples of Sri Ramakrishna* (St. Louis: Vedanta Society of St. Louis, 1997), 519.

67. Annadananda, *Swami Akhandananda,* 28.

68. *Divine Play,* 854.

69. *Divine Play,* 900.

70. Nikhilananda, *Vivekananda: A Biography* (Calcutta: Advaita Ashrama, 1964), 36.

71. Ashis Nandy also examines Brahmo disdain for the "intricate web of ceremony and form" (16): Ashis Nandy, "Sati: A Nineteenth-Century Tale of Women, Violence, and Protest," in *At the Edge of Psychology* (Oxford: Oxford University Press, 1980), 1–32. I am grateful to Sudipta Sen of the History Department, University of California, Davis, for this point.

4. Vivekananda and His Travels

1. For such "lateral connections," see Juliet Mitchell, *Siblings: Sex and Violence* (London: Polity, 2003), 31.

2. Diana L. Eck, *India: A Sacred Geography* (New York: Three Rivers Press, 2012), 1–42.

3. Sister Nivedita, The Master as I Saw Him, in *The Complete Works of Sister Nivedita*, ed. Pravrajika Atmapranam, 2nd ed., 5 vols. (Kolkata: Advaita Ashrama, 2016), 1:63 (hereafter *CWSN*).

4. Prathama Banerjee, *Elementary Aspects of the Political: Histories from the Global South* (Durham, NC: Duke University Press, 2020), 36–39.

5. Rajagopal Chattopadhyaya, *Swami Vivekananda in India: A Corrective Biography* (New Delhi: Motilal Banarsidass, 1999), 83, recounts that as early as 1888 he was set on the "regeneration of my motherland," a report which suggests how difficult it is to assess these retrospective remarks.

6. Jung Hyun Kim, "Rethinking Vivekananda through Space and Territorialised Spirituality, c. 1880–1920" (PhD diss., University of Cambridge, History Faculty, 2017), 42.

7. Swami Vivekananda to Pramadadas Mitra, December 30, 1889, Epistles–2nd Series, XIV, vol. 6, *Complete Works of Swami Vivekananda*, 10 vols., https://en.wikisource.org/wiki/The _Complete_Works_of_Swami_Vivekananda (hereafter *CWSV*).

8. Rent: Nikhilananda, *Vivekananda: A Biography* (Calcutta: Advaita Ashrama, 1964), 81; cook's pay: Mahendranath Gupta, *Sri Ramakrishna Kathamrita*, 5 vols. (Calcutta: Kathamrita Bhawan, 1902–1932), www.kathamrita.org/kathamrita, vol. 2, 442 (hereafter *Kathamrita*).

9. *Kathamrita*, 2:443.

10. *Kathamrita*, 2:457.

11. Swami Mumukshananda, "The Genesis of the Ramakrishna Mission," in *The Story of Ramakrishna Mission: Swami Vivekananda's Vision and Fulfilment*, ed. Swami Prabhananada (Kolkata: Advaita Ashrama, 2006), 224. In this telling, it was "a huge fire of logs."

12. Swami Gambhirananda, ed., *The Apostles of Shri Ramakrishna* (Calcutta: Advaita Ashram, 1982), 30.

13. See Chapter 3.

14. Nikhilananda, *Vivekananda*, 83.

15. Sondra L. Hausner, *Wandering with Sadhus: Ascetics in the Hindu Himalayas* (Bloomington: Indiana University Press, 2007), 64–65.

16. See Shyamali Chowdhury, *Chronological Account of the Events in the Parivrajaka Life of Swami Vivekananda (July 1890–May 1893)* (Kolkata: Ramakrishna Mission Institute of Culture, 2015), 135–187 (hereafter Chowdhury, *Parivrajaka Life*).

17. For example, Vivekananda, Turiyananda, Saradananda, and others lived together in the neighborhood of Hrishikish. See Swami Yatiswarananda and Swami Prabhavananda, *The Eternal Companion: Life and Teachings of Swami Brahmananda*, rev. ed. (Chennai: Sri Ramakrishna Mission, 2016), 47.

18. Chowdhury, *Parivrajaka Life*, 25–30; Chattopadhyaya, *Swami Vivekananda in India*, 88.

19. See Chapter 3.

20. Swami Aseshananda, *Glimpses of a Great Soul: Portrait of Swami Saradananda* (Chennai: Sri Ramakrishna Math, 1982), 20–1. E. M. Forster partly set *A Passage to India* (1924) in these caves, as Santanu Das at All Souls, University of Oxford, has reminded me.

21. Aseshananda, *Glimpses of a Great Soul*, 21. The quotation come from an unpublished autobiography of Swami Abhedananda.

22. Hausner, *Wandering with Sadhus*, 43.

23. Ramakrishna K. Rao and Anand C. Paranjpe, "'Yoga Psychology': Theory and Application," in *Psychology in the Indian Tradition*, ed. Rao and Paranjpe (Cambridge, UK: Foundation Books, 2008), 186–216.

24. Cited in Shamita Basu, *Religious Revivalism as Nationalist Discourse: Swami Vivekananda and New Hinduism in Nineteenth-Century Bengal* (New York: Oxford University Press, 2002), 31.

25. *Kathamrita*, 3:491.

26. This, too, is said to have derived from Vedic fire rituals.

27. Nikhilananda, *Vivekananda*, 84; Gambhirananda, *The Apostles of Shri Ramakrishna*, 31

28. *Swami Ramakrishnananda, as We Saw Him: Reminiscences of Monastic and Lay Devotees* (Chennai: Sri Ramakrishna Math, 2012), 9.

29. Jeffrey Kripal, *Kali's Child* (Chicago: University of Chicago Press, 1998), 91.

30. Gambhirananda, *The Apostles of Shri Ramakrishna*, 31.

31. Aruneya Upanishad: It is a minor text in the larger corpus and is classified as a Sannyasa Upanishad; *Narada-Parivrajaka Upanishad*. For a wonderful account of the renouncer undertaking, see Sondra Hausner, *Wandering with Sadhus*, 3, 62, 95–96, 103. Other references can be found in Wendy Doniger with Brian K. Smith, trans., *The Laws of Manu* (New York: Penguin Books, 1991), 121; the classic text remains Patrick Olivelle, *The Asrama System: The History and Hermeneutics of Religious Institution* (New Delhi: Munshiram Manoharlal Publishers, 2004).

32. Nick Sutton of the Hindu Studies Centre, Oxford, gave me his translations from the *Moksha-dharma* section of Book 12 (Shanti-parvan) of the Mahabharata, chapter 2, passage entitled *Bhrigu-Bharadvaja-Samvada*. This passage, however, relates to the third stage of life, when a householder gradually withdraws from temporal activities to become a "forest-dweller." See Patrick Olivette, *The Asrama System*, 11, 25, 65, 108, 112, 142, 179, and 201.

33. Asim Chaudhuri, *Vivekananda's Loving Relationships with His Brother Disciples—A Striking Example of Divine Love's Human Manifestations* (Burbank, CA: Chaudhuri Publications, 2019), 281.

34. Chattopadhyaya, *Swami Vivekananda in India*, 80.

35. Santanu Das, *Touch and Intimacy in First World War Literature* (Cambridge, UK: Cambridge University Press, 2005), 1–32.

36. Chaudhuri, *Vivekananda's Loving Relationships*, 123

37. Swami Vivekananda to Pramadadas Mitra, February 19, 1890, Epistles–2nd Series, XXII, vol. 6, *CWSV.*

38. Swami Annadananda, *Swami Akhandananda: An Apostle of Sri Ramakrishna*, trans. Shri Narayan Chandra Bhattacharya (Calcutta: Advaita Ashrama, 1993), 68.

39. Annadananda, *Swami Akhandananda*, 70, 71, 77–86.

40. This is called *purusa*; see Rao and Paranjpe, "Yoga Psychology" for the metapsychology of yoga.

41. Gambhirananda, *The Apostles of Shri Ramakrishna*, 257.

42. Gambhirananda, *The Apostles of Shri Ramakrishna*, 209.

43. Holding one's breath was called *kumbhaka*. See *Kathamrita*, 4:454.

44. Hausner, *Wandering with Sadhus*, 55–57.

45. See Caroline Bynum, *Holy Feast and Holy Fast: The Religious Significance of Food to Medieval Women* (Berkeley: University of California Press, 1987).

46. More recent accounts of this "passage" suggest that once sannyasa is attained, the basic needs of the body are acknowledged. Agehananda Bharat, *The Ochre Robe* (London: Allen and Unwin, 1961), 152–153 and 234.

47. Swami Aseshananda, *Glimpses of a Great Soul: A Portrait of Swami Saradananda* (St. Louis, MO: Vedanta Society of St. Louis, 1982), 22.

48. Chattopadhyaya, *Swami Vivekananda in India*, 87.

49. Swami Ritajananda, *Swami Turiyananda: Life and Teachings* (Madras: Sri Ramakrishna Math, 1963), 32.

50. Swami Shivananda, *Letters for Spiritual Seekers: Letters of Swami Shivananda*, trans. Swami Lokeswarananda (Mayavati: Advaita Ashrama, 1995), 14.

51. Shivananda, *Letters for Spiritual Seekers*, 15; both letters date from 1889.

52. Swami Chetanananda, *They Lived with God: Life Stories of Some Devotees of Sri Ramakrishna*, 2nd ed. (Kolkata: Advaita Ashrama, 2006), 139–150.

53. Shivananda, *Letters for Spiritual Seekers*, 16.

54. Shivananda, *Letters for Spiritual Seekers*, 25.

55. Quoted in Annadananda, *Swami Akhandananda*, 72.

56. Chattopadhyaya, *Swami Vivekananda in India*, 97; Chowdhury, *Parivrajak Life*, 3–13, for chronology. The "four corners" are known as *dhams*; the "sacred land," as *punyabhumi*.

57. Eck, *India: A Sacred Geography*, 7–16.

58. I thank D. Gellner for this choice of words. Eck, *India: A Sacred Geography*, 145–146, 171–173.

59. Eck, *India: A Sacred Geography*, 10; also, Eck's translation of the Skanda Purana, 6, 45.

60. Diana L. Eck, *Banaras: City of Light* (Harmondsworth, UK: Penguin Books, 1983), 35.

61. Swami Vivekananda, "From the Diary of a Disciple," Conversations and Dialogues, II, vol. 7, *CWSV*.

62. See Chapter 2.

63. Swami Yatiswarananda and Swami Prabhavanda, *The Eternal Companion: Life and Teachings of Swami Brahmananda* (Mylapore: Sri Ramakrishna Math, 2016), 42

64. Swami Vivekananda to Pramadadas Mitra, December 30, 1889, Epistles–2nd Series, XIV, vol. 6, *CWSV*.

65. Swami Vivekananda, "Address of Welcome at Almora and Reply," Lectures from Colombo to Almora, vol. 3, *CWSV*; he first went in 1890.

66. Swami Vivekananda to Sister Christine, August 5, 1896, Letters–5th Series, XCVIII, vol. 9, *CWSV*.

67. Vivekananda, "From the Diary of a Disciple."

68. Temperature: from Swami Vivekananda, "Prose Sketch of the Life of Pavhari Baba," February 6, 1890, Writings: Prose, vol. 4, *CWSV*.

69. Swami Vivekananda to Balaram Basu., February 6, 1890, Letters–5th Series, I, vol. 6, *CWSV*.

70. Swami Vivekananda to Balaram Basu, February 7, 1890, Epistles–2nd Series, XIX, vol. 6, *CWSV*. See also Swami Gambhirananda, *Life of Swami Vivekananda by His Eastern and Western Disciples*, 6th ed. (Calcutta: Sri Gouranga Press Private Ltd., 1960), 228–234.

71. Nikhilananda, *Vivekananda*, 94.

72. Swami Vivekananda to Saradananda and Kripananda, July 7, 1890, Epistles–2nd Series, XXXIV, vol. 6, *CWSV*.

73. Sister Nivedita, Notes of Some Wanderings with the Swami Vivekananda, in *CWSN*, 1:306.

74. Swami Vivekananda, "Footnotes to 'The Imitation of Christ,'" Writings: Prose, vol. 9, *CWSV*.

75. "Footnotes to 'The Imitation of Christ,'" Writings: Prose, vol. 9, *CWSV*, shows how he used the Bhagavad Gita and the Gospels to compare the *Imitation* to them.

76. Swami Vivekananda, "A Preface to *The Imitation of Christ*," Writings: Prose, vol. 8, *CWSV*, translated from an original Bengali writing of the Swami in 1889.

77. Swami Suddhananda, in *Reminiscences of Swami Vivekananda*, 3rd ed. (Calcutta: Advaita Ashrama, 1983), https://www.ramakrishnavivekananda.info/reminiscences/316_ss.htm (hereafter *Reminiscences*).

78. Vivekananda, "A Preface to *The Imitation of Christ*."

79. Chowdhury, *Parivrajaka Life*, is masterly in this regard.

80. Chattopadhyaya, *Swami Vivekananda in India*, esp. 80–88.

81. Chattopadhyaya, *Swami Vivekananda in India*, 82.

82. Quoted in Chattopadhyaya, *Swami Vivekananda in India*, 84.

83. Chattopadhyaya, *Swami Vivekananda in India*, 84.

84. Haripada Mitra, www.vivekananda.net/PDFBooks/Reminiscences/Haripada.html.

85. Chattopadhyaya, *Swami Vivekananda in India*, 93.

86. Chattopadhyaya, *Swami Vivekananda in India*, 82.

87. Chowdhury, *Parivrajaka Life*, 22–23; Shivananda, *Letters for Spiritual Seekers*, 20.

88. Chattopadhyaya, *Swami Vivekananda in India*, 88.

89. Quoted in Chattopadhyaya, *Swami Vivekananda in India*, 83.

90. Chowdhury, *Parivrajaka Life*, 23.

91. For more on his revelations, see Nikihilananda, *Vivekananda*, 98.

92. Swami Vivekananda, "Practical Vedanta, Part I," presented November 10, 1896, in London, "Practical Vedanta" and Other Lectures, vol. 2, *CWSV.*

93. Gwilym Beckerlegge, "Swami Vivekananda's Iconic Presence and Conventions of Nineteenth-Century Photographic Portraiture," *International Journal of Hindu Studies* 12 (2008): 11, 27.

94. Chattopadhyaya, *Swami Vivekananda in India*, 120–121.

95. Beckerlegge, "Swami Vivekananda's Iconic Presence," 7–12.

96. See Chapter 13.

97. Itty Abraham, *How India Became Territorial: Foreign Policy, Diaspora, Geopolitics* (Palo Alto: Stanford University Press, 2014), 28–33. How much this came from British colonial technologies and cartography, how much from his pilgrimages, and how much from interacting with these "rulers" is hard to judge.

98. Sumathi Ramaswamy, *The Goddess and the Nation: Mapping Mother India* (Durham, NC, Duke University Press, 2010), 136–149, studies the origins of "geo-piety" and the uneasy relationship between the anthropomorphic (Mother India) and the cartographic (associated with British conquest).

99. Kim, "Rethinking Vivekananda," 36.

100. Swami Vivekananda to Haridas Viharidas Desai, September 1894, Epistles–4th Series, XXIX, vol. 8, *CWSV*; in this letter, he thanks Desai for writing to G. W. Hale, a Harvard professor, establishing Vivekananda's bona fides.

101. Kim, "Rethinking Vivekananda," 24; C. A. Bayly, *Origins of Nationality in South Asia: Patriotism and Ethical Government in the Making of Modern India* (New Delhi: Oxford University Press, 1998), 98–99, 101–103.

102. Quoted in Chattopadhyaya, *Swami Vivekananda in India*, 91.

103. Guest of the Dewan: Chattopadhyaya, *Swami Vivekananda in India*, 95; meeting the prince: Kim, "Rethinking Vivekananda," 42.

104. Sister Nivedita, Notes of Some Wanderings, *CWSN*, 1:291.

105. Nikhilananda, *Vivekananda*, 119.

106. Kim, "Rethinking Vivekananda," 49.

107. Chattopadhyaya, *Swami Vivekananda in India*, 93.

108. Nikhilananda, *Vivekananda*, 104.

109. See Chapter 12.

110. See Swami Vivekananda, "Aryans and Tamilians," Writings: Prose, vol. 4, *CWSV.* For more context, Romila Thapar, "The Theory of Aryan Race and India: History and Politics," *Social Scientist*, 24 (1996): 3–29.

111. Kim, "Rethinking Vivekananda," 56–57.

112. See Chapter 12.

113. There are various views of when and where Vivekananda meditated at Kanyakumari; the Order seems to favor the story of the "rock hill, jutting out of the sea near Madhava Tirtha and Pitri Tirtha." It is said that he swam across to this rock and stayed for three days: Chowdhury, *Parivrajaka Life*, 173–174.

114. Confided this revelation: Swami Sunirmalananda, *Alasinga Perumal: An Illustrious Disciple of Swami Vivekananda, A Saga of Commitment, Dedication and Devotion to the Guru* (Chennai: Sri Ramakrishna Math, 2012), 79.

115. Swami Vivekananda to Ramakrishnananda, March 19, 1894, Epistles–2nd Series, XLI, vol. 6, *CWSV*. By using the word "Chandala," he was suggesting something potentially radical.

116. Ibid.

117. Swami Vivekananda, "Address at the Final Session," presented September 27, 1893, in Chicago, *Addresses at the Parliament of Religions*, vol. 1, *CWSV*.

118. For more on Karma yoga, see Chapter 12.

119. David Washbrook, *The Emergence of Provincial Politics: The Madras Presidency* (Cambridge, UK: Cambridge University Press, 1976), 212.

120. Susan M. Nelid, "Colonial Urbanism: The Development of Madras City in the Eighteenth and Nineteenth Centuries," *Modern Asian Studies* 13 (1979): 217–246.

121. He also admired the "great Ramanuja," another important theological figure, key to the creation of "qualified monism." and central to the development of bhakti.

122. Swami Vivekananda, "Reply to the Madras Address," Writings: Prose, vol. 4, *CWSV*.

123. See Chapter 1.

124. Anand Kumar V, "Swami Vivekananda, Mahakavi Bharathi and Triplicane, Madras," blog post, *Anand's Blog, AP Legal Chambers*, https://aplegalchambers.wordpress.com. His paper was read out during the sessions.

125. Another was Dewan Bahadur Raghunatha Rao, a civil servant and later of the Indian National Congress.

126. Sunirmalananda, *Alasinga Perumal*, 76.

127. Sunirmalananda, *Alasinga Perumal*, 78. He apparently spoke on Vyasa, Valmiki, and Kalidasa.

128. Sunirmalananda, *Alasinga Perumal*, 78.

129. Sunirmalananda, *Alasinga Perumal*, 80–81.

130. K. S. Ramaswami Sastri, in *Reminiscences*, https://www./ramakrishnavivekananda.info/reminiscences/098_ksrs.htm.

131. G. S. Bhate, in *Reminiscences*, https://www.ramakrishnavivekananda.info/reminiscences/052_gsb.htm.

132. We will never know whether he sported the turban to associate himself with Ram Mohun Roy, who he always admired; he is shown wearing this headgear in 1887 when an impoverished young monk in Baranagar, the only one to do so among the disciples. Gaurav Kalra, "Politics of Posture and Sartorial Sagacity: The Construction of Ascetic Masculinity in Vivekananda's Photographs and Posters," n.d., Tasveer Ghar: A Digital Archive of South Asian Popular Visual Culture, http://www.tasveergharindia.net/essay/politics-ascetic-vivekananda.html.

133. *Kathamrita*, 1:229.

134. Swami Vivekananda to Ramakrishnananda, March 19, 1894, Epistles-Second Series, XLI, vol. 6, *CWSV*.

135. See Chapter 11.

136. Swami Brahmananda et al., *Spiritual Talks by the First Disciples of Sri Ramakrishna* (Mayavati: Advaita Asharam, 1936), 5; these remarks were said to be repeated by the Holy Mother.

137. Swami Vivekananda to Alasinga Perumal, October 27, 1894, Epistles–1st Series, XXI, vol. 5, *CWSV*.

5. The World's Parliament of Religions

1. Swami Sunirmalananda, *Alasinga Perumal* (Chennai: Sri Ramakrishna Math, 2012), 83.

2. A Timeline of Important Events in Swami Vivekananda's Life, Advaita Yoga.org, 1891–92. http://www.advaitayoga.org/advaitayogaarticles/vivekanandatimeline.html.

3. It was called the Suddha Dharma Mandalam.

4. Rajagopal Chattopadhyaya, *Swami Vivekananda in India: A Corrective Biography* (New Delhi: Motilal Banarsidass, 1999), 107.

5. See Swami Purnatmananda, ed., *Reminiscences of Sri Sarada Devi by Monastics, Devotees and Others*, trans. Maloti Sen Gupta (Kolkata: Advaita Ashrama, 2004), 9 and Chapter 13; after his return, he purified himself in the Ganges before visiting the Holy Mother.

6. Swami Vivekananda to Alasinga Perumal, February 11, 1893, Epistles–4th Series, vol. 8, XI, in *Complete Works of Swami Vivekananda*, 10 vols., https://en.wikisource.org/wiki/The_Complete_Works_of_Swami_Vivekananda (hereafter *CWSV*); he impugns the reliability of the southern raja and says his plans had been "dashed to the ground"; Chattopadhyaya, *Swami Vivekananda in India*, 107.

7. Quoted in Swami Chetanananda, *Sri Sarada Devi and Her Divine Play* (St. Louis, MO: Vedanta Society of St. Louis, 2015), 187.

8. Quoted in Chetanananda, *Sri Sarada Devi and Her Divine Play*, 187.

9. Margaret Noble remarked: "you should see the chivalrous feeling that the monks have for [Sarada]." See Sister Nivedita to Nell Hammond, May 22, 1898, *Letters of Sister Nivedita*, collected and ed. Sankari Prasad Basu, 2 vols. (Kolkata: Advaita Ashrama, 2017), vol. 1, no. 4. For Vivekananda and Sarada, see *Sri Sarada Devi and Her Divine Play*, 197–209. These stories suggest her centrality to everything he did.

10. Swami Vivekananda to Diwanji Saheb, May 1893, Epistles–4th Series, XIII, vol. 8, *CWSV*.

11. The official exchange rate was 15 rupees to a £1 sterling, so he went with £266. The average monthly wage for a skilled carpenter in Calcutta was 15 rupees a month; Chattopadhyaya, *Swami Vivekananda in India*, 107.

12. John. R. Haller Jr., "Charles Bonney and the World's Parliament of Religions," *Distant Voices: Sketches of a Swedenborgian Worldview* (London: Swedenborg Society, 2017), 161.

13. Asim Chaudhuri, *Swami Vivekananda in Chicago: New Findings* (Kolkata: Advaita Ashrama, 2012), 54. For images, see *World's Columbian Exposition of 1893*, Paul V. Galvin Library Digital History Collection, Illinois Institute of Technology, https://library.iit.edu/find/articles/by-content/digital-collections/577.

14. Brian A. Hatcher, *Eclecticism and Modern Hindu Discourse* (New York: Oxford University Press, 1999), 47–70. On page 57, Hatcher suggests that the eclecticism of the fair mirrored Vivekananda's thought.

15. John P. Burris, *Exhibiting Religion: Colonialism and Spectacle at International Expositions, 1851–1893* (Charlottesville: University of Virginia Press, 2001), 86–122.

16. See Henry Em, *The Great Enterprise: Sovereignty and Historiography in Modern Korea* (Durham: Duke University Press, 2013), 60.

17. Judith Snodgrass, *Presenting Japanese Buddhism to the West: Orientalism, Occidentalism, and the Columbian Exposition* (Chapel Hill: University of North Carolina Press, 2003), 29–43. Remnants of the pavilion are at the Chicago Art Institute.

18. Jung Hyun Kim, "Rethinking Vivekananda through Space and Territorialised Spirituality" (PhD diss., University of Cambridge, 2018), 74.

19. Kim, "Rethinking Vivekananda," 86.

20. Kim, "Rethinking Vivekananda," quoted on 88.

21. Burris, *Exhibiting Religion*, 105; for the politics of display, Carol. A. Breckenridge, "The Aesthetics and Politics of Colonial Collecting: India at World's Fairs," in *Comparative Studies in Society and History* 31 (1989): 195–216.

22. Justin Nordstrom, "Utopians at the Parliament: The World's Parliament of Religions and the Columbia Exposition of 1893," *Journal of Religious History* 33, 2009: 348–365; and Richard Hughes Seager, *The World's Parliament of Religions: The East-West Encounter, Chicago, 1893* (Bloomington: Indiana University Press, 1995).

23. Somenath Mukherjee, *The Ships of Vivekananda* (Kolkata: Advaita Ashrama, 2013), 24.

24. Anagarika Dharmapala from Sri Lanka loved the courtesies of racial equality in this "floating world."

25. See Tamson Pietsch, "A British Sea: Making Sense of Global Space in the Late-Nineteenth Century," *Journal of Global History* 5 (2010): 423–446.

26. "Here is a man": Quoted in Gopal Stavig, *Western Admirers of Ramakrishna and His Disciples* (Kolkata: Advaita Ashrama, 2010), 413.

27. See Chapter 6.

28. Mary Louise Burke, *Swami Vivekananda in the West: New Discoveries, His Prophetic Mission*, 4th ed. (Calcutta: Advaita Ashrama, 1992), 1:59.

29. Swami Vivekananda to "brother disciples," September 25, 1894, Epistles–2nd Series, XLVII, vol. 6, *CWSV.*

30. Haller, "Charles Bonney and the World's Parliament of Religions," 162.

31. Haller, "Charles Bonney and the World's Parliament of Religions," 162.

32. Haller, "Charles Bonney and the World's Parliament of Religions," 162.

33. Sarah Pike, *New Age and Neopagan Religions in America* (New York: Columbia University Press, 2004), 48–49; Robert W. Delp, "Andrew Jackson Davis and Spiritualism," in *Pseudo-Science and Society in Nineteenth-Century America,* ed. Arthur Wrobel (Lexington: Kentucky University Press, 1987), 100–121, and Catherine Albanese, *A Republic of Mind and Spirit: A Cultural History of American Metaphysical Religion* (New Haven, CT: Yale University Press: 2007), 206–220.

34. Quoted in Albanese, *A Republic of Mind and Spirit,* 141.

35. Vincent Roy-DiPiazza, "'Ghosts from Other Planets': Plurality of Worlds: Afterlife, and Satire in Emanuel Swedenborg's *De Telluribus in mundo nostro solar*" (1758), *Annals of Science* 77, no. 4 (2020): 8–12.

36. Haller, "Henry James Sr., and Ralph Waldo Emerson," *Distant Voices,* 1–46.

37. Haller, "Henry James Sr., and Ralph Waldo Emerson," 163.

38. Barrows, 1:18.

39. Tomoko Masuzawa, *The Invention of World Religions, or, How European Universalism was Preserved in the Language of Pluralism* (Chicago: Chicago University Press, 2005), 121–146.

40. John Henry Barrows, *The World's Parliament of Religions: An Illustrated and Popular Story of the World's First Parliament of Religions, Held in Chicago in Connection with the Columbian Exposition of 1893,* 2 vols. (Chicago: Parliament Publishing Co., 1893), 1:18 (hereafter Barrows).

41. Barrows, 1:61.

42. Dharmapala in "Diary Leaves of the Buddhist Representative to the World's Parliament of Religions in Chicago," *Return to Righteousness: A Collection of Speeches, Essays, and Letters of the Anagarika Dharmapala* (Colombo: Anagarika Dharmapala Birth Centenary Committee, Ministry of Education and Cultural Affairs, Ceylon, 1965), 707.

43. Chattopadhyaya, *Swami Vivekananda in India,* 136–137.

44. Walter R. Houghton, *Neely's History of the Parliament of Religions and Religious Congresses at the World's Columbian Exposition,* 5 vols. (Chicago: Neely, 1894) (hereafter Houghton), 1:47.

45. Barrows, 1:107.

46. Barrows, 1:107.

47. See Muhammad Abdullah Al-Ahari, ed., *The Islam Papers: The 1893 World Parliament of Religion* (Chicago: Magribine Press, 2011); see also Barrows, 1:68–69, and 70–73 respectively.

48. Houghton, 1:40.

49. Barrows, 1:28; printed in the published volume, but they were uttered at the Christian Endeavour Convention in New York.

50. See Chapter 8 for Green Acre; and John Henry Barrows, *Christianity, the World-Religion: Lectures Delivered in India and Japan* (Chicago: A. C. McClurg, 1897); he even noted Vivekananda's triumphal return: 440–441.

51. Derek Michaud, ed. "A Brief History of the 1893 World's Parliament of Religion," in *The Boston Collaborative Encyclopedia of Western Theology, Interfaith Observer,* July 9, 2015, http://www.theinterfaithobserver.org/journal-articles/2015/7/9/a-brief-history-of-the-1893 -worlds-parliament-of-religions.html.

52. Barrows, 1:26.

53. Houghton, 1:45–46.

54. Houghton, 1:69.

55. Houghton, 1:40.

56. Houghton, 1:42.

57. "A Letter in Behalf of the Armenians," in Barrows, 1:130.

58. Al-Ahari, *The Islam Papers;* this little volume suggests how finite was the Islamic "presence."

59. George Washburn, "The Points of Contact and Contrast between Christianity and Mohammedanism," in Barrows, 1:570, 578; Washburn was stationed in Constantinople.

60. Merciful God: Mrs. Eliza R. Sunderland, "Serious Study of All Religions," in Barrows, 1:631; "fire and sword": Chunder Mozoomdar, "The Brahmo-Somaj," in Barrows, 1:350.

61. Barrows, 1:440.

62. Barrows, 1:445; see also Snodgrass, *Presenting Japanese Buddhism,* 172–197.

63. Barrows, 1:448.

64. The contact was not all negative. Soyen Shaku met Paul Carus, the editor of the Open Court Publishing company, and then sent D. T. Suzuki to stay with Carus. Together they launched Zen in the West; J. Snodgrass, "Publishing Eastern Buddhism: D. T. Suzuki's Journey to the West," in *Casting Faiths: Imperialism and the Transformations of Religion in East and Southeast Asia,* ed. Thomas David DuBois (London: Palgrave, 2009), 46–72.

65. Swami Vivekananda to Alasinga Perumal et al., July 10, 1893, Epistles–1st Series, III, vol. 5, *CWSV.*

66. Vivekananda to Alasinga et al., July 10, 1893.

67. Vivekananda to Alasinga et al., July 10, 1893.

68. Vivekananda to Alasinga et al., July 10, 1893. To reinforce this message, he used the same words on March 11, 1898, in Calcutta when introducing Nivedita's lecture "The Influence of Indian Spiritual Thought in England," Swami Vivekananda, Lectures from Colombo to Almora, vol. 3, *CWSV.*

69. Shingon and Tendai temples in Japan still use the Ranjana script, brought with Buddhism from India, via China, for writing mantras on funerary monuments and offerings; I thank David Gellner of All Souls College, Oxford, for this information.

70. Rev. Philips of Madras, "The Ancient Religion of India and Primitive Revelation." Like so many others, he considered the oldest texts to be the purest, the implication being that Hinduism had irretrievably degenerated. Houghton, 1:104.

71. Houghton, 1:165.

72. Sudipta Sen of the University of California, Davis, reminded me of this important connection. Basu, *Religious Revivalism,* 43, explains how such metaphysical tendencies were deemed to make Indians unable to write "scientific" history.

73. See Chapter 12.

74. Chattopadhyaya, *Swami Vivekananda in India,* 135. There is a different tally in J. V. Nash, "India at the World's Parliament of Religions," *Open Court* 47 (1933): 217–230; on 218, he only cites thirteen.

75. He first read it during a hospital stay in in Japan in 1889, *Dharmapala Diaries,* typescript, Archives of the Mahabodhi Society, Colombo, Sri Lanka, March 5, 1889.

76. Stephen R. Prothero explains in *The White Buddhist: The Asian Odyssey of Henry Steel Olcott* (Bloomington: Indiana University Press, 1996) how this was subject to Western "modification"; also see Anne M. Blackburn, *Locations of Buddhism: Colonialism and Modernity in Sri*

Lanka (Buddhism and Modernity) (Chicago: University of Chicago Press, 2010); and David L. McMahan, *The Making of Buddhist Modernism* (Oxford: Oxford University Press, 2008).

77. M. Roberts, "For Humanity, For the Sinhalese. Dharmapala as Crusading Bosat," *Journal of Asian Studies* 56 (1997): 1006–1032. See Anagarika Dharmapala, *The Bodh-Gaya Temple Case* (Calcutta: Caxton Press, 1895); Steven Kemper, *Rescued from the Nation: Anagarika Dharmapala and the Buddhist World* (Chicago: Chicago University Press, 2015), 256–282; Alan Trevithick, *The Revival of Buddhist Pilgrimage at Bodh Gaya: Anagarika Dharmapala and the Mahabodhi Temple* (New Delhi: Motilal Banarsidass, 2006); David Geary, *The Rebirth of Bodh Gaya: Buddhism and the Making of a World Heritage Site* (Seattle: University of Washington Press, 2017).

78. Thomas A. Tweed, *The American Encounter with Buddhism, 1844–1912: Victorian Culture & the Limits of Dissent* (Chapel Hill: University of North Carolina Press, 1992), 26–110.

79. "Speech of Dharmapala," Barrows, 1:95; for Ashoka, orientalism, and archaeology, see Charles Allen, *Ashoka: The Search for India's Lost Emperor* (London: Little Brown, 2012).

80. Dharmapala phrased it this way: "And when Darwin shows us life passing onward and upward through a series of constantly improving forms toward the Better and the Best, . . . what is this again but the Buddhist doctrine of Karma and Dharma" in "Buddhism and Modern Science," Ananda Guruge, *Return to Righteousness:* A Collection of Speeches, Essays and Letters of the Anagarika Dharmapala (Colombo, Sri Lanka: Ministry of Cultural Affairs & Information, 1965), 19.

81. Guruge, *Return to Righteousness,* 405–406.

82. James R. Moore, *Post-Darwinian Controversies: A Study of the Protestant Struggle to Come to Terms with Darwin in Great Britain and America, 1870–1900* (Cambridge, UK: Cambridge University Press, 1979); see especially 77–100, 217–298.

83. *Dharmapala Diaries,* April 21, 1893, Archives of the Mahabodhi Society, Colombo, Sri Lanka.

84. Houghton, 1:611. In one letter from Vivekananda, he is addressed as Narasimhacharya.

85. Cited with kind permission of Eijiro Hazama, "'Neo-Advaita' Reconsidered: The Intellectual Relationship between Manilal N. Dvivedi and M. K. Gandhi" (paper, British Association for South Asian Studies Annual Conference, Durham University, UK, April 4, 2019).

86. Barrows, 1:328–329.

87. This did not preclude his also representing a Vaishnava and two other orthodox organizations; see Amiya Sen, "Aggressive Hinduism: Ecumenical, Evangelist and Expansive," in *Colonial Hinduism* (Oxford Centre for Hindu Studies, forthcoming), cited with kind permission of the author.

88. See Chapter 7. See also Bruce F. Campbell, *Ancient Wisdom Revived: A History of the Theosophical Movement* (Berkeley: California University Press 1980), 8–20; Antoine Faivre, *Theosophy, Imagination, Tradition: Studies in Western Esotericism* (Albany: State University of New York Press, 2000); Isaac Lubelsky, *Celestial India: Madame Blavatsky and the Birth of Indian Nationalism* (Sheffield, UK: Equinox, 2012); J. Barton Scott, "Miracle Publics: Theosophy, Christianity, and the Coulomb Affair," *History of Religions* 49 (2009): 172–196.

89. Mark Bevir, "Theosophy and the Origins of the Indian National Congress," *International Journal of Hindu Studies* 1–3 (2003): 104–105; Wouter J. Hanegraaff, *New Age Religion and Western Culture: Esotericism in the Mirror of Secular Thought* (Albany: State University of New York Press, 1998), 448, for the final official objectives of the Theosophical Society, 1896.

90. Kemper, *Rescued from the Nation,* 52–115.

91. A. Trevithick, "The Theosophical Society and its Subaltern Acolytes (1880–1986)," *Marburg Journal of Religion* 13 (2008): 16–27 shows how European mentors kept their South Asian disciples in thrall.

92. Traditions: Hanegraaff, *New Age Religion,* 448–455.

93. Houghton, 1:610.

94. Susan Bayly, *Caste, Society and Politics in India from the Eighteenth Century to the Modern Age* (Cambridge, UK: Cambridge University Press, 1999), 182–183.

95. Houghton, 1:611.

96. Robert Frykenberg, "The Emergence of Modern 'Hinduism' as a Concept and as an Institution: A Reappraisal with Special Reference to South India" and H. Von Stietencron, "Hinduism: On the Proper Use of a Deceptive Term," in *Hinduism Reconsidered,* eds. G. D. Sontheimer and H. Kulke (reissued New Delhi: Manohar, 1997), 29–50. The term "Hindu" is ancient and of variable in meaning, while "Hinduism" was more recent, but remained slippery. It could become nothing more than reference to a native civilization; see Peter van der Veer, *Religious Nationalism: Hindus and Muslims in India* (Berkeley: University of California Press, 1994), 134.

97. David Gellner, "Hinduism—None, One or Many?" *Social Anthropology,* 12 (2004): 367–371.

98. Julius Lipner, *Hindus: Their Religious Beliefs and Practices,* 2nd ed. (London: Routledge and Kegan Paul, 2010), 1–23.

99. Lipner, *Hindus,* 99.

100. See Chapters 9 and 12.

101. Swami Vivekananda, "Response to Welcome," September 11, 1893, Addresses at the Parliament of Religions, vol. 1, *CWSV.*

102. Vivekananda, "Response to Welcome," vol. 1.

103. Vivekananda, "Response to Welcome," vol. 1.

104. For this idea restated, see Bhagavad Gita, https://www.holy-bhagavad-gita.org/chapter/18/verse/66, which is translated as "Abandon all varieties of *dharmas* and simply surrender unto me alone. I shall liberate you from all sinful reactions; do not fear."

105. Swami Vivekananda, "Why We Disagree," September 15, 1893, Addresses at the Parliament of Religion, vol. 1, *CWSV.*

106. Vivekananda, "Why We Disagree."

107. Swami Vivekananda, "The Hindu View of Life," *Brooklyn Times,* December 31, 1894, in Reports in American Newspapers, vol. 2, *CWSV.*

108. Swami Vivekananda, "Paper on Hinduism," September 19, 1893, Addresses at the Parliament of Religions, vol. 1, *CWSV.* All quotations from this paragraph are taken from this source.

109. All quotations from this paragraph in Vivekananda, "Paper on Hinduism."

110. See George W. Stocking Jr., *Race, Culture and Evolution: Essays in the History of Evolution* (New York: Free Press, 1968), 195–233.

111. Vivekananda, "Why We Disagree."

112. They went mostly to Cranganore (now Kodungallur), an ancient port near Cochin. Point discussed with Sudipta Sen of Davis, University of California.

113. Peter van der Veer, *The Modern Spirit of Asia: The Spiritual and the Secular in China and India* (Princeton: Princeton University Press, 2013), 85.

114. Swami Vivekananda to Alasinga, November 2, 1893, Epistles–1st Series, V, vol. 5, *CWSV.*

115. Swami Vivekananda to Alasinga, November 2, 1893.

116. Swami Vivekananda to Alasinga, November 2, 1893.

117. Swami Vivekananda to G. G. Narasimhachariar, January 11, 1895, Epistles–1st Series, XXIX, vol. 5, *CWSV.*

118. Cited in Burke, *Swami Vivekananda in the West,* vol. 1, 112; from the *Dubuque Iowa Times* of September 29, 1892, and in "At the Parliament of Religions," *Reports in American Newspapers,* vol. 3, *CWSV.*

119. Swami Vivekananda, "Religion Not the Crying Need of India," Newspaper Reports, vol. 9, *CWSV.*

120. Swami Vivekananda, "What the East Needs," Newspaper Reports, vol. 9, *CWSV.*

121. References cited in Burke, *Swami Vivekananda in the West,* vol. 1, 128.

122. Swami Vivekananda, "Buddhism: The Fulfilment of Hinduism," September 26, 1893, Addresses at the Parliament of Religions, vol. 1, *CWSV*. He did, however, believe that the Buddha fell within the Hindu embrace (Buddha was considered an incarnation of Vishnu). Later, he spoke of a "degraded Buddhism," however, and was disillusioned by what he encountered in Sri Lanka. See Swami Vivekananda to Mrs. Bull, May 15, 1897, Epistles–3rd Series, XXXIX, vol. 7, *CWSV*.

123. Swami Vivekananda, "Address at the Final Session," September 27, 1893, Addresses at the Parliament of Religions, vol. 1, *CWSV*.

124. Barrows, 1:171.

125. Chauduri, *Swami Vivekananda in Chicago*, 131 and 171.

126. *Dharmapala Diaries*, September 12, 1893, Archives of the Mahabodhi Society, Colombo, Sri Lanka.

127. Burke, *Swami Vivekananda in the West*, vol. 1, 87–90; the newspaper reports are error-filled; e.g., they say he was a Brahmin.

6. Women East and West

1. See my book *Lourdes: Body and Spirit in the Secular Age* (Harmondsworth, UK: Allen Lane, 1999), passim.

2. Mary Tappan Wright, "Vengeance of History," n.d., http://www.vivekananda.net/ReminiscenesOnSwami/MaryTappanWright.html.

3. Gopal Stavig, *Western Admirers of Ramakrishna and His Disciples* (Kolkata: Advaita Ashrama, 2010), 348.

4. Swami Vivekananda to Alasinga Perumal, August 20, 1893, Epistles–1st Series, vol. 5, IV, *CWSV*.

5. Vivekananda to Alasinga, August 20, 1893.

6. Vivekananda to Alasinga, August 20, 1893.

7. See Alice Sheppard, "From Kate Sanborn to Feminist Psychology: The Social Context of Women's Humor, 1885–1985," *Psychology of Women Quarterly* 10 (1986): 155–170.

8. Sheppard, "From Kate Sanborn to Feminist Psychology," quoted 158.

9. Mary Tappan Wright, "Mrs. Mary Tappan Wright to her mother," August 29, 1893, www.vivekananda.net/LettersToVivekananda.html.

10. Kate Sanborn, *Abandoning an Adopted Farm* (New York: D. Appleton and Company, 1894), 13–14; she writes at length about his impact, 8–14.

11. See Catherine Hall, *Civilising Subjects: Metropole and Colony in the English Imagination, 1830–1867* (Chicago: Chicago University Press, 2002), which deals with the Caribbean, but touches on similar themes; Antoinette Burton, *At the Heart of the Empire: Indians and the Colonial Encounter in Late-Victorian Britain* (Berkeley: University of California Press, 1998); Peter Mandler, "'Race' and 'Nation' in Mid-Victorian Thought," in *History, Religion, and Culture: British Intellectual History, 1750–1950*, ed. Stefan Collini, Richard Whatmore, and Brian Young (Cambridge, UK: Cambridge University Press, 2000), 224–244, stresses civilizational over "racial" arguments in understanding Indian "otherness"; Elleke Boehmer, *Indian Arrivals 1870–1915: Networks of British Empire* (Oxford: Oxford University Press, 2015); and Somak Biswas, "Passages through India: Indian Gurus, Western Disciples and the Politics of Indophilia, 1890–1940" (PhD diss, University of Warwick, 2020), 120–155. Large-scale migration to the West Coast only began in the 1890s, especially to California.

12. Wright, "Mrs. Mary Tappan Wright to her mother," www.vivekananda.net/LettersToVivekananda.html. Both quotations are from this source.

13. Mary Louise Burke, *Swami Vivekananda in the West: New Discoveries, His Prophetic Mission*, 4th ed. (Calcutta: Advaita Ashrama, 1992), 1:49; quotation from the *Daily Gazette*, August 29, 1893.

14. Russell E. Richey, "Religious Organization in the New Nation," in *The Cambridge History of Religions in America, 1790-1945,* vol. 2, ed. Stephen J. Stein (Cambridge, UK: Cambridge University Press, 2012), 98-101.

15. Peter Thuesen, 'Theological Controversies, 1790-1865," in *The Cambridge History of Religions in America, 1790-1945,* vol. 2, ed. Stephen J. Stein (Cambridge, UK: Cambridge University Press, 2012)143.

16. Clare Midgley, "Transoceanic Commemoration and Connections between Bengali Brahmos and British and American Unitarians," *Historical Journal* 54 (2011): 787; see also Chapter 8.

17. See Chapters 7 and 8.

18. See Chapter 14.

19. Swami Vivekananda to the Hale sisters, July 26, 1894, Epistles–4th Series, XXIV, vol. 8, *CWSV.*

20. Swami Vivekananda to Haripada Mitra, December 28, 1893, Epistles–1st Series, VI, vol. 5, *CWSV,* translated from Bengali.

21. See Pravrajika Prabuddhaprana, *Saint Sara: The Life of Sara Chapman Bull: The American Mother of Swami Vivekananda* (Dakshineswar: Sri Sarada Math, 2002), 106-108, 255-226; Andrew C. Rieser, *The Chautauqua Moment: Protestants, Progressives, and the Culture of Modern Liberalism, 1874-1920* (New York: Columbia University Press, 2003), 15-46 and 161-206; see also Austin Warren, "The Concord School of Philosophy," *New England Quarterly* 2 (1929): 199-233; Bruce Ronda, "The Concord School of Philosophy and the Legacy of Transcendentalism," *New England Quarterly* 82 (2004): 575-607.

22. See Chapter 8.

23. Swami Vivekananda to Alasinga Perumal, August 20, 1893, Epistles–1st Series, IV, vol. 5, *CWSV.*

24. Burke, *Swami Vivekananda in the West,* quoted 110, from the *Chicago Inter Ocean* of September 20, 1893.

25. Burke, *Swami Vivekananda in the West,* 116.

26. Burke, *Swami Vivekananda in the West,* 196. This was not universally the case; see M. N. Srinivas, *The Remembered Village,* 2nd ed. (New Delhi: Oxford University Press 2012), 317-360.

27. Susan Bayly, *Caste, Society and Politics in India from the Eighteenth Century to the Modern Age* (Cambridge, UK: Cambridge University Press, 1999), 182-183.

28. See C. J. Fuller, "Gods, Priests and Purity: On the Relations between Hinduism and the Caste System," *Man* 14 (1979): 459-476, especially 461.

29. Frank Trentmann, "Beyond Consumerism: New Historical Perspectives on Consumption," *Journal of Contemporary History* 39 (2004): 373-401.

30. Edwin S. Gaustad and Leigh Schmidt, eds., *The Religious History of America: The Heart of the American Story from Colonial Times to Today* (New York: HarperOne, 2004), 236-238; and Dana Logan, "Commerce, Consumerism, and Christianity in America," abstract, Oxford Research Encyclopaedias (December 19, 2017), https://doi.org/10.1093/acrefore/9780199340378.013.414.

31. John Corrigan, *Business of the Heart: Religion and Emotion in the Nineteenth Century* (Berkeley: University of California Press, 2002), 12-40 and 207-230.

32. Quoted in Burke, *Swami Vivekananda in the West,* 213. Report in the *Iowa State Register,* December 3, 1893.

33. Carrie Tirado Bramen, "Christian Maidens and Heathen Monks: Oratorical Seduction at the 1893 World's Parliament of Religions," in *The Puritan Origins of American Sex: Religion, Sexuality, and National Identity in American Literatures,* ed. Tracy Fessenden, Nicholas F. Radel, and Magdalena J. Zabrowska (New York: Routledge, 2001), 191-220.

34. Constance Towne, in Swami Suddhananda, *Reminiscences of Swami Vivekananda,* 3rd ed. (Calcutta: Advaita Ashrama, 1983), https://www.ramakrishnavivekananda.info/reminiscences /246_ct.htm (hereafter *Reminiscences*).

35. Ida Ansell, in *Reminiscences,* https://www.ramakrishnavivekananda.info/reminiscences /362_ia.htm.

36. E. T. Sturdy, in *Reminiscences,* https://www.ramakrishnavivekananda.info/reminiscences /294_ets.htm.

37. Cornelia Conger, in *Reminiscences,* https://www.ramakrishnavivekananda.info/remini scences/130_cc.htm.

38. S. E. Waldo, in *Reminiscences,* https://www.ramakrishnavivekananda.info/reminiscences /113_sew.htm.

39. "Glowing eyes": Eric Hammond, in *Reminiscences,* https://www.ramakrishnavivekananda .info/reminiscences/291_eh.htm; heavy dark eyes: Maud Stumm, in *Reminiscences.*

40. Fincke, in *Reminiscences.*

41. Mrs. Alice M. Hansbrough, "Sunday, March 23, 1941," in *Reminiscences,* https://www .ramakrishnavivekananda.info/reminiscences/other_02_amh.htm.

42. Hansbrough, "Sunday, March 23, 1941."

43. Emma Calvé, quoted from private papers, in Swami Vidyatmananda, *Vivekananda in Europe* (Mayavati: Advaita Ashrama, 2012), 275.

44. "Six feet two": Sanborn, *Abandoning an Adopted Farm,* 8–9; Garibaldi or Napoléon: Gwilym Beckerlegge sets aside these stereotypes in "Swami Vivekananda's Iconic Presence and Conventions of Nineteenth-Century Photographic Portraiture," *International Journal of Hindu Studies* 12 (2008): 21.

45. Sister Christine, in *Reminiscences,* https://www.ramakrishnavivekananda.info /reminiscences/146_sc.htm.

46. For more on these dynamics, see Parama Roy, *Indian Traffic: Identities in Question in Colonial and Postcolonial India* (Berkeley: University of California Press, 1999), 118–127.

47. Max Weber, *Charisma and Disenchantment: The Vocation Lectures,* ed. Paul Reitter and C. Wellmon (New York: *New York Review of Books,* 2020), xviii–xiv. See also Joshua Derman, "Max Weber and Charisma: A Transatlantic Affair," *New German Critique* 113 (2011): 51–88.

48. The only later trace of her comes in letters in 1926–1927 to Nadia Boulanger, the eminent French composer, conductor, and teacher, available at the Bibliothèque nationale de France.

49. Subsequent quotations come from this text, Finke, in *Reminiscences.*

50. Swami Vivekananda to Mr. Manmatha Nath Bhattacharya, September 6, 1894, Epistles–3rd Series, XXIII, vol. 7, *CWSV.*

51. Swami Vivekananda to Haripada Mitra, December 28, 1893, Epistles–1st Series, VI, vol. 5, *CWSV.*

52. Swami Vivekananda to H. H. Maharaja of Khetri, 1894, Epistles–2nd Series, XL, vol. 6, *CWSV.*

53. Swami Vivekananda to Haripada Mitra, December 28, 1893, Epistles–1st Series, vol. 5, *CWSV.*

54. Swami Vivekananda to Mrs. G. W. Hale, March 16, 1894, Letters–5th Series, XIII, vol. 9. *CWSV.*

55. See Chapter 4.

56. Swami Vivekananda to "Sisters" of the Hale family, July 31, 1894, Epistles–2nd Series, XLIV, vol. 6, *CWSV.*

57. See Wendy Gamber, *The Female Economy: The Millinery and Dressmaking Trades, 1860–1930* (Chicago: University of Illinois Press, 1997), 138.

58. Swami Vivekananda to "Sisters" of the Hale family, July 31, 1894, Epistles–2nd Series, XLIV, vol. 6, *CWSV.*

59. Vivekananda to "Sisters," July 31, 1894.

60. Swami Vivekananda to Mr. Manmatha Nath Bhattacharya, September 5, 1894, Epistles–3rd Series, XXIII, vol. 7, *CWSV.*

61. Vivekananda to Bhattacharya, September 5, 1894.

62. Ashis Nandy, *The Intimate Enemy: Loss and Recovery of Self* (New Delhi: Oxford University Press, 1983), 8, 24–5, 47, 51.

63. Swami Vivekananda to Mrs. G. W. Hale, July 23, 1894, Letters–5th Series, XXV, vol. 9, *CWSV*.

64. Swami Vivekananda to "Sisters" of the Hale family, July 31, 1894, Epistles–2nd Series, XLIV, vol. 6, *CWSV*.

65. Swami Vivekananda to Mrs. G. W. Hale, May 14, 1894, Letters–5th Series, XX, vol. 9, *CWSV*.

66. "Armadillas": Swami Vivekananda to Mrs. G. W. Hale, August 28, 1894, Letters–5th Series, XXX, vol. 9, *CWSV*; "body conscious": Swami Vivekananda to Mr. Manmatha Nath Bhattacharya, September 5, 1894, Epistles–3rd Series, XXIII, vol. 7, *CWSV*.

67. Vivekananda to Bhattacharya, September 5, 1894.

68. See Chapter 10.

69. Swami Vivekananda to Alasinga Perumal, July 1, 1895, Epistles–1st Series, XLIII, vol. 5, *CWSV*.

70. Stumm, in *Reminiscences*.

71. J. J. Goodwin, St. Louis Vedanta Society, June 28, 1897; for the full run of letters, see Swami Chetanananda, "With Swamiji in India: J. J. Goodwin's Letters from India about Vivekananda," in Swami Shuddhidananda, *Vivekananda as the Turning Point: The Rise of a New Spiritual Wave* (Kolkata: Advaita Ashrama, 2013), 480–490.

72. Tanika Sarkar, *Hindu Wife, Hindu Nation, Community, Religion, and Cultural Nationalism* (Bloomington: Indiana University Press, 2001), 23–52.

73. Tanika Sarkar, *Rebels, Wives, Saints: Designing Selves and Nations in Colonial Times* (London: Seagull Books, 2009), 284–285.

74. Sarkar, *Rebels, Wives, Saints*, 1–2; and Chandrika Kaul, "England and India: The Ilbert Bill, 1883: A Case Study of the Metropolitan Press," *Indian Economic and Social History Review* 30 (1993): 413–436, for British investment in amending it.

75. Sarkar, *Rebels, Wives, Saints*, 45; 133n34; she observes that even though lower-caste widows were allowed to remarry, they, too, often disdained such practices.

76. Sarkar, *Hindu Wife, Hindu Nation*, 23–52.

77. Sarkar, *Hindu Wife, Hindu Nation*, 42; Sarkar, *Rebels, Wives, Saints*, 192–228; Krupa Shandilya, *Intimate Relations: Social Reform and the Late Nineteenth-Century South Asian Novel* (Evanston, IL: Northwestern University Press, 2017): 20–37. Bankim's exaltation of *sati* was in tension with the often heroic stature of his female characters; see Sudipta Kaviraj, *The Unhappy Consciousness: Bankimchandra Chattopadhyay and the Formation of Nationalist Discourse in India* (New Delhi: Oxford University Press, 1995), passim, and Sarkar, *Hindu Wife, Hindu Nation*, 135–162.

78. Protap Chunder Mazoomdar, *The Life and Teachings of Keshub Chunder Sen* (Calcutta: J. W. Thomas Baptist Mission Press, 1887), 204–211.

79. Mazoomdar, *Life and Teachings of Keshub Chunder Sen*, 265.

80. Mazoomdar, *Life and Teaching of Keshub Chunder Sen*, 264, 265.

81. Swami Vivekananda to Mr. Manmatha Nath Bhattacharya, September 5, 1894, Epistles–3rd Series, XXIII, vol. 7, *CWSV*.

82. Swami Vivekananda to Saradananda, December 23, 1895, Epistles–4th Series, LXV, vol. 8, *CWSV*.

83. Swami Vivekananda, "II: The Loss of Shraddha in India and Need of Its Revival–Men We Want–Real Social Reform," from the private diary of Shri Surendra Nath Sen, January 22, 1898, Conversations and Dialogues, vol. 5, *CWSV*.

84. These were the *shradda* rites.

85. Swami Vivekananda, VIII (From the Diary of a Disciple, translated from Bengali), March or April 1897, Conversations and Dialogues, vol. 6, *CWSV*; this is a record of a private conversation.

86. In 1884, Rukhmabai, a low-caste, educated woman, sought to release herself from an unsuitable marriage claiming lack of consent. See Sarkar, *Hindu Wife, Hindu Nation*, 48–49 and 207, and Padma Anagol, *The Emergence of Feminism in India, 1850–1920* (Farnham, UK: Ashgate, 2005), 187–196; these debates raged on in different forms during the interwar, see Mrinalini Sinha's excellent *Specters of Mother India: The Global Restructuring of an Empire* (Durham, NC: Duke University Press 2006), and Ishita Pande, *Sex, Law and the Politics of Age: Child Marriage in India, 1891–1937* (Cambridge, UK: Cambridge University Press, 2020), 1–71; Pande gives the most conceptually sophisticated account to date.

87. Meera Kosambi, "Girl Brides and Socio-legal Change: Age of Consent Bill (1891) controversy," *Economic and Political Weekly* 26, no. 31 (August 3–10, 1991): 1857–1868.

88. For the debate, see also Charles H. Heimsath, 'The Origin and Enactment of the Indian Age of Consent Bill, 1891," *Journal of Asian Studies* 21 (1962): 491–504; Meredith Borthwick, *The Changing Role of Women in Bengal* (Princeton: Princeton University Press, 1985) describes expanding horizons and domestic possibilities; Dagmar Engels, "The Age of Consent Act of 1891: Colonial Ideology in Bengal," in *South Asia Research* 2 (1985): 107–134; Mrinalini Sinha, "The Age of Consent Act: The Ideal of Masculinity and Colonial Ideology in Nineteenth-Century Bengal," in *Shaping Bengali Worlds, Public and Private*, ed. Tony K. Steward (East Lansing: Asian Studies Center at Michigan State University, 1989), 99–127; for women's emerging role in this controversy, see Padma Anagol-McGinn, "The Age of Consent Act (1891) Reconsidered: Women's Perspectives and Participation in Child-Marriage Controversy in India," *South Asia Research* 12 (1992): 1–19; for the quotation, Swami Vivekananda to Rakhal Chandra Ghosh (later Swami Brahmananda), 1895, LXXI, Epistles–2nd Series, vol. 6, *CWSV*.

89. Swami Vivekananda, "Women in India." Reports in American Newspapers, vol. 3, *CWSV*, published in the *Detroit Free Press*, March 25, 1894.

90. Swami Vivekananda, "Mother-Worship," Notes of Class Talks and Lectures, vol. 6, *CWSV*; he made no mention of shifting ideas concerning conjugal intimacy.

91. Swami Vivekananda, "Women of India," delivered at the Shakespeare Club House in Pasadena, California, on January 18, 1900, Lectures and Discourses, vol. 8, *CWSV*.

92. Sankar, *The Monk as Man: The Unknown Life of Swami Vivekananda* (Gurgaon: Penguin, 2015), cited on 3.

93. See Swapna M. Banerjee, "Debates on Domesticity and the Position of Women in Late Colonial India," *History Compass* 8, no. 6 (2010); Anagol, *Emergence of Feminism in India, 1850–1920*, especially 181–209; for global connections, see Barbara N. Ramusack, "Cultural Missionaries, Maternal Imperialists, Feminist Allies: British Women Activists in India, 1865–1945," *Women's Studies International Forum* 13, no. 4 (1990): 309–321; Antoinette M. Burton, "The White Woman's Burden: British Feminists and 'the Indian Woman,' 1865–1915," *Women's Studies International Forum* 13, no. 4 (1990): 295–308; and Mrinalini Sinha, "'Chathams, Pitts, and Gladstones in Petticoats': The Politics of Gender and Race in the Ilbert Bill Controversy, 1883–1884," in *Western Women and Imperialism: Complicity and Resistance*, ed. Nupur Chaudhuri and Margaret Strobel (Bloomington: Indiana University Press, 1992).

94. Rosalind, O'Hanlon, trans., *A Comparison between Women and Men: Tarabai Shinde and the Critique of Gender Relations in Colonial India* (New Delhi: Oxford University Press, 1994).

95. Swami Vivekananda, "The Education That India Needs," Translation: Prose, written to Shrimati Saralâ Ghosal, April 24, 1897, vol. 4, *CWSV*.

96. Sarkar, *Rebels, Wives, Saints*, 199, and Julius Lipner, introduction to Bankimchandra Chatterji, *Anandamath, or the Sacred Brotherhood* (Oxford: Oxford University Press, 2005), 3–126.

97. See Chapter 12; in a talk given in Cambridge, Massachusetts, in 1894, he mentioned another Bankim novel, *Rajasimha* (1882) about the Rajput princess Chârumati, or Rupamati.

98. Sarkar, *Hindu Wife, Hindu Nation,* 51; Rachael Fabish, "The Political Goddess: Aurobindo's Use of Bengali *Sakta* Tantrism to Justify Political Violence in the Indian Anti-Colonial Movement," *South Asia: Journal of South Asian Studies* 30 (2007): 269–292.

99. Swami Vivekananda, "Mother-Worship," Notes of Class Talks and Lectures, vol. 6, *CWSV.*

100. Swami Vivekananda, "Reply to the Address of Welcome at Pamban," Lectures from Colombo to Almora, vol. 3, *CWSV.*

101. See, for example, Swami Vivekananda to Mohammed Sarafaraz Husain, June 10, 1898, 2nd Series, CXLII, vol. 6, *CWSV.*

102. See Ramaswamy, *The Goddess,* especially, 117–151.

103. Shamita Basu, *Religious Revivalism as Nationalist Discourse: Swami Vivekananda and New Hinduism in Nineteenth-Century Bengal* (New York: Oxford University Press, 2002), 124–126.

104. Dipesh Chakrabarty, *Provincializing Europe: Postcolonial Thought and Historical Difference,* new ed. (Princeton: Princeton University Press, 2009), 228–232.

105. Sankar, *The Monk as Man,* 7.

106. Sankar, *The Monk as Man,* 12.

107. Sankar, *The Monk as Man,* also in Swami Tathagatananda, *Swami Vivekananda's Devotion to His Mother Bhuvaneshwari Devi* (Kolkata: Advaita Ashrama, 2014), 20.

108. Sankar, *The Monk as Man,* 12.

109. Sankar, *The Monk as Man,* 50–51.

110. Vivekananda's paternal uncle Gyanadasundari ousted his mother. The case was finally settled on June 28, 1902, just before he died, after the uncle paid financial compensation. For a timeline, see Sankar, *The Monk as Man,* 40–42.

111. Swami Vivekananda to Sara Bull, December 12, 1899, Epistles–2nd Series, CL, vol. 6, *CWSV.*

112. Sankar, *The Monk as Man,* 53.

113. Swami Vivekananda to H. H. Raja of Khetri, November 22, 1898, Letters–5th Series, CXXVIII, vol. 9, *CWSV.*

114. J. T. F. Jordens, *Dayananda Sarasvati: Essays on His Life and Ideas* (New Delhi: Oxford University Press, 1978), 116–120.

115. Jordens, *Dayananda Sarasvati,* 128.

116. For more on the campaign, see Sarkar: *Rebels, Wives, Saints,* 13–68.

117. Vivekananda, "Women of India."

118. Sarkar, *Rebels, Wives, Saints,* 121–152; for an example of the resistance to this view, see 115–118.

119. Burton, *At the Heart of the Empire,* 72–110, recounts her complex relationship with her English "sisters"; for an excellent account see Gauri Viswanathan, *Outside the Fold: Conversion, Modernity, and Belief* (Princeton: Princeton University Press, 1998), 118–152.

120. Pandita Ramabai, *American Encounter: The Peoples of the United States (1889),* trans. and ed. Meera Kosambi (Bloomington: Indiana University Press, 2003), 22–23.

121. Meera Kosambi, "Indian Response to Christianity, Church and Colonialism: Case of Pandita Ramabai," *Economic and Political Weekly,* October 24–31, 1992: 61–69; Amagol-McGinn discusses Ramabai's views in "The Age of Consent Act (1891) Reconsidered," 103, 104n, 108, 110.

122. Sarkar, *Rebels, Wives, Saints,* 13–68; see also Chitra Sinha, *Contesting Patriarchy* (Oxford: Oxford University Press, 2012), 7–8, 13; for more on Roy, see Ashis Nandy, "Sati: A Nineteenth Century Tale of Women, Violence and Protest," *At the Edge of Psychology,* 1–31.

123. Vivekananda, "The Manners and Customs of India" (*Minneapolis Tribune,* December 15, 1893), Newspaper Reports, Part 1: American Newspaper Reports, vol. 9, *CWSV.*

124. Faisal Devji, *The Impossible Indian: Gandhi and the Temptation of Violence* (London: Hurst & Co., 2012), 107–118.

125. Sarkar, *Rebels, Wives, Saints,* 29. She mentions the way notions of "consent" opened up the possibility of an individual legal subjectivity for women on page 140.

126. Lucy Evangeline Guinness, *Across India at the Dawn of the Twentieth Century* (London: Religious Tract Society, 1898), quoted on 145.

127. Pandita Ramabai, *A Testimony* (Kedgaon, Poona: Ramabai Mukti Mission, 9th ed., 1968), 13.

128. Swami Vivekananda, "Child Widows of India" (*Daily Eagle,* February 27, 1895), Reports in American Newspapers, vol. 2, *CWSV.*

129. Vivekananda, "Women of India."

130. Sharleen Mondal, "Hindu Widows as Religious Subjects, Revival in Colonial India," *Journal of Women's History* 29 (2017): 110–136.

131. Swami Vivekananda to "Friends" [his disciples in Madras], January 24, 1894, Epistles– 1st Series, VII, vol. 5, Swami Vivekananda, VIII (From the Diary of a Disciple, translated from Bengali), Conversations and Dialogues, vol. 6, *CWSV.*

132. K. Sundarama Iyer, in *Reminiscences,* https://www.ramakrishnavivekananda.info/remini scences/o57_ksi.htm.

133. Swami Vivekananda to "Dear Brothers" [brother-disciples of Swamiji], 1894, Epistles, 2nd Series, vol. 6.

134. Bal Gangadhar Tilak, in *Reminiscences,* https://www.ramakrishnavivekananda.info /reminiscences/o2o_bgt.htm.

135. Swami Saradananda, *Sri Ramakrishna and His Divine Play,* trans. Swami Chetanan- anda (St. Louis, MO: Vedanta Society of St. Louis, 2003), 764–765 (hereafter *Divine Play*), 679; the dishes in Bengali are *nadu* and *charchari.*

136. For the "butter thief," see Chapter 2.

137. "Repetition of the mantra": *Divine Play,* 680; pulling her rosary: In India, a rosary could be as simple as a string of beans or beads and was used to count prayers.

138. *Divine Play,* 680.

139. *Divine Play,* 681.

140. *Divine Play,* 681.

141. Mahendranath Gupta, *Sri Ramakrishna Kathamrita,* 5 vols. (Calcutta: Kathamrita Bhawan, 1902–1932), www.kathamrita.org/kathamrita, 2:4 (hereafter *Kathamrita*), 2:354.

142. Swami Chetanananda, *Sri Sarada Devi and Her Divine Play* (St. Louis, MO: Vedanta So- ciety of St. Louis, 2015), 137–138.

143. Chetanananda, *Sri Sarada Devi and Her Divine Play,* 141.

144. Chetanananda, *Sri Sarada Devi and Her Divine Play,* 144.

145. She claimed that Ramakrishna told her to keep her jewelry.

146. Chetanananda, *Sri Sarada Devi and Her Divine Play,* 171.

147. Brahmachari Akshaychaitanya, *The Compassionate Mother: The Oldest Biography of Sri Sarada Devi* (Kolkata: Advaita Ashrama, 2009), 118.

148. Trishia Nicole Goulet, *The Lives of Sarada Devi: Gender, Renunciation, and Hindu Poli- tics in Colonial India* (PhD diss., University of Manitoba, Religion Department, 2010), 50.

149. Swami Tapasyananda, *Sri Sarada Devi, The Holy Mother* (Madras: Sri Ramakrishna Math, 1977), 97.

150. Goulet, *The Lives of Sarada Devi,* 218.

151. See Swami Saradeshananda, *The Mother as I Saw Her: Reminiscences of Holy Mother Sri Sarada Devi,* trans. J. N. Dey (Madras: Sri Ramakrishna Math, 1982), and Swami Purtnat- mananda, *Reminiscences of Sri Sarada Devi,* trans. Maloti Sen Gupta (Mayavati: Advaita Ash- rama, 2004); see also Swami Gambhirananda, *Holy Mother, Sri Sarada Devi* (Mylapore, Madras: Sri Ramakrishna Math, 1977), 395–425.

152. For a different and fuller translation, see Vivekananda, *Amba Stotram: Hindi Translation by Sagar Pitroda,* Archive.org, https://archive.org/details/AmbaStotramBySwamiVivekanandaSanskritHindiEngTranslationBySagarPitroda.

153. Meena Khandelwal, *Women in Ochre Robes: Gendering Renunciation* (Albany: SUNY Press, 2004), 187, Narasingha Prosad Sil, *Divine Dowager: The Life and Teachings of Saradamani, the Holy Mother* (Selingsgrove, PA: Susquehanna University Press, 2003), 50.

7. Magic, Science, Transcendence

1. Swami Vivekananda, "Miracles," Interviews (*Memphis Commercial,* January 15, 1894), vol. 5, in *Complete Works of Swami Vivekananda,* 10 vols., https://en.wikisource.org/wiki/The_Complete_Works_of_Swami_Vivekananda (hereafter *CWSV*).

2. Swami Vivekananda, "Miracles," Reports in American Newspapers (*Evening News,* February 17, 1894), vol. 3, *CWSV*.

3. Mary Louise Burke, *Swami Vivekananda in the West: New Discoveries, His Prophetic Mission,* 4th ed. (Calcutta: Advaita Ashrama, 1992), vol. 1, cited 209.

4. John Zubrzycki, *Empire of Enchantment: The Story of Indian Magic* (London: Hurst, 2018), 99.

5. Shruti Kapila, 'The Enchantment of Science in India," *Isis* 101 (2010): 120–132; Akeel Bilgrami, "Occidentalism the Very Idea: An Essay on Enlightenment and Enchantment," *Critical Inquiry* 32 (2006): 381–411; and his enlarged *Secularism, Identity, and Enchantment* (Cambridge, MA: Harvard University Press, 2014).

6. See Chapter 8 for William James, and Chapter 14 for the collaboration between Nivedita and Jagadish Chandra Bose.

7. Kapila, "Enchantment of Science in India," 125–126.

8. Swami Vivekananda, "The Mission of the Vedanta," Lectures from Colombo to Almora, vol. 3, *CWSV*.

9. Gyan Prakash, *Another Reason: Science and the Imagination of Modern India* (Princeton: Princeton University Press, 1999) analyses this audacious endeavor, passim.

10. See Gillian Beer, *Open Fields: Science in Cultural Encounter* (Oxford: Oxford University Press, 1996), especially, 242–272.

11. Swami Vivekananda, "The Real Nature of Man," delivered on June 21, 1896, in London, Jnana-Yoga, vol. 2, *CWSV*.

12. Zubrzycki, *Empire of Enchantment,* 52.

13. Mahendranath Gupta, *Sri Ramakrishna Kathamrita,* 5 vols. (Calcutta: Kathamrita Bhawan, 1902–1932), www.kathamrita.org/kathamrita, 2:145 (hereafter *Kathamrita*); Ramakrishna had scornfully condemned a magician "buried and . . . in a grave for many years," who emerged when his tomb was unlocked.

14. "Never divulged this": *Sri Saradananda, Sri Ramakrishna and his Divine Play,* 867.

15. *Kathamrita,* 4:453.

16. *Kathamrita,* 4:476.

17. *Kathamrita,* 4:493; the name of the physician is rendered as Doctor Sarkar in the *Kathamrita.*

18. Pratik Chakrabarti, *Western Science in Modern India: Metropolitan Methods, Colonial Practices* (New Delhi: Permanent Black, 2004), 146–179. See also Lal Sircar, *Moral Influences of Physical Science* (Calcutta: Anglo-Sanskrit Press, 2004), 151.

19. Chakrabarti, *Western Science in Modern India,* 146–179, and Makarand Paranjape, "Science, Spirituality and Modern India," in *Science, Spirituality and the Modernization of India,* ed. Makarand R. Paranjape (London: Anthem Press, 2012), 3–14; and Prakash, *Another Reason,* interestingly, Sircar endorsed phrenology (with reserve) and homeopathy, 56–57.

20. Nikhilananda, *Vivekananda: A Biography* (Calcutta: Advaita Ashrama, 1964), 18.

21. Nikhilananda, *Vivekananda*, 18.

22. Asim Chaudhuri, *Vivekananda's Loving Relationships with His Brother Disciples—A Striking Example of Divine Love's Human Manifestations* (Burbank, CA: Chaudhuri Publications, 2019), 122.

23. Swami Saradananda, *Sri Ramakrishna and His Divine Play*, trans. Swami Chetanananda (St. Louis, MO: Vedanta Society of St. Louis, 2003), 764–765 (hereafter *Divine Play*).

24. Swami Vivekananda, "Pratyahara and Dharana," Raja-Yoga, vol. 1, *CWSV*.

25. Thomas Green, "'The Spirit of the Vedanta': Occultism and Piety in Max Müller and Swami Vivekananda's Interpretation of Ramakrishna," *Numen* 64, nos. 2–3 (2017): 244; trans. by Green.

26. See Chapter 8.

27. Gananannth Obeyesekere, *The Awakened Ones: Phenomenology of Visionary Experience* (New York: Columbia University Press, 2012), 325–341; and Joy Dixon, *Divine Feminine: Theosophy and Feminism in England* (Baltimore: Johns Hopkins University Press, 2001), 21–24.

28. I thank Julia Mannherz of Oriel College for reminding me of these important points.

29. For Olcott, see Obeyesekere, *Awakened Ones*, 351–354; Stephen R. Prothero, *White Buddhist The Asian Odyssey of Henry Steel Olcott* (Bloomington: Indiana University Press, 1996); Stephen Prothero, "Henry Steel Olcott and 'Protestant Buddhism,'" *Journal of the American Academy of Religion* 63 (1995): 281–302.

30. Wouter J. Hanegraaff, *New Age Religion and Western Culture: Esotericism in the Mirror of Secular Thought* (Albany: State University of New York Press, 1998), 448–455, 470–472.

31. Antoine Faivre, *Theosophy, Imagination and Tradition: Studies in Western Esotericism* (Albany: State University of New York Press, 2000), 27–28; on 8, he explains how they embraced both Western esotericism and all religions in a universal subjectivity.

32. Dayananda broke with them in 1881; Peter van der Veer, *Imperial Encounters: Religion and Modernity in India and Britain* (Princeton: Princeton University Press, 2001), 55–56.

33. Accused of political engagement by the Raj, the Arya Samaj endorsed Universalism to underscore its putatively "religious" character. See C. S. Adcock, *The Limits of Tolerance: Indian Secularism and the Politics of Religious Freedom* (Oxford: Oxford University Press, 2013), 86–113.

34. Van der Veer, *Imperial Encounters*, 55.

35. Henry Steel Olcott, *The Buddhist Catechism* (Madras: Theosophical Publishing Society, 1915), Project Gutenberg, https://www.gutenberg.org/ebooks/30216; Henry Steel Olcott, *Old Diary Leaves*, 1:300; Henry Steel Olcott with Hikkaduve Sumangala, *A Buddhist Catechism According to the Canon of the Southern Church* (Colombo, Ceylon: Theosophical Society, Buddhist Section, 1881). For Dharmapala's links, see Steven Kemper, *Rescued from the Nation: Anagarika Dharmapala and the Buddhist World* (Chicago: Chicago University Press, 2015), 52–115; and Anne M. Blackburn, *Locations of Buddhism: Colonialism and Modernity in Sri Lanka (Buddhism and Modernity)* (Chicago: University of Chicago Press, 2010), especially 104–142.

36. David L. McMahan, *The Making of Buddhist Modernism* (Oxford: Oxford University Press, 2008), 99–101.

37. Rom Harré, "Positivist Thought in the Nineteenth Century," in *The Cambridge History of Philosophy, 1870–1945*, vol. 1, ed. Thomas Baldwin (Cambridge, UK, Cambridge University Press, 2003), 7–26.

38. Mishka Sinha, "Chapter VII: Proliferation: Sanskrit's Golden Age at Harvard," in *What the Thunder Said: A History of Sanskrit in Britain and the United States, 1828–1939*, manuscript copy cited with kind permission of the author.

39. James Allard, "Idealism in Britain and the United States," *The Cambridge History of Philosophy, 1870–1945*, vol. 1, ed. Thomas Baldwin (Cambridge, UK: Cambridge University Press,

2012), 59; Sandra Den Otter, *British Idealism and Social Explanation: A Study in Late Victorian Thought* (Oxford, UK: Clarendon Press, 1996), especially chapters 3 and 4.

40. Hanegraaff, *New Age Religion*, 443–455.

41. H. P. Blavatsky, *The Secret Doctrine: The Synthesis of Science, Religion and Philosophy*, vol. 1, *Cosmogenesis* (New York, Penguin, 2016), 357.

42. Swami Vivekananda, "Ramakrishna: His Life and Sayings," Translation: Prose, vol. 4, *CWSV*. Translation of a review of *Ramakrishna: His Life and Sayings* by Professor Max Müller,

43. Van der Veer, *Imperial Encounters*, 74.

44. Gauri Viswanathan, "The Ordinary Business of Occultism," *Critical Inquiry* 27 (2000): 29–30.

45. Barton Scott, "Miracle Publics: Theosophy, Christianity, and the Coulomb Affair," *History of Religions* 49 (2009): 172–196.

46. A. Trevithick, "The Theosophical Society and Its Subaltern Acolytes (1880–1986)," *Marburg Journal of Religion* 13 (2008): 16–17; Gregory Tillett, *The Elder Brother: A Biography of Charles Webster Leadbeater* (London: Routledge and Kegan Paul, 1982), especially 77–90.

47. Obeyesekere, *Awakened Ones*, 345–351.

48. Trevithick, "Theosophical Society and its Subaltern Acolytes," 1.

49. Swami Vivekananda, "Stray Remarks on Theosophy," Writings: Prose, vol. 4, *CWSV*.

50. Vivekananda, "Stray Remarks on Theosophy."

51. See Chapter 8; Max Müller, "A Real Mahatman," *Indian Mirror*, December 6 and 10, 1897; *Vivekananda in Indian Newspapers, 1893–1902: Extracts from 22 Newspapers and Periodicals*, ed. with intro. by Sankari Prasad Basu (Calcutta: Dineshchandra Basu, Basu Bhattacharyya, 1969), 109–116 (hereafter Basu).

52. Swami Vivekananda, "Stray Remarks on Theosophy," Writings: Prose, vol. 4, *CWSV*.

53. Swami Vivekananda to Alasinga Perumal, January 23, 1896, Epistles–4th Series, LXIX, vol. 8, *CWSV*.

54. See Green, "'The Spirit of the Vedanta,'" n15; Sarah Dadswell, "Juggler, Fakirs and Jaduwalahs: Indian Magicians and the British Stage," *New Theatre Quarterly* 23 (2007): 3–24; Zubryzycki, *Empire of Enchantment*, 109–146.

55. Swami Vivekananda to Alasinga Perumal, January 23, 1896, Epistles–4th Series, LXIX, vol. 8, *CWSV*.

56. Jung Hyun Kim, "Rethinking Vivekananda through Space and Territorialised Spirituality" (PhD diss., University of Oxford, 2018), 48–54.

57. Swami Vivekananda to Alasinga Perumal, July 11, 1894, Epistles–1st Series, XI, vol. 5, *CWSV*.

58. Swami Vivekananda to Alasinga Perumal, August 31, 1894, Epistles–1st Series, XIII, vol. 5, *CWSV*.

59. Swami Vivekananda "To My Brave Boys," November 19, 1894, Writings: Prose, vol. 4, *CWSV*.

60. Swami Vivekananda to Alasinga Perumal, January 12, 1895, Epistles–1st Series, XXX, vol. 5, *CWSV*; Jung Hyun Kim, "Rethinking Vivekananda through Space and Territorialised Spirituality, c. 1880–1920" (PhD diss., University of Cambridge, History Faculty, 2017), 51–54.

61. Cited in Linda Prugh, *Josephine MacLeod and Vivekananda's Mission* (Chennai: Ramakrishna Math, 2001), 61.

62. Swami Vivekananda, "My Plan of Campaign." delivered at Victoria Hall, Madras, Lectures from Colombo to Almora, vol. 3, *CWSV*.

63. Swami Vivekananda to Mrs. Ole Bull, May 5, 1897, Epistles–3rd Series, XXXIX, vol. 7, *CWSV*.

64. Mrs. Alice M. Hansbrough, in *Reminiscences of Swami Vivekananda*, 3rd ed. (Calcutta: Advaita Ashrama, 1983) (hereafter *Reminiscences*), https://www.ramakrishnavivekananda.info /reminiscences/other_02_amh.htm.

65. Kemper, *Rescued from the Nation*, 52–115.

66. Gandhi: Gandhi, *An Autobiography: The Story of My Experiments with Truth*, trans. Mahadev Desai (Boston: Beacon Press, 1993), 264; Kathryn Tidrick, *Gandhi: A Political and Spiritual Life* (London: I. B. Tauris, 2006), 11–19; Nehru: Jawaharlal Nehru, *An Autobiography* (Harmondsworth: Penguin Books, 2004), 16–17. Besant is the author of *The Ancient Wisdom: An Outline of Theosophical Teachings* (London: Theosophical Publishing Society, 1899).

67. Swami Vivekananda to Mary Hale, September 13, 1894, Epistles–4th Series, XXVIII, vol. 8, *CWSV.*

68. Swami Vivekananda to "brother disciples," December 25, 1894, Epistles–2nd Series, XLVII, vol. 6, *CWSV.*

69. Eric Caplan, *Mind Games: American Culture and the Birth of Psychotherapy* (Berkeley: California University Press, 2001), 61–83.

70. Heather D. Curtis, *Faith in the Great Physician: Suffering and Divine Healing in American Culture, 1860–1900* (Baltimore: Johns Hopkins University Press, 2007), 51–80.

71. See also Catherine L. Albanese, *Nature Religion in America: From the Algonkian Indians to the New Age* (Chicago: Chicago University Press, 1990) and Robert C. Fuller, *Alternative Medicine and American Religious Life* (New York, Oxford University Press, 1989), especially chapters 1 and 2.

72. Brian C. Wilson, *Dr. John Harvey Kellogg and the Religion of Biologic Living* (Bloomington: Indiana University Press, 2014), 30–62; Kellogg ultimately broke with the Church, 106–133.

73. See Chapter 9.

74. For examples, see Stephen Gottschalk, *Rolling Away the Stone: Mary Baker Eddy's Challenge to Materialism* (Bloomington: Indiana University Press, 2006), 50–51, 61.

75. Editions: Amy Voorhees, "Writing Revelation: Mary Baker Eddy and Her Early Editions of 'Science and Health,' 1875–1891" (PhD diss., Religious Studies, University of California, Santa Barbara, 2013), 223; for *Science and Health*, see 209–233; Gillian Gill regards the "1875 text . . . as one of the loneliest books ever written," in *Mary Baker Eddy* (Reading, MA: Perseus Books, 1998), 217; see also 209–233.

76. See Maria H. Frawley, *Invalidism and Identity in Nineteenth-Century Britain* (Chicago: Chicago University Press, 2004), 12–63 for the "borderland status" of long-term illness.

77. Donald F. Duclow, "William James, Mind Cure, and the Religion of Healthy-Mindedness," *Journal of Religion and Health*, 41 (2002): 45–56.

78. Hanegraaff, *New Age Religion*, 485.

79. Hanegraaff, *New Age Religion*, 485.

80. Voorhees, "Writing Revelation," 42, 43.

81. Frank Podmore, "Mary Baker Eddy" in *Mesmerism and Christian Science: A Short History of Mental Healing* (Cambridge, UK: Cambridge University Press, 2011), 267. Podmore mentions that Eddy's first advertisement as a healer appeared in 1868, in the spiritualist paper the *Banner of Light.*

82. Voorhees, "Writing Revelation," 39. It resulted in a libel trial in the 1890s. See Gottschalk, *Rolling Away the Stone*, 274.

83. She endorsed equality between men and women, but she did not, like Elizabeth Cady Stanton, see Christianity as inherently patriarchal: Amy B. Voorhees, "Mary Baker Eddy, the Woman Question, and Christian Salvation: Finding a Consistent Connection by Broadening the Boundaries of Feminist Scholarship," *Journal of Feminist Studies in Religion* 29 (2012): 5–25; Kathi Kern, *Mrs. Stanton's Bible* (Ithaca, NY: Cornell University Press, 2001); Gary Dorrien, *The Remaking of Evangelical Theology* (Louisville, KY: Westminster John Knox, 1998), 1–6, 13–14.

84. Gary Dorrien, *The Making of American Liberal Theology: Imagining Progressive Religion, 1805–1900*, vol. 1 (Louisville, KY: Westminster John Knox, 2001), especially ch. 2.

85. The interest continued in the 1780s with the Asiatic Society of Bengal.

86. See Philip Goldberg, *American Veda: From Emerson and the Beatles to Yoga and Medita-tion: How Indian Spirituality Changed the West* (New York: Three Rivers Press, 2010), 32–38, 42–46; Alan Hodder, "Asian Influences," in *The Oxford Handbook of Transcendentalism,* ed. Joel Myerson, Sandra Harbert Petrulionis, and Laura Dassow Walls (New York: Oxford University Press, 2010), 27–37.

87. Goldberg, *American Veda,* 32–38; this essay is in Ralph Waldo Emerson, *Self-Reliance, the Over-Soul and Other Essays* (Claremont, CA: Coyote Canyon Press, 2010), 55–69; see also Ar-thur Versluis, *American Transcendentalism and Asian Religion* (New York: Oxford University Press, 1993), 51–79; Sara Pike, *New Age and Neopagan Religions in America* (New York: Columbia University Press, 2004), 49–50. Hanegraaff, in *New Age Religion,* 238, explains that Emerson still viewed Eastern religions with some disdain, despite incorporating their ideas.

88. Goldberg, *American Veda,* 31.

89. The impact was great in India as well; see Chapter 1 for Vivekananda's learning of the Over-soul in Calcutta.

90. Goldberg, 33, quoting the *Dictionary of the History of Ideas.* Through Neoplatonism, Americans resisted the dualistic aspects of Plato's thought, speaking of "the One," favoring Plo-tinus, a third-century Roman Egyptian, whose metaphysics explained how Jesus could be both God and man.

91. Frederick C. Dahlstrand, *Amos Bronson Alcott: An Intellectual Biography* (Rutherford, NJ: Fairleigh Dickinson University Press, 1982), 213.

92. Madeline R. Harding, "Vedanta and Christian Science," *Prabuddha Bharata,* 33 (1928): 117; Swami Abhedananda, who received these indications secondhand, said that there were four epi-graphs to do with Vedanta, later all deleted. This piece reveals how much Indians prized such citations.

93. Gill, *Mary Baker Eddy,* 332–333, 335.

94. Quoted in Gottschalk, *Rolling Away the Stone,* 142; and quoted in Claire Hoertz Bada-racco, *Prescribing Faith: Medicine, Media, and Religion in American Culture* (Waco, TX: Baylor University Press, 2007), 87; these disciples established the Church of New Thought in Chicago; Amy B. Voorhees, "Understanding the Religious Gulf Between Mary Baker Eddy, Ursula N. Gestefeld, and Their Churches," *Church History* 80 (2011): 798–831.

95. Swami Vivekananda to "brother disciples," December 25, 1894, Epistles–2nd Series, XLVII, vol. 6, *CWSV.*

96. Vivekananda to "brother disciples," December 25, 1894; Hugh B. Urban, *The Economics of Ecstasy: Tantra, Secrecy and Power in Colonial Bengal* (Oxford: Oxford University Press, 2001), 181; and Sarkar, *Writing Social History,* 315, 320–322; Ramakrishna knew their doctrines and practices and was often discontented with their views; his relationship to them, Kripal argues, remained unresolved: *Kali's Child,* 122–125, 225.

97. Mary Baker Eddy, *Science and Health,* chapter 18, titled "Fruitage" (Boston: Christian Sci-ence Board of Directors, 2006), 600–700, speaks of the healings.

98. Swami Vivekananda to Adhyapakji (Prof. John Henry Wright), May 24, 1894, Epistles–3rd Series, XXI, vol. 7, *CWSV.*

99. Swami Vivekananda, "The Teacher of Spirituality." Addresses on Bhakti-Yoga, vol. 4, *CWSV.*

100. Vivekananda, "The Teacher of Spirituality."

101. Swami Vivekananda to "Friend" (Edward Toronto Sturdy), October 31, 1895, Epistles–4th Series, LVII, vol. 8, *CWSV.*

102. Dhruv Raina and S. Irfan Habib, "The Moral Legitimation of Modern Science: Bhadralok Reflections on Theories of Evolution," *Social Studies of Science* 26 (1996): 9–42, but especially 9.

103. Romila Thapar, "The Theory of Aryan Race and India: History and Politics," *Social Scien-tist,* 24 (1996): 3–29; she shows how important "race" was even before Darwinism to "Aryanism," East and West.

104. Theodor Eimer maintained that variation (especially in moles) was restricted, which suggested that natural selection could not apply in the way Darwin had suggested. Joseph Thomas Cunningham attacked August Weismann's neo-Darwinism, which set forth that only the "germ cells" (gametes) were responsible for inheritance. Others argued that, like crystals, species developed in a certain pattern according to internal laws. See Igor Popov, "Orthogenesis versus Darwinism: The Russian Case," *Revue d'histoire des sciences,* 61, no. (2008): 220, and Mark A. Ulett, "Making the Case for Orthogenesis: The Popularization of Definitely Directed Evolution (1890–1926)," *Studies in History and Philosophy of Biological and Biomedical Sciences* 45 (2014): 124–132. Notions of inherited characteristics remained strong in social science as well; see George W. Stocking Jr., *Race, Culture and Evolution: Essays in the History of Evolution* (New York: Free Press, 1968), 234–269.

105. He wrote to his friend Alasinga, "Lord knows how and when the crystal will form," in Swami Vivekananda to Alasinga Perumal, May 28, 1894, Epistles–1st Series, X, vol. 5, *CWSV.*

106. Pratik Chakrabarti, *Inscriptions of Nature: Geology and the Naturalization of Antiquity* (Baltimore: Johns Hopkins University Press, 2020), 107; see also David. L. Gosling, "Science and the Hindu Tradition," *Zygon* (2012): 575–588; Mackenzie Brown, *Hindu Perspectives on Evolution, Darwin, Dharma, and Design* (London: Routledge, 2012), 131–154.

107. Swami Vivekananda, "The Cosmos: The Macrocosm," delivered in New York, January 19, 1896, Jnana-Yoga, vol. 2, *CWSV.*

108. D. H. Killingley, "Yoga-Sutra IV, 2–3 and Vivekananda's Interpretation of Evolution," *Journal of Indian Philosophy* 18 (1990): 151.

109. James R. Moore, *Post-Darwinian Controversies* (Cambridge, UK: Cambridge University Press, 1979); see especially 77–100; 217–298; Swami Vivekananda, "The Reality and the Shadow," Notes of Class Talks and Lectures, vol. 6, *CWSV.*

110. Swami Vivekananda, VIII, Conversations and Dialogues, vol. 7, *CWSV.*

111. Vivekananda, VIII, Conversations and Dialogues.

112. Kapila, "Enchantment of Science in India," passim, and Raina and Habib, "Moral Legitimation of Modern Science," 29.

113. Swami Vivekananda, "Evolution," Notes from Lectures and Discourses, vol. 5, *CWSV.*

114. He was not alone; see Shruti Kapila, "Self, Spencer, and Swaraj: Nationalist Thought and Critiques of Liberalism, 1890–1920," *Modern Intellectual History* 44 (2007): 109–127.

115. Vivekananda, "Evolution."

116. "Born criminal": Daniel Pick, *Faces of Degeneration: A European Disorder, c. 1848–1918* (Cambridge, UK: Cambridge University Press, 1989), 109–152; killing evil-doers: Swami Vivekananda, VIII, Conversations and Dialogues, vol. 7, *CWSV.*

117. See Mark Maguire, "The Birth of Biometric Security," *Anthropology Today* 25, no. 2 (April 25, 2009): 9–14.

118. Swami Vivekananda, "The Atman: Its Bondage and Freedom," Jnana-Yoga, vol. 2, *CWSV.*

119. Gandhi famously said, "To lose patience is to lose the battle." Quoted in N. B. Sen, ed., *Wit and Wisdom of Gandhi, Nehru, Tagore* (New Delhi: New Book Society of India, 1968), 365. See Uday Singh Mehta, "Gandhi on Democracy, Politics and the Ethics of Everyday Life," in *Political Thought in Action,* ed. Kapila, F. Devji (Cambridge, UK: Cambridge University Press, 2013), 88–106.

120. Vivekananda, "Evolution,"

121. Vivekananda, "Evolution."

122. Brown, *Hindu Perspectives,* 144.

123. Vivekananda, "The Atman: Its Bondage and Freedom."

124. Killingley, "Yoga-sutra IV," 153.

125. Darwin held no special place for "Man Place in Nature" and believed that people were subject to the same natural laws as animals. For Thomas Huxley, see Killingley, "Yoga-sutra IV,"

154; In contrast, Alfred Russell Wallace, who had "co-discovered" natural selection, argued that the "moral and higher intellectual nature of man" did not originate by any "law of evolution"; see Peter Raby, *Alfred Russel Wallace: A Life* (Princeton: Princeton University Press, 2001), quoted 202.

126. This meant something very different to Pantanjali; Killingley, "Yoga-Sutra IV," 157.

127. Vivekananda, "Evolution."

128. Akhandananda, recognized the error: "'Man progresses birth after birth; he has no retrogression such as being reborn as beasts and other creatures'—and [he] asked me not to talk about it anywhere." Swami Akhandananda, *Service of God in Man* (Chennai: Sri Ramakrishna Math, 2013), 121–122.

129. Brown, *Hindu Perspectives*, 139–140; Clifford Geertz, in his *Agricultural Involution: The Process of Ecological Change in Indonesia* (Berkeley: California University Press, 1963), used the term to describe a nonprogressive kind of monoculture.

130. Vivekananda, "The Cosmos and the Self," Notes from Lectures and Discourses, vol. 5, *CWSV.*

131. Ernst Haeckel, *The History of Creation: Or, the Development of the Earth and its Inhabitants by the Action of Natural Causes*, trans. and ed. E. Ray Lankester (New York: D. Appleton and Company, 1880), 10–11.

132. Swami Vivekananda, talk delivered on August 5, 1895, "Recorded by Miss S. E. Waldo, a Disciple," Inspired Talks, vol. 7, *CWSV.*

8. Green Acre, William James, and Raja Yoga

1. A sapling from the original pine was transported from Green Acre and planted at Ridgely, though it later died; I thank Swami Chetanananda for this information.

2. Swami Vivekananda to the Hale sisters, Epistles–2nd Series, July 31, 1894, XLIV, vol. 6, in *Complete Works of Swami Vivekananda*, 10 vols., https://en.wikisource.org/wiki/The_Complete _Works_of_Swami_Vivekananda (hereafter *CWSV*).

3. Ruth Harris, 'Vivekananda, Sarah Farmer, and Global Spiritual Transformations in the Fin de Siècle," *Journal of Global History* 14 (2019), 179–198.

4. This did not mean they abandoned all Christian beliefs, however.

5. Catherine Tumber, *American Feminism and the Birth of New Age Spirituality: Searching for the Higher Self, 1875–1915* (Lanham, MD: Rowman & Littlefield, 2002), 123.

6. Pravrajika Prabuddhaprana, *Saint Sara: The Life of Sara Chapman Bull: The American Mother of Swami Vivekananda* (Dakshineswar: Sri Sarada Math, 2002), 8.

7. See Chapter 1.

8. Catherine Albanese, *A Republic of Mind and Spirit: A Cultural History of American Metaphysical Religion* (New Haven, CT: Yale University Press: 2007), 160–163.

9. Leigh Eric Schmidt, in *Restless Souls: The Making of American Spirituality from Emerson to Oprah* (New York: Harper San Francisco, 2005), argues that these spiritual innovations may have offset the intermittent intolerance of Evangelicalism.

10. S. Farmer, "The Green Acre Ideal," 1898, 2, in Archives of the National Spiritual Assembly of the Bahá'ís of the United States, Wilmette, IL, https://bahai-library.com/uhj_bahai_archives _texts.

11. See *Lewis G. Janes: Philosopher, Patriot, Lover of Man* (Boston, James H. West, 1902); see also "Comparative Religion Notes," *Biblical World* 8 (1896), 166.

12. Schmidt, *Restless Souls*, 195–196.

13. Margaret R. Ford, *Sarah Farmer*, unpublished memoir, Baha'i Archives, https://bahai -library.com/uhj_bahai_archives_texts.

14. Einar Haugen, *Ole Bull: Norway's Romantic Musician and Cosmopolitan Patriot* (Madison: University of Wisconsin Press, 1993).

15. Sister Nivedita to Josephine MacLeod, March 29, 1901, *Letters of Sister Nivedita,* collected and ed. Sankari Prasad Basu, 2 vols. (Kolkata: Advaita Ashrama, 2017), vol. 1, no. 167. Nivedita explained how a bronze statue of Bull was to be unveiled in Bergen on May 17, Constitution Day, when Norwegians protested the union with Sweden.

16. Prabuddhaprana, *Saint Sara,* quoted on 57.

17. Emma Calvé, *My Life,* trans. Rosamon Gilder (New York: D. Appleton and Company, 1922), 185–194.

18. Prabuddhaprana, *Saint Sara,* 59.

19. Babbitt's translations: Prabuddhaprana, *Saint Sara,* 58; "For hatred": Irving Babbitt, *Dhammapada, Translated from the Pali with an Essay on Buddha and the Occident* (Oxford, Oxford University Press, 1936), 3.

20. Thomas A. Tweed, *American Encounter with Buddhism, 1844–1912: Victorian Culture & the Limits of Dissent* (Chapel Hill: University of North Carolina Press, 1992), 26–47.

21. Prabuddhaprana, *Saint Sara,* 59.

22. When Sara Bull was in contact with Savage, he was publishing his *Poems of Modern Thought* (London: Williams and Norgate, 1884); he later wrote *Life Beyond Death: Being a Review of the World's Beliefs on the Subject* (New York: G. P. Putnam's Sons, 1905).

23. Tumber, *American Feminism,* 10–65.

24. Ann Braude, *Radical Spirits: Spiritualism and Women's Rights in Nineteenth-Century America* (Boston: Beacon Press, 1989), 41.

25. R. F. Foster, *W. B. Yeats: A Life,* vol. 1, *The Apprentice Mage* (Oxford: Oxford University Press, 1997), 147–8; Mriganka Mukhopadhyay, "Mohini: A Case Study of a Transnational Spiritual Space in the History of the Theosophical Society," *Numen* 67 (2020): 165–190.

26. C. A. Bayly, "India, the Bhagavad Gita and the World" and Mishka Sinha, "The Transnational Gita," in *Political Thought in Action: The Bhagavad Gita and Modern India,* ed. Shruti Kapila and Faisal Devji (Cambridge, UK: Cambridge University Press, 2013), 1–24, 25–47.

27. Mohini M. Chatterji, *The Bhagavad Gita, or the Lord's Lay: with Commentary and Notes, as Well as References to the Christian Scriptures* (Boston: Houghton Mifflin Company, 1887), 6; in Mohini's text, the biblical references are cited as footnotes. I have altered their position.

28. Prabuddhaprana, *Saint Sara,* quoted on 66.

29. Thomas Merton, *The Seven Storey Mountain* (London: SPCK, 2009), 191–199; and Romain Rolland, *The Life of Vivekananda and the Universal Gospel,* vol. 2 (Almora: Advaita Ashrama, 1947), 395–396, suggests how India might revivify Christian mystical traditions.

30. Richard Hodgson: He had first been involved with the Society for Psychical Research in Britain, and then secretary of the American organization; music: Richard Hodgson to Sara Bull, Boston, June 24, 1887, and her response June 24, 1887; Sara Bull Collection, Vedanta Society of San Francisco.

31. Prabuddhaprana, *Saint Sara,* quoted on 67.

32. Tumber, *American Feminism,* 25. Chautauqua assemblies were named after a lake in southwest New York; the name was Native American in origin.

33. Quoted in Prabuddhaprana, *Saint Sara,* 89.

34. Prabuddhaprana, *Saint Sara,* 90.

35. Prabuddhaprana, *Saint Sara,* 90.

36. Schmidt, *Restless Souls,* 194.

37. Ford, *Sarah Farmer,* 1.

38. See Chapters 8, 9, 14.

39. See Joy Dixon, *Divine Feminine: Theosophy and Feminism in England* (Baltimore: Johns Hopkins University Press, 2001), 168–171.

40. Mrs. J. H. Morrison to Sara Bull, December 19, 1894, Archives of the Vedanta Society of Northern California.

41. "Swami's Pine": Linda Prugh, *Josephine MacLeod and Vivekananda's Mission* (Chennai: Ramakrishna Math, 2001), 304; "Bodhi Tree": Schmidt, *Restless Souls,* 194.

42. Franklin Benjamin Sanborn, *Henry D. Thoreau* (Houghton Mifflin: Boston, MA, 1882), 126.

43. Gopal Stavig, *Western Admirers of Ramakrishna and His Disciples* (Kolkata: Advaita Ashrama, 2010), 354.

44. Henry David Thoreau, *Oxford World's Classics: Walden,* ed. Stephen Fender (Oxford: Oxford University Press, 1999), 265.

45. Thoreau, *Walden,* 266.

46. Robert W. Delp, "Andrew Jackson Davis and Spiritualism," in *Pseudo-Science and Society in Nineteenth-Century America,* ed. Arthur Wrobel (Lexington: Kentucky University Press, 1987), 100–121 and Sara Pike, *New Age and Neopagan Religions in America* (New York: Columbia University Press, 2004), 48–49.

47. Emmanuel Swedenborg, *Heaven and Its Wonders and Hell,* trans. John C. Ager (West Chester, PA: Swedenborg Foundation, 2009), 352.

48. Emmanuel Swedenborg, *A Swedenborg Sampler,* trans. G. F. Dole, Linda Hyatt Cooper, and Jonathan S. Rose (West Chester, PA: Swedenborg Foundation, 2011), 9.

49. Swami Vivekananda, "The Divinity of Man," Reports in American Newspapers (*Detroit Free Press,* February 18, 1894), vol. 3, *CWSV.*

50. Vivekananda, "The Divinity of Man."

51. Horatio W. Dresser, *Spiritual Health and Healing* (New York: Thomas Y. Crowell, 1922), 160.

52. Dresser, *Spiritual Health and Healing.*

53. Swami Vivekananda to Sara Bull, January 3, 1896, Letters–5th Series, LXXXI, vol. 9, *CWSV;* he hesitated before he accepted, per Rajagopal Chattopadhyaya, *Swami Vivekananda in India: A Corrective Biography* (New Delhi: Motilal Banarsidass, 1999), 362.

54. Ralph Waldo Trine, *In Tune with the Infinite: Or, Fullness of Peace, Power and Plenty* (New York: Dodd, Mead and Company, 1897), 15.

55. Trine, *In Tune with the Infinite,* 16.

56. Swami Vivekananda, "The Aim of Raja-Yoga," Notes from Lectures and Discourses, vol. 5, *CWSV.*

57. Trine was a special correspondent for the *Boston Daily,* reporting on conferences and symposia, and hence on Vivekananda. See John R. Haller Jr., *Distant Voices: Sketches of a Swedenborgian Worldview* (London: Swedenborg Society, 2017), 216.

58. Swami Vivekananda to Mary Hale, June 22, 1895, Epistles–4th Series, XLVI, vol. 8, *CWSV.*

59. Swami Vivekananda to the Hale sisters, July 31, 1894, Epistles–2nd Series, XLIV, vol. 6, *CWSV.*

60. Sister Christine, in Swami Suddhananda, *Reminiscences of Swami Vivekananda,* 3rd ed. (Calcutta: Advaita Ashrama, 1983), http://ramakrishnavivekananda.info/reminiscences/146_sc .htm (hereafter *Reminiscences*). She explained that his employer was Pond's Lecture Bureau.

61. Mrs. Alice M. Hansbrough, in *Reminiscences,* https://www.ramakrishnavivekananda .info/reminiscences/other_02_amh.htm.

62. Prabuddhaprana, *Saint Sara,* 93.

63. See Shinjini Das, *Vernacular Medicine in Colonial India: Family, Market and Homoeopathy* (Cambridge: Cambridge University Press, 2019).

64. Swami Vivekananda, to Shri Pramadadas Mitra, March 21, 1899, Epistles–4th Series, III (translated from Bengali), vol. 8, *CWSV.*

65. Mesmerism: Alison Winter, *Mesmerized: Powers of Mind in Victorian Britain* (Chicago: Chicago University Press, 1998), 187–212; climate: Swami Vivekananda to Mary Hale, December 27, 1899, Epistles–4th Series, CXLIII, vol. 8, *CWSV*.

66. Swami Vivekananda, "Matter for Serious Thought" (translated from Bengali), vol. 6, Writings: Prose and Poems (Original and Translated), vol. 6, *CWSV*.

67. Swami Vivekananda, "Psychic Prana," Raja-Yoga, vol. 1, *CWSV*; at Harvard, however, he denied that Advaita had anything to do with "self-hypnosis" during questioning; see Swami Vivekananda, "I: Discussion at The Graduate Philosophical Society of Harvard University," Questions and Answers, vol. 5, *CWSV*.

68. Fuller, *Alternative Medicine*, 66–90.

69. Swami Vivekananda to Josephine MacLeod, August 3, 1899, CXXXVIII, vol. 8, *CWSV*; William Passey of Oxford pointed out this possible allusion.

70. Swami Vivekananda to Mary Hale, September 1899, Epistles–4th Series, CXLIII, vol. 8, *CWSV*. See also Holly Folk, *The Religion of Chiropractic: Populist Healing from the American Heartland* (Chapel Hill, NC: UNC Press, 2018), 186.

71. Swami Vivekananda to the Hale Sisters, July 31, 1894, Epistles–2nd Series, XLIV, vol. 6, *CWSV*.

72. Catherine L. Albanese, in *Nature Religion in America: From the Algonkian Indians to the New Age* (Chicago: Chicago University Press, 1990), passim, reveals how these categories were often overlapping.

73. Swami Vivekananda, "The Religion of India," Notes of Lectures and Classes, vol. 9, *CWSV*.

74. See Dermot Killingley, "Manufacturing Yogis: Swami Vivekananda as a Yoga Teacher," in Mark Singleton and Ellen Goldberg, *Gurus of Modern Yoga* (Oxford: Oxford University Press, 2013), 18–34.

75. Mishka Sinha, *What the Thunder Said: A History of Sanskrit in Britain and the United States, 1828–1939* (forthcoming), manuscript cited with kind permission of the author.

76. Mishka Sinha, "Orienting America: Sanskrit and Modern Scholarship in the United States, 1842–1894," in *Debating Orientalism*, ed. Zaid Elmarsafy, and Anna Bernard, David Atwell (Basingstoke, UK: Palgrave Macmillan, 2013), 71–93, and Mishka Sinha, *What the Thunder Said: A History of Sanskrit in Britain and the United States, 1828–1939* (forthcoming), manuscript cited with kind permission of the author.

77. Sinha, *What the Thunder Said*.

78. Prabuddhaprana, *Saint Sara*, 182.

79. Swami Vivekananda to Mrs. Ole Bull, May 8, 1896, Letters–5th Series, XCII, vol. 9, *CWSV*.

80. Prem Shankar and Uma Parameswaram, "Swami Vivekananda and William James in the History of Transpersonal Psychology," *Annals of the Bhandarkar Oriental Research Institute* 67, no. 1 / 4 (1986): 117–124, especially 120.

81. William James, "Lecture IV: The One and the Many," *Pragmatism: A New Name for Some Old Ways of Thinking* (Cambridge: Cambridge University Press, 2014), 152–153.

82. James, *Pragmatism*, 153–154.

83. "Psychologically profound": Robert C. Fuller, *Americans and the Unconscious* (Oxford: Oxford University Press, 1986), 79.

84. Janet Oppenheim, *The Other World: Spiritualism and Psychical Research in England, 1850–1914* (Cambridge, UK: Cambridge University Press, 2004), 110–135.

85. Haller, *Distant Voices*, 1–47.

86. James, *Pragmatism*, 12.

87. James, *Pragmatism*, 9.

88. William James, *Essays in Psychical Research*, ed. Robert A. McDermott (Cambridge, MA: Harvard University Press, 1986); for Mrs. Piper, see 79, 187, 394, 398, 400, 442, 492, 494.

89. Krister Dylan Knapp, *William James: Psychical Research and the Challenge of Modernity* (Chapel Hill: University of North Carolina Press, 2017), 186–198.

90. "Will to believe": The name of a lecture James published in 1896 in *New World* 5 (1896), 327–347; dramatic potential: Knapp, *William James*, 175.

91. James, "The Confidences of a "Psychical Researcher," in *Essays in Psychical Research*, 374.

92. Stephanie L. Hawkins, in "William James, Gustav Fechner, and Early Psychophysics," *Frontiers of Physiology*, 2 (2011): 1–10, maintains that Fechner's "wave theory" shaped his view of the "mother-sea of consciousness"; the metaphor was much closer to Ramakrishna's.

93. Dale Riepe, "A Note on William James and Indian Philosophy," *Philosophy and Phenomenological Research* 28 (1968): 587.

94. Moncure D. Conway, "Memories of Max Müller," *North American Review* 171, no. 529 (December 1900): 884–893.

95. Swami Vivekananda to the Hale sisters: May 5, 1895, Epistles–2nd Series, XLII, vol. 8, *CWSV*.

96. Swami Vivekananda to Mary Hale, May 30, 1896, Epistles–2nd Series, LXXVI, vol. 8, *CWSV*.

97. Swami Vivekananda, "On Professor Max Müller," Writings: Prose, vol. 4, *CWSV*; June 6, 1896, published in the *Brahmavadin*.

98. Thomas H. Green, *Religion for a Secular Age: Max Müller, Swami Vivekananda and Vedanta* (London: Routledge, 2016), 79–112.

99. Max Müller, "A Real Mahatman," *Nineteenth-Century* 40 (1896): 306–319.

100. "A very nice man": Prabuddhaprana, *Saint Sara*, 183.

101. Swami Vivekananda to "Frankincense" (Mr. Francis H. Leggett), July 6, 1896, Epistles–2nd Series, CII, vol. 6, *CWSV*.

102. Vivekananda, "On Professor Max Müller."

103. Jason A. Josephson-Storm, *The Myth of Disenchantment: Magic, Modernity, and the Birth of the Human Sciences* (Chicago: University of Chicago Press, 2017), 107–124.

104. See Thomas Green, "'The Spirit of Vedanta": Occultism and Piety in Max Müller and Swami Vivekananda's Interpretation of Ramakrishna," *Numen* 64 (2017): 229–257.

105. Max Müller, *Ramakrishna: His Life and Sayings* (London: Theosophical Publishing Society, 1898), 129.

106. Müller, *Ramakrishna*, 183.

107. William James, *The Varieties of Religious Experience* (New York: Viking Penguin, 1982), 361, 365.

108. William James, *The Correspondence of William James*, vol. 9, ed. Ignas K. Skrupskelis and Elizabeth M. Berkeley (Charlottesville: University Press of Virginia, 1992–2004), 544, September 17, 1901, to Alice James.

109. It was later included in Swami Vivekananda, "The Real and the Apparent Man," *Jnana-Yoga* (1907), vol. 2, *CWSV*; lecture given in New York on February 16, 1896, and again in London on June 21, 1896.

110. William James, *Varieties*, 513–514. He cites Swami Vivekananda, "The Open Secret," "Practical Vendata" and Other Lectures, vol. 2, *CWSV*; this lecture was given in Los Angeles on January 5, 1900. He also cites Swami Vivekananda, "Practical Vedanta: Part IV," "Practical Vendata" and Other Lectures, vol. 2, *CWSV*, given in London on December 18, 1896 (though James notes 1897), and Vivekananda, "The Real and Apparent Man."

111. Calvé, *My Life*; she told Vivekananda: "I cling to my individuality . . . I don't want to be absorbed into the Eternal Unity!": 187–188.

112. James, *Correspondence of William James*, vol. 8, 487, January 11, 1899, to William Sloane Kennedy. Knapp also uses these quotations in *William James*, 276–280.

113. James, *Correspondence of William James*, vol. 8, 491, January 28, 1899, to James Ward.

114. Knapp, *William James*, 276–280.

115. See Swami Vivekananda, "The Basis for Psychic or Spiritual Research," Lectures and Discourses, vol. 4, *CWSV*.

116. G. William Barnard, *Exploring Unseen Worlds: William James and the Philosophy of Mysticism* (Albany: State University of New York, 1997), 237–244, suggests that James was targeting academic neo-Hegelianism, not Eastern religion.

117. Swami Vivekananda, "Dhyana and Samadhi," Ch. VII in Raja-Yoga, vol. 1, *CWSV.*

118. Swami Vivekananda, "Introductory," Raja-Yoga, vol. 1, *CWSV.*

119. Swami Vivekananda, "Preface," Raja-Yoga, vol. 1, *CWSV.*

120. 'Swami Vivekananda, "Prana," Raja-Yoga, vol. 1, *CWSV.*

121. Vivekananda did not, however, reject pranayama or avoid discussion of the kundalini.

122. These qualities are homologous with caste divisions, albeit from a Brahmin point of view: sattva, is associated with Brahmins; rajas, with Kshatriyas; and tamas, with Dalits.

123. David Gordon White, *The Yoga Sutra of Patanjali: A Biography* (Princeton: Princeton University Press, 2014), 31–32.

124. The term he used was *moksha.*

125. White, *Yoga Sutra,* 48.

126. White, *Yoga Sutra,* 1.

127. As early as 1885, Blavatsky spoke of prana, of notions of "ether," 'astral light," and "magnetic fluid," as essential to her communication with her mahatmas. H. P. Blavatsky, *The Secret Doctrine: The Synthesis of Science, Religion and Philosophy,* vol. 1: *Cosmogenesis* (New York: Penguin, 2016). For references to "prana," see, for example, 109, 112, 1036, 1039, 1240; "ether," 242–244; *"an lumen sit corpus, nec non?,"* 370–373; for "astral light," 55–57; and for "magnetic fluid," 56, 81, and 391–392. Nor were Colebrooke's and Müller's fears entirely fantasy; William R. Pinch, *Warrior Ascetics and Indian Empires* (New York: Cambridge University Press, 2006) describes how sadhus claimed exceptional powers and turned to violence, for example, 196–197, 211–212, and 238–248; Zubrzycki, *Empire of Enchantment,* describes the "rope trick," 5.

128. They could fend off hunger, their bodies became indestructible, etc.

129. Swami Vivekananda, "Patanjali's Yoga Aphorism—powers," Raja-Yoga, vol. 1, *CWSV.*

130. The Sanskrit terms were *pratyahara, dharana,* and *dhyana.*

131. Elizabeth de Michelis, *A History of Modern Yoga* (London: Continuum, 2004), 150.

132. Vivekananda, "Prana," Raja-Yoga.

133. Julia Mannherz, "Popular Occultism in Late Imperial Russia" (PhD diss., History Faculty, University of Cambridge, 2005), 187–189.

134. See Anna Pokazanyeva, "Mind within Matter: Science, the Occult, and the (Meta) Physics of Ether and Akasha," *Zygon, Journal of Religion & Science* 51 (2016): 318–346; Swami Vivekananda, "The Ether," Writings: Prose and Poems (Original and Translated), vol. 9, *CWSV;* anonymous article in February 1895 issue of *New York Medical Times;* see also Imogen Clarke, "The Ether at the Crossroads of Classical and Modern Physics," in Jaume Navarro, *Ether and Modernity: The Recalcitrance of an Epistemic Object in the Early Twentieth Century* (Oxford: Oxford University Press, 2018), 14–25; she focuses on 1909–1914, when reputable physicists continued to use this term.

135. Sam Halliday, "Electricity, Telephony, Communication," in *Late Victorian into Modern (Oxford Twenty-First Century Approaches to Literature),* ed. Laura Marcus, Michèle Mendelsohn, and Kirsten E. Shepherd-Barr, (Oxford: Oxford University Press, 2014), 597–609.

136. Vivekananda, "Introductory," *Raja-Yoga.*

137. Josephson-Storm, *The Myth of Disenchantment,* 107–124.

138. Swami Vidyatmananda, *Vivekananda in Europe* (Kolkata: Advaita Ashrama, 2012), passim.

139. Swami Vivekananda to Sister Christine, September 15, 1900, Letters–5th Series, CLXXXIV, vol. 9, *CWSV.* They seemed to return there together, see in Swami Vidyatmananda, *Vivekananda in Europe,* 44–45.

140. Nile Green, "Breathing in India, c. 1890," *Modern Asian Studies* 42, nos. 2–3 (2008): 283–315.

141. Isabel Margesson, in *Reminiscences,* https://www.ramakrishnavivekananda.info/reminiscences/380_im.htm.

142. Josephine MacLeod, in *Reminiscences,* https://www.ramakrishnavivekananda.info/remini scences/228_jm.htm.

143. Ida Ansell, in *Reminiscences,* https://www.ramakrishnavivekananda.info/reminiscences /362_ia.htm.

144. Margesson, in *Reminiscences.*

145. Green, "Breathing in India, c. 1890," and, as Green suggests, also tamed the wildness of the Indian holy man.

146. Swami Vivekananda, "The Aim of Raja-Yoga," Notes from Lectures and Discourses, vol. 5, *CWSV.*

147. Quoted in White, *Yoga Sutra of Patanjali,* 116.

148. Swami Vivekananda, "The First Steps," Raja-Yoga, vol. 1, *CWSV;* Mark Singleton, *Yoga Body: The Origins of Modern Posture Practice* (Oxford: Oxford University Press, 2010), 70–75, and Swami Gambhirananda, ed., *The Apostles of Shri Ramakrishna* (Calcutta: Advaita Ashrama, 1982), 132.

149. *Kathamrita,* 2:326.

150. This is called the kundalini.

151. Vivekananda, "Prana," Raja-Yoga.

152. Swami Vivekananda, "Control of the Psychic Prana," Raja-Yoga, vol. 1, *CWSV.*

153. From Mrs. George Roorbach's reminiscences of Camp Taylor, California, May 1900, quoted in Swami Vivekananda, "Sayings and Utterances," *CWSV* 9.

154. Prakash, *Another Reason,* 127.

155. See Chapter 12.

156. Swami Vivekananda, talk delivered on August 3, 1895, "Recorded by Miss E. Waldo, a disciple," Inspired Talks, vol. 7, *CWSV.*

157. Swami Vivekananda to Mary Hale, September 17, 1896, Epistles–4th Series, LXXXV, vol. 8, *CWSV,* in which he advocated celibacy to her.

158. Swami Vivekananda, "From the Diary of a Disciple," XVIII, Conversations and Dialogues, vol. 7, *CWSV.*

159. Swami Vivekananda, Sayings and Utterances. no. 85, vol. 9, *CWSV.* For the quotation, see Sister Nivedita, "Glimpses in the West," The Master as I Saw Him, in *The Complete Works of Sister Nivedita,* ed. Pravrajika Atmapranam, 2nd ed., 5 vols. (Kolkata: Advaita Ashrama, 2016), 1:158.

160. Peter van der Veer, *The Modern Spirit, of Asia: The Spiritual and the Secular in China and India* (Princeton: Princeton University Press, 2013), 173–178 highlights this "embodied nationalism," as does Joseph S. Alter, *The Wrestler's Body: Identity and Ideology in North India* (Berkeley: University of California Press, 1992) and especially his *Yoga in Modern India: The Body between Science and Philosophy* (Princeton: Princeton University Press, 2021), passim.

161. Alex Wolfers, "Born like Krishna in the Prison-House: Revolutionary Asceticism in the Political Ashram of Aurobindo Ghose," *South Asia: Journal of South Asian Studies* 39 (2016): 525–545; for Aurobindo, see Chapter 15.

162. As Green suggests in "Breathing in India," 302, Vivekananda was an important innovator, but the twentieth century brought others; see Hazrat Inayat Khan, *Sufi Teachings,* vol. 8: *The Sufi Message* (New Delhi: Motilal Banarisidass, 1990), 49–56; see also Peter Heehs, *The Lives of Aurobindo* (New York: Columbia University Press, 2008), for example, 146–150.

9. Female Devotees and the Labors of the Guru

1. Swami Vivekananda to Mrs. G. W. Hale. June 28, 1894, Letters–5th Series, XXII, vol. 9, in *Complete Works of Swami Vivekananda,* 10 vols., https://en.wikisource.org/wiki/The_Complete_Works _of_Swami_Vivekananda (hereafter *CWSV*).

2. Swami Vivekananda to Sara Bull, June 7, 1895, Epistles–2nd Series, LXVII, vol. 6, *CWSV.*

3. He wrote: "American Indians were in this country for thousands of years, and a few handfuls of your ancestors came to their land. What difference they have caused in the appearance of the country! Why did not the Indians make improvements and build cities, if all were equal?" Swami Vivekananda, "The Ideal of Karma-Yoga," Karma-Yoga, vol. 1, *CWSV.*

4. Sister Christine, "The Master and the Message," in Swami Suddhananda, *Reminiscences of Swami Vivekananda,* 3rd ed. (Calcutta: Advaita Ashrama, 1983), http://ramakrishnavivekananda .info/reminiscences/146_sc.htm (hereafter *Reminiscences*).

5. Pravrajika Vrajaprana, *A Portrait of Sister Christine* (Kolkata: Ramakrishna Mission Institute of Culture, 1996), 4. Quoting an unpublished manuscript held at the Sarada Convent, Santa Barbara, 1927.

6. Vrajaprana, *A Portrait of Sister Christine,* 1.

7. The following blog has the most complete information on Libbie Dutcher that I have been able to find: Vivekananda Abroad: A Postcard Pilgrimage, https://vivekanandaabroad.blogspot .com/2018/04/thousand-island-park-wellesley-island.html#!/2018/04/thousand-island-park -wellesley-island.html.

8. We know little of Libbie Dutcher's religious influences, but she may have known of the "Holiness" movement in Methodism; see Russell E. Richey, *Methodism in the American Forest* (Oxford: Oxford University Press, 2015), 121–163; for the importance of forest sites, 164–176.

9. Sister Christine, "The Disciples at Thousand Island Park," in *Reminiscences.*

10. Sister Christine, "Disciples at Thousand Island Park."

11. Sister Christine, "Disciples at Thousand Island Park."

12. Sister Christine, "Disciples at Thousand Island Park."

13. For mentions of Swami Abhayananda, see *Letters of Sister Nivedita,* collected and ed. Sankari Prasad Basu, 2 vols. (Kolkata: Advaita Ashrama, 2017), vol. 1 (hereafter *LSN*). Nivedita portrays her as self-centered and careless of Vivekananda's teachings; other evidence suggests that her lecturing helped her attain badly needed funds.

14. Sister Christine, "Disciples at Thousand Island Park."

15. Sister Christine, "Disciples at Thousand Island Park."

16. Swami Vivekananda to Sara Bull, February 14, 1895, Epistles–2nd Series, LX, vol. 6, *CWSV.*

17. Swami Vivekananda to Sara Bull, April 25, 1895, Epistles–2nd Series, LXIV, vol. 6, *CWSV.*

18. Leon Landsberg to Sara Bull, July 10, 1894, Archives of the Vedanta Society of Northern California (hereafter VSNC).

19. Swami Vivekananda, "Freedom," Karma-Yoga, vol. 1, *CWSV.*

20. Swami Vivekananda, talk delivered on July 3, 1985, "Recorded by Miss S. E. Waldo, a Disciple," Inspired Talks, vol.7, *CWSV.*

21. Notions of dharma were undergoing revision during his time, per Amiya P. Sen, *Explorations in Modern Bengal c.1800–1900: Essays on History, Religion and Culture* (New Delhi: Primus Books, 2010), 121–165; see also its conclusion.

22. I thank Sudipta Sen for explaining this to me.

23. Julius Lipner, *Hindus: Their Religious Beliefs and Practices,* 2nd ed. (London: Routledge and Kegan Paul, 2010), 89, 103–125; 126–147.

24. See Chapter 12.

25. Sister Christine, "Disciples at Thousand Island Park."

26. Swami Vivekananda, talk delivered on August 1, 1895, "Recorded by Miss S. E. Waldo, a Disciple," Inspired Talks, vol. 7, *CWSV.*

27. Swami Vivekananda, "Who is a Real Guru?" Notes from Lectures and Discourses, vol. 5, *CWSV.*

28. A. Srinivasa Pai, in *Reminiscences,* https://www.ramakrishnavivekananda.info/remini scences/106_asp.htm.

29. Sister Christine, "Training a Disciple," in *Reminiscences.*

30. "You should love the terrible and the painful as well," Swami Vivekananda, "Notes Taken Down in Madras, 1892–3," Notes of Class Talks and Lectures, vol. 6, *CWSV*.

31. Sister Christine, "Training a Disciple."

32. Sister Christine, "Disciples at Thousand Island Park."

33. Sister Christine, "Disciples at Thousand Island Park."

34. Sister Christine, "Disciples at Thousand Island Park." Hawthorne and Margaret Fuller also tired of the "communal spirit."

35. Sister Christine, "Disciples at Thousand Island Park."

36. Sister Christine, "Disciples at Thousand Island Park."

37. It remains unclear whether he distinguished between Indians and "white" women in terms of their possibility for spiritual elevation. Clearly, he discovered no one as holy or godly as Sarada Devi while abroad.

38. See Chapter 14.

39. Sister Christine, "Disciples at Thousand Island Park."

40. Sister Christine, "Disciples at Thousand Island Park."

41. Sister Christine, "The Guru," in *Reminiscences*.

42. S. E. Waldo, in *Reminiscences*, https://www.ramakrishnavivekananda.info/reminiscences /113_sew.htm.

43. Sister Christine, in *Reminiscences*.

44. Sister Christine, in *Reminiscences*.

45. Sister Christine, in *Reminiscences*.

46. Mary C. Funke, in *Reminiscences*, https://www.ramakrishnavivekananda.info/remini scences/251_mcf.htm.

47. Sister Christine, in *Reminiscences*.

48. Sister Christine, in *Reminiscences*.

49. Sister Christine, in *Reminiscences*.

50. Sister Christine, in *Reminiscences*.

51. S. E. Waldo, in *Reminiscences*.

52. Swami Vivekananda, talk delivered on June 19, 1895, "Recorded by Miss S. E. Waldo, a Disciple," Inspired Talks, vol. 7, *CWSV*.

53. Swami Vivekananda, talk delivered on June 30, 1895, "Recorded by Miss S. E. Waldo, a Disciple," Inspired Talks, vol. 7, *CWSV*.

54. Swami Vivekananda, talk delivered on June 25, 1895, "Recorded by Miss S. E. Waldo, a Disciple," Inspired Talks, vol. 7, *CWSV*.

55. Swami Vivekananda, talk delivered on June 26, 1895, "Recorded by Miss S. E. Waldo, a Disciple," Inspired Talks, vol. 7, *CWSV*.

56. Swami Vivekananda, talk delivered on July 1, 1895, "Recorded by Miss S. E. Waldo, a Disciple," Inspired Talks, vol. 7, *CWSV*.

57. See Chapter 12.

58. Prathama Banerjee, *Elementary Aspects of the Political: Histories from the Global South* (Durham, NC: Duke University Press, 2020), 31.

59. Swami Vivekananda, Conversations and Dialogues, XXX, vol. 7, *CWSV*.

60. Vivekananda, Inspired Talks, June 26, 1895.

61. T. Gregory Garvey, ed., *The Emerson Dilemma: Essays on Emerson and Social Reform* (Athens: University of Georgia Press, 2001), passim.

62. I borrow from Robert D. Priest, "The 'Great Doctrine of Transcendent Disdain,' History, Politics and the Self in Renan's Life of Jesus," *History of European Ideas* 40 (2014): 761–776.

63. "Violent attempts": Swami Vivekananda, talk delivered on June 30, 1895, "Recorded by Miss S. E. Waldo, a Disciple," Inspired Talks, vol. 7, *CWSV*.

64. Swami Vivekananda, talk delivered on June 24, 1895, "Recorded by Miss S. E. Waldo, a Disciple," Inspired Talks, vol. 7, *CWSV*.

65. Vivekananda, Inspired Talks, July 1, 1895.

66. Swami Vivekananda, talk delivered on July 2, 1895, "Recorded by Miss S. E. Waldo, a Disciple," Inspired Talks, vol. 7, *CWSV*.

67. Swami Vivekananda, talk delivered on July 10, 1895, "Recorded by Miss S. E. Waldo, a Disciple," Inspired Talks, vol. 7, *CWSV*.

68. Swami Vivekananda, talk delivered on July 27, 1895, "Recorded by Miss S. E. Waldo, a Disciple," Inspired Talks, vol. 7, *CWSV*.

69. Sister Nivedita to Josephine MacLeod (hereafter JM), January 30, 1899, *LSN*, vol. 1, no. 17, 44.

70. Sumana Shashidhar and Shashidhar Belwadi, *The Firebrand: Warrior Monk of India* (self-published, 2003). Indian newspapers referred to him in these "fighting" terms; see Shubho Basu and Sikata Banerjee, "The Question for Manhood: Masculine Hinduism and Nation in Bengal," *Comparative Studies of South Asia, Africa and Middle East* 26 (2006): 476–490.

71. Romain Rolland, *L'Inde (Un échange fructueux)* (Paris: A. Michel, 1960), 192.

72. Linda Prugh, *Josephine MacLeod and Vivekananda's Mission (Chennai: Ramakrishna Math, 2001)*, 277–278, cites her health and Vivekananda's response to his own bedridden state. See also Swami Vivekananda to Josephine MacLeod, November 8, 1901, Epistles–1st Series, CXIII, vol. 5, *CWSV*.

73. Prugh, *Josephine MacLeod*, 30–31.

74. Prugh, *Josephine MacLeod*, 423; Frances later divorced her husband and returned to Ridgely to live with her children.

75. See Frances Leggett, *Late and Soon* (London: John Murray, 1968).

76. Sara Bull to her daughter Olea, undated (but from 1898), from Bally on the Ganges (near Calcutta), VSNC. They read together Emerson's *Method of Nature* (first published 1836), which to her seemed the "most glorious call to life."

77. See Chapter 1.

78. Prugh, *Josephine MacLeod*, 15; Dora Roethlesberger had led Josephine and Betty to Vivekananda, 25.

79. Prugh, *Josephine MacLeod*, 14–15.

80. Josephine MacLeod, in *Reminiscences*, https://www.ramakrishnavivekananda.info /reminiscences/228_jm.htm.

81. I thank Linda Prugh for this information.

82. Prugh, *Josephine MacLeod*, 14–16.

83. Leggett, *Late and Soon*, 169.

84. Prabuddhaprana, *Tantine, The Life of Josephine MacLeod, Friend of Swami Vivekananda* (Dakshineswar: Shri Sarada Math, 1990), 132.

85. MacLeod, in *Reminiscences*.

86. MacLeod, in *Reminiscences*.

87. Sister Nivedita to JM, *LSN*, vol. 1, June 25, 1899, no. 51.

88. Swami Vivekananda to Josephine MacLeod, August 3, 1899, Epistles–4th Series, CXXXVIII, vol. 8, *CWSV*.

89. Sister Nivedita to JM, June 25, 1899, *LSN*, vol. 1, no. 51.

90. See Ayon Maharaj, "The Challenge of the Oceanic Feeing: Romain Rolland's Mystical Critique of Psychoanalysis and his Call for a 'New Science of Mind,'" *History of European Ideas* 43 (2017), 474–493; and Henri and Madeline Vermorel, *Freud et Romain Rolland. Correspondance 1923–1936* (Paris: Presses Universitaires de France, 1993), 249–285.

91. Josephine MacLeod to Sara Bull, November 26, 1899, VSNC.

92. He met Sarah Bernhardt in America in 1896 and again in Paris in 1900 during the Exposition Universelle; see Swami Pavitrananda, "Vivekananda and Sarah Bernhardt," in *Vedanta for the Western World,* ed. Christopher Isherwood (London, Unwin books, 1963), 24–26.

93. Emma Calvé, *My Life,* trans. R. Gilder (New York: D. Appleton and Company, 1922), 188.

94. Prugh, *Josephine MacLeod,* 39, 151.

95. Swami Vivekananda to Mary Hale, March 17, 1900, Epistles–3rd Series, vol. 7, *CWSV.*

96. Prugh, *Josephine MacLeod,* quoted on 374–375.

97. Mrs. Alice M. Hansbrough, in *Reminiscences,* https://www.ramakrishnavivekananda.info /reminiscences/other_02_amh.htm.

98. Maud Stumm, in *Reminiscences,* https://www.ramakrishnavivekananda.info/remini scences/263_ms.htm.

99. Hansbrough in *Reminiscences.*

100. Prabuddhaprana, *Tantine,* 135–136.

101. "Think in symbols": Sister Nivedita to JM, July 4, 1904, *LSN,* vol. 1, no. 292; "cosmic heart": Prabuddhaprana, *Tantine,* 136.

102. See Chapter 6.

103. See Chapter 6.

104. Mrs. S. K (Roxie). Blodgett, in *Reminiscences,* from a letter dated September 2, 1902, to Josephine MacLeod.

105. Cornelia Conger, in *Reminiscences,* https://www.ramakrishnavivekananda.info/remini scences/130_cc.htm.

106. Sister Nivedita to JM, November 11, 1899, *LSN,* vol. 1, no. 76.

107. MacLeod, in *Reminiscences.*

108. Sister Nivedita to Sara Bull, August 3, 1900, *LSN,* vol. 1, no. 143.

109. Swami Vivekananda to Sister Nivedita, October 1, 1897, Epistles–4th Series, CX, vol. 8, *CWSV.*

110. For Charcot, see Georges Didi-Huberman, *Invention of Hysteria: Charcot and the Photographic Iconography of the Salpêtrière,* trans. Alisa Hartz (Cambridge, MA: MIT Press, 2003).

111. Lisa Appignanesi and John Forrester, *Freud's Women* (London: Phoenix, 2005), 63–167; see Richard Kluft, "Freud's Rejection of Hypnosis," pt. 1, *American Journal of Clinical Hypnosis* 601 (2018), 307–323.

112. John Forrester, "Contracting the Disease of Love: Authority and Freedom in the Origins of Psychoanalysis," in *The Anatomy of Madness: People and Ideas, Essays in the History of Medicine,* vol. 1, ed. W. F. Bynum, R. Porter and M. Shepherd (London: Tavistock, 1985), 255–270.

113. Freud's engagement with eastern religions (and indirectly to Ramakrishna and Vivekananda) is reassessed in William B. Parsons, *Freud and Religion: Advancing the Dialogue* (Cambridge, UK: Cambridge University Press, 2021), 152–187.

114. Sigmund Freud, *The Standard Edition of the Complete Psychological Works of Sigmund Freud,* vol. 12, *1911–1913,* trans. James Strachey, (London: Hogarth Press, 1958); see "The Dynamics of Transference," 97–108; "Observations on Transference-Love," 157–171.

115. S. E. Waldo, in *Reminiscences.*

116. Shruti Kapila, "Self, Spencer and *Swaraj:* Nationalist Thought and Critiques of Liberalism, 1890–1920," *Modern Intellectual History* 4, no. 1 (2007): 108.

10. The Pains and Pleasures of Love in America

1. Varun Rana, "I Want to Hold Your Hand," *Paper Magazine,* April 28, 2020, and Caroline and Filippo Osella, "Friendship and Flirting: Micro-Politics in Kerala, South India," *Journal of the Royal Anthropological Institute* 4 (1998): 190–192.

2. Asim Chauduri, *Vivekananda's Loving Relationships with His Brother Disciples—A Striking Example of Divine Love's Human Manifestations* (Burbank, CA: Chaudhuri Publications, 2019), 309–311; Swami Vijnanananda was famous for winning a contest with Ramakrishna, who believed the disciple had wrestled with Krishna in another life.

3. See Chapters 2–4.

4. Swami Vivekananda to Sister Nivedita, October 1, 1897, Epistles–4th Series, CX, vol. 8, in *Complete Works of Swami Vivekananda,* 10 vols., https://en.wikisource.org/wiki/The_Complete _Works_of_Swami_Vivekananda (hereafter *CWSV*).

5. Swami Vivekananda, "The Real Nature of Man," Jnana-Yoga, vol. 2, *CWSV*. This lecture was first delivered in London in 1896.

6. Swami Vivekananda, "On the Vedanta Philosophy," Notes from Lectures and Discourses, vol. 5, *CWSV*.

7. D. W. Winnicott, *The Child, the Family and the Outside World* (Middlesex, UK: Penguin, 1973), 86–87 and 194; Adam Phillips, *Winnicott* (Cambridge, MA: Harvard University Press, 1988).

8. Swami Vivekananda, "The Religion of Love," Notes of Class Talks and Lectures, vol. 8, *CWSV*; notes of a lecture delivered in London on November 16, 1895.

9. Swami Vivekananda, talk delivered on July 31, 1895, "Recorded by Miss S. E. Waldo, a disciple," Inspired Talks, vol. 7, *CWSV*.

10. S. K. Blodgett, in Swami Suddhananda, *Reminiscences of Swami Vivekananda,* 3rd ed. (Calcutta: Advaita Ashrama, 1983), http://ramakrishnavivekananda.info/reminiscences/358_skb.htm (hereafter *Reminiscences*).

11. Kirstin Johnston Largen, *Baby Krishna, Infant Christ: A Comparative Theology of Salvation* (Maryknoll, New York: Orbis Books, 2011), 23–102.

12. Swami Vivekananda, "Human Representations of the Divine Ideal of Love," Para-Bhakti or Supreme Devotion, vol. 3, *CWSV*.

13. Kimberly VanEsveld Adams's *Our Lady of Victorian Feminism: The Madonna in the work of Anna Jameson, Margaret Fuller and George Eliot* (Athens, Ohio University Press, 2000) underscores the importance of Marianism.

14. See Victoria Ford Smith, "Dolls and Imaginative Agency in Bradford, Pardoe and Dickens," *Dickens Studies Annual,* 40 (2009), 171–197.

15. Sister Devamata, in *Reminiscences,* https://www.ramakrishnavivekananda.info/remini scences/121_sd.htm.

16. Josephine MacLeod, in *Reminiscences,* https://www.ramakrishnavivekananda.info/remini scences/228_jm.htm.

17. J. Ransome Bransby, in *Reminiscences,* https://www.ramakrishnavivekananda.info/remini scences/other_05_jrb.htm; and Mrs. S. K. Blodgett, in *Reminiscences,* https://www.ramakrishna vivekananda.info/reminiscences/358_skb.htm. From a letter to Josephine MacLeod, September 2, 1902.

18. Maud Stumm, in *Reminiscences.* https://www.ramakrishnavivekananda.info/reminiscences /263_ms.htm.

19. Blodgett, in *Reminiscences,*

20. Ida Ansell, in *Reminiscences,* https://www.ramakrishnavivekananda.info/reminiscences /362_ia.htm.

21. Sister Christine, "Swami Vivekananda as I Saw Him," in *Reminiscences.*

22. Sister Christine, "Swami Vivekananda as I Saw Him."

23. David Gellner of All Souls, Oxford, helped me with this idea.

24. Josephine Macleod to Sister Nivedita, December 20, 1899, Archives of the Vedanta Society of Southern California (hereafter VSSC).

25. Swami Vivekananda, from San Francisco, to Mrs. Leggett (Josephine's sister), March 17, 1900, Epistles–3rd Series, XLVIII, vol. 7, *CWSV*.

26. Swami Vivekananda to Mrs. Leggett, September 3, 1900, Epistles–2nd Series, CLXIII, vol. 6, *CWSV*. This letter speaks of "James" and may refer to the Harvard philosopher, but probably concerns "Janes," the head of the Brooklyn Ethical Association.

27. Swami Vivekananda to Sister Christine, November 10, 1899, Letters–5th Series, CLI, vol. 9, *CWSV*; he does not describe the food.

28. Swami Vivekananda to Sara Bull, November 12, 1899, Letters–5th Series, CLIII, vol. 9, *CWSV*.

29. Swami Vivekananda to Sister Nivedita, November 15, 1899, Epistles–2nd Series, CXLIX, vol. 6, *CWSV*.

30. Vivekananda to Sister Nivedita, February 15, 1900.

31. Swami Vivekananda to Mary Hale, March 16, 1899, Epistles–4th Series, CXXXVI, vol. 8, *CWSV*.

32. Swami Vivekananda to Josephine MacLeod, June 14, 1901, Epistles–1st Series, CV, vol. 5, *CWSV*.

33. Swami Vivekananda to Josephine MacLeod, November 8, 1901, Epistles–4th Series, CXIII, vol. 8, *CWSV*.

34. Asim Chaudhuri, *Vivekananda's Loving Relationships with His Brother Disciples—A Striking Example of Divine Love's Human Manifestations* (Burbank, CA: Chaudhuri Publications, 2019), quoted on 56.

35. Swami Vivekananda to Alasinga Perumal, January 23, 1896, Epistles–4th Series, LXIX, vol. 8, *CWSV*.

36. Swami Vivekananda, "The Absolute and the Manifestation," Jnana-Yoga, vol. 2 *CWSV*, first delivered in London, 1896.

37. Swami Vivekananda, "An Interesting Correspondence," Writings: Prose and Poems, vol. 8, *CWSV*.

38. Paramahansa Yogananda, *Autobiography of a Yogi* (New Delhi: Rupa Publications, 2017), 129.

39. Yogananda, *Autobiography of a Yogi*, 208.

40. Mrs. Alice M. Hansbrough, in *Reminiscences*, https://www.ramakrishnavivekananda.info/reminiscences/other_02_amh.htm.

41. Hansbrough, in *Reminiscences*.

42. MacLeod, in *Reminiscences*.

43. Sister Nivedita to Josephine MacLeod (hereafter JM), June 25, 1899, *Letters of Sister Nivedita*, collected and ed. Sankari Prasad Basu, 2 vols. (Kolkata: Advaita Ashrama, 2017), vol. 1, no. 51.

44. Sister Devamata, in *Reminiscences*.

45. Sudipta Sen of University of California, Davis, offered this terminology.

46. Frances Leggett, *Late and Soon* (London: John Murray, 1968), 123.

47. Leggett, *Late and Soon*; Frances quotes her mother's letter on the same page.

48. Swami Vivekananda to Mrs. G. W. Hale, June 28, 1894, Letters–5th Series, XXII, vol. 9, *CWSV*.

49. Vedanta Society of Northern California; news of the gift of the coat appears in Sara Bull to Leon Landsberg, February 2, 1895.

50. Sister Christine, "Reminiscences of Swami Vivekananda," in *Reminiscences*, https://www.ramakrishnavivekananda.info/reminiscences/146_sc.htm.

51. Leon Landsberg to Sara Bull, April 16, 1895, Archives of the Vedanta Society of Northern California (hereafter VSNC).

52. Landsberg to Bull, April 16, 1895.

53. Swami Vivekananda, "Who is a Real Guru?" Notes from Lectures and Discourses, vol. 5, *CWSV*.

54. Leon Landsberg to Sara Bull, April 16, 1895.

55. Landsberg to Bull, April 16, 1895.

56. Swami Vivekananda to Mary Hale, May 30, 1896, Epistles–4th Series, LXXVI, vol. 8, *CWSV*.

57. Ida Ansell, in *Reminiscences*.

58. Leon Landsberg to Sara Bull, April 16, 1895.

59. Swami Vivekananda to Josephine MacLeod, June 1895, Epistles–4th Series, XLIV, vol. 8, *CWSV*.

60. Vivekananda to MacLeod, June 1895.

61. Leon Landsberg to Sara Bull, November 22, 1895, VSNC.

62. *Kathamrita*, 1:152.

63. Ansell, in *Reminiscences*.

64. Pravrajika Prabuddhaprana, *Saint Sara: The Life of Sara Chapman Bull: The American Mother of Swami Vivekananda* (Dakshineswar: Sri Sarada Math, 2002), quoted on 136.

65. Tramp: Leon Landsberg to Sara Bull, May 23, 1895, VSNC.

66. Leon Landsberg to Sara Bull, August 27, 1895, VSNC.

67. Leon Landsberg to Sara Bull, June 19, 1895, VSNC.

68. Landsberg to Sara Bull, November 1, 1895, VSNC.

69. Josh Getzler of St Hugh's College, Oxford, kindly helped me with this verse.

70. Leon Landsberg to Sara Bull, November 22, 1895, VSNC.

71. Quoted in Prabuddhaprana, *Saint Sara*, 160.

72. Prabuddhaprana, *Saint Sara*, quoted on 162–163, and 168.

73. Chetanananda, "With Swamiji in India": J. J. Goodwin's Letters from India about Vivekananda," in Swami Shuddhidananda, *Vivekananda as the Turning Point: The Rise of a New Spiritual Wave* (Kolkata: Advaita Ashrama, 2013), 480–490.

74. Prabuddhaprana, *Saint Sara*, 169.

75. Prabuddhaprana, *Saint Sara*, 169.

76. Sara Bull to Leon Landsberg, undated letter, VSNC.

11. The Pains and Pleasures of Love in Great Britain

1. Swami Shivananda, *Letters for Spiritual Seekers: Letters of Swami Shivananda*, trans. Swami Lokeswarananda (Mayavati: Advaita Ashrama, 1995), 36–37, May 13, 1893, written more than a year before the World Parliament.

2. Swami Vivekananda to Edward Toronto Sturdy, April 24, 1895, Epistles–4th Series, XL, vol. 8, in *Complete Works of Swami Vivekananda*, 10 vols., https://en.wikisource.org/wiki/The_Complete_Works_of_Swami_Vivekananda (hereafter *CWSV*).

3. Vivekananda to Sturdy, April 24, 1895.

4. See Ayon Maharaj, "Swami Vivekananda's Vedantic Critique of Schopenhauer's Doctrine of the Will," in *Philosophy East & West* 67 (2017): 1192.

5. Swami Vivekananda to Edward Toronto Sturdy, 1895, Epistles–4th Series, LXIII, vol. 8, *CWSV*. See also Swami Vivekananda, "A Study of the Sankhya Philosophy," "Practical Vedanta" and Other Lectures, vol. 2, *CWSV*.

6. Swami Vivekananda to Josephine MacLeod, September 1895, Epistles–4th Series, LII, vol. 8, *CWSV*.

7. Vivekananda to MacLeod, September 1895.

8. Vivekananda to MacLeod, September 1895.

9. Vivekananda to MacLeod, September 1895.

10. Swami Vivekananda to Mrs. Bull, October 6, 1895, Epistles–2nd Series, LXXXIV, vol. 6, *CWSV*; Sturdy's translation from the Sanskrit is *Nakada Sûtra: An Inquiry into Love (Bhakti-Jijnâsâ)* (London: Longman, 1896); it was dedicated to Vivekananda.

11. Swami Vivekananda to Edward Toronto Sturdy, October 1895, Epistles–4th Series, LXIII, vol. 8, *CWSV*.

12. Swami Vivekananda to Edward Toronto Sturdy, October 31, 1895, Epistles–4th Series, LVII, vol. 8, *CWSV*.

13. Vivekananda to Sturdy, October 31, 1895.

14. Marie Louise Burke (Sister Gargi), *Swami Trigunatita: His Life and Work* (Calcutta: Advaita Ashrama, 1997), 173–198.

15. Swami Vivekananda to Sara Bull, December 8, 1895, Epistles–4th Series, LXXXVIII, vol. 8, *CWSV*. This letter was written in New York after his return from Britain.

16. Amrita M. Salm, *Mother of Mayavati: The Story of Charlotte Sevier and Advaita Ashrama* (Kolkata: Advaita Ashrama, 2013), 32.

17. See Chapter 12

18. Swami Vivekananda to Edward Toronto Sturdy, December 16, 1895, Epistles–4th Series, LXIV, vol. 8; see Chapter 12 for this new discipline. For more about time, see Sumit Sarkar, *Beyond Nationalist Frames: Postmodernism, Hindu Fundamentalism, History* (Calcutta: Permanent Black, 2002), 10–37.

19. "Blessed and Beloved": Swami Vivekananda to Edward Toronto Sturdy, January 16, 1896, Epistles–4th Series, LXVIII, vol. 8, *CWSV*.

20. Vivekananda to Sturdy, January 16, 1896.

21. Swami Vivekananda to Sara Bull, May 8, 1896, Letters–5th Series, XCII, vol. 9, *CWSV*.

22. Swami Vivekananda to Sara Bull, August 19, 1897, Letters–5th Series, CXXXIII, vol. 9, *CWSV*.

23. Swami Tathagatananda, *The Vedanta Society of New York: A Brief Survey* (New York: Vedanta Society of New York, 2000), 133, and 136–189.

24. Swami Vivekananda to Sara Bull, December 8, 1895, Epistles–4th Series, LXXXVIII, vol. 8, *CWSV*.

25. Swami Vivekananda to Sara Bull, September 4, 1899, Epistles–4th Series, CXLI, vol. 8, *CWSV*.

26. Swami Vivekananda to Edward Toronto Sturdy, September 14, 1899, Epistles–4th Series, CXLII, vol. 8, *CWSV*. This "other friend" was probably Mrs. Ethel Mary Ashton Jonson, an aspiring playwright who wrote under the name of Dorothy Leighton. Vivekananda spelled the name "Johnson."

27. Catherine L. Albanese, "Physic and Metaphysic in Nineteenth-Century America: Medical Sectarians and Religious Healing," *Church History* 55 (1986): 489–502.

28. Swami Vivekananda to Edward Toronto Sturdy, September 14, 1899, Epistles–4th Series, CXLII, vol. 8, *CWSV*.

29. Vivekananda to Sturdy, September 14, 1899.

30. Vivekananda to Sturdy, September 14, 1899.

31. Swami Vivekananda to Edward Toronto Sturdy, November 1899, Epistles–3rd Series, XLIV, vol. 7, *CWSV*.

32. Gwilym Beckerlegge suggests that Müller's feminism may have annoyed Vivekananda; see *The Ramakrishna Mission: The Making of a Modern Hindu Movement* (Oxford: Oxford University Press, 2000), 180–201.

33. Mahendranath Datta, *Swami Vivekananda in London*, trans. Swami Yogeshananda (Chennai, Vivekananda Kendra Prakashan Trust, 2015); this translation deletes Mahendranath's interpretations of the miraculous.

34. Swami Vivekananda, "On Professor Max Müller," Writings: Prose, vol. 4, *CWSV*; June 6, 1896, published in the *Brahmavadin*.

35. Edward Toronto Sturdy, "Friends," December 23, 1899; St. Louis Vedanta Society; this letter goes on for six and a half pages (typewritten).

36. Sturdy, "Friends," December 23, 1899.

37. Basu, *Amrita Bazar Patrika,* August 25, 1894, 38; *Tribune* of Lahore, May 19, 1895, 71.

38. Basu, *Indian Christian Herald,* September 11, 1894, 51.

39. Somak Biswas gives a detailed account of Vivekananda's attempts to legitimize himself, in "Passages through India: Indian Gurus, Western Disciples and the Politics of Indophilia, 1890–1940" (PhD diss, University of Warwick, 2020), 213–220.

40. Swami Vivekananda, "My Plan of Campaign," Lectures from Colombo to Almora, vol. 3, *CWSV.*

41. Mrs. Alice M. Hansbrough, in *Reminiscences of Swami Vivekananda,* 3rd ed. (Calcutta: Advaita Ashrama, 1983), https://www.ramakrishnavivekananda.info/reminiscences/other_02 _amh.htm (hereafter *Reminiscences*), explains how he believed he had fallen ill from a cook at a Chinese restaurant whose "bad character" had polluted the food.

42. Sturdy to MacLeod, December 23, 1899, Vedanta Society of St. Louis.

43. See Chapter 7.

44. Swami Vivekananda to Edward Toronto Sturdy, undated, Epistles–4th Series, CXLVI, vol. 8: *CWSV.*

45. Vivekananda to Sturdy, undated.

46. Vivekananda to Sturdy, undated.

47. Sara Farwell also wrote to Sara Bull on August 28, 1899, "The Swami's smoking was a stumbling block to me," Archives of the Vedanta Society of Northern California.

48. Vivekananda to Edward Toronto Sturdy, February 13, 1896, Epistles–1st Series, LVII, vol. 5, *CWSV.*

49. Swami Vivekananda, "The East and the West—Food and Cooking," Writings: Prose and Poems, vol. 5, *CWSV.*

50. Gandhi, *An Autobiography: The Story of My Experiments with Truth,* trans. Mahadev Desai (Boston: Beacon Press, 1993), 55–58.

51. Hansbrough, in *Reminiscences.*

52. Salm, *Mother of Mayavati,* 15.

53. Swami Vivekananda to Sister Christine, August 5, 1896, Letters–5th Series, XCVIII, vol. 9, *CWSV.*

54. Salm, *Mother of Mayavati,* 42, and Pravrajika Vrajaprana, *"My Faithful Goodwin"* (Kolkata, Advaita Ashrama, 3rd printing, 2015).

55. Swami Vivekananda to Alasinga Perumal, March 23, 1896, Epistles–1st Series, LIX, vol. 5, *CWSV.*

56. Swami Vivekananda to Shrimati Sarala Ghosal, April 6, 1897, Epistles–1st Series, LXXIV, vol. 5, *CWSV.*

57. Swami Vivekananda, "Is Vedanta the Future Religion?" Lectures and Discourses, vol. 8, *CWSV,* delivered in San Francisco on April 6, 1900.

58. Salm, *Mother of Mayavati,* 81.

59. Salm, *Mother of Mayavati,* 103.

60. Quoted in Salm, *Mother of Mayavati,* 83. I do not know who decorated the room and whether it was stripped of images under Vivekananda's orders.

61. Lizelle Reymond, *The Dedicated: A Biography of Nivedita* (New York: John Day, 1953), 9. It is hard to know how much to depend on Reymond's work. Sometimes there is corroborating evidence, other times, the account seems more fanciful. She had early access to Nivedita's papers through Josephine MacLeod.

62. Sister Nivedita, "Barisal," Glimpses of Famine and Flood in East Bengal in 1906, *The Complete Works of Sister Nivedita,* ed. Pravrajika Atmapranam, 2nd ed., 5 vols. (Kolkata: Advaita

Ashrama, 2016), 4:461 (hereafter *CWSN*). She mentions Ireland but focuses on the difference—everyone eats rice in Barisal, while in Ireland the poor ate potatoes, the rich, wheat.

63. Sister Nivedita to Josephine MacLeod (hereafter JM), July 14, 1910, *Letters of Sister Nivedita*, collected and ed. Sankari Prasad Basu, 2 vols. (Kolkata: Advaita Ashrama, 2017), vol. 2, no. 690 (hereafter *LSN*).

64. Pravrajika Amalaprana, ed., *More Letters of Sister Nivedita* (Kolkata, Sri Sarada Math, 2016), 31; see also, Jayati Gupta, "Many Journeys, Many Selves: The Travels of Margaret Elizabeth Noble," *Studies in Travel Writing* 20 (2016): 176–189.

65. Sister Nivedita to Mrs. Ole Bull, March 5, 1899, *LSN*, vol. 1, no. 25.

66. "Sister Nivedita, A Chronology: 1867–1911," *LSN*, 1:31.

67. Swami Kritarthananda, "Nivedita: A Blend of Strength and Softness," in *Sister Nivedita: Offered to India* (special number), *Prabuddha Bharata* 122 (2017): 43–44.

68. Somenath Mukherjee, "Nivedita and her Times" in *Sister Nivedita: Offered to India* (special number), *Prabuddha Bharata*, 122 (2017): 140.

69. Sister Nivedita, "The Christ Child," Miscellaneous Articles, *CWSN*, 5:371–373. She moved again, this time to Chester, where she worked between 1889 and 1891.

70. Sister Nivedita, "Hag Ridden: Jane Nuttall, Herbalist," Miscellaneous Articles, *CWSN*, 5:374–378.

71. Sister Nivedita, "A Visit to a Coal Mine," Miscellaneous Articles, 379–385.

72. Sister Nivedita, "A Page from Wrexham Life," Miscellaneous Articles, *CSWN*, 5:421.

73. Sister Nivedita, "Papers on Women's Rights—No. 1," Miscellaneous Articles, *CWSN*, 5:388.

74. Mukherjee, "Nivedita and Her Times," 137–141.

75. G. Beckerlegge, "The 'Irishness' of Margaret Noble / Sister Nivedita," in *Sister Nivedita: Offered to India*, 118–146, and Malachi O'Doherty, "Nivedita," 224–234, in *Sister Nivedita: Offered to India*.

76. Sister Nivedita, "Review of *Mutual Aid* by Peter, Prince Kropotkin," Biographical Sketches and Reviews, *CWSN*, 5:299–302.

77. Sister Nivedita, The Master as I Saw Him, *CWSN*, 1:17–19.

78. Sister Nivedita, The Master as I Saw Him, 1:20.

79. Sister Nivedita, The Master as I Saw Him, 1:20.

80. Sister Nivedita, The Master as I Saw Him, 1:23.

81. Sister Nivedita, "How and Why I Adopted the Hindu Religion," *CWSN*, 2:460.

82. Sister Nivedita to Mr. S. K. Ratcliffe, July 6, 1910, *LSN*, vol. 2, no. 685.

83. Sister Nivedita to Mrs. Eric Hammond, June 5, 1898, *LSN*, vol. 1, no. 5.

84. Sister Nivedita, The Master as I Saw Him, *CWSN*, 1:23.

85. Sister Nivedita, The Master as I Saw Him, 1:28.

86. Sister Nivedita, The Master as I Saw Him, 1:28–29.

87. Sister Nivedita, The Master as I Saw Him, 1:33.

88. Sister Nivedita, The Master as I Saw Him, 1:32.

89. Swami Vivekananda to Sister Nivedita, June 7, 1896, Epistles–3rd Series, XXXVI, vol. 7, *CWSV*.

90. Swami Vivekananda to Sister Nivedita, July 29, 1897, Epistles–3rd Series, XLII, vol. 7, *CWSV*.

12. Vivekananda Returns

1. Swami Vivekananda, "We Help Ourselves, Not the World," Karma-Yoga, vol. 1, *CWSV*.

2. Occasionally, he alluded to a temple or the need for an educational center; sometimes he spoke on religious topics, which were more focused.

3. Swami Vivekananda, "First Public Lecture in the East," lecture at Colombo, January 1897, Lectures from Colombo to Almora, vol. 3, *CWSV*.

4. Swami Vivekananda, "Reply to the Address of Welcome at Paramakudi," Lectures from Colombo to Almora, vol. 3, *CWSV.*

5. Vivekananda, "Reply to the Address of Welcome at Paramakudi."

6. Prathama Banerjee, *Elementary Aspects of the Political of the Political: Histories from the Global South* (Durham, NC: Duke University Press, 2020), 32.

7. Swami Vivekananda, "The Mission of the Vedanta," Lectures from Colombo to Almora, vol. 3, *CWSV.*

8. Vivekananda, "The Mission of the Vedanta."

9. Swami Vivekananda, "Vedanta in Its Application to Indian Life," Lectures from Colombo to Almora, vol. 3, *CWSV.*

10. Swami Vivekananda, "The Mission of the Vedanta," Lectures from Colombo to Almora, vol. 3, *CWSV.*

11. Swami Vivekananda, "My Plan of Campaign," Lectures from Colombo to Almora, vol. 3, *CWSV.*

12. Vivekananda, "My Plan of Campaign."

13. Swami Vivekananda, "The Future of India," Lectures from Colombo to Almora, vol. 3, *CWSV.*

14. Swami Vivekananda, "Reply to the Address of Welcome at Madras," Lectures from Colombo to Almora, vol. 3, *CWSV.*

15. Shamita Basu, *Religious Revivalism as Nationalist Discourse: Swami Vivekananda and New Hinduism in Nineteenth-Century Bengal* (New York: Oxford University Press, 2002), 95–102

16. Sailendra Nath Dhar, *A Comprehensive Biography of Swami Vivekananda* (1975–6) (Chennai: Vivekananda Kendra Prakashan, 2012), 1:23–24.

17. Swami Vivekananda, "Memoirs of European Travel I," Translation of Writings, vol. 7, *CWSV.*

18. Swami Vivekananda, "On the Bounds of Hinduism," *Prabuddha Bharata*, April, 1899, Interviews, vol. 5, *CWSV.*

19. Swami Vivekananda, "IV (Selections from the Math Diary)," Questions and Answers, vol. 5, *CWSV.*

20. Basu, *Religious Revivalism,* 102–111.

21. Lectures and Discourses, Swami Vivekananda, "Women of India," Lectures and Discourses, vol. 8, *CWSV.*

22. Swami Vivekananda to Mary Hale, November 1, 1896, Epistles–2nd Series, CXII, vol. 6, *CWSV.*

23. Bhupendranath Datta, *Swami Vivekananda, Patriot-Prophet: A Study* (Calcutta: Nababharat Publishers, 1954); for a selection of views, see 222, 230–231, 241–243.

24. See Chapter 7.

25. Vivekananda, "My Plan of Campaign" and "The Mission of the Vedanta."

26. Vivekananda, "My Plan of Campaign" and "The Mission of the Vedanta."

27. Basu, *Religious Revivalism,* 113–115.

28. Basu, *Religious Revivalism,* 48.

29. Vivekananda, "The Future of India."

30. Swami Vivekananda, Sayings and Utterances, no. 25, vol. 9, *CWSV.*

31. Vivekananda, "Vedanta in Its Application to Indian Life."

32. See Chapter 6.

33. Vivekananda, "Selections from the Math Diary."

34. Swami Vivekananda, XXX, Conversations and Dialogues, vol. 7, *CWSV.*

35. Vivekananda, "The Future of India."

36. Vivekananda, "The Future of India."

37. Swami Vivekananda to Mary Hale, January 30, 1897, Epistles–2nd Series, CXXI, vol. 6, *CWSV.*

38. Swami Vivekananda to Mary Hale, April 28, 1897, Epistles–2nd Series, CXXIII, vol. 6, *CWSV.*

39. Swami Vivekananda to Sara Bull, February 25, 1897, Epistles–2nd Series, CXXII, vol. 6, *CWSV.*

40. Vivekananda to Sara Bull, February 25, 1897.

41. Swami Vivekananda to Mary Hale, January 30, 1897, Epistles–2nd Series, CXXI, vol. 6, *CWSV.*

42. Swami Vivekananda to Sara Bull, March 26, 1897, Letters–5th Series, CVI, vol. 9, *CWSV.*

43. Swami Vivekananda to Mary Hale, April 28, 1897, Epistles–2nd Series, CXXIII, vol. 6, *CWSV.*

44. Paul Hacker, "Schopenhauer and Hindu Ethics," in *Philology and Confrontation: Paul Hacker on Traditional and Modern Vedanta,* ed. Wilhelm Halbfass, trans. D. Killingley (Albany: New York University Press, 1995), 211–237; there are many who maintain that without Western influence, especially the work of Deussen, Vivekananda would not have advocated his vision of service. In *Religious Revivalism,* Basu also argues that the "Brahmo Reformation" underpinned this view, 185–186.

45. Political theorist Jyotirmaya Sharma, author of *Restatement of Religion: Swami Vivekananda and the Making of Hindu Nationalism* (New Haven, CT: Yale University Press, 2013) also tends in this direction; see 52, 195–196.

46. Banerjee, Elementary *Aspects,* 28.

47. Basu, *Religious Revivalism,* 180–185.

48. Elizabeth de Michelis, *A History of Modern Yoga* (London: Continuum, 2004), 73–80, 97–99, 109. She writes, "Despite Datta's repudiation of Brahmoism, his nation-regenerating programme . . . will ultimately turn out to be cast very much in the form of Sen's missionary enterprise."

49. See Chapter 15.

50. Gwilym Beckerlegge, "Swami Vivekananda and Seva," in *Swami Vivekananda and the Modernization of Hinduism,* ed. William Radice (New Delhi: Oxford University Press, 1998), 180.

51. Carey Anthony Watt, *Serving the Nation, Cultures of Association, and Citizenship* (New Delhi: Oxford University Press, 2005), 32.

52. "Charity": Beckerlegge, "Swami Vivekananda and Seva," Radice, 158–173; Queen Victoria: Swami Vivekananda to Rakhal, June 14, 1897, Epistles–2nd Series, CXXVIII (translated from Bengali), vol. 6, *CWSV.*

53. Swami Vivekananda, "The Practice of Religion," delivered at Alameda, California, March 18, 1900, Notes of Class Talks and Lectures, vol. 6, *CWSV.*

54. Gwilym Beckerlegge, *Swami Vivekananda's Legacy of Service: A Study of the Ramakrishna Math and Mission* (Oxford: Oxford University Press, 2006), 188–192, and Beckerlegge, "Swami Vivekananda and Seva," 188–189; he especially credits Swaminarayan.

55. Swami Vivekananda, "To My Brave Boys," delivered at Alasinga, California, November 19, 1897, Writings: Prose, vol. 4, *CWSV;* and Vivekananda, The Future of India"; see also Beckerlegge, "Swami Vivekananda and Seva," 188–189.

56. William R. Pinch, *Warrior Ascetics and Indian Empires* (New York: Cambridge University Press, 2006), passim.

57. 'Swami Vivekananda to Pramadadas Mitra, February 19, 1890, Epistles–Series 2, XXII (translated from Bengali), vol. 6, *CWSV.*

58. Swami Vivekananda, "Notes Taken Down in Madras, 1892-3," Notes of Class Talks and Lectures, vol. 6, *CWSV.*

59. Beckerlegge, *Swami Vivekananda's Legacy of Service*, 9–11, especially for the reformulation of these traditions.

60. Basu, *Religious Revivalism,* 151.

61. Swami Vivekananda to Pramadadas Mitra, March 3, 1890, Epistles–2nd Series, XXV (translated from Bengali), vol. 6, *CWSV*.

62. See Chapters 3, 4, and 12.

63. Swami Vivekananda, "The Absolute and Manifestation," Jnana-Yoga, vol. 2, *CWSV*.

64. Wilhelm Hablfass, *India and Europe: An Essay in Philosophical Understanding* (New Delhi: Motilal Banarsidass, 1990), 235–236.

65. See Chapter 2.

66. Basu, *Religious Revivalism,* 75

67. Swami Vivekananda to Alasinga Perumal, August 20, 1893, Epistles–3rd Series, IV, vol. 5, *CWSV*.

68. Julius Lipner, *Hindus: Their Religious Beliefs and Practices,* 2nd ed. (London: Routledge and Kegan Paul, 2010), 341.

69. Amiya P. Sen, *Explorations in Modern Bengal, c. 1800–1900: Essays on History, Religion and Culture* (New Delhi: Primus Books, 2010), 104.

70. Faisal Devji, "Morality in the Shadow of Politics," 107–126, and Shruti Kapila, "A History of Violence," 177–199, in *Political Thought in Action: The Bhagavad Gita and Modern India,* ed. Shruti Kapila and Faisal Devji (Cambridge, UK: Cambridge University Press, 2013).

71. Swami Vivekananda, "Each Is Great in His Own Place," Karma-Yoga, vol. 1, *CWSV*.

72. C. A. Bayly, "India, the Bhagavad Gita and the World," 1–24, and Mishka Sinha, "The Transnational Gita," 25–47, in *Political Thought in Action,* ed. Kapila and Devji. Vivekananda spoke of Kant's theory of mind, but not the categorical imperative.

73. Sen, *Explorations in Modern Bengal,* 104. Basu, *Religious Revivalism,* argues that national unity needed to be achieved in the "highest" form of Hindu thought as form of cultivating "modernity," 77–78.

74. Sen, *Explorations in Modern Bengal,* 48–49.

75. Both quotations: Swami Vivekananda, "Karma in Its Effect on Character," Karma-Yoga, vol. 1, *CWSV*.

76. Vivekananda, "Each Is Great in Its Own Place."

77. 'Vivekananda, "Karma in its Effect on Character."

78. He disdained such plaudits: Swami Vivekananda to G. G. Narasimhachariar, January 11, 1895, Epistles–3rd Series, XXIX, vol. 5, *CWSV*.

79. Banerjee, *Elementary Aspects,* 27. She is the one who uses the term "anti-social."

80. Swami Prabhananda, "The First Phase of Ramakrishna Movement (1872 to 1905: Laying the Foundation)," in Swami Lokeswarananda et al., *The Story of Ramakrishna Mission: Swami Vivekananda's Vision and Fulfilment* (Kolkata: Advaita Ashrama, 2006), 240–241.

81. Asim Chaudhuri, *Vivekananda's Loving Relationships with His Brother Disciples—A Striking Example of Divine Love's Human Manifestations* (Burbank, CA: Chaudhuri Publications, 2019), 159.

82. Swami Vivekananda to "brother-disciples of Swamiji," 1894, Epistles–2nd Series, XLV, vol. 6, *CWSV*.

83. Vivekananda to the "brother-disciples of Swamiji," 1894.

84. Vivekananda to the "brother-disciples of Swamiji," 1894.

85. Akhandananda, *Service of God in Man* (Chennai: Sri Ramakrishna Math, 2013), 62.

86. Swami Vivekananda to Akhandananda, March or April 1894, Epistles–2nd Series, LV (translated from Bengali), vol. 6, *CWSV*.

87. Beckerlegge, *Swami Vivekananda's Legacy of Service,* 206–220, gives an excellent survey.

88. Georgina Brewis, "'Fill Full the Mouth of Famine': Voluntary Action in Famine Relief in India 1896–1901," *Modern Asian Studies* 44 (2010): 897–899.

89. Brewis, "'Fill Full the Mouth of Famine,'" 898.

90. Swami Vivekananda, "Practical Vedanta: Part I," "Practical Vedanta" and Other Lectures, vol. 2, *CWSV*.

91. Vivekananda, "Practical Vedanta: Part I."

92. Vivekananda, "Practical Vedanta: Part I."

93. Vivekananda, "Practical Vedanta: Part I."

94. Vivekananda, "Practical Vedanta: Part III," "Practical Vedanta" and Other Lectures, vol. 2, *CWSV*.

95. Akhandananda, *Service of God in Man*, 32.

96. Akhandananda, *Service of God in Man*, 32.

97. Watt, *Serving the Nation*, 16.

98. Swami Vivekananda to his brother-disciples at Alambazar Monastery, Epistles–2nd Series, LVI, vol. 6, *CWSV*, probably written in the summer of 1894.

99. Swami Vivekananda, "Our Duty to the Masses," Writings: Prose, vol. 4, *CWSV*, written from Chicago to H. H. the Maharaja of Mysore on June 23, 1894.

100. Swami Vivekananda to Shri Haridas Viharidas Desai, November (?) 1894, Epistles / Letters–4th Series, XXXIV, vol. 8, *CWSV*. Desai was the enlightened administrator who had instituted many reforms in the Junagadh state, as well as creating and improving Hindu pilgrimage sites.

101. Swami Vivekananda, "Practical Vedanta: Part I," "Practical Vedanta" and Other Lectures, vol. 3, *CWSV*.

102. Swami Vivekananda, "Address at the Rameswaram Temple on Real Worship," Lectures from Colombo to Almora, vol. 3, *CWSV*. Interestingly, he uses Shiva as the god in the poor. More typically he spoke of Daridra Narayan, or "Vishnu in the poor."

103. Swami Vivekananda, XXIV, Conversations and Dialogues, vol. 7, *CWSV*.

104. Geoffrey Russell Searle, *The Quest for National Efficiency: A Study in British Social and Political Thought, 1899–1914* (Berkeley: University of California Press, 1971).

105. Swami Vivekananda, "Reawakening of Hinduism on a National Basis," Interviews, vol. 5, *CWSV*; originally published in *Prabuddha Bharata*, September 1898.

106. His ideas on race were complex, as I will show in my next volume.

107. Susan Bayly, *Caste, Society and Politics in India from the Eighteenth Century to the Modern Age* (Cambridge, UK: Cambridge University Press, 1999), 144–186.

108. Swami Prabhananda, "The First Phase of Ramakrishna Movement," in Swami Lokeswarananda et al., *The Story of Ramakrishna Mission*, 244–245.

109. Swami Prabhananda, "The First Phase of Ramakrishna Movement," in Swami Lokeswarananda et al., *The Story of Ramakrishna Mission*, 253.

110. Began to: Swami Vivekananda to "brother-disciples of the Alambazar Math," (summer of?) 1895, Epistles–2nd Series, LXXIII, vol. 6, *CWSV*, to forbid the monks: Swami Vivekananda to "Members of the Alambazar Math," written in Caversham, Reading, April 27, 1896, Epistles–3rd Series, XXXII, vol. 7, *CWSV*.

111. Vivekananda, Brahmananda, Premananda, Yogananda, Niranjananda and Purna (Pourna Chandra Ghosh).

112. Ungratefully reticent: Swami Purnatmananda, "Swamis Brahmananda, Premananda, Turiyananda, and Saradananda—Breaking New Ground," in Swami Lokeswarananda et al., *The Story of Ramakrishna Mission*, 109–110; or have married: Chauduri, *Vivekananda's Loving Relationships*, 73, 93.

113. Swami Vivekananda, "The Social Conference Address," Writings: Prose, vol. 4, *CWSV*.

114. Swami Vivekananda, "The Religion of Love" (notes on a lecture delivered in London on November 16, 1895), Notes of Class Talks and Lectures, vol. 8, *CWSV*.

115. Swami Vivekananda, "The Ideal of a Universal Religion," "Practical Vedanta" and Other Lectures, vol. 2, *CWSV*.

116. Purnatmananda, "Swamis Brahmananda, Premananda, Turiyananda, and Saradananda," 109–115.

117. Swami Lokeswarananda et al., *The Story of Ramakrishna Mission,* 247.

118. Swami Vivekananda, "Sankhya and Vedanta," "Practical Vedanta" and Other Lectures, vol. 2, *CWSV*.

119. Chaudhuri, *Vivekananda's Loving Relationships,* 94–95.

120. Swami Apurvananda, *Swami Vijnanananda (A Short Life and Spiritual Discourses)* (Allahabad: Sri Ramakrishna Math, 1984), 7–8.

121. Swami Chetanananda, *How a Shepherd Boy Became a Saint* (St. Louis, MO: Vedanta Society of St. Louis, 2015), 113, 116–117.

122. Like Vivekananda, he was au fait with debates on the occult; see his *Life beyond Death: A Critical Study of Spiritualism,* 9th ed. (Kolkata: Ramakrishna Vedanta Math, 2013).

123. See Swami Aseshananda, *Glimpses of a Great Soul: A Portrait of Swami Saradananda* (St. Louis, MO: Vedanta Society of St. Louis, 1982).

124. Swami Vivekananda, Conversations and Dialogues, X, vol. 7, *CWSV*; the disciple may have objected also to a magazine for householders as being too worldly.

125. Swami Shivananda, *Letters for Spiritual Seekers: Letters of Swami Shivananda,* trans. Swami Lokeswarananda (Mayavati: Advaita Ashrama, 1995), 10.

126. *Swami Ramakrishnananda, As We Saw Him* (Chennai: Sri Ramakrishna Math, 2012), 10–20; Vivekananda obliged: Swami Ritajananda, *Swami Turiyananda: Life and Teachings* (Madras: Sri Ramakrishna Math, 1963), 50–64.

127. Marie Louise Burke (Sister Gargi), *Swami Trigunatita: His Life and Work* (Calcutta: Advaita Ashrama, 1997), 131–172; this work had already begun, see Ritajananda, *Swami Turiyananda,* 64–89.

128. Chaudhuri, *Vivekananda's Loving Relationships,* 322.

129. Somak Biswas, "Passages through India: Indian Gurus, Western Disciples and the Politics of Indophilia, 1890–1940" (PhD. diss, University of Warwick, 2020), 209–213, especially 236–243.

130. Swami Vivekananda to Shashi, written (beginning of?) 1895, Epistles–2nd Series, LXXV, vol. 6, *CWSV*.

131. Swami Vivekananda to "Members of the Alambazar Math," written at Caversham, Reading, April 27, 1896, Epistles–3rd Series, XXXII, vol. 7, *CWSV*.

132. Swami Vivekananda, Conversations and Dialogues, XVIII, vol. 7 *CWSV*.

133. "History—Sri Srada Math," http://www.srisaradamath.org/history5.php.

134. Brewis, "Fill Full the Mouth of Famine," 887–918; and Ira Klein, "When the Rains Failed: Famine, Relief and Mortality in British India," *Indian Economic and Social History Review* 21 (1984): 185–214; there is perhaps such a huge range of millions because of a lack of accurate records.

135. Beckerlegge, *Swami Vivekananda's Legacy of Service,* chapters 2, 9, and especially chapter 10.

136. See Chapter 3.

137. Jefferson Ellsworth Scott, *In Famine Land: Observations and Experiences in India during the Great Drought of 1899–1900* (New York and London: Harper, 1904), 29.

138. Vaughan Robinson Nash, a notable journalist quoted in Scott, *In Famine Land,* 14.

139. Brewis, "Fill Full the Mouth of Famine," 903.

140. Watt, *Serving the Nation,* 7.

141. Gokhale, for example, established the Servants of India.

142. Brewis, "Fill Full the Mouth of Famine," 908.

143. Brewis, "Fill Full the Mouth of Famine," 911.

144. Sharleen Mondal, 'Hindu Widows as Religious Subjects, Revival in Colonial India, *Journal of Women's History* 29 (2017), 110–136; Mondal examines this phenomenon during Swadeshi, 1905–1907.

145. Lajpat Rai, *Arya Samaj: An Account of Its Origins, Doctrines and Activities: With a Biographical Sketch of the Founder* (London: Longmans, Green, 1915), 217; Navtej Singh, *Starvation and Colonialism: A Study of Famines in the Nineteenth-Century British Punjab 1858–1901* (New Delhi: National Book Organisation, 1996), 156.

146. Watt, *Serving the Nation*, 82–83.

147. Watt, *Serving the Nation*, 7, 83–85

148. Burke, *Swami Trigunatita*, 59–60.

149. Burke, *Swami Trigunatita*, 354.

150. Burke, *Swami Trigunatita*, 365.

151. Burke, *Swami Trigunatita*, 367.

152. Akhandananda, *Service of God in Man*, 2–3.

153. Akhandananda, *Service of God in Man*, 144–145.

154. Akhandananda, *Service of God in Man*, 142.

155. Akhandananda, *Service of God in Man*, 155.

156. Akhandananda, *Service of God in Man*, 162. I thank Diwakar Acharya for precision on this word.

157. Akhandananda, *Service of God in Man*, 163.

158. Akhandananda, *Service of God in Man*, 163.

159. Swami Vivekananda to Akhandananda, June 15, 1897, Epistles–2nd Series, CXXVIII, vol. 6, *CWSV.*

160. Swami Vivekananda to Sister Nivedita, July 23, 1897, Epistles–3rd Series, XLI, vol. 7, *CWSV.*

161. Swami Vivekananda to Rakhal, September 30, 1897, Epistles–4th Series, CVII, vol. 8, *CWSV.*

162. Swami Vivekananda to Rakhal, July 10, 1897, Epistles–2nd Series, CXXX, vol. 6, *CWSV.*

163. Akhandananda, *Service of God in Man*, 127.

164. Swami Prabhananda, "The First Phase of the Ramakrishna Movement," in *Story of Ramakrishna Mission*, 247–248.

165. Swami Vivekananda to Josephine MacLeod, April 18, 1900, Epistles–2nd Series, CLVIII, vol. 6, *CWSV.*

166. Faisal Devji, *The Impossible Indian: Gandhi and the Temptation of Violence* (London: Hurst & Co, 2012), 105–118.

167. Swami Vivekananda, "Sannyasa: Its Ideal and Practice," Lectures from Colombo to Almora *CWSV*; this was not a lecture, but an entry in the Math Diary dated June 19, 1899.

168. Vivekananda, "Sannyasa: Its Ideal and Practice."

13. The Clinch

1. See Chapter 11.

2. Others, such as Mirabehn, became part of Gandhi's intimate circle, and Mirra Alfassa, who became Aurobindo's Shakti.

3. Sister Nivedita, Notes of Some Wanderings with the Swami Vivekananda, in *The Complete Works of Sister Nivedita*, ed. Pravrajika Atmapranam, 2nd ed., 5 vols. (Kolkata: Advaita Ashrama, 2016), 1:284 (hereafter *CWSN*).

4. Lizelle Reymond, *The Dedicated: A Biography of Nivedita* (New York: John Day, 1953), 75, records that he ate with Dalits and was also caring for more novices.

5. Sister Nivedita, Notes of Some Wanderings, *CWSN*, 1:284–285.

6. Reymond, *The Dedicated*, 80–81.

7. Reymond, *The Dedicated*, 88–89.

8. Akhandananda, *Service of God in Man* (Chennai: Sri Ramakrishna Math, 2013), 128.

9. Sister Nivedita to Mrs. Eric Hammond, May 22, 1898, *Letters of Sister Nivedita*, collected and ed. Sankari Prasad Basu, 2 vols. (Kolkata: Advaita Ashrama, 2017), vol. 1, no. 4 (hereafter *LSN*).

10. Sister Nivedita to Mrs. Eric Hammond, June 5, 1898, *LSN*, vol. 1, no. 5.

11. Sister Nivedita to Mrs. Eric Hammond, September 2, 1898, *LSN*, vol. 1, no. 7.

12. Sister Nivedita to Mrs. Eric Hammond, June 5, 1898, *LSN*, vol. 1, no. 5.

13. Sister Nivedita, Notes of Some Wanderings, *CWSN*, 1:293.

14. Sister Nivedita, The Master as I Saw Him, *CWSN*, 1:82.

15. Sister Nivedita to Mrs. Eric Hammond, May 22, 1898, *LSN*, vol. 1, no. 4.

16. Sister Nivedita to Mrs. Eric Hammond, August 7, 1898, *LSN*, vol. 1, no. 6.

17. Sister Nivedita, The Master as I Saw Him, *CWSN*, 1:94.

18. Sister Nivedita to Mrs. Eric Hammond, August 7, 1898, *LSN*, vol. 1, no. 6.

19. Sister Nivedita to Mrs. Eric Hammond, August 7, 1898.

20. Narasingh Prosad Sil, *Prophet Disarmed: Vivekananda and Nivedita* (Clayton, Australia: Monash University, 1997) has also written on this episode.

21. Sister Nivedita to Josephine MacLeod (hereafter JM), January 18, 1900, *LSN*, vol. 1, no. 106.

22. Swami Vivekananda, "Kali the Mother," Writings: Poems, vol. 4, *CWSV*.

23. Sister Nivedita to unknown correspondent, October 13, 1898, *LSN*, vol. 1, no. 9.

24. Sister Nivedita to unknown correspondent, October 13, 1898, *LSN*, vol. 1, no. 9.

25. Sister Nivedita to unknown correspondent, October 13, 1898, *LSN*, vol. 1, no. 9, and *LSN*, vol. 1, no. 10.

26. Sister Nivedita to unknown correspondent, October 13, 1898, *LSN*, vol. 1, no. 9, and *LSN*, vol. 1, no. 10.

27. Prathama Banerjee, *Elementary Aspects of the Political: Histories from the Global South* (Durham, NC: Duke University Press, 2020), 41.

28. Sister Nivedita to unknown correspondent, October 13, 1898, *LSN*, vol. 1, no. 10.

29. Sister Nivedita to unknown correspondent, October 13, 1898, *LSN*, vol. 1, no. 10.

30. Banerjee, *Elementary Aspects*, 41.

31. Sister Nivedita to unknown correspondent, October 13, 1898, *LSN*, vol. 1, no. 10.

32. I thank D. Gellner for explaining the game to me.

33. Sister Nivedita to JM, January 30, 1899, *LSN*, vol. 1, no. 17.

34. Sister Nivedita to JM, February 21, 1899, *LSN*, vol. 1, no. 20.

35. Sister Nivedita to JM, May 28, 1899, *LSN*, vol. 1, no. 45.

36. Sister Nivedita to JM, February 21, 1899, *LSN*, vol. 1, no. 20.

37. Sister Nivedita to JM, January 1, 1899, *LSN*, vol. 1, no. 12.

38. Sister Nivedita to JM, February 15, 1899, *LSN*, vol. 1, no. 19.

39. Swami Purnatmananda, ed., *Reminiscences of Sri Sarada Devi by Monastics, Devotees and Others*, trans. Maloti Sen Gupta (Kolkata: Advaita Ashrama, 2004), 108–109.

40. Sister Nivedita, The Web of Indian Life, *CWSN*, 2:13.

41. Sister Nivedita, The Web of Indian Life, 2:2.

42. Sister Nivedita, The Web of Indian Life, 2:14.

43. Sister Nivedita to Mrs. Eric Hammond, March 9, 1899, *LSN*, vol. 1, no. 26.

44. Sister Nivedita to Mrs. Hammond, March 9, 1899.

45. Purnatmananda, *Reminiscences of Sri Sarada Devi*, 9. The Hindu goddess Bangala is one of the ten representations of Shakti [Dasa Mahavidya] of which Kali is one.

46. Purnatmananda, *Reminiscences of Sri Sarada Devi*, 9.

47. Sister Nivedita to Mrs. Eric Hammond, May 22, 1898, *LSN*, vol. 1, no. 4.

48. Sister Nivedita, The Master as I Saw Him, 1:106.

49. Sister Nivedita, The Master as I Saw Him, 1:106.

50. Sister Nivedita, The Master as I Saw Him, 1:107.

51. Sister Nivedita to JM, April 6, 1899 (second part of letter begun April 5), *LSN*, vol. 1, no. 34.

52. Sister Nivedita to Sara Bull, April 19, 1899, *LSN*, vol. 1, no. 37.

53. David Arnold, *Colonizing the Body: State Medicine and Epidemic Disease in Nineteenth Century India* (Berkeley: California University Press, 1993), 200–239.

54. Prerna Agarwal, "The Government Will Come to Its Senses," quoted in *The India Forum*, May 1, 2020, https://www.theindiaforum.in/article/government-will-come-its-senses.

55. Agarwal, "The Government Will Come to Its Senses,"

56. This is from a document found among Nivedita's papers and claims to be an account of an English lady's experience in Calcutta during the plague. Sister Nivedita to JM, May 4, 1898, *LSN*, vol. 1, no. 28.

57. Gyan Prakash, *Another Reason: Science and the Imagination of Modern India* (Princeton: Princeton University Press, 1999), 134–136 especially.

58. David Arnold, "Touching the Body: Perspectives on the Indian Plague, 1896–1900," in *Subaltern Studies V: Writings on South Asian History and Society,* ed. Ranajit Guha (New Delhi: Oxford University Press, 1987), 55–90, 396–400.

59. J. Catanach, "'The Gendered Terrain of Disaster'? India and the Plague, c. 1896–1918," *South Asia: Journal of South Asian Studies* 30, no. 2 (2007): 241–267; British men also attacked South Asian servants.

60. Rajnarayan Chandavarkar, "Plague Panic and Epidemic Politics in India, 1896–1914," in *Epidemics and Ideas: Essays on the Historical Perception of Pestilence,* ed. Terence Ranger and Paul Slack (Cambridge, UK: Cambridge University Press, 1992), 203–240; Chandavarkar adjusts Ranger's argument here.

61. Sister Nivedita to JM, March 23, 1899, *LSN*, vol. 1, no. 31.

62. Sister Nivedita to JM, March 23, 1899.

63. Both quotes in Sister Nivedita to JM, April 5, 1899, *LSN*, vol. 1, no. 34.

64. She also said drugs, but it was not clear which she meant.

65. Sister Nivedita, "The Plague in Calcutta," *CWSN*, 5:210–213.

66. Sister Nivedita to JM, April 8, 1899, *LSN*, vol. 1, no. 35.

67. Sister Nivedita to JM, April 9, 1899, *LSN*, vol. 1, no. 36.

68. Swami Vivekananda to Josephine MacLeod, April 29, 1898, Epistles–4th Series, CXVII, vol. 8, *CWSV*.

69. Sister Nivedita, "Plague and the Duty of Students," *CWSN*, 5:217–220.

70. All citations from Swami Vivekananda, "The Plague Manifesto," Writings: Prose, vol. 9, *CWSV*. See also Shamita Basu, *Religious Revivalism as Nationalist Discourse: Swami Vivekananda and New Hinduism in Nineteenth-Century Bengal* (New York: Oxford University Press, 2002), 157, explains, however, that after his return in 1897, Vivekananda prioritized "practical" measures against famine and plague rather than singing the Sankirtan.

71. Sister Nivedita to JM, Easter Week, 1904, *LSN*, vol. 2, no. 286.

72. Chandavarkar, "'Plague Panic,'" 203.

73. "Banish fear and weakness": Sister Nivedita, The Master as I Saw Him, *CWSN*, 1:119. For more on aggression, see Chapter 15.

74. Sister Nivedita, The Master as I Saw Him, 1:119.

75. Sister Nivedita, The Master as I Saw Him, 1:119.

76. Lucy Evangeline Guinness, *Across India at the Dawn of the Twentieth Century* (London: Religious Tract Society, 1898), 256.

77. Sister Nivedita to JM, January 1, 1899, *LSN*, vol. 1, no. 12.

78. Sister Nivedita, "Kali and Her Worship," *CWSN*, 2:418–433.

79. Sister Nivedita, "Kali, and Her Worship," 2:425.

80. Sister Nivedita, "Kali, and Her Worship," 2:426.

81. Sister Nivedita, "Kali, and Her Worship," 2:427.

82. Sister Nivedita, Kali the Mother, 1:479.

83. Quoted in Eaven Boland, *Object Lessons: The Life of the Woman and the Poet in Our Time* (New York: W. W. Norton, 1996), 102.

84. Sister Nivedita, Kali the Mother, *CWSN*, 1:478.

85. Sister Nivedita, "Kali, and Her Worship," 2:428.

86. Sister Nivedita, "Kali, and Her Worship," 2:428.

87. Sister Nivedita to JM, February 15, 1899, *LSN,* vol. 1, no. 19.

88. Sister Nivedita to JM, February 21, 1899, *LSN,* vol. 1, no. 20.

89. Sister Nivedita to JM, February 21, 1899.

90. Sister Nivedita to JM, February 21, 1899.

91. Sister Nivedita to JM, February 21, 1899.

92. Sister Nivedita to JM, May 28, 1899, *LSN,* vol. 1, no. 45.

93. Sister Nivedita, "Copy of Talk," May 29, 1899, *LSN,* 1:156.

94. Sister Nivedita to JM, February 15, 1899, *LSN,* vol. 1, no. 19.

14. Education, "Divine Play," and the Nation

1. See Amiya P. Sen, ed., *An Idealist in India: Selected Writings and Speeches of Sister Nivedita* (Chennai: Primus Books, 2016), 1–45.

2. Kristen D. Nawrotzki, "Froebel Is Dead; Long Live Froebel! The National Froebel Foundation and English Education," *History of Education* 35 (2006): 209–223; Jane Read, "Free Play with Froebel: Use and Abuse of Progressive Pedagogy in London's Infant Schools, 1870–c. 1904," *Paedgogica historica* 42 (2006): 299–323.

3. Sister Nivedita, "Teaching the Three R's on Modern Principles," On Education, in *The Complete Works of Sister Nivedita*, ed. Pravrajika Atmapranam, 2nd ed., 5 vols. (Kolkata: Advaita Ashrama, 2016), 5:11 (hereafter *CWSN*).

4. Sister Nivedita, "Teaching the Three R's," 5:3.

5. Sister Nivedita, "Hints on Practical Education," On Education, *CWSN* 5:41.

6. In later years, "Cookie" would teach art to other friends of Vivekananda at Ridgely Park.

7. Lizelle Reymond, *The Dedicated: A Biography of Nivedita* (New York: John Day, 1953), 48.

8. Sister Nivedita, "The Story of Kali," Kali the Mother, *CWSN* 1:514.

9. Donald W. Winnicott, "Communicating and Not Communicating Leading to a Study of Certain Opposites," *The Maturational Processes and the Facilitating Environment: Studies in the Theory of Emotional Development* (London: Routledge, 1990), 187.

10. Sister Nivedita, "The Story of Kali," 1:515.

11. Sister Nivedita to Josephine MacLeod (hereafter JM), August 2, 1899, *Letters of Sister Nivedita,* collected and ed. Sankari Prasad Basu, 2 vols. (Kolkata: Advaita Ashrama, 2017), vol. 1, no. 60 (hereafter *LSN*).

12. Sister Nivedita, "An Indian Study of Life and Death," *CWSN* 2:278.

13. Sister Nivedita, "An Indian Study," 2:279.

14. Sister Nivedita, The Master as I Saw Him, *CWSN* 1:89.

15. Swami Chetanananda, "Holy Mother and Sister Nivedita," in *Sister Nivedita: Offered to India* (special number) *Prabuddha Bharata*, 122, no. 1 (January 2017): 24.

16. S. Saralabala Sarkar, *Nivedita as I Saw Her* (Calcutta: Sister Nivedita Girls' School, 1999), 29–30.

17. Swami Saradananda, *Sri Ramakrishna and His Divine Play*, trans. Swami Chetanananda (St. Louis, MO: Vedanta Society of St. Louis, 2003), 209.

18. Sister Nivedita, "Occasional Notes on Education," On Education, *CWSN*, 5:66.

19. Sister Nivedita to Swami Akhandananda, July 28, 1903, *LSN*, vol. 2, no. 249.

20. Sister Nivedita to Akhandananda, July 28, 1903.

21. Sister Nivedita to Akhandananda, July 28, 1903.

22. Sarkar, *Nivedita as I Saw Her*, 25.

23. Sister Nivedita to JM, May 21, 1899, *LSN*, vol. 1, no. 44.

24. Sister Nivedita to Mrs. Eric Hammond, September 2, 1898, *LSN*, vol. 1, no. 7; and Sister Nivedita to Mr. Ebenezer Cooke, September 18, 1898, *LSN*, vol. 1, no. 8.

25. Sister Nivedita to JM, May 21, 1899.

26. Sister Nivedita to JM, May 21, 1899.

27. Both quotes in Sister Nivedita to JM, July 5, 1899, *LSN*, vol. 1, no. 54.

28. Sister Nivedita to JM, July 5, 1899.

29. Sister Nivedita to JM, July 15, 1899, *LSN*, vol. 1, no. 56.

30. See Chapter 11.

31. "Unpublished Letters from Sister Nivedita to Anna Geddes," *Prabuddha Bharata* 120 (2015), 18–19.

32. Sister Nivedita to JM, October 9, 1899, *LSN*, vol. 1, no. 70.

33. Sister Nivedita to JM, November 11, 1899, *LSN*, vol. 1, no. 76. Mrs. Ethel Mary Ashton Jonson was disinclined to support Nivedita's efforts in Britain as well. Ashton Jonson was part of the circle around Sturdy and Henrietta Müller, Sara Bull collection, July 23, 1899, Vedanta Society of Northern California (hereafter VSNC).

34. He explained this virtue in Swami Vivekananda, "Steps to Realisation" Lectures and Discourse, vol. 1, *CWSV*.

35. Sister Nivedita to JM, October 9, 1899, *LSN*, vol. 1, no. 70.

36. See Chapter 9.

37. Sister Nivedita to Sara Bull, November 10, 1899, *LSN*, vol. 1, no. 75.

38. Sister Nivedita to JM, November 16, 1899, *LSN*, vol. 1, no. 78.

39. Sister Nivedita to JM, November 16, 1899.

40. "Platitudes": Sister Nivedita to JM, December 4, 1899, *LSN*, vol. 1, no. 86.

41. Cited in Prabuddhaprana, *Tantine: The Life of Josephine MacLeod, Friend of Swami Vivekananda* (Dakshineswar: Shri Sarada Math, 1990), 91.

42. Louise W. Knight, *Jane Addams: Spirit in Action* (New York: W. W. Norton, 2010). For reference to her work in sanitation, 97; for world peace, 135; for child development, 129.

43. Sister Nivedita to JM, January 18, 1900, *LSN*, vol. 1, no. 106.

44. Sister Nivedita to JM, November 16, 1899, *LSN*, vol. 1, no. 78.

45. Sister Nivedita to Sara Bull, November 25, 1899, *LSN*, vol. 1, no. 83.

46. Bull supported her: Sister Nivedita to JM, September 1, 1899, *LSN*, vol. 1, no. 68.

47. Sister Nivedita to Sara Bull, December 6, 1899, *LSN*, vol. 1, no. 88.

48. Sister Nivedita to JM, January 9, 1900, *LSN*, vol. 1, no. 102. Smaller towns like Ann Arbor often had more generous audiences: Sister Nivedita to JM, January 3, 1900, *LSN*, vol. 1, no. 103.

49. Sister Nivedita to JM, June 9, 1900, *LSN*, vol. 1, no. 132.

50. Sister Nivedita to JM, January 16, 1900, *LSN*, vol. 1, no. 105.

51. See articles on her talks in Prabuddhaprana, *Sister Nivedita in Contemporary Newspapers* (Dakshineswar: Sri Sarada Math, 2017).

52. Sister Nivedita to JM, December 6, 1899, *LSN,* vol. 1, no. 87.

53. "Anglo-Saxon type": Sister Nivedita to JM, December 6, 1899, *LSN,* vol. 1, no. 87; "Humanity and Freedom": Sister Nivedita to JM, December 6, 1899, *LSN,* vol. 1, no. 87.

54. Sister Nivedita to Vivekananda, March 13, 1900, *LSN,* vol. 1, no. 116. She quotes Norman Wyld, another disciple of Geddes's.

55. Sister Nivedita to Swami Vivekananda, March 13, 1900.

56. See her letter of September 15, 1900, to Anna Geddes, for example. Her later letters to Anna express greater disenchantment; see "Unpublished Letters from Sister Nivedita to Anna Geddes," *Prabuddha Bharata* 120 (2015): 497–501.

57. Sister Nivedita to Swami Vivekananda, March 13, 1900, *LSN,* vol. 1, no. 116.

58. Helen Meller, *Patrick Geddes: Social Evolutionist and City Planner* (London: Routledge, 1990), 34–38, 41–42.

59. E. Cumming, "Patrick Geddes: Cultivating the Garden of Life," in *Patrick Geddes: The French Connection,* ed. Francis Fowle and Belinda Thomas (Oxford: White Cockade Publishing, 2004), quoted on 21.

60. Rachel Haworth, "Patrick Geddes' Concept of Conservative Surgery," *Architectural Heritage* 11 (2000): 37–42.

61. Sister Nivedita, Civic Ideal and Indian Nationality, *CWSN,* 4:218, 230–234; she praised instead medieval European cities for their cathedrals.

62. Sister Nivedita to JM, September 22, 1910, *LSN,* vol. 2, no. 712.

63. Sister Nivedita to JM, July 31, 1910, *LSN,* vol. 2, no. 694.

64. Sister Nivedita to Swami Vivekananda, March 13, 1900, *LSN,* vol. 1, no. 116.

65. Patrick Geddes, quoted in Murdo MacDonald, "Finding Nivedita from a Scottish Point of View," in *Sister Nivedita: Offered to India* (special number) *Prabuddha Bharata,* 122, no. 1 (January 2017): 163; see also Sudipta Sen's excellent, *Ganges: The Many Pasts of an Indian River* (New Haven, CT: Yale University Press, 2019).

66. Sister Nivedita to Swami Vivekananda, March 13, 1900, *LSN,* vol. 1, no. 116.

67. Patrick Geddes and J. Arthur Thomson, *Evolution* (New York, Henry Holt and Company, 1911), 113.

68. Sister Nivedita to JM, January 28, 1900, *LSN,* vol. 1, no. 109.

69. Sister Nivedita, The Web of Indian Life, *CWSN* 2:9. She credited Romesh Chunder Dutt with encouraging the project. A J. C. Hudson spoke about it: Sara Bull on July 25, 1905, VSNC.

70. Geddes drew upon Élisée Réclus, whose work remains key to eco-anarchism even today.

71. Sister Nivedita, Quoted in Editor's Preface, *Queen,* August 24, 1904, *CWSN,* 2: x.

72. Sister Nivedita, Quoted in Editor's Preface, *Detroit Free Press,* July 24, 1904, *CWSN,* 2: x–xi.

73. Prabuddhaprana, *Sister Nivedita in Contemporary Newspapers,* 83–84.

74. Sister Nivedita, Quoted in Editor's Preface, *Athenaeum,* 1904, *CWSN,* 2:xi.

75. Sister Nivedita, Quoted in Editor's Preface, *Church Times,* August 19, 1904, *CWSN,* 2:xi. These critiques took on even greater force in the interwar period; see Mrinalini Sinha, *Specters of Mother India: The Global Restructuring of an Empire* (Durham, NC: Duke University Press 2006).

76. Sister Nivedita, Quoted in Editor's Preface, *Church Times,* August 19, 1904.

77. Prabuddhaprana, *Sister Nivedita in Contemporary Newspapers,* 80–83.

78. Sister Nivedita to JM, August 18, 1900, *LSN,* vol. 1, no. 145.

79. Sister Nivedita to JM, July 1, 1900, *LSN*, vol. 1, no. 137.

80. Sister Nivedita to JM, July 1, 1900.

81. Sister Nivedita to JM, July 1, 1900.

82. Sister Nivedita to JM, July 1, 1900.

83. Sister Nivedita to Sara Bull, August 13, 1900, *LSN*, vol. 1, no. 143.

84. Sister Nivedita to JM, March 7, 1901, *LSN*, vol. 1, no. 164.

85. Sister Nivedita to JM, August 22, 1900, *LSN*, vol. 1, no. 146.

86. Swami Vivekananda to Nivedita, August 25, 1900, CLXI, Epistles–2nd Series, vol. 6, in *Complete Works of Swami Vivekananda,* 10 vols., https://en.wikisource.org/wiki/The_Complete _Works_of_Swami_Vivekananda (hereafter *CWSV*).

87. We know from a letter from Josephine Macleod to Sara Bull, December 21, 1899, VSNC, that Vivekananda had been engrossed in a work by Élisée Relcus, *The Earth and Its Inhabitants* (New York: D. Appleton and Company, 1898), while in California.

88. See Patrick Geddes, "Conservative Surgery," in *Patrick Geddes in India,* ed. Jacqueline Tyrwhitt (London: Lund Humphries, 1947), 40–59.

89. Sister Nivedita, "Unpublished Letters of Sister Nivedita to Anna Geddes," *Prabuddha Bharata* 120 (August 2015), 499.

90. Sister Nivedita to JM, August 29, 1900, *LSN*, vol. 1, no. 147.

91. Sister Nivedita, The Master as I Saw Him, *CWSN* 1:155.

92. Sister Nivedita, The Master as I Saw Him, 1:155.

93. Sister Nivedita, The Master as I Saw Him, 1:156; Swami Vivekananda, "A Benediction," Writings: Prose and Poems (Original and Translated), vol. 6, *CWSV.*

94. Sister Nivedita, The Master as I Saw Him, 1:156.

95. Sister Nivedita to JM, April 25, 1899, *LSN*, vol. 1, no. 123.

96. Sister Nivedita to JM, April 25, 1899.

97. Sister Nivedita to Sara Bull, April 26, 1899, *LSN*, vol. 1, no. 125.

98. Sister Nivedita to Sara Bull, April 26, 1899.

99. Sister Nivedita to JM, August 22, 1900, *LSN*, vol. 1, no. 146.

100. Sister Nivedita to JM, November 15, 1900, *LSN*, vol. 1, no. 155.

101. Sister Nivedita to Dr. and Mrs. Jagadish Chandra Bose, November 5, 1900, *LSN*, vol. 1, no. 154.

102. Sister Nivedita to Dr. and Mrs. Bose, November 5, 1900.

103. Sister Nivedita to Dr. and Mrs. Bose, November 5, 1900.

104. Susmita Chatterjee, "Acharya Jagadis Chandra Bose: Looking beyond the Idiom," in *Science, Spirituality and the Modernization of India,* ed. Marakand R. Paranjape (London: Anthem Press, 2009), 79–80.

105. Gyan Prakash, *Another Reason: Science and the Imagination of Modern India* (Princeton: Princeton University Press, 1999), 19–21.

106. Sister Nivedita to JM, November 15, 1900, *LSN*, vol. 1, no. 155.

107. Sister Nivedita to JM, April 3, 1909, *LSN*, vol. 2, no. 547.

108. Ashis Nandy, "Defiance and Conformity in Science: The Identity of Jagadis Chandra Bose," *Science Studies* 2 (January 1972): 65–66.

109. Naveeda Khan, "Patrick Geddes in India: Town Planning, Plant Sentience and Cooperative Evolution," *Environment and Planning: Society and Space* 29 (2011): 840–856.

110. I thank Sudipta Sen for this point.

111. Patrick Geddes, *The Life and Work of Sir Jagadis C. Bose* (London: Longmans Green and Co., 1920); Bose had become known between 1894 and 1899 for his work on microwaves and for extending James Clerk Maxwell's studies in electromagnetic radiation. He had produced radio waves at tiny wavelengths (a millimeter) so their properties could be studied.

112. Geddes, *Life and Work of Sir Jagadis C. Bose,* 33.

113. Sister Nivedita to JM, January 20, 1903, *LSN,* vol. 2, no. 221.

114. Subrata Dasgupta, *Jagadish Chandra Bose and the Indian Response to Western Science* (New Delhi: Oxford University Press, 1999), 128; C. Mackenzie Brown, "Jagadish Chandra Bose and Vedantic Science," in *Science and Religion: East and West,* ed. Yiftach Fehige (London: Routledge, 2016), 107; for less radical, but similar statements, see also Susmita Chatterjee, "Acharya Jagadish Chandra Bose," in *Science and Religion,* 65–95.

115. Quoted in Chatterjee, "Acharya Jagadis Chandra Bose," 65; see also Nandy, "Defiance and Conformity in Science," 31–85.

116. Quoted in Geddes, *Life and Work of Sir Jagadis C. Bose,* 96.

117. Quoted in Geddes, *Life and Work of Sir Jagadis C. Bose,* 97.

118. Jagadish Chandra Bose, "The Response of Inorganic Matter to Mechanical and Electrical Stimulus," in *Acharya J. C. Bose: A Scientist & Dreamer,* ed. Prantosh Bhattarcharyya and Meher Engineer, vol. 1 (Calcutta: Bose Institute, 1996), 205–217 (quotation, 209).

119. Paranjape, "Science, Spirituality and Modernity in India," 4; and Prakash, *Another Reason,* 229–230.

120. Siladitya Jana, "Sister Nivedita's Influence on J. C. Bose's Writings," *Journal of the Association for Information Science and Technology* 66 (2015): 645–650.

121. Sister Nivedita, "Review of *Is Matter Alive?* by J. C. Bose," *CWSN* 5:289–298.

122. Jana, "Sister Nivedita's Influence on J. C. Bose's Writings."

123. Sister Nivedita to Sara Bull, February 10, 1904, *LSN,* vol. 2, no. 273.

124. "The Plant as Machine." review of Jagadish Bose, "Plant Response as a Means of Physiological Investigation," in *Nature* (January 31, 1907): 313.

125. Nandy, "Defiance and Conformity in Science," 63–65.

126. Sister Nivedita to Sara Bull, February 21, 1907, *LSN,* vol. 2, no. 439. I have not been able to discover the review.

127. Nandy, "Defiance and Conformity in Science," 44; his reformist father was a theist; his mother, a devotee of the Mother Goddess.

128. Sister Nivedita to JM, May 4, 1899, *LSN,* vol. 1, no. 34.

129. Sister Nivedita to JM, May 4, 1899.

130. Sister Nivedita to JM, November 1, 1900, *LSN,* vol. 1, no. 153.

131. Taking root: Sister Nivedita to JM, December 25, 1900, *LSN,* vol. 1, no. 158; "walking into blindfold": Sister Nivedita to JM, January 11, 1901, *LSN,* vol. 1, no. 160.

132. Sister Nivedita to JM, January 4, 1902, *LSN,* vol. 1, no. 159.

133. Sister Nivedita to JM, January 4, 1902.

134. Sister Nivedita to JM, January 4, 1902.

135. Sister Nivedita to JM, June 10, 1901, *LSN,* vol. 1, no. 170.

136. Sister Nivedita to JM, June 10, 1901.

137. Sister Nivedita to JM, June 10, 1901.

138. Sister Nivedita to JM, July 19, 1901, *LSN,* vol. 1, no. 173.

139. Sister Nivedita to JM, July 19, 1901.

140. She first published "Lambs among Wolves: Missionaries in India" in *Westminster Review,* 158 (1902), 414–430; also available under same title in *CWSN,* vol. 4, 509–532.

141. Sister Nivedita to JM, April 14, 1903.

142. Going further: Sister Nivedita to JM, April 14, 1903; "About India": Sister Nivedita to JM, July 19, 1901, *LSN,* vol. 1, no. 173.

143. Sister Nivedita to JM, July 19, 1901.

144. Sister Nivedita to JM, October 3, 1901, *LSN,* vol. 1, no. 177; both quotes are from this source.

145. Sister Nivedita to JM, October 3, 1901.

146. Sister Nivedita to JM, October 3, 1901.

147. Sister Nivedita to JM, October 3, 1901.

148. Sister Nivedita, "Mukti: Freedom," Religion and Dharma, *CWSN* 3:380–383.

15. Femininity, the National Idea, and Politics

1. Swami Vivekananda to Sister Christine., March 16, 1897, Letters–5th Series, CV, vol. 9, in *Complete Works of Swami Vivekananda,* 10 vols., https://en.wikisource.org/wiki/The_Complete _Works_of_Swami_Vivekananda (hereafter *CWSV*).

2. Swami Vivekananda to Mary Hale, April 28, 1897, Epistles–2nd Series, CXXIII, vol. 6, *CWSV*.

3. Swami Vivekananda to Mrs. Ole Bull, April 4, 1898, Letters–5th Series, CXX, vol. 9, *CWSV;* to Sister Christine, June 21, 1902, Epistles–4th Series, CCXXVII, vol. 8, *CWSV*.

4. Swami Vivekananda to Swami Brahmananda, July 13, 1897, Epistles–4th Series, XCVIII, vol. 8, *CWSV*.

5. Dyspepsia afflicted him for years; see Swami Vivekananda to Sister Christine, January 26, 1899, Letters–5th Series, CXXXII, vol. 9, *CWSV*.

6. "Nervous body": Swami Vivekananda to Sister Nivedita, November 15, 1899, Epistles–2nd Series, CXLIX, vol. 6, *CSWV;* not to write to him: Swami Vivekananda to Swami Brahmananda, November 21, 1899, Epistles–4th Series, CL, vol. 8, *CWSV*.

7. Swami Vivekananda to Mary Hale, August 27, 1901, Epistles–1st Series, CX, vol. 5, *CWSV*.

8. Sankar, *The Monk as Man: The Unknown Life of Swami Vivekananda* (Gurgaon: Penguin, 2015), 49.

9. "Sister Nivedita: A Chronology: 1867–1911," *Letters of Sister Nivedita,* collected and ed. Sankari Prasad Basu, 2 vols. (Kolkata: Advaita Ashrama, 2017), 1:38 (hereafter *LSN*).

10. Sister Nivedita to Josephine MacLeod (hereafter JM), July 10, 1902, *LSN,* vol. 1, no. 193.

11. Sister Nivedita to JM, July 10, 1902, *LSN,* vol. 1, no. 193.

12. Sister Nivedita to JM, May 25, 1902, *LSN,* vol. 1, no. 187.

13. Sister Nivedita to JM, May 25, 1902.

14. Sister Nivedita to JM, September 14, 1902, *LSN,* vol. 1, no. 207.

15. In this, I disagree with Reba Som, *Margot: Sister Nivedita of Swami Vivekananda* (New York: Viking, 2017), 105, because of subsequent events.

16. Sister Nivedita to Mr. and Mrs. Eric Hammond, August 28, 1902, *LSN,* vol. 1, no. 204.

17. Sister Nivedita to Swami Brahmananda, July 18, 1902, *LSN,* vol. 1, no. 196.

18. "Sister Nivedita to the Editor of *The Indian Mirror,*" *LSN,* Appendix—1902, no. 28, 1:530.

19. *Indian Mirror,* July 31, 1902, *Vivekananda in Indian Newspapers, 1893–1902: Extracts from 22 Newspapers and Periodicals,* ed. with intro. by Sankari Prasad Basu (Calcutta: Dineshchandra Basu, Basu Bhattacharyya, 1969), 226 (hereafter Basu).

20. Sister Nivedita to Swami Brahmananda, July 18, 1902, *LSN,* vol. 1, no. 196.

21. See *Indian Mirror,* July 31, 1902, Basu, 226.

22. "Vivekananda Memorial Meeting," *Indian Mirror,* September 20, 1902, Basu, 228.

23. Sister Nivedita to JM, July 24, 1902, *LSN,* vol. 1, no. 197.

24. Reports of these speeches are in Newspaper Reports of Speeches and Interviews, in *The Complete Works of Sister Nivedita,* ed. Pravrajika Atmapranam, 2nd ed., 5 vols. (Kolkata: Advaita Ashrama, 2016), 5:324–330 (hereafter *CWSN*).

25. Sister Nivedita to JM, August 21, 1902, *LSN,* vol. 1, no. 202.

26. Sister Nivedita to Sara Bull, December 12, 1906, *LSN,* vol. 2, no. 428.

27. Sister Nivedita to JM, July 24, 1902, *LSN,* vol. 1, no. 197.

28. Sister Nivedita to JM, July 24, 1902.

29. She was ambivalent about Sarala Ghosal, and believed that Cornelia Sorabji, a lawyer, social reformer, and writer, was a spy for the British.

30. Tanika Sarkar, *Rebels, Wives, Saints: Designing Selves and Nations in Colonial Times* (London: Seagull Books, 2009), 257.

31. Sister Nivedita to JM, August 24, 1905, *LSN*, vol. 2, no. 365.

32. Sister Nivedita to JM, July 24, 1902, *LSN*, vol. 1, no. 197.

33. Sister Nivedita to JM, July 24, 1902.

34. Sister Nivedita, The Master as I Saw Him, *CWSN*, 1:50.

35. Sister Nivedita to JM, August 21, 1902, *LSN*, vol. 1, no. 202.

36. Sister Nivedita to JM, October 1, 1902, *LSN*, vol. 1, no. 209.

37. Sister Nivedita to JM, October 1, 1902.

38. Sister Nivedita to JM, October 1, 1902.

39. Sister Nivedita to JM, July 24, 1902, *LSN*, vol. 1, no. 197.

40. Quoted in Lizelle Reymond, *The Dedicated: A Biography of Nivedita* (New York: John Day, 1953), 272.

41. Sister Nivedita to JM, February 1, 1905, *LSN*, vol. 2, no. 330.

42. *Indian Mirror,* October 2, 1902, Basu, 232.

43. Sister Nivedita to JM, July 24, 1902, *LSN*, vol. 1, no. 197.

44. Sister Nivedita to JM, January 21, 1904, *LSN*, vol. 2, no. 268.

45. Sister Nivedita to Sara Bull, December 12, 1906, *LSN*, vol. 2, no. 428.

46. Sister Nivedita to JM, April 24, 1907, *LSN*, vol. 2, no. 451.

47. Pankaj Mishra, *From the Ruins of Empire: The Revolt against the West and the Remaking of Asia* (London: Allen Lane, 2012), chapters 2 through 6.

48. "Okakura Kakuzo's 'Nostalgic Journey to India and the Invention of Asia,'" in *Nostalgic Journeys: Literary Pilgrimages between Japan and the West,* ed. Susan Fisher (Vancouver: CJR, Japan Research Series, 2001), 119–132.

49. Rustom Bharucha, *Another Asia: Rabindranath Tagore and Okakura Tenshin* (New Delhi, Oxford University Press, 2006). See photographic inserts between 136 and 137.

50. Partha Mitter, *Art and Nationalism in Colonial India, 1850–1922: Occidental Orientations* (Cambridge, UK: Cambridge University Press, 1994), 263; for the wider discussion, 262–266.

51. Bharucha, *Another Asia,* 5.

52. Mitter, *Art and Nationalism,* 265.

53. Bharucha, *Another Asia,* 123–130.

54. Sister Nivedita to JM, June 15, 1902, *LSN*, vol. 1, no. 190.

55. Kakuzo Okakura, *The Ideals of the East with Special Reference to the Art of Japan* (London, John Murray, 1903), xi.

56. K. N. Panikkar, "From Revolt to Agitation: Beginning of the National Movement," *Social Scientist* 25 (1997), 34; see also C. A. Bayly, 'The Origins of Swadeshi (home industry): Cloth and Indian Society, 1700–1930," in Arjun Appadurai, *The Social Life of Things: Commodities in Cultural Perspective* (Cambridge, UK: Cambridge University Press 2013), 285–322.

57. Swami Vivekananda to Sister Nivedita, April 4, 1901, Letters–5th Series, CXCIII, vol. 9, *CWSV.*

58. Sister Nivedita to Sara Bull, July 23, 1901, *LSN*, vol. 1, no. 174. Sister Nivedita to JM, August 7, 1902, *LSN*, vol. 1, no. 200; and Panikkar, "From Revolt to Agitation," 34. She defended him stoutly against a younger generation's criticism in the *Modern Review;* see Sister Nivedita, "Romesh Chandra Dutt," Biographical Sketches and Reviews, *CWSN*, 5:261–265.

59. Romesh Chunder Dutt, *The Economic History of India under Early British Rule: From the Rise of the British Power in 1758 to the Accession of Queen Victoria,* vol. 1 (London: Kegan Paul, Trench, Trübner & Co., 1902) and *The Economic History of India in the Victorian Age, 1837–1900,* vol. 2 (London: Kegan Paul, Trench, Trübner & Co., 1904). For more on Indian economic thought,

see Sumit Sarkar, *The Swadeshi Movement in Bengal, 1903–1908* (New Delhi, Permanent Black, 2011), 81–86; and Prakash, *Another Reason*, 146.

60. Sister Nivedita to JM, February 28, 1902, *LSN*, vol. 1, no. 178. In this letter she waits to learn more about Josephine's trip to Ajanta.

61. Okakura, *Ideals of the East*, xvi.

62. German archaeology and historical thought were central to such claims: A. Sartori, "Beyond Culture-Contact and Colonial Discourse: 'Germanism in Colonial Bengal'" in *An Intellectual History for India*, ed. Shruti Kapila (Cambridge, UK: Foundation Books, 2010), 68–84, especially 71–75.

63. Culture as a whole: Dipesh Chakrabarty, *Provincializing Europe: Postcolonial Thought and Historical Difference*, new ed. (Princeton: Princeton University Press, 2009), passim; "mere outpost": Okakura, *Ideas of the East*, xiv.

64. Okakura, *Ideas of the East*, xv.

65. Swami Vivekananda, "The Abroad and the Problems at Home," *The Hindu*, Madras, February 1897, Interviews, vol. 5, *CWSV*.

66. Okakura, *Ideals of the East*, 1.

67. Okakura, *Ideals of the East*, 7.

68. Okakura, *Ideals of the East*, 8.

69. Sister Nivedita to JM, August 14, 1902, *LSN*, vol. 1, no. 201.

70. Pekka Korhonen, "The Geography of Okakura Tenshin," *Japan Review* no. 3 (2002): 107–127 (especially 110); the author does not say, however, where it was found.

71. "Japan and Korea'" in the *Modern Review* in *CSWN*, 5, 242–243; for Gandhi, Thomas Weber, and Akira Hayashi's "The Japanese Connection," https://www.mkgandhi.org/articles /mahatma-gandhi-the-japanese-connection.html; consulted May 13, 2021.

72. Sister Nivedita to JM, July 28, 1902, *LSN*, vol. 1, no. 199.

73. Sister Nivedita to JM, October 11, 1902, *LSN*, vol. 1, no. 210.

74. Sister Nivedita to JM, December 9, 1903, *LSN*, vol. 2, no. 259.

75. Sister Nivedita to JM, December 9, 1903.

76. She thought Protestantism "dry" and dismissed Charles Paul Sabatier's work on St. Francis as "so fearfully Protestant [. . .] so little of the Catholic aroma!" See Sister Nivedita to JM, February 24, 1904, *LSN*, vol. 2, no. 275.

77. Claire Masurel-Murray, "Conversions to Catholicism among Fin de Siècle Writers: A Spiritual and Literary Genealogy," *Cahiers victoriens et édouardiens* 76 (2012): 105–125.

78. Sister Nivedita to JM, December 6, 1905, *LSN*, vol. 2, no. 378.

79. Sister Nivedita to JM, November 25, 1903, *LSN*, vol. 2, no. 257.

80. Sister Nivedita to JM, April 14, 1903, *LSN*, vol. 2, no. 236.

81. Sister Nivedita to JM, August 11, 1904, *LSN*, vol. 2, no. 302.

82. Sister Nivedita to JM, Wednesday in Easter Week 1904, *LSN*, vol. 2, no. 286.

83. "Little power": Sister Nivedita to JM, Wednesday in Easter Week 1904, *LSN*, vol. 2, no. 286; "force and fire": Sister Nivedita to JM, November 6, 1904, *LSN*, vol. 2, no. 315.

84. For a selection, see Sister Nivedita to JM, August 22, 1900, *LSN*, vol. 1, no. 146; Sister Nivedita to Sara Bull, July 20, 1901, *LSN*, vol. 1, no. 173; Sister Nivedita to Sara Bull, December 17, 1903, *LSN*, vol. 2, no. 260; Sister Nivedita to JM, May 2, 1909, *LSN*, vol. 2, no. 552; there are still more.

85. This term first appears in Sister Nivedita to JM, February 7, 1899, *LSN*, vol. 1, no. 18, when Nivedita signs off her letter to Josephine as "your absent childe." It is used even more frequently in *LSN*, vol. 2, and last appears in Sister Nivedita to JM, April 2, 1911, *LSN*, vol. 2, no. 743.

86. She called her real mother, Mary Noble, "little mother," a title common for Bengalis, but one which may also have signified her diminished stature in comparison to her "adopted" mothers.

87. Sister Nivedita to JM, April 23, 1903, *LSN*, vol. 2, no. 239.

88. Sister Nivedita to Mrs. Abala Bose, May 18, 1902 (or 1903), *LSN,* vol. 1, no. 185.

89. Sister Nivedita to Mrs. Bose, May 18, 1902 (or 1903).

90. Sister Nivedita, The Web of Indian Life, *CWSN,* 2:18.

91. Sister Nivedita, The Web of Indian Life, 2:18.

92. Sister Nivedita, "Family Life and Nationality in India," *CSWN,* 2:497.

93. Sister Nivedita to JM, December 9, 1903, *LSN,* vol. 2, no. 259; she wrote *Studies from an Eastern Home,* published posthumously in 1913, to describe their lives together. Sister Nivedita, Studies from an Eastern Home, *CWSN,* 2:293-398.

94. Sister Nivedita to JM, December 28, 1910, *LSN,* vol. 2, no. 728. For more on Gopaler Ma, see Sister Nivedita, Studies from an Eastern Home, 2:361-363.

95. Sister Nivedita to JM, August 5, 1909, *LSN,* vol. 2, no. 582.

96. Sister Nivedita to Sarada Devi, December 11, 1910, *LSN,* vol. 1, no. 725.

97. Pankaj Mishra, *From the Ruins of Empire,* chapters 2, 3, and 5.

98. Georges Sorel, *Réflexions sur la Violence: Édition définitive suivie du plaidoyer pour Lénine* (Paris: M. Rivière, 1946); Michael Curtis, *Three against the Third Republic: Sorel, Barrès and Maurras* (Princeton: Princeton University Press, 1959), 45-63.

99. Semanti Ghosh, *Different Nationalisms: Bengal 1905-1947* (New Delhi: Oxford University Press, 2016), 21.

100. Richard I. Cashman, *The Myth of the* Lokamanya *Tilak and Mass Politics in Maharashtra* (Berkeley: California University Press, 1974).

101. Sarkar, *Swadeshi Movement in Bengal,* 30-39 and 53-63, which remains the best book on the subject.

102. Shruti Kapila, *Violent Fraternity: Indian Political Thought in the Global Age* (Princeton: Princeton University Press, 2021), 16.

103. See Peter Heehs, *The Lives of Aurobindo* (Chichester, UK: Columbia University Press 2008), especially 101-158.

104. Kapila and Devji, *Political Thought in Action,* especially chapters 3, 4, 6, and 9.

105. Kapila, *Violent Fraternity,* 130-162; Devji, *Impossible Indian,* 105-118; Akeel Bilgrami, "Gandhi's Religion and its Relation to his Politics," in *The Cambridge Companion to Gandhi,* ed. Judith M. Brown and Antony Parel (Cambridge, UK: Cambridge University Press, 2011), 93-116.

106. Sister Nivedita to Mr. and Mrs. S. K. Ratcliffe, December 1, 1909, *LSN,* vol. 2, no. 624.

107. Sister Nivedita to JM, November 7, 1906, *LSN,* vol. 2, no. 423.

108. Striking students: She also spoke about national education, Sarkar, *Swadeshi,* 137-138; Bengali language:

109. Nonetheless, both switched sides later, Semanti Ghosh, *Different Nationalisms,* 32, 44-47.

110. Ghosh, *Different Nationalisms,* 32-33.

111. Sister Nivedita to JM, April 14, 1903, *LSN,* vol. 2, no. 236.

112. "Shifting constancy": Sister Nivedita, The Web of Indian Life, 2:195; "ethical passion": Sister Nivedita, The Web of Indian Life, 2:208.

113. Sister Nivedita, The Web of Indian Life, 2:201.

114. "Sister Nivedita: A Chronology: 1867-1911," 1:41.

115. Ghosh, *Different Nationalisms,* 47-48, 59.

116. Sarkar, *Swadeshi,* 357.

117. Sister Nivedita, Glimpses of Famine and Flood in East Bengal in 1906, *CWSN,* 4:449.

118. Sister Nivedita, Glimpses of Famine and Flood, 4:457.

119. Sister Nivedita, Glimpses of Famine and Flood, 4:479.

120. For a quotation that encapsulates the view that everything in India that was British or Islam was "foreign," see Rabindranath Tagore quoted in Sudipta Kaviraj, *The Invention of Private Life: Literature and Ideas* (New York: Columbia University Press, 2015), 87.

121. Shankari Prasad Basu, *Vivekananda O Samakalin Bharatbarsha* [Vivekananda and Contemporary India], Basu, 6:70–82

122. "Bharate Vivekananda," September 20, 1908, in *Bande Mataram*.

123. Basu, *Vivekananda O Samakalin Bharatbarsha*, 85–94.

124. Sarkar, *Swadeshi*, 397–399

125. See Chapter 13.

126. Ghosh, *Different Nationalisms*, 53, and Sarkar, *Swadeshi*, 359.

127. Swami Vivekananda, "Karma in Its Effect on Character," Karma-Yoga, vol. 1, *CWSV.*

128. Sister Nivedita, "Brahmin and Kshatriya," On Hindu Life, Thought and Religion, *CWSN*, 5:89.

129. "Activity" over "passivity": Sister Nivedita, Aggressive Hinduism, *CWSN*, 3:492. Vivekananda used the notion of "aggression" in religion, but the term "aggressive Hinduism" seems to come from this 1905 pamphlet. Hindus did not just "ape" Christian athletic models, because Americans took on Indian forms of exercise. Joseph S. Alter, "Indian Clubs and Colonialism: Hindu Masculinity and Muscular Christianity," *Comparative Studies in Society and History* 46 (2004): 497–534. Hindu character: Sister Nivedita, Aggressive Hinduism, 3:495.

130. Sister Nivedita, "Aggressive Hinduism," 3:495.

131. Sarkar, *Swadeshi*, 402. Her connection to Aurobindo was important. See Elleke Boehmer, *Empire, the National, and the Postcolonial, 1890–1920: Resistance in Interaction* (Oxford: Oxford University Press, 2002), 79–124.

132. Sarkar, *Swadeshi*, 401.

133. Sarkar, *Swadeshi*, 399. See also Peter Heehs, *Nationalism, Terrorism, Communalism: Essays in Modern Indian History* (New Delhi: Oxford University Press, 2000); *The Bomb in Bengal: The Rise of Revolutionary Terrorism in India, 1900–1900* (New York: Oxford University Press: 1994), 222, and *The Lives of Sri Aurobindo* (New York: Columbia University Press, 2008), 59–63; "Foreign Influences on Bengali Revolutionary Terrorism, 1902–1908," *Modern Asian Studies* 28 (1994): 533–556, and his "The Maniktala Secret Society: An Early Bengali Terrorist Group," *Indian Economic & Social History Review* 29 (1992): 349–370; also, Barbara Southward, "The Political Strategy of Aurobindo Ghosh: The Utilization of Hindu Religious Symbolism and the Problem of Political Mobilization in Bengal," *Modern Asian Studies* 14 (1980): 353–376.

134. Sister Nivedita, "An Indian Study of Love and Death," *CWSN*, 2:280.

135. Sister Nivedita, "An Indian Study of Love and Death," 2:280.

136. Sister Nivedita, Civic Ideal and Indian Nationality, *CWSN*, 4:323 and 326.

137. Shilarna Stokes, *Playing the Crowd: Mass Pageantry in Europe and the United States, 1905–1935* (PhD diss., Columbia University, New York, 2013), 54–113; https://player.bfi.org.uk/free/film/watch-sherborne-pageant-1905-online.

138. Sister Nivedita to JM, July 25, 1907, *LSN*, vol. 2, no. 415.

139. See Gérard Toffin, *La fête-spectacle: Théâtre et rite au Népal* (Paris: Éditions de la Maison des Sciences de l'homme, 2010).

140. Sister Nivedita, Hints on National Education in India, *CWSN*, 4:412.

141. Sister Nivedita, Studies from an Eastern Home, *CWSN*, 2:304.

142. Referring to Hindu Orthodoxy was complex and controversial, see, for example, Heehs, *The Lives of Sri Aurobindo*, 186–187.

143. Ghosh, *Different Nationalisms*, 54; Bipin Chandra Pal later became a "federalist."

144. Ghosh, *Different Nationalisms*, 53–59.

145. Sarkar, *Swadeshi*, 381–386, 390.

146. Sister Nivedita to E. B. Havell, March 3, 1910, *LSN*, vol. 2, no. 657. For context see Mitter, *Art and Nationalism*, 222, 267–339, and Tapati Guha-Thakurta, *The Making of New 'Indian' Art* (Cambridge, UK: Cambridge University Press, 1992), 146–184 and 185–225.

147. Sister Nivedita to JM, December 9, 1903, *LSN*, vol. 2, no. 259; she also mentioned Ellora in this quotation.

148. Mitter, *Art and Nationalism*, 221. See also Sister Nivedita, "Havell on Indian Painting," *Indian Art, CWSN*, 3:33–37.

149. Aimée Brown Price, *Puvis de Chavannes* (New Haven, CT: Yale University Press, 2010), 2 vols.

150. Frances Fowle, "The Franco-Scottish Alliance: Artistic Links between Scotland and France in the late 1880s and 1890s," *Patrick Geddes: The French Connection*, ed. Frances Fowle and Belinda Thomas (Oxford: Alden Press, 2004), 27–46.

151. Sister Nivedita to Sara Bull, December 12, 1906, *LSN*, vol. 2, no. 428.

152. Sister Nivedita, "Abanindra Nath Tagore, *Bharat Mata*," Indian Art: Appreciations, *CWSN*, 3:57.

153. Sister Nivedita, "Abanindra Nath Tagore, *Bharat Mata*, 57.

154. She is dressed as a *sadhvi*, a Sanskrit word for a female renouncer.

155. Sarkar, *Rebels, Wives, Saints*, 209.

156. Sister Nivedita, "Nanda Lal Bose, *Sati*," Indian Art: Appreciations, *CWSN*, 3:66.

157. Sister Nivedita, "Jules Breton, *Peasant Girls*," Indian Art: Appreciations, *CWSN*, 3:92.

158. Sister Nivedita, "Puvis de Chavannes, *Sainte Geneviève Watching over Paris*," Indian Art: Appreciations, *CWSN*, 3:85.

159. Sister Nivedita, Studies from an Eastern Home, 2:285–386.

160. Sister Nivedita, Studies from an Eastern Home, 2:297.

161. Sister Nivedita, Civic Ideal and Indian Nationality, 4:277.

162. Sister Nivedita, Civic Ideal and Indian Nationality, 4:278.

163. See Mitter, *Art and Nationalism*, 267–339, and Guha-Tahkurta, *The Making of New Indian Art*, 146–184 and 185–225.

164. Sumathi Ramaswamy, *The Goddess and the Nation: Mapping Mother India* (Durham, NC: Duke University Press, 2010), 251.

165. Sister Nivedita, "The Vajra as a National Flag," On Political, National, and Social Problems, *CWSN*, 5:166–167.

166. Sister Nivedita, "The Vajra as a National Flag," 5:167–168. For more on the flag, see Ramaswamy, *The Goddess and the Nation*, 251. Nivedita wrote: "Unfortunately, I took the Chinese War Flag as my ideal, and made it black on red. This does not appeal to Indians—so the next is to be yellow on scarlet," Sister Nivedita to JM, February 8, 1905, *LSN*, vol. 2, no. 332.

167. Sister Nivedita to JM, July 25, 1906, *LSN*, vol. 2, no. 415; she was also designing a medal for schools and wished to imprint the same symbol.

168. Chakrabarti, *Provincializing Europe*, 234–235.

169. Sister Nivedita to JM, June 2, 1907, *LSN*, vol. 2, no. 456.

170. Sister Nivedita to JM, December 13, 1906, *LSN*, vol. 2, no. 429.

171. Sister Nivedita to JM, December 18, 1906, *LSN*, vol. 2, no. 430.

172. Sister Nivedita to JM, June 9, 1907, *LSN*, vol. 2, no. 458.

173. Sister Nivedita to JM, November 21, 1906, *LSN*, vol. 2, no. 424.

174. Sister Nivedita to JM, June 8–9, 1907, *LSN*, vol. 2, no. 457.

175. Sister Nivedita to JM, June 8–9, 1907.

176. Sister Nivedita to JM, June 9, 1907, *LSN*, vol. 2, no. 458.

177. See Sister Nivedita, "The Recent Congress," On Political, Economic, and Social Problems, *CWSN* 5:160–162.

178. Aurobindo Ghosh, *Sri Aurobindo on Himself*, 2011, 91, https://www.aurobindo.ru.

179. Sister Nivedita to Mr. and Mrs. S. K. Ratcliffe, November 3, 1909, *LSN*, vol. 2, no. 618.

180. Sister Nivedita to Mr. and Mrs. S. K. Ratcliffe, March 10, 1910, *LSN*, vol. 2, no. 659.

181. Prabuddhaprana, ed., *Sister Nivedita in Contemporary Newspapers* (Dakshineswar: Sri Sarada Math, 2017), 244.

182. Prabuddhaprana, *Sister Nivedita in Contemporary Newspapers,* 49.

183. Aurobindo Ghosh, *Sri Aurobindo on Himself and on the Mother* (Pondicherry: Sri Aurobindo Ashram, 1953), 429 and 92.

184. Bipin Chandra Pal, "Sister Nivedita (Character Sketch)," *Indian Nationalism: Its Principles and Personalities* (Madras: S. R. Murthy, 1918), 228–238.

185. "Sister Nivedita: to the editor of *The Indian Mirror,*" July 5, 1901, Basu, 217. Repeatedly, Nivedita's work on Kali received compliments, with the *Indian Mirror* in July 1901 remarking that it was "a standing monument of her deep learning, avowed faith, and literary finish."

186. Ghosh, *Sri Aurobindo on Himself,* 25.

187. "Sister Nivedita on the Plague in Calcutta": to the editor of *The Indian Mirror,* March 28, 1899, Basu, 211.

188. "Filthiest bustis": "Sister Nivedita on the Plague in Calcutta," 224; "thoroughly surpassed": the *Indian Mirror,* March 6, 1902, Basu, 219.

189. "Sister Nivedita & the Late Swami Vivekananda," *Mahratta,* October 5, 1902, Basu, 401.

190. Pal, "Sister Nivedita (Character Sketch)" 238.

191. Faisal Devji, of St. Antony's College, Oxford, offered me these thoughts.

16. Malign Influence and Harrowing Deaths

1. Sister Nivedita to Mr. S. K. Ratcliffe, July 21, 1909, *Letters of Sister Nivedita,* collected and ed. Sankari Prasad Basu, 2 vols. (Kolkata: Advaita Ashrama, 2017), vol. 2, no. 576 (hereafter *LSN*).

2. Sister Nivedita to Sister Devamata, September 8, 1909, *LSN,* vol. 2, no. 593. Semiblindness was seen as result of American adulteration of the mustard oil used for bathing and cooking.

3. Sister Nivedita to unknown recipient, August 11, 1909, *LSN,* vol. 2, no. 585. Sister Nivedita claimed she said to Sarada Devi, "The Whole of India is yours!"

4. Sister Nivedita to Josephine MacLeod (hereafter JM), November 3, 1907, *LSN,* vol. 2, no. 472.

5. Sister Nivedita to Dr. Cheyne, March 4, 1908, *LSN,* vol. 2, no. 489.

6. Sister Nivedita to Mr. and Mrs. S. K. Ratcliffe, November 4, 1908, *LSN,* vol. 2, no. 514.

7. Sister Nivedita to Mr. and Mrs. Ratcliffe, November 4, 1908.

8. Sister Nivedita to Mr. and Mrs. S. K. Ratcliffe, December 1, 1909, *LSN,* vol. 2, no. 624.

9. Bhupendranath Datta, *Swami Vivekananda, Patriot-Prophet: A Study* (Calcutta: Nababharat Publishers, 1954); he writes of a George Freeman, born George Fitzgerald, who was notoriously anti-Semitic and who may have been the conduit for these ideas. Freeman was dedicated to Irish revolution and may have also been involved in attempts to incite revolution in British-ruled India.

10. The report was delivered on March 9, 1905, and finally canceled on July 12, 1906.

11. Sister Nivedita to Mr. S. K. Ratcliffe, August 25, 1910, *LSN,* vol. 2, no. 704.

12. Sister Nivedita to Mr. Ratcliffe, August 23, 1910.

13. Swami Vivekananda, "Vedanta as a Factor in Civilisation," Lectures and Discourses, vol. 1, *Complete Works of Swami Vivekananda,* 10 vols. Vivekananda, https://en.wikisource.org/wiki/The_Complete_Works_of_Swami_Vivekananda (hereafter *CWSV*). He did say once that the "Western world is governed by a handful of Shylocks" when he returned to India, Swami Vivekananda, "Reply to the Address of Welcome at Paramakudi," Lectures from Colombo to Almora, vol. 3, *CWSV;* and spoke of "modern, sharp Jew" in "Maya and the Evolution of the Conception of God," Jnana-Yoga, vol. 2.

14. Sister Nivedita to Mr. S. K. Ratcliffe, August 25, 1910, *LSN,* vol. 2, no. 704; the reference to the "stay-at-homes" is Sister Nivedita to JM, November 3, 1907, *LSN,* vol. 2, no. 472.

15. Sister Nivedita to Mr. and Mrs. S. K. Ratcliffe, September 14, 1910, *LSN,* vol. 2, no. 710.

16. Sister Nivedita to Mr. S. K. Ratcliffe, September 14, 1911, *LSN,* vol. 2, no. 780: "I am by nature political. . . . Even religion is to me too much an instrument for throwing Humanity into the furnace and remoulding huge masses and areas of men! Sometimes I think I am altogether material and secular and haven't a grain of the real thing in me!"

17. Sister Nivedita to Mrs. Wilson, May 15, 1909, *LSN,* vol. 2, no. 556.

18. Sister Nivedita to Mrs. S. K. Ratcliffe, July 6, 1910, *LSN,* vol. 5, no. 585.

19. Sister Nivedita to JM: July 10, 1902, *LSN,* vol. 1, no. 193; October 11, 1902, *LSN,* vol. 1, no. 210; and November 23, 1907, *LSN,* vol. 2, no. 880.

20. Sister Nivedita to Mrs. Roethlesberger, April 23, 1903, *LSN,* vol. 2, no. 240.

21. Sister Nivedita to JM, March 17, 1904, *LSN,* vol. 2, no. 279.

22. Sister Nivedita to JM, July 22, 1908, *LSN,* vol. 2, no. 500. She continued to seek this intervention regarding Bose's niece, Savitri, who was dying. See Sister Nivedita to JM, August 19, 1909, *LSN,* vol. 2, no. 588; and October 20, 1909, *LSN,* vol. 2, no. 614.

23. Sister Nivedita to Mrs. Wilson (Nim), September 15, 1909, *LSN,* vol. 2, no. 597.

24. Sister Nivedita to Mrs. Francis Leggett (Betty), September 19, 1909, *LSN,* vol. 2, no. 601.

25. Sister Nivedita to JM, September 29, 1909, *LSN,* vol. 2, no. 605.

26. Sister Nivedita to Mrs. Wilson, August 11, 1909, *LSN,* vol. 2, no. 586.

27. Swami Vivekananda to H. H. Maharaja of Khetri, 1894, Epistles–2nd Series, XL, vol. 6, *CWSV.*

28. Sister Nivedita to Mr. and Mrs. S. K. Ratcliffe, November 3, 1909, *LSN,* vol. 2, no. 618.

29. Sister Nivedita to Mr. and Mrs. Ratcliffe, November 3, 1909.

30. "Fancy—Himself [Dr. Bose] tells me that one of the pleasant little methods of the police here is to put a towel over your face and then pour a stream of water continuously till you put up your hand to confess." Sister Nivedita to Mr. and Mrs. S. K. Ratcliffe, September 22, 1910, *LSN,* vol. 2, no. 713.

31. Sister Nivedita to JM, October 20, 1909, *LSN,* vol. 2, no. 614.

32. Pravrajika Prabuddhaprana, *Saint Sara: The Life of Sara Chapman Bull: The American Mother of Swami Vivekananda* (Dakshineswar: Sri Sarada Math, 2002), 456.

33. Sister Nivedita to JM, April 18, 1907, *LSN,* vol. 2, no. 450.

34. Prabuddhaprana, *Saint Sara,* 123–124.

35. Sister Nivedita to JM, August 4, 1910, *LSN,* vol. 2, no. 695.

36. Sister Nivedita to JM, July 31, 1910, *LSN,* vol. 2, no. 605.

37. For another account, see, Jacqueline Brady, "Wise Mother? Insane Mother?: Sara Chapman Bull and the Disarticulated Subjectivities of Turn-of-the Century Motherhood," in *Disjointed Perspectives on Motherhood,* ed. Catalina Florina Florescu (Lanham, MD: Lexington Books, 2013), 201–216.

38. Prabuddhaprana, *Saint Sara,* 399; "from [Olea's] childhood to babyhood, I was compelled to renounce so much, leaving her with those I loved and whom I was serving in my absence."

39. Sister Nivedita to JM, October 18, 1899, *LSN,* vol. 1, no. 71.

40. Prabuddhaprana, *Saint Sara,* 445.

41. Sister Nivedita to JM, October 8, 1908, *LSN,* vol. 2, no. 506.

42. Sister Nivedita to Mrs. Wilson (Nim), September 15, 1909, *LSN,* vol. 2, no. 597.

43. Sister Nivedita to JM, February 24, 1910, *LSN,* vol. 2, no. 654.

44. This information was given to me by Prabuddhaprana in a conversation in Sri Sarada Math, Dakshineswar.

45. Prabuddhaprana, *Saint Sara,* 485.

46. Sister Nivedita to Mr. K. Ratcliffe, October 14, 1910, *LSN,* vol. 2, no. 719.

47. Prabuddhaprana, *Saint Sara,* 491.

48. Sister Nivedita to JM, January 4, 1910, *LSN,* vol. 2, no. 722.

49. Sister Nivedita to JM, October 14, 1910, *LSN*, vol. 2, no. 718.

50. Sister Nivedita to JM, December 4, 1910, *LSN*, vol. 2, no. 722.

51. Prabuddhaprana, ed., *Sister Nivedita in Contemporary Newspapers* (Dakshineswar: Sri Sarada Math, 2017), 179.

52. Sister Nivedita to JM, December 19, 1910, *LSN*, vol. 2, no. 726.

53. Sister Nivedita to JM, December 19, 1910.

54. Sister Nivedita to JM, December 26, 1910, *LSN*, vol. 2, no. 727.

55. Sister Nivedita to JM, December 26, 1910.

56. Sister Nivedita to JM, December 28, 1910, *LSN*, vol. 2, no. 728.

57. Sister Nivedita to Mr. S. K. Ratcliffe, January 12, 1911, *LSN*, vol. 2, no. 730.

58. Prabuddhaprana, *Sister Nivedita in Contemporary Newspapers*, 157, and Stephen Prothero, "Hinduphobia and Hinduphilia in United States Culture," in *The Stranger's Religion: Fascination and Fear*, ed. Anna Lännström (Notre Dame, IN: Notre Dame University Press, 2004), 13–37.

59. Two copies of the final will and two codicils are available in docket no. 87864 in the archives of York Country Register of Probate in Alfred, Maine. I would like to thank Linda Waite for sending me photographs of these documents and her kind attention to this matter. The will is dated April 5, 1906.

60. Prabuddhaprana, *Sister Nivedita in Contemporary Newspapers*, 166; this was the contention of Ralph Bartlett to Emma Thursby on April 18, 1911.

61. Prabuddhaprana, *Sister Nivedita in Contemporary Newspapers*, 158.

62. Prabuddhaprana, *Sister Nivedita in Contemporary Newspapers*, 167–168.

63. Disguised as a maid: Prabuddhaprana, *Sister Nivedita in Contemporary Newspapers*, 198.

64. Prabuddhaprana, *Sister Nivedita in Contemporary Newspapers*, 171.

65. Prabuddhaprana, *Sister Nivedita in Contemporary Newspapers*, 170.

66. Prabuddhaprana, *Sister Nivedita in Contemporary Newspapers*, 176.

67. Prabuddhaprana, *Sister Nivedita in Contemporary Newspapers*, 155.

68. Prabuddhaprana, *Sister Nivedita in Contemporary Newspapers*, 155. She was also shocked to see their betrayal: Sister Nivedita to Mr. and Mrs. S. K. Ratcliffe, August 31, 1911, *LSN*, vol. 2, no. 769.

69. I have never been able to find out how, exactly, the estate was distributed after her death.

70. Sister Nivedita to JM, July 4, 1911, *LSN*, vol. 2, no. 757.

71. Sister Nivedita to Mr. S. K. Ratcliffe, July 6, 1911, *LSN*, vol. 2, no. 758.

72. Sister Nivedita to Mr. S. K. Ratcliffe, July 20, 1911, *LSN*, vol. 2, no. 760.

73. Sister Nivedita to Mr. S. K. Ratcliffe, July 28, 1911, *LSN*, vol. 2, no. 761.

74. Sister Christine to JM, October 16, 1911, *LSN*, vol. 2, Appendix, no. 77.

Conclusion

1. Swami Vivekananda, "My Plan of Campaign," Lectures from Colombo to Almora, vol. 3, *CWSV*.

2. Shamita Basu, *Religious Revivalism as Nationalist Discourse: Swami Vivekananda and New Hinduism in Nineteenth-Century Bengal* (New York: Oxford University Press, 2002), passim.

3. I thank D. Gellner for this insight; while condemning Brahmanical prerogatives, Vivekananda seems to have retained some aspects of "hierarchical incorporation"; see Peter van der Veer, *The Modern Spirit of Asia: The Spiritual and the Secular in China and India* (Princeton: Princeton University Press, 2013), 120–121.

4. Swami Vivekananda to "My Dear Friend," June 10, 1898, Epistles–2nd Series, CXLII, vol. 6, *CWSV*.

5. Prathama Banerjee, *Elementary Aspects of the Political: Histories from the Global South* (Durham, NC: Duke University Press, 2020), 25–42.

6. Van der Veer, *Modern Spirit,* 171.

7. Swami Vivekananda to Shri Haridas Viharidas Desai, November (?) 1894, Epistles–4th Series, XXXIV, vol. 8, *CWSV.*

8. I thank Sudipta Sen for these thoughts.

9. Aurobindo: "Bharate Vivekananda," *Bande Mataram,* September 20, 1908; Andrews: Martin Gilbert, *Servant of India: A Study of Imperial Rule, from 1905–1910, as Told through the Correspondence and Diaries of Sir James Dunlop Smith* (London: Longmans, 1966), 87.

10. Gandhi, for example, had Margaret Slade, also known as Mirabehn, the daughter of an admiral, who became his British "daughter." Aurobindo similarly had the French Jewish Mirra Alfassa as his most devoted follower.

Acknowledgments

During the very long time I took to write this book, I incurred many debts to both individuals and institutions. Five years ago, I was elected to a Senior Research Fellowship at All Souls, a post that provides a unique mixture of calm and intellectual stimulation. I am also grateful to a range of archives and institutions. The Vedanta Society of Northern California allowed me full access to its papers, and I am particularly indebted to the archivist, Sister Dharmaprana. I would also like to thank Swami Tattwamayananda, who gave me an early, valuable lesson in the society's vision of the relationship between dualism and nondualism in Hinduism. I am equally grateful to Swami Sarvadevananda and Brother Jnana Chaitanya of the Vedanta Society of Southern California, in Hollywood, for letting me read manuscripts, and for their hospitality. Darshann in the archives helped me locate documents and photographs. While in Southern California, I also met Asim Chaudhuri, who later shared his unpublished manuscript with me, and was put into contact with Gopal Stavig, who helpfully sent along some materials. Rosanne Adams, the archivist at Green Acre, Maine, guided us around the site, gave permissions for images, and showed us documents, while her colleague Roger Dahl in Wilmette, Illinois, has always been helpful in providing material from the Baha'i Archives.

Swami Chetanananda, author of many works and translations about the Ramakrishna-Vivekananda movement, welcomed me to the St. Louis Vedanta Society and let me read and cite letters from the Friends Collection. I am grateful for the afternoon we spent discussing the origins of Vedanta in America and Hindu devotion to Kali and hope that, despite his reservations, he will not be disappointed with my book. In St. Louis, I met Linda Prugh (Uma) of the Kansas City Vedanta Society, who then read an early draft of the manuscript. Her remarks led me back to the sources and made me reconsider aspects of my interpretation, while also sparing me many errors. I was very touched by the time and trouble she took in helping me.

Swami Sarvapriyananda at the New York Vedanta Society allowed me to reproduce images, and Swami Vidananda at the Ramakrishna-Vivekananda Center of New York gave prompt and generous help. He also contacted Swami Suparnanandaji at the Vivekananda Institute in Kolkata, who allowed me to reproduce a photograph of the kantha embroidery held at the Ramakrishna Mission Institute of Culture; Swami Suparnanandaji was also vital in arranging a meeting with the General Secretary at Belur Math, Swami Suviranandaji Maharaj, who extended a warm welcome to me and my husband. Despite our amicable meeting, I was not granted entry to the archives and, like so many other historians, hope that the original manuscripts will someday become available. Kahini Ghosh was a wonderful and efficient research assistant who continued to work on this project even after I left India, despite her busy schedule. I was grateful to Santanu Dey, who invited me to talk to students at the Ramakrishna Mission Vidyamandira on Vivekananda's relationship to American religion. Swami Narasimhananda published a version of this lecture in the *Prabuddhabharata,* and Sandipan Sen kindly sent me a copy of his dissertation on Vivekananda and development.

I would also like to thank Professor Parul Chakrabarti of the J C Bose Science Heritage Museum. Although the museum was closed, she still allowed me to visit the building and gardens, where I was able to view Bose's remarkable scientific instruments and get a sense of how he blended research, teaching, and home life.

Pravrajika Prabuddhaprana at Sri Sarada Devi Math shared her knowledge of Sara Bull. Her recent edited compilation of the newspaper coverage of Sister Nivedita has been invaluable in writing the last part of this book. I was glad to have met Ayon Maharaj while at Belur and to know of his work.

Sujit Sivasundaram was an early counselor who helped me arrange a trip to Sri Lanka before I decided to concentrate on Vivekananda and India. Partha Mitter in Oxford knows a great deal about everything Bengali, and his work on art and Nivedita as well as his impressions of Vivekananda were important to me. Nick Sutton of the Hindu Studies Centre allowed me to cite his translations, and Sondra Hausner gave me valuable advice and bibliographic help throughout this process. Mishka Sinha's unpublished manuscript on Sanskrit in America was crucial in understanding Vivekananda's relations with Harvard academics. Lucien Wong and especially Amiya Sen generously supplied me with their very recent and clarifying work on the history of Vaishnavism in Bengal. Julia Mannherz corrected mischaracterizations and nuanced ideas in the chapters on science, religion, and magic, while querying important terms. Diwakar Acharya at All Souls was always ready to answer questions on Indian religion and Hindu sacred texts. Rustom Bharucha was a lively interlocutor in Kolkata and journeyed with me to Dakshineswar; while there, he encouraged me to be bolder in my interpretation of Sister Nivedita.

Somak Biswas—who writes on themes not too dissimilar to my own—has been a remarkable interlocutor, stimulating, challenging, and always himself. He has also been fastidious in looking at and checking translations for me. Will Passey did an extraordinary amount of research during the early stages of the manuscript and caught some of Vivekananda's allusions to English poetry that I missed.

The book would never have been completed without Debdatta Sen and his family. He and his wife, Panchali, hosted me and my husband in Kolkata and introduced us to a wonderful array of people. Sujaya Sen took me to an all-night concert of Indian classical music in Kolkata. Without this experience I would not have understood the importance of music to Ramakrishna and Vivekananda. Aniruddh Chari kindly invited us to visit the Anchor and Hope Lodge, where Vivekananda had his early brush with Freemasonry. Jayanta Sengupta, secretary and curator at the Victoria Memorial Hall, explained more about the museum, its activities, and the history of Calcutta.

I am grateful to Sharmila Sen of Harvard University Press for reading the manuscript, working so hard on my behalf, and thinking so seriously about how to reach readers who had never heard of Vivekananda. I am also very grateful to members of her team, especially Heather Hughes and more recently Olivia Woods, who have been so attentive. At the last minute, Kate Brick at the Press astonished me with her kindness by volunteering to help with editorial checking. Iris Bass, the copyeditor, was tireless in verifying details and even responded to the book's content in her comments. Cecilia MacKay as always was a wonderful and indefatigable picture researcher, sensitive to text and to image. Special thanks go to my agent, Rebecca Carter, whose intelligence and care I value.

Finally, and most important, I have benefited from wonderful and generous commentary. Edward Berenson, a colleague in French history who knew nothing about Vivekananda, reassured me after reading the manuscript that others without previous knowledge of the subject might be interested in the book. Tanika Sarkar encouraged me throughout and read two of the chapters—her remarks were especially important in helping me think again about Hindu-Muslim relations. Gary Gerstle, despite his own pressing deadlines, found time to read the chapters on America and Britain; he offered several vital suggestions on improving the emotional logic of the narrative. Santanu Das read two-thirds of the book; his lively commentary and intellectual response as a literary scholar and Brahmo were just what I needed. David Gellner repeatedly offered to read the manuscript and returned it with a running commentary of questions, thoughts, and corrections, providing a bibliography of pertinent anthropological works that enriched the text. Both he and Santanu are wonderful colleagues at All Souls.

I cannot thank Sudipta Sen enough for his intellectual engagement, much of which I have incorporated into my text and cited. He has a rare scholarly sensibility, which he shared unstintingly and enthusiastically through his deep knowledge of Bengali culture and society. Sudipta Kaviraj, a reader for Harvard University Press who unveiled himself, understood so well what I was trying to do. Shruti Kapila, another reader, was also in touch. She offered brilliant and provocative thoughts; she is simultaneously open and lavish in her support. I have now known Faisal Devji for over ten years, and he has been my mainstay at Oxford during this intellectual journey. He, too, read parts of the book, but even more he opened my mind and continues to do so.

Lyndal Roper has been an intellectual collaborator for forty years, and I am constantly surprised by our ability to renew and explore this connection. I was grateful for her enthusiasm, which partly came thanks to Arnand Narsey, and her willingness to read parts of it repeatedly. I must thank Iain Pears, my husband, who, as always, spent many hours talking and thinking with me over the years of this book's gestation and spent wonderful weeks with me in India. As always, he encouraged me to take the unconventional path, even when naysayers suggested that I should not do this project. And he backed up endless inspiration with practical help, spending hours away from his own work editing and reading drafts. It is to him and to our decades together that I dedicate this book. Finally, I want to thank my children, Mike and Alex, who were captivated by the people in this story. I am delighted that they continue to love history.

Errors and missteps no doubt remain despite this wealth of advice and aid.

Illustration Credits

Every effort has been made to contact all copyright holders. The publisher will be pleased to amend in future editions any errors or omissions brought to their attention.

I.1   Castle Kernan, Madras, built 1842. © Gemini Prostudio / Dreamstime.com.

I.2   Vivekananda at the World Parliament, Chicago, 1893. Wikimedia Commons.

I.3   Modi pays his respects to Vivekananda, 2017. AP / Shutterstock.

1.1   Raja Ram Mohun Roy. Portrait by Rembrandt Peale, 1833. Oil on canvas. Courtesy of the Peabody Essex Museum, Salem, MA. Museum purchase, 1999.137982.

1.2   Keshub Chandra Sen with his disciples and ektara. Reproduced from *Sri Ramakrishna: A Biography in Pictures*, Advaita Ashrama, Kolkata, 1976.

2.1   Dakshineswar temple, Calcutta. Photograph by Francis Frith. Historic Images / Alamy Stock Photo.

2.2   Kali statue, Dakshineswar Temple. Reproduced from *Sri Ramakrishna: A Biography in Pictures*, Advaita Ashrama, Kolkata, 1976.

2.3   Kali and Shiva, Bengali illustration, c. 1885–1890. Heritage Image Partnership Ltd. / Alamy Stock Photo.

2.4   Chaitanya. Statue in Mayapur Temple, West Bengal. Vrindavan Lila / flickr, CC BY-ND 2.0.

2.5   Ramakrishna. Reproduced from *Sri Ramakrishna: A Biography in Pictures*, Advaita Ashrama, Kolkata, 1976.

2.6   Tota Puri. Reproduced from Monika Mitra, *Sree Digambar Baba*, Sachindra Kumar Mitra, 1994.

2.7   Sarada Devi. Reproduced from *Vivekananda: A Biography in Pictures*, Advaita Ashrama, Kolkata, 1966.

4.1   The "Haunted House," Baranagar. Reproduced from *Vivekananda: A Biography in Pictures*, Advaita Ashrama, Kolkata, 1966.

4.2   The Monks at Baranagar, 1887. Reproduced from *Vivekananda: A Biography in Pictures*, Advaita Ashrama, Kolkata, 1966.

4.3 Victoria Terminus, Bombay, photograph, c. 1900s. Metropolitan Museum of Art, New York. Gift of Matthew Dontzin, 1985. CC0.

4.4 Vivekananda as mendicant. Reproduced from *Vivekananda: A Biography in Pictures,* Advaita Ashrama, Kolkata, 1966.

4.5 Ajit Singh, Raja of Khetri. Reproduced from *Vivekananda: A Biography in Pictures,* Advaita Ashrama, Kolkata, 1966.

4.6 Rameswaran Temple. Reproduced from H. F. Helmolt, *The World's History,* Vol. 2, William Heinemann, London, 1904.

4.7 Cape Comorin, with the Rock Memorial to Vivekananda in the middle. CPA Media Co. Ltd. / TopFoto.

4.8 Parthasarathy Temple, Madras. Photograph, 1858. Canadian Centre for Architecture, Montreal.

5.1 View toward the Administration Building, Chicago World's Columbian Exposition, 1893. C. D. Arnold and H. D. Higinbotham, *Official Views of The World's Columbian Exposition,* C. B. Woodward Co., Saint Louis, 1893 / Wikimedia Commons.

5.2 Interior of the Japanese Pavilion at the Chicago World's Columbian Exposition. Reproduced from *Portfolio of the World's Fair,* The Werner Company, Chicago, 1893.

5.3 Exterior of the East Indian Pavilion at the Chicago World's Columbian Exposition. Reproduced from C. D. Arnold & H. D. Higinbotham, *Official Views of The World's Columbian Exposition,* C. B. Woodward Co., Saint Louis, 1893.

5.4 Vivekananda meets Mrs. Hale in Chicago after sleeping in a box. Kantha embroidery. Museum of the Ramakrishnan Mission Institute of Culture, Golpark, Kolkata. Courtesy of Iain Pears.

5.5 The Hale Sisters. Reproduced from *Vivekananda: A Biography in Pictures,* Advaita Ashrama, Kolkata, 1966.

5.6 Union Stockyards, Chicago. Suhling & Koehn Co., Chicago / Wikimedia Commons.

5.7 Virchand Gandhi, Dharmapala *(slightly behind)* and Vivekananda, Chicago, 1893. Reproduced from *Vivekananda: A Biography in Pictures,* Advaita Ashrama, Kolkata, 1966.

5.8 Helen Blavatsky and Henry Steel Olcott. Wikimedia Commons.

6.1a–c Vivekananda in three different garbs. Reproduced from *Vivekananda: A Biography in Pictures,* Advaita Ashrama, Kolkata, 1966.

6.2 The beach at Magnolia, near Gloucester, Massachusetts. Postcard, c. 1900. The Miriam and Ira D. Wallach Division of Art, Prints and Photographs: Photography Collection, The New York Public Library. "Bathing Beach, Magnolia, Mass." *The New York Public Library Digital Collections.* 1903–1904. https:// digitalcollections.nypl.org/items/510d47d9-a4a6-a3d9-e040-e00a18064a99.

6.3 Bhuvaneshwari Devi. Reproduced from *Vivekananda: A Biography in Pictures,* Advaita Ashrama, Kolkata, 1966.

6.4 Pandita Ramabai. Reproduced from Pandita Ramabai Sarasvati, *The High Caste Hindu Woman,* Jas. B. Rodgers Printing Co., Philadelphia, 1887.

6.5 Gopaler Ma. Reproduced from *Sri Ramakrishna: A Biography in Pictures,* Advaita Ashrama, Kolkata, 1976.

7.1   Haeckel's Development of the embryo: hog, calf, lamb, and human. Ernst Haeckel, *The History of Creation: Or, the Development of the Earth and Its Inhabitants by the Action of Natural Causes,* D. Appleton and Company, New York, 1880 / Wellcome Collection, London / CC BY 4.0.

8.1   Vivekananda at Green Acre, 1894. Courtesy of Eliot Baha'i Archives, Eliot Maine.

8.2   Sarah Farmer and followers. Courtesy of Eliot Baha'i Archives, Eliot Maine.

8.3   Sara Chapman Bull. Reproduced from *Vivekananda: A Biography in Pictures,* Advaita Ashrama, Kolkata, 1966.

8.4   Ole Bull's villa, Lysøen Island, Norway. Dag Fosse / KODE.

9.1   Boldt Castle, Heart Island, New York. Louise Heusinkveld / Alamy Stock Photo.

9.2   Dutcher House, Wellesley Island. Courtesy of Iain Pears.

9.3   Libbie Dutcher in her studio. Courtesy of Ramakrishna-Vivekananda Center of New York.

9.4   Josephine MacLeod in older age. Reproduced from *Vivekananda: A Biography in Pictures,* Advaita Ashrama, Kolkata, 1966.

9.5   Ridgely Park, c. 1900. Reproduced from *Vivekananda: A Biography in Pictures,* Advaita Ashrama, Kolkata, 1966.

10.1   Vivekananda in Pasadena, California. Reproduced from *Vivekananda: A Biography in Pictures,* Advaita Ashrama, Kolkata, 1966.

10.2   Alasinga Perumal. Reproduced from *Sri Sarada Devi: A Biography in Pictures,* Advaita Ahsrama, Kolkata, 1988.

11.1   Edward Sturdy's fireplace at Norburton House, with Sanskrit inscription, "There is no higher law than truth." Courtesy of C. F. Dunn.

11.2   Mayavati Ashrama, Uttarakhand. Reproduced from *Vivekananda: A Biography in Pictures,* pub. Advaita Ashrama, Kolkata, 1966.

11.3   Dungannon. Photograph, nineteenth century. National Library of Ireland, Dublin / flickr.

12.1   Vivekananda in Calcutta, 1897. Reproduced from *Vivekananda: A Biography in Pictures,* Advaita Ashrama, Kolkata, 1966.

13.1   Nivedita on a street sign, Kolkata, 2019. Courtesy of Iain Pears.

13.2   The four travelers: Josephine MacLeod, Sara Bull, Vivekananda and Sister Nivedita. Reproduced from *Vivekananda: A Biography in Pictures,* Advaita Ashrama, Kolkata, 1966.

13.3   The route to Amarnath, 1920. Reproduced from *Vivekananda: A Biography in Pictures,* Advaita Ashrama, Kolkata, 1966.

13.4   The ice lingam. Reproduced from *Vivekananda: A Biography in Pictures,* Advaita Ashrama, Kolkata, 1966.

13.5   On the houseboat. Reproduced from *Vivekananda: A Biography in Pictures,* Advaita Ashrama, Kolkata, 1966.

13.6   Khir Bhawani Temple, c. 1880s. Reproduced from *Vivekananda: A Biography in Pictures,* Advaita Ashrama, Kolkata, 1966.

13.7   Sarada Devi and Nivedita. Reproduced from *Sri Sarada Devi: A Biography in Pictures,* Advaita Ahsrama, Kolkata, 1988.

14.1   Nivedita in her self-designed habit. Reproduced from *Vivekananda: A Biography in Pictures,* Advaita Ashrama, Kolkata, 1966.

14.2   Examples of Froebel's gifts. Courtesy of Kiyoshi Togashi.

14.3   Patrick Geddes. Mary Evans Picture Library.

14.4   Geddes's Valley Plan, from Victor Brandford and Patrick Geddes, *The Making of the Future: The Coming Polity,* pub. Williams and Norgate, 1919. Photo © British Library Board / Bridgeman Images.

14.5   Jagadish Chandra Bose at the Royal Institution, 1897. Mattwo Omied / Alamy Stock Photo.

15.1   Okakura Kakuzo, c. 1905. Photo © Isabella Stewart Gardner Museum, Boston, MA / Bridgeman Images.

15.2   Nivedita with Gopaler Ma as she lay dying. Matteo Omied / Alamy.

15.3   Sherborne Pageant, 1905: The Death of Ethelbald. Reproduced from *The Bystander,* June 7, 1905.

15.4   Bodhisattva of Compassion. Wall painting in Ajanta, Cave 1, 5th century CE. Tuul and Bruno Morandi / Alamy Stock Photo.

15.5   Abanindranath Tagore, *Bharat Mata,* painting, 1905. Niday Picture Library / Alamy Stock Photo.

15.6   Nandalal Bose, *Sati,* gold wash and tempera on paper, 1907. National Gallery of Modern Art, New Delhi.

15.7   Pierre Puvis de Chavannes, *Ste. Genevieve Overlooking Paris,* 1898. Reproduced from the author's collection.

Index

Page numbers in italics refer to photographs.